WITHDRAWN BY THE
UNIVERSITY OF MICHIGAN

Plato's Republic

STANLEY ROSEN

Plato's Republic

A STUDY

Yale University Press
New Haven &
London

To the genuine Leo Strauss

Published with assistance from the Louis Stern Memorial Fund.
Copyright © 2005 by Yale University.
All rights reserved.
This book may not be reproduced, in whole or in part, including illustrations, in any form (beyond that copying permitted by Sections 107 and 108 of the U.S. Copyright Law and except by reviewers for the public press), without written permission from the publishers.

Set in Sabon type by Keystone Typesetting, Inc.

Printed in the United States of America.

Library of Congress Cataloging-in-Publication Data
Rosen, Stanley, 1929–
Plato's Republic : a study / Stanley Rosen.
p. cm.
Includes bibliographical references and index.
ISBN 0-300-10962-8 (alk. paper)
1. Plato. Republic. I. Title.
JC71.P6R67 2005
321'.07—dc22
2005044011

A catalogue record for this book is available from the British Library.

The paper in this book meets the guidelines for permanence and durability of the Committee on Production Guidelines for Book Longevity of the Council on Library Resources.

10 9 8 7 6 5 4 3 2 1

Contents

Preface   vii

Introduction   1

Part One

1   Cephalus and Polemarchus   19
2   Thrasymachus   38
3   Glaucon and Adeimantus   60

Part Two

4   *Paideia* I: The Luxurious City   79
5   *Paideia* II: The Purged City   109
6   Justice   139
7   The Female Drama   171

Part Three

8 Possibility 201

9 The Philosophical Nature 227

10 The Good, the Divided Line, and the Cave: The Education of the Philosopher 255

Part Four

11 Political Decay 305

12 Happiness and Pleasure 333

13 The Quarrel between Philosophy and Poetry 352

14 The Immortal Soul 377

Epilogue 389

Notes 397

Index 405

Preface

The following interpretation of the *Republic* is the result of some fifty years of reflection and numerous graduate seminars offered at Penn State University, the Scuola Superiore in Pisa, and Boston University, as well as invited lectures at a wide range of academic institutions and conferences, too many to acknowledge. I learned something important on each of these occasions and benefited from too many teachers, colleagues, and students to name them all. One name stands out, that of Leo Strauss, and it is important to acknowledge this influence, especially today when so many absurd accusations are being leveled against him, not infrequently by those who have highhandedly appropriated his doctrines and methods, but more often by those who have simply distorted his teaching or reduced it to vulgarity. It is especially incumbent upon me to make this acknowledgment because I disagree with his interpretation of the *Republic* on important points and find it lacking in technical detail on such crucial topics as the doctrine of Ideas. Strauss's lectures on Plato require modification and development, but they constitute an essential step in my own understanding of the dramatic structure of the dialogues. As a small token of my esteem for Strauss as a teacher and scholar, I dedicate this book to his memory.

Whereas the book is addressed to professors and students alike, I have made a special effort to write in a style that is compatible with that of Socrates himself, certainly not in depth or literary genius, but in the sense that he strives to render himself intelligible to students as well as professors. Very few Greek terms appear in the text, and always with a translation as well as some kind of explanation of their importance. Notes have been kept to a minimum because of the length of the text. I have, however, tried my best to mention those whose views intersect with or are parallel to my own, or who derive some importance for my study because of my disagreement with their own approach to Plato. But the book is already too long to allow extensive debate with the secondary literature.

I wish to express my gratitude to David Botwinik for his gracious and expert assistance in the electronic preparation of the manuscript. Nor can I pass by in silence the generous support of my research by John Silber, Dennis Berkey, and Jon Westling, all of Boston University.

Introduction

I

Plato's *Republic* is one of those works in the history of philosophy that is both excessively familiar and inexhaustibly mysterious. It has been studied endlessly by a wide range of readers, specialists and amateurs alike, and has become a canonical document of Western civilization. No one would expect to find Hegel's *Science of Logic* or Kant's *Critique of Pure Reason* as the text in a Great Books discussion group or even as required reading in an undergraduate humanities course. But the *Republic* is at home in both settings, or, if not quite at home, certainly not entirely out of place. It addresses the most important question that a human being can raise: What is the good life? And, despite the presence of occasional technical passages, the dialogue is composed in such a way as to seem to speak directly to a wide audience of intelligent and serious persons who exhibit a philosophical spirit but are not necessarily philosophical adepts.

There can be little doubt that the wide appeal of the *Republic* is largely due to its artistic brilliance. The task of the philosophical student, however, is not only to enjoy but also to understand. It is now acknowledged by competent Plato scholars that we cannot arrive at a satisfactory appreciation of his philosophical teaching if we ignore the connection between the discursive argument on the one hand and the dramatic form and rhetorical elements of the text on the other. The *Republic* is Plato's most universal dialogue, and despite the long-standing quarrel between philosophy and poetry, the presentation of that quarrel takes place in an idiom that combines both sides of the human spirit. To combine, of course, is not to dissolve but to fit together. I shall therefore proceed on the assumption that the hermeneutical battle has been won and does not need to be refought. Let me just say as a matter of form that I agree with those for whom the successful interpretation of a Platonic dialogue depends, among other things, upon careful attention to such topics as these: the dramatic setting, the character and intelligence of the main interlocutors, the difference between the rhetoric of living conversation and scientific or analytical discourse, the use of irony or, as is especially appropriate in a political conversation, urbanity, and the appeal to myth or allegory in order to reunite elements of the whole that have been displaced or disenfranchised by the piecemeal inspection of individual "arguments" (a word that has a dramatic as well as a logical meaning).

Of special importance is the fact that the rhetoric of conversation requires us to attend to the use of logically faulty arguments. The *Republic* is not a treatise on politics but a dramatic portrait of people conversing about the connection between justice and the good. When we converse, especially on a topic that arouses as much excitement as does politics, and that requires modes of persuasion other than the purely logical, we do not simply exchange arguments crafted for validity, as though we were doing exercises in a logic textbook. Our analysis of the aforementioned conversation needs to be guided by a consideration of the role of the particular argument in the overall intentions of the author. And this task in turn is rendered especially difficult because the author, Plato, no more appears in his dramas than does Shakespeare in his. In the absence of direct guidance by Plato, we have to infer his intentions from the guidance of the drama itself. Plato speaks in the story he tells, not in the arguments he assigns to his dramatis personae.[1]

This is not to say that we interpreters are excused from the task of analyzing the many arguments, sound or defective, that Socrates employs in his construction of the just (or shall we say ostensibly just) city. But we can no longer assume without deeper reflection that the faults of the Socratic argument, when these appear, are unintentional blunders in logic. Nor can we automatically identify Plato's views with those expressed by Socrates. Most difficult of all, we cannot assume naively that Socrates himself believes everything he says. If philosopher-kings are authorized to tell medicinal lies for the good of the city, why should the teacher of philosopher-kings not permit himself such medicine for the good of his pupils?

But there is a further complication. In the *Republic*, Socrates seems to agree with his analytically oriented contemporary admirers that poetry is conceptually inferior to philosophy. From this inferiority, Socrates infers that the charm of poetry constitutes a great danger to the political authority of the philosopher. The philosopher, one could say, uses poetical rhetoric for purposes of persuasion, but at least his or her rhetoric is informed by the truth. According to Socrates, the philosopher seeks truth, hates above everything else the lie in the soul that is rooted in self-deception, and is guided by a pure cognitive vision of the Platonic Ideas or eternal archetypes of the particulars of the domain of genesis. The poet, on the other hand, so the story goes, has no access to the Ideas but produces copies of the items of genesis, or what one could call simulacra (images of images). The poet thus deludes us into believing that he or she knows the truth, and this illusory knowledge is more attractive to the general populace than is the rigorous and genuine truth of philosophy. To make a long story short, if they are not checked, the poets will become the unacknowledged legislators of society, thereby usurping a role that ought to be filled by philosophers.

We are therefore faced with the peculiar situation in which Socrates speaks with what seems to be great frankness but in an idiom that he has himself identified as an illusion of the truth. We must not forget that although Socrates is presented as narrating the dialogue to an unnamed audience, Plato conceals himself as the imitator of the entire conversation. The *Republic* is no less a mimetic poem than are the *Iliad* and the *Odyssey*. Furthermore, despite the explicit distinction between the use of images of the truth and access to the truth itself by way of the dialectic of Platonic Ideas, Socrates makes it clear that he is speaking in the *Republic* to novices, however gifted some of them may be, and accordingly, he says that he cannot tell the full truth about the doctrine of Ideas, in particular about the culminating or grounding Idea of the Good, which is brought down to the level of the present conversation with the assistance of the image of the sun. The entire presentation is saturated with rhetoric and myth, and therefore with the imagery of poetry. These are said to stand to the truth as do reflections in pools and mirrors to the objects of reality. The divided line, on which the lowest segment is assigned to images, is itself an image.

It follows from these considerations that the famous quarrel between philosophy and poetry is the surface of a deeper argument. It is safe to say that no one who possesses the poetical gifts of Plato could fail to see the inadequacy of the account of poetry given by Socrates in the *Republic*. Not only does Socrates make use of poetry and myth in expounding his fundamental claims, he also continues to cite the poets, and in particular, Homer, as experts on human nature long after the moral and epistemic criticism of poetry has been presented. The expulsion of the mimetic poets from the just city is itself unjust in one sense, although it is indispensable for political purposes, once we accept the need for the unmitigated rule of reason.

The poetic account of human nature cannot possibly be as defective as Socrates presents it. But the great power of poetry requires that it be placed under the jurisdiction of the philosophers for the good of the city. If we think this through, it leads to the subordination of philosophy to justice, and hence to politics. In order to found and live within the just city, philosophers must suppress the poetical side of their nature, or what comes to the same thing, submit it to constant censorship and the degradation of poetry into political ideology. It is no empty paradox to say that the price of entrance for genuine philosophers into the just city is expulsion or purgation of their previous decadent selves.

This point can be made about philosophers by way of a reference to Nietzsche, who says in his Notebooks, "I am as well as Wagner the child of this time, that is to say, a décadent; except that I grasped it; except that I resisted it. The philosopher in me resisted it. This is what most deeply occupied me."[2] I suggest that the *Republic* is Plato's account of his struggle against decadence. In the name of this struggle, he not only expels the great poets from the purified city in speech but also advocates a complete transformation of traditional Greek life. In other words, Nietzsche is the prophet of the coming of Zarathustra, and so three steps removed (as Plato would calculate) from the society of the superman. To repeat an earlier observation, neither Socrates nor Plato would be able to dwell within the just city they describe, without sacrificing an essential element of their nature. The *Republic* could not be published in the just city it ostensibly recommends, nor could Socrates conduct investigations among the guardians that are designed to move them to critical thinking about the human soul.

This hypothesis also provides a possible solution to what is perhaps the most vexing of hermeneutical problems for the study of Plato. Many readers of the *Republic* have come to the conclusion not only that the Socratic recipe for a just city is unworkable and undesirable but also that Plato was aware of this fact. On this reading, the *Republic* is a kind of satire that illustrates the bad consequences of extremism in the pursuit of justice. This is in many ways an attractive hypothesis, but it has at least one serious defect. Socrates without exception professes admiration for his revolutionary political proposals, and he ends up with a very qualified but nevertheless explicit assertion that the city is possible. The question arises: Why would he lie? If there is some other hidden political doctrine that Socrates wishes to protect from vulgar eyes, why proceed by recommending in the strongest terms a city that one privately regards as radically defective? And how could such a shocking city protect the traditional city of Athens against the dangerous thoughts it engenders?

If anything is being satirized in the *Republic*, it would seem to be the political consequences of the rule of philosophers. I would state the point as follows. On what has sometimes been called the Straussian view (a portmanteau expression for the students of Leo Strauss), which I myself accepted for many years, Plato intends us to understand that Socrates is aware of the radical shortcomings and even in at least some cases the unjust consequences of his major proposals for constructing a truly just city. The moral of the satire is then the impossibility of extreme efforts to institute perfect justice. But this could have been presented directly, with an associated defense of a moderate aristocratically inclined democracy in the manner of Aristotle. The "exoteric" surface of the Socratic argument is so contrary to Greek practice generally, and the views of the Athenian establishment in particular, that what I shall call the Aristotelian solution, which is the natural consequence of a philosophical repudiation of philosophical tyranny, would have been widely accepted.

The revolutionary nature of the *Republic* in my opinion lies not in its exposure of the dangers of extremism in the name of justice but in the frank, shockingly open statement by Socrates of what is required if we take seriously, and follow consistently, the political implications of philosophical wisdom. Socrates (and so Plato) makes it quite clear that the rule of wisdom is tyrannical, and that it cannot tolerate words or deeds, laws or traditional institutions, and certainly political theories that impinge upon its rule. In this sense, modern enemies of Plato's political thought, of whom the most prominent in our time is no doubt Karl Popper, are correct in their objections, although they are ingenuous or let us say insufficiently rigorous in their consideration of the political consequences of theoretical truth. In Popper's case, this is probably due to his conviction that we can establish the falsehood of a proposition but not its truth. This conviction may well be more compatible with democracy in the modern sense of the term than the conviction that genuine philosophers know the truth. The argument of the *Republic* on the other hand is that, if we did know the truth, we would be led to support a city very much like the one constructed in the *Republic* under the leadership of Socrates.

I think, therefore, that it is quite mistaken to say that Socrates (and so Plato) wishes to recommend a prudent accommodation of philosophy to the views of the many. Instead, he exposes the views of the few to the many, and in so doing he invents political philosophy. I do not intend this latter term to represent academic theorizing in secluded philosophical circles. By attempting to convert members of the political establishment to the life of reason, Socrates not only commits treason against the city of Athens but also prepares the way for what is today called "ideology." These consequences follow whether or not the *Republic* is a satire. The historical irony of the fate of the *Republic* is that it illustrates Plato's conception of the cyclical nature of human life: a work intended to found a new mode of political life by bringing philosophy down from the heavens and allowing it to walk in the cities of humankind is the first step on the road that leads finally to the repudiation of Platonism and the rule of poets and those whom Plato would have regarded as sophists.

It is not impossible to give a moderate formulation to this state of affairs. We can say that Socrates (and so Plato) wished the reader to see that philosophy, in order to carry out the conditions for its own rule, leads to tyranny. The dialogue, properly understood, prevents us from overlooking the fact that truth by its nature intends to suppress falsehood. Today we avoid this unpleasant implication by relativizing truth, above all, political truth, in such a way as to respect all parties to the dispute, including those who are false or unjust. Plato does no such thing. There are no anti-Platonists in the just city. But Plato also shows us, in another side to the same story, that there is no final reconciliation between theory and practice. An extreme version of the best is self-destructive. In brief, as is suggested by Plato's three voyages to Sicily, his revolutionary politics is not only a purging of decadence but also a powerful portrait of his temptation to rule, regardless of how dangerous that temptation may be.

Some of my readers may regard this interpretation as an anachronistic imposition of a Nietzschean theme onto Plato. I reply that it shows how deeply Nietzsche learned from Plato. But one thing that Nietzsche did not learn is that every attempt to enact the truth in human affairs without compromise leads to the reversal of that truth. The result of having learned this lesson is to retreat backward into one degree or another of decadence. Socrates does not state this truth in the *Republic*, but it follows from what he does say. Aristotle, the third of this great trio, safeguards moderation, and so tradition, by separating philosophy from politics. He thus fails to mention the most radical aspects of Plato's regime in his review of other regimes in the *Politics*.

I therefore suggest that the implied teaching of the *Republic* is that the desirability of bringing philosophy into political life outweighs the dangers implicit in the frankness that such an effort entails. This is, of course, true only at certain moments and places in history. One could not imagine such an enterprise to be successful in cultures like those of medieval Islam and its Hebrew component, in which the religious and political atmosphere presents an insuperable obstacle to frankness. Plato's example shows us that it was possible to initiate a revolution in speech in his own time, not, to be sure, the revolution described within the *Republic*, but the one of which we are ourselves the long-term consequences. That we have reverted to decadence does not negate the enrichment of our history by philosophy but rather exhibits the impossibility of preserving virility. The same message appears within the laws of the beautiful city in the form of the decay of rules or customs governing breeding and mating.

In sum, the accommodation of the *Republic* is not to the spokesmen for the many, which is to say that it is not political. Instead, the accommodation is to the few, or the few as they were in their youth, like Glaucon and Adeimantus, who must be tested by the conversation in order to determine their fitness for philosophy. This is the peculiarity of the *Republic*: to speak out on the most dangerous of things and to exercise restraint or a rhetoric of indirection in the discussion of that which seems least likely to endanger the city, real or imagined. In slightly different terms, what Socrates calls dialectic enters the city surreptitiously, and it must do so in order to make the city safe for philosophy. In exchange for this safety, philosophy offers to the city a foundation for justice that is exaggerated in the account of the beautiful city but in its more sober version is verified by the course of Western history.

We should therefore resist the temptation to bring to bear the heavy artillery of contemporary philosophical analysis on the presentation in the *Republic* of those passages that most resemble an ancestral version of basic problems of epistemology and ontology. The purpose of the *Republic* is not to found these disciplines, a task that is left to other dialogues, but rather to sustain in the minds of Glaucon and Adeimantus the possibility of a philosopher-king. In the *Republic*, Socrates is in the business not of training epistemologists or ontologists but of seeking recruits who will advance the entrance of philosophy into the city, not just as a covert invader but as an instrument for the transformation of the city, a transformation in which philosophy will play a decisive role in the enrichment of human life. This is a dangerous enterprise, but it is worth the risk, at least in the eyes of Plato. To this I add that one should not make the mistake of taking the revolutionary message of the *Republic* as Plato's total political teaching, or even as designed to establish an open and progressive society, in the modern sense of those terms. A philosophical society is for Plato a closed society that protects its citizens from the sickness of the human soul. Plato's revolution is intended to defend us against nature, not to master it.

I said above that the conversation in the *Republic* is accommodated primarily to Glaucon and Adeimantus. This is true in the action of the dialogue, which depends upon potential guardian-auxiliaries to make possible the founding of the just city by expelling everyone over the age of ten and turning over power to the philosopher or philosophers. The austerity of Adeimantus must be channeled into something higher than moral outrage by the eros of

8   Introduction

Glaucon. The technical arguments or themes, like those of the doctrine of Ideas and the divided line, are developed just far enough to sustain that process.

In sum, without excessive exaggeration, one could suggest that what is surely one of the most famous works of philosophy ever produced does not possess unambiguously the nature of a philosophical work, as that nature is defined within the work itself and as it is understood by most professional philosophers. It would be more accurate to say that the *Republic* (and not only the *Republic*) is an advertisement for philosophy, in terms that are intelligible to the companions of Socrates, and in particular to Glaucon and Adeimantus. This is to say that within the dialogue, Socrates addresses primarily guardians, not philosopher-kings. The eros of Glaucon and the spiritedness (*thumos*, which also means "anger") of Adeimantus must be persuaded to obey the *logos* of Socrates. The interpreter, however, is not a character within the dialogue but views it from the outside. I mean by this that we are not excused from the obligation to acquire a philosophical understanding of this advertisement for philosophical revolution. Let us be especially careful that our understanding is of Plato's advertisement, not our own.

Despite anything I have said thus far, there will still be readers who believe that I have not gone far enough in absolving Plato from practicing esotericism or saying different things to different members of his audience. Unfortunately for them, such practice is obvious in the Platonic dialogues, and in fact it underlies the structure of the just city, not to mention the dialogue itself. One has only to remember the discussion in the *Phaedrus* of philosophical rhetoric as the accommodation of speech to the nature of the interlocutor or, within the *Republic*, the licensing of medicinal and even noble lies for the good of the city to see that contemporary objections on this point are naive and anachronistic. Those who hold this view may be highly moral persons, but they have simply not read the text before them. We can meet such critics halfway by reiterating that there is no way in which to introduce a revolution while concealing the acts in which the revolution consists. Whatever may be true of the citizens who have received their entire education within the just city, the founders of the city, represented here primarily by Glaucon and Adeimantus, have to know what they are supposed to do, whether or not they understand adequately why they must do it.

I come back now to the question of whether Socrates believed in the justness of the city he constructed. If he did not, there would have been no point in recommending it, since its nature is to alienate popular support rather than to attract it, nor could one understand it as a mask for the introduction of a still more bizarre paradigm of the just city. Precisely upon the hypothesis of esotericism, the utility of the Socratic city is that it really is just, in the strictest sense of the term, but that it is too strict to be adopted by human beings. If the argument for perfect justice is a reductio ad absurdum, then the exemplary city must really be just, even as it leads us inexorably to injustice. There is then no esotericism with respect to the founding of the city, only once it is founded. Let me emphasize that this statement is meant to apply to the *Republic*, not necessarily to other Platonic dialogues.

Yet another question is whether Socrates fully believes that philosophers will not seek political power in actual cities unless they are compelled to do so. What is meant here by compulsion? Who compelled Socrates to engage in his revolutionary conversation with Glaucon, Adeimantus, and the other members of his audience or, what comes to the same thing, who compelled Plato to write the *Republic*? Who or what compelled Plato to make repeated efforts to establish a philosophical city in Sicily at the urging of Dion and Dionysios? As I read it, the *Republic* forces us to reflect upon the necessity of a philosophical intervention into political life, not just for the sake of the city but also for that of philosophy itself. By bringing philosophy down from the heavens to the cities of humankind, Socrates invests it with political responsibility and thereby, far from being a conservative, founds the radical Western tradition according to which justice must be pursued by doctrinal construction. For this decisive reason, his teaching is much closer to that of the modern progressive spirit than is that of Aristotle, the true conservative. And it is the twentieth century that gives the clearest evidence of the extreme danger in the Platonic teaching.

In sum, the *Republic* is on my view more an unsuccessful catharsis of the philosophical compulsion to rule than a satire on the excessive pursuit of justice, although it is also the latter. But more than either of these, the *Republic* is Plato's solution to the problem of how to rule at second hand, as the creator and teacher of rulers. What we now call the participation of "intellectuals" in politics is a distant and deteriorated consequence of genuine Platonism. When philosophy seeks to bend the city to its will, it turns inevitably into ideology and tyranny. From this standpoint, we can regard the contemporary effort of the biological sciences to transform human nature as the "postmodern" version of Platonism, in which the rhetoric of scientific progress replaces the altogether less politically persuasive doctrine of the vision of Platonic Ideas. History as it were triumphs over eternity, but the motivation is the same: to protect humanity against nature. It seems heretical to attribute this view to Platonism, in however degenerate a form, but the point follows directly from the doctrine of the natural division and illness of the human soul, and the correlative thesis that this illness can be cured only by philosophical psychiatry.

The dialogue form has been chosen to give each reader his or her due, or justice, and this can be done only through the rule of philosophers. But the institution of philosophical rule leads to disaster, and Socrates never says anything of the kind. Instead, Plato shows us dramatically how philosophy, in its attempt to acquire political power, is transformed into tyranny. It seems exceedingly odd to write a long and intricate work to express the reverse of one's own viewpoint or the absurdity of what one claims fervently to wish for.[3] But Plato has done something different. It is not what he wishes for that is absurd but the means required for its achievement. In this way, the general approach to the *Republic* made notorious by Leo Strauss is justified, or at the least defended from the charge of absurdity. I have made modifications in the Straussian reading, some of which Strauss would no doubt have rejected. However this may be, the center of my own reading lies in the recognition of a political temptation to which philosophers are destined to succumb as soon as they undertake to deviate from tradition and to reconstruct the foundations of the just city, whether in speech alone or in acts as well.

It should be noted that the self-destructive character of fanaticism is implicit throughout Aristotle's practical writings, which purport to generalize upon the common views of prudent and experienced men of affairs. Aristotle's celebration of common sense seems to confirm the orthodoxy of what is vulgarly referred to as the secret teaching of the *Republic*. It is the public teaching that shocks and offends, and it is precisely this public teaching that Aristotle rejects in his own treatment of ethics and politics. It would be very strange if Plato concealed a more sensible view of politics by the public presentation of a more extreme and even impossible set of recommendations. Surely it would have been more effective to compose a judicious critique of fanaticism than a mad recommendation of extremism, if Plato's intention in the *Republic* were indeed to praise moderation in the pursuit of justice.

For the reasons just given, I suspect that Plato did in fact believe the explicit teaching assigned to Socrates in the *Republic*, namely, that justice requires the purification of theology, the subordination of art to the good of the city, the abolition of the family, and the rule of philosophers. But this is to say that the only psychiatric therapy powerful enough to cure the sickness of the human soul is in fact so powerful that it destroys the patient, like some of the wonder drugs of the medicine of our own epoch. To put this in another way, the successes of politics stem from the fact that the city is an artifact, not a natural growth. To the extent that the city exists by nature, it reflects accurately the sickness of the human soul, that is, its division against itself. If it were possible to overcome this inner division by art, whether political or philosophical, the result would be a new type of human being: either a monster or an angel, and therefore not a human being at all. Plato shows us in the *Republic* the alternative of the monster.

2

I turn now from hermeneutical generality to the particularities of Plato's dramatic construction. According to the ancient tradition, Plato wrote thirty-five dialogues and a set of thirteen letters. Modern scholars have raised doubts about the authenticity of some of the dialogues, but their evidence and arguments have themselves been doubted, and for our purposes we can ignore these restrictions. So far as I know, Leo Strauss was the first contemporary scholar to study carefully the titles of the dialogues as well as to expand upon the role of the dramatic form already remarked upon by others, including Heidegger, Paul Friedländer, and H. G. Gadamer.[4] Strauss's discussion of the titles is suggestive but inconclusive. It will be safer to begin with the title of the dialogue that is our major concern: *Politeia*, usually translated as "Republic" but better rendered by "regime," a translation made popular by Strauss, or perhaps as "polity." The *politeia* is the soul of the city, and as such, the basis of its laws. For Socrates, it is also the context within which philosophy emerges and is the great rival to philosophical authority. As we shall see in due course, the range of the dialogue is expressed metaphorically in the ascent from the cave beneath the city to the so-called Platonic Ideas that dwell somewhere beyond the heavens. Otherwise put, the dialogue begins with a descent from the upper city of Athens down into the Piraeus, the harbor, and it ends, in the myth of Er, with a rather different descent from the doctrine of Ideas to Hades. The *Republic* is dramatically comprehensive; it deals with heaven and hell and all things in between.

Before I turn to the dramatic setting and the characters in our drama, I want to mention another distinction made famous by Leo Strauss, that between narrative and performed dialogues. According to Socrates in the *Republic* (III. 393a3ff.), in narratives it is easier to determine the views of the speakers, since they speak directly, in their own name, and not as characters in a play. There is, however, a problem with this distinction. Some dialogues are narrated from one standpoint and performed from another. This is especially true of dialogues with prologues in which someone agrees to recount, or to have read aloud his or her written record of, a conversation that took place at a previous date. Suffice it to say that the *Republic* is a narrated dialogue. We shall thus have access at various points to Socrates's account of his own responses or inner thoughts during the conversation that he narrates. The device of the prologue raises its own problems, such as how to correct for the possibly faulty memories or personal limitations of the narrator of the main conversation. Again, this issue does not arise in the case of the *Republic*. What does arise is the question of the audience to whom Socrates is speaking. Why should we assume, for example, that he accommodates his views to the characters with whom he converses within the dialogue, whereas he reveals frankly his personal or inner thoughts to the unnamed audience to which the dialogue is recounted?

In one sense, the *Republic* is a monologue. No one is presented directly as speaking, other than Socrates himself. But Socrates recounts in great detail a complex conversation that he had with, or in the presence of, ten other persons. I shall come back shortly to the question of the identities of these ten characters. The immediate question is why Socrates is represented as recounting the conversation about the just city to an anonymous audience, that is to say, to no one. Are we meant to infer that the *Republic*, like Nietzsche's *Thus Spoke Zarathustra*, is a book for everyone and no one? Simply to launch a trial balloon, I shall observe that both works are addressed to no one among the contemporaries of the main speaker; Zarathustra is not the superman but the prophet of the coming of the superman, and Socrates, as he makes clear in the Platonic corpus, is unwilling to participate in politics and, given his peculiar nature, he is incapable of doing so. Socrates is thus the "prophet" of the philosopher-king but not one himself. The same cannot be said of Plato, whose prophecy is the founding of the just city as well as the announcement of its decline. On the other hand, both works are addressed to everyone; this constitutes their universality. The founding of a just city concerns all human beings, albeit in different ways. The less global point, but one of considerable importance for understanding the *Republic*, is that it is narrated by Socrates, though in such a way that he assumes the identities, and utters the speeches, of everyone in the dialogue, which is accordingly also mimetic. This *polupragmosunē*, or minding of everyone's business, the opposite of justice as defined in the *Republic*, is exceeded only by Plato's silent invention of the entire Socratic monologue.

In the *Republic*, the main interlocutor (apart from Socrates himself) is without doubt Glaucon, who is erotic and spirited or brave, as well as highly intelligent, but who lacks the austerity of his brother Adeimantus that is the necessary restraint upon erotic madness. Glaucon is better suited for the role of auxiliary or soldier than to be a philosopher-king. This is to say that he makes an excellent disciple of the founding father. He is a lieutenant in a revolution but not a general or strategist. The theoretical or strategic dimension of revolution intrigues him, but what he requires is a rhetorical description of philosophy, not the real thing. He needs to know only enough to channel his enthusiasm into the correct political outlets. In slightly different terms, what the citizen of a well-constructed city needs to know is not necessarily the same as what the founding fathers need to know. But we must not make the mistake of thinking that Glaucon and Adeimantus are "founding fathers." They do not need to know what Socrates knows. The account that Socrates gives to these young men (not to mention the other participants in the discussion) is not necessarily the same as the one he would give to Plato and Xenophon.

The dialogue takes place in the Piraeus, the harbor of Athens, rather than within the city itself, and under cover of night, almost entirely in the home of a foreign resident (*metic*) named Cephalus. I note in passing that his name means "head" in Greek, and he is of course the head of the house in which the main conversation takes place, although, as we shall see in due course, he transmits that position to his sons very early in the dialogue with Socrates. There is also a certain excitement in the dramatic event, namely, the festival of Bendis, which we are told is being celebrated for the first time. There will be banqueting and no doubt drinking, as well as another novelty, a torch race on horseback. In short, the atmosphere is charged with spectacle, novelty, and conviviality. The main part of the conversation will thus as it were be camouflaged by the general carnival spirit, just as the dramatic location in the Piraeus, in the home of a foreigner, indicates a detachment from the authority of Athenian custom and law. To this I add that Aristotle warns us in the *Politics* about the political dangers of harbors, which serve as an entrance of novelty into the city. Finally, as we shall see shortly, Socrates is reluctant to join the gathering in the home of Cephalus but succumbs to the playful threat of force, as well as the enthusiasm of Glaucon. It seems fair to say that the dramatic setting conveys a mixture of frankness and dissimulation, as is appropriate to political conspiracies.[5]

Plato increases the tension of the dramatic scene by selecting interlocutors for Socrates who were involved, either as direct participants or as victims, in the tyranny of the Thirty, led by Critias, who does not appear in the *Republic* but who plays a leading role in the dialogue *Charmides*, in which he is presented as the lover of Charmides, Plato's uncle, and also in the *Critias*, the sequel to the *Timaeus*. He was thus a member of the extended Socratic circle. The democratic resistance to the tyranny was based in the Piraeus, and there was a decisive battle near the temple of Bendis, at which Critias was killed. Lysias and Polemarchus, the two sons of Cephalus, participated in the resistance to the tyranny and were put to death by it, whereas Charmides died as a supporter of the Thirty. The cast of characters evokes the tyranny of the Thirty but does not consist in their supporters alone. On the other hand, Socrates was disliked by the democrats and owed his death in large part to them or their representatives. We should also note that the ten characters (other than Socrates) in the *Republic* are evocative of the authority established by the Thirty tyrants in the Piraeus and known as the Ten. In sum: the dramatic setting of the *Republic* is a peculiar anticipation of the reign of the Thirty tyrants. To the extent that Socrates is the founder and lawgiver of the just city, he replaces Critias, the chief tyrant. It would not be surprising to find a certain similarity between some of his speeches (and deeds) and tyranny. And despite the subsequent allegiance between the house of Cephalus and the antityrannical democratic faction, there is a very strong denunciation of democracy in the *Republic*, to which, as Leo Strauss points out, no one objects.[6]

Let us reflect for a moment on the significance of the dramatis personae in the *Republic*. It is immediately obvious that whether or not all the main speakers were themselves politically active, they were soon to be overwhelmed by political events. Socrates's own condemnation to death was influenced by the conviction of his enemies that he was sympathetic with tyrants. I regard it as extremely unlikely that the members of Socrates's audience would not have been stimulated in their own political ambitions by conversations like the one created for the *Republic*. But these possible influences to one side, the main point is clear: we cannot avoid being caught up in political upheavals even if we lack political ambitions. And if we describe utopian revolutions to a group of political zealots, we can hardly fail to incur some responsibility for their subsequent acts. Socrates does not inoculate his audience against violence by making the leaders of his wished-for city philosophers. In the first place, these rulers are also soldiers and entirely devoted to ideological purification of the most brutal sort. Second, we are all prepared to identify ourselves as philosophers when the occasion demands it. Clever people enjoy the dangers of cleverness. In sum, the unwillingness of the philosopher to participate in political rule is contradicted by political speech, and it is not manifestly just to stir others to dangerous actions while refusing any responsibility for one's own words.

To continue with the main characters in the *Republic*, Glaucon and Adeimantus are Plato's brothers. It is important to note that Socrates goes down to the Piraeus with Glaucon, whereas he encounters Adeimantus in the company of Polemarchus. I quote a short passage from Xenophon's *Memorabilia*: "Glaucon, the son of Ariston, was attempting to become an orator, desiring to take a leading role in the city although he was not yet twenty years old. None of his relatives or friends was capable of restraining him, although he was dragged from the platform [*bēma*] and made a laughing-stock. Socrates took an interest in him for the sake of Plato and Glaucon's son Charmides [this Glaucon is Plato's grandfather, and Charmides is his uncle] and was alone able to check him" (III. 6, 1). In the continuation, Socrates describes Glaucon as possessed by "the desire for fame [*tou eudoksein*]" (III. 6. 16). There is no indication anywhere, so far as I know, that Socrates had a similar interest in Adeimantus. The difference between the two brothers will emerge as we penetrate into the heart of the dialogue. In order to set his ambition in its proper light, I note that it is the erotic and spirited Glaucon who is the interlocutor in most of the passages dealing with radical innovation and the most difficult philosophical topics. I quote an observation by Leo Strauss with respect to the two speeches attacking justice: "Glaucon's speech makes use of poetry; Adeimantus' speech is so to speak nothing but an indictment of poetry."[7]

Next to the two brothers, Thrasymachus is certainly the most important speaker. He was a well-known teacher of rhetoric. Ferrari notes in his glossary to the Griffith translation: "In Plato's *Phaedrus* (267c) he is credited with particular expertise in the manipulation of strong emotions and in mounting and dispelling accusations."[8] Strauss interprets him as a caricature of the angry city but asserts that his anger or spiritedness "is not the core of his being but subordinate to his art."[9] Cephalus is a wealthy resident alien who came to Athens at the invitation of Pericles, presumably because of his knowledge of the weapons industry; in any case, his sons managed a munition factory.[10] Polemarchus is his son and is said in the *Phaedrus* (257b) to have taken up philosophy. I shall have more to say about these characters as we proceed.

To sum up, the *Republic* is in the first instance a narrated dialogue in which Socrates recounts the whole story to an unnamed audience. The atmosphere corresponds to the theme: We are in the midst of novelty, excitement, and revolution. Just as the dramatic setting evokes the atmosphere of the glory of the Athenian democracy prior to the tyranny of the Thirty, so the discussion itself is a kind of treason against the democracy, a treason in which daring and revolutionary proposals, deeply antidemocratic, are made about the founding of the just city. Our first inclination would be to assume that the title signifies the main theme of the work. This may need to be qualified, but it is a plausible hypothesis. If it is correct, then we can also say that the wide variety of topics in the dialogue are all presented from the standpoint of the question of the regime. We are now ready to turn directly to the text.[11]

PART One

I

Cephalus and Polemarchus

1

The theme of descent plays an important role in the dramatic structure of the *Republic*.¹ To note only the obvious, Socrates and Glaucon descend from Athens to the Piraeus at the very beginning of the dialogue; Book Seven begins with a descent from the sunlight into the cave of shadows that represents the subpolitical nature of the human soul; the dialogue closes with an account of the descent of Er into Hades. Each of these descents is described in considerably greater detail than the outstanding example of ascent to the Idea of the Good, or more properly, to its surrogate, the image of the sun. Nevertheless, it makes sense to say that the dialogue as a whole is the story of the attempt by Socrates to rise from the Piraeus to the Idea of the Good, and then to descend via the account of the deterioration of cities and the final discussion of poetry, immortality, and the myth of Er. The first question to be answered is thus why this attempt is not made from Athens proper. Why, in other words, do we need to descend before we can ascend from our initial level?

The descent to the Piraeus takes place at night, as Socrates explains, "both in order to pray to the goddess and at the same time because I wanted to see in what way they would conduct the festival, since this was the first time it was being celebrated" (327a1–3). The goddess in question is Bendis, a Thracian deity who has been accepted into the Athenian religious practice. The date, based upon the evidence of ancient inscriptions, is presumably somewhere between 431 and 411, in the early or middle stages of the Peloponnesian War, with Athens at the peak of its power. But the dialogue takes place in the harbor rather than in the main precincts of the city, and in the home of Cephalus, a resident foreigner rather than a legal citizen. The light is artificial (as it will be later in the allegory of the cave), and the dramatic occasion is more like a carnival than an exhibition of political might. We are detached from the city at its peak and are encouraged to a more spontaneous mode of conversation, one that is more appropriate to the shadows cast by firelight than to the splendor of political and military rhetoric.

Socrates is prepared to observe, but not to participate in, a ceremony dedicated to a foreign goddess. He says that the Thracian performance was no less fitting than that of the Athenians. He does not say that the Thracian god is the equal of the Olympians. We shall see in due course that Socrates sharply criticizes the poetical, and in particular the Homeric, presentation of the Greek gods in the early stages of the dialogue, when he is discussing the musical education of the young guardians (Book Two). He regularly praises only "the" god, who is marked by unchanging goodness and so by freedom from human attributes. Still later, however, in Book Five, when Socrates is legislating the manner in which guardians who have died in defense of the city must be buried and commemorated, the Greekness of the city is emphasized, and the god is identified as Apollo. Let us say for the moment that Socrates's attitude toward the gods is flexible.

The descent is not only from the city to the harbor and from daylight to firelight, it also brings philosophy into a zone of freedom, privacy, and openness to what is foreign. The indefinite temporal reference to "yesterday" reminds us that the Athens of which Plato writes has disappeared. "Once upon a time" there was a glorious city called Athens and a remarkable man called Socrates. The glory of Athens has dissolved, and we are left with our memories. The task of the philosopher is now to recollect not so much the actual history of Athens as the inner truth of that city, and what it implies with respect to political possibility. In other words, the reader of the *Republic* has two tasks: to bear witness to the revolutionary proposal that politics be placed in the charge of philosophers, and to understand the sense in which the proposal has succeeded as well as the sense in which it has failed.

The personality of Glaucon is an essential clue to the answers to these two questions. To state the main point at the outset, Glaucon's ambition is required to encourage Socrates to articulate the "ideology" of the revolution. As is appropriate to the nature of a soldier, Glaucon is described by Socrates as "always most manly" (II. 357a2), which Griffith translates rather weakly as "extremely determined . . . in everything he does." In addition, much is made of his erotic nature (II. 368a2–3; III. 403a4–5; V. 468b9–12; V. 474c8ff. and esp. d4 and passim). Finally, Glaucon urges Socrates to take up dangerous questions when the latter is reluctant to do so (see III. 414c8, V. 451b2, and VI. 506d2 for examples).[2] There is one other important point to make in this connection. When Socrates wishes to return home, despite the strong request by Polemarchus to remain in the Piraeus, it is Glaucon who officially overrules Socrates's reticence (I. 328b2–3). Erotic and brave guardians are required during the founding of the city and not merely as ingredients within it. Socrates is not delivering a lecture on political theory to a group of scholarly specialists. Regardless of whether he believes that the city is possible, it cannot be built without eros as well as *thumos* (spiritedness). To give only a single example, Glaucon will have to oversee the rustication of everyone over the age of ten, a step described in Book Eight as essential to the founding of the city. But more generally, he encourages the philosopher to engage in the process of preparing for the revolution, which could not be carried out by theoretical persons alone.[3]

In sum, there are two different aspects to the contribution of Glaucon. He is the external stimulus that moves Socrates to engage in the founding of the beautiful city, and he represents some of the essential characteristics of the guardian class within the city itself. Philosophers cannot become kings without lieutenants like Glaucon. I do not believe that Adeimantus is a soldier so much as a potential high-ranking official, such as the state censor of poetry and the fine arts. As we shall see later in connection with judges and physicians, the division of the guardian class into rulers and soldiers is not complete.

2

Polemarchus sends his slave boy to grab Socrates's cloak from behind and to convey his order that Socrates and Glaucon wait; "Polemarchus" means "warlord" in Greek. At a pivotal point in the dialogue, Polemarchus will grab the cloak of Adeimantus from behind. The two will conspire to force Socrates to discuss at length the community of women and children, upon which the possibility of the just city depends (V. 449b1–c5). The importance of Polemarchus is twofold. First, he shows the connection between justice and compulsion. Second, as the heir of Cephalus, he resuscitates the argument that his father has bequeathed to him. This will become clear as we proceed. Meanwhile, we note that what is being offered here is pleasure; there is no question initially of so momentous a conversation as the one to come. When Socrates asks if Polemarchus and his companions may not be persuaded to release Glaucon and himself, Polemarchus replies: "How could you persuade us if we don't listen?" (327c12). Glaucon agrees that there is no way to persuade those who don't listen. He is already disposed to remain, and when he is told of the impending banquet and the novel torch race on horseback, as well as the prospect for conversation with many young men, Glaucon says, "It seems to be necessary that we stay" (328b2). Glaucon himself is about to be persuaded to converse with Socrates rather than with young men, as a result of which he gets neither a banquet nor the chance to see the new torch race.

The atmosphere in the Piraeus is a mixture of convention and novelty. Socrates and his companions withdraw from this atmosphere to the privacy of the house of Cephalus. It would be tempting to describe this transition as yet another descent into pure convention. And yet, the conversation cannot take place in the streets or public squares, which are crowded with revelers and sightseers. On the other hand, if Cephalus had remained present for the entire evening, the conversation as we have it could not have taken place. Cephalus provides shelter for a conversation in which he cannot participate, and which he bequeaths to his sons. They are, so to speak, sons of the bourgeoisie who can be persuaded to consider alternatives to the society that nurtured them. Their education, family connections, and leisure make them potential revolutionaries.

The scene has now been set for the first step in the revolution in speech: the examination of Cephalus. It is a striking feature of the dialogue that the investigation of justice begins with a consideration of old age and the approach of death, or in other words with the imminent departure of the individual soul from political existence. One of the crucial assumptions underlying the construction of the just city in the *Republic* is that justice is the same in the individual soul and the city. The city, we shall be told, is the soul writ large, and therefore justice is easier to see in its political than in its private manifestation. I have already mentioned the lack of an analogy between the epithumetic part of the soul and the class of workers, each of whom possesses a tripartite soul. We shall have further occasion to question the soundness of this analogy between the city and the soul. Even though the analogy does not hold good, it is easy to see that we could not recognize justice in the city unless we had first discerned it in the soul.[4] It may be, of course, that justice is more fully visible in the city than in the soul. But that would not affect the priority of the soul. It is the soul's desire for justice that leads to the founding of the city. To desire justice, after all, is to possess a pretheoretical awareness of what it is, even if one cannot furnish a fully articulate definition. It makes no sense to say that the city desires justice and therefore produces the individual person. The dramatic setting of the *Republic* exhibits this simple priority. The pursuit of justice begins with an interrogation of a private person, one who is not even a citizen of Athens but a resident alien. And it focuses on the most personal aspects of human existence: sexuality and death.

The same general point is illustrated by Aristotle when he makes the *Nicomachean Ethics* prior to the work on *Politics*. It should also be noticed that Aristotle distinguishes between the virtue of the gentleman on the one hand and that of the citizen or statesman on the other.[5] In the *Republic*, Plato makes no such distinction; instead, the "vulgar" virtue of the nonphilosopher is contrasted with the epistemic virtue of the philosopher (VI. 500d4–9, VII. 518d9–e3). This contrast is refined by Aristotle into the distinction between theoretical and practical virtue. But this difference between the two thinkers, important as it is in its own right, does not alter the fact that neither of them affirms the priority of the city to the individual person in the investigation of justice. It is true that we cannot live a fully human and so just life except in a city, or that the city completes private life just as art completes nature. But this is to say that the city is for the sake of the individual citizen, and, more precisely, for the sake of the citizen's capacity to live a happy life. The question we are about to study is whether the just or the unjust life is happier. Our main concern is thus with the condition of the individual soul, and the entire treatment of politics is introduced for the sake of making the inquiry easier to carry out. The unsatisfactoriness of this procedure will become evident in the difficulty faced by Socrates when he is asked whether the guardians of the just city are happy. To anticipate, his answer will be that we are concerned with the happiness of the city, not of some part of its citizenry. But this goes directly counter to the emphasis throughout upon individual happiness.

Our examination proper of the good life begins with the question of a good death. It should, however, be noted that Cephalus does not provide us with the most profound insight into the relation between justice and death. He is not a tragic hero but a kind of pagan Everyman. Justice is his narcotic; it serves to numb the transition from life to death. In slightly different terms, Cephalus is unsuited, by age and character, to play a role in political revolution. He has often been taken as a decent representative of conventional morality who is not up to the dangerous perturbations of philosophical investigation. Up to a point, I think that this is correct. But it should be added that Cephalus is not necessarily wrong to avoid philosophical reflection upon the comforts of tradition. The principle that motivates him will be found once more in the political rhetoric of the just city with respect to death and immortality. On this set of topics, the beliefs to be inculcated into the guardians are simply a development of those that govern Cephalus's last days. For this reason, the transition from the man of convention to the philosopher is not simply an ascent but also a circle.

So much by way of anticipation. Let us now turn to the details of the conversation with Cephalus.⁶ Neither he nor his sons are members of the Socratic circle. The presence of the philosopher in Cephalus's home is unusual, like the torch race by horseback (328b9, c6). Socrates is of course familiar with the sons of Cephalus, but tonight it will be necessary for him to negotiate their detachment from the father, who, as just noted, represents convention but also the preparation for death, not revolution. As a resident alien, Cephalus is an epiphenomenon of Athenian splendor. And as an old man, his interest lies fundamentally with himself and his family, which is an extension of himself. Cephalus is crowned with a wreath and has just performed a sacrifice. He looks quite old to Socrates, who has not seen him in some time. Cephalus alludes to his age almost immediately. He is too old to make the trip to Athens easily, and Socrates is rarely in the Piraeus. Cephalus then adds another note of compulsion to go with the restraint imposed upon Socrates by his son. Socrates must come more often. "I want you to know that as the other pleasures, those connected with the body, wither away, the desires and pleasures of speech are augmented" (328d2–4).

Cephalus is primarily interested in pleasure, and were he younger, he would prefer the pleasures of the body to those of the soul. Temperance has been forced upon him by the infirmities of age, but he is able to transform this disability into an occasion for pleasure rather than pain. Cephalus continues: "Don't do otherwise, but associate with these young men and come hither to us as to friends and your own family" (328d4–6). Friendship and family are the two main components of private life. Cephalus speaks as if he is attempting to assimilate Socrates into his own family and is using the young men as bait to tempt Socrates to visit him more frequently. On second thought, this congeniality can hardly be more than a pretended interest in the sort of conversation for which Socrates is famous. What is probably of greater importance to Cephalus is that if Socrates were to come more often to visit him, this would be an added incentive to his sons and their friends to spend time in their father's company. The young are interested in a conversation quite different from the kind that Cephalus would prefer. In his reply, however, Socrates ignores the young men and says, "I delight in talking to the very old" (328d7; cf. the reference to pleasure at e4). He means by this those who, because of their extreme age, are about to step over the threshold from life to death. They are a long way further ahead on a road that we too will probably have to travel. Socrates asks whether the journey to death is rough or smooth. "Is it a difficult time of life? How do you find it?" (328e6–7).

In pressing home Cephalus's nearness to death, Socrates runs the risk of discomfiting his host. The old man replies with an oath: "By Zeus!" This is the first oath in the dialogue; we normally swear when we are excited or upset. Cephalus's reply suggests the enthusiasm of the religious convert or, perhaps even better, of someone who is pleased with his own gracious response to enforced bodily temperance (328d7–329a1). He follows his oath with an account of the conversations of old men about the pains of extreme age. Most of them complain about the lost pleasures of youth, in particular, sex, drinking, and feasting. Others complain that the old are mistreated by their relatives. Cephalus, however, denies that his aged friends have correctly identified the roughness of old age. It is caused not by the loss of physical vigor but by the *tropos* (way or character) of the man (329d3). Let us look at this more closely.

According to Cephalus, if old age were to blame for the difficulties just cited, then he and all those who have reached his age would be making the same complaints. But he has met others who do not, most notably the dramatist Sophocles. This suggests that the number of old men with temperate characters is considerably smaller than the number of those who succumb to the deprivations of extreme age with lamentations of lost pleasure (note *hoi pleistoi* at 329a4). Cephalus once asked Sophocles if he were still capable of sexual intercourse with a woman. Sophocles replied: "Hush, man [*anthrōpe*]! Most joyfully did I escape it, as though I had run away from a raging and savage master" (329c1–4; cf. d1: "many mad masters"). This is the first of a number of negative remarks in the dialogue about eros, which conclude as they begin, namely, by identifying eros as a tyrant. The choice of Sophocles to introduce the topic is interesting, since his dramas have canonized the private and public destructiveness of the violation of sexual taboos. In his regulations on sex in the just city, Socrates will attempt to exclude incest between parent and child, but not between brother and sister. More generally, the abolishment of the family violates traditional Greek views on the most personal of all relations.

There is thus a disagreement between Socrates and Sophocles, or let us say between philosophy and poetry, on the nature of the sacred. Equally striking is Socrates's association of eros with philosophy in a way that is very similar to the argument in the *Symposium* and *Phaedrus*, which contain the fullest statement of the abstraction from the body and an ascent to the love of pure forms. One could say that in these two dialogues, the private is replaced by the universal, but certainly not by the public life of politics. The *Republic*, on the other hand, subordinates the private philosophical eros, and its culmination in the universal, to the need for a philosopher-king. This adds to the strangeness of the *Republic*, and to the confusion stemming from the simultaneous praise and denunciation of eros. It is not simply that the bodily eros is contrasted unfavorably with the eros of the soul. Even further, the first is necessary to the virility of the city even though it poses the greatest threat to its survival, whereas the second seems to be placed in the service of the city precisely because it points beyond it.

According to Cephalus, it is not the debilitated body but a defective character that makes the loss of sex, drinking, and feasting so hard to bear. "If one is well-ordered and calm, even old age is only moderately painful." Otherwise life is hard for the young as well as the old (329d3–6). Cephalus does not use the word, but we can take this speech to be an endorsement of temperance (*sōphrosunē*). Even though justice is somehow the main theme of the dialogue, temperance is the first of the four cardinal virtues to be praised. It is the one virtue that Cephalus shares with the guardians of the just city. Later we shall see that it is difficult to distinguish justice from temperance. Meanwhile, Socrates enjoys the remarks of Cephalus and wishes to stimulate him to say more. He thus introduces an objection: many will say that it is not character but money that allows one to bear the burdens of old age. Cephalus agrees that they have a point, but he defends his view with a quotation from Themistocles. A resident of Seriphos abuses Themistocles by attributing his fame to the city of Athens rather than to his own excellences. Themistocles replies: "If I had been a Seriphean, I would not be famous, but neither would you if you had been an Athenian" (330a1–3). In other words, money is necessary, but it is useful only to the person with a temperate character. Cephalus explains: Those who are not wealthy and have a bad character will bear old age with difficulty. On the other hand, a good character overcomes poverty and makes old age bearable, but "not altogether easy." Finally, the wealthy man with the wrong character will be altogether miserable (329d7–330a6). The unstated premise is that there are decent men with money who will bear old age well. Cephalus does not add in their case that even with money, old age is not altogether easy. He is determined to present his own situation as favorably as possible.

Instead of pursuing the general topic of wealth, Socrates somewhat abruptly asks whether Cephalus has inherited most of his fortune or earned it (330a7–8). This is a bit rude, as was Socrates's remark about the proximity of Cephalus to death. But the latter takes no offense; he clearly derives pleasure from talking about himself, thereby showing how well he handles the burdens of extreme age. Cephalus is vain, but he may also be whistling in the dark, that is, trying to buttress his own morale by exhibiting himself as the model of good character. The closeness of vanity to tyranny is suggested by small details in the opening scene. See for example the statement at 328c6ff.: If I were younger, *we* would go more often to the city to visit you, and then it would not be necessary for you to come here. Cephalus presumably keeps a tight rein on his sons, a rein of money. Polemarchus applies a different rein to Socrates when he orders him to stay in the Piraeus, but the general character trait is the same in both members of the family.

The topic of moneymaking is closely connected to that of sexual pleasure. Later in the discussion, Socrates will speak of the desires of the body in two main ways, first, with respect to sex and, second, as the faculty devoted to moneymaking. Thus the workers in the just city are collectively known as the moneymaking class; they play no part in the governing of the city. The genuine citizens and rulers do not engage in moneymaking. Sexual desire, on the other hand, is very noticeably present among the guardians and has to be catered to in one way and regulated in another. The link between sex and money is in part obvious, since possession of wealth makes sensual gratification much easier. To bring out the deeper link, consider Cephalus's financial status. He has in effect earned little or nothing and falls between his grandfather and his father in net worth. The grandfather inherited about as much as Cephalus now possesses, and he multiplied it many times. Cephalus's father, on the other hand, spent most of the surplus and left him with a little less than he has now. So Cephalus maintained his inheritance but did not dramatically increase it; he had enough to live a life of pleasure without dissipating the entire estate. Socrates says that he raised the question because Cephalus did not seem to him to be excessively fond of money. In other words, Cephalus is a temperate hedonist. People who make money, says Socrates, are twice as attached to it as are those who inherit it. "For just as poets are fond of their poems and fathers of their sons, so too people who make money take it very seriously as their own product as well as for the sake of their use, as do the others" (330c3–4).

Underlying this argument is the metaphor of making money and poems as a kind of sexual reproduction. People love most what they produce as an extension of themselves. This has important political consequences. First, poetry, together with its near relatives, myth and rhetoric, is closely associated with patriotism. One thinks of national epics, anthems, and the rhetorical expression we give to our strong feeling for our own neighborhood, our local sports heroes, and so on. It would be absurd to celebrate one's country in mathematical equations. Second, patriotism, as the word indicates ("fatherland" — the same general point applies to "motherland") is connected to sexual reproduction, at first symbolically (sprung from the womb of one's native soil) and then literally (love of the ancestors, one's immediate family, one's wife and children). The root of eros is self-reproduction and self-extension in the products of one's work, whether physical or mental. This is why Socrates, who wishes to replace love of one's own by love of the good, will criticize, censor, and even expel poetry from his new city. On the other hand, as I have already emphasized, he will identify the love of the truth, and in particular of the Platonic Ideas, with an eros that is not a love of oneself and (in the *Republic* at least) does not culminate in the production of children of the soul.

Self-love is inseparable from the desire for immortality. We want to live on because death quenches that which we love most: ourselves. Socrates replaces personal immortality, and so self-love, with love of the Ideas, in particular (in the *Republic*) the Idea of the Good. In politics, this is represented by the wished-for city, in which the genuine citizens (philosopher-kings and soldier-guardians) have everything in common. This community takes the political form of the suppression of private property; even women and children are in common. It is radically expanded in the philosophical or theoretical domain to transform our love of our beliefs into the desire for knowledge of the whole. My beliefs are mine; they may or may not be yours. But knowledge and the truth are the same for everyone who is capable of acquiring them. Philosophers have even their thoughts in common to the extent that they gaze upon the Ideas. This is, incidentally, the main reason why mathematics is so important a part of the education of the guardian and kingly class. Mathematics turns us away from the world of the body and so of particularity and self-love. As we shall see, mathematics is not the vision of the Ideas but a pedagogical propaedutic to that vision, which is associated with what Socrates calls "dialectic." How useful this is to politics is another question.

3

Once Cephalus's moderation as a moneymaker has been established, Socrates asks: "What do you suppose to be the greatest good that you have enjoyed through the possession of much money?" (330d1–3). Whereas there is frequent mention of badness or bad things in the first part of the discussion with Cephalus (e.g., "evils" [*kakōn*] appears at 329b2), this is the first appearance in the dialogue of the word *good* (*agathon*): 330d2). It is of course true that one cannot discuss evil, badness, harshness, madness, and tyranny without tacitly referring to their opposites as good things. Nevertheless, it is striking that there is no explicit reference to the good until now. In other words, its introduction marks a transition in the conversation with Cephalus. Hitherto we took it for granted that temperance and money were good things. But this is too vague. There are many goods associated with wealth. Which is the best? To say this in another way, Socrates often argues that none of the things we praise, such as wealth, health, and even wisdom, is good in itself but must be good for us who desire them.[7] Goodness in this sense is usually understood to mean benefit or utility. We shall see the connection between goodness and utility later.

Cephalus says that his response to this question may be controversial. Closeness to the moment of death brings with it fears that the myths about Hades may be correct, namely, that one is punished there for injustices committed in this life. This is the first appearance of words that express justice in any form (330d8: *adikēsanta*: injustice is mentioned before justice). Apparently Cephalus did not worry about injustice before he reached extreme old age; conversely, he must not have been excessively concerned with justice. I do not mean to suggest that Cephalus is unusually unjust; he is a conventional man and no doubt believes that obedience to the law is the same as justice. On the other hand, he must have spent a fair amount of money, presumably on one form of pleasure or another, since his estate is not much larger than when he inherited it. It would be wrong to describe Cephalus as a libertine, but neither is he truly temperate. Let us say that he is a moderate hedonist who spends within his means. But he cannot have been without faults, since he fears that he has injustices to correct before he dies.

Cephalus implies that temperance is useful for prolonging pleasure and mitigating pain, but the end is pleasure, not temperance. Justice is also useful for removing the pain of punishment after death or, more modestly, for mitigating our fear of punishment after death while we are still alive. In short, justice, like temperance, is valued for the pleasures it brings. And Cephalus is concerned with injustices to his fellow citizens, not in their political guise but as private persons. After emphasizing the connection between justice and sweetness of life with a quotation from Pindar, Cephalus goes on to say: "For I hold the possession of money to be most important, not for every man, but for him who is decent and orderly" (331a11–b1). Cephalus's interpretation of decency and order is interesting; money is of greatest use in making amends for unwilling deceptions and lies in this life. One can discharge these debts without owing anything to a god (a sacrifice) or a mortal (a debt) and thus can die without being terrified of punishment to come. That is, one will have "pleasant and good hope" (331a2). I note that, even in this vulgar sense, decency and orderliness have a connection to temperance.

If our fraudulent acts and lies were intended, then we must be unjust. Cephalus does not mention whether this injustice can be erased through the judicious use of money. And presumably the genuinely temperate person would not have committed these injustices, although this point is not entirely evident. On balance, one would have to say that where there is smoke, there is probably fire. Cephalus would not fear involuntary deceptions or lies if he had behaved with full decency and orderliness. But the main point, again, is that justice, like temperance, is for the sake of pleasure. And we remain within the horizon of the private life; certainly nothing that has been said thus far could lead us to suspect that the conversation is shortly going to expand into the construction of a just city. But we are a step closer to this expansion, thanks to the introduction of justice. Temperance is addressed primarily to oneself, whereas justice so to speak is an extension of temperance to others.

Socrates now generalizes Cephalus's statement by asking whether it is true that justice is simply telling the truth and paying one's debts, or whether it is sometimes the case that this behavior is unjust. His example is that of someone who borrows a weapon from a person of sound mind but who refuses to return it to the same man if he has become mad; nor would it seem to be just to tell the whole truth to a madman (331c1–d1). I note first a certain ambiguity in this example. Justice may well be paying one's debts and speaking the truth, but we may not owe the return of property or the truth to a madman. For example, physicians may withhold part of the truth from their patients for their own good. Still more generally, some version of Socrates's objection could be applied, I suspect, to any plausible definition of justice. To anticipate, Socrates is going to define justice as "minding one's own business" ("doing one's own thing": *ta heautou prattein*). But what is one's business? Does this not vary from context to context?

Strictly speaking, we would need a wise man to tell us what is our business in each circumstance of life, a point that is made by the Eleatic Stranger in the *Statesman* (295a10–b5). Since this is impossible, we require laws; but these in turn must be subject to equity, and in fact, the legal process is a branch of the hermeneutics of *Dasein*, as Heidegger calls it. There is, then, reason to doubt whether justice can be satisfactorily defined in a single formula. But Polemarchus defends the definition that has been associated with his father by Socrates. Cephalus supported his conception of justice with a quotation from Pindar; Polemarchus follows with a passage from a poem by Simonides (331d4–5). There will be a good deal of citation from the poets in this dialogue, despite the notorious criticism of poetry that leads finally to the expulsion of mimetic poets from the just city. It would be distinctly odd to cite mathematicians or dialecticians on justice and goodness. Poets are the acknowledged experts on the states of the individual human soul. Philosophy "corrects" the poetic account, not because it is mistaken but because poets do not seek to change human behavior but rather seek to celebrate and understand it as it is.

Cephalus bequeaths the argument to his son, since he himself must now attend to the sacrifices. The symbolism is obvious; at this point, the conversation leaves the dimension of social conventions and turns to argument. At 331e1 Socrates refers to Polemarchus as "the heir to the *logos*." This word could mean "conversation" but is normally reserved for more disciplined discourse. Cephalus laughs and exits, in a way reminiscent of Pontius Pilate. Laughter and *logos* are normally unrelated. One cannot demonstrate or refute by laughing, which is rather a type of rhetorical attack, designed to make us ashamed to hold a view that the opponent rejects. Polemarchus is much more serious than his father, and he does not laugh.

Let us sum up. The definition of justice attributed to Cephalus is: speak the truth and pay your debts. Polemarchus supports his father's definition by citing his own "noble" (or "beautiful") version of it, namely, that justice is to give to each man what is owed (331e3–4). Apparently Polemarchus senses a certain crudeness in Cephalus's version.[8] In addition, "nobly" is not the same as "truly," and in fact, Polemarchus omits "not lying," or, as Socrates rephrases it, "telling the truth," from the Cephalus definition. This is the first hint in the dialogue that lying may not be incompatible with justice.

Socrates repeats the objection he made to Cephalus about returning property to a madman who will make harmful use of it. This irritates Polemarchus, who swears "By Zeus" (332a9), just as his father did at 329a1 in beginning his statement on old age and intemperance. Polemarchus's interpretation of Simonides is as follows: we owe good to our friends and bad (*kakon*) to our enemies (332a7–b8). Perhaps Polemarchus assumes that lies are something bad and thus owed to enemies. This point will assume considerable importance somewhat later in the dialogue. Meanwhile, Socrates unfolds a complicated argument in order to show that Simonides spoke in a riddle, as poets do (332b9). Note that Socrates also swears at c5 in the name of Zeus. The riddle to be examined is the claim that it is just to give the fitting or what is owed to each person, that is, good to our friends and bad to our enemies.

Socrates begins with two examples, medicine and cooking. The first owes drugs, food, and drink to the body, whereas cooking owes seasoning to cooked food (which contains meat or fish: 332c5–d1). The word for cooked food (*opson*) will assume great importance in the actual construction of the city in Book Two. There is something very odd about these examples. An art is not obligated to do anything. What one can say is that if it is a genuine art, that is, if it is practiced correctly, then it does so-and-so and does not do thus-and-such. This behavior is "correct" in the sense that to practice the art is simply to engage in that behavior. The behavior becomes just or unjust depending upon how or for what purpose it is practiced by the artist, for example the physician. One might say that the physician owes the patient good treatment but not that medicine owes the body drugs. But why does the physician owe the patient good treatment? Not because of anything intrinsic to the art of medicine but because of an agreement with the patient. For example, the physician is charging a fee for his services.

There are two ambiguous elements in the present example. First, Socrates's argument about the madman exhibits the previously noted point that an act is good if and only if it has good consequences, certainly not if the consequences are bad. The correct performance of the art, for example in treating a patient, is not "good" in the sense that justice is good. "Good consequences" are those that are beneficial rather than harmful. Nor can one leave it at this, since some benefits accrue to unjust acts, such as money to a bank robber. The kind of benefits at issue must be those that are just. We must therefore understand what we mean by "justice" *before* we attempt to define it. This is a good example of what Socrates means by knowledge as recollection.

Second, justice is not a transaction between an art and its material, such as medicine and the body, but between human beings. There are two kinds of justice, corresponding to public and private transactions. One of the most difficult questions about justice is whether political justice is the basis for private justice or vice versa. I have already suggested the following simple consideration. It is the need of the person for justice that leads to the foundation of the city. Once the city comes into existence, it plays a decisive role in modifying the private conception of justice. But it never entirely replaces it. In the last analysis, we judge the justice of laws and customs on the basis of our own perception of the fair or equitable. This is much more fundamental than the sense of private justice that obtains in fulfilling a professional contract, such as the one in which a physician accepts a fee for the attempt to cure a patient of a disease.

In this light, let us consider the apparently absurd example of the cook who owes sauce to the meat. This differs from the example of medicine in the following important way. At a strictly technical level, medical treatment is intimately connected with the pursuit of health by the nature of the two items, medicine and the body. But there is no natural reason for putting sauce on meat, since we can eat without sauce, and we would probably be better off if we did so. In fact, Socrates's first version of the just city omits not only sauce or relish from cooking but meat as well. We put sauce on meat as a matter of convention, not nature. One might object that meat with sauce tastes better than meat without it, but this raises the question of necessary or healthy conventions and those that are derived from excessive sophistication or decadence. Otherwise put, it raises the question of good and bad pleasures. In particular, it raises the question whether the city without meat or sauce is not better because closer to nature than the luxurious city that sanctions seasoning and cooked flesh. By not raising these questions, Socrates remains at the level of Cephalus in his opening analysis of Polemarchus's definition of justice.

The second stage of the argument with Polemarchus starts from the thesis that justice is doing good to friends and harm to enemies. Socrates now varies his original question. Previously he established that the art of medicine is best able to give what is owed to the body. This step did not directly invoke justice but referred instead to technical competence. The patient is not as such the physician's friend, any more than sauce is the friend of meat. In the second step of the argument, the physician is identified as the one who is best able to do good to sick friends and bad to enemies. This is no longer simply a technical question, even though, or rather precisely because, the physician is also best able to do harm to his sick friends. This might be technical incompetence, but it could also be injustice. The crucial addition to the examples is that of friendship and enmity. This is not the same as technical responsibility. And to say the least, it is much more difficult to know what we owe to our friends and enemies than it is for the technician to know what is owed to the things or persons upon which the art is applied. As a technician, the physician must use the best knowledge of his art that is available to him, regardless of whether he likes or dislikes the patient, or even whether he is treating a complete stranger (332d3–e5).

I repeat the sequence: First, technical obligation; second, the obligation of justice to do good to friends and harm to enemies. Now the third step: Socrates asks for the circumstances under which physicians, pilots, and just men are useful. Once again we are at the margin of utilitarianism. Utility is clearly an essential ingredient of the good or the just. No sane person would argue that the good is harmful or for that matter that it is neither beneficial nor harmful. The difficult question, of course, is what we mean by "beneficial" and "harmful," and this rests upon some awareness of goodness and justice.

All three examples (the physician, the pilot, the just man) are concerned with preserving the lives of one's friends, more specifically, with the care of the body. The physician is useless when no one is sick, and the pilot is useless when one is not on a sea voyage. In other words, the utility of these arts depends upon their enactment. The case of justice is at least partly different; the just man is useful in war and peace, as are farming and shoemaking (332e6–333a13). So it seems that we can classify the arts into two categories: those that are useful in danger but not in safety, and those that are useful in both. I am not going to analyze this minutely but shall say only that medicine and piloting are useful even when not curing or sailing; for example, physicians must teach medicine, and pilots must instruct novices in the art of navigation.

The least we can say is that for Polemarchus the tacit equation of goodness and utility is not something that requires a comment. No doubt he would agree with my previous remark that the good, whatever else it is, must be beneficial; it makes no sense to say that we are harmed or for that matter unaffected by the good. In times of peace, justice is useful with respect to contracts (*sumbolaia*), for which term Socrates substitutes *koinōnēma* (see Bloom's note to this term in his edition), which brings out the communal basis of contracts (333a12–14). Socrates begins, as usual, with technical utility. When two people agree to play draughts, who is more useful in setting up the pieces on the board, the just man or the skilled player? Polemarchus admits that it is the latter. I note first that this agreement to play draughts is not really a contract or a communal partnership. We don't sign contracts to play games unless we are professionals. But let that pass. Socrates will put pressure on Polemarchus by restricting the utility of justice, and he does so by defining "useful" as a consequence of technical knowledge. Furthermore, the knowledge is specific: playing draughts, house building, playing the harp. With these examples, Socrates maneuvers Polemarchus into giving a comparable specific dimension in which justice is useful. He says that justice is useful in money matters, but it is easy for Socrates to construct examples in which, once again, we require technical expertise rather than justice, for example, when buying a horse. Polemarchus reluctantly agrees, but he has been tricked. Knowledge of horses is useful for making one's selection and setting the price, but justice is required for the enforcement of the contract. Experts on horses may also be unjust, just like physicians in the previous set of examples. Polemarchus should have realized that technical knowledge is not the same as justice (333a12–c4).

Justice seems to be useful when money is not being used but is being kept under deposit. Socrates applies the same reasoning to another set of examples and forces Polemarchus to agree that justice is useful only for guarding things that are not being used. He then adds: justice could not be a very serious thing if it is useful only for useless things. This is false reasoning, and it is not compatible with the conclusion at 332e6–333a14 that justice is useful at all times, for example in war as well as peace. Certainly it is also useful when the various *technai* are not being employed. Even accepting the premise that underlies this stage of the argument, it is essential to the subsequent use of things that they be safely preserved while not being used. Guardianship is thus an intrinsic component of justice; hence the need for the police department, armies, and the guardian class in the beautiful city (333c5–e5).

Socrates now makes use of an earlier point about technical knowledge. He who possesses it can use it to benefit or to harm. The correct inference here would be that justice is not technical knowledge but the decision to use it for good rather than for bad reasons. One of his examples requires a comment.

The good guardian of an army is he who can also steal the enemy's plans; if therefore the just man is clever at guarding money, he will also be clever at stealing it. Again, the correct inference would be that justice is the decision not to steal money. As to stealing the enemy's plans, the governing hypothesis is that justice is doing good to one's friends and harm to one's enemies. It is therefore not unjust to steal the plans in question (333e6–334a9).

It should be clear by now that Socrates is playing with Polemarchus. Is he treating him unjustly? Certainly he is using bad logic to confuse the young man, but this confusion is presumably for his own good, since it will open him up to the subsequent discussion. This presumption, however, rests in turn upon the premise that Polemarchus could not be persuaded to surrender his defective view of justice by sound reasoning. It also introduces the possibility that Polemarchus's definition is not defective, and so could not be refuted by sound reasoning. Both these possibilities will play a central role throughout the dialogue. To anticipate, they arise from the question why Socrates proceeds for the most part with defective arguments.

Socrates continues to play with Polemarchus by attributing falsely to him the view that "justice is a kind of stealing for the benefit of one's friends and the harm of one's enemies," a thesis that he also attributes to Simonides and Homer (334a10–b6). In fact, all that Polemarchus has admitted is that justice is useful for guarding things that are not being used, and that he who possesses technical knowledge can use it to benefit or to harm friends or enemies. As Socrates admits, the just man will benefit friends and harm only his enemies. It is therefore a gross exaggeration to refer on this basis to the just man as a thief. Polemarchus is actually much closer to the standard view of justice than Socrates is to refuting him. It is Socrates who introduces the technical examples, not Polemarchus, who is struggling to express the notion of justice as the ends to which we apply our technical knowledge. No one could deny that it is just to benefit one's friends (although there may be some ambiguous particular cases concerning what is truly beneficial). The serious question is whether it is also just to harm one's enemies. We shall see later whether Socrates does not himself adhere to Polemarchus's definition when he arrives at his own definition of justice as "minding one's own business." Is it not precisely my business to benefit my friends and harm my enemies? To take only one example, when Socrates argues that we must expel gifted mimetic poets and send them to the neighboring city, is he not harming or attempting to harm those who are at least potential enemies?

Socrates is not yet finished with poor Polemarchus, who no longer knows what he means and swears to Zeus in his perplexity (334b7). But he holds on to his definition of justice, despite the attack to which Socrates has subjected it. The next step in the attack is to point out that we are sometimes mistaken about the identity of our friends and enemies. Therefore, we may benefit our enemies and harm our friends. Socrates suggests that this shows a defect in Polemarchus's definition. But this does not seem to be right. It is one thing to accept Polemarchus's definition and another to have correctly identified one's friends and enemies. One could say that it is impossible to be just if one does not know this, and furthermore, since we cannot know it in each case, the city is forced to make laws that define who are our political friends and enemies. This passage raises yet another problem. Is justice the actual doing of good to our friends and the like or is it the *intention* to act in this way? It is usually said that there is no conception of a good will in Plato. I reserve judgment and suggest that we keep our eyes open for such a distinction (334b7–d8).

After some further discussion, Polemarchus asks to change his original definition by expanding on the difference between friends and enemies. A man who seems to be, and is, *chrēston* is a friend, whereas the one who seems to be, but is not, *chrēston* is not a friend; and so too with the enemy. The Greek word means "useful" but can also mean "good" (334e10–335a2). Socrates then proceeds to the last step in his interrogation of Polemarchus. He holds that to harm dogs and horses is to make them worse with respect to the particular excellence of being a dog or a horse. Polemarchus agrees to the further conclusion that if a man is harmed, he becomes worse with respect to the excellence of being human. Since justice is human excellence, to harm someone is to make him more unjust. Socrates uses the word *aretē* here, which can mean moral virtue or some natural excellence (335b8–d2). Also, Socrates assumes without argument that justice is human excellence. But there is a more obvious difficulty. In time of war or when treating criminals, it is often necessary to harm human beings. If Socrates's inference were to be accepted, we would all be pacifists and the entire judicial system would be radically changed. In fact, Socrates argues elsewhere that punishment makes criminals worse rather than better. Later in the conversation he will allow for the execution of hardened criminals. But what are we to do in time of war with enemy troops who are threatening to slaughter our families and fellow citizens?

Socrates has now led Polemarchus to agree that the just man never harms anyone, friend or enemy. He attributes the contrary view to various persons, none of whom can be rightly said to be wise (335d11–336a8). Socrates and Polemarchus are now partners in the war against the thesis that justice is doing harm to one's enemies; but nothing has been said to repudiate the first part of the definition, namely, that justice is doing good to one's friends. The question is still open whether one owes nothing to one's enemies or ought to do good to them as well.

Thrasymachus is straining at the leash, but before we allow him to speak, let us recapitulate the discussion with Polemarchus. The definition of justice as doing good to one's friends and harm to one's enemies is rejected by Socrates on the following grounds. First, the just man is useless except with useless things, that is, things that are not being used. But this is nonsense, because guarding is not useless, as will become evident from the later discussion of the guardian class. Furthermore, justice is not simply guarding but also the act of returning what belongs to someone else. If we add the qualification that the return is just only when the original owner is of sound mind and character, it must be added that we mean by "friend" someone who is of sound mind and character. When friends go mad, our relation to them changes, and justice becomes medicinal. A madman is not as such our friend. Third, when we buy something, it is the expert who benefits us, not the just man. This is true if and only if the expert gives us his genuine or correct opinion, and it is this honesty that constitutes justice, not the technical opinion itself. Fourth, whoever is clever at guarding is also clever at stealing, so the just man is a thief. But again, justice is precisely the decision not to use one's expertise in order to steal. Physicians would make excellent murderers, but that does not mean that murder is part of medicine. Finally, people become worse in their defining virtue when they are harmed. This may or may not be true, but even if it is, what do we do in time of war, faction, or with respect to criminals? To this I add that sometimes doing good to our friends is doing harm to our enemies, for example, saving the city in time of war or our neighbor from attack by robbers. Or to take nonviolent examples, we are often forced to choose between benefiting one friend rather than another. Is the failure to benefit not very close to the actual doing of harm?

Socrates is going to shift later from the technical model to a very general definition of justice, for which there is no special art, as shoemaking is the art of the shoemaker, and so on. Furthermore, it soon becomes clear that if we consider an art or craft in itself, it is neither just nor unjust; what counts for justice is the end to which the technique is applied. *Technē* is clearly detached from, or disregards, the justice or injustice of its action. Why then does Socrates begin with these examples? The most obvious answer is that he wishes to confuse Polemarchus, not out of a desire to cause mischief but to get him to rethink his own thesis. Later in the discussion, this same confusion will appear as follows. Justice is minding one's own business, but one's business is not simply performing one's art, as Socrates will argue. Justice is performing one's art well, that is, to benefit one's friends rather than to harm them. It is entirely implausible to argue that we benefit our friends simply by doing the task that the city has assigned to us. So we are not done with Polemarchus's definition. At least half of it is correct. We still have to decide what to do with our enemies. In sum: Polemarchus is not just a curtain-raiser in the great drama of the problem of justice. He is, rather, the problem itself.

2

Thrasymachus

I

We are now prepared to turn from Polemarchus ("warlord") to Thrasymachus (literally, "bold in battle"). This Platonic joke has more than one resonance. The definitions of justice offered by the two have in common the invocation to harm one's enemies. It will become evident that Thrasymachus, if he is consistent with his stated beliefs, has no genuine friends. Socrates will claim in Book Six that he and Thrasymachus have become friends, "although we were not previously enemies" (498c9–d1). I find this qualification dubious, especially in view of Thrasymachus's graceless and ill-tempered submission to refutation by Socrates. It is at least an open question whether Socrates can persuade Thrasymachus. In the *Gorgias*, he was, after all, unable to succeed with Callicles, a man whose views are similar to those of Thrasymachus. Thrasymachus's surrender is more likely due to shame than to persuasion. To say this in another way, the philosopher-kings in the just city are unable to govern directly the desires and passions of the moneymaking class but depend upon the compulsion exercised by the soldiers or auxiliaries (a subset of the guardian class). Shame is the most effective form of compulsion in the case of professors who are shown to be incompetent.

Certainly Thrasymachus is driven by vanity to make a forceful and condescending eruption in the conversation. He has been restrained for some time by his companions, but at last he breaks through and launches himself upon Socrates like a wild beast (336b1–6). He demands that Socrates cease to babble like a child and also to ask questions but not to answer them. In fact, Thrasymachus admits that Socrates has led the discussion to some positive results, in particular, that he has associated justice with the needful, the beneficial, the profitable, and so on, but he himself will not accept these as genuine answers to the question "What is justice?" Thrasymachus demands that Socrates speak more plainly and precisely (336c1–d4). Why does he make this objection? He does so because he takes Socrates to claim that justice is that which is beneficial for all, whereas Thrasymachus is about to hold that justice is the benefit of the strong (338c1–2). Thrasymachus substitutes the strong and the weak for Polemarchus's friends and enemies. Both take it for granted that the just is the performance of beneficial deeds; neither person recognizes a sense of justice as good independently of benefit. But Polemarchus also takes it for granted that friendship is a good. He would never suggest that justice is doing good to one's enemies, and there are no other categories in his exposition. Are friends good because they benefit us, or do we benefit them because they are good? However Polemarchus would answer this question, there is no room for friendship in Thrasymachus's definition, although there is a place for enemies. If justice is the interest of the strong, then they have the right to take away the benefits of the weak. But this is true even among the strong; the strongest have the right to take away the benefits of the less strong. In other words, if might makes right, then life is a perpetual war of each against all, as Hobbes teaches: we are all enemies. If there is such a thing as friendship, it is an allegiance to dominate others; the moment there is a shift in the balance of power, friends become enemies and enemies friends. Today we call this realpolitik.

Socrates tells the unknown audience of his monologue that he was so frightened by Thrasymachus's assault that he could barely avoid being struck dumb. However the audience may have responded to this claim, Thrasymachus himself is under no illusion. He breaks into laughter and identifies Socrates's response as an example of his habitual irony (337a1–2). It is worth noting that Socrates preserves his modesty before the silent audience. He does not say "I decided to pretend that I was afraid of Thrasymachus in order to lull him into carelessness" or something of that sort. If the narrated dialogue makes it possible for us to eavesdrop on the silent thoughts of the main speaker, then it is implausible to say that the speaker is being ironical toward himself. I think that Socrates probably is afraid, although not to the extent that he claims. He is initially afraid that he cannot refute Thrasymachus, just as he fails with Callicles in the *Gorgias*. It is not Thrasymachus personally who frightens him but the thesis that might makes right. I suggest that in order to refute this thesis, one must have a conception of justice as the good that is independent of, although related to, the conception of the just as the beneficial. It is true that the just must be beneficial. But there are so many different kinds of benefit (for example, benefit to friends, to citizens, to mankind at large, and so on) that these must be rank-ordered. Some benefits are better than others. But what is the standard by which we rank them? Is it not "the good?" This cannot be defined in turn as the just or the beneficial without circularity. There may in fact be no noncircular definition of justice.

Socrates says that Thrasymachus's injunction against using benefit and its synonyms is like refusing to explain the number 12 as reached by 2 times 6, 3 times 4, and so on. The point of this analogy is that justice is indeed benefit, but that there are various ways of analyzing its structure. The disanalogy is that whereas 2 times 6 is not better than 4 times 3 for reaching 12, some benefits are better, that is, more just, than others. There is also the question of whether all forms of benefit are types of justice. In the midst of further sparring, Thrasymachus demands that Socrates pay a penalty for having been taught the correct definition. He refers to this penalty as monetary recompense. The expression can have a legal meaning, but in general it refers to paying a debt. In the present context, there can be little doubt that Thrasymachus wishes to receive a fee (thereby metaphorically classifying himself in advance with the moneymakers of the wished-for city or the epithumetic part of the soul). Socrates offers to repay Thrasymachus by learning from him if his definition of justice is superior to those that have been given previously. But this is not enough for professionals like Thrasymachus. When Socrates indicates that he is currently out of funds, Glaucon speaks for the group by saying that they will contribute the fee (337a8–d10). Once more Glaucon comes to the aid of Socrates.

It is too soon to develop the point, but we should at least mention that this passage raises the question of the class to which certain practitioners of *technē* like physicians, judges, and specialists in music and rhetoric will belong in the just city. One might assume that they are guardians, but nothing is said about the education of the highest class to suggest that it includes these arts. If the artists of this sort are permitted to charge a fee, then they must be classified with the farmers and workers. But this associates with the desires of the body those arts that are most particularly addressed to the care of the soul, either entirely or in part, as in the case of medicine.

To continue, Thrasymachus then says that "the just is nothing other than *to tou kreittonos sumpheron*" (338c2–3). As Bloom points out in his note to the passage, *kreittōn* means "better" or "stronger" but can also mean "good."[1] What is useful is clearly beneficial; strength provides the principle for rank-ordering the different types of utility. But why should strength be better than weakness? This question makes no sense to Thrasymachus. That is how the world works: the strong prevail. Now let us go step by step through the presentation of his position. Socrates first asks: If athletes benefit from eating a lot of meat, does that mean that it is just for weaker people to eat the same amount? Thrasymachus is outraged at this attempt to make fun of his thesis. He does not say so, but we can say on his behalf that weak people cannot benefit from large amounts of meat precisely because they are not strong enough. But the problem is that it is better for weak people to eat less. The question thus becomes: How can it be to the advantage of the stronger that weak people eat less? Is it because this leaves more meat for the strong? This seems dubious, but it gains in credibility when we shift from meat to power. And this in turn depends upon the truth of the premise that too much power, like too much meat, is bad for weak persons. It is certainly to the advantage of the strong that the weak are content with little power. We can generalize this analysis by noting that there are two types of utility or benefit, one for the strong and one for the weak. What counts for Thrasymachus is the benefit of the strong; the weak do not interest him. So for him justice is not simply benefit or utility but the utility of the strong. In other words, the strong are able to take what they want, whether this be much or little. And the weak have to make due with the leftovers.

In sum, the strong are better *because they are stronger*. There is no underlying moral argument or insight but rather a denial of the relevance of moral arguments or insights. Might makes right. Or so Thrasymachus might have argued. But he rejects the example of meat eating as a caricature of his actual definition, which is now rephrased. In every city there is a ruling group that sets up the laws, and these define what is just. But the members of the group establish laws that enforce their will, that is, are to their own advantage. "This is what I say, o best of men; in all cities, the same thing is just: the utility of the established ruling body" (338e6–339a2).

Let us spell out the elements of this claim. Justice is expressed in laws, and laws are established by the ruling class to its own advantage. It makes no difference which type of regime we examine; the same is true for all. I have already referred to Hobbes in connection with Thrasymachus. For both, human life is the manifestation of power; this is also the view of Nietzsche. Moral doctrines or conceptions of justice that recommend restrictions on the manifestation of power have been invented by the weak for their own protection, but they cannot appeal to any authority for the enforcement of these doctrines besides their own strength, and this is to confirm the view that might makes right, not to refute it.

There is, however, another way to look at Thrasymachus's definition. We can add the qualification that justice is what is actually in the interest of the stronger, not simply what the latter desires. In other words, we require knowledge in order to determine what is truly to our benefit. We thus define "might" in the formula "might makes right" to mean "ability to determine as well as to obtain one's good." This is not the Hobbesian or the Nietzschean view, since for both, desire, or will, determines what is beneficial or good. Take a simple example that apparently contradicts our modification of "might makes right." It seems that health is by nature better than sickness for the strong and the weak alike. But the strong will sacrifice their health for the sake of victory in war. If it is up to us to determine what is good, then we cannot leave this determination to the will to power. In addition, this raises the question of whether we can leave it to nature.

In order to refute Thrasymachus, Socrates must show that justice, in the sense of a restriction upon the autonomy of power, is beneficial to all. This thesis can be argued in three different ways. First, one can simply define the just as the legal, but this is obviously defective, since some laws are seen to be unjust. Second, one can appeal to a moral sense, a religious revelation, or some kind of intuitive perception of the just. But this seems arbitrary and eventually reduces to the question of which formulation of the intuition, and so on, is accepted in one's own community. Once more, the just is the legal. Third, one can claim that justice is the expression of what is correctly known to be beneficial. But it is not so easy to explain what one means by knowledge of the good; in attempting to do so, we inevitably make use of some intuited sense of "good" as a criterion for rank-ordering the various empirical or biological or "natural" benefits. This is of course why, in the modern epoch, the rights of the individual person were made higher than those of the state. Justice for the individual person comes to mean something negative: restricting the power of the state so as to allow for the free development of the individual, that is, for his or her choice of benefits. In other words, instead of defining and rank-ordering benefits, we say that such an evaluation is entirely personal; the only thing the state can do is to interfere as little as possible with our making that evaluation. I would describe this as a shift from substantive to formalist doctrines of justice.

It is very important to see that Socrates cannot point to the actual practice of politics as evidence against the thesis of Polemarchus. Cities always benefit their friends and harm their enemies. With all due qualification, this is exactly what the just city will do. At the level of foreign relations, there is no practical difference between the definition of Polemarchus and that of Thrasymachus. Inside the city, the Thrasymachean thesis is easier to attack on political grounds, since it is not uncommon for members of the ruling class to pass laws that seem to benefit their constituency rather than themselves. But it is extremely uncommon, to say the least, to find politicians and legislators who abstain from harming the interests of their political enemies. And if we identify the stronger as those whose will prevails in the political process, then Thrasymachus can argue that whatever the motives of the stronger, their conception of the advantageous triumphs. Thrasymachus's position becomes stronger when we turn to the international arena. Cities, like modern nations, pursue their own interest as far as their power allows. The least that can be said is that there is a difference between internal affairs and foreign relations on this point. More generally, there is a difference between the public and the private, since we are more likely to seek our own interests through strength when dealing with those who are not our friends or members of our family. To look ahead, this consideration will have an important bearing on the soundness of the analogy between the city and the soul, upon which the bulk of the dialogue depends.

2

Let us begin again. According to Thrasymachus, justice is the interest of the stronger. He is referring not to the physical strength of the individual person but to members of the ruling class in the city: "Does not the ruling element in each city dominate?" "Certainly," Socrates replies. Thrasymachus goes on to assert without argument that "in all cities, the same thing is just, namely, what benefits the established rule" (338d10–339a2). He makes no distinction between types of regime, such as democracies or tyrannies. How one comes to power is initially of no importance; what counts is that everywhere people in power determine what is just on the basis of their self-interest. Otherwise put, there is no basis for justice until the city is established. In what will be called by seventeenth- and eighteenth-century thinkers the state of nature, might makes right. In the city, the brute expression of the will to power is mitigated by the laws. When laws are present, we can speak of justice and injustice, but this means very little more than to say that, in the city, the will to power is "rationalized" and becomes more efficient.

Socrates begins his refutation of Thrasymachus by accusing him of self-contradiction. Thrasymachus claims that justice is the interest of the stronger. It follows that, in order to be just, the weaker must obey the commands of the stronger and act in their interest. But if the rulers mistakenly command what is not advantageous to themselves, the weaker are required by justice to act unjustly (339a5–e8). The proper inference from this would seem to be that one must know one's interest; strength alone is not sufficient. But before

Thrasymachus can introduce this clarification, Cleitophon engages in what at first seems like a mistaken defense of the Thrasymachean argument. In an exchange with Polemarchus, Cleitophon attributes to Thrasymachus the thesis that justice is what seems to the stronger to be to his advantage (340b6–8). Cleitophon must mean by this that with respect to the advantageous, what seems so, is so. In this case, there is no knowledge of what is genuinely advantageous, and this is altogether unacceptable to Thrasymachus, who in his own way is a champion of *technē*. He therefore rejects Socrates's restatement of the point with considerable indignation by denying that he calls a man "stronger" at the moment when that man is making mistakes (340c6–7). Before I comment directly on this passage, let me put it into a general context.

The problem is for Thrasymachus as follows. What sort of knowledge teaches us our advantage? It cannot be the power to persuade, because without knowledge of the beneficial, one may easily be led to persuade others to do what is disadvantageous to oneself. But technical knowledge can be used well or badly; it may lead to our disadvantage as well as our advantage. The entire problematic thus looks ahead for its solution to the distinction between *technē* and philosophy. We require a kind of knowledge of the useful and the useless that is not technical, and therefore not neutral with respect to justice and injustice. If this kind of knowledge cannot be found, then the point introduced but not developed adequately by Cleitophon will be unrefuted. The incoherence of Thrasymachus's attempt to associate technical knowledge with the interest of the strong is not proof that there is a philosophical or nontechnical solution to the problem. When the point is fully developed, it will lead Socrates to the most obscure part of his own teaching: the Idea of the Good. No one should therefore assume that, simply by introducing the need for knowledge, Socrates has refuted Thrasymachus. Instead, he has tacitly issued a promissory note to provide us with a sense of knowledge of justice, and so of what is genuinely advantageous to us. The main part of his effort will be met with in Books Five through Seven.

To continue with our analysis, by denying that he intended to include among the stronger anyone who is in the process of making a mistake, Thrasymachus assimilates the ruler to the artist and craftsman. To the extent that the stronger are functioning as ruler, artist, or craftsman, they cannot err. Mistakes are made by human beings who, at that moment, either lack or have forgotten the requisite knowledge. "The one who errs does so through a lack of knowledge [*epistēmē*], in which error he is not a craftsman. So a craftsman, a wise man, or a ruler never makes a mistake at the moment he is ruling" (340d2–e5).[2] Thrasymachus drives home the point by giving what he calls the most precise formulation of his position: "The ruler, insofar as he is a ruler, does not make mistakes, and not making mistakes, he sets down what is best for himself, and this is what the one being ruled must do" (340e7–341a2).

In this passage, Thrasymachus accepts the extension of the "ruling–being ruled" relation to the arts and crafts. In so doing, he identifies ruling as an art, and so as a type of knowledge. But there is a serious problem in his procedure, which was clearly visible in the conversation with Polemarchus. Arts and crafts are knowledge of how to produce something, not of how to use artifacts to one's personal advantage. One might have expected Socrates to make this point in response, but he chooses a different and more obscure line of attack. The simpler approach (What kind of knowledge shows us the advantageous?) would lead us directly to the difference between technical knowledge and practical judgment, and so to a line of argument that is first developed extensively by Aristotle. To take this path, however, would be to bypass the entire discussion of the Ideas and their associated method of dialectic, including the need for a *technē* to perform the "turning around" of the soul toward the Ideas (VII. 518d3–7). It is much too soon to study these issues in detail, but they had to be introduced in order to explain Socrates's behavior with Thrasymachus. In sum, Socrates will attempt to overcome the split between *technē* and knowledge of the good, or as Aristotle might put it, the difference between theory and practice.

Let me now introduce a much simpler distinction that will help us in our analysis of this section of the argument. The artist uses his art to produce an artifact, which may be, but normally is not, used by the artist himself. In most cases, then, we must add to the first three elements a fourth: use. These are not the only factors involved in technical production, but they are the most important ones, especially for our purposes. We can easily see, with the aid of this quadripartition, that the identification of ruler and ruled in the artistic process is not simple. Furthermore, to speak of the "advantage" of the art or the artifact is to use the term in a metaphorical rather than a literal sense; strictly speaking, it is the artist and the user who gain or lose. Things and modes of production have advantages and disadvantages for the persons who make or use the artifacts. Advantages and disadvantages correspond to purposes and judgments, not to the instruments by which these are carried out. If I say "this tool has the advantage over that one for the following purpose," I mean that its use is advantageous to me, because without me or someone else, there would be no purpose and so no advantage. In sum: there is a difference between technical and intentional purpose. But this means that there is a difference between technical and political advantage. What is useful for producing an artifact of a certain kind may or may not be useful for those who make and/or use it.

I turn now to 341c4ff. According to Thrasymachus, the ruler in the most precise sense does not make any mistakes and is thus the stronger whose interests must be attended to by the weaker, who are ruled. He has already prepared the way for Socrates to take him to mean that there is an art of ruling analogous to medicine or grammar. It is presumably this art that corrects our natural desires on the basis of a correct determination of the advantageous. Socrates begins his interrogation by referring to the art of medicine. In this case, the advantageous is in one sense immediately clear; it is the curing of illness and the establishment of good health. I shall come back in a moment to the sense in which it is not clear. Socrates next establishes that the physician in the precise sense is not a moneymaker but one who cares for the sick. He adds that the pilot in the precise sense of the term is so called "because of his art and through his ruling over the sailors" (341d3). There are advantages for the sailors as well as for the pilot; the key point here is that it is advantageous for both that the pilot rule over the sailors. Nothing is said about moneymaking in connection with the pilot, but it surely figures in the purposes of the pilot and his crew as much as it does in those of the physician. However, we may grant Socrates that the art as art, whether it be medicine or piloting, is not for the sake of moneymaking but rather for the sake of producing its artifact in a technically competent manner. Moneymaking, as well as the here unmentioned pride in workmanship or performance, are along with other motives the concern of the artist, not qua artist but qua human being, or, more precisely, citizen.

It is easy to see the political penumbra of the discussion of art. Not so easy is to see the connection between the rule of the art over the process of production or the artifact, on the one hand and, on the other, the rule of the statesmen over their fellow citizens. Making a good technical product is not the same as, although it may obviously be connected with, acting to the advantage of oneself or others. As I have already noted, Socrates does not take up this issue in the present context. Instead, he argues that the sole advantage of each of the arts is to be as perfect as possible (341d10–11). He means by this not that the arts literally gain advantage to themselves by trying to function perfectly but that, as Thrasymachus has already asserted, it is the nature of art to be as perfect as possible. The function is advantageous to the artist and the users, not to the art. One could say that it is advantageous to me to eat a ripe pear rather than a rotten one, but there is no comparable advantage to the pear. Similarly, it is advantageous to me to purchase a pair of well-made shoes, but no advantage accrues to the art of shoemaking from carrying out its function. Nor can we say that shoemaking rules over the shoe; it is rather the shoemaker who rules over the shoe through the instrumentality of the art of shoemaking.

This should be kept in mind, because Socrates frequently speaks as if the art itself possesses advantages and exercises the ruling art over the artifact.

The sense of perfection here is illustrated by the case of medicine. We start with the human body, which is defective in the sense that it suffers from illnesses that require a physician's attention. The art of medicine is accordingly developed to furnish the body with the beneficial, namely, a restoration to good health. But the art of medicine itself does not require some other art to correct an inner defect and thereby consider its own advantage. Let us note carefully that Socrates, like Aristotle, apparently accepts Thrasymachus's own premise to the effect that the art qua art cannot err. From a contemporary epistemological standpoint, the premise is odd. We think of the arts as constantly changing and, in the case of modern scientific technology, as steadily improving. What is technically correct today may be recognized tomorrow as an error. But in the view endorsed by Thrasymachus, art is to be understood as genuinely manifested in its success only. To take a humble example, the style in footwear may change from time to time, but the purpose of footwear in general will always be achieved by the genuine master of shoemaking.

In the case of the physician, the art of medicine is manifested in the curing of an illness, and to the extent that this does not take place, the art is absent as well. The art of shoemaking is manifested in the successful production of a pair of shoes; if the job is botched, the art is once more absent. And so too with the art of ruling. The art qua art has no defects and thus requires no services from some other art. But neither is the art reflexive; it does not attend to its own needs in carrying out its function. On the contrary, the art of medicine attends to the needs of the sick body, the art of horsemanship attends to the needs of the horse by making it better suited for racing, and so on. Each art attends to the needs of that of which it is the art (342a1–c10).

Entirely apart from any differences between the ancient and the modern view of the arts, the interpretation defended by Thrasymachus has the odd consequence that the person who fails to cure one disease, even though he or she is an expert therapist in other cases, is not acting as a physician. But this seems counterintuitive. A failure in one case does not negate the possession of the art, especially if that failure is due to lack of appropriate knowledge by all physicians of the period. It seems that Thrasymachus is implicitly close to the Aristotelian view, cited previously in note 2, that the end of an art and the capacity of the artist to fulfill that end are both determinable independent of the perfectibility of technical procedures.

Socrates wishes to infer from the preceding argument that the art of ruling benefits the subjects, not the ruler. One could object that the practice of an art is often, and in a way always, for the benefit, that is, the improvement, of the art itself. I have just explained why Socrates and Thrasymachus would reject this way of looking at the arts. But even if we put this objection to one side, we have to distinguish between the advantage that accrues to the artist, say the physician, through the acquisition of honor, pride in his work, or a fee, and the advantage that accrues to the sick body, which is changed into a healthy one. In general, it could be simultaneously true that an art is perfect in itself and seeks the advantage of its product, and that rulers use the arts for their own advantage. Unfortunately for his own argument, Thrasymachus does not see this, and Socrates does not call it to his attention. The compatibility of the two conditions is rooted in a distinction between two senses of "beneficial." Rulers benefit themselves in a sense quite different from the benefit bestowed upon their objects by the arts. Arts may undergo technical progress, but this is to the benefit of human beings, in particular to the ruler who enforces his or her will on the city, not to the arts.

Socrates takes a different line. He addresses the advantage that accrues to the artist in an oversimplified way by introducing the art of moneymaking. The second kind of advantage (that accrues to its object) is not the result of an "intention" by the art, say medicine, as distinct from the artist. We may say that we are grateful to the art of medicine when it cures us of a disease, but it is actually the physician who has cured us, whether out of pecuniary motives, pride in his metier, or for some other reason. To translate this into political terms, the ruler uses the art of ruling not to benefit that art but rather for the sake of himself and his subjects. It is poetic license to say that the art of ruling looks to the welfare of the ruled. Medicine, for example, can be used to torture and mutilate as well as to heal. This may be a misuse of medicine on moral grounds, but not for technical reasons. Similarly, the art of ruling, on the basis of the new argument that Thrasymachus is forced to accept, tends to the advantage of the ruler as well as the ruled. Ruling has to do with the proper function of the city, and this affects the welfare of both ruler and ruled. And the same is true in all the other arts. The artist is benefited by his art, as is the person who uses the artifact. Socrates tries to conceal the first kind of benefit by arguing that the art is not benefited, and then by blurring the distinction between artist and art.

Just as the ruler is not the art of ruling, so too the art of ruling is not the same as the art of shoemaking, piloting a ship, or curing the sick. The shoemaker does not wear the shoes that he makes for his customer, and the physician does not enjoy the good health he produces in his patient. The pilot, it is true, makes the same trip that his passengers make, but not for the same reason. The ruler, on the other hand, cannot practice his art without benefiting or suffering directly from it; he and his subjects are equally at the mercy of the proper functioning of the city. And perhaps even more important, the very nature of ruling is to be just or unjust; this is not true of the other arts. This seems to entail that we shall not find the art of ruling by sticking to the usual run of technical examples. Ruling is used only metaphorically in conjunction with these arts. To this I add that it does not guarantee that we shall discover the art of ruling by discovering the definition of justice. There may in fact be no art of ruling, if to be an art is to be neutral whereas to rule is to be just or unjust. Aristotle may have been right in distinguishing between art and *phronēsis*, or practical judgment. This distinction is blurred in Plato because of the prominence of the model of *technē* in the discussion of philosophical knowledge, and because of Plato's failure to distinguish practice from production. But it is not entirely absent.

So Thrasymachus has been defending two separate arguments thus far in the first book of the *Republic* His first argument is that justice is in the interest of the stronger, namely, those who can impose their wills upon others and thus satisfy their desires. His second argument is that strength is technical knowledge. By this, of course, he does not mean that politics is medicine or something of the sort, he means that there is an art of ruling. It is plausible to infer that he has in mind the art of oratory. The question is how to connect these two arguments. What is needed is a more subtle analysis of the art of ruling. This analysis will lead to the necessity of combining strength and knowledge.

3

Thrasymachus once more loses his temper and becomes abusive; he says that Socrates requires a wet nurse to wipe his nose. In other words, Socrates babbles like a small child. He is so naive as to suppose that herdsmen tend their herds for the sake of the brutes rather than for that of the masters and themselves. This tripartition (ruler, herdsman, herd) anticipates the division of the just city into three main classes. I am not going to analyze all of Thrasymachus's examples. Suffice it to say that he seems here to return to his initial statement that justice is the interest of the stronger. The identification of justice and *technē* is not mentioned. All of Thrasymachus's examples involve money, physical possessions, or corporeal punishments; there is no reference to the soul. Having been tripped up by the argument from *technē*, Thrasymachus now seems to lose his way in an outburst of anger, in which he shifts from the definition of justice to the praise of injustice. This is the third argument that Thrasymachus advances, and it is in contradiction, at least on the surface, to the claim that justice is the interest of the stronger. There can be no doubt that Thrasymachus's anger leads him to replace justice with injustice. He does of course say at 343c1ff. that justice is "another man's good, the advantageous for the stronger and the ruler."³ But he soon shifts from the argument that justice is the interest of the stronger to the claim that injustice, if it is on a grand scale that allows one to gain more than one's share (*pleonektein*: 344a1), is more advantageous than justice and enables its practitioner to achieve the greatest happiness (*eudaimonestaton*: 344a5). So strength is now associated with injustice and weakness with justice. Common to both these arguments, and deeper than either, is Thrasymachus's praise of might. When one's power is at a certain height, the distinction between justice and injustice disappears.⁴

Thrasymachus next falls back on a more blunt statement of his initial opinion. Justice means giving each person his fair share. But human beings desire more than their share, and those with the power to acquire it will do so. Only the weak defend justice, and they would repudiate it if they could. It is therefore not strictly correct to say that justice is the advantageous for the stronger, one should instead assert that the advantageous has a stronger claim on our desire than does justice. Furthermore, Thrasymachus does not say that there is no such thing as justice, only that it is weak. But neither does he say that the strength of injustice transforms it into justice. He says rather that injustice is stronger than justice within the human animal. Man is the animal who conceives of justice but disregards it whenever he can. This being so, force is required not only to impose injustice but *also to impose justice*. If Thrasymachus is indeed sympathetic to the cause of justice, then he will be led to support a class of warrior-guardians within the city. In other words, the real disagreement between Thrasymachus and Socrates is not on the need for police to enforce justice but on the nature of philosophy. Or rather, Thrasymachus wishes to replace philosophy with oratory, that is, political rhetoric. In one last formulation, Socrates must claim that justice is advantageous for everyone, but he cannot demonstrate that everyone possesses knowledge of what is advantageous for oneself. In a word, the philosopher will be forced to impose justice, and this will require both knowledge of the good and the rhetorical power to persuade others. If Socrates and Thrasymachus are going to become friends, Socrates will need to exercise his own rhetorical powers on the professor of oratory. The friendship is not, as we say today, "personal." In my opinion, however, it is not the type represented by Thrasymachus but rather those like Glaucon, Adeimantus, and Polemarchus that will be indispensable to the founding of the beautiful city. And this is why we shift from Thrasymachus to Glaucon and Adeimantus in the remaining books of the dialogue. Thrasymachus is a prototype; he is not totally unjust, but his nature is insufficiently refined to make him politically reliable in the higher echelons of the city.

Thrasymachus is prepared to leave after this outburst. Socrates indicates the roughness of Thrasymachus's character (as if proof were still required) by comparing him to an attendant in a public bath who pours a torrent of water (that is, speech) on us all at once and then departs. Note that it is not Socrates who persuades Thrasymachus to stay; "those who were present forced him to remain and to furnish an argument for the things that had been said" (344d1–5). In so doing, they exemplify the definition of justice as dependent upon force but not identical with it. This is connected to the fact that Socrates was also forced to give his comprehensive *logos* although he wished to return to his home. Socrates "begs" (*edeomēn*: 344d5) Thrasymachus to stay. Just as Gorgias, in the dialogue bearing his name, must intervene to persuade Callias to continue his conversation with Socrates, so here it is not Socrates to whose rhetoric Thrasymachus responds.

As I have already suggested, Thrasymachus is shamed into remaining; he is a professor of rhetoric and cannot refuse to finish the argument without casting doubt among the other members of the audience on his professional competence. When the superiority of Socrates becomes unmistakable, Thrasymachus will pretend to continue responding in order not to incur the anger of the others. But this in itself is an admission of defeat. Thrasymachus must pay his debt, and in so doing he either gives up the principle that might makes right or admits his own weakness.

The force applied to Thrasymachus reminds us of the beginning of the dialogue, where Polemarchus uses the threat of force to gain Socrates's continued company. It would be virtually unthinkable to imagine an appeal to force in discussions of mathematics or philosophical dialectic. As Leo Strauss used to say, there are no oaths in Euclid. Especially interesting in the present context is the connection between force and friendship. Aristotle says that friendship makes justice superfluous.[5] The law compels us to be just, whereas friendship makes justice voluntary. The point should not be exaggerated, but Socrates is responding to political considerations as well as acting to moderate Glaucon's eros for the sake of his friendship with Plato.

Thrasymachus, on the other hand, will lose the advantage of his *technē* if the city is founded. His oratory will be replaced by that of the philosopher-kings. The most he can hope for is to make himself useful in regulating the moneymakers, but only if he entirely changes his views on justice and renders himself subservient to the guardians. But the other members of the group, who are younger than Socrates and Thrasymachus, are also more political than the two technicians, and they are eager to become guardians. This is not, I think, Thrasymachus's ambition; he prefers the life of the tyrant (see 344a6–7).

Socrates next restates briefly the disagreement at which they have arrived.

He asks Thrasymachus whether he believes that those who truly rule the city do so voluntarily. Thrasymachus replies: "By Zeus, I do not believe it; I know it well" (345e2–3). Socrates then returns to the rule of the various arts over their productions, and he holds, with Thrasymachus's agreement, that each art benefits what it rules. For example, medicine benefits not itself but the body. I have already pointed out that this is only figuratively true; art has no intentions, only a function. In some cases, it is the artist who supplies the intention, as for example in medicine, where the physician, for whatever reason, desires to cure his patient by means of the art of medicine, which could nevertheless be used to harm people in other circumstances. In other cases, as for example carpentry, the intention of the artist is to produce a good artifact and thereby to benefit himself, whether in money or reputation. But whether the product of the art of carpentry is used for just or unjust reasons depends not on the carpenter but rather upon those who in fact use what he has produced, for example, a gallows.

Socrates disregards honor in his claim that if technicians benefit from something in common, it is not from their particular *technē* but from *mistharnētikē*. This word can be translated as "the art of moneymaking;" Socrates calls it a *technē* at 346c10 (345e5–346c11). Apart from the fact that money is not the only advantage that comes from technical production, Socrates speaks as if the benefit accruing to the artist is the same as that accruing to the art. Strictly speaking, art does not make money; the artist does, through the instrumentality of art. Previously Socrates argued that the art as such requires nothing outside itself to complete it. He was silent about the artist. But now the attempt to assert the self-sufficiency of the arts cannot be carried through. Socrates is forced to refer to the artist, that is, the rulers. In other words, they are not content with the mere practice of their arts but charge a fee. This reminds us that the independence of the arts qua arts has nothing directly to do with justice, which is a relation between persons, more particularly, fellow citizens (and in the limit-case, with oneself), not between medicine and the body or shoemaking and a pair of shoes. Socrates continues to ignore this crucial point and to concentrate upon the inner structure of *technē* in his refutation of Thrasymachus. But his conclusion is defective: "No art or kind of rule provides for its own benefit . . . it provides for and commands the one who is ruled, looking to the advantage of the weaker, but not that of the stronger" (346e3–7). The defect is now evident. Whereas no art looks to its own advantage, artists do. And in particular, rulers cannot make proper use of the art of ruling without benefiting themselves as well as their subjects.

This is enough to show that even if ruling is an art, it is unlike all the other arts that Socrates has introduced thus far. This art cannot be practiced except by considering one's own advantage as well as that of the citizenry. The political art resembles philosophy in that it takes care of the whole — even the cosmos is, as it were, regulated by religious laws and customs. But we have not shown that justice is equivalent to the benefit of the stronger or that it licenses unqualified *pleoneksia* (having more than one's share). In other words, the art of ruling includes justice, as medicine and shoemaking do not. It is therefore advantageous to the weak as well as the strong. From this standpoint, Socrates's refutation of Thrasymachus is also a refutation of himself. Or rather, Socrates's argument allows us to see that the art of ruling is not a *technē*. But he does not say this explicitly. This leaves it open whether we are correcting Socrates or inferring his covert meaning.

Two more points in this connection. First, in all actual cities, the rulers are given more than the ruled. The surplus may not consist in cash, but there will always be perquisites of political office that are not offered to private citizens. In Socrates's city, the rulers are given less than the ruled. It is not quite true to say that they have nothing at all, because the best are given special breeding rights. In other words, sexual eros cannot be suppressed in the way that love of private property can be. It is the desire to have more that corrupts politicians in actual cities and leads to the diatribe of Thrasymachus. The suppression of private property is at the very center of Socrates's full-length refutation of Thrasymachus. That is, it is not a refutation at all but a granting of the force of Thrasymachus's argument and the attempt to deal with it.

Second, Socrates distinguishes between the wage-earning art and the others. There is something peculiar about wage earning; it benefits the ruler (or artist) rather than the art itself or its productive activity. Socrates mentions three kinds of wages that are demanded by the prospective ruler: money, honor, or a penalty if he should not rule. At this point Glaucon speaks for the first time since 337d9, where he offered to contribute to the fee demanded by Thrasymachus for introducing his own definition of justice. He says that he now understands two of the kinds of wages, namely, money and honor, but not the third (347a7–9). Socrates replies rather harshly that Glaucon does not understand the wages of the best, who govern only through unwillingness to be ruled by a worse man. Note that Glaucon is well aware that the love of honor and the love of money are said to be, and are, reproaches. But this has not stopped him from seeking to participate in politics (347a10–b4).

Socrates says that if there were a city of good men, they would fight for the privilege of not ruling, just as in actual cities there is a fight for political power. He adds that this would make it plain "that a genuinely true ruler does not by nature seek his own benefit, but that of the ruled" (347d2–6). This is not persuasive. It is certainly to one's advantage not to be ruled by inferiors.

Socrates adds that in such a city every perceptive person would rather be benefited by another than take the trouble of benefiting another. If so, this shows that self-interest is a part of goodness. But presumably the good city is the one that Socrates is about to construct. He will claim that, in this city, philosophers are obligated to rule or that they have a duty to the whole city that outweighs their personal inclinations. In other words, this obligation outweighs the selfishness of private good, which is not the same as that of political life.[6]

Socrates does not pursue the difference between private and public good but turns instead to Thrasymachus's claim that the life of the unjust man is stronger (that is, better, more advantageous) than that of the just man. He first discusses the issue with Glaucon, who says that in his opinion the life of the just man is more profitable (or "advantageous": *lusitelesteron*: 347e7). Glaucon was not persuaded by Thrasymachus's list of the good things that come from injustice and strongly agrees that he wants to refute the professor of oratory (348a1–5). He also accepts Socrates's claim that if they list separately the goods that accrue on either side, they will have need of judges to pass a verdict on their counting and measuring, whereas if they try to come to agreement through conversation, then they will be both judges and pleaders (348a7–b5). This is a striking passage. First, agreement is no sign of correctness; the conflicting parties will still need some kind of judge to determine whether this agreement is sound or not. Second, it seems distinctly unjust for persons to plead their case before themselves. In short, agreement avoids trouble but does not establish soundness. Otherwise put, there is something "political" about mutual persuasion.

Socrates now turns back to Thrasymachus, who, incidentally, did not agree to agree; this was done by Glaucon. There is still some fight left in Thrasymachus. He continues to hold that complete injustice is more profitable (*lusitelesteran*) than complete justice. However, he denies that justice is a virtue and injustice an evil; the reverse, he says, is true. But in his next statement, he modifies this bold answer: Justice is not an evil but extreme noble simplicity (foolishness: 348c12). We may think ahead for a moment to the noble lie upon which the founding of the beautiful city will be said to depend. Thrasymachus comes rather close to referring to justice as a noble lie; it would be compatible with his position to say that for the weak (that is, the citizens) to believe this noble lie is to the advantage of the stronger (that is, the rulers). As to injustice, he denies that it is an evil and calls it instead "good counsel" (348d1–2).

According to Thrasymachus, injustice is profitable, a mark of excellence or strength (what he obviously means by *aretē*), and prudence (*phronimos*: able to give good counsel). He does not deny that petty crime, like purse snatching, can be profitable if one gets away with it, but it is not worth mentioning. What concerns him is complete injustice, and this can take place not on the private level but only in politics, through the subjugation of cities and tribes (348d5). This point is very important for the transition from private happiness (Cephalus) to the just city. To paraphrase Socrates, the public is the private writ large. The question for Thrasymachus is not the understanding of the human soul but the greater opportunity for profit. As Socrates is going to argue, the second depends upon the first.

Socrates says next that Thrasymachus is not joking but is rather expressing his true opinion when he calls justice a vice and injustice noble and strong, as well as a virtue and wisdom (348e9–349a2). If so — and Thrasymachus claims that it is so — then it is highly unlikely, as some have argued, that Thrasymachus is really on the side of justice and is outraged by injustice. But that is not our main concern. Much more important is Thrasymachus's reply that it makes no difference whether he is joking or stating his opinion; in either case, Socrates must refute the argument. And Socrates agrees (349a9–b1). This has a bearing on the so-called hermeneutical problem with respect to the Platonic dialogues. We cannot prove that Socrates is joking or serious. But we can easily show that he adjusts his speeches — in the first instance, his questions — to the nature of his interlocutor. The search for agreement is not the same as logical demonstration.

3

After attributing seriousness to Thrasymachus, Socrates launches the next stage of his refutation. The just man wishes and claims to deserve more than the unjust man but not the just man, whereas the unjust man will wish and claim to deserve more than both the just and the unjust man (349b6–c10). This is ambiguous. We might be inclined to say that the just man does not wish to get more than the unjust man, since that would make him unjust as well. What he wants is his due. The verb *pleonektein* is employed in this passage; it means "having more than" or "to gain an advantage." Socrates continues: the just man tries to have the advantage over the unlike (that is, the unjust), whereas the unjust man tries to have the advantage over the like and the unlike (that is, the unjust and the just). As this is understood by Thrasymachus, the unjust man is like the prudent and good man, whereas the just man is not (349d6–7). Socrates now returns to the arts and gets Thrasymachus to agree that the musical man is *phronimos*, that is, able to give good counsel about music, whereas the unmusical man is not. And a similar conclusion holds for the medical man (349d12–350a5).

Socrates gives two examples. The musical man — presumably the one with knowledge of the musical *technē*—does not try to get the advantage over and claim to be worth more than another musical man with respect to the tuning of a lyre, but he makes this claim about the unmusical man. Socrates here assumes that technical knowledge is the same in both musicians and that there is just one way to tune a lyre, but this is dubious. Musicians often compete with one another on technical points, and the correct adjustment of the strings is surely dependent in part on taste, the acoustics of the auditorium, and so on.

A similar situation obtains in the case of the medical man. Physicians engage very frequently in rivalries concerning the correct diagnosis of a disease or the best way to treat it. Socrates ought to say here that rivalry and the desire to have more is inherent in the artist, and so in the physician, not the art of medicine. The physician wants to get the better of the nonmedical man in the sense of depriving him of the right to practice medicine. To "get the better of" means here "to have one's technical knowledge obeyed," as opposed to being treated by ignorance. And this is true of all the *epistēmai*, a word that Socrates uses as interchangeable with *technai*. The person who lacks knowledge, however, if he were obeyed, would gain more than both the knower and the one who does not know (and whose advice is not followed: 350a6–b2). In other words, the ignorant man wishes to take away patients from the knower but also wishes to treat those who are ignorant of medicine, like himself.

Socrates's argument is appealing, but it suffers from the same shortcoming as the other arguments from technical knowledge. First, *technē* is not justice but only an instrument that may be used either justly or unjustly. Second, it has not been shown that the ignorant man, namely, one who tries to practice an art that he does not possess, is unjust. At most, it has shown that he is ignorant. But, third, this admission is not incompatible with either of Thrasymachus's two main claims, namely, that justice is the interest of the stronger and that extreme injustice is better than justice. This point is not immediately obvious, because we would all prefer to have competent physicians rather than frauds, and so too in the case of the other arts. Furthermore, there is normally a criterion for distinguishing between the competent artist and the fraud: the excellence or utility of the product. But the fact that we prefer competent doctors to frauds does not contradict the claim that justice is in the interest of the stronger. Precisely if knowledge is art, it presumably makes its possessor stronger than the fraud. But that does not in itself make him just. He must still use his technical knowledge justly.

This is the real flaw in Thrasymachus's argument. By insisting that art never errs, and by defining the art of ruling as the flawless application of technical knowledge for one's own advantage, Thrasymachus is forced to acknowledge that the possessor of technical knowledge is stronger than the ignoramus. And this in turn is given two different interpretations. On the first, justice is in the interest of the stronger, so the interests of the technician are the aim of justice. On the second, extreme injustice is superior to justice of any kind. "Interest of the stronger" is here no longer defined in terms of technical knowledge but rather of pure force. The acts of the tyrant as described by Thrasymachus have nothing directly to do with the possession of technical knowledge, unless one takes the art of ruling to be that of the tyrant. On both these alternative interpretations, we are required to admit that justice is a manner of using an art, not simply practicing that art. What looked like the great advantage of introducing knowledge has turned out to be an obstacle in the path of our inquiry, because the wrong conception of knowledge is being used, namely, that of *technē*. This section of the argument leads Thrasymachus to blush (350d2–3). His shame is merited, but this does not mean that Socrates has covered himself with glory.

Thrasymachus claims that he has not been persuaded, but he is too embarrassed to continue the attack. He asks permission to speak at length, or else to continue giving short and docile answers to Socrates's questions. Socrates replies as though no alternative had been offered. In other words, he says that he will continue questioning and thus does not give Thrasymachus a chance to speak at length. This is a clear case of *pleoneksia* (350c12–e10). Socrates reiterates the equivocal thesis that wisdom and virtue are together justice; it will therefore easily be seen that justice is stronger than injustice. However, he shifts to the question of the just city. If justice is wisdom, then it will make a city stronger; as Socrates restates the point, the city must have power together with justice (351b6–9). Obviously justice is not sufficient to make the city stronger in comparison with its neighbors. In other words, we see once again that knowledge without persuasion is deficient in power.

This leads to an important new point. If the members of an unjust city were unjust to each other, this would weaken their power. Injustice produces hatred and factions among free men as well as slaves; even a band of robbers or pirates must practice justice among themselves in order to carry out their desire to have more than the others. And Socrates extends his conclusion to individual men whose souls have become infected with injustice; Thrasymachus agrees with some reservation so as not to make trouble (351c7–e8). I note again that none of this establishes the nature of justice as technical knowledge. Instead, it supports the argument that even those with technical knowledge are required to be just in order to gain their own advantage. This passage serves another important purpose; it anticipates the subsequent analogy between the city and the soul. Injustice sets a man at odds with himself and thereby prevents him from acting. It is true that ignorance of medicine prevents us from acting to cure our diseases, just as ignorance of shoemaking will prevent us from making shoes. But this is not injustice. Life without shoes and medicine is no doubt harsh, but it may be just.

There is another curious feature of Socrates's claim, which he proceeds to develop at some length. He emphasizes that the unjust city, group, or even individual is hindered from action and becomes the enemy of everyone, those whom it is like and those whom it is not like. But this need not be true. So long as justice is practiced among themselves, thieves and other unjust persons may well be able to act unjustly toward the others with impunity. And the same is true of the individual person. He can be unjust to others as long as he is not immobilized by inner factions (352c3–8). Socrates makes a persuasive case for partial justice, that is, justice toward friends but not toward enemies. His argument thus turns out to reestablish the definition of justice presented by Polemarchus, namely, doing good to friends and harm to enemies.

This brings us finally to the question of whether the just live better and happier lives than the unjust. For the argument is not about some chance question but rather about how we should live our lives (352d5–6). In other words, the political investigation to follow is in the service of the question about the individual, and the investigation of the just city is due to the ostensible analogy between the soul of the individual person and the structure of the city. It is of course true that for Socrates the best life can be lived only within a city, but that does not alter the order of importance of the two investigations. Contrary to what we usually hear about the Greeks in general and the Socratic school in particular, the public is for the sake of the private. This is in fact obvious, once we realize that individuals but not cities are philosophical or happy.

Socrates next establishes that the work of each thing is what it alone can do, or do more beautifully than anything else (353a10–11). We can see with the eyes only and hear with the ears alone. We can trim a branch with a dagger or leather cutter, but not as well as with a pruning knife. So in addition to the work of each thing, there is an *aretē*, or excellence (and not a moral virtue). The excellence of the eye is to see beautifully or finely; the excellence of the ears is to hear beautifully; and so on. In each case, there is both a particular excellence without which the work of the thing could not be carried out and a *kakia*, that is, the privation of the excellence (not a moral vice). Socrates extends this claim to the soul. Its work is to manage, rule, and deliberate; above all, the job of the soul is to live (353d3–10).

Thrasymachus agrees that the soul cannot accomplish its work without its proper excellence. Socrates then asserts that a bad soul necessarily rules and manages badly, while a good soul does all things well. Since they also agreed that justice is virtue of the soul and injustice is vice, the just man will have a good life and the unjust man will have a bad one (353d9–12). In fact, they agreed that justice is the excellence of the soul to itself and its friends or allies, no doubt a major conclusion but not the entire thesis that Socrates tries to establish. For it has not been proven that injustice toward one's enemies is not a part of the good and happy life. So long as "good" means "excellence" of function rather than "moral virtue," there is room for Thrasymachus to maneuver.

This is in effect admitted by Socrates in the last paragraph of Book One. Socrates did not establish initially the definition of justice but considered particular cases. One wants to reply that there is no other way to arrive at a definition of anything, including justice, except by considering particular cases. But we have certainly not arrived at such a definition, in large part because of equivocation on words like virtue, wisdom, learning, and knowledge; in particular, technical knowledge. Therefore we have not established that the just man is happier than the unjust man. And in fact, to claim this as a rule is to fly in the face of experience (354a12–c3). It is therefore possible for Glaucon and Adeimantus to praise injustice and argue for its superiority to justice, as they will do in the next book.

3

Glaucon and Adeimantus

I

Socrates assumes that the refutation of Thrasymachus is now complete, and with it, the conversation recorded in Book One. "Complete" means here not success but failure. As Socrates puts it, they have failed to arrive at a definition of justice. This may be so, but we have found considerable agreement among the main speakers with respect to the claim that justice is doing good to your friends and harm to your enemies. Polemarchus put this forward explicitly, and it is implied by the Thrasymachean view that justice is the interest of the stronger, as that view was corrected by Socrates. Even the unjust man must practice justice with his friends and allies, but he does so in order to defeat his enemies, namely, all those whose cooperation is not required for his striving to have more than others. Socrates has praised justice but, as he admits, has failed to define it. Therefore he has not shown that it is unjust to harm one's enemies. The argument that was supposed to establish this claim holds that we make things worse by damaging them, but there are obvious cases in which we cannot avoid damaging others, as for example in time of war and with respect to incorrigible criminals.

At a more subtle level, we can also suggest that there are many occasions in which it is impossible to do good to one friend without harming another. A simple example: professors often have to recommend one of their graduate students for a fellowship or a job, even though to do so is to harm the prospects of their other students who are applying for the same award. The fact that one person deserves the award more than others does not alter the fact that, in order to do justice, we have to deprive friends of a benefit. In cases like these, justice is the harming of friends. It thus seems impossible to define justice as always doing good to one's friends and harm to one's enemies. But are there any cases in which justice requires us to do good to our enemies? One can agree that sometimes this redounds to our advantage by making the enemy better, and so friendlier. But it is not uniformly true, as our other examples (crime, war) have shown.

The net result is that even the widely accepted principle championed by Polemarchus is not a precise definition of justice. What has to be shown is that what looks like harm from a superficial point of view always turns out to be a benefit from a deeper analysis. But this sounds dubious at best and would require case-by-case analyses, most of which would undoubtedly lead to controversy and make the administration of justice impossible. This leads to the corollary that even if we could find an acceptable definition of justice, it would often, and perhaps almost always, be necessarily arbitrary in the decisions it validates. One more observation before we turn to Book Two. The conversation in Book One is conducted on the assumption that every participant knows enough about the nature of justice to defend or attack it. They are, of course, all residents of cities and therefore familiar with the usual views on the topic. But the point cuts deeper; whatever the reasons for which we enter into communal life, the need for justice arises spontaneously from our dealings, private and public, with one another. In this sense, the definition of justice cannot be a purely technical artifact that is intelligible only to specialists. It must answer to the needs that give rise to a variety of formal definitions.

Glaucon, who could be called the father of the *logos* because of his insistence upon remaining in the Piraeus, plays that role still more explicitly at the beginning of Book Two. He is, as Socrates says, *aei andreiotatos*, "always most brave" or "manly" (357a2–3), and he is unwilling to rest content with the refutation of Thrasymachus. That is to say: Glaucon grasps intuitively that the refutation was not convincing. I do not mean by this that he recognizes the invalidity of Socrates's arguments and his use of ambiguous, even equivocal terms without sufficient analysis. But he sees that Socrates has yet to prove that justice is in every way superior to injustice (357a4–b2). Under Glaucon's preliminary interrogation, Socrates agrees that there are three kinds of good. Note his terminology here. He first refers to *toionde ti agathon*, "a something of suchlike kind" or, in smoother English, "a good of such a kind that" we choose to possess it (357b5). This sounds like Aristotle's *toionde ti* as modifying *tode ti*, "this thing here of such and such a kind." At 357c5, Glaucon replaces "a sort of good" with *triton ti eidos* ("a third kind of form"), and he asks whether Socrates "sees" it. This is our first introduction to the language of the so-called Platonic Ideas, which springs from the everyday act of discerning shapes, patterns, forms, or looks that allow us to distinguish one thing from another.

We like some things for themselves alone, some for themselves and what follows from them, and finally, some for what follows from them, but not for themselves. An example of the third kind is gymnastics, which is painful in itself but leads to good condition. Socrates had claimed that the just man is happier as well as wiser and better than the unjust man. He now adds that justice is something that belongs to the most beautiful class, namely, things that the man who is going to become blessed likes for themselves and for what comes out of them. Glaucon is sympathetic to the thesis that justice is a good of the second kind, but he is not persuaded. The reason he gives, again, is not the inadequacy of the technicalities of Socrates's argument but the fact that it is not acceptable to the many (*tois pollois*: 358a4). The many argue that what counts is the appearance of justice, not the reality. So long as we are not caught and punished, it is better to be unjust than just. We can thus do good to ourselves (as we understand it) and harm to everyone else, without losing our friends. Now Socrates had actually addressed this claim previously, when he said that the unjust soul does its work badly, while the just soul does it well (I. 353d9–13). This argument is a direct anticipation of the subsequent conclusion that justice is the harmony of the soul. The argument is rejected by the many, either because they regard injustice as the proper management of the soul or because the attractions of the soul are outweighed by the allure of unrestricted material possessions. In either case, the outcome is the same.

Why is it a matter of such concern to Glaucon what the many believe? If Glaucon is a passionate friend of justice, as both he and Socrates claim that he is, the contrary views of the many should be of little interest to him. We are entitled to infer from what follows that Glaucon is himself tempted by the views of the many. In the actual city, these views are of great importance to someone who aspires to political prominence. This inference is supported by the previously cited passage in Xenophon's *Memorabilia* concerning Glaucon's oratorical, and so political, ambitions. At a deeper level, however, it is supported by the ambiguous nature of Socrates's own defense of justice. It looks as if one is forced to use invalid arguments in the defense of justice; that is to say, one must use the rhetorical device of pretending to demonstrate something that cannot be demonstrated. Finally, if the many cannot be persuaded by argument, or even by the rhetorical appearance of argument, then they must be compelled to be just. This is exactly what Socrates will recommend in the founding of the just city.

This leads Glaucon to demand that Socrates demonstrate the desirability of justice for itself alone, regardless of what the consequences may be. Strictly speaking, this is impossible, and we shall see that Socrates never fulfils his assignment on this point. Even if justice is the harmony of the soul, the consequences of that harmony in one's actions are different from the consequences of disharmony. Healthy persons behave quite differently from sick ones. Almost equally plain, although difficult to prove, is that it would be impossible to act with complete justice and be regarded everywhere as unjust, or vice versa. For example, someone who is completely just would necessarily do certain things that reveal him or her to be at least partly just, and this impression would be strengthened by his or her never being seen to perform unjust acts. Justice apart from all acts is at most an abstraction, something like the Idea of Justice, which makes its subterranean appearance in Glaucon's unrealistic demand. If the extreme demand made by Glaucon must be fulfilled in order to persuade the many of the complete superiority of justice to injustice, then that persuasion is impossible to accomplish.

What would it mean to suppose that the best case is to be regarded as just while actually being unjust? We acquire the appearance of justice because it is useful for tricking our fellow human beings. And this in turn is because everyone thinks that a just man is more honorable, more moral, and safer to deal with than an unjust man. This can be restated more harshly as the conviction that it is to our own advantage to deal with just rather than unjust persons. But this in turn comes very close to saying that we believe justice to be superior to injustice. We can deny this by holding that one must be just only to one's friends, but this is enough to overthrow the argument of the many and return us to Polemarchus's definition. In sum, it is not better for us to be uniformly unjust, since the consequences will soon become apparent, to our subsequent disadvantage. But neither is it better for others that we be uniformly unjust, for reasons that do not require stating.

The many have obviously heard this argument before; it is nothing more than conventional wisdom. Why has it not persuaded them? I suggest that it is because desire is stronger than reason, and passion is stronger than desire. Furthermore, the desires and passions of the body are stronger, and so more persuasive, than the desires and passions of the soul, at least in the case of the many (and one should remember that the Socratic analysis of the love of honor links it closely with tyranny or the love of money and erotic pleasure). One thing is undeniable, and this is the thesis that Socrates will uphold when he begins the task of constructing the just city. Desire (and passion) must be controlled by reason, but this is possible only through the mediation of spiritedness.

There is another point to be made about Glaucon's terminology in this passage. At 358b4–6, Glaucon demands of Socrates: "I desire [*epithumō*] to hear what each is [*ti t' estin hekateron*] and what power it has [*kai tina echei dunamin*] by itself alone [*auto kath' hauto*] in the soul." In other words, there are desires of the soul as well as of the body. Second, Glaucon refers to hearing rather than to vision. We see forms but we hear definitions and arguments. Third, Glaucon introduces further aspects of the technical terminology of the doctrine of Platonic Ideas. Frequently in the dialogues, the question "What is it?" is answered by identifying the thing's power. All these expressions are rooted in everyday language, although they are given a special meaning by Socrates and his students. Glaucon then offers to praise the unjust life with all his might, not because he accepts this estimate but because he wants to hear Socrates counter with the highest praise of the superiority of the just life. Again, Glaucon says that he wants to hear justice praised *auto kath' hauto* (358d2). He does not repeat this phrase with respect to the praise of injustice, but I shall let that pass in view of the general remark at b4, quoted above.

Socrates is delighted: "What would anyone with intelligence prefer to hear discussed again and again?" (358d7–8). In other words, the conversation that follows is not the last word on the topic of justice, which must be discussed again and again because no *logos* is strong enough to persuade the many, even if we assume that Socrates's *logos* is strong enough to persuade the few. Glaucon will begin by telling us what the many say (e3: *phasin*) justice is and whence it originated (358e1–2); he leaves out a reference to power.

2

The first point establishes that the many regard injustice as good and justice as bad by nature. But the bad that arises from being treated unjustly is much greater than the good that arises from acting unjustly to others. When this becomes evident, those who can neither prevent injustice to themselves by their own efforts nor practice it in dealing with others deem it useful to make a compact with each other neither to act nor to be treated unjustly (358e3–359a2). In other words, the many regard laws as necessary evils; Glaucon here retains Thrasymachus's earlier point that laws are established by the weak to protect themselves against the strong. If we were all strong, however, it is not difficult to see that laws would still be needed, whatever the many believe. Since not all people are equally strong, the scale of relative strength now becomes the basis for distinguishing between the stronger and the weaker. Political compacts are still necessary, and not merely for self-defense, since the acquisition of money, power, and pleasure is dramatically accelerated within a flourishing city. We should also note that the many put justice in the intermediate category between what is best (doing justice with impunity) and what is worst (being treated unjustly with no possibility of revenge). It is therefore not completely bad, even on the extreme assessment of the many.

Glaucon illustrates his point by telling the story of a shepherd, Gyges, who acquires a ring that makes him invisible. Gyges uses this power to seduce the queen, kill the king, and take over the throne (359e3–360b2). I note in passing that the queen raises no objections to any part of Gyges's plan. Glaucon then says that if there were two such rings, one owned by the just man and the other by the unjust, the just owner would behave exactly the same as the unjust. He concludes that this story is "a great proof that no one is willingly just but is compelled to be so, on the grounds that it is not a good in private, for whenever each person believes himself to be capable of acting unjustly, he does so" (360c5–8). Now in fact this story proves nothing whatsoever. It illustrates a view that Glaucon attributes to the many, a view that rests upon the premise that justice is not a "private" or intrinsic good, or in other words, that there are no just persons.

One could certainly say that there is enough empirical evidence to make Glaucon's contention worth taking very seriously. That Socrates takes it seriously is plain from the fact that in constructing his city, he places the desires under the control of the guardian class (spiritedness directed by reason). In fact, Socrates differs from the many on one point only. He believes that there are philosophers who are just by nature; in slightly different terms, he holds that moral virtue is identical with reason or (in the proper sense of the term) knowledge. The same point will be made at the end of the dialogue, in the myth of Er. Those who possess demotic or nonphilosophical virtue cannot be counted upon to choose a just life in their next reincarnation.

To use Socrates's expression, Glaucon polishes up his verbal portrait of the just and the unjust man as if each were a statue (361d4–6). In fact, he has less to say about the just man, and in the continuation, after describing the consequences of appearing to be just, Glaucon omits entirely the just man who appears to be unjust. The reference to statues underlines the previous use of language that leads to the doctrine of Ideas. We are to consider someone who is a man of perfect justice in himself but who is regarded by the external world as entirely unjust, and we are to contrast him with the perfectly unjust man who is regarded by everyone else as perfectly just. Glaucon then says that he will contrast the life of each—in other words, he will attribute the worst consequences of injustice to the just life, while the unjust life is to be linked to the best consequences of the perfectly just life. Let us examine the first case. The concealed unjust man (as I shall call him) rules the city because he appears to be just. Second, he marries and gives his children in marriage to whomever he wishes. Third, he makes contracts and agreements with whomever he wants, from which he benefits doubly because he does not hesitate to be unjust. When he enters into private and public contests, he wins and gains more than his enemies do. In getting more, he is wealthy and does good to his friends and harm to his enemies. Furthermore, he makes more sacrifices to the gods and takes better care of them than does the concealed just man. It is therefore likely that the concealed unjust man will be dearer to the gods than the other (362b2–c8).

This is a rich passage. Glaucon (speaking on behalf of the many) organizes the advantages of injustice around three goods: power or honor, sex, and money. Nothing is said about whether injustice is advantageous to philosophy. The official reason for this silence is no doubt because we are considering the views of the many. The unjust man is also able to bribe the gods, who are thus presented as themselves unjust. It is not entirely clear why Glaucon says that the unjust man will be given the rule of the city because he appears to be just. One can easily imagine cases in which the politically powerful would prefer to have someone in office who is himself unjust, or at least who does good to his friends and harm to his enemies. And indeed, Glaucon attributes to the concealed unjust man precisely this quality. It is quite interesting how this definition of justice keeps reappearing in the conversation. Here, of course, it is associated with perfect injustice, and we may assume that the friends of the unjust man are also unjust, or at least that they will be rewarded at the expense of those who are partly if not entirely just. But this does not alter the fact that the unjust man is good to his friends, and this goodness is not compatible with perfect badness. Socrates's argument about justice among thieves comes into play here. Human life is such that complete injustice is impossible, even among tyrants. Or let us say that even if complete injustice is possible, it is not possible to avoid doing good to one's friends, that is, it is impossible to have no friends in any sense of the term, however debased. I note one other consequence. Glaucon asks us to assume that the gods are unjust, that is, they favor the extremely unjust persons who give them greater honors. The injustice of the gods, however, will not be perceived, since the injustice of their favorites is by hypothesis concealed and looks rather like complete justice. As I noted a moment ago, Glaucon does not add a portrait of the concealed just man who is regarded as perfectly unjust. He is more interested in extreme injustice, because it is this that raises difficulties for just persons.

At this point, Adeimantus breaks into the conversation, not in order to demand that Glaucon describe the just man who seems to be entirely unjust but instead to consider the statements of those who praise justice and condemn injustice. Whereas Glaucon makes a statue or paradigm of perfect injustice, Adeimantus is concerned with what people actually say. He is more down to earth than his spirited brother and wishes to make clearer what Glaucon said (*saphesteron*: 363e4). Whereas Glaucon cites Aeschylus twice (361b7, 362a8–b1), and himself speaks poetically, he does not draw special attention to poets for their praise of injustice. Adeimantus, on the other hand, not only quotes the poets but even singles them out for harsh criticism, in the first instance the noble Hesiod and Homer (363e8). As to the substance of what people actually say, in prose or poetry (363e6–364a1), Adeimantus follows fairly closely the charges made by his brother. The poets render more articulate the views of the many. One noteworthy difference: Adeimantus explicitly links temperance with justice; Glaucon describes acts of intemperance (seducing the queen) but does not name them as such, nor, despite the importance of sex in his account, does he emphasize the connection between pleasure and injustice. Sex figures in his account as an instrument for gaining or solidifying political power. I do not mean to imply by this observation that Glaucon is ignorant of the pleasures of sex; the reverse will be established soon. But these pleasures seem to be private rather than public; I mean by this that, somewhat like Alcibiades, Glaucon can distinguish between the private pleasures of sex and the use of sex to gain political advantage. In his speech about injustice, Glaucon is concerned with the latter.

If I am not mistaken, Glaucon never uses the word *pleasure* in his account of the advantages that are said to accrue to the perfectly unjust man. Instead, he concentrates on political power, triumphing over one's enemies and rivals, and "having more" (*pleoneksia*). Adeimantus also leaves out any important references to pleasure (he refers to "pleasurable games" for the purification of sins at 364e6–365a1) and leaves it to us to infer his austerity from the connection between temperance and justice.[1] Early in his speech, he notes that intemperance and injustice are said to be "pleasant" or "sweet" (*hēdu*) to acquire, whereas temperance and justice are said to be noble but hard and painful (*epiponon*) to acquire. In addition, Adeimantus emphasizes the bad consequences of poetry for justice (see especially 364c5–365a3), and he is very much concerned with temperance. It seems fair to infer that Adeimantus is more austere than Glaucon and more concerned with conventional morality.

In sum, Adeimantus directs his criticism especially at the poets because they make a powerful contribution to the corruption of the many. For the many, the poets are "wise" (365c1) and the spokesmen for the gods (365d6–366b2).

This point will be retained by Socrates when he turns to the founding of the just city, except of course that Socrates will replace the poets by the philosophers. It should also be noted that the paradigmatic criticism of the poets as formulated by Adeimantus has little if anything to do with their imitative function or the difference between art and theory (that is, with what is today called "ontology"). The main point is that the poets do not elevate the many but debase them through the persuasiveness of their rhetorical powers. Adeimantus is concerned with moral virtue, not "being." Since he is obviously very familiar with the great poets, Adeimantus is well aware that their language is much richer and deeper than the speeches of the many. But this is of interest to him only as a sign of the poet's power to persuade. He gives a one-sided account of poetry, but the side that he brings out—the poets pander to the worst elements of the many—is central for justice. We shall return on more than one occasion to this topic; here I note only that the demands of justice do not coincide easily with the notion that justice requires freedom of speech.

I mention in passing that Adeimantus attributes to the many (and so to the poets) a willingness to entertain the possibility that the gods do not exist (365d7–e1). It should be obvious, but it is worth stating, that "atheism" was not restricted in classical antiquity to the occasional philosopher. We should also notice Adeimantus's remark at 366c6–d1 that prepares us for a more detailed formulation by Socrates: "Unless someone despises injustice thanks to his divine nature or avoids it through the acquisition of knowledge, none of the rest [of mankind] is willingly just." The continuation of this passage is also an anticipation of the myth of Er, in which the soul of the man who was conventionally just in his previous existence, when offered the first choice of the next incarnation, at once chooses the life of the tyrant.

Adeimantus summarizes his speech with a powerful plea to Socrates that he show not only that justice is stronger but also that it is more praiseworthy than injustice because of the inner effects of each upon the soul, regardless of their external consequences (note that at 367b4 Adeimantus uses a variation on the expression previously introduced by Glaucon to refer to justice in itself: *autē di' hautēn*). Socrates expresses his admiration for the two young men, first by praising their father and then by quoting the opening line of a poem written for Glaucon by his lover (367e6–368a5). This is an implicit contrast between political and private eros. Even more striking is the fact that nothing is said of Adeimantus's lovers, if indeed he has any. Glaucon is erotic and spirited, but Adeimantus is sober and virtuous. Both are necessary for the founding of the just city.

Socrates admires the nature of the two brothers (367e6), namely, their ability to praise injustice and blame justice even though they do not believe in the truth of their own arguments. Glaucon and Adeimantus thus have the ability to make the better argument look like the worse and the worse like the better. This is a criticism that has been leveled against sophists and philosophers alike. Socrates assumes that the brothers have not been persuaded by their own words because of his general familiarity with their characters; "on the basis of your speeches, I would distrust you" (368a7–b3). It follows from this that if one does not know the character of a speaker, it is prudent to distrust him, at least if he is speaking about justice, virtue, and politics. Contemporary analytical philosophers sometimes refer to "the principle of charity" when discussing the properties of language, namely, that one must assume that our interlocutors are expressing their views truly. A much less naive principle would be that of the politics of suspicion. More like the principle of charity is the widespread assumption among modern and contemporary students of Plato that he could never lie or conceal his views because he is a philosopher, a word that the moderns use here in a sense that derives from the biblical rather than the pagan tradition. Glaucon and Adeimantus, to come back to the text, provide us with our first extended example of the need to detach one's personal beliefs from a theoretical investigation. An ability to argue well for what one does not believe, is a philosophical virtue, provided that it is used by persons of good character. This point is spelled out by Socrates in terms of the noble lie, which we shall meet in a later passage.

3

Glaucon and Adeimantus ask Socrates to refute the arguments they have put forward on behalf of the superiority of injustice to justice. Socrates says that he is incapable of doing so, since his refutation of Thrasymachus did not persuade them. In other words, the speeches by the two brothers did not break new substantive ground but gave eloquent testimony to the opinions of the many, and in particular to the more eloquent rendition of these views by the poets. Nevertheless, it would be impious (*oud' hosion*) for Socrates not to come to the assistance of justice when it is being defamed (368b3–c3). "Glaucon and the others" beg Socrates to proceed and not to desert the discussion "but to track down what each [justice and injustice] is, and to speak the truth about the respective benefits of each" (368c4–7). Glaucon is again given precedence in the exhortation to Socrates, who acquiesces and begins the next stage of the investigation as follows: Just as it is easier to read large letters first and then to proceed to their smaller replicas, "if they happen to be the same," so it would be helpful to the present investigation if we could find a version of justice larger than the individual soul (368d7).

I call attention to a suggestive point in this passage. Socrates does not assert unequivocally that the city is the soul writ large. He says first that if someone were to direct us to larger letters that were "perhaps" (*pou*) the same as the smaller, this would facilitate our task (368d5). A few lines later, he predicates the utility of the larger letters "if they should happen to be the same" as the smaller ones (368d7). This is not to overlook the fact that he argues henceforward as though the two sets of letters, that is, justice in the soul and justice in the city, were the same. But no proof is ever given of this isomorphism, which is instead a basic assumption that governs the entire discussion of the founding of the just city. We are required to ask what the just city would look like if there were no such isomorphism. In other words, it would be necessary to write a second dialogue. Although we must be primarily concerned with the existing *Republic*, the shadow of the unwritten sequel will fall across these pages on more than one occasion.

At this point, Adeimantus rather than Glaucon responds to Socrates. It is he who agrees to Socrates's suggestion that since justice is within the individual person and also in the city, whereas the city is larger than the person, "perhaps there would be more justice in the bigger and it would be easier to examine closely. If you wish, let us first investigate in the cities what kind of thing justice is. Next we can examine in this way the interior of each individual person, and look for the likeness of the bigger in the look [*idea*] of the smaller" (368e7–369a3). The underlying assumption is then that there is more of the same justice in the city than is contained in the soul. Unfortunately, in order to determine that the kinds of justice are the same, one would have to inspect the smaller version first. But if the smaller version is accessible, then the reference to the city seems to be unnecessary. A number of other objections have been raised against the ostensible analogy between the city and the soul, but it will be easier to consider them when we have been introduced to the structural details of the analogy. I shall mention here only the most obvious of the structural difficulties. Whereas each of the three parts of the soul is said to correspond to a political class within the city, it is clear that every citizen will have all three parts of the soul. For the analogy to hold, workers should lack intelligence and spiritedness, auxiliaries should be without intelligence and desire, and the philosopher-kings should have neither spiritedness nor desire.

We should first notice Socrates's use of the word *idea* in speaking of the nature of justice within the individual person. Socrates does not use this word in conjunction with the justice of the city. This is in keeping with the main theme of the dialogue, namely, to determine which is happier, the life of justice or that of injustice. The original of justice is in the soul; the copy lies in the city. This last is a *homoiotēs*, a likeness or a resemblance of the *idea* of justice in the personal soul. Implicit here is the question of whether a likeness is or can be the same as its original. This question arises in particular with the introduction of the doctrine of the so-called Platonic Ideas; but in its preliminary form, the question has to do with the appropriateness of drawing inferences about the soul from an inspection of the city. As we proceed in our analysis, we shall find that we make constant use of our knowledge of the soul in order to bring the city into existence. If there were not first individual souls or persons, there would be no cities, but the reverse is not true. The priority of the soul to the city suggests that it may be misleading to take the larger city as a more accessible version of the soul. Each of us is closer to his or her personal soul than to the external city. One might reply that the soul is shaped decisively by the particular city in which it lives, but the particular city is itself an interpretation of what it is to be a human being, namely, an ensouled person. And this is true of Socrates's just city as well.

In other words, the priority of the soul to the city would not be negated by the claim that justice is primarily a political virtue. The key point is that political virtue makes no sense when expressed in exclusively impersonal terms. Even political realism, or the view that all personal rights are suspended when required for the welfare of the city, rests upon the assumption that the city is necessary, not for itself as a collection of buildings and laws but in order that its citizens may prosper, that is, have the means to live justly. Nor do we have to read the laws of the city we inhabit in order to discover what is meant by justice. On the contrary, as Socrates would insist, we decide whether the laws of the city are themselves just or unjust. But there is no way to do this by comparing these laws with others. This leads to an infinite regress. The only way to avoid such a regress is by recognizing that laws are judged by their consequences for the lives of our citizens. We must first decide what is a just life for the individual person before we can begin to write laws sensibly.

Adeimantus goes on to agree that if we watch a city coming into existence in speech, we shall "probably" see the genesis of its justice and injustice, and this allows the "hope" that we shall see more easily what we are looking for (369a5–b1). I note the underlying assumption that we can start to build a city without knowing what justice is, and that the latter will appear at a certain point in the construction. We assume this because we already know from our experience of cities that they contain justice. That is to say, we already know what justice is; otherwise we could not recognize it when it appears. And this in turn suggests that we do not need to define justice in order to know what it is; we are acquainted with justice by virtue of our humanity. The founding of a city, however simple, is itself already the expression of the desire for justice.

Adeimantus announces on behalf of the other interlocutors that the investigation is to continue (see Bloom's note to *eskeptai* at 369b4). This usurpation of power stems from his initial fervor in denouncing the immorality of poetry. That is to say, Adeimantus is the representative or, better still, the symbol of justice as temperance. But his defense of temperance is so to speak intemperate, and this is because one cannot defend the temperance of the body without restricting the poetic power to persuade. The different dramatic significance of the two brothers will shortly become clearer still as Socrates, with Adeimantus's assistance, constructs the first city, in which temperance approaches extreme austerity. Socrates is forced to deviate from this city by Glaucon, who protests against the simplicity of the citizen's meals.

Socrates begins by stating that the city comes into existence because each of us is not self-sufficient or, literally, self-ruling (*autarchēs*) but is, rather, extremely needy. In the *Symposium*, Diotima tells Socrates that eros is born of cleverness and poverty. The city, it seems, is born of poverty only; to anticipate, Socrates will omit mention of sexual eros in the first city until the very end of his exposition. I shall return to this point shortly. Meanwhile, Socrates says that the city originates when one man takes on another for one need and yet another man for another need; since there are many needs, the process leads to a gathering of many into one. The language seems to rule out the possibility that one man can fulfil several needs; in other words, the division of labor is present at the outset (369b4–c5). This will shortly be made explicit.

The principle of the division of labor is itself based upon the perception that it is more efficient to distribute tasks in accord with ability or for the sake of efficiency. But this perception already contains the notion of justice, namely, the customs or regulations by which tasks are distributed and goods are exchanged. The division of labor is the most primitive manifestation of minding one's own business, which will eventually be offered by Socrates as the definition of justice. The latter does not come into view in the course of building the city; it is the act of founding itself. The city is a one out of many but is a unity in which the constituent elements do not disappear. The individual citizens derive their nature as citizens through membership in the city, which itself exists as something separate from, even if it is the defining characteristic of, its members. From this standpoint, the city resembles a Platonic Idea, as do all similar collections. One could say that the city in speech is something like the Idea of the city.

We turn now to the construction of the city in speech, which, Socrates says, is made by "our need" (369c10). According to Socrates, the first and greatest of needs is food, second is housing, third is clothing, and so on. One man will attend to the acquisition of food, a second to housing, and so on; each will give a share of what he acquires or produces to his fellow citizens "because he believes this to be better for himself" (369c7). The city originates in selfishness rather than in friendship or sympathy. Strikingly enough, the selfishness is that of the body, yet there is no reference to women or eros until the very end of the construction of the so-called city of need. "The neediest city," as Socrates refers to it, will be made up of four or five men, each of whom satisfies through his labor one of the four or five primary necessities of human existence. In this way, the body is taken care of (369d1–e1). This city expands steadily as we recognize the need for further workers. Once it is completed, and Socrates begins to look for justice and injustice within it, he mentions children for the first time (372b6–c1), emphasizing the point that as few as possible will be produced, in order to avoid war and poverty. Yet even here explicit reference to women is absent. This downplaying of sex is a hint of the problem it poses for a just city. The neediest city comes closest to resolving that problem, but in a way that no one would accept. To say this in another way, the assimilation of women into men, which will lie at the heart of the fully developed Socratic city, has a natural limitation: the production of children. In the discussion of the neediest city, women are so to speak invisible, but they will soon come to light as the discussion progresses.

Since human beings differ from one another by nature, they also differ in the kind of work they can best perform. Adeimantus and Socrates thus agree on the natural basis of what we can call the division of labor: "one man, one art" (370b5–6). In this way, each man can concentrate on his proper work and act at the right moment rather than shift from task to task, thereby running the risk of neglecting all tasks at a critical time. Each product of work will be more plentiful and beautiful, as well as easier, when each workman produces in accord with nature and at the right moment (369e2–370c2). I emphasize that prepolitical need produces the city by laying down procedures for the assignment of distinct occupations and the exchange of goods. In other words, need "needs" justice. Without these preliminary arrangements, there is no city.

Socrates goes on to observe that more than four workers will be required if we are to make the neediest city. He lists a number of common occupations, including carpenters, smiths, shepherds, farmers, merchants, and those who deal in trade with other cities. All these occupations, which arise from a need to preserve and tend the body, fall within the class of farmers and laborers, neither of which will participate in any significant way in the governing of the city in its final form. And of course, there are no guardians, whether philosophers or soldiers. The first city thus consists exclusively of the lowest class of the final city. And the extreme downplaying of the role of sex in the first city is connected with the absence of philosophy. This is also the place to point out that at first Socrates is constructing the basic elements of any city whatsoever.

At a certain point, however, he is faced with decisions that point in the direction of a very particular and idiosyncratic city. Furthermore, Socrates is about to call the neediest city the true city. If this is so, then political life, which is almost completely absent from the first city, is not fully in accord with nature. But the last stage, or the city of philosopher-kings, is also not natural, because it can only come into existence by the efforts of a philosopher who enforces the suppression of the natural desire to possess and favor one's own children, and this is the basis of monogamy as well (370c7–371e6).

Not only sex but also what could be called friendship and community are introduced by Socrates in the moderately expanded version of the neediest city in connection with banqueting and singing to the gods, or in other words, leisure as opposed to work (372a5–c1). The city was originally founded because of the work of self-preservation, yet it is immediately obvious that such a city could not survive. In the second stage of the founding of the city, the difficulty is removed by the addition of women at the last moment. As Socrates describes it, one could very well infer that sex is restricted to the occasion of religious celebrations, in order to keep the number of births low enough to avoid poverty and war.

The addition of necessary occupations entails a substantial increase in population over the original four or five. But the result is more like the expansion of a business association than the genesis of a city. Socrates himself calls attention to this point. In the course of discussing the exchange of goods, which leads to the creation of a market, commerce, and money, he reminds Adeimantus that this was why they "produced a community in order to build a city" (371b5–6). Socrates has remained entirely silent thus far about rulers, the duties of citizenship, and the structure and function of government. Needless to say, there has been no mention of philosophy (and so theoretical science) or the fine arts. There is, however, an important shift in the description of the city. Thanks to its increase in size, with the concomitant expansion of production and distribution, of which perhaps the crucial step is the invention of money, the city seems to have opened itself to the rise of intemperance, or let us say to the erosion of temperance. Socrates seems to have thought of this problem, because in beginning his description of the lives of the men of the city, he presents a picture of austerity. To take the crucial example, they will eat bread made of barley and wheat and will drink wine. As Glaucon is about to protest, there is no meat or sauce in their diet, and the other aspects of their lives seem equally primitive. On the other hand, they will sing of the gods, which means that poetry, if not professional poets, will be present in the city, and with it, religion. And this is the last point introduced into the construction of a relatively austere city, a city that will be unacceptable to Glaucon but to which Adeimantus has raised no objections. All of this points to the central role of eros in the *Republic*, or more precisely to the political need to restrict eros, a need that cannot be fulfilled because eros, as it were, is needier, that is, more exigent, than justice.

That there is a transition in the discussion is made very clear by Glaucon's interruption. He has nothing to say about the virtual silence about women, nor does he complain about the restrictions on "sweet intercourse," perhaps because it does not rule out homosexual contacts. Curiously enough, his complaint is about the cuisine: "But it looks as if you have these men feasting without relish [or sauces]." Socrates replies: "You speak the truth. I forgot that they will have relish," and he proceeds to list salt, oil, cheese, and various vegetables, fruits, and berries or nuts. But this still does not satisfy the hungry Glaucon, who compares the cuisine to food fit for pigs (372c2–d5). Perhaps he is thinking of the banquet which was promised by Polemarchus but which has been postponed indefinitely by the conversation. In any case, Glaucon is not at all content with the austere regime that satisfied his brother. He wants couches and tables, as well as relishes and desserts in the current fashion. The word *opson* means in general cooked food, and (according to the dictionary of Liddell, Scott, and Jones) it meant fish in Athens. Neither Socrates nor Glaucon refers explicitly to meat or flesh, but such a reference seems to be implied by Glaucon's distaste for Socrates's own vegetarian interpretation of the term (372d6–e1).

Socrates says that as he now understands it, they are in the process of constructing a luxurious (*truphōsan*) city (372e3). There is a certain ambiguity concerning how many cities have been constructed thus far. It seems that everything from the city of four or five technicians through to Glaucon's intervention counts as one developing city, but there is a break in the exposition when it is recognized that many more specialists than four or five will be required. This leads to an expansion of the neediest city, which is not identified as a new city but which differs in being less austere and in the acknowledgment of children and so, by inference, of women. In my opinion, it would be plausible to say that Socrates is not constructing truly separate cities here but is building up the city step by step. But if we continue with the traditional reference to separate cities, thus far we have two or three, depending upon how we divide. That is, it will depend upon whether the neediest city is distinct from the city that includes women; the luxurious city is distinct in either case.

This imprecision is typical of Plato. More immediately important is Socrates's assertion that, in his opinion, the true city is the healthy one that they have just described (namely, the neediest city in its full version: 372e6–7), but that the growth of justice and injustice can be conveniently observed in the evolution of the luxurious city. Socrates implies that the healthy city is possible and even desirable, despite the absence of philosophy and, in any serious sense of the term, of politics. It remains to be seen how we are to characterize the luxurious city. Let us say only that in this city, luxury is accompanied by philosophy and war, and so by fever or illness (372e8). The peaceful life of the true, austere, and healthy city (372c1, d2) is about to be lost by another kind of neediness or necessity, namely, the necessity of desire, of which the deepest and most pervasive form is eros.

PART Two

4

Paideia *I: The Luxurious City*

I

Thus far I have been speaking of the construction of the neediest city, which in its developed form is called by Socrates the healthy or true city (372e6–7). When Socrates asks Adeimantus whether this city is now complete, he replies "perhaps" (371e11). The true city contains very few amenities, restricted sexual reproduction, and, in short, no luxury, which is why Glaucon says that it is a city fit for pigs (372d4–5). There is some poetry (hymns to the gods), but obviously no philosophy. We must also ask why Socrates calls this the true and healthy city, and in particular how this could be so in comparison to the city of philosopher-kings. It is helpful to remember that something like the neediest city must have existed in the first stages of the process leading to the development of cities as Socrates and his contemporaries knew them. The philosophical city, on the other hand, has never existed and probably never could exist. But this cannot explain why "true" is associated with so primitive a community, in which there is no philosophy and no discernible political activity. Nor does it take into account Socrates's statement that the just city is a paradigm laid up in heaven. This is of course a metaphor, but it serves to associate the just city with the paradigms called Ideas.

The first city was founded with the assistance of the austere Adeimantus, and it is a kind of caricature of his nature. The second city is brought into being by Glaucon's denunciation of the absence of luxury in the first. The city of pigs, as Glaucon characterizes Socrates's healthy, peaceful, and true city, is expanded not only in size but through the admission of flesh eating, together with relishes and sauces that are not made simply of fruits, nuts, and the like. We shall also require couches to recline on, tables from which to dine, and "perfume, incense, courtesans, and cakes." Socrates goes on to add artworks made of precious metals, as well as music, poetry, dancing, theater, and the craftsmen associated with these arts. The luxurious and feverish style of life now requires the addition of servants like wet nurses and beauticians, and also of physicians, who were apparently unnecessary in Adeimantus's city (372e4–373d3).

The luxurious and feverish city contains the full panoply of the fine arts that was missing from the city of pigs. Physical ornamentation and the presence of courtesans indicate the greater diversity of erotic contacts as well. And Socrates goes beyond relish to indicate that the luxurious city includes the consumption of meat; there will now be need of swineherds to tend to the pigs that were absent from the city of pigs (373c4–6). This cultivation of the appetite in turn raises the need for additional land for pasture and tillage. Our citizens will now be forced to take part of their neighbors' land, and they in turn to occupy ours, if they engage in the unlimited acquisition of money, beyond what is necessary. They will therefore go to war with each other (373e2), and this is another decisive difference between the two cities: meat eating, poetry and the fine arts, extended sexuality, and war are all instances of luxury. So far, there is no mention of philosophy, but it will eventually be introduced into the feverish city.

We must now come back to the question of the difference between the true city and what we should presumably call the false city. At the least, one can say that the distinction shows the innate defect in human cities; they are destroyed by their most attractive features. The true city suffices for a life of health and peace, but at the price of the cultivation of the soul. The luxurious city cultivates the arts and will allow the practice of philosophy, but at the price of the health of the body. This is no doubt oversimplified, since for Socrates, art and philosophy can lead to the corruption of the soul. But the general point holds good. One cannot quite say that Socrates speaks here as an admirer of Sparta, because war is associated with luxury. There is nevertheless something Spartan about his initial austerity and neglect of the intellect and artistic sensibility. We could be drawn to the conclusion that the city of pigs is for Socrates the *natural* city, in the sense that it covers the indispensable minimum of physical wants. The great difficulty, of course, is how a city can be natural that excludes philosophy. And the answer can only be that there is an intrinsic conflict between philosophy and politics. This leads in turn to the inference that nature is split in half within the human breast. Philosophy is necessary for those who are by nature philosophers, yet it is not only unnecessary but dangerous as well for the nonphilosophers. One final remark in this vein. The neediest city is subnatural rather than natural, by which I mean that it exhibits the lowest stratum of characteristically human nature, a stratum that is itself grounded in the nonhuman animals. The question of the subnatural will arise when we come to the allegory of the cave in Book Seven.

Socrates does not reject Glaucon's request to introduce luxury into the city. He accepts the need to go beyond the so-called true city, which is both subpolitical and subnatural, if not *unnatural*, because human beings will not consent to maintain their lives at that level of simplicity. And perhaps no harm will come to us from the introduction of luxury, since our primary intention is to discover the nature of justice, which is "perhaps" visible within a luxurious city (372e3). This statement, which is made in order to placate Glaucon, will be minimized to a considerable extent by later developments, in which the city is purged of its excessive luxury. It is, I think, plain that Socrates, faced with a choice, would also choose not to live in the true city. Its truth lies in the representation of the limits that would have to be set upon human nature in order to maintain a happiness that is undisturbed by desire, in particular, erotic desire. As it is, however, the limits are unenforceable. In order to be at peace, human beings must cease to be fully human. Speaking very generally, political life in the full sense is a consequence of the impossibility of transforming human beings into brutes. In the just city that Socrates is about to construct, the attempt to effect this transformation is not entirely lacking, but it is partly obscured by a parallel attempt to transform human beings into gods, or let us say "supermen." This double attempt leads to tension and even contradiction in the simultaneous indulgence and restriction of the two forms of eros, sexual and philosophical. I have already referred to the sexual contradiction; as to philosophy, it is in one sense encouraged to flourish, and, indeed, to rule the city, but in another, it is subjected to a severe and unspoken restriction: all the philosophers must be "Socratics."

We can therefore say that Socrates expresses the common philosophical desire to engage in the extreme form of philosophical activity, which includes the exclusion of all views other than his own. This is the desire to rule, or better, to encompass the whole. But in order to carry out this attempt, he must transform the city into a Socratic tyranny, or sacrifice the very justice that he attributes to the city. I would therefore modify the Straussian view that the main purpose of the *Republic* is to show the dangers entailed by an excessive pursuit of justice. This is a subsidiary purpose. The main purpose is to show the impossibility of the full satisfaction of philosophical eros.[1] This is to say that the philosopher both desires and does not desire to rule, or in other words that there is no more unity in the philosophical nature than there is in the city.

To summarize the entire stretch of the discussion to this point, the city does not exist by nature in any simple or straightforwardly honorific sense. It arises from physical need. At first glance, these needs seem to be deceptively simple. But the very principle of the division of labor (one man, one art) leads to the multiplication of arts, hence to the need for more citizens, and so to the steady increase in the complexity of human existence. The very process by which we take care of physical desire leads to its increase, not its restraint. It is this process that takes us out of what the early modern thinkers will call the state of nature.

2

Let us now return to the pursuit of justice. The first virtue to be given prominence was that of temperance, already associated with Cephalus. The next is courage, which comes to light very naturally in connection with a consideration of war. Socrates first calls attention to the fact that whether war is good or bad, we have discovered its origin, namely, those things in the city that most of all produce private and public evils (373e4–7). Socrates does not tell us what those things are. We have been discussing the expansion of the city, or to say the same thing in another way, the multiplication of desire. As we just saw, desire cannot be restrained below a certain level, and when our desires exceed our possessions, we must go to war to acquire additional sources of satisfaction. And the same, of course, is true of other cities, which will attack us or try to defend themselves against our incursions. War is thus built into the very structure of politics; there is no such thing as perpetual peace. We can say that war is bad because it brings mutilation, death, and other less violent forms of discomfort. But we can also say that war is good because we are driven by our natures to acquire and protect the necessities of existence. One could object that it is a main purpose of the *Republic* to advocate the limitation of desire, but this does not alter the basic claim, as Socrates's own exposition makes entirely explicit. To mention only the most obvious point, one of the three general classes of the just city consists of warriors who mediate between intelligence and desire.[2]

The underlying sequence of thought is that when temperance fails, as it must, human beings have need of courage in order to expand their possessions and so to satisfy their desires. The need for an army will increase the size of the city dramatically. This is guaranteed by the principle of one man, one job, because the number of special tasks and different weapons required by an army is considerable. Furthermore, we cannot simply turn our citizens into soldiers when war occurs, because war is itself an art or profession. One must possess the requisite nature for it, and one must practice the attendant skills (373e9–374e9).

Socrates anticipates his later terminology by saying that it is now our task to select the nature that is suitable for guarding the city. He attributes greater urgency to the art of war than to any of the other occupations. The reason for this is obvious. If the purpose of the city is to protect the indispensable needs of the body, and if these needs overshoot the boundary of what is necessary thanks to the very processes through which we satisfy them, then the art of war is the greatest preserver of the body and underlies all other attempts to care for its needs. Since the soul cannot exist without the body, war or the capacity to make war is also the greatest preserver of the soul.

We must not be cowardly in attempting to select the warlike nature (374d3, e11). Socrates means, first, that we must not shirk at the seriousness of this task but, second, that we should be brave enough to address it in a playful manner. This at least is how I understand his turn to the nature of the dog, which supplies him with the paradigm of the military man. More precisely, Socrates compares the noble young dog with the well-born young man and establishes that for the purposes of guarding there is no difference in their natures. If this is true, then spiritedness and courage are the only powers of the soul that soldiers require; their intelligence may be limited to the ability to obey their master's orders. But who are these masters? It looks as though the officers will come from the subclass of philosopher-kings. As to the bodies of the warriors, in both cases, canine and human, they must have sharp senses, speed, and strength. This analogy cannot possibly be taken literally, as is evident from the previous discussion, to the effect that good soldiers require both the knowledge (*epistēmē*) of how to use their weapons and practice in how to use them (374d5–7). The separation of spiritedness from intelligence is plausible in the case of dogs, but it makes no sense when applied to human beings (and this point will come up again when we arrive at the creation of the three classes of the city in keeping with the analogy between the city and the soul).

Still, there is a certain plausibility in saying that both dogs and soldiers must be spirited and courageous. But consider the situation if we substitute some other animal, say a bear, for the dog. Bears, tigers, and other wild animals may be both spirited and courageous, but they differ from the dog precisely in that the latter has been bred and trained to his tasks by human beings; this is what we mean by the difference between tame and wild animals. In many cases the wild animal can destroy the tame one simply through greater strength, but dogs can also be trained to die in the protection of their masters, and sometimes this tenacity allows them to prevail over stronger opponents. In other words, what we require here is not just spiritedness and courage but also loyalty. If this were not true, human beings would prefer to be guarded by bears and tigers rather than by dogs. The question is why loyalty is a characteristic of the great majority of dogs (unless they are wild) and of so few, if any, wild beasts — and then only if they have been subjected to training.

In sum, a dog is already a pseudosoldier; we have trained the dog in the light of our image of the soldier. It would therefore be circular to argue that our image or paradigm of the soldier comes from observation of noble dogs. To say that a dog is "noble" is already to refer to its breeding and training. I am no specialist in the relative intelligence of animals, but dogs are unusually useful to human beings precisely because they can be bred and trained, and this susceptibility cannot be due simply to the spiritedness or courage of the dog. At least part of it must be due to the dog's intelligence. We cannot go wrong, however, in emphasizing the word *loyalty*.

But this is not quite the main point. In approaching it, I note in passing that extreme spiritedness is not synonymous with, but is the foundation or cause of, courage (375a11–b3).[3] As to the point itself, Socrates raises the danger that the soldier, precisely because he is strong and courageous, will attack us and our friends as well as our enemies. How can we find human beings who are both gentle to their friends and harsh to their enemies? In other words, how can we produce an army that does good to its friends and bad to its enemies? Once more the definition of justice defended by Polemarchus comes into view, and fittingly enough, in connection with war. The soldiers have been separated from the rest of the citizen body, so we cannot quite say that justice for the entire city is doing good to friends and bad to enemies. But the inference is tempting. There can be no doubt, however, that the importance of war guarantees the importance of Polemarchus's definition of justice.

A gentle spirit seems to be opposed by nature to a fierce one (375c7–8), yet our guardians require both attributes. The problem is solved, however, as soon as we think back to the noble dog, who is "by nature" inclined to be gentle to those whom it knows and the opposite to those whom it does not know. Socrates infers from this that the combination of characters is possible and not contrary to nature (375e1–8). At no point does Socrates give an example of a human being who exhibits this combined nature. The possibility of a guardian class, namely, of soldiers who are both good to friends and harsh to enemies, is affirmed by recourse to the behavior of dogs. But dogs, to repeat, are bred and trained by human beings; they are by nature wild. If the analogy holds, then good soldiers are artifacts of training, that is, they are artificial, not natural. This will become of great importance later, when Socrates discusses the relations between spiritedness and intelligence. Spiritedness or courage is not in itself enough to produce loyalty; this must be accomplished by intelligence. The numerous references to nature in this whole passage are therefore misleading and incomplete. Human beings no less than puppies must be trained for the occupation of the guardian. And what is true of guardians is certainly true of the other arts and crafts. We can thus conclude that it will be necessary for the intelligent portion of the city to train the rest to perform their proper tasks, that is, to mind their own business. In short, justice is a product of intelligence. Socrates knows as well as Aristotle that people must be trained, that is, habituated to be virtuous. But he requires that this training be administered by intelligence or the philosopher, a conclusion that Aristotle wishes to avoid.

In sum, we can breed dogs to be fierce toward strangers and gentle to friends because we ourselves exhibit this inclination. The apparent problem about the opposition between fierceness and gentleness is an illusion; these two attributes are directed toward two different objects: strangers and friends. Also of great interest is the connection between strangers and enemies. This connection is important for politics as well as in our private life. The unknown may be dangerous. More precisely, friendship intersects with familiarity; we become accustomed to the familiar, and this in turn often leads to the feeling of security if not friendship. Familiarity and the ensuing security are inferior forms of friendship, but they are necessary for human life. And this necessity once more sustains the plausibility of the definition of justice as doing good to one's friends and bad to our enemies: that is, every stranger is a potential enemy.

Socrates develops the need for familiarity by continuing his analogy between the guardian and the dog. He says that the guardian must be not only spirited (courageous) but a philosopher as well. The dog exhibits this philosophical nature by becoming angry when it sees someone it does not know, whereas if it knows the person, it greets him warmly. All other questions to one side, if this is correct, then philosophers must be fierce toward strangers and affectionate or friendly to people whom they know, that is, are familiar with. No doubt the familiarity of philosophers with one another is quite different from that of dogs with human beings. It can also be aroused by reading someone's writings or hearing an account of them. The key point is that knowledge produces gentleness and ignorance produces harshness. There is, then, a link between philosophy and the definition of justice as doing good to one's friends and harm to one's enemies. Some philosophical doctrines may be quite harmful to the city. Again: strangers or the unknown present a challenge and a warning of possible dangers. Socrates makes this connection explicit by saying that if someone is to be gentle to his own and those known to him, he must be a philosopher. He does not add the second clause, namely, that one must also be harsh toward what belongs to another and is not known to one. This is in keeping with my earlier remark that the second clause is the more difficult of the two (375e9–376c3).

The entire discussion on this point is playful, another attribute of noble puppies. Since Socrates is forced to depend upon the nature of dogs in order to prove that his description of the nature of the guardian is not a contradiction, one must suspect that a deeper analysis would raise serious difficulties. The difficulties are indicated by Socrates's equation of familiarity with knowledge (note the shift from *sunēthēs te kai gnōrimous* at 375e3 to *katamathein* at 376b4). Dogs are gentle with people whom they "know" in the sense of being familiar with them. But this is a far cry from philosophical knowledge. Furthermore, it is anything but obvious that gentility depends upon such knowledge. Problems like this arise when we attempt to analyze the human soul by dividing it into definite and separate functions or properties. This will become still more apparent when we take up the analogy between the city and the soul in greater detail.

Socrates sums up this stage of the discussion as follows: "Whoever is going to be a noble and good guardian of the city [that is, a "gentleman"] will be by nature a philosopher, spirited, swift and strong" (376c4–5). On the basis of Socrates's model (the dog), swiftness and strength are easy to understand. Spiritedness raises a bit of a problem, since it corresponds to the virtue of courage, but the connection between fierceness and gentleness cannot be explained by recourse to spiritedness alone. If courageous men are gentle to their friends, it is not because they are spirited but because their ferocity has been tamed by familiarity, the political imitation of friendship. Most difficult of all is the attribute of being philosophical. Knowledge does not come from spiritedness. In fact, the exact relation between courage and wisdom is not entirely clear. If we are harsh toward strangers, it is because we fear them in some way; the barking dog may be brave, but its bravery is called into play by concern for the danger that the stranger represents to its pack. In other words, the dog as it were knows that it does not know, and this stimulates fear as well as courage. I do not wish to suggest that courage is superfluous to philosophy, or even that fear predominates over courage. My point is that for Socrates, the brave man knows what to fear and what not to fear. Courage, in other words, is at bottom knowledge or philosophy. But this is not the same thing as being a soldier or guardian. We must not forget that the discussion is not about the philosopher-king at this point but rather about the nature of the warrior. Socrates prepares for the later discussion by combining the courage of the warrior with the philosophical temperament of the dog. But the discussion rests upon an equivocation in the meaning of knowledge or the act of knowing. It would have been much better to say that the spiritedness of the dog or soldier depends upon the knowledge and wisdom of the philosopher.

3

Given the nature of the warrior or guardian, how are we to educate him? (Note that women have not yet played any but a peripheral role in the discussion.) At this point Adeimantus intervenes and takes up the role of interlocutor. He and Socrates agree that the question of education is crucial to the success of their main goal: to find out how justice and injustice enter into the city. They are about to tell a myth (*en muthō muthologountes*) and thereby to educate the guardians in speech (*logō*: 376c7–e1). The two main parts of education are music for the soul and gymnastics for the body. Music is first in order because it includes speeches, and young children are obviously exposed to speeches before they enter into a regime of gymnastics. We might expect Socrates to say that children must first become familiar with true speeches. But he is not thinking here of the assertions of everyday life. It is poetry and myth that are crucial to education. These tales provide the child with a general account of the lives of humans and gods, and in the form that we communicate them to children they are largely false (377a1–2).

Although Socrates begins this section with the distinction between true and false speeches and tales, he shifts very quickly to the distinction between myths that are noble (377b6) and those that are not (377b10–c2). Socrates does not say that noble myths for children are true. Noble myths are obviously those that have been constructed to cultivate nobility in the still plastic nature of the child's soul; if such myths are "true," it is of course not in the same sense as are propositions of everyday life, the arts, and philosophy. One may perhaps think of a contemporary myth like that of Santa Claus or the tooth fairy. Socrates, of course, is especially interested in the myths about the gods that are told by the great poets. The plasticity of the young soul makes it essential that it not be exposed to ignoble myths: the beginning of every work is the most important part (377a12). We must therefore begin by "supervising," that is, censoring, the makers of myths and admitting only those myths that are noble. Since the "lesser" myths told by nurses and parents to children are copies of the "greater" myths told by the poets, they too must submit to censorship.

Adeimantus is entirely sympathetic to this conclusion, and to its consequence that the educators of the city must scrutinize the works of the poets like Homer and Hesiod, but also those of others, who told false myths (377d4–6). The problem here seems to be not so much that the myths are false as that these poets "did not lie nobly" (377d8–9). This is compatible with 377a4–7, where Socrates says that all myths told to children are "on the whole false." It also prepares us for the subsequent introduction of the famous noble lie, a passage that has caused difficulties for many readers of the *Republic*. In the present passage, Socrates is making a much less controversial point, but one with far-reaching consequences. Infants and children are deeply stamped by the kinds of stories and songs to which they are subjected. Many if not most contemporaries would be made uneasy by talk of censorship, but the perception of the problem is today widespread and much debated. One may disagree with Socrates, but this much is clear. Socrates does not define freedom as license. Edifying falsehoods are an essential ingredient in education.

Who will be in charge of the censorship, and so of the construction of noble lies for the young? It is obvious that in the first instance the authority lies in the founding fathers, more precisely, in Socrates. We must first produce noble guardians before we can entrust them with the responsibility of educating their children. Socrates is taking the first step in preparing Glaucon and Adeimantus to be soldier-guardians. Adeimantus, as we saw previously, represents the austerity that is a necessary ingredient in the founding of the city. Whereas Glaucon is moved by political ambition, Adeimantus is moved by anger at immorality. But his conception of morality does not include a prohibition against noble lies; the good is, as it were, higher than the true.

The biggest lie on the biggest subject was told by Hesiod, who in the *Theogony* describes how Kronos came to power by castrating his father Ouranos and was deposed by Zeus in his turn. Socrates says that even if these stories were true they should not be told to the thoughtless young, because they are not noble lies (377e7). If they must be told, it should be as "unspeakable secrets" and with much ceremonial preparation. There is an interesting reference to the pig; the sacrifice required as preparation to hear the ignoble Hesiodic myth must not be a common animal like the pig but something much more difficult to find. One thinks here of the pigless city of pigs. But this aside, what is so terrible about the myths of Hesiod? They seem to sanction the view that one may perform the extremes of injustice, in particular, punish the unjust deeds of one's father in every way, without wrongdoing; in so acting, we shall simply be imitating the god (377e6–378a6). Socrates's city is not so revolutionary as to reject conventional morality entirely; the Greeks generally deprecated the mistreatment of parents, in particular, murder and incest. There is no reference to incest in the passages cited by Socrates. The overthrow of the father is central here, because it symbolizes the violent overthrow of human rulers and governments. In general, the sanctity of the parents is also the sanctity of tradition. However revolutionary Socrates's city may be, if it is going to endure, its institutions must themselves become the basis of tradition.

In the new tradition, there can be no talk of gods making war against gods, which is not true (378c1) but, more important, is ignoble or shameful. That this is more important than truth is clear from Socrates's next point. "If we are somehow to persuade the guardians that no citizen was ever angry with another and that to be so is not holy [*hosion*]," they must be indoctrinated with this belief from earliest childhood, and as they grow older, the poets must be forced to write stories very much like that training. It is manifestly false that citizens were never angry with one another, but it is politically important for this belief to be held by the guardians. Obviously it will not be held by the founding fathers, or those who have come to maturity before the founding of the city (378c1–d3). Passages like these show the naïveté of those who flinch from the perception of the role of lying in politics. From a political standpoint, nobility is higher than truth.

Myths about mistreatment of their parents by the gods or their fighting wars with one another must all be excluded from the education of the guardians. This is true whether the stories are endowed with secret meanings or not (378d6), since children are too young to detect them, where they exist. The myths that Socrates sanctions do not have secret meanings, except in the sense that they have been concocted to train the young guardians in nobility. They may also be false; obviously this falseness must be concealed from children or the point of telling such tales would be entirely lost.

Adeimantus wants to know which myths may be told to the children of the guardian class; Socrates replies that we at present are not poets but founders of a city (378e4–379a4). As we shall see, this is rather misleading, since Socrates uses the language of craftsmanship and artistic production throughout his account of the founding; see for example 376d9, where our present discourse is compared to the telling of a myth. Still, we may grant Socrates that his task is not to write poems for the educational curriculum but to describe the "models" (*tupoi*) according to which the poets must mythologize, in particular, the models of "theology" (*theologia*), literally, the account of the gods. This is ambiguous; it seems that what we need to know are the types of permissible stories about the gods, not their true nature. It is after all going to become rather clear that Socrates does not believe in the Olympian gods; if they do not exist, then their models are themselves myths. We need to know which kinds of myth are politically salutary. In sum, Socrates does seem to be making myths; what he is not doing is writing in verse.

At this point I interpolate an important observation. It has become gradually more evident that, in turning to the education of the soldiers, Socrates is no longer building a model for the construction of any city whatsoever. Every city must have farmers, carpenters, and so on, and their function is much the same in each case. But whereas every city must have an educational program of some sort, the one described by Socrates is radically idiosyncratic and goes against the customs of his contemporaries in what could only be called a revolutionary manner. Indeed, most of our contemporaries, and perhaps we ourselves, find it shocking or absurd. This means that Socrates is not just constructing a city step by step, in anticipation of justice eventually turning up. On the contrary, he is making use of a certain conception of how human beings should live, and so too a certain conception of justice. This follows from the definition he will reach eventually of justice as minding one's own business. We cannot mind our own business unless we know what it is; as usual, virtue is for Socrates knowledge. At the very least, Socrates must know why it is just to repudiate the theology (a term that Plato is apparently the first Greek to use) and moral training accepted by his fellow Athenians.

To return to the text, the first theological point that Socrates makes is that "the god must always be presented as he is" (379a7). I note that Socrates shifts from the plural to the singular; this is a preparation for the abandonment of the Olympians and the other gods of mythology. Socrates does not say why this is so, and it certainly does not follow from his previous elevation of nobility or goodness above the truth. The reason seems to be the nature attributed to the god by Socrates: Adeimantus agrees that the god is genuinely (or truly: *tō onti*) good and hence must be spoken of as such (379b1–2). Why should we accept this? The answer is obvious: because it is politically salutary. Whether the belief is true or false, it is noble to believe in a good god. That is to say, such a god serves as a model for the inclination on the part of the young guardians to act nobly themselves. If the god happened to be bad, surely Socrates would not allow us to speak the truth on this point. In general, one can say that philosophers agreed with Socrates on this question until the full spread of the modern Enlightenment.

There follows a short argument to the effect that what is good does not produce anything harmful (surely a dubious proposition), and what is not harmful cannot be bad. Therefore, what never does anything bad cannot be the cause of the bad. Adeimantus next agrees that the good is beneficial, thereby reminding us of the utilitarian element we discovered in the previous discussion of justice; as beneficial, it is the cause of doing good. Hence it cannot be the cause of the bad. Socrates does not say that there are two gods, one good and one bad, but he refers to one god who causes those few things that are good for human beings. We must seek for other causes (plural) of the many bad things (379b1–c8). No original conception of what is good and bad is introduced here by Socrates. The shift back to the singular "god" suggests that unity and goodness refer to a higher ontological level than do courage and temperance. This is conjectural; what cannot be denied is that the shift in terminology occurs as I have described it.

Socrates is in the process of developing a radical critique of Greek theology as part of his intention to revise conventional views of good and bad. But he cannot simply repudiate the entire Greek experience of these attributes, because it is this everyday, commonsensical experience that provides us with our perceptions of the good and the bad. For example, everyone knows what it means to be benefited, but very few would share Socrates's understanding of the beneficial and the harmful. In order to revise traditional morality and theology, Socrates must begin by accepting what is after all obvious: No one prefers to be harmed rather than benefited. Whereas the good may be something more than benefit, it is also and indisputably beneficial. In short, a new interpretation of the good and the bad cannot contradict the views that are universally held on this question. If it can, it will destroy the very phenomena it purports to explain.

The view that the god causes the good and nothing but the good is unusual by everyday Greek standards, but it is nevertheless a modification of the traditional view that good and bad things come from the gods. The shift from gods to "the god" is more unusual still. It is plausible to argue that if the god is good, he will do no harm. But why should there be one god rather than many? Perhaps the answer is that if there are two or more gods, this leaves room for disagreement on the nature of the good. In this case, there will be degrees of goodness, and therefore relative badness, in the domain of the divine. Finally, I note that on Socrates's view, life is primarily bad; there are very few things that are good for human beings (379c4–6). This apparently holds true within the just city as well.

All passages in poetry that assign responsibility to the gods for human evils must therefore be banished. The reason for this is not one of piety alone but rather is political as well. If the poet should say "that bad men were wretched because they needed punishment, and that by paying the penalty they were benefited by the god, one must let it stand" (380b4–6). But if the laws are to be well observed, we must strenuously prevent anyone "in our own city" from saying that god causes an evil, and this prohibition extends to the old as well as the young. It refers to speech in meter or without meter, since to say such a thing would be neither pious nor advantageous for us, nor would these statements harmonize with one another (3380b4–c3). Socrates expresses himself in such a way as to leave it unclear whether his piety is defined by his political goals or whether it serves as the paradigm for a politically sound education. In either case, the theology sanctioned by piety is radically revolutionary by the standards of Greek tradition.

Adeimantus gives his vote for this new law, and Socrates turns to a second theological point. The god is not a wizard who changes himself from one look (*idea*) to another. The word *idea* appears twice in this passage, and *eidos* once; there is also a reference to *morphē* (shape). It is therefore not surprising that Socrates speaks here of "the" god; stated as concisely as possible, there cannot be two Ideas of anything, least of all, of the Good. This is another step in the preparation of the doctrine of Platonic Ideas (380d1–6). It is more difficult to accept than the first law, as is plain from Adeimantus's inability to say whether the god remains always the same or changes his form. Socrates argues as follows: To exit from one's *idea* is to change, either by oneself or through something else. Whatever is in the best condition is least likely to be altered or changed. Socrates gives examples from natural bodies, the soul, and finally "compounds" (*ta suntheta*), that is, artifacts. The best bodies are least affected by nourishment and labor, and the healthiest and strongest plants are best able to resist excessive heat. The bravest and most intelligent soul is least likely to be disturbed and altered by external forces. And so too for compounds, such as tools, houses, and clothing; the best made last the longest (380d7–381a10). This argument overlooks things that are both the best of their kind and also fragile; that is to say, it assumes that "best" means "lasts longest." But this is what has to be proved.

Throughout this section of the argument, Socrates assumes that "everything that is in fine shape [*kalōs echon*], by nature, art, or both, is least able to be transformed into something else." Since the god and whatever belongs to him are altogether in the best shape of anything, the god is least likely to have many shapes (381b1–7). No argument is offered to prove the existence of the god, which is taken for granted throughout the dialogue. Socrates adds that nothing wants to change itself for the worse; hence the god could not willingly change himself, since any such change would be for the worse (381c3–5). Socrates is silent here about the possibility of the god being changed by some external force (cf. 380d8–e1). Since the god is both good and produces the good alone, it remains possible that the cause of evil is stronger than the god and can change him. I do not find it surprising that Socrates is once more forced to rely upon faulty arguments. One could complain about this if and only if sound arguments were readily available.

The next point is extremely important, in view of Socrates's tolerance thus far toward noble lies. He asserts that god would not wish to lie, either verbally or in deed, by producing a false image (*fantasma*). Adeimantus does not know whether this is true, whereas he had no such doubts about the immorality of the conduct traditionally ascribed to the Greek gods. He continues in his ignorance when Socrates indicates that "all gods and humans hate the true lie, if one can use this expression." What Socrates means is that no one will intentionally lie to the best part of himself about the best things. In other words, the true lie is one that is told to one's own soul about the beings (*peri ta onta*). But this does not preclude telling lies to others (382b1–6). And if the god exists, there is no obvious reason why he would not lie to human beings for their own good.

To repeat, the true lie is the ignorance in the soul of the man who has been lied to about the nature of the beings. It does not include deceiving others for their own good. Such deception is carried out not through ignorance but by speech that is accommodated to the exigencies of politics and war. This kind of lie is a medicine (*pharmakon*), and as such it is useful in dealing with enemies and so-called friends, namely, those who do evil through madness. And with respect to mythology, that is, the stories about the gods, we do something useful when we do not know the truth by bringing falsehood into as close an accord with the truth as possible. This plainly means that if we do not know the truth, we can make it up, that is, lie, in accord with our own best understanding of what our guardians should believe (382c6–d4).

Finally, Socrates tries to establish that the god contains no lying poet, that is, will not lie. Socrates holds that the god has no motive to lie, neither through ignorance of ancient things or fear of enemies nor because of the folly or madness of his friends (382d5–e11). He omits here the very point that we just noticed about human beings. The god might lie for our own good, out of his own goodness. This is suppressed, I suggest, because it has dangerous political implications. If the god lies, even for our own good, who is to interpret his words? This problem emerges at the very beginning of the rise of biblical hermeneutics; it is well illustrated by Spinoza's claim that God spoke to human beings *ad captum vulgi* (in a way accommodated to the intelligence of the crowd).

We have now established, according to Socrates, that the god is unchanging and entirely truthful. These two conclusions serve as the basis for the censorship of poetry and are intended to make it as reverential and as divine as possible. The three main theoretical points in this long discussion of the gods are that the eternal and unchanging is better than the transient and changing; that noble or medicinal lies are permitted to human beings when speaking to others, and in particular within the political context; and that the god causes the good only. Nothing has been said thus far about the cause of the bad. Finally, when speaking of unity, goodness, and truthfulness, Socrates regularly uses the singular "the god," whereas in speaking of courage and temperance he shifts to the plural "the gods."

4

We have moved in the course of Book Two from the true to the luxurious or fevered city, thanks to the need to gratify Glaucon's insistence upon comfort. The luxurious city is never explicitly called the false city, but it is at the least a sick version of political life. Nor could one say that this sickness is unnatural; it springs directly from the nature of desire. It would be more accurate to call the true city unnatural, in the first instance because philosophy could not arise within it. By calling the full version of the city feverish, Socrates shows that unqualified talk of living in accord with nature is naive. It is true that the censorship of the poets is already a big step toward the mitigation of the luxuriousness of the city. Socrates will later note that we have purged the city of much of its luxury and that we should continue this process (III. 399e5–8). But he does not say that we have cured the city of its fever. The human being could achieve peace only by not living in accord with nature, namely, by restricting his or her physical appetites to those of the pig, in Glaucon's telling metaphor. And the situation with respect to the development of the soul would be equally primitive. In other words, peace and health are available only to small troops of primitive humans. By developing our natural faculties, we produce war and fever.

In the course of discussing the education that is required in the fevered city, Socrates modifies his procedure by designing a program of music and gymnastics, in particular a purified version of myth, that is designed to moderate the fever and in effect eliminate much of the luxury. That is, he deviates at this point from a general discussion of the origin of the city to the construction of a very special city. It is only within this special city that philosophy enters into the discussion. Philosophy is related to but later than the origin of war. All cities must have warriors, but not all cities require philosophy. In ordinary cities, the warriors are told what to do by tradition, belief, and common sense, and their attention is directed outside the city toward actual and potential foreign enemies. Unless we are dealing with a tyranny, the regulation of domestic violence and lawbreaking is either handled by a different body, which we call the police, or, if the two, police and warriors, are one and the same, once more by law and custom. In the Socratic city, law and custom are replaced, that is to say, produced, by philosophy.

To look at Book Two from a slightly different angle, since life is fundamentally war, the work of the guardian or soldier class is more important than that of the other arts (374c2–3 and d8–e2). Therefore, Socrates turns to the question of the proper nature and education of the guardians, which he does not do in the case of the other arts and crafts. But there is something odd about this stage in the construction of the city. According to the analogy between the city and the soul, we should be able to find justice in any city. But Socrates proceeds directly to a very special kind of city, in which the education of the guardians is entirely novel and is especially concerned with the formation of their beliefs about the gods. The question of censorship and the telling of medicinal or noble lies is thus introduced as a military issue. Nothing is said about the education of the artisans, craftsmen, farmers, merchants, and laborers. As to the philosopher-kings, they have not yet been mentioned, but we can safely say that they would be aware of the difference between noble and shameful stories about the gods, and the need for suppressing the latter. They are already prefigured in the person of Socrates, who is the prime mover in the founding of the city. The guardian-soldiers (also called "auxiliaries") are thus not the sort whom we find in the average city, but to the extent that they resemble any others, it is the Spartans, not the Athenians, to whom they can be compared.

A question is raised by the shift from the luxurious city to the special training of the soldiers, which in turn leads to, or is itself the first step in, the repudiation of that city, and so too in the construction of the just or Socratic city. Suppose that Socrates had proceeded to articulate the luxurious city and thus to describe the construction of cities as they are. Would he then have found justice? It would seem that he could not, if justice is indeed minding one's own business. Justice in this special Socratic sense thus depends upon a revolutionary reform of actual cities, based upon his understanding of what constitutes the good life. Socrates obviously has this conception of the good life in mind before he initiates his political revolution. That is, the Socratic conception of justice is part and parcel of his conception of the good life for the individual person. It is this knowledge of the human soul that permits him to set out upon the task of constructing the just city. Once more we see that knowledge of justice in the soul is prior to, and determines, the nature of justice in the city.

The first point in the education of the guardians is to make them honor the gods (Socrates shifts to the plural) and ancestors as friends. As we saw previously, this depends upon the belief that gods cause nothing but the good, and therefore that they are perfectly just. The second point has to do with courage, the cardinal virtue of the guardian-soldier. Temperance, the first virtue to be discussed, is present, if at all, in a muted form within the luxurious and feverish city. The extreme form of temperance that characterized the true city is not needed, and is impossible, in a city that could actually be suited to human beings rather than pigs. But courage is not muted; it is required in its extreme form in the luxurious city. This is because fear of death, the extreme form of cowardice, presents the greatest risk to the efficacy of the guardians, who must be fearless in the face of death and choose it rather than suffer defeat or be enslaved (386a1–b3). I note that courage does not seem to be involved in the belief in the complete goodness and justice of god. But it is visible just beneath the surface; if we can count on the goodness of god, then we are better able to face death. Sound practice depends upon salutary theory. This shows that the need to instill courage is already present in the luxurious city on its own terms, whereas the need for temperance is not. There is a more direct transition from courage to political revolution than from temperance.

If I am not mistaken, there were eight distinct quotations from the poets on the topics of the goodness, unchangeability, and honesty of god, together with one extended reference to Hesiod. In the beginning of Book Three, the number of quotations increases, and at the same time Socrates shifts from "the god" to "gods." It would be difficult and cumbersome to develop exact statistics, but the general trend is clear. For example, there are twelve quotes from the poets on the fear of death alone in the short stretch from 386c3 to 388e8, not counting allusions to a word or phrase. There are fourteen more quotations from the poets on various points requiring censorship from 389a5 to 393a5. Throughout this section, Adeimantus is the interlocutor. It seems reasonable to infer that the topics under discussion by means of these quotations require greater attention in the training of the guardians than do those discussed in Book Two. No argument is required to sustain the inference that the fear of death is a much greater evil for professional soldiers than are unsound views on the unchanging nature of the deity. In taking up this point, Socrates emphasizes the need to purge the poetical representations of Hades as a place of punishment. We must replace such stories with speeches and writings of "the opposite type" (387c9). This does not mean that we are to praise Hades as the place in which bravery is rewarded. Socrates has just excluded this by stating that it is neither true nor beneficial for fighting men to believe in Hades (b10–c1), although it is "poetical and pleasant for the many" to hear about the domain of the dead (387b2–3). The soldiers must be taught that for the decent man, death is not a terrible thing (387d5–6)

This is an interesting passage. At first glance we would not expect the many to enjoy hearing the poets speak in a frightening manner about death and the hereafter. But poetry in particular, and art in general, has the capacity to make us enjoy what is intrinsically frightening or even evil. One of the greatest blessings of poetry is the transmutation of terror into exaltation. This holds good especially among "the many," that is, those who are not guardians.

Fighting men, however, do not have the luxury of fearing death as they plunge into battle. I do not see why some soldiers could not be inspired by poetry to acts of heroism, but the possibility of harming their morale is greater if the poems accentuate the terrifying side of death. Courage is aroused in those who believe themselves to be facing death, and even dying, for the sake of their god. But this form of "theology" never appears in Plato; it is characteristic of the prophetic religions. Finally, I have suggested throughout this section that the shift from the singular "god" to the plural "gods" has something to do with the shift from the discussion of the nature of the deity to discussion of courage and temperance, and so with death and sex. In connection with these topics, theoretical correctness is superfluous. Even worse, it is ineffectual. This point will recur later in the discussion.

Our own fear (387c4, 6) of weakening the morale of the guardians, and so inducing fear in them, justifies the expansion of censorship to traditional views on death. We must also exclude all references to famous persons lamenting the death of a son, relative, or comrade (387d1–10). Somehow this prohibition strikes me as the most unnatural of Socrates's innovations. To believe in the perfect goodness of god requires, perhaps, naïveté; to be brave in battle is laudatory in itself. But not to mourn one's dead son or friend on the ground that death is not an evil is, I think, to depreciate the goodness of life. And to make life so unimportant is to make political existence unimportant. This ambivalence, namely, the emphasis on the good life and so too on the importance of the city, on the one hand, and the depreciation of human existence, on the other, goes very deep in Plato.

The mourning of Achilles for Patroclus or of Priam for Hector must therefore be suppressed. But even more important, so too must be the lamentation of Thetis for her son, Achilles, since she is a goddess, or of Zeus for his son Sarpedon (388a5–d1). These passages move us precisely because they transform into sublime language experiences and suffering that are central to the human condition. Socrates is not in the process of creating a city that is best by nature but in the process of attempting to transform human nature for the sake of justice. It is therefore not true that in order to find justice we have only to trace the development of the city, any city at all, since cities are all a magnified portrait of the human soul. On the contrary, in the course of building the city, Socrates is changing human nature. If this were not so, he could have looked for justice in the structure of Athens or Sparta. It follows that no actual city is just, precisely if all are the soul writ large, that is, the soul as it is by nature, before it has been transformed by the philosopher. Socrates does not follow nature; he draws upon it in order to modify it. At least that is the practical intention of his conversation in the *Republic*.

Adeimantus readily agrees to the next restriction: The guardians should not be lovers of laughter. The reason given by Socrates is that he who lets himself go in strong laughter seeks a strong change. This is not very clearly expressed, but it seems to mean that strong laughter is the sign of a volatile personality that requires purging. All poetic texts that express "the unquenchable laughter of the gods" must therefore be suppressed (388e5–389b1). As is well known, Socrates laughs only twice in the dialogues, both times in the *Phaedo*, which deals with the fear of death and shows the philosopher's immunity to this emotion. To this we can add that Socrates is never shown as crying, and this point is connected to the previous condemnation of lamentations for the dead. We can therefore anticipate that comedy and tragedy will not be present in Socrates's city. The reason is of course not that Socrates fails to appreciate the power of poetry and drama but that this power, when left to itself, is greater than that of the laws and customs of the city.

We have already established that lies are useless to the gods, whereas the same is not the case for human beings. It is useful to tell lies in order to do good to our friends and harm to our enemies (II. 382c6–d3). Socrates now refines the previous point as follows: "It is fitting for the rulers of the city, if for anyone at all, to lie about enemies or citizens for the benefit of the city, whereas no one else may make use of lies at all" (III. 389b7–9). In the previous discussion, nothing was said about rulers; we were talking about the gods on the one hand and guardians or soldiers on the other. Now Socrates restricts medicinal and useful lying to the rulers (389b7). Hitherto the two groups were not identified; in the present passage, Socrates leaves out guardian-soldiers, who must presumably take their orders from the rulers. The upshot of this passage is that the rulers are like doctors who assuage political illness by telling useful lies. It will later be confirmed that this is the right interpretation. At 414d2–3, Socrates says: "I shall try to persuade first the rulers and the soldiers, and next the rest of the city" that they are all fashioned in the bosom of the earth, and that those who are fit to rule had gold mixed into their composition, whereas the potential guardians contain silver and the working classes iron and bronze.

It is safe to say that the rulers, who are philosophers, will not be persuaded of the truth of the noble lie but will accept it because of its nobility or usefulness. As to the auxiliaries, nothing that Socrates says gives us any reason to doubt that they can be persuaded. Furthermore, by saying "I shall try to persuade them" Socrates makes it clear that the guardian-soldiers are not the source of the lie. The philosopher-king, or rather the founding father, will instead try to arrange the education of the various classes in the city, among them the auxiliaries, in such a way as to produce belief, or at least acquiescence, in the noble lie. Coming back to 389b7ff, the discussion of lying once more supports Polemarchus's definition of justice. But the private citizen (*idiōtēs*) is excluded from the privilege of using medicinal lies; this is reserved for the experts, namely, the "physicians" of the city, who are the rulers (later to be identified as the philosopher-kings; compare the poetic citation at 389d2–3).

Throughout Books Two and Three the discussion of courage is closely associated with the topic of lying. The reader can hardly fail to see that the inculcation of courage is made to depend heavily upon the medicinal and noble use of lying. Incidentally, utility and nobility are not synonymous, but they come very close together in Socrates's development of the point. It is noble to be of use to, that is, to foster the preservation of, the city. This suggests that the city is just, and that it alone is just, since it has to be constructed from the bottom up by means of deviations, many of them revolutionary, from all actual cities. Once more doubt is cast on the thesis that the city is the soul writ large. The thesis may be correct if it means that sick cities mirror sick souls. But if the city does not mirror a healthy soul, then we shall not find justice in it, as Socrates suggested that we would. The conclusion is that, in order to find a just soul, we must construct a just city, because human beings are sick by nature, and they can be healed only through the modification of that nature by philosophers. Plato is thus not quite as far removed from modern constructionist philosophy as is usually claimed.

Having finished with courage, Socrates turns next to *sōphrosunē*, "temperance" or "moderation," a virtue normally associated with the physical appetites. Glaucon, who is both extremely erotic and requires luxurious dining, falls far short of the austerity exhibited by Adeimantus, who appropriately enough continues as the main interlocutor. We should recall, however, that Glaucon is also extremely courageous. Why was he not the interlocutor during the discussion of courage? The answer, I think, has already been given. For Socrates, the topic of courage is very closely connected to that of lying, and thus to the censorship of the poets. Glaucon is less concerned, if at all, with the amorality of the poets, and his courage seems to derive from a source other than poetry. Otherwise put, his courage differs from that of Adeimantus in that it is motivated in particular by political ambition and more generally by a love of audacious conversation. The love of honor, in extreme cases like Glaucon, and still more so like Alcibiades, can supervene over the fear of death. Socrates seems to have exaggerated the need to purify poetry of all attributions of that fear to gods and noble men. In any case, we shall not be surprised to find Glaucon as the interlocutor during the most philosophically difficult parts of the dialogue.

Socrates begins the treatment of temperance "for the multitude," more precisely its youthful portion (389e7, 390a4), by defining it as obedience to one's rulers and also as oneself ruling the pleasures of drink, sex, and food (389d7–e3). The first attribute is not usually associated with temperance; it would seem to be closer to justice. This is the first hint that temperance could replace justice, a point that will come up when we assign the virtues to their respective functions in the city. The guardians are here associated with the multitude and sharply distinguished from the rulers of the city. No reference was made to the multitude in the previous discussion of the education of the guardians with respect to courage. This is undoubtedly because the multitude (the farmers, workers, and the like) will not be permitted to serve in the army or police force. But they must be temperate, at least in the sense of obeying their rulers, if the city is to survive.

Gods, demons, and heroes must not be presented by the poets as being intemperate in sex or fond of money (389e4–390c8). Sex and money go regularly together in the *Republic* because the latter is essential in the gratification of all one's appetites, and of course not only one's sexual appetite. To these, Socrates adds excessive cruelty and disregard for the dignity of the dead bodies of one's opponents. It should be noted that Achilles is frequently criticized in the discussion of courage in Book Three. He is a prime example of someone whose bravery is closely associated with intemperance.[4] We are not to believe that acts of violence and outright evil could be performed by heroes, that is, children of the gods. Again, in this part of his exposition, Socrates speaks of gods in the plural. The treatment of courage and temperance is not as theoretical as that of the unity, eternity, and goodness of god. When Socrates comes in Book Five to speak about the burial and commemoration of those soldiers who have fallen in defense of the city, he will once more speak of "the gods," with Apollo leading the way.

Having dealt with gods, demons, and heroes, we ought next to take up permissible and impermissible ways of speaking about human beings. But we cannot do so at this point, because the speeches we wish to condemn are those that attribute happiness to the unjust and misery to the just, as well as those that define justice as what is good for another but disadvantageous to oneself. In order to know which speeches are to be made about human beings on this point, we must first know what justice is. So this part of the purification of the education of the guardians cannot be completed here. Presumably this will not interfere with the construction of the city, since we need to complete it in order to see where justice is contained within it. Socrates's résumé also implies that we do not attribute justice to gods, demons, and heroes. In addition, it is not clear why he restricts impermissible speeches to those that praise injustice.

There is, then, something unclear at this transitional point in Book Three. Perhaps the simplest way to bring this out is by asking how we shall recognize justice when it appears, if we do not know what it is. Did we not in fact understand a good bit about it, enough to refute Cephalus, Polemarchus, and Thrasymachus? Or did we only seem to have refuted them? The latter conclusion is implied by the regular recurrence of the definition of Polemarchus. On the other hand, there seems to be no problem with respect to courage and temperance, at least as these apply to superhuman beings. Finally, if the gods are good and the cause of everything good for human beings, are they not the cause of justice as well as being themselves just (392a3–c5)?

5

We are now through with the content of speeches and turn to the question of *lexis*, that is, how we speak: style or diction (392c6–8). Adeimantus has trouble in grasping what this means, and Socrates begins his explanation with the help of Homer. Tellers of tales or poets narrate events past, present, and future. Narratives are simple or imitative. In the former, the poet speaks directly; in the latter, he pretends to be the speaker. We can also say that the poet hides behind imitation of others but shows himself directly in narrative (392c9–394b2). This last point, however, is not as obvious as Socrates implies, since there is no reason why a narrative cannot also conceal the author. We have only to think of the Platonic dialogues, in particular the *Republic*. Are we seriously to believe Socrates when, in narrating the speeches and deeds within the dialogue, he tells his unknown audience that he is frightened of Thrasymachus? And what of Plato, who narrates all of the *Republic* by disguising himself as Socrates? In other words, Socratic narrations are Platonic imitations.[5]

These difficulties to one side, there is something illuminating about Socrates's distinction. We are closer to the speaker in narrative than in imitation, since the author distinguishes between himself and the other characters in the first case but not in the second. Socrates illustrates his point by transcribing the opening of the *Iliad* into prose narrative; he omits the meter because, he says, "I am not poetic" (393d1). At II. 369c9–10 he invites Adeimantus to make a city from the beginning and then says that it is made by our need. At II. 378e7 he tells Adeimantus that they are at present not poets but builders (*oikistai*) of the city. The two cases are different. In the first, Socrates distinguishes between writing poetry and making a city; in the second, the distinction is between writing with or without meter. The same verb (*poiein*) is used for making and for writing poetry in meter. For the sake of clarity, let me use the verb *to make* in the sense of producing something that did not previously exist and *to poeticize* in the sense of writing poetry. This gives us a very narrow definition of poetry, but it is in accord with Socratic usage. The key point is now that the city does not exist by nature but must be constructed by human beings. At first glance, poetry is a species of making, since the poem did not exist before it was produced. But there is no reason why the poem cannot imitate something that exists, or even transmit some understanding of what it imitates. In sum, whether or not he is a poet, Socrates is certainly a maker, and although Plato does not write in meter, he is obviously both.

The imitator adapts his speech as much as possible to the person he is imitating, but there is no reason why the narrator cannot conceal himself, whether or not he does so by imitating some character in his narrative. So it turns out that the distinction between narrated and imitative dialogues is not as clear as we could have wished. Socrates says that comedies and tragedies are entirely imitations — the author pretends to be the speakers, and there are no assertions by the author in between these speeches — whereas poems may be either narrative or imitative or both (394b8–c5). We have to decide which of these styles of poetry are to be admitted into our city, in particular whether we shall allow tragedies and comedies. Thus far we have only agreed that poetry must be censored, if it is to be admitted at all.

This leads to the question of whether the guardians should be imitators. According to Socrates, it follows already from the original principle of the division of labor that they should not. But the principle said that each man should do the one job for which he is best suited. What if this job should be that of an actor? The answer seems to be that the same actor cannot imitate many things as well as he can imitate one thing (394e8–10), but this is an argument for the development of many specialized actors, not the abolition of the theater. One can grant that such a system would be cumbersome and require an enormous expansion of the number of actors. But the whole point is wrong; trained actors can imitate a wide variety of human types. Some skilled actors can imitate kings and presidents so as to make them more convincing than the actual incumbents. It is no doubt correct that one cannot be a professional soldier and pursue a career of acting at the same time, but this is not because of any defect in imitation. We must first decide whether we want skilled imitators, and so drama, in our city. A much better argument against the theater would parallel the critique of epic and lyric poetry; the drama is too powerful an influence on human passions to be sanctioned by a city that places a high value on temperance. Temperance, we recall, is said by Socrates to be in the first instance obedience to the rulers. But why can we not have a theater of political propaganda?

Socrates could reply to all of this that the example of one man imitating many others is in itself too dangerous for our city, which is built upon the principle of one man, one job. If he takes this line, then he seems to be obligated to exclude all of poetry from the city. Mimetic poetry is out, for the reason already given. But narrative poetry is also mimetic; the narrative poet pretends to give an accurate account of speeches and deeds past, present, and future; in other words, he imitates through his own narration the narratives and actions of others. As we move forward, Socrates's position on poetry will undergo change; as he says at 394d8–9, they will go "wherever the *logos*, like a wind, carries us."

In the course of applying the principle of one man, one job, Socrates elicits Adeimantus's agreement to the statement that the same person cannot imitate well in both tragedy and comedy (395a1–7). We cannot avoid recalling that at the end of the *Symposium* (223d2–6) Socrates is compelling the drunken Agathon (a tragedian) and Aristophanes (the comedian par excellence) to admit that the same man knows the art of writing tragedy and comedy. I can only suggest here that Plato is such a man, as were Homer and Shakespeare, among others. One could hardly be said to have understood the human soul, and so to be a philosopher, if one does not grasp both "the tragedy and the comedy of life as a whole" (*Philebus* 50b3). In the *Republic*, Socrates is determined to apply the principle of the division of labor as completely as possible. He will make an important exception in one crucial case, the education of the philosophers, who must understand all aspects of knowledge and statesmanship. It is already obvious from the act of constructing the city that Socrates himself does not obey the principle of one man, one job, nor can one say that his sole job is philosophy. Socrates makes it quite clear that whereas the philosophers must rule, philosophy is something distinct from ruling.

Why is the division of labor so important to Socrates? It clearly has to do with the attempt to divide the soul and the city into three parts. This in turn is rooted in the need to separate the rulers from the ruled; the just city does not fall under Aristotle's definition of political life as ruling and being ruled. Aristotle means that every citizen does both, not that each function is fulfilled by a separate class. If the three parts of the soul cannot be sharply separated from one another, then of course the just city is impossible. But is it desirable? Is it a city that every intelligent and just person should wish for? We are not ready to address this question in any detail. One more point in this series. The division of labor is a separate question from that of the decision to admit or to expel poetry in general and tragedy and comedy in particular. As ruled by philosophy, the city must express the principle that each person acts, either directly or indirectly, through knowledge, whether technical or political. This is just one way of saying that the city is to be as unified as possible by the spirit of philosophy. And thus the entire tragedy and comedy of human life is constructed by the philosopher, that is to say, Socrates or, more profoundly, Plato. In such a city, the poets become superfluous, not because they do not understand the soul at all but because they are skilled at eliciting the heterogeneity of human nature. In the philosophical soul, the intellect rules spiritedness and passion. In poetry, which is a much more accurate imitation of actual life than is philosophy, spiritedness and passion rule over the intellect.

Socrates summarizes the situation as follows. Human nature is cut up into small pieces; that is, each person "is unable to imitate many things nobly or to do the things themselves of which the imitations are likenesses" (395b3–6). This assertion has not yet been established. Poetry is itself an art like medicine or carpentry in the sense that one must master a method in order to excel at it. But the particular nature of poetry is such that the master artist can indeed imitate many things nobly or beautifully. This is something different from being able actually to practice the various arts at a high level of achievement. The question remains whether the master poet performs a function that is necessary in the city. Socrates himself refers regularly to the great poets and dramatists as witnesses to the various types of human nature. After all, the poet does not claim to be a carpenter or a physician but claims rather to teach us something about what it is to be human. It is on this point that the poet and the philosopher are rivals. The philosopher-king in Socrates's city wishes to restrict the heterogeneity and plasticity of human nature, not to celebrate or portray it. The restriction or even abolishment of poetry is part of the price we pay for the sake of a healthy city, and hence one in which justice is guaranteed. The poet shows us instead how difficult, not to say rare, justice is in the actual city. This is a part of the early conditioning of the potential guardians. But it has no place in a truly just city as conceived by Socrates. In this city, artistic freedom is replaced by propaganda. The properly educated guardians are entrusted exclusively with the task of being "demiurges of the freedom of the city" (395b8–c1); but this freedom is itself subordinated to justice. Socrates and his two main interlocutors are "makers" of the city; in the course of carrying out this production, they also become the craftsmen of freedom, which is defined by the rulers and defended by the soldiers, who are actually demiurges at second hand.

Now Socrates says that if the guardians are to be permitted to imitate at all, they may only imitate men who are "courageous, moderate, holy, free, and so forth," and never the opposites of these, such as slaves or those who behave slavishly or are mad. Socrates also rules out the imitation of the smith's craft or that of rowing a trireme; he seems to be thinking here of humble crafts that are associated with slavishness. Next comes bestiality; the guardian must not imitate the noises made by animals and also not the sounds of nature, such as the crashing of the sea or the sound of thunder (395c3–396b9). Throughout this part of Book Three, what Socrates opposes is the imitation of many things on the one hand and of base things on the other. In one important sense, the guardians will have to imitate the model or paradigm of their class, which we are in the process of constructing. Imitations of the noble and good are permitted; the several attributes of the noble and good man are elements in a single personality rather than expressions of diversity. This seems to be compatible with the admission of some mimetic poets into the city (see 398a8–b1). The status of the poets as a class in the Socratic city is not consistently formulated; in Book Ten, Socrates will say that they were entirely expelled.

This point is amplified in the immediate sequel in such a way as to give support to my earlier assertion that narrative itself is, or can be, a species of imitation. The noble and good man narrates "whenever he must say something" (396c1). When he comes to speak of the speeches and deeds of a noble and good man, he will not be ashamed to do so as if he were himself that man (396c5–d1). This is not quite clear; Socrates means that to give an account of a good man, we must ourselves enter into his character by the act of endorsing it. We speak of such a man as someone we would be glad to emulate. And this must never be done of persons of the reverse character. The entire passage presents speech as narration, and narration of human beings as an imitation of them. It is not clear whether we must forbid all speech about evil, mad, or slavish persons or whether, as seems more reasonable, we are free to condemn them. Socrates is primarily concerned here not with the telling of stories but with the speeches and deeds by which we directly live our lives. The imitations in question are not roles played by the guardians in narrative dramas but the practice of nobility and goodness. Socrates presents his point here in a confusing way, because he is also thinking about the problem of the poet or actor who plays many parts. In sum, there will be a little bit of imitation in every narration (396e4–8), but when it comes to what is shameful, we must refuse to imitate it, whether in narrative or in direct action. And if we are free, or even obligated, to condemn the shameful, it is implied here that we must somehow imitate what we refuse to imitate. There is no way in which to understand what it is to be evil without reproducing that character in our own souls. We cannot just turn away from the shameful without knowing what it is, and we cannot know what it is without feeling its baseness within ourselves. This point will come up later when Socrates discusses the experience required of judges.

There are then two kinds of style, narrative and mimetic. To this, Socrates now adds harmony and rhythm. The proper way of telling stories, in addition to what has previously been said, is to make few variations. This is because the citizens of our city are temperate and stick to a single task; this leads to uniformity of temperament and the absence of manifold personalities. Hence there will be no need to engage in many deviations of style or musical modes (cf. 397b6–c1 with d10–e4). The opposite speech is required for complex personalities, but these have been barred from our city and in effect identified with vice. As Adeimantus puts it, he supports just one style of speaking, namely, "the unmixed imitator of the decent" (that is, with no part of the imitation of the indecent: 397d4–5). From the standpoint of contemporary Athens, our citizens will be simple and boring, that is, not pleasant to boys and their teachers as well as to the great crowd, who enjoy diversity (397d6–8). Justice requires noble simplicity, and so boring citizens. There is no place for the modern psychological novel in this city, and, more to the point, none for ancient poetry or drama. Everyday discourse replaces much of poetry, and this discourse is almost entirely about the virtuous citizen. In a word, ordinary speech, as well as what is left of poetry, is patriotic propaganda. Once again the influence of the Spartan paradigm is unmistakable.

The next exchange shows us something very striking about the conception of justice that underlies the entire discussion of the guardian class. "If a man would come to us in our city who is able through wisdom to become everything whatsoever and to imitate all things, and would wish to exhibit himself and his poems," we would pay him homage and send him to another city, "while we ourselves would make use of a more austere and less pleasant poet and mythologist for the sake of benefit [*ōphelias*], who would imitate for us the speech of the decent man" and not at all that of the opposite (398a1–b5). Justice does not prevent us from sending the pleasant and complex, and so unjust and vicious, poet to another city, which, precisely because differing so sharply from ours, is already corrupt. We are required to do good to our friends only, and again it seems that we may do harm to our enemies, as one may refer to all cities other than our own. This point is also of importance to the question of whether the Socratic city is possible, since it could exist only by insulating itself from the art, customs, and even speeches of its neighbors, despite contact through trade and war.

Adeimantus agrees that we have probably finished our discussion of music as it deals with speeches and storytelling. It remains only to treat of song and melody; Socrates asks whether what we need to say about them is not obvious to everyone on the basis of what we have already said, if there is to be harmony between the two parts of the investigation. At this point, no doubt out of restlessness at the prospect of listening to more austere talk about music, Glaucon laughs (398e7). This should make us think of the denunciation of the love of laughter at 388d3–e7, with which Adeimantus, who is not given to laughing, entirely agreed. Glaucon says that he is apparently not one of "everyone," that is, he is not able to provide the needed speech about music, although he has a suspicion. A few lines later, Socrates indicates the reason for the dramatic shift from Adeimantus; Glaucon is a musical man (398e1). He will be more suited to the rather technical discussion that follows. Adeimantus is too austere to be a poetical man, but his austerity is just the attribute needed for him to serve as Socrates's partner in the radical censorship of poetry.

The first point to be made about music is that melody consists in speech, harmony, and rhythm. The speech of music must follow the same model as narration, and the modes of harmony and rhythm must conform to these models as well. We must exclude all musical modes that are appropriate for wailing, lamentation, drunkenness, softness, idleness, and drinking parties (398c11–399a2). The Lydian and Ionian modes are thus excluded, and this leaves, according to Glaucon, the Dorian and Phrygian modes as suitable to warriors. Socrates purports not to know the modes but infers that we are to retain those that imitate the speeches and deeds of courage on the one hand and moderation on the other. Glaucon then confirms that these are precisely the two modes just mentioned (399a3–d10). This in turn has consequences for the regulation not only against panharmonic, that is, complicated, modes but also against the manufacture of musical instruments that are suited to the performance of such songs, like the flute and the many-stringed instruments that imitate it. We are left with nothing but the lyre and the cither for the city and the pipe for shepherds.

As Socrates puts it, in choosing Apollo and his instrument (the cither) over Marsyas and his instruments (the flute and its many-stringed imitations), we have done nothing new. Glaucon and Socrates then interchange oaths. Glaucon: "By Zeus! We don't seem to me to have done so." Socrates: "By the dog, it escaped our attention that we have once more purged what we previously called the luxurious city." To which Glaucon adds: "That was temperate [*sōphronountes*] of us" (399e1–7). We can now understand the previous shift from Adeimantus to Glaucon more precisely. In addition to being an expert on music, Glaucon is marked by intemperance; it was on his account that the luxurious city was introduced. But Glaucon has been rendered more temperate by the discussion of the education of the guardians. His eros is in the process of being shifted from the pleasures of the body to those of the soul. Needless to say, this does not mean that he is being transformed into Adeimantus. We shall be given further indications of Glaucon's sexual eros, but his primary function in the *Republic* is to guard Socrates against the dangers that arise from the introduction of radical political points and to encourage him to discuss the innovations in the education of the philosopher-kings. The exchange of oaths is itself a sign that temperance is not unmitigated. It belongs to the behavior of the guardians within the just city but not so much to the speeches of the founding fathers.

Socrates says that we have purged our city of luxury; he means that we have applied a specific purge in the case of poetry and music, but we are not yet done (399e8: "let's purge the remainder"). This does not mean that we are going to return to the city of pigs, that is, the large version of the so-called neediest city. Nor does Socrates yet say that it is no longer feverish. But we may assume that the fever is being mitigated. The purgation was performed not by attention to physical appetite but to the regulation of poetry and music. As Shakespeare says, "Music hath charms to soothe the savage breast." Perhaps the most important aspect of temperance for Socrates is obedience to one's rulers, and this is inculcated in childhood by myths and songs.

5

Paideia *II: The Purged City*

I

We are in the midst of applying purges to the luxurious city by establishing regulations for the education of the guardians. These regulations are intended to moderate courage by temperance. The process is tantamount to narrowing our focus from the origin of all cities to the construction of the just or Socratic city. In Book Two, Socrates argued that the noble dog is proof that fierceness toward enemies and gentleness toward friends can exist in the same soul by nature. But fierceness and gentleness are not the exact equivalents of courage and temperance. The doggish attribute of fierceness is triggered by ignorance of strangers, not by knowledge. And something analogous can be said of their gentleness, which is a result of habituation and familiarity, not knowledge of who are their true friends. A dog could be gentle to a tyrant or a hardened criminal. What we want to know here, however, is whether courage and temperance can be combined in human beings. Socrates has not yet presented us with the answer, but it has to do with the analogy between the city and the soul.

The next step is to consider rhythm. Once again, we are to reject subtle and complex rhythms — virtuosity is not virtue — in favor of those that are compatible with an ordered and courageous life (399e8–11). Glaucon is aware of the various rhythms but cannot say which are compatible with a virtuous life on the one hand and vicious lives on the other. This is interesting because it shows, together with one or two earlier passages, that Glaucon, despite his innate musicality, has hitherto not attended to the political or ethical implications of art, something with which his brother, who is not said to be or presented as musical, is much concerned.

Socrates seems to be better informed about rhythms than he implied, but for the first time in the conversation he says that we shall turn over the details of the topic to an outside expert, in this case Damon, a theoretical (and perhaps practical) musician "who developed a theory of the influence of the different modes and rhythms of music on the emotions, hence of its importance in the education of character."[1] This shows that the philosopher-kings, and indeed the founding fathers, cannot be entirely self-reliant in the construction of the city. Specialists are necessary wherever *technē* is involved. The task of the statesman is obviously to be able to discriminate among rival experts. Music is so fundamental to the construction of the city that a knowledge of the models of human behavior should suffice in choosing our adviser. The technical details of the art are less important from this standpoint than knowledge of the connection between temperance, say, and simple, unexciting harmonies.

Socrates in effect says that we must find technicians who have good natures and can therefore "track down the nature of what is noble and graceful" (401c4–5). Nevertheless, there is a serious problem here. Part of the problem arises from the sheer need to consult experts, who after all are not guardians but what will later be identified as members of the class of workers, farmers, and so on. How can we be sure that their natural goodness is strong enough to regulate *technē* by the needs of virtue? Furthermore, *technē* is inseparable from change. It is plausible to assume that the just city will have to keep its armaments at the level of those of its opponents. And here technical expertise is independent of good character. This point will become sharper when the question is raised about the growth of the city. It is one thing to say that we shall allow no changes in the kinds of music that are to be performed in our city. It is something else again to extend that prohibition to the arts of war. And this leads to other changes that threaten the stability of the polity.

To continue, the manner of the style and speech of music follows the *ēthos*, that is, the custom or disposition of the soul: the character. And this applies not merely to music but to all the arts, which must be subjected to regulation so as to foster the production of the good disposition and to prevent the introduction of the opposite. Socrates speaks here of the impression of good or bad images onto the souls of the young guardians (401b1–c1). In other words, life is imitation, whether of virtuous or vicious models, and this extends to our narrative speech. In particular, the citizens of the just city will not be allowed to grow up spontaneously, for this allows the impression of licentious, illiberal, and ungracious images (401b5). By "illiberal" is meant that which is unbecoming to the character of the gentleman; a free man is not the slave of the passions (cf. 402a1). The models of virtue are the preliminary representation of what will become the doctrine of Platonic Ideas.

This suppression of spontaneity is one of the most striking differences between ancient and modern political philosophy. The modern celebration of spontaneity is also expressed by making freedom the highest principle. In the modern sense, of course, freedom does not mean the independence of the city or state from outside authority, it means something much closer to the independence of the individual citizen from the authority of the city or state. Both conceptions of freedom can be carried to a fatal extreme, as when the independence or autonomy of the political organization requires the complete subordination of the citizens to the government or, alternatively, when the excessive spontaneity of the individual citizens leads to the crippling if not dissolution of the government. The just city to be constructed by Socrates moves toward the first fatal extreme, and the late-modern democracy runs the risk of the second. It should be immediately added, however, that thanks to modern technology the pseudospontaneity of the apolitical individual resident, who can scarcely be called a citizen, makes it possible for a small minority of persons effectively to control the government, and the nature of modern civilization is such as to guarantee that this will occur. One has only to think of the "noble lie" that purports the government is responsive to the voice of the people. The inaccessibility of modern technology to Socrates requires that he depend upon the restriction of the size of his city as well as upon the complete control of education from infancy on. Finally, as I mentioned earlier, all philosophers in the Socratic city are themselves Socratics; there is no spontaneity among the ruling class and none among the philosophers.

To continue, Socrates emphasizes once more that musical education is of the highest importance (401d5–6), to which we may add that this is all the more reason to regard the trust to be placed in Damon as a sign of trouble. But the main point here is a comparison between reading and knowing the forms (*eidē*) of temperance, courage, liberality, and magnificence (402c2–3). We learn to read by mastering the alphabet and then discerning the individual letters as they are contained in various combinations. This is not entirely persuasive, since it could be argued that we do not read letters as such but rather words. The letters are not meaningful in themselves, only as constituents of a referring expression, as epistemologists say today. For example, the *c* in "courage" stands for an ingredient not of the attribute of courage but rather of the symbol that we use to designate the name of the attribute. The name has no meaning except by convention, and this meaning does not derive from the letters with which we spell the name. Socrates either does not notice or chooses to ignore this difficulty. He adds that we cannot recognize images of the letters in water or mirrors prior to knowing the letters themselves, which is certainly true (Bloom translates *grammata* as "writings" rather than "letters," which is what the word normally means; he thereby obscures the point I am discussing). Of course, a written letter c is also an image of the original letter. Socrates does not go into detail here, but what he means is that we discern the original as that which is expressed by all accurate images. In other words, the original is like a Platonic Idea, and all physical manifestations of the letter are images of that original or model. This point is discussed at length in the *Sophist*. Socrates will return to it later, but never in the technical detail that the issue requires (402a7–b8).[2]

With respect to music, our mastery of this art requires that we know the forms of temperance and so on, as well as their opposites, in whatever type of life they present themselves. In other words, the virtues and vices are like letters, which, once we recognize them, will allow us to understand the compounds in which they occur, namely, human lives. But the analogy limps for more than one reason. In the first place, vices are the opposite of virtues, but there are no letters that are the opposite of letters. Second, to know the form of temperance is to know temperance, whereas to know the letter *c* is not to know the virtue of courage. One could perhaps say that the virtues and vices are the "letters" of human life, but in view of the limited possibility of associating units of meaning with letters, one would be wiser to say that virtues and vices are the words that constitute the sentence of a life of such-and-such a kind. Oddly, classical Greek seems to lack a separate word for *word*; certainly Socrates neglects to introduce it here. *Logos* and *rēma* can mean "word," but their range of senses is too broad to supply what is needed here.

In the present context, these considerations are a bit fussy, but they are of great importance for the larger topic of the Platonic Ideas. I shall therefore repeat the difficulty. An image of the original of, say, courage or temperance is an instance of courage or temperance. If there were originals or models of these virtues, it would be genuinely useful to know them, since they would serve as the basis for identifying the images, as these appear in actual human beings. Or so it might be claimed. But an image of a letter is an image of an image or simulacrum, namely, of the physical shape that stands for a unit of sound. The letter does not make transparent or bring before the eye of the soul the original letter, which has no shape or essential form because it is a conventional device, meaningless in itself and of interest only as an element within an alphabet, used for building up words. To borrow a term from Saussure, it marks a difference; as such, it is somehow poised between being and nonbeing. Finally, let us assume for the sake of argument that there is an original letter, for example, *c*, which is by definition not an image of itself. In this case it can be neither written nor spoken, but it seems to be impossible to define a sense of knowing the original letter that does not assign physical attributes to it, and so transform it into an image.

I have gone into these details because Socrates is obviously preparing us for a more extensive discussion of the Ideas. At the present moment we need only the very imprecise and very general analogy between originals and images. Virtues and vices are the building blocks or elements of character, and as such they may be compared loosely to letters, which are the building blocks of words—and the latter are mysteriously not mentioned by Socrates; Bloom supplies the English expression "combinations in which [letters] turn up," which does not appear in the Greek (402a8–b2); Griffith is more daring and says "words" twice, thereby overinterpreting "all things in which it [the letter] is scattered" (*en hapasin hois estin peripheromena*) and *out' en smikrō out' en megalō* as "neither in small nor in large words." Unfortunately, the word *words* is absent from the text. Perhaps we may invoke the principle of charity at this point and allow that it is words to which everyone, Socrates and his translators, are referring. But the text is a curious one.

To sum up, we shall never be musical unless we can identify or become acquainted with (*gnōrizōmen*: 402c5) the forms (*eidē*) of the virtues and their opposites. The form of the virtue is an element in the model of a noble and good life, whereas the form of a vice is an element in the model of a shameful and bad life. Virtuous and vicious speeches and deeds are images of the respective elements; taken altogether, they define the nature of the actual life. There is one cautionary note that must be struck here. Socrates says that there are forms of the virtues and of their opposites (402c4). But vices are privations of virtues; for example, the vice opposite to justice is injustice. In the subsequent discussion of the Ideas, Socrates does not extend them to negations or privations of an entity, property, or relation. It also makes no sense to speak of Ideas of negative concepts, because Ideas are not concepts. We shall return to this point in the proper place.

In the meantime, I want to emphasize the vagueness of Socrates's description of how acquaintance with the originals allows us to become virtuous (to put vice to one side for the moment). Do we first see the form or model and then observe its image in the deeds and speeches of actual life? If this is so, then recognition of a virtue is independent of our experience of it, which seems paradoxical. But if we first see the image, how can we identify it correctly without an antecedent knowledge of the original? If we see both simultaneously, what accounts for this double vision of form and image in our encounter with the actual particular? We can suggest that the form illuminates its particular manifestation, but this does not explain how forms can exist in particulars. Finally, assuming that we see both, how does that serve to make us virtuous? What is the link between identifying the form of courage, or for that matter the model of the virtuous life, and actually being courageous or living virtuously? Socrates claims that a life in which the virtues of the soul coincide with the forms of virtue, so that both participate in the same model (*tupou*), is the most beautiful sight that anyone could see. He then establishes that the most beautiful is the most lovable. But instead of identifying the lover as the virtuous man, he says that it is the musical man who would most love this sight. This assumes that music is understood as already defined and regulated by a commitment to virtue. It also implies that Glaucon, who is musical, loves, or could love, such a sight more than Adeimantus, who is not musical. In other words, we must first know the model of the desired life and then construct a system of education rooted in the sovereign importance of music, which, through its beauty and power to impress itself upon the human soul over a long period of training, will produce love of virtue in the properly educated musical man (402d1–9).

It thus turns out that there is a close connection between eros and music (as 402d6–9 shows). The musical man is the lover par excellence of the beautiful soul. What Socrates does not prove, but simply assumes, is that the virtuous soul is the most beautiful. The premise that actually functions here is that persons of a certain nature can be habituated to love virtue. This is not to deny that some few may be by nature attracted to virtue, but Socrates's entire argument demonstrates that the number is too small to serve as the basis of a just city.

Glaucon says that the musical man would not love someone who had a defect in the soul sufficient to untune its harmony. But if the soul is sound and there is some bodily defect, he might be willing to overlook it, thanks to his wish for "clinging fondly to" (*aspazesthai*), or in other words delighting in or loving, the person in question (402d10–e1). Socrates replies that he understands: Glaucon now has, or had previously, such a boy—that is, a sweetheart—and Socrates grants the point. We can love defective bodies if the soul is harmonious. At least we can if we are like Glaucon. The two agree next that excessive pleasure has nothing in common with temperance, but instead, as Glaucon says, it drives us out of our minds as much as does pain. Furthermore, it is related to insolence and licentiousness rather than to any of the virtues. It comes as no surprise to learn that Glaucon cannot think of a greater or sharper pleasure than that of sex, nor one that is more manic (402e2–403a6).

In response, Socrates elicits immediate agreement from Glaucon that the "correct eros is to love by nature the orderly and beautiful in a temperate and musical way" (403a7–9). There is something surprising about Glaucon's ready acquiescence in this definition, given his extremely erotic nature. He agrees that the excessive or mad pleasure must not be allowed to have anything in common with the correct erotic relationship between lover and boy. The lover may kiss, associate with, and touch the boy as if he were his own son, and then only if the boy allows it. Glaucon swears by Zeus to show his excited conviction of the dangers of eros and the need to restrict it as Socrates describes. But this restriction applies to the guardians of the just city, which is coming into existence in speech, not deeds. The intensity of the pursuit of justice, that is, the attractiveness of the conversation, leads Glaucon to make concessions for others, and for imaginary beings at that, which he would not necessarily make for himself. But whatever the merits of this conjecture, the main point is clear. Music institutes virtue through the purging and refining of eros (403a10–c3). This is an important indication of the fact that the educational system diminishes the luxury that was initially attributed to the city under construction.

2

Socrates announces that the topic of music has been completed as it should be, namely, in the erotic love of the beautiful (403c4–7). We can now turn to gymnastics, the second major part of education. This portion of the argument presents us with fewer difficulties than did the discussion of music. It is also immediately clear that rigorous physical exercise is incompatible with indulgence in the luxuries of the body. Socrates begins by maintaining that it is not a useful or sound body that makes a soul good, but the reverse. We can therefore avoid excessive detail by turning the care of the body over to the intellect, that is, to the intellect that has been and is undergoing the harmonious musical education. Otherwise stated, the details of gymnastic training are deducible from the model of the virtuous life. More precisely, since we are discussing the education of the guardians, the training must focus on the exigencies of war and stasis. We are producing not professional athletes but soldiers, and not just any soldiers but those who are suited to the protection of justice (403c8–e3).

The training of athletes institutes "sleepy habits," that is, it prepares the body for just one task, performance in gymnastics and other competitions. Soldiers, on the other hand, must be prepared for a wide range of physical conditions. But this does not lead Socrates to recommend a complex gymnastic training. The best gymnastic, which prepares in particular for war, must be related to the simple music in which the soul is trained. Interestingly enough, Homer is cited here as an authority, whereas he was rejected, along with the other poets, or at least sharply criticized, in connection with the gods and the human soul. A second striking feature of this step in the discussion is that Glaucon is now sufficiently disciplined to exclude excessive luxury or complications in cooking (403e4–404c9). Homer never makes mention of the eating of relishes (*hēdusmata*) by warriors, whereas Glaucon originally protested against the rude cuisine and eating arrangements of the true city by calling attention to the omission of relish (*opsos*: I. 372c3). Whether because of his good nature or because he is easily impressed by the flow of the argument, Glaucon is the instrument for a further purging of luxury from the beautiful city.

In the sequel, Socrates emphasizes the connection between sex and food by prohibiting the guardians from possessing Corinthian mistresses as well as Attic sweets. A simple regime is best for body as well as soul; as one could express it, the virtue most analogous to harmony is temperance. Refinement leads to licentiousness and illness, and this in turn to a profusion of law courts and hospitals. The greatest sign of a bad and shameful education is the need for eminent physicians and judges, not only for the lower class and craftsmen but for those who have been liberally raised. Socrates indicates that it would be shameful for the guardians not to judge themselves but be forced to use an imported justice, thereby making others their masters and judges. In other words, the guardians are sufficiently separated from the workers that the latter are like residents of another city. Aristotle complains in the *Politics* about precisely this feature of Socrates's polity; it is several cities rather than a unified city.[3] Socrates never explains how a city can survive with such separation between the rulers and the ruled. The lower class apparently lives a life very much like that of the residents of ordinary cities, except that the guardians exist like an armed camp within the city walls, in order to prevent stasis and to defend the city from external enemies.

After a brief denunciation of the life spent in litigation, Socrates launches into an attack on contemporary medicine, which has introduced new modes of treatment and new names for old diseases. Its essential defect is that it keeps the sick person alive beyond the point at which he or she can perform his or her specific job, a performance upon which good laws depend. The difference between the ancient medicine of the Asclepiads and that of more recent practitioners like Herodicus is that the former understood the connection between health and politics, whereas the latter did not. Asclepius thus possessed the same knowledge of prolonging life as did his successors, but he kept it hidden. This is an extremely important point and shows how Socrates, like Aristotle after him, assumes that art in general, and medicine in particular, has a natural end which is independent of technical progress and serves to regulate it. All arts are capable of indefinite progress, but this would dissolve the stability of the city. More precisely, health is the end of medicine, but not the preservation of life through continuous treatment. Life is worth living only so long as we can fulfill our function, do our work rather than spend all our time in the hands of physicians. Death, as Socrates puts it, is the mortal disease that can be drawn out but not cured (405b6–406c8). The notion of the sanctity of life under any circumstances is alien to him.

Socrates argues next that the Asclepiad principle is valid for the rich as well as the poor. He takes it as self-evident that a carpenter, for example, cannot afford to engage in medical cures that do not bring him back to sound health and leave no time for his work. He therefore stops treatment and either cures himself or dies, and in the latter case is freed from his troubles. But what of the rich, who can afford continuous medical attention? The answer is indicated with a quotation from the poet Phocylides: he who already has the means for his livelihood should practice virtue (406d1–407a8). And this is incompatible with the life of the valetudinarian or perpetual invalid. Once again, a poet is cited as an authority.

Glaucon points out that excessive care of the body, if it goes beyond gymnastics, causes trouble for us in managing our household during wars, and also in the fulfillment of our peacetime political obligations. For Socrates, however, the greatest defect of this excess is that it raises difficulties for learning, thinking, and caring for oneself, that is, for one's soul. Obsession with bodily health leads to tension and dizziness in the head, which is blamed on philosophy. This is an obstacle to the exercise of virtue, but its main defect is that it interferes with learning and thinking. In other words, our highest work is thinking, not practicing the moral virtues (407b4–c5).

Socrates reinforces his portrait of what Glaucon calls a "political Asclepius" with further references to Homer concerning the medical practice of the great physician's sons, who continue their father's subordination of their art to politics. As Bloom says in his note to this passage, Socrates alters Homer in order to emphasize the limits on the care of the body, even that of a hero. On the other hand, Pindar, Aeschylus, and Euripides are criticized for saying that Asclepius was persuaded by gold to cure a rich man who was virtually dead (407c7–408c4). It should by now be obvious that Socratic hermeneutics, as applied to poetry, is governed by the same political interest that he attributes to Asclepius. Furthermore, some passages in the poetic canon are politically sound, whereas many more are not. Homer in particular seems to be safer speaking about human beings in general, and their arts in particular, than he is about the gods and heroes. But we should not try to apply this standard rigidly; the point is rather Socrates's extreme flexibility in rejecting or accepting the words of the poets and dramatists. It is therefore false to say that the poets are ignorant of the human soul. But they are dangerous to Socrates because they expose the evil and shamefulness of the soul as well as its goodness and nobility. The poets tell us more than Socrates wants the guardians to know about human beings, and certainly more than they can safely hear about the gods. But whereas traditional theology is unnecessary in the just city, the same cannot be said for knowledge of human beings. The poets are therefore useful to us as we construct our city, but once we are finished, there is little if any room in the city for them. They must be transformed into propagandists.

Glaucon continues to insist that we shall need good physicians in our city (408c5), despite his apparent acquiescence in the temperate life of the guardians and in Socrates's praise of what could be called minimal medicine. I think that there is a subterranean connection between this passage and his original, silently withdrawn, insistence upon a sophisticated cuisine. Glaucon has a certain inclination toward comfortable living that seems to be related to his erotic nature. This eros has certainly not as yet been (if it ever will be) diverted to the Platonic Ideas. Having been deprived, as it were, of relishes and Attic sweets, on the one hand, and sexual relations with beautiful boys, not to mention Corinthian courtesans, on the other, Glaucon shifts his appetite for bodily pleasure to the demand for many good physicians.

But Socrates continues to apply the purge to Glaucon's corporeal hedonism. Glaucon takes it as obvious that the best physicians are those who have treated the most persons, healthy as well as sick, just as the best judges are those who have associated with all kinds of natures. Socrates takes up the two parts of this opinion in order. The statement about physicians is not entirely clear. Physicians would become most clever if in addition to learning from childhood the art of medicine, they associated with as many sick bodies as possible; it is not uninteresting that Socrates omits reference to sick souls. These would presumably be cured by philosophy rather than psychiatry. Next Socrates recommends that erstwhile physicians themselves suffer all diseases and be not entirely healthy by nature. This is surely an odd requirement; for one thing, it would seem to make perpetual invalids out of the physicians and thus violate Socrates's earlier principle that the constantly sick cannot perform their work and should be allowed to die. Socrates offers the following explanation. Physicians "do not use the body to treat the body. If they did, it would not be allowable for a doctor's body ever to be diseased. No, they use the mind to treat the body, and it is not permitted for a mind which has become diseased, and is still in bad shape, to treat anything successfully" (Griffith translation: 408e1–5).

In other words, the physicians can undergo, and thus gain experience of, diseases via the body, which leaves their mind unaffected and so able to make use of their corporeal experience to treat other sick bodies. There is no good reason for Socrates to assume that the soul or the mind can be kept free of bad consequences from bodily disease and in particular, one must say, free from undergoing all bodily diseases. He himself has just told us otherwise (407b4–c5). This passage is very dark (408d10–e5). One difficulty that is never addressed directly is the class membership of physicians. Medicine seems to be neither an art like the arts relegated to the moneymaking class nor a duty of the guardians. On balance, it seems best to assume that physicians, like judges, will come from the guardian class, but that the experience of illness and injustice that they require will be largely derived from the moneymaking class.

Let us turn to the case of judges, who differ from physicians in ruling a soul with the soul. In other words, we pass judgment with the intellect and our general experience of human beings, not with our body. But what is judged in the accused is not his body, or even the physical act with which he has been charged, but the state of his soul. It is therefore altogether a mistake to submit the soul of an erstwhile judge to the joint rearing and familiarity with bad souls from childhood up, and to allow it to commit all unjust deeds in order to gain experience in discerning the unjust deeds of others. It is obvious that if a judge acts in this way, he will himself be unjust—or if not entirely obvious, certainly very likely. It is too frivolous to suggest that the potential judge could be raised with the understanding that he commit all injustices not for their own sake but in order to become thoroughly familiar with them for the sake of his future duties. Let us grant Socrates the deleterious consequences of such an upbringing. But is the case really so different from that of the physician? The physician must arrive at a comprehensive experience with diseases, but there seems to be no need for him to be sick himself. Instead, he must practice the art of medicine. A judge must acquire knowledge of injustice, but this does not require him to act unjustly; in fact, that is forbidden. What is needed is observation of injustice, the analogue to the physician's observation of diseases. Socrates in effect grants this, with the qualification that the judge must not be exposed to injustice as a child and young man. He must be a "late learner of injustice," so as to have already formed a good character, but not too late to prevent him from building up the body of experience that his art requires (409a1–b2).

The general point here is that the physician and the judge must become thoroughly acquainted with illness and health, on the one hand, and injustice and justice, on the other. In both cases, the soul must be kept healthy throughout. How, then, will it acquire the necessary experience of illness or injustice without being corrupted? I add to what has already been said that in the arts, including medicine, one may learn the techniques without corrupting the soul, especially if that soul has been properly educated in music and gymnastics, because *technē* is morally neutral. It is harder to learn about injustice without oneself becoming unjust, but it is not impossible. In the first place, the judge must spend much of his time studying the law; this in itself provides him with negative knowledge of injustice as violation of the law. As to the development of one's knowledge of human nature, this is a question of insight together with experience. It is taught by life, not by artists or technicians. That is to say, one must come into contact with unjust persons over a long period of time. But these persons will be recognized as unjust only by someone with a healthy soul, namely, as Socrates says, with a properly educated soul. The more difficult question arises: Must there not be injustice in the just city, and a good deal of it, if our judges are to acquire the necessary knowledge? The answer with respect to the workers and farmers is certainly in the affirmative, and despite Socrates's earlier unwillingness to bring up judges from the lower class, he will be obligated to send judges down from the guardian to the lowest class for the sake of their education. But there will be injustice in the guardian class as well, and this is guaranteed by the violation of the mating laws, to mention no other cause.

In sum, badness cannot know virtue, whereas virtue in an educated soul will in time come to know both itself and badness (409d6–e2). Glaucon agrees that the beautiful city must have laws establishing arts of medicine and judging such as we have now described. Both will take care of the souls and bodies of citizens who are naturally good. Previously Socrates had said that medicine treats sick bodies, and granted that injustice is the illness of the soul, it would be fair to say that the art of the judge takes care of sick souls. But this is not what Socrates says here. In order to be treated or cared for, one must have a good nature. In other words, our physicians and judges will tend to those illnesses that affect even persons with good natures. It is impossible to eliminate illness and injustice, even in a city that has been constructed for the sake of justice. As to persons with bad natures, both arts, medicine and justice, will let die those with bad bodies and will actually murder those with bad souls (409e4–410a4). Socrates's language is ambiguous; the stronger interpretation takes him to say that both medicine and judging act in tandem, or on the same principles. The weaker interpretation has it that medicine lets those die who are not naturally good, if their bodies are bad, in other words, hard to cure or capable only of the state of perpetual invalidism; the judges, on the other hand, put to death corrupted natures with incurable souls. On either reading, the subordination of the arts to the purpose of the city is manifest. We may also be meant to infer the existence of mental and physical illnesses that affect people with good natures who are members of the guardian class. In fact, this seems to be a virtual certainty in the case of bodily illness.

3

The arts of medicine and judging belong neither to music nor to gymnastics. We learned previously that simplicity in music produces temperance in souls, whereas in gymnastics it produces health in bodies (404e4–6). Since temperance is a virtual synonym for health in the soul, it seems that medicine and judging are required only with the advent of illness. This is much clearer in the case of medicine than judging, since not all judicial cases fall under the criminal law. In the passage just cited, Socrates goes on to say that it is a clear sign of a bad education if eminent doctors and judges are required not just for the vulgar and the craftsmen but also for those who have received a liberal education. The section that we have just traversed makes it more than likely that we shall need physicians and judges for the guardian class. But they must themselves be members of that class, and not have risen up from the vulgar. We have also learned that there are two kinds of persons, those of a good nature and those of the opposite type. The diseases of the good-natured persons should be treated, whereas persons of a bad nature should be allowed to die or actually be put to death. A person of a good nature, in accord with what we have learned thus far, is courageous and temperate. Such a person can obviously fall victim to many diseases of the body to which bad natures are also susceptible. But a good-natured or virtuous person cannot fall victim to diseases of the mind, since these diseases are the opposites of the virtues of courage and temperance, and people of this sort do not have good natures and would not be members of the guardian class. Why, then, do we need judges for the guardian class? Obviously there is some defect in the reasoning I have just summarized. It must be that whereas members of the guardian class ought to be of good natures, difficulties will arise that no amount of precaution or assiduity in education will be able to prevent. There will be sick souls in the guardian class, perhaps from violations of the mating laws, or for some other, not yet identified reason. In other words, there will be intemperance and cowardice from time to time in the guardian class. Socrates does not make this explicit but buries it in a mass of details that we must sort out for ourselves.

If the guardians stay within the limits of simple music, they will require physicians only in the case of necessity. This last must refer to the aforementioned bodily diseases to which all human beings are subject. Second, simple music engenders temperance, and with it absence of need for the art of the judge (410a5–10). The judge is needed in the case of injustice. Therefore, either there is no injustice in the guardian class and judges are superfluous, or the musical education is a failure. Socrates seems to deny both of these alternatives. But this leads to a contradiction. In fact, there is injustice as well as physical illness in the guardian class, and this cannot be entirely eliminated by the proper musical training. The just city is thus not perfectly just, only as just as possible.

Socrates says that gymnastics was established for the sake of the soul, not the body, namely, to stimulate spiritedness rather than bodily strength. Those who devote themselves to gymnastics but avoid music become savage and hard, whereas those who do the opposite become soft and gentle. The savagery comes from the spirited element of the soul; it is thus an exaggeration of courage. We might expect Socrates to attribute softness and gentleness to a defect in courage, thus arriving at an Aristotelian schema of two extremes, both vices, and virtue in the middle. Instead, he says that tameness belongs to the philosophical nature, an expression that probably means something like "musical" or "cultivated" rather than "philosophical" in the technical sense of the term. In any event, tameness seems to be an attribute of this part of the soul, which, if it is properly reared, becomes gentle and orderly. One must assume that the philosophical nature belongs primarily to the intellectual function of the soul, but it is not quite satisfactory to refer to this function as gentle and orderly, because of the erotic nature of philosophy, a topic that will soon move to center stage. On the other hand, the erotic soul becomes gentle and orderly through the proper musical education, and it is to this aspect of things that Socrates is directing his attention (410b10–e3).

In sum: the spirited element becomes savage if it is not properly reared, whereas the correct training produces courage. The philosophical nature becomes either gentle and orderly or excessively soft, depending upon its nurture. The extreme or defective condition comes respectively from too much gymnastics and no music, or too much music and no gymnastics. The guardian, like the noble dog, requires both courage and gentleness. But since the virtuous mean (if I may call it such) depends in both cases upon the right music, it seems far-fetched to look to the dog as the paradigm of the guardian. The gentleness of dogs was described as directed toward friends through habituation or familiarity, not music. But there is a more important ambiguity. What Socrates calls here "the philosophical nature" seems rather to correspond to temperance (consider 399b3–c4). This in turn is described as a virtue of the guardian class. But in the next stage of the discussion, temperance is associated with *epithumia* (desires and passions). And this part of the soul is the original of the class of farmers and workers. I am of course not denying that the guardians must be reared to temperance. My point is that this virtue belongs to the soul altogether, and not just to one part. Socrates seems to be connecting music to the intellect, but in fact he does not do so. Instead, for example, of referring to wisdom, the virtue that is coordinate with courage and temperance, he uses the ambiguous phrase "philosophical nature."

Socrates concludes that the soul of the properly educated guardian is a harmony of fierceness and gentleness, and is therefore temperate and courageous. Since wisdom has not yet been mentioned, it would seem not to be necessary for the acquisition of the aforementioned virtues. It is the founding fathers or philosopher-kings who must be wise, in order to devise the proper nurture and education of the guardian class. Socrates reiterates his strictures against the flute as a major contributor to the excessive softening of the soul. The avoidance of music and philosophy, on the other hand, produces not merely excessive fierceness but also weakness, deafness, and blindness of the soul. Once again, philosophy is associated with temperance, gentleness, and orderliness. This helps us to clarify the initial reference to philosophy. Those who are fierce rather than courageous have defective intellectual powers. In terms of a later stage in the argument, such a spiritedness is unable to listen to or obey the commands of the philosopher-kings. As the present passage shows, the separation of the three powers in the soul (intellect, spiritedness, and desire) is not the total isolation of each. Spirit and desire must be sufficiently intelligent to carry out their roles within the city, and the same is true of the individual soul (410e4–411d6).

To conclude, some god gave to human beings the two arts of music and gymnastics, not for the soul and the body but for the spirited and the philosophical aspects of human nature. Once again, the philosophical is associated with the spirited part of the soul, although the implication is that it belongs to the intellectual part as well. As will in fact soon become explicit, spiritedness and intellect are more closely related than are spiritedness and desire. But the connection between spiritedness and philosophy is introduced only toward the end of the section we have been studying. However we identify it, the philosophical part requires gymnastics so as not to become too soft. Gymnastics thus contributes to both courage and temperance, which cannot be acquired through music alone (411d7–412a3).

Although the main line of the discussion about music and gymnastics is more or less clear, there are a number of small but crucial points at which confusion enters. One confusion is that whereas the great majority of technicians and craftsmen must belong to the third, or moneymaking, class, this cannot be true of the musicians and gymnasts who train the young guardians, and it certainly cannot be true of physicians and judges. Furthermore, we began this entire discussion with respect to the education of the warriors or guardians. Are they also to be experts on weaponry and the various arts of manufacturing and improving them? Or is their sole expertise the use of these weapons and implements of war? It seems reasonable to say that courage does not depend on a knowledge of how to make weapons, but surely some technical skills are required of the excellent soldier. A third difficulty: What is the exact difference between temperance and gentle orderliness? And how is this related to philosophy, which as it were slips into the conversation at a late stage, and without any clarification? Finally, I remind the reader that we were originally supposed to build a city, that is, any city, in order to find justice in it. But very soon in his discussion, Socrates transforms the goal into the founding of a rather peculiar city; more precisely, he sets out to found the just city in order to find justice within it, and thus to learn its nature. But this is circular.

All these questions emerge from the principle of one man, one job, itself a questionable assumption but one that is taken for granted throughout the *Republic*. Among the many problems that this principle raises is the fact that the soldier-guardians, who are indispensable to the preservation of the city, will not participate in its rule. This seems to justify Aristotle's complaint that we are not building a city at all. If the soldiers (often referred to as auxiliaries), together with the members of the working class, are ruled but do not rule, whereas the philosopher-kings rule but are not ruled (except of course during childhood and youth), then strictly speaking there are no citizens in this city in the full sense of the word, as Aristotle defines it, a definition that certainly accords with the standard Greek view. A citizen is one who rules and is ruled.[4]

4

We are now ready to shift our attention to the upbringing of the rulers. Socrates says by way of transition that he who most beautifully mixes gymnastics with music, thereby bringing the greatest measure (*metriōtata*) into the soul, is the most musical and well tempered (or "harmonious": *euarmostaton*: 412a4–7). As we have seen, music is given primacy over gymnastics, the main function of which is the negative one of preventing the soul from becoming too soft. Socrates entirely minimizes the part played by gymnastics in the health of the body; gymnastics, like music, is primarily for the sake of the spirited and philosophic part of the soul. We speak of the most musical man, not of the greatest gymnast, as best ordered. It is something like this man who will be needed to oversee (that is, supervise) our city, if it is going to be saved (412a9–10).

It is self-evident that the rulers will come from the guardian class, since it is here that we find the most musical persons. The rulers must be older than the ruled, and they must be the best among them. Equally obvious, they must be the most prudent (*phronimous*) and powerful (*dunatous*) and, in particular, protectors of the city. The word *kēdemonas* can also be translated as "those who care for" the city; *kēdos* carries with it the sense of emotional attachment. Socrates says that those care most for the city who love it, and he loves it most who believes that the same things are advantageous to himself and to it, so that when one prospers, the other does as well (412b8–d8). This passage should be taken together with the assertion in II. 369b5–d2 that the city comes into existence through our need, and that the first and greatest of our needs is for the necessities of life. Otherwise stated, the city originates in the desire for self-preservation; love of the city must come later. At I. 330b8–c6 Socrates says that people are fond of things that they themselves have made. The reason for this is plainly because they love themselves, and so by extension their own works. And as the present passage shows, we love what we associate with our own advantage. In sum, self-love is the root of patriotism. This conclusion is hardly different from that of the founders of modern political philosophy. What is unusual about Socrates's approach is that he plans to bring about as close a unity as possible between the guardians and the city. But since the guardians have little or nothing in common with the workers, it is with their own class, that is, with themselves, that they are to be unified. This is another way in which the attempt to unify leads instead to division.

Human beings do not have to be persuaded to love themselves. But they must be persuaded to hold that self-love is the same as love of the city. To begin with, this persuasion entails the "banishing" of the contrary opinion. In other words, the same censorship of the poets that we studied previously must be extended to the opinions of the guardians on the origin of the city. Before introducing the device of the noble lie, which is the mainspring or foundation of the control to be exercised over the beliefs of the guardians, Socrates explains how we shall test the youthful members of this class for strength of memory, that is, the ability to remember "that they must always do what seems best for the city," a belief that Socrates calls a *dogma* (see Bloom's note). He goes on to describe the training and testing of the memory of potential rulers in very flowery language, but we shall not hesitate to call the process by the name of what Socrates says is the cause of forgetting true opinions: bewitchery. As so bewitched, namely, as perfectly harmonious and entirely convinced of the identity between his own advantage and that of the city, the ruler will be "most useful" to both (413c1–e5).

At this point, there is a shift in terminology. Those whom we previously referred to as guardians (*phulakas*) will now be called "auxiliaries and helpers [*epikourous kai boēthous*] of the dogmas of the rulers" (414b4–6). "Guardian" will be reserved in its full sense for the rulers (414a1, b1–2). The shift is required because we are in the process of distinguishing between rulers and ruled, that is, between philosopher-kings and soldiers. The auxiliaries are as it were second-class guardians, and they will not receive the advanced education to which the potential philosophers are submitted. If there is a difference between ruler and ruled, then it would seem necessary that they differ in their understanding of what it means to do everything for the benefit of the city. In other words, the best of the guardians become the rulers because they are the most useful to themselves and the city. Given the separation of work in accord with the differing abilities of individual persons, the inferior guardians will devote all their working lives to war. They will thus not be in a position to lay down policy or conduct the process of government on a daily basis. This is why they are called auxiliaries and helpers. In a word, they must carry out the orders of the rulers, not share in the process of deciding the basis of the utility of their orders. Ruling is one form of utility; obeying or being ruled is another.

We thus arrive at one of the most controversial passages in the *Republic*. I am sorry to say that the controversy arises from inattentive reading of what is plainly stated, and, indeed, was stated previously. There is no room here for academic romanticism, which hesitates to believe that philosophers tell lies. We should take solace in the fact that Socrates has already distinguished between the lie in the soul and the medicinal lie that is required for the advantage of the city.

Socrates asks "whether we could not somehow contrive one of those lies that come into existence through necessity of which we spoke just now, telling one particular noble lie that will persuade maximally the rulers themselves, but if not, the rest of the city" (414b8–c2). The lie is related to a Phoenician (hence not to a Greek) myth and describes something, says Socrates, that has happened many times before but not in our own time. By speaking in this way, he both underlines his own originality and at the same time appeals to the mythical past as a basis for sanctifying his own myth. He adds that it might not be possible today, and would require much persuasion. When he hesitates to state the lie, Glaucon encourages him: "Speak, and don't be afraid" (414c11). Socrates's reticence shows the difference between philosophy and soldiering. There is a difference in the type of courage required by each. Glaucon obviously wishes to give the impression that no one will harm Socrates for telling his audacious fib. That is, Glaucon will protect Socrates from harm and speaks out boldly, as befits a soldier. Socrates is brave enough to tell the lie, but he tries to soften the blow by hesitating and doubting his own daring.

When he does speak out, Socrates takes it upon himself to tell the lie, which he hopes will persuade the entire city, but first of all the rulers and soldiers, namely, that the rearing and education they received in the city were like dreams. In fact, they were being fashioned and reared under the earth, and their weapons and other equipment were being made for them. At the completion of the job, their mother earth sent them up. The native land must be defended like a mother and nurse, and the fellow citizens are to be regarded as brothers and born of the earth. One curiosity is that nothing is said here of the father, nor is the city itself mentioned in this passage. There is also no mention of sisters. Despite his desire to persuade everyone of this lie, Socrates is thinking here primarily of a brotherhood of soldiers for whom courage is rooted in self-love.

I interrupt the analysis of the details to make a comment about the passage in general. At the beginning of Book Seven, Socrates will recount an image or allegory in which human existence is likened to imprisonment within a cave. The subterranean content of the discussion of the noble lie is of primarily political importance, whereas the allegory of the cave could be called "psychological" to the extent that it deals with the condition of the human soul in its ascent from images and shadows to a vision of the pure Ideas. Finally, in Book Ten, we shall make another descent below the surface of the earth in order to cast light upon the problem of personal immortality. The connection between subterranean or (what I shall later call) subnatural and normal existence is a kind of development of the original descent from Athens to the Piraeus, where the reader encounters the spirit of Socrates, but also of some of the most politically active Athenians of the period just prior to the rapid decline of the great city. In discussing the relevant passages, we shall have to come to some understanding of the fundamental importance in the *Republic* of the metaphor of descent and its connection to the two great themes of birth and death, as these themes bear upon the question of the genesis of the city.

To come back to the noble lie, Glaucon is not surprised at Socrates's reticence in speaking of it, but he has no objection to a fuller account. All those who inhabit the city are certainly brothers. The god shaped them; in so doing, he mixed gold in some, silver in others, and iron and bronze in the remainder. Thus were born the rulers, the auxiliaries, and the farmers and demiurges, respectively. The city is now mentioned and the father is identified; he is "the god" who replaced the Olympians in the purification of theology. But the citizenry continue to be addressed as "brothers," with no mention of sisters. This is noteworthy in view of the subsequent discussion of the role of women in the top two classes.

By separating the roles of the mother and father in the manufacture of citizens, Socrates de-eroticizes their origin. As one could put this, *poiēsis* replaces genesis. Something almost identical occurs in the allegory of the cave, in which eros is entirely absent. This replacement is not restricted to the first generation; otherwise, the souls of subsequent generations would not be covered by the terms of the myth, which are essential for establishing the unity of the guardian class. Strictly speaking, under the terms of the noble lie, women, or let us say sexual intercourse and reproduction, would be unnecessary. At this point, the myth clearly breaks down. The next point to be made introduces the fundamental problem of sexual eros, and so too women are unmistakably alluded to but not mentioned explicitly. Since everyone in the city is related, although people will breed for the most part with others of their own particular metal, it will happen from time to time that miscegenation will occur; children will be produced by parents of different metallic natures. In this case no pity must be shown, and each child must be placed within the class to which its own mixed nature most closely corresponds. It is easy to see that at this stage of the argument, either the noble lie is no longer operative or else the citizens will be expected to believe that they have dreamed not only their childhood but also their sexual relations with one another, and that they continue to be produced in the bosom of the earth. This is simply too cumbersome to take seriously. For example, if our sexual life is a dream, why must rules be passed to regulate whom we take as sexual partners? More pressing, perhaps, the adults will watch the children being born as a result of sexual relations, and there will be no sign of infants springing from the earth. The more we think about it, the more the "mechanism" of the noble lie is seen to be defective. Its value is symbolic, not paradigmatic.

Socrates assumes that the majority will breed true without explaining why; presumably propinquity is responsible. Incidentally, if this part of our life is a dream and we are fashioned in the earth, why not have the god implant a repugnance in us for breeding with members of another class? It is plain that human sexual desire cannot be completely regulated by god or man. Socrates will later introduce laws to enforce this erotic uniformity, laws that will eventually be disregarded, thereby leading to the destruction of the city. It is, however, apparent from the very beginning, as the lie makes clear, that sex is the great danger to the stability of the city. Socrates then asks Glaucon whether he has a "device" (*mēchanē*: cf. 414b8) for persuading the citizens of this myth. Glaucon replies that he has nothing for the first generation, but as for those who come afterward. . . . He does not actually finish the thought, but Socrates takes his point (414c6–d5).

Details aside, this is a straightforward statement of the need for lying and what is today called "brainwashing." We do Plato no favors by trying to blur his meaning in a way that is compatible with contemporary morality. To do this is to conceal from ourselves Plato's conception of the price to be paid for the establishment of a just city. Plato's contemporary enemies come closer to the mark when they accuse him of fostering a tyranny in the *Republic*. I think that this is also wrong, but it is understandable and closer to the text. The philosopher feels the desire to rule the entire city, with no restrictions placed upon superior knowledge and judgment. From time to time, philosophers in actual cities will succumb to this desire, but the results will be bad, as they were in the case of Plato's own trips to Sicily. The *Republic* is in part a daydream in which Plato imagines what it would be like to be a beneficent despot. Those who are not tempted by the prospect of exercising this power are not genuine philosophers; but neither are those who succumb to that temptation. This last remark will seem extreme or absurd to those contemporaries for whom philosophy has become almost exclusively a technical enterprise, but if we are honest with ourselves, we see the same desire at work, albeit in a much lower way, in the academic feuding of different schools of philosophy. The expulsion of rival viewpoints is in the best cases an expression of the wish for the truth to triumph, and in the worst, of the will to power. We need not surrender to the excesses of Nietzsche in order to see that the first comes dangerously close to the second.

The remainder of Book Three is devoted to a description of the communal life of the auxiliaries, who are described as "temperate and courageous athletes of war" (416d8–e1). They dwell in an armed camp that is located in a place convenient for them to march out against internal or external enemies. Their education is designed to prevent them from attacking their fellow citizens like wolves instead of protecting them like noble dogs. In addition, they will have no private property or right to privacy that protects them from unannounced entrance by any of their companions into the room they occupy. Meals suited to temperate soldiers will be served in common at the expense of the city. They will be allowed no human money, since they possess divine gold and silver within their souls. Such is the communal existence of the soldier-guardians and (presumably) the potential philosophers who are being educated to rule. By attempting to remove every source of difference, Socrates wishes to make it easier for the guardians to identify with the city; privacy is replaced by publicity. But if this identification occurs, do not the guardians cease to be human beings (416d3–417b9)?

Something like this must have occurred to Adeimantus, who, no longer restrained by the austerity that led him to criticize popular mythology, opens Book Four with an appropriate question. How will Socrates defend himself against the charge that he is not making the guardian class very happy? For the guardians have been deprived of money, large houses, and the benefits of private life that normally belong to those who in effect own the city. Instead of being blessed, they sit in the city like mercenaries and do nothing but keep watch (419a1–420a1). It looks as though we have returned to Socrates's argument in Book One that justice is useful only for *guarding* property, not using it. Socrates adds to Adeimantus's list the fact that the guardians serve for no recompense other than food. Since they receive no wages, they cannot make private trips or buy gifts for courtesans, or in general indulge any expenditures they wish, a liberty that is attributed to the happy (420a2–7).

The unstated assumption underlying Adeimantus's question is that happiness is not a matter of belief. Sometimes we say that so-and-so believes himself to be happy but is not. Yet even in these exceptional cases we make it clear that the belief fails to conceal the absence of happiness. We associate happiness in the first instance with the gratification of our personal wishes. Adeimantus implies that these wishes will arise even in the just city, and even among those who have been educated to identify their own interests with those of the city. Socrates begins his reply as follows: "It would not be surprising if these men, such as they are, are the happiest of all, but we did not construct the city with this in mind, that one tribe [*ethnos*] among us will be outstandingly happy, but rather so that the whole city will be as happy as possible" (420b4–8).

The city was constructed in order to find the origin and nature of justice, and thereby to determine which life, the just or the unjust, is in itself the happiest (e.g., I. 361c4–d3). The entire controversy, from the contribution of Cephalus through the long speeches by Glaucon and Adeimantus, was addressed to the question of personal happiness, that is, the happiness of the individual human being. It is therefore not correct to say that our aim was to produce a city that is as happy as possible. What we can say is that if the city is the soul writ large, we are constructing it for the sake of making more visible the condition of the soul. Furthermore, it is extremely doubtful that the conception of a happy city makes any sense apart from the question of the happiness of its constituent "tribes," as Socrates calls them. If the special happiness of the guardians is not crucial, then neither is the happiness of the other two classes. In this case, the happiness of the city depends upon some special arrangement of its parts. We should note also that if we succeed in constructing a happy city, this will not in itself prove the city to be just. To assume that it does is to beg the question, namely, of which life is happiest.

If we grant the analogy between the city and the soul, then if the city is happy, so too must be the soul. This will mean in turn that happiness is not a characteristic of one part of the soul but of the order of all the parts. And this is what Socrates will argue at a later stage, although he has already prepared for this argument by his analysis of the harmony of the parts of the soul through temperance and courage. Harmony is the representation of the health of the soul, whereas disharmony is the mark of sickness. If we make the extremely plausible assumption that health is more conducive to happiness than illness, it follows that the just (and so both harmonious and healthy) life is happier than the unjust life. Whether "happier than" excludes unhappiness entirely is of course another question.

This reflection shows us that the order of the parts in the city is not the same as the order of the parts in the individual soul. The well-ordering of the parts of the city supposedly leads to a happy city, but a happy city may have unhappy citizens, and these may well coincide with all or part of the guardian class. But the well-ordering of the parts of the soul produces a guardian, that is, an individual human being of a certain type, and one whose happiness remains to be established. Everything comes down to the simple question: Can a healthy person be unhappy? And the answer to this question is certainly yes. We know this from our own experience, but it also follows from the regular Socratic argument that nothing, including health, is a blessing unless it is used for good purposes.

In developing this point, Socrates says that our purpose is not to make the guardians the happiest of human beings, or for that matter the farmers and workers; he does not mention the rulers, but we can assume that they are still included within the general class of guardians, together with the auxiliaries (see 421b6–c1). Our purpose, to continue, is rather to keep separate from the guardians everything that will spoil their nature and so make them less or not at all fitted to preserve the city. We must consider whether our city as a whole is happy, and to this end we must "compel and persuade" (ibid.) the auxiliaries and guardians to do the same, and so too all the residents of the city. Socrates seems to have confused happiness with justice throughout this argument. Everything that has been said so far is compatible with the thesis that the city can be just but not happy or, alternatively, happy but not just. Is it not, for example, unjust to compel and persuade the guardians to ignore their private happiness for the sake of the happiness of the city as a whole? But if they are not happy, then the claim that the harmony of the soul is health and justice does not in itself establish the identity of these two attributes with happiness.

In his discussion of happiness, Socrates mentions fine clothing together with feasting and drinking as things that might make the farmers and craftsmen happy but would damage them as workers and technicians, thereby damaging the city as well. The underlying premise, again, is that the city prospers when each person does his or her own work well. The work of the guardians is to guard, not to enjoy private wealth and indulgences that would interfere with their capacity to protect the city. Socrates goes on to say that a worker who becomes wealthy neglects his craft and so becomes a worse practitioner, whereas poverty makes it impossible for him to buy tools, so that his own work deteriorates, as does the training of his sons. He concludes that "from both of these, poverty and wealth, the products of the arts become worse, and so too do the artists" (421e4–5). Note that this argument does not apply to the guardians themselves, who will have no property, and so be neither rich nor poor. Their role is to guard against these conditions ever creeping unnoticed into the city (421e7–8). The arts of the extended guardian class, which includes both rulers and auxiliaries, are to govern and preserve the city, or as one might say, to reproduce it continuously. The guardians do not make shoes or houses; they make the city.

The difference between the two classes may be considered from the standpoint of the harmony of the soul. At III. 412a4–7 Socrates says: "We would say correctly that the man who makes the most beautiful mixture of gymnastics and music, thereby bringing the soul to complete measure, is fully musical and well harmonized, far more so than the man who tunes the strings of an instrument." Such a man is required as a ruler; if he does his job properly, then the craftsmen will be neither rich nor poor. This may well prevent them from the two kinds of deterioration just noted by Socrates, but it does not in itself guarantee that they will work at the highest possible level. Remember that the workers are not perfectly harmonized in their own souls; this is why they must be supervised by the ruler. Through this submission, the city, but not each citizen, becomes harmonious. The workers are deficient in courage and moderation. Since they are not allowed to become rich, is it not likely that they will work just hard enough to avoid the extreme poverty against which Socrates warns? Or even more likely, will they not strive to accumulate wealth behind the backs of the guardians?

It should be emphasized that harmony is not justice. Socrates has not yet identified the definition of this cardinal virtue but limited himself to courage and temperance. Those who have looked ahead will of course know that, in fact, Socrates is building toward the definition of justice as "doing one's own work" or "minding one's own business." His conception of justice is already implied in the principle of the division of labor. If we make this explicit, then we can say that personal happiness in the conventional sense is sacrificed for the sake of the conditions of justice, and an untraditional sense of justice at that. If we put to one side the philosopher-kings, who have not yet made their official appearance, then we can say of guardians and workers alike that they have been "shaped" to perform a single task, and that Socrates dedicates them to the pursuit of joy through work.

I must confess that I for one do not find a single feature in this forced and unnatural analysis to legitimate Socrates's claim that the city will be happy, to say nothing of the citizens. Little wonder that the city of the *Republic* has been subjected to such harsh criticism by modern and contemporary readers of the most varied political persuasions. What needs to be explained is admiration for such a city. And this leads directly to the question of Socrates's intention. Did he seriously believe that his city is just, happy, and something that reasonable persons could wish for? Or is it a satire on the foolishness of the dream of perfect justice? My suggestion is that the rule of philosophy is for Plato just, but that the resulting city is not one that would be desirable or lead to the happiness of its citizens. There is in fact a conflict between justice and happiness; the first restricts our desires, whereas the second entails their satisfaction. Justice is a necessary evil; it is the good of another, not of oneself. One could perhaps say that the real noble lie in the *Republic* is the claim that justice in itself makes us happy. The harmonious soul is one that attends primarily to its own inner health and happiness, not to that of the city. In short, the *Republic* is both seriously intended by Plato and also a demonstration of the impossibility of a truly philosophical city. The tension between the need for and the inaccessibility of philosopher-kings is not a literary paradox but the pulse of human existence. Our claim to love justice beyond everything else is a noble lie.

In terms introduced by Socrates, does it make sense to sacrifice the personal happiness of the citizens for the sake of a dubious happiness of the city? And if we are told that there is no sacrifice inasmuch as the citizens of actual cities are not actually happy, because they live their lives in a lack of harmony and justice, we must ask in reply if it is not unjust to enforce harmony, or whether harmony as conceived by Socrates is not itself already unjust. Those who bridle at the necessity of lying to everyone in the city in order to preserve justice are perhaps right after all. Is not a city based upon fairy tales itself a fairy tale?

5

Now let us pick up once more the thread of the argument. Socrates says that wealth produces luxury, idleness, and innovation, whereas poverty produces illiberality and wrongdoing as well as innovation (422a1–3). One might add to this that wealth also produces more wealth, and more important, it brings about the conditions for the improvement of technology. Even the art of shoemaking, to take Socrates's favorite example, can be improved through the manufacture of better equipment and materials. But it is not an increase in labor and money as such that worries Socrates; his real target is innovation, which he says is also caused by poverty. Let us first be clear that poverty does not normally lead to an improvement in production or the performance of any art, including that of war, although in this last case exigency may give a special impetus to courage. Revolution is the innovation induced by poverty, and this is fundamentally the desperation of the desire to become wealthy. I realize that revolutionaries may justify themselves initially on more modest grounds, namely, as motivated by the desire for a fair share. But what seems fair tends to expand in the course of the rebellion's increasing success, and most dramatically in the aftermath of victory.

On the whole, I think it is fair to say that wealth is more desirable than poverty, just as health is more desirable than illness, and success than failure. For Socrates, however, this traditional evaluation, one that he might well make himself in another context, is not satisfactory. A wealthy city soon attracts enemies from the outside as well as corrupting those on the inside. A poor city is relatively easy to conquer but not so desirable an acquisition, unless for special purposes like those of strategic location. Our city comes much closer to poverty than to wealth, and Socrates supplements this advantage with the following device. First, he assumes that the guardians of his city are the best trained in the arts of war and, like the champion boxer, will fight easily against two rich, fat nonboxers (422b6–8). This is singularly unconvincing; there is no reason why rich cities cannot have very good soldiers; Athens is the outstanding example. And of course they will have more and better-equipped troops than the city under construction. Something more is required. If our city has two enemies, we can send the guardians to the rulers of one and ask for their help in defeating the other, for which service they may keep all the gold and silver, as well as the other property of the vanquished foe (422d1–7). The obvious difficulty with this plan is that there is nothing to keep our wealthy ally from conquering the third city and then us. Socrates is unduly reliant upon the good training of local troops. He also omits the possibility that the beautiful city will have several potential enemies. The negotiations required in actual circumstances to avoid defeat by such stratagems would strain the cunning of a Metternich.

In any event, Socrates indicates how far he is willing to go in order to preserve his city by discussing the problem of size. Real cities are each a many, not a one; in particular, there are two warring parties in every actual city, the rich and the poor. If we try to deal with these cities as though each were a unity, we shall fail. But if we approach them as a many and offer the money, property, or even lives of one group to the other, we shall always have many allies and very few enemies (423a2–5). This is an odd passage; it is not clear whether Socrates advocates offering the money of a city that attacks us to a potential ally, or instructs us to play upon the division between the rich and the poor in a potential enemy. What is clear is that, as we saw previously when Socrates recommended that we send marvelous mimetic poets to a neighboring city, he has no hesitation in corrupting other cities. Justice is limited in principle to our dealings with our fellow citizens. There may well be certain common practices, based upon unwritten laws and mutual advantage, that regulate the behavior of cities toward each other. But these are subordinate to, and for the sake of, the preservation of the city, which supervenes over all considerations of what would today be called international relations. We are allowed to destroy our neighbors if this is necessary for the preservation of the beautiful city.

Socrates is necessarily imprecise when it comes to the question of the proper size of the city. He says that so long as it is "temperately ordered" (*sōphronōs etachthē*) as it was before, it will be the greatest city, not in numbers but in truth (423a5–7). This passage makes evident a point that we have had occasion to notice previously. The greatness of the city does not depend upon justice, which has not yet been introduced, but rather upon temperance, a virtue that Socrates extended to cover obedience to the rulers (III. 389d9–e2). I shall return to this at the appropriate place. It is enough to say here that there is some link between minding one's own business (as justice will be defined) and temperance.

With respect to size, Socrates allows the city to grow up to the point at which it is willing to be one (423b9–10). Socrates and Adeimantus both acknowledge the difficulty of this task, which of course requires the strict regulation of sex. Socrates reminds Adeimantus that children must be taken from their parents and placed in the class to which they belong by nature. He touches lightly on a corollary that will later assume central importance in the arrangement of the city. The possession of women, marriage, and procreation must be arranged as far as possible in accord with the proverb that friends have all things in common (423e5–424a2). Adeimantus accepts this without hesitating, although he is soon to have second thoughts. As will be made explicit, this principle applies only to the (extended) guardian class. The rule clearly has to do with the goal of unity, and the unification of the feeling of brotherhood and family with love of the city. It should be easy to see that the principle raises more problems than it solves, since it asks us to establish neither complete promiscuity nor strict application of the traditional Greek views on marriage, legitimate sexual intercourse, and the importance of the bloodline in establishing citizenship.

Socrates summarizes the question of the size of the city with an ambiguous simile. If there are no innovations in music and gymnastic, and hence in the education and rearing of the guardians, then "the regime [*politeia*], once it has been well launched, will be augmented like a circle" (424a4–5). I take this to mean that it will fluctuate in size but never change in its nature. But it is also possible that Socrates refers to an augmentation of virtue, thanks to the steady improvement of successive generations. We should note here that the prevention of innovation in music is singled out as crucial to the preservation of the circular development of the city, a point that Socrates makes via a citation from Damon to the effect that changes in musical style bring about changes in the greatest political laws (424c3–6). No such remark is made about gymnastics. Adeimantus reiterates Socrates's warning about the political influence of music, a view that he held with great fervor in the criticism of the poets.

With this settled, Socrates turns to a number of important topics for which it would be inappropriate to establish particular laws. He cites the well-ordering of the games of young boys, the various forms of respect for one's elders, business and contractual dealings with tradesmen and artisans, the appointment of judges, and so on (425a2–d6). On these last topics, Adeimantus says that it is not worth giving orders to gentlemen. To this, Socrates asks ironically if it is "gracious" of corrupted persons to regard as their greatest enemy the man who tells them the truth about licentiousness, namely, that unless one gives up drinking, overeating, sex, and idleness, one will not be cured by drugs, burning, cutting, or odes and charms. We are not surprised to hear Adeimantus deny strongly the graciousness of a condemnation by one who says something good. Socrates adds, just to accentuate the point, that Adeimantus is not one who praises such men. "No, by Zeus!" Adeimantus replies. One can see that it would have been somewhat more difficult to have this conversation with Glaucon.

According to Socrates, we are now at the end of our task of legislating for "us," that is, for the human residents of the city. There remain the affairs of the gods, to which we shall turn next. Let me now make some summary remarks about the human side of the founding and legislation. The reader will note that we have concentrated upon education, and hence upon music and gymnastics, but not at all upon the countless daily details of human intercourse that require some form of legislation. Socrates says that in a bad city such laws are useless, whereas in a good city they may easily be found by the gentlemen (427a2–b2). To this I add the following remark. In the *Republic*, our primary goal is to inspect the nature of the soul, in order to determine whether the just or the unjust life is the happiest for the individual person. We have come very close to the assertion that the just life is not necessarily the happiest, but that whether or not it is, what counts is the happiness of the city. There is thus a curious disjunction in the flow of the argument. What started out as an inquiry into individual happiness has culminated in the subordination of the happiness of the individual soul to that of the city. As Socrates himself implies, there may be unhappy persons in a happy city. If this is so, however, then the analogy between the city and the soul cannot hold.

The Purged City 137

We are, of course, not really at the end of our legislative duties, as will become clear at the beginning of Book Five. Socrates is plainly hoping to avoid a detailed discussion of the principle of women and children in common, which he mentioned in passing a short while ago. But he has also not introduced the extremely puzzling principle of the need for philosopher-kings, together with the discussion of their education. Up to this point, the conversation has been difficult at moments but in no way beyond the grasp of Socrates's audience. As gentlemen, they could all arrange for the legislation required on the countless points of daily political life. Differently stated, men like Glaucon and Adeimantus (to say nothing of the others) could be counted on to finish the legislative task as hitherto defined, provided that they had been subjected from birth to the education in music and gymnastic which we have now composed. Glaucon represents courage and Adeimantus represents temperance. It only remains for the two to be "harmonized" or "unified."

All this having been said, it remains true that a failure to carry out the details of legislation tends to obscure the countless practical difficulties in establishing a city as imagined by Socrates. This detailed legislating would be contrary to the spirit of the conversation. Our goals are lofty, and it would be a constriction of our vision to get bogged down in vulgar detail. But on the other hand, politics is largely vulgar detail, even when the goals are lofty. Let us say simply that there are advantages and disadvantages to speaking at the general level, or in restricting oneself to the main structural features of the city. The key point, I think, whether one calls it an advantage or a disadvantage, is that we fail to take into account the endless obstacles to the preservation of a city that requires, on the one hand, the greatest sacrifices of the individual to the city and, on the other, constant brainwashing so as to convince everyone, the guardians included, that disadvantages are actually advantages. Socrates requires a citizenry who are devoted to the task of deluding themselves into believing that their city is the model of justice and that its happiness is theirs. In my view, it is psychologically impossible to imagine the guardians, as they and their education have so far been described, as capable of legislating and governing the Socratic city. That this was also Plato's view is proved by the introduction of the philosopher-kings. But this will bring with it another set of problems. My main claim at the moment is that Adeimantus's statement, encouraged and accepted by Socrates, that gentlemen will know how to take care of the details of legislation is false, if it means that they can do so while remaining gentlemen of the type described. Neither courage nor temperance is the same as political intelligence, or let us say the characteristic required to govern a city. Let the difficulty of choosing suitable judges stand as a satisfactory example of the insoluble problem set by Socrates.

A final remark. One might reply to my observations that I have missed the point, and that the intention of Plato is to provide us with a model of the best or most beautiful city, a model to which actual cities can only approximate, but which they need in order to strive in the right direction. Furthermore, the model has not yet been fully constructed. Thus, for example, we may expect the shortcomings of the guardians to be supplemented by the virtues of the philosopher-kings. But it is this reply that misses the mark. I am in the process of denying that the Socratic city is indeed the model of the just city. More fully expressed, I claim that the rule of philosophy is just, but that the attempt to exercise it leads to injustice. The question is not one of the degree to which we are able to approach the Socratic model in practice. It is rather the case that we cannot move one step toward the actualization of the model without setting into motion circumstances that contradict the model. In order to make this claim fully plausible, however, I must analyze the entire dialogue. We have to see for ourselves how these destructive consequences follow from each step in the argument.

By way of summary, let me give just one important example of the overall problem. The guardians, exemplars of temperance and courage, are, not to beat about the bush, deficient in practical intelligence. Their efficacy, as far as it goes, depends upon the preposterous assumption that the citizens of the city will be kept always at the highest possible level of control by the rulers. Furthermore, they will be spending the bulk of their time, once they have completed their education, in the practice of war. If we honor the principle of one man, one job, the auxiliaries will have no time and will not be permitted to attend to actually legislating, governing, and tinkering with the forms of education. All this work must be performed either by the worker-farmer-merchant class or by the philosopher-kings. The first possibility is ruled out at once by the baseness of the members of the lowest class. But how will the philosophers be educated to supplement courage and temperance with practical intelligence? Is the art of legislation a corollary of the study of mathematics and dialectic? Where will time be found to acquire enough practical understanding of everyday life to engage in legislation? By the time the philosophers become kings, they have spent a lifetime in learning things that have no direct utility to the statesman or legislator.

6

Justice

I

The city has been founded, and with it, the human side of legislation is complete. But what of the gods and our dealings with them? When Socrates engaged in criticism of the poets, he used the singular *ho theos* to refer to the unity, unchangeableness, and veracity of the genuine deity, whereas in speaking about the courage and temperance of the auxiliaries, he referred to the gods in the plural. It looks at first as if Socrates has not thought through, or speaks with extreme carelessness about, the question of the number of the gods. The best way to handle this apparent contradiction between the one and the many is by inferring that the official theology is monotheistic, although the traditional deities may be invoked when this is useful to regulate the behavior of the citizens. At a deeper level, courage and temperance are detached from the philosophical conception of the deity. In any event, Socrates never explains or even calls attention to this theological dualism.

In the next section of the conversation, Socrates speaks entirely in a traditional religious mode. When it comes to temples, services and sacrifices, funerals, and so on, "we know nothing, and in founding the city, we shall not be persuaded by anyone else, if we have any sense, nor shall we make use of any other interpreter than that of hereditary custom. This god [i.e., Apollo at

Delphi: IV. 427b2–3] is doubtless the ancestral interpreter for all human beings and he passes judgment while seated at the navel in the middle of the earth" (427b8–c4).

Once again, it looks as if there is a certain discordance between the first and the second discussion of the gods. Whereas tradition was initially rejected and then tacitly reinvoked, it is here accepted unreservedly. We can, however, reconcile the two passages as follows. When Socrates speaks of human behavior, he allows himself to advert to apparent polytheism as the need arises. The present discussion is of religious practice, and in a way that connects this theme to the earlier discussion of courage and temperance. Despite the rule of philosophers, the city requires a religious basis for everyday life. But why did Socrates not invent new traditions and practices in conformity with the "theoretical" argument of Books Two and Three? I suspect that it is because the theological doctrine of the first discussion is too austere to serve as a basis for everyday political life. The god of the philosophers is one, but the citizen-soldiers require a more personal creed to sustain them in the presence of death.

Another implication of the present discussion, which will be stated explicitly at V. 470e4–6, is that the city Socrates and his companions are founding is Greek; hence the traditional forms of religious practice will be Greek as well. More generally, the institution of the *polis* is Greek, not barbarian; thus barbarians can be transformed into Greeks by organizing them into a city. This is what Socrates means when he says that Apollo is interpreter and judge "of all human beings." At a deeper level, it is what he will mean when he says at VI. 497a3–5 that philosophy cannot accomplish the greatest things without a suitable polis. And this is why Socrates will go so far as to say that philosophy could come to power "in some barbaric place" (VI. 499c9). Should it do so, the barbarian place will be transformed into a city by the adoption of the very proposals we are now studying. But this is an extreme case; Socrates clearly believes that the best situation will be to found the city in Greece and with Greeks. Even though the actual founding of the just city begins, as we shall see later, with the expulsion of everyone over the age of ten from the boundaries of the city (VII. 540e5), the children are already habituated to Greek myth. And this is better than being forced to build a city with children who are indoctrinated into the ways and beliefs of the barbarians.

Socrates now asks Adeimantus to find adequate lights for his brother and the other speakers, in order that they may search out justice and injustice in the completed city. Glaucon intervenes at this point with a rather sharp rebuke ("You're talking nonsense"). Socrates, he says, is attempting to turn over to others a task that he had undertaken for himself, on the grounds that it is not holy for him to fail to come to the aid of justice when it is attacked in his presence. Socrates accepts the reminder but says that the others must look as well. Glaucon's boldness has thus saved Socrates from impiety (427d1–e4).

The first step is to assume that, since our city has been correctly built, it is perfectly good and is therefore wise, courageous, temperate, and just. There is no "deduction" of these attributes from a higher knowledge of the good; Socrates takes the point as obvious. Otherwise put, he never proves that the four traditional virtues are sufficient to found a city. But what would such a proof look like? Actual cities grow up in stages, but not from a finite set of discrete virtues. We could also object, however, that it is premature to assume that our city is just, since we do not yet officially know what justice is. If we do not know the definition of justice, how shall we recognize it in our inspection of the completed city? Socrates says that if we are looking for one of four parts of anything at all, and identify three as something else, then the remaining part is what we are looking for. This is obviously false. The fourth part will be justice if and only if justice is present in the city and our division or identification of the parts has been exhaustive. Despite Socrates's assurance that we have completed the city, no definition of the rulers has been given. We do not yet know what kind of education they must receive in order to separate them from the auxiliary-guardians (427e6–428a10). Finally, we began to investigate the steps necessary for the origin of any city whatsoever but shifted to the construction of the best city when we turned to the education of the rulers and soldiers. At this point, Socrates must have known what justice is, and he could have learned this only from his knowledge of the human soul.

One might object that Socrates has in fact introduced the rulers at III. 413c5ff, where he says that the best guardians can be picked out as those who remember most firmly their conviction that they must always do what seems best for the city. Various exercises and games will be established for the youthful guardians, all of them designed to test the strength of this conviction. But we need something more than this conviction in a ruler. We require the intelligence and wisdom that is suitable to decide in each case what is indeed best for the city. The best of the guardians are adamant in their loyalty to the city, and their souls exhibit the most complete harmony of courage and temperance, but this hardly makes them statesmen, especially when we remember that Socrates includes obedience to the rulers as a part of temperance (III. 389d9–e2).

To come back to Book Four, Socrates draws the following account of wisdom out of Glaucon. I note that Socrates opens this account with the assertion that there is something odd (*atopon*) about the wisdom of the city (428b1). This wisdom is identified as "good counsel" (*euboulia*), which, says Socrates, is a kind of knowledge (*epistēmē*). He distinguishes this knowledge from other forms, all of which concern specific arts like carpentry, toolmaking, and farming. One wonders at this point why Socrates devoted so much time to arguments based upon the technical nature of knowledge. It should, after all, have been obvious from the beginning that statesmanship, the royal art, is nothing like shoemaking or carpentry. But it is, or should be, equally obvious that good counsel is not the same as the martial art. It is not the same as the harmony of courage and temperance. The best guardians, as so far described, would perhaps be suitable as the officer class of the army. But it is the civilians who rule the military (428b3–c10).

Socrates next identifies as the skill of the guardians the knowledge that counsels us about the city as a whole, in its dealings with itself and other cities. Those who possess this knowledge will be a small minority. It is by no means irrelevant to note that *euboulia* corresponds to what Aristotle calls *phronēsis*, or practical judgment. Aristotle apparently differs from Plato in denying the need for philosopher-kings. But at this point in the *Republic*, despite one or two occurrences of the word *philosophy*, no mention has been made of the need for philosopher-kings. Socrates apparently wishes to avoid this point, just as he skirted the principle of women and children in common, and he might justify himself by saying that thus far they have been concerned with the origin or location of justice within the structure of the city, not with the possibility of such a city. The philosopher-king enters into the discussion at the point at which Socrates is forced to reply to the question of this possibility (428c11–429a4).

Socrates says that we have found wisdom, "I do not know in what way" (429a5), in the supervisory and ruling part of the guardian class, namely, those few guardians who possess the wisdom of good counsel. If this is to be taken seriously, then it looks as if philosophy in the full sense of the term, and so too the peculiar education of the philosopher-kings, to which we shall turn later, as well as topics like the Platonic Ideas and the structure of knowledge (the divided line), are strictly speaking unnecessary to the pursuit of justice. But this conclusion is much too strong. What is true is that Socrates postpones for as long as possible a detailed discussion of the two most controversial features of his city: the rule of philosophy and the abolition of the family, having instead women and children in common. *Euboulia* is satisfactory for the governing of ordinary cities, as is taught by Aristotle in his practical writings. But taken by itself, it will not do for our city as Socrates is in the process of describing it. We also, and indeed primarily, require philosophy, or the apprehension of the Platonic Ideas.

The radical difference between Plato's *Republic* and Aristotle's *Politics* is that the former is a striking expression of philosophical madness, whereas the latter is a sober treatise. When Aristotle summarizes the main argument of the *Republic*, he leaves out any mention of the philosopher-kings and their outlandish education, thereby silently correcting Platonic excess. But the intentions of master and student are not the same. Plato is writing not as a guide to the practical statesman but in order to spell out the implications of the rule of philosophy. In the explicit argument, Socrates holds that this rule is required for the sake of genuine justice. He grants that life in the philosophical city would be distasteful to those who were not raised in accord with its customs and laws. But that is no argument against the justice of the city. A much deeper problem is that of happiness. When we come to the relevant passages, I believe we shall find that Socrates tries to finesse the problem with rhetoric. The main point has already been introduced; what counts is the happiness of the *city*, not that of the individual citizens. As I understand Plato's intentions, we are meant to see that talk of a happy city is absurd, and that the citizens cannot be made happy by what we today call brainwashing, or, in a more salubrious expression, by being brought up to know no other life than the one to which they have been assigned within the just city.

The richness of the *Republic* cannot be properly appreciated without distinguishing between Plato and Socrates. Socrates speaks for those philosophers who have no political ambition and wish to live a life of quiet speculation. Inside the just city, the native-born philosophers will be compelled to rule by their ostensible sense of justice. This would apply to Socrates as well, were he born into such a city. But in the case of Plato, who went to Sicily three times, whereas Socrates never attempted such a dramatic political role, the *Republic* is (to repeat an earlier expression) a daydream about the unity of theory and practice. The details of this unification are often, perhaps always, ineffectual and sometimes absurd, but this does not lessen the attractiveness of the prospect of philosophical rule. In this very specific sense, those who make a comparison between Plato's foray into politics and Heidegger's abortive career as a Nazi functionary are not entirely wrong. Plato's *Republic* is a dangerous book because it presents a highly dramatic argument for the tyranny of truth. It is simply untenable to regard it either as a straightforward utopia or as a concealed repudiation of philosophical zeal in the pursuit of justice. In an age in which philosophy has been replaced by science and technology, the danger of the tyranny of truth should be more, not less, visible than in classical antiquity.

Socrates goes on to say that courage has been discovered in the soldier class, to which he adds that this part makes the city as a whole courageous. I repeat the point: it is the soldier (or extended guardian) class, and only this class, in which we look for courage. At the same time, if the analogy between the city and the soul were sound, we would have to look for courage in the spirited element of the members of all three classes. Perhaps Socrates would reply that the courageous element in the worker class is minimal. In any case, if we follow the literal argument, the rest of the city need not be courageous. More precisely, it is not decisive whether the citizens other than the guardians are courageous or cowardly. This is in accord with the earlier inference that the whole city is wise if a small part is wise, namely, the rulers. There is something here that should make us uneasy. If only a few possess prudence, then of course the many must be ruled by force, whether this be physical or rhetorical. In other words, noble and medicinal lies are required because of the paucity of good counsel. One must admit that something like this situation obtains in most if not all actual cities (or modern nations, for that matter). But it is not self-evident that good counsel can be effectively administered by force and fraud. We have considerable evidence that bad counsel can be imposed in this way. But by limiting the ruling class to a fraction of the guardians, Socrates leaves the great majority of the city outside the political horizon of concern. How, then, is it possible for them to be forced into practicing virtue? Will their lack of wisdom not inevitably corrupt the execution of the wisest laws? This is especially worrisome with respect to courage, for it is surely false that a whole city is made brave by the bravery of its warriors.

In expanding upon the inculcation of courage, Socrates employs a striking image that summarizes much of what is crucial in his treatment of the city. We must preserve in the guardians the opinions produced by law through education; this process is like that of dyers who prepare a fabric to receive a color that will not bleach or be washed out by cleaning. This was the function of our education in music and gymnastic. In other words, we the founding fathers have arranged for the souls of the guardians to be stained with the dye of obedience to the regime. If we have succeeded, there is no room for independent judgment or (as Bloom indicates in his note to the passage) the challenging of conventional opinion. This raises another practical problem. The dye of obedience must be applied to the guardians from infancy onward. This means that it will also be applied to the souls of the future philosopher-kings. But will this not make them courageous rather than wise? A soul that has been dyed with a fixed color cannot alter its shade with the circumstances of daily political life (429d4–430c2).

We are to call the courage just discovered "political." It is steadfastness with respect to the laws of the city, or more fully, the power and preservation, through all circumstances, of correct opinion and the laws concerning what is terrible and what is not (430b2–4). If Glaucon wishes, we can give a more beautiful account of courage on another occasion. The present one will do for our purpose, which is to discover justice (430c3–6). This is another indication of a point I made previously about the incompleteness of the account of the city. Socrates seems to be prepared now to skip the identification of the source of temperance in the city and to proceed directly to justice, but Glaucon will not be satisfied with such haste. As recently as III. 410e10, Socrates said that the soul that exhibits the proper harmony between music and gymnastics, and so between softness and fierceness, is both temperate and courageous. In the present passage, Socrates says that temperance is more like a symphony (that is, accord) and harmony than are the others, and by others he presumably means wisdom and courage, the two virtues identified thus far. The difference between courage and temperance is as follows. Courage is primarily the refusal to deviate from what the laws tell us is best for the city; temperance is "a certain order [*kosmos*] of some pleasures and mastery of desires" (430e6–7).

Temperance is also presented as the subordination of the worse part of the soul to that part which is by nature better. In the case of the city, temperance is the mastery of the desires of the many and the bad by the desires and prudence of the few who are of the more decent kind (431c9–d2). Furthermore, in our city, the rulers and the ruled have the same opinion about who should rule, and for this reason, as I pointed out previously, the city is temperate. When this mastery of vulgar desire and agreement about ruling and being ruled are both present, then the whole city is temperate, and not just one part, as was the case with wisdom and courage. In other words, wisdom exists in the wise, courage exists in the brave, but temperance is a kind of double virtue. It exists in those who can subordinate the lower desires to the higher ones, and this is temperance properly or customarily speaking. But it also exists in the other two virtues, wisdom and courage (431e10–432a9).

This last mode of existence is virtually equivalent to the enforcement of the principle one man, one job. The temperate city is one in which each part does its own work in the best possible way. It is a city in which the whole and its parts all mind their own business. As we are about to see, this makes temperance hard if not impossible to distinguish from justice.[1] We might also refer to temperance as harmony, accord, order, and measure, qualities that seem to do the work of justice and thus to make it superfluous. If this is too extreme, let us say that justice is the music of the soul, and hence of the city, which is the soul writ large.

Now we proceed like hunters to track down justice, and, lo and behold! (*Iou iou*), it has been rolling around at our feet from the very beginning (432d2–3). Justice, Socrates suggests, is nothing other than the practice of minding one's own business, that is, one man, one job (433a1–b1). Justice is what is left over after we have discovered temperance, courage, and prudence (Socrates uses *phronēsis* here as interchangeable with *sophia*: cf. 433d8): "It is this which furnished the power to all of these so that they could come into existence, and which preserved them once they had done so, for as long as it is present within the city." Otherwise put, the existence of the city depends upon the justness of the principle that each person has one task that he or she can perform better than any other, and that this natural gift is what should determine one's place in the harmony of ruler and ruled. It is therefore obvious that we must know this fact about the human soul before we set out to construct a just city. It is, however, not at all self-evident that each of us can do one thing better than anything else. But even if we grant this point, it remains to be shown that our political function should be determined by this skill. Is it not possible, and not only possible but necessary for the existence of a just city, that farmers, for example, may possess enough prudence to participate in the process of governing the city? In order to make his point, Socrates must argue that prudence, in the sense of practical judgment, is not sufficient as a qualification for ruling, but that one must be wise in the highest sense of the term, that is, one must be a philosopher in order to be a competent king. And so the conflict between sober and mad politics is introduced into the overall argument.

2

Justice, to repeat, is minding one's own business and avoiding *polupragmosunē*, busying oneself with many things and so minding someone else's business (433d1–5). It would be hard to say which of the four cardinal virtues is most important to the city; Socrates refers to them as all on a par (*enamillon*: 433d7–9). He then establishes that the rulers in the city will judge lawsuits. This confirms our earlier conjecture that judges come from the guardian class, but it does not resolve all the difficulties arising from the need of the judges to have much experience with evil. Their sole duty is to determine that no one have what belongs to others or not have what belongs to him. But this means that each citizen must fulfill the function of the class to which he or she has been assigned. Socrates makes it explicit here that members of the lowest class are free to change their occupations and even to practice two crafts. What would cause great damage to the city is the shift of citizens from one class to another. It is obvious that the main point of the tripartition of the city is to separate rulers and soldiers from everyone else as well as from each other. Evidently life in the third class will be the same as it is in all actual cities, so far as physical labor, farming, commerce, and the arts and crafts are concerned (434a3–c2). Henceforward, unless there is some specific reason for not doing so, I shall for the sake of simplicity refer to the third class as that of the moneymakers, a term that Socrates himself employs at 434c7–8.

There is something unsettling about the division of the city into three distinct classes. For one thing, we turned to the city because it is supposed to be the soul writ large. Thus the parts of the city should have exhibited in a more visible way the parts of the soul. But Socrates did not look to actual cities; instead, he has constructed a radically innovative polity on the basis of his antecedent convictions concerning the nature of the soul. For example, Socrates said that human nature is cut up into small pieces, or in other words that people excel at different tasks. He could not have inferred this simply from noticing that in actual cities there is a division of labor, since this could be due to the artificial customs and laws of the city itself. To make the same point in a different way, Socrates criticizes actual cities because they are not in conformity with the best or healthy order of the individual soul. This inference depends both upon knowledge of actual cities and also knowledge of the soul. Otherwise one could argue that the order of the soul is not independent but is rather an artifact of the city in which one happens to live.

In sum, it is of course extremely helpful, and perhaps indispensable, to have experience of human behavior in actual cities. But in order to modify this behavior in a model of the best city, one must have a criterion of rank-ordering of polities that is itself based upon our understanding of the human soul and what is best for it. This is the same problem that faces modern political philosophers of the state of nature; for example, Rousseau. But it cannot be solved by looking first at the city and attempting to deduce from it the nature of the soul, because we cannot be certain that the soul revealed by the actual city is not a product of that city. How, then, are we to separate the soul from its political context? An inability to answer this question leads directly to the interpretation of human existence as a political or social construction.

There is a further point to be made about the present passage. Since workers must work and soldiers must fight, it follows that all the acts of government will be carried out by the rulers. For example, as we just learned, they will serve as judges in lawsuits. The judge is someone who has as his business seeing to it that all parties in a dispute get their fair share. In that sense, he does his own job or minds his own business by minding the business of everyone who comes before his jurisdiction. It is easy to see that this must be true of every political responsibility that affects the city as a whole, with respect either to itself or to other cities. The rulers, in practicing their own occupation, are directly concerned with minding the business of the others. They are the paradigmatic exemplars of *polupragmosunē*.

To continue, justice in the city is the minding by each class of its business or doing its own task: ruling, war, or moneymaking. We are now to compare this with the soul of the individual person; if the two agree, then we may be sure that we have found justice (434d2–435a1). This passage makes plain the circularity of Socrates's reasoning. As I have just noted, if we can see the soul of the human being well enough to verify that it is isomorphic to the structure of the city, then we do not need to construct a city in order to see the soul. We could look directly at the soul. Conversely, if the soul is not visible independently of the city, then we could never determine that the latter is the larger copy of the former. Since most of our views about the soul are acquired in cities, the soul must be visible as it is in itself, despite the fact that it so to speak wears the garments of a citizen, and a citizen in one actual or historical state or another.

One way to formulate this suggestion is to say that cities must magnify, but not mirror, the structure of the soul. There must be something about cities, or more generally, political life, that enables us to see the individual souls at work, but this is not possible if the city mirrors the soul. For in this case, different cities will mirror different orders in the soul. There is no such thing as *the* city; even the just city is a model of one kind of city, in which the citizens are altered so as to conform with its customs and laws. And these customs and laws were devised by such-and-such properties of the soul. What we want is to be able to see those properties themselves, not their political expression, and to see how their effects are to be rank-ordered. Only if we can see this shall we be in a position to construct "the best" or the truly beautiful city.

This task is not as difficult as it might initially appear. In fact, there could be no basis upon which we judge cities, or ostensibly ideal constitutions, other than our interpretation of the good life; and this is primarily a matter of the order of the individual soul, and only secondarily of the construction of a city that makes the good life possible. If there is no human nature, and so no naturally superior rank-ordering of the attributes of the soul, then all attempts to prefer one city over another are entirely arbitrary. This thesis may seem attractive to an age of historical relativism, but it makes no empirical sense, as those who have lived part of their lives in tyrannies and dictatorships will be happy to testify.

A man differs from a city, says Socrates, only in that one is smaller than the other. Hence the man will be the same as the just city "with respect to the form itself of justice" (*kat' auto to tēs dikaiosunēs eidos*: 435b1–2). No matter how we look at the matter, the identification of man and city (except for size) is clearly an exaggeration. I shall not repeat all the objections I have raised to the soundness of the analogy but shall restrict myself to the main points. Cities are not alive in the biological sense, and their parts are not organically unified. If an individual soul is courageous, it is so as an entirety. But the city, according to Socrates, is courageous if the soldiers are, regardless of the rest of the population. And a similar point holds good for the three other cardinal virtues. Thus the workers correspond to the desiring element in the soul, which requires to be moderated by the auxiliary-soldiers or spiritedness. But this is the exercise of compulsion, not the expression of temperance. A city will thus be temperate if the rulers and soldiers are, even when most of the citizens are not. And it is obvious that a city is wise if its rulers are, even though the rest of the citizenry lacks wisdom, whereas a wise man is so in the harmony and wholeness of his soul. Finally, a just man does not act in opposition to his desires but, again, as a harmonious totality of the soul.

Socrates seems to treat the principle of the division of labor as defining the structure of the soul as well as the city. This entails that the parts of the city must correspond to parts of the individual soul. But whereas courage in the soul is located in spiritedness, in the city it is located in a class of persons, each of whose soul contains intellect, spiritedness, and desire. But the soul as a total structure is not a larger version of one part of the soul. Cities can neither be happy nor engage in philosophy. Nothing I have just said is intended to deny that there is any utility in the analogy between the city and the soul. But it makes no sense to speak of "sameness."[2]

I note parenthetically that in the passage just discussed, Socrates in effect makes use of the terminology of the doctrine of Platonic Ideas when he speaks of "the form of justice itself." But Socrates has referred to "forms" on several previous occasions. The terminology is not particularly technical or extraordinary; it takes for granted that we cannot describe particular things except as instances of some particular kind of thing. Ordinary language takes for granted the conception of *the* cow or *the* horse, which is neither this nor that cow or horse but expresses truly what each is. In other words, the speaker of ordinary language, contrary to what some would claim, practices metaphysics by distinguishing implicitly between the existence of particular things and the being of abstract entities. Ordinary language is based upon the distinction between being and existence, without which it would be impossible, since it depends upon reference to, and identification of, particulars as *what* they are. It remains for the metaphysician to render this distinction explicit by introducing the required terminology.

One can therefore understand that if we see the same form of justice in the city and the soul, they are identical with respect to justice, however much they may differ in all other ways. This does not mean that the concrete manifestation of justice is the same in all cases for the city and the soul, only that justice is present in both. The point is easier to see in arithmetic. Everyone would agree that if we see two apples and two stones, they are the same with respect to their twoness (provided that we do not cut them in half). The number two is the standard by which we call these otherwise quite different things the same. Anyone who denies the existence of two is talking nonsense, as he or she would if asserting that the existence of the number two (not the symbol) is the same as the existence of the apples and the stones. Similarly, "apple" is that with respect to which four apples are called the same. It would be absurd to deny that there is any such thing as *the* apple, but equally absurd to claim that the existence of *the* apple and the four pieces of fruit must be the same. *The* apple, for example, does not grow on trees and is not edible. But neither do instances of the fruit we call apples come into existence when we invent the term or define the concept "apple."

To come back to the analogy between city and soul, according to the initial hypothesis, the individual human being is wise, courageous, temperate, and just because he or she exhibits the same forms in the soul as are exhibited in the city. Socrates has also taken it for granted that the forms are contained or visible within analogous parts; in other words, the rulers, who exemplify wisdom in the city, are analogous to the intellect in the private soul, the auxiliaries or soldiers are analogous to spiritedness, and the moneymakers are analogous to the faculty of desire. There are some problems here. First, it is surely absurd to suggest that soldiers and rulers have no desires. What Socrates means is of course that these desires are controlled by the intellectual part of the soul, through the instrumentality of spiritedness. But the fact remains that if all three classes have desires, then it cannot be the moneymakers alone who are isomorphic to the desiring part of the soul. Furthermore, as Bernard Williams has pointed out, there is also no reason to assume that the moneymakers are uniformly persons of uncontrollable desires.[3] Second, as I observed earlier, it is unreasonable to hold that the courage of the moneymakers is politically irrelevant. Socrates does not deny that they may be courageous, only that this courage is essential to the salvation of the city. I think that this is manifestly wrong. The courage of the military cannot supervene over the cowardice of the populace at large, as history has shown on numerous occasions. But if the courage of the city does not lie in one class alone, then the soldier class cannot be the large image of spiritedness in the individual soul. It can only be the most important site of courage. Third, since temperance and justice are harmonies, they must lie within all three parts of the city. In this case, it is impossible that each is contained within a single part of the soul alone, as Socrates himself noted. And as I pointed out, it may even be impossible to distinguish between the two. The correlation of parts of the city with analogous parts of the soul seems to work best with wisdom. It would be very much in keeping with the entire argument to say that it strongly implies the distinction between wisdom, on the one hand, and what Socrates will call the "demotic virtues," on the other (see VI. 500d4–9). In terms of the present analogy, the sense is that the intellect rules over the rest of the soul, and in that way over the body, including the body politic.

We should emphasize that the individual members of the three classes of the city each have a complete soul. In other words, the individual ruler has not only intellect but also spiritedness and desire; the soul of the auxiliary possesses intellect and desire as well as spiritedness, and the moneymakers have intellect and spiritedness as well as desire. Yet, as a member of one and only one class, each person exemplifies wisdom, courage, or temperance. Thus, for example, the ruler is not simply a large copy of the intellect in his own soul; he is, rather, preeminent in intelligence; and a similar point holds for each of the other two types of person. Or as we can also put it, the form of wisdom is exhibited by the ruling soul, but it is not necessarily exhibited in the intellect of each particular soul. In fact, it cannot be exhibited in the soul of the soldier or the moneymaker. In short, the three parts of the city do not mirror the three faculties of the soul, but each part of the city is identified as the political function to be performed by persons of such-and-such a type.

Socrates raises none of these or other problems; but he hints at their existence by saying that they will never find out with precision, on the road they have been traveling, if the soul contains the three forms thus far identified. There is another road, longer and more time consuming, that we would have to take. But perhaps we can reach our destination in a way that is up to the level of our present mode of inquiry (435c9–d5). So the present discussion is not at all sufficient for the philosopher (see VI. 504b1–d3), although it satisfies Glaucon. Once they have reached agreement on this point, Socrates goes on to ask whether the three forms and characters (*ēthē*) have not been acquired by the city from persons of the same type. Thus spiritedness has come in from those with characters like those of the Thracians, Scythians, and other northerners, the love of learning from those resembling the residents of the moderate zone (Attica), and the love of moneymaking from persons like the Phoenicians and Egyptians (see Bloom's note to the passage). Glaucon agrees that this is so.[4]

The implication is that the individual attributes or characters are derived from geography, that is, from nature rather than convention or custom. In other words, Socrates does not mean to make the absurd claim that intelligence is a characteristic to be found exclusively in the moderate climate of Attica, but rather he means that the moderate climate favors the development of intellectual prowess (435e1–436a4). That is, nature distinguishes three main human types, and the city is constructed from members of all three. And this in turn seems to support the hypothesis that the distinct powers of the soul perform distinct tasks (ruling, protecting, desiring), but not at all that each person performs one task only. Again, the power of the soul is analogous not to the individual person as a whole but to the peculiar excellence of each of the three classes.

But now Socrates says that it is hard to know if we perform the three separate functions of ruling, soldiering, and making money or desiring with separate parts of the soul, or whether each function is fulfilled by the soul as a whole. This question seems to cast doubt on the analogy of the city and the soul, which up to now has sustained virtually the entire argument. If we do everything with the whole soul, then there is no basis in human nature for justifying the tripartite division of the city. Socrates begins with the attempt to determine if the three powers of the soul are the same as or different from each other. If the first alternative is established, presumably we shall have proved that the soul acts as a whole (436a8–b4).

In this inquiry, Socrates employs what has sometimes been called the principle of noncontradiction. "It is plain that the same thing will neither do nor suffer opposites with respect to the same part and in relation to the same thing" (436b8–c1). We normally think of a contradiction as holding between two propositions, but the reason why one proposition contradicts another is because the two simultaneously affirm and deny that one thing is another or that a property belongs to an owner (and note that the logical subject stands in the proposition for the ontological substance). Socrates's formulation refers directly to the way things function, not to the statements we make about those functions. This is quite important, and the same point holds for Aristotle, because it distinguishes the Socratic school from modern logical nominalism. For modern logicians, the proposition is primary; for the ancients, the beings about which we propose are primary.

Socrates gives three examples, of which we need examine only the first. If a person stands still and moves his hands and his head, we cannot say that he both moves and is still but rather that he moves one part of himself and remains motionless in another part. Socrates shifts here to what we can say, but it is plain that this in turn is determined by what is the case (436c8–437a2). Unfortunately, Socrates makes a logical mistake in the sequel. He confuses contradiction, that is, opposition of two things such that the affirmation of one is the negation of the other, and vice versa, with contrariety. Take the example of desire and nondesire. Desire is defined as the soul's embracing or reaching out to grasp what it wants; not desiring is the soul's thrusting away or driving out of itself that which is not desired. But these are not opposites, because both can be rejected or avoided in favor of quiescence, namely, neither desiring nor not-desiring but remaining indifferent. It remains to be seen how serious this mistake is to his argument. The next point shifts ground. Socrates asks whether, when we are thirsty, we desire drink or a particular kind of drink, for example, hot or cold. Glaucon replies in effect that thirst is by nature the desire for drink, whereas the kind of drink we desire depends upon the circumstances; for example, a cold drink in hot weather and a hot drink in cold weather (437d2–e8). This requires a small but crucial modification. Desire for drink is desire for good drink, not for a drink that will poison us, and so too with food or anything else that we desire.

Socrates generalizes the preceding point in a way that is difficult for Glaucon to understand. I simplify it as follows. Whatever is a desire for something is related to that thing. Things that are just themselves, for example, hunger and thirst, are related to things that are just themselves, for example, food and drink. As we saw previously, hunger is not by nature for a steak but for any good food, and good means "capable of assuaging hunger." But hunger for a steak is hunger of a certain kind, and it arises from custom, experience, the weather, and so on. Hunger for a steak is related to steak, not just to food as such (438a1–b2). This point can be extended. The greater is greater than the less, the much greater than the much less, the double than the half, and so on. That is, the greater is just what it is, and not much greater or twice as much. Hence it is related simply to the less, and not to the much less or one-half. And so too with knowledge. Knowledge itself is knowledge of learning itself or in general, whereas knowledge of building houses is knowledge of carpentry. Socrates summarizes the general point as follows: if we take all those things that are related to something else, some of these things are simple or unqualified, such as hunger or thirst or knowledge, and other things are compounded or qualified, such as hunger for a steak or thirst for a hot drink or knowledge of carpentry. The simple things are related to simple things, and the compound things are related to compound things.

This distinction is now connected to the point about opposites. We have stipulated that the same thing will not do or suffer opposites at the same time and in the same way. If a man is thirsty, he is drawn to drink by a certain power or function of the soul. But if he is drawn away from drink while he suffers from thirst, it must be by some other power or function. Socrates does not mention a case of conflicting desires, for example, cases in which someone is drawn away from drink by a stronger desire for sex. He refers to cases in which the desire for drink is negated by a command of the intellect, here called *logismos*, or calculation (439a1–d3). Socrates might reply to us that when we are pulled by two different desires, it is calculative reason that decides between the two, but I do not find this persuasive. At the very least, reason is here dominated by desire, say, sexual desire. Socrates wishes to establish that if the intellect pulls us back from that to which we are drawn by desire, then as agents of opposing motions, these two must be different parts of the soul. In this context, it seems to be assumed that the intellect masters desire by itself, without the mediation of spiritedness. If this were unqualifiedly true, then the analogy between the city and the soul would break down, since there would be no need for auxiliary guardians to enforce the commands of reason (439d4–e1).

Despite this difficulty, it is initially plausible to suggest that intellect and desire are two different functions of the soul, since the former can restrain or master the latter (and of course the latter can master the former, if the soul lacks harmony or temperance). The problem with the suggestion is that it makes no allowance for what I shall call intellectual desire; to take the most important case, it makes no allowance for philosophical eros, which will soon figure heavily in the discussion of the nature of the rulers. More generally, if we factor out the element of desire from reason, then what motive is left for the soul to act on purely rational or calculative grounds? Considerations of this sort tend to support the view that the soul acts as a unity or totality of its powers, if we take it as rational or genuinely human. Where reason is either absent or too rudimentary to take command, then no doubt desire rules. But in so doing, it speaks for the whole soul, as in the case of beasts. Socrates referred a few lines previously to desire leading us like beasts to drink (439b4–5); the simile is understandable, but to be *like* a beast is not the same as to be a beast. Just as the intellect feels desire, so desire is subject to reason. I am not referring here to cases in which desire is restrained by force or a countervailing desire. In order to be commanded by reason, desire must be reasonable to a degree. Otherwise the commands will not be understood.

In order to begin to meet this objection, Socrates must establish that desire is not rational at all. But this requires it to be controlled through some ally of the intellect that is not itself intellectual. This ally will turn out to be spiritedness. But Socrates still cannot explain why spiritedness, which is different from reason, should be amenable to it, or why reason, which is independent of desire, should *want* to employ the services of spiritedness in order to master desire. Let us now look at the claim that spiritedness is a distinct part of the soul. Instead of starting with terminological distinctions, Socrates tells us a story. A man named Leontius was walking up to Athens from the Piraeus when he passed the place where the public executioner had deposited some corpses. He desired to look at them, but was at the same time disgusted by the prospect and turned away from it. "For a while he struggled and covered over his face, but being mastered by desire, he opened his eyes wide and, running toward the corpses, said [to his eyes], 'Look, you damned wretches; fill yourself up with this beautiful sight!'" (439e6–440a3).

Socrates claims that the story shows that anger (*tēn orgēn*: the attribute of spiritedness) can make war against the desires as one thing opposed to another single thing. But the story certainly does not show that anger or spiritedness is separate from and opposed to the intellect; the opposite is suggested by the fact that Leontius speaks to his eyes. Socrates goes on to say that we often see people reproaching themselves for having succumbed to desire contrary to calculation. But even as he tells it, we reproach ourselves *and* our spirit is aroused against that in us which is doing the forcing (440a8–b2). The reproach is clearly a consequence of calculation, which must itself be angry; otherwise the inner conflict would not occur. The spirit is apparently affected by the anger of calculation and becomes its ally against the desires; but we never see the reverse, namely, the anger of spiritedness making common cause with the desires to do something that *logos* has forbidden (440a5–b5). If intelligence commands, then it must prefer one act to another; and this is hard to distinguish from the desire that one's preference be enacted. It is difficult to believe that spiritedness acts spontaneously in the cause of reason or calculation. Even worse, surely Socrates is mistaken to say that anger never sides with the passions. Just think of the anger of the alcoholic when he or she is deprived of whiskey. A final observation: *thumos* produces anger as well as courage, but the two are not the same. It would seem that anger transforms courage into foolhardiness; at the least, we do not say that anger acts in subordination to the intellect.

Suppose we were to conclude, on the basis of arguments like those I have presented, that the soul acts in all cases as a whole rather than through separate parts. After all, if the parts are really separate, then it becomes hard to understand how they affect one another. Does this require us to modify the political argument? We would certainly need to reject the highly artificial and paradox-prone thesis that the city is the soul writ large. To state only the most obvious problem, the city must divide up its populace into different roles, each of which will be played by the unified action of the various individual souls. Thus the farmer or the artisan will calculate, desire, and be angry in various ways, even while performing one general type of work: moneymaking. In other words, we still need rulers, soldiers, and workers (whether or not these alone are moneymakers), but these separate functions will not correspond to three separate powers of the soul. We shall have to distinguish between jobs or roles within the polity on the one hand and types of human character on the other. A unified individual soul is not a homogeneous monad but a specific harmony of elements that results in a wide range of human types, in which one or another of the psychic powers may predominate over the other two, which do not cease to be present and functioning simply because they are subordinate to the first.

3

The story of Leontius is part of the examination of the unity or multiplicity of the soul. By "unity," of course, I do not mean homogeneity. No one disputes that reason, spiritedness, and desire are different conditions of the individual soul. We can also grant that it is helpful to the analysis of everyday life to say that two of these conditions cooperate against the influence of a third. Socrates refers to this quarrel as "the civil war [*stasis*] of the soul" (440e4–6). But we use the term *stasis* to refer to a conflict in which the participants are citizens of the same city. And the unity of the city is restored upon the resolution of the conflict, even if the regime has changed. The analogy between the city and the soul can be misleading here, because the participants in a civil conflict are individual persons, each of whom possesses all three conditions of the soul. The conditions themselves are not individual persons but rather states that are enabled to act in various combinations thanks to the underlying unity of the soul. I can be angry with myself, not because I am two people but because my spiritedness is a function of the same unity as my reason and desire.

As is especially obvious in modern philosophy, the legitimate attempt to "analyze" the soul, psyche, or mind, however we call it, carries with it the great defect that it renders the unity of the soul inaccessible from the outset. To analyze is to divide. And the consequences of division are to dissolve the apparent evidence of unity in our immediate experience. To pursue this topic would take us from our path and into the domain of the philosophy of mind that deals with problems of self-identity. Suffice it to say that the most reasonable hypothesis on unity and multiplicity is the one that makes our experience intelligible. If we are divided within ourselves in the way that a city is divided into its citizens, this does not prove that the citizens are not unified by the laws and customs of the city. This unification, however, is clearly not the same as the unity of the person, because it lacks self-consciousness. It is not cities but citizens who are aware of inner conflicts between, say, anger and desire. As to the citizens or individual persons, we have to ask whether it makes more sense to speak of the soul as an articulated unity or a compound of disparate properties.

Each one of us will have his or her own preference as to the right choice on this delicate point, but as students of the *Republic* it is our primary duty to observe that the analogy between the city and the soul, and the correlative acceptance of the division of labor, leads Socrates to exaggerate the separateness of the conditions of the soul in such a way as to politicize inner harmony. I mean by this that the harmony of the soul is explained as arising through the pacification and training of its several parts, rather than as furnished by nature. Human beings, with the exception of a lucky few, are born ill and divided against themselves. There is no question here of a naive injunction to "live in accord with nature." On the contrary, human nature must be healed and united by the medicine of philosophy. In my view, even if we accept this psychiatric interpretation of philosophy, it is not possible to discern stasis within the soul except on the basis of a pre-analytical awareness of underlying unity. The parts at war with one another are parts of the same unity. This is granted by Socrates from the outset, since he speaks of the individual soul, but it is contradicted by the main thrust of his analysis.

However this may be, on Socrates's account, spiritedness or anger is higher than desire because it is akin to intellect. I also raised the question of how intelligence by itself can desire anything to be accomplished, or prefer the reasonable to the unreasonable. Socrates speaks as if there is an inclination in reason toward the reasonable, an inclination that is distinct from desire and somehow resembles a human soul within the soul, an agent that employs spiritedness to bend the passions or desires to its will. In other words, if intellect were really separate from spiritedness and desire, then the active part of the soul would be irrational. It seems, then, that the soul acts as a whole, although whether its actions are rational will depend upon the relative strength of its several functions. The main point is that a soul is not human if *logos* does not function in every decision to act or not to act. One cannot speak of "decision" without referring to intellect. As to involuntary or instinctual inclinations, these are not intentional acts, and so they express our animal rather than our human nature.

To come back to spiritedness, Socrates holds that the nobler a man is, the angrier he will be with himself for doing injustice, and the less capable will he be of feeling anger toward someone whom he is treating unjustly (440a8–c5). Justice, we recall, is minding one's own business or having one's own possessions but not those of another. It is, however, intellect that determines the business of each person and so too what things are his or hers. If spiritedness were separate from intelligence, it could not know what is just, and so its anger would be random, not to say motivated by desire. Spiritedness seems something like righteous indignation as Socrates describes it, but anger is base as well as noble, as is already implied by the comparatives in the passage just cited. If the degree of nobility or baseness is determined by the extent to which spiritedness forces desire to submit to reason, then once more reason or intellect is the criterion of nobility. The analysis is the same in the case of the man who becomes angry when he believes himself to be treated unjustly by another. Socrates says that this man will not cease to obtain justice until he succeeds or death intervenes, or until he is called in by the *logos* within him like a dog by the shepherd and calmed down (440c7–d3). But a man knows that he has been treated unjustly by engaging in calculation, at however rudimentary a level, and thus determining that someone has taken what belongs to him.

There is an alternative interpretation, however, and this is to say that there is a difference between perceiving justice and perceiving injustice. Socrates holds that if someone punishes us justly, the nobler we are, the less angry we feel. He attributes anger only to cases in which we ourselves are being treated unjustly. This is certainly too restricted, since we often are roused to anger by the injustice of others toward people whom we do not know personally. As to ourselves, there would be very little occasion to be angry when we are treated justly by the law courts or our friends and fellow citizens. But the noble man is also not angry at the just punishment of an unjust man other than himself, since no further injustice is being perpetrated. The doing of justice, to ourselves or others, quenches rather than inflames anger. On the other hand, to be aroused by the perception of injustice is in fact to become angry. I believe that this interpretation is plausible as far as it goes, but it fails to explain how we perceive justice and injustice. It seems that there is one possibility only: The intellect defines justice as minding one's own business or possessing what belongs to oneself, where these conditions have been settled by the rational calculation of what each type of person is worth and what is his or her own business. These definitions follow from an understanding of what is useful for the city. Unfortunately, they are circular, since what is useful for the city is what enables us to live a just, and so noble, life. We seem to be left with the result that there is no explanation for the nobility of justice, although anger at being treated unjustly can perhaps be explained by recourse not to the intellect but to desire.

However we look at it, there is a serious problem here. No one of the three powers of the soul, as Socrates explains them, is clearly equipped to perceive the nobility, beauty, or intrinsic goodness of justice and the baseness of injustice. Spiritedness comes closest to the perception of injustice, since the latter makes us angry. That is, spiritedness knows when we have less than we deserve, or is capable of understanding this when it is explained by *logos*. Socrates takes the anger of spiritedness against injustice to be noble, but he says nothing about the joy of spiritedness at the doing of justice. The utility of justice is something that we can understand, but our sense of its nobility is not rational or calculative. I can understand that I am pleased by the nobility of justice if and only if "understanding" is redefined in a way that goes beyond *logos* in the sense of *logismos*.

To come back to the main thread of the argument, Socrates concludes that spiritedness, whereas it looked initially like a relative of desire, has been found to be an ally of intellect.[5] We must now see whether it is the same as or different from its ally. The question is rather quickly settled. We see that young children are spirited from birth, whereas they come to calculation later, and in the case of the many, much later, and some seem never to possess it. The same is true of beasts, and it is attested by Homer with respect to Odysseus, who calms down his anger by the faculty of calculation (441a5–c2). Socrates now sums up the long analysis of the three parts of the soul, which he takes to correspond to the three classes in the city. The private man is wise in the same way and about the same thing that the city is wise. This refers to *euboulia*, or good counsel, which is obtained by calculative intelligence. Second, the city is courageous because of the same thing and in the same way that the private man is courageous. This refers to spiritedness or anger. Note that anger toward injustice is not mentioned in this context. But anger is silently assimilated to courage. No explicit mention is made of desire; instead, Socrates says that in all other things with respect to virtue, the same is true as in the case of calculation and spiritedness. Assuming this to refer to desire, the fourth point is that both the individual person and the city are just in the same way, namely, because each of the three classes minds its own business. I repeat once again that this is very close to temperance, which includes obedience to the rulers and is a harmony of all three parts of the soul. For whatever the reason, Socrates does not mention temperance here in conjunction with desire (441c4–e2).

It is, then, appropriate for intelligence to rule and spiritedness to obey it. The education that mixes music and gymnastics will regulate the order or harmony of intelligence or wisdom and spiritedness or courage, so that each is in the best condition. Again, there is no mention of desire or temperance, which latter was evoked by Glaucon at 399e7 in conjunction with a purging of the luxurious city through the proper music and again by Socrates at 402e3ff. as the opposite of extreme (that is, erotic) pleasure. In this context, temperance is once more connected to order and music (403a7–8). Incidentally, the regulation of sex is associated with music, whereas the avoidance of drunkenness and bad or excessive diet is made part of gymnastic training (403e4–404d10). At 404e3–5, Socrates says that simplicity in music produces temperance in the soul, whereas in gymnastics it produces health in bodies. The overall argument thus associates temperance with the order, harmony, and simplicity of the soul, although regulation of food and drink is due to the proper gymnastics. But this is explained by the fact that gymnastics has as its primary end the training of the soul.

Why is temperance left out in the present passage? My own guess is that it has to do with the emphasis upon justice in the immediate context. Where justice is present, temperance is unnecessary, and vice versa. This is because temperance is also a making-do with one's own possessions and minding one's own business. The temperate man has an orderly soul and is a member of the guardian class. But to speak of temperance as an independent virtue akin to wisdom, courage, and justice is to invoke thoughts of the traditional sense of the control of bodily appetite. Socrates wishes to redefine temperance as a characteristic virtue, connected with the orderliness and harmony of the soul, which is the ruler of the body. He thus reminds us that the mixture of music and gymnastics produces the proper "harmony" for the job of supervising the desiring part of the soul, which is by far the largest and the most insatiable for money (442a4–7). The working or moneymaking class is the only one that has no intrinsic virtue; temperance is imposed from above, that is, by the guardians. We thus see that the mixture of gymnastics and music is a harmony of fierceness and softness that produces both courage and temperance.

Socrates goes once more through the list of virtues and their faculties in the soul. As expected, courage corresponds to spiritedness, and wisdom to the intellect. Temperance is now defined not as control over sex, food, and drink but as the friendship and harmony of "these parts, when the ruling part and the two ruled parts are of the same opinion, namely, that the calculating part ought to rule, and they [spiritedness and desire] form no factions against it" (442c10–d1). It is not quite clear that "these parts" refers to all three parts of the soul rather than to wisdom and courage only. But let us assume that the context suggests this meaning. The harmony of music and gymnastics produces temperance, which is itself a harmony of intelligence, spiritedness, and desire. Otherwise put, temperance is the communal agreement in the soul that the calculative intelligence ought to rule. This seems to be very similar to justice. But perhaps we can distinguish them as follows. The proper education produces temperance, which in turn produces obedience to intelligence, and justice is the manner in which intelligence carries out its dictates. However, once we have the harmonious obedience to the rule of intelligence, justice understood as law is in effect replaced by friendship, that is, the friendship of the parts of the soul on the one hand and of the classes of the city on the other. Finally, let us once more notice that Socrates speaks of the parts of the soul as though they were separate citizens, and instead of unity, he refers to harmony.

We thus receive the impression of an ordering of separate parts, rather than of a unity of distinguishable faculties.

Socrates then reviews the "vulgar" conceptions of justice (*ta phortika*) and finds that the just man as we have now defined him is incapable of unjust acts like stealing deposits, robbing temples, or committing adultery. In other words, the model of justice as constructed by the founding fathers of the beautiful city coincides with traditional views of justice, and not at all with the cynical and corrupt understanding. As Kant will observe much later, it would be a surprise if philosophy produced a new conception of justice. Its task is rather to verify the validity of the common conception of ordinary life. This lends support to my earlier analysis of the impossibility of deriving justice or nobility from theoretical concepts. We can demonstrate that justice is useful, but not that it is noble (442d7–443a11).

We now seem to have achieved our goal of finding a model for, and the origin of, justice. Justice, as we have determined, is minding one's own business. And *technē* turns out to be an image (*eidōlon*) of justice; hence the utility of the early examples of shoemaking, carpentry, and so on. The utility here is as a model not of calculation or intelligence but of minding one's own business, that is, as the saying goes, of the shoemaker sticking to his last, and so too with all the other craftsmen, in order that the best artifacts be produced. Hence Socrates's advocacy of the principle of one man, one job. Internal justice, of course, is the order and harmony within the soul, in which each faculty, intelligence, spiritedness, and desire, minds its own business . The just man is thus a friend to himself, since all three parts of his soul are in complete harmony, and therefore he is temperate. Socrates elicits Glaucon's agreement that it would not be a lie to claim that we have now found justice in the city and in the individual human being (443b1–444a10). One more point here; let us note that at 443d7 Socrates says that if there are more than three parts, the soul will harmonize the others with the three we have mentioned. This is another indication that the conversation, with all its length and intricacy, is not exhaustive or completely rigorous.

It follows from what has been said that injustice is the existence of factions within the soul, or rebellion by one part against the whole. Socrates states emphatically that the rebellious part is by nature fit to be a slave to the ruler (444b4–5). In other words, even within the just soul, there is a disjunction or split that underlies, and makes necessary, the harmony of its parts. Whereas Socrates spoke a moment ago of becoming one's own friend through the order of justice and self-rule (443d5), he now refers to the natural order within the soul as that of master and slave. This means that the soul cannot be a unity or have a single form. The "natural" condition of the soul is from the first that of disharmony; more precisely, there is a separation or disharmony within the very harmony of the three parts of the soul. The situation is much worse in the case of the unjust man, since his soul is disharmonious and contrary to the natural order. This passage is very important, because it raises the difference between friendship and mastery. For example, Aristotle regards friendship as higher than justice because the former does not require compulsion; one could say that this is the difference between temperance and justice in the *Republic*. Otherwise put, for Socrates, there is no genuine friendship between intellect and desire; even in the just man, peace is preserved by the force of spiritedness (444b1–8).

Socrates proceeds in the verification of the definition of justice by introducing the analogy between health and sickness. We produce health in the body by establishing the natural order of mastery and obedience among its parts, whereas sickness is the relation of ruling and being ruled that is contrary to nature. So too justice is the natural relation of mastery among the parts of the soul, and injustice is the reverse. I call attention to the following difficulty. It is fairly straightforward to identify health and sickness in the body. But the identification of the proper order in the soul, and so too of justice and injustice, depends upon our understanding of justice. This has to be supplied by intuition, custom, or revelation; justice cannot be established by the logical analysis of concepts or through a deduction from first principles. What is to one man cancer is so to another as well. But what is sickness of the soul for Socrates may be for someone else the expression of strength and the verification of the principle that might makes right (444c5–d12).

If we grant the analogy between justice and health, it seems to be self-evident that the just life is superior to the unjust life, since no one prefers sickness to health. Socrates speaks of virtue (*aretē*) rather than simply of justice when he says that the former is a certain health, beauty, and good condition of the soul, whereas vice is sickness, ugliness, and weakness (444d13–e2). Despite Glaucon's conviction that the superiority of justice is now proved, Socrates says that it would be laughable if they did not persevere. The emphasis in this passage is on visual imagery; they are now well situated to see that there is one form for virtue, presumably the one that they have just mentioned, and an unlimited number of forms of vice, of which four are worthy to be remembered. The *skopia*, or lookout point, from which they can inspect the forms of virtue and vice is an anticipation of the lookout point from which the philosophers will gaze upon the Platonic Ideas (445a5–c4).

It seems as though we are about to make a study of the types of regime that correspond to the five forms of the soul. Socrates identifies the form of virtue with the regime of the city they have just constructed. If one man rules, it is a monarchy; if more than one, an aristocracy. The laws will be much the same in both versions of this virtuous regime (445c5–e4). At this point, Book Four ends, and Socrates is interrupted in his itinerary at the beginning of Book Five.

4

Socrates is just about to discuss the four kinds of bad and mistaken regimes, now that we have constructed the single form of virtue that corresponds to the good regime. Since the good regime does not exist, it is plain that for Socrates, all actual cities are sick, ugly, and in bad condition. As one could also put it, if the philosopher does not start from scratch and bring into existence the virtuous city, human beings will pass their lives in a way that is contrary to nature. "Nature" here means not "what is" but "what ought to be," if human beings are to live the best possible life. Except for the extreme case, then, human life is contrary to nature, and the human animal is divided against itself in the disorderliness and stasis of its soul. Humankind is by nature sick, and only the transformation of nature by philosophy can make it healthy. This transformation makes use of natural elements, especially human beings of particular types; but it produces the correct order of these types, or the harmony that is best by nature. In this sense, Plato's *Republic* is a utopia. It exists nowhere but must be constructed by the art of the philosopher. This constructive element in Plato's political philosophy is regularly missed by commentators, who have become prisoners of the orthodox view that constructivism is a feature of modern thought and does not occur in antiquity. The "unnaturalness" of nature is closely related to the previously noted fact that the human soul exhibits the master-slave structure, both in the healthy and in the unhealthy person. There is then no master-slave "dialectic" in Plato that, as in Hegel, overcomes this innate disjunction at a higher level of development. In this context, there is no development in Plato, or no "history" in the modern sense of the term.

As was pointed out by Leo Strauss, Book Five begins with a dramatic action that reminds us of the very beginning of Book One.[6] The conversation comes about when Polemarchus orders his slave boy to detain Socrates. The slave boy does so by taking hold of Socrates's cloak from behind and conveying the command of his master (I. 327b4). Glaucon speaks on behalf of Socrates, and the two are persuaded to remain in the Piraeus for a banquet and torch race that, so far as we know, they did not attend. The banquet is replaced by conversation and the novelty of the torch race by that of the beautiful city. In Book Five, Polemarchus, who is sitting at a little distance from Adeimantus, reaches out and grasps the latter's cloak from above. They consult while Socrates is talking and agree not to let him go. They are referring to the community of women and children, which Socrates mentioned in passing but did not develop (IV. 423e4–424a2).

Polemarchus is the active party in both passages. In Book One, Socrates is accompanied by Glaucon; in Book Five, he is conversing with Glaucon. When Socrates mentioned the community of women and children, he was talking with Adeimantus, who had no questions or objections to making the proposal. Presumably he has been moved by Polemarchus to raise a demand for clarification. We should also remember that just as Socrates is accompanied by Glaucon on his trip to the Piraeus, Adeimantus is already present with Polemarchus and some others. Polemarchus, whose name means "warlord," defends the thesis that justice is doing good to one's friends and harm to one's enemies. Glaucon and Adeimantus do not present a preliminary definition of justice but instead propound powerful criticisms of the view that the just life is happier than the unjust life. Polemarchus has a strong view on the nature of justice as he enters into the conversation; Socrates at least claims that it will be necessary to engage in the construction of the wished-for city in order to find out what justice is.

I infer from these observations, first, that Polemarchus and Socrates bring out the common view of justice on the one hand and the philosophical modification of that view on the other. Socrates and Polemarchus agree that justice is doing good to one's friends; they disagree on the justness of doing harm to one's enemies. Glaucon and Adeimantus are much more impressed by Thrasymachus's argument than was Polemarchus, who says nothing in response to it. This is a mistake on his part, since Thrasymachus is also committed to doing good to one's friends and harm to one's enemies. He is refuted because he cannot explain to Socrates how he knows who are his friends and who are his enemies. But he provides a strong incentive to Plato's brothers to carry forward the conversation, and in order to do so, they paint a deeper portrait of the advantages of injustice than Thrasymachus could offer. They are able to do so because they are not bound to a defense of technical knowledge but appeal instead to spiritedness and desire. The difference between the two brothers seems to be that Glaucon feels the force of the thesis that might makes right, whereas Adeimantus is outraged by it. We should not be too hasty in assuming that Adeimantus is superior to Glaucon in this respect. Outrage against injustice is virtuous, but in a conventional manner. To feel the attraction of injustice is part of the process by which eros is transformed from tyranny into philosophy.

Second, there is something wrong with Socrates's presentation of justice in

Books Two to Four. Socrates is free to criticize conventional notions of eros in these books, and thus to satisfy the austerity of Adeimantus. But he has not been willing to give a full account of the erotic structure of the just city, and so to cater to the nature of Glaucon, no doubt because one cannot consider eros thoroughly without rising up to philosophy, a step that, for all his intelligence, Glaucon cannot take. Socrates is compelled to go into these matters by two people who are radically less erotic than Glaucon, and who are puzzled by the shocking advocacy of women and children in common. I add here that Adeimantus takes time to feel the shock, but Glaucon never feels it. Perhaps because of his extreme pederasty, Glaucon has no qualms about the transformation of breeding into a political function. It is an interesting question why Glaucon does not protest against the restrictions placed upon pederasty itself. No doubt he has been carried away for the time being by the excitement of the founding of the city, which satisfies his political spiritedness.

Third and more briefly, the interruption by Polemarchus and Adeimantus shows us that persons of a lower erotic level cause more trouble in political revolutions precisely because they are more conventional. Glaucon's eagerness to open all difficulties to discussion is the other side of his immunity to shock. This has good but also bad consequences. The important point here is that Glaucon is not an obstacle to Socrates, once we have negotiated the refutation of Thrasymachus and the main investigation is under way. That is to say, he does not slow down the conversation but does require that Socrates accommodate his views to the level of Glaucon's apprehension. In other words, speeding up is here a kind of slowing down. In sum, Socrates is caused trouble by persons of a lower type who force him to introduce the most difficult discussion of philosophy, including eros and the Ideas, and also of the political organization of sexual relations. Glaucon causes him no trouble over the introduction of philosophy, yet it is primarily for Glaucon's sake that Socrates would have been silent about philosophy. For, as Socrates will tell us later, potential philosophers who are spoiled by political ambition in their youth turn out extremely badly, and thus give rise to the widespread bad opinion of philosophy. Glaucon, in short, is an inferior version of Alcibiades. Adeimantus and Polemarchus will soon forget what they have heard, or relegate it to a memory of a stimulating conversation. But Glaucon is likely to remember, and with bad consequences both for himself and the city.

In Book One, a slave boy pulls at Socrates's cloak. In Book Five, the slave's master pulls at the cloak of Polemarchus's friend, Adeimantus. In the first case, the question is whether Socrates should be allowed to leave for home, and so not talk at all. In the second case, it is a question of whether Socrates should be allowed to continue talking but also of suppressing a necessary part of his speech. In the second but not the first case, there is a political faction formed against Socrates consisting of Polemarchus and Adeimantus; it is soon joined by Glaucon and Thrasymachus. Perhaps more interesting is the fact that at crucial moments Socrates is forced to speak when he does not wish to do so. His construction of the just city is not simply voluntary. He is compelled to defend justice by his piety (that is, not simply for the protection of his young companions), but once he begins this defense, he has to accommodate it to the several and different elements in his audience. At a more general level, I have suggested that what compels Socrates to speak is the political ambition that is intrinsic to philosophy, even when it goes against the temperament of individual philosophers.

Although Polemarchus evidently initiates the faction, it is Adeimantus who speaks out with the complaint that Socrates "has robbed us of an entire form [*eidos*] of the argument [*logos*], and not the least important one," so as to avoid the trouble of going through it (449c2–5). The accusation of injustice against Socrates is not entirely playful. As I have suggested, he tries to make his case without broaching or dwelling upon exceptionally difficult elements. To repeat the main point, Socrates hoped for an easy acquiescence in the community of women and children because it is the most shocking of his various novel proposals, especially to someone like Adeimantus. It is also the most difficult to enforce, because it rests upon comprehensive regulation of sexual reproduction. The maxim that friends have everything in common is intended to camouflage the shock of these new sexual arrangements, which go against standard Greek political beliefs and, even more important, moral and religious opposition to adultery and incest.

It is therefore not surprising that Socrates's interlocutors, stimulated by Adeimantus, demand particulars. They employ legal terminology, as though Socrates has been arrested and will be tried for robbery, not merely to chastise him for passing by the difficult part of the argument but as a sign of the challenge that argument poses for *nomos*. Leo Strauss calls attention to the fact that Thrasymachus is now a member of the polity constituted by the conversation (450a5–6).[7] The political and legal setting of the decision concerning the continuation of the discussion suggests that philosophy will be subordinated to political compulsion. This suggestion will gain strength from the subsequent assertion that philosophers will have to be compelled to rule in the beautiful city. Philosophy is itself marked by an inner disharmony between the desire to rule and the desire not to rule. To say that philosophy is compelled to rule is to say that it compels itself, as is exhibited by Socrates's own assertion of the necessity of that compulsion.

Socrates says in his defense that the demand by his judges to discuss the community of women and children raises a swarm of problems, and that it would have been much easier to listen to arguments "in due measure" (450b1–5). At IV. 435c4–d4, Socrates raised the question of whether the soul has the three forms they have identified. This is a difficult question that cannot be adequately answered if they follow the road on which they are now traveling. A longer way would be required, but Glaucon is content to continue as they have begun, and so to arrive at an answer that is along the level of the discussion to this point. On the other hand, neither he nor his companions are content to follow the extremely short road of mentioning the community of women and children without further development. It is obvious that the question of sex and reproduction is much more pressing politically than the number of the parts of the soul. But furthermore, if we do not require precision with respect to the parts of the soul, then we must assume that the analogy of the city and the soul has itself been stated imprecisely, as a convenience to the presentation of the broad structure of the city.

Many (but not all) of the most important topics seem to have been reserved for the middle books of the *Republic*. But this can hardly have been done to conceal them from the attention of careless readers, as Strauss's hermeneutical principle suggests. On the contrary, we have just studied the various dramatic devices by which Plato calls sharply to our attention the importance of what follows. This importance, of course, is entirely compatible with the fact that we are still presumably on the "shorter way." As we shall see in the section on the Platonic Ideas, Socrates has to balance the consideration of his audience's capacities with the need to bring into the open the theoretical presuppositions of the just city, something that Aristotle, for example, can avoid, if only because he does not require philosophers to be kings. In sum, there is no consistently moderate presentation of an immoderate political teaching. Speaking of Strauss, he also holds that in the *Politics* Aristotle fails to mention the topics of Books Five to Seven because they are unnecessary for the discussion of politics. This may be true for Aristotelian political philosophy, but it cannot be true of Plato. I stated earlier that there is something wrong with Socrates's presentation of the argument in Books Two to Four. What is wrong is that he constructs a city that requires philosophy to be king for its very existence, but without introducing philosophy. The result is not just that of having taken a shortcut but rather that of deviating from the main path. Books Five to Seven put us squarely back onto the main path.

To be sure, philosophy is not explicitly at issue in the transitional scene that we are now examining; the topic at issue is sex. But the transition from sex to philosophy is easy to see. The guardians must be trained to sacrifice private sexual needs to the unity and goodness of the city. These needs are both bodily and spiritual, and the proper training of the body is obviously dependent upon the proper training of the soul. What unifies the souls of human beings is not sexual love for bodies but the higher erotic desire for pure forms. The pleasures of the body are peculiar to the individual, whereas the pleasures of the intellectual part of the soul are common to all competent persons, and to one degree or another, to all human beings. The pure intellectual contemplation of the Platonic Ideas is thus the highest expression of the unity of the philosopher-kings, whereas the community of women and children is the highest expression of the unity of the soldier-guardians. The latter is essential to, but insufficient for, the management of the city. Stated as briefly as possible, the community of the instruments of bodily pleasure does not unify the pleasures of individual persons. The soldiers can be unified, if at all, only by the philosopher-kings. This also explains why all philosophers in the just city are Platonists. There are no schools or conflicting ideologies in that city. And the foundation for this uniformity of doctrine is the vision of the Ideas, which are not speeches, and so not concepts or predicates, but the transdiscursive domain about which we talk. Plato's claim is that either we see the Ideas or we do not, but even though we see them through a glass darkly, we cannot be mistaken; and this, of course, is Aristotle's doctrine as well.

I have anticipated certain topics in order to clarify the significance of the shift that we are now negotiating. The energetic Glaucon asserts that the proper measure for anyone with brains is to spend his whole life listening to speeches of this sort. He does not say "speaking," because this is mainly the prerogative of Socrates (450b6–7). Listening is less fatiguing than speaking; therefore Glaucon urges Socrates not to become fatigued in stating his opinions about the community of women and children and the rearing of the children in that most difficult time, between birth and education. Glaucon seems to have forgotten that a good bit was said on this topic during the discussion of the censorship of poetry and music, but he now wants Socrates to concentrate upon the formation of infants and "preschoolers," as we would say. This is undoubtedly because he is concerned with the treatment of infants who will have no private family to look after their rearing.

Socrates begins by warning Glaucon that his proposals are more dubious than anything that has yet been said. It may not be possible to carry them out, and even if possible under the most favorable conditions, there will be doubts whether they would be the best arrangements. Glaucon tries to encourage Socrates by promising him a receptive audience, but this adds to the latter's hesitation. One is safe and confident when speaking of things that one knows before an audience of prudent friends. But it is frightening and perilous to make speeches concerning things that one doubts and is still investigating. The problem is not that of becoming a laughingstock but rather that of misleading one's friends along with oneself (450d8–451a4). This passage should inoculate us against the mistake of taking what follows as anything but a hypothesis or, better, what the Germans call a *Gedankenexperiment*. The common notion of Plato as an "absolutist" or dogmatic thinker must be modified by Socrates's hesitations and qualifications. In other words, the level of confidence among philosophers in their own views is much lower outside the just city than within it. But this has to do with the utopian nature of the constructed city. It is an axiom that the rulers are genuine philosophers, and hence wise, whereas Socrates describes himself as knowing only that he does not know.

Socrates prostrates himself before nemesis; in other words, he is prepared to take the consequences if he should be wrong. It is better to run the risk of unintentional murder than to deceive about beautiful, good, and just matters of the law, and still better to run that risk with enemies than friends. This is an amusing passage, since it reminds us again of the notion of justice as doing good to one's friends and harm to one's enemies. Socrates comes a step closer to this definition than hitherto by saying that it is better to harm enemies than friends. Still, it would be highly beneficial to our friends if we should succeed in speaking correctly or truly, and this is the risk that Socrates takes (451a4–b1). Glaucon laughs, presumably because he is exhilarated at the thought of what is to follow, but perhaps also because he is amused by the idea of pardoning Socrates of the charge of murder should his argument bring harm to his audience (451b2–5). In either case, the laughter is a sign of his high spirits and great confidence in Socrates, but also of his lack of concern for the possible danger of the argument to follow.

The man who has been acquitted of a murder charge is innocent before the law. Therefore, Socrates can continue with impunity if not entire confidence in what he will say. I want to emphasize the very elaborate nature of the transition from Book Four to Book Five. What follows is both doubtful and dangerous. Socrates and his audience have banded together to form a city where initially there was faction. In this way, laws (borrowed from Athens) now exist to legitimate the dangerous shift to the most revolutionary elements of the Socratic political program. Athens, or let us say the actual city, is as it were used as a cover for proposals that would quickly lead to its destruction. This aspect of the transitional scene is of course highly rhetorical, but it is so precisely because the danger is real. Putting the issue of sex to one side for a moment, we are taking the path that will make philosophers kings, even though, as we shall see, it is highly dubious whether there are any philosophers in the paradigmatic sense that Socrates employs to identify the future rulers of his city. The twentieth century is unusually rich in examples of the dangers that follow from giving political power to pseudophilosophers or ignoble sophists. In so doing, however, it reiterates, consciously or not, an important and pervasive message of the *Republic*.

7

The Female Drama

I

We saw in the previous chapter that Socrates does not mind making a laughingstock of himself (V. 451a1), and that Glaucon laughs at the thought of releasing Socrates from the charge of having murdered his friends (451b2). In the passage running from 452a2 to d7 there are seven further occurrences of *geloia* (laughter) and its cognates, as well as one occurrence of "charming jests" (452b7), one of acting a comedy (452d1), and one of acting playfully rather than seriously (452e6). It looks as though Plato wishes to facilitate our journey into danger with laughter rather than seriousness. As we shall see shortly, much of the laughter is stimulated by the suggestion that women should engage in the same education as men, in particular, wrestle naked with old men as well as youths. Socrates also begins with a metaphor from the theater: Now that the male drama has been completed, it is perhaps appropriate to turn to the female (451c1–3). Bloom conjectures in his note to this passage that Socrates is alluding to Aristophanes's *Ecclesiazusae*, "which also proposed the emancipation of women and communism." This may also account for the frequency of references to laughter. Since it is more difficult to be angry when one is laughing, Socrates tries to blunt the offensive aspects of his proposal about women by beginning with its humorous side.

The theme of the male drama was to produce guardians of the herd (451c8). This metaphor reduces the status of the moneymaking class to that of brutes and of the guardians to dogs. The only fully human beings in the just city are the rulers. In the same idiom, Socrates asks whether the females of the guardian dogs guard, hunt, and do everything else in common with the males, or stay indoors as though weakened by bearing and rearing the puppies. The answer is that they share the work in common with the males, with allowance for the difference in their physical strength. This passage refers us back to the example of the noble dog, which was intended to show that the combination of gentleness to friends and fierceness to enemies is not contrary to nature. I remind the reader that this is the equivalent to Polemarchus's definition of justice as doing good to friends and harm to enemies (452d1–e2).

Since the females have the same tasks, they must also receive the same education as the males. At this point, Socrates shifts from dogs to human beings. Women must be trained in the same music and gymnastics as are the men, since the two sexes have the same aim: to be warriors. And this has laughable consequences, prominent among them the aforementioned sight of women wrestling naked with young men, but also with the older wrinkled ones who love gymnastics but are not pleasant to the eye. One wonders immediately whether this part of the education may not stimulate sexual desire in ways that are harmful to the city. Socrates does not refer directly to this problem but instead says that we must disregard the jokes made in response to the comic aspect of the new gymnastics procedures. He is presumably referring here to those who will be informed of the innovations, rather than to those within the new city who have been educated since infancy to accept them as normal. This is how Glaucon understands him at 452b4 ("as things now stand"). These jokesters must be told not to mind their own business, that is, not to write comedies about the education of women. This is an extremely interesting passage, since it shows that "minding one's own business" is too general to serve as a definition of justice. As Bloom notes, minding one's own business (writing comedies) is unjust because it ridicules the laws and encourages disobedience (451e3–452c5).

It was once regarded as shameful and laughable by the Greeks to see men exercising naked, as it currently is to the barbarians. But following the lead of the Cretans and the Lacedaimonians (regularly regarded in Plato as the best governed of the Greeks), this prejudice has been overcome. Once it became clear that it was better to wrestle naked than clothed, what seemed absurd to the eye disappeared in the light of what was revealed by arguments (*en tois logois*). "And this showed that only a fool supposes anything to be laughable other than the bad" (to which Socrates adds "senseless" in the next sentence).

In sum, what is laughable is to regard the beautiful (or noble) from any standpoint other than what is good (452c6–e2).

In a famous passage in the *Laws*, the Athenian Stranger says that only the divine is serious; the human being has been created as a plaything of the gods. We are, however, compelled to take human affairs seriously (VII. 803b3ff.). The *Republic*, I think it is fair to say, is much more amusing than the *Laws*; the Athenian Stranger lacks the Attic urbanity that is so much a part of Socrates's style. The playfulness of the *Laws* is presented with great seriousness, by one sober old man to two others. But the seriousness of the *Republic* tends to be presented playfully, as is suited to the nature of an ironist lecturing under the protection of an erotic and high-spirited youth. Not even the austere Adeimantus is able to bring the conversation down to the level of sobriety that characterizes the *Laws*. I would go so far as to say that the *Republic* appeals at once to every intelligent reader, even to readers who sharply reject the desirability of the Socratic city, whereas the *Laws* is an acquired taste. The most obvious sign of the difference between the two works, apart from the natures of the interlocutors, is that the *Republic* leaves out the boring detail of legislation, whereas the *Laws* presents it to the point of stupefaction.

The *Republic* is exciting, like political revolution itself. The *Laws*, if one dare say it, is boring, like the comprehensive legislative process itself. I do not mean to belittle the *Laws* and would defend its boring nature as an essential ingredient in the teaching of the dialogue. But as we read the *Republic*, it is difficult not to laugh on numerous occasions, despite the injunction against laughter in the Socratic city. The message of the *Republic* is that seriousness can be acquired only through playfulness, when we are dealing with youths, as we must in a revolutionary plot. In one last formulation, the *Republic* is a great work of art, something like a modern novel; its brilliance, wit, and psychological insight are all immediately visible to a wide range of readers. The *Laws* may or may not be a great work of art, but it cannot compete with the *Republic* in brilliance and wit, and its psychological insights are much less obvious although not absent.

Let me repeat: there is no doubt that Socrates wants to make the citizens of his city serious, in the double sense of being responsible or decent as well as not prone to laughter. But since most persons are bad or possess disharmonious souls, they will regard the beautiful from some standpoint other than the good. They are therefore both laughable and themselves prone to laughter. Athens is a city filled with laughter. Nor should we forget the "unquenchable laughter of the gods" (in Homer's expression: *Iliad* I. 599), who live a life of blessedness by the standards of the average Greek, but whose speeches and deeds as reported by the poets are condemned by Socrates. In sum, if we apply the highest philosophical standards, it is human life and its divine idealization that is laughable. But one cannot quench laughter with seriousness alone. Those who laugh must be charmed by a higher laughter.

We are now ready to listen to the argument, whether from someone who is playful or someone who is serious, against the claim that the female human nature can share in all, some, or none of the tasks of the male nature, in particular, of course, the task of war. As it turns out, the argument is rather simple, and runs as follows. We originally agreed that each person should mind what is his or her own business according to nature. Since the nature of women differs considerably from that of men, it is contrary to nature to assign the same tasks to the two sexes. Glaucon is unable to refute this argument on the spot and asks Socrates to do so. It is fair to say that for the nonphilosophical Glaucon, the "look" of woman is identical with her *morphē*, or physical shape, which is commonly taken to possess a function different from that of the male. Socrates hesitates to argue against the traditional view because he will be forced to reduce the most significant and universally recognized difference between men and women to a secondary characteristic. In so doing, Socrates shows how philosophy deviates from the obvious surface of nature. Before we turn to his attempt to refute the commonsensical majority opinion, let us notice that nothing in the earlier argument excluded the possibility that women could be soldiers. The relevant differences in nature, so far as the construction of the just city is concerned, are those that distinguish each of the three classes from the other two. Socrates has therefore not contradicted himself, as he is accused of doing by his hypothetical critic at 453c2–3. It remains to be shown how the physical differences between men and women affect the capacity of the latter to be soldiers (452e4–453d3).

Socrates could be expected to reply with a reference to the model of the dog, which presumably already showed that females can be guardians. Instead, he makes the obvious point, to which I have just alluded, that not all natural differences are significant for imposing a difference in work, that is, in one's own business. Less obvious is the reason for the sudden eruption of technical terminology in 454a1–9, a passage that we have to examine rather closely. Here is a translation: " 'How splendid, Glaucon,' I said, 'is the power of the art of disputation [*tēs antilogikēs technēs*: literally, the art of contradiction].' 'In what way?' 'Because,' I said, 'many people seem to me to fall into it unwillingly, and believe that they are engaging in dialectic rather than eristic, because they are unable to consider what has been said by dividing it up in accordance with forms [*kat' eidē diairoumenoi*]. They look for contradiction in the literal sense of what has been said, using eristic, not dialectic, with one another.' "

The general purpose of this rather pompous language is reasonably clear. The art of formal division has been introduced at this point in order to assist us in changing our attitude toward the natural division of human beings into men and women. Needless to say, this distinction is not going to be abolished. Instead, we are going to alter its significance in the economy of human life. As the term *dialectic* is used in this passage, it cannot possess the narrow and technical sense of what will later be called reasoning with the use of Ideas alone. In the first place, Socrates has not yet introduced that technical sense of the term. But second and more important, Platonic Ideas do not vary in themselves, however much we vary the perspective from which we view them. The Idea of the cow never looks like the Idea of some other animal, whereas we may very well mistake one individual animal for a representative of another class. But cows, horses, and human beings as well may be considered from various standpoints in the exercise of diaeresis.

To take the case in point, men and women differ completely with respect to the role they play in sexual reproduction, but this difference is going to be called politically irrelevant. What counts politically is aptitude. It would be a difficult task to try to determine which Platonic Ideas play a role in the proper classification of human aptitudes. In particular, it is far from clear that there is an Idea of philosophical aptitude, or even of *the* philosopher. Diaeresis in this context is thus relative to the intention of the investigator and resembles what we call today "conceptual analysis." On the other hand, as the necessary preliminary to dialectic in the precise sense, diaeresis must mean the art of dividing complex formal structures into the pure Ideas out of which they are woven together. If this is what Socrates means here by dialectic, then he must be saying that the sexual difference is not a formal distinction in the nature of the human being, whereas differences in intellectual and spiritual aptitudes are such distinctions. On balance, the first alternative seems the more plausible interpretation, but the passage is excessively condensed and very difficult.

Glaucon expresses no surprise at Socrates's formulation, whereas he will have trouble with the doctrine of Ideas. As an educated Athenian, he is familiar with disputation and eristic, both of which include the attempt to derive a contradiction from the views of one's opponent. This is of course also a procedure that will be familiar to those who frequent the law courts. The point of eristic is to win, not to establish the truth, and the method is to reduce the opponent to silence. The art of finding a contradiction is not restricted to eristic; Socrates makes wide use of it throughout the dialogues. But there is no reason to assume that Socrates's companions would be familiar with diaeresis and dialectic. They must parse the second half of the above statement as the contrast to disputation and eristic. They are assisted in this task by the increasing references to "forms" (*eidē*) or looks. A look is superficially the visual organization of the parts of a thing by which we identify and reidentify it. It is that to which we refer when we say that "X looks like Y." In identifying X, we do not identify it with Y but rather distinguish between the two. This is the basis for perceiving a sameness of look. If one cow looks like another, this does not mean that the two cows are the same cow, it means that both exhibit the form of the cow. When we have isolated the look of each referential element in a statement, we have arrived at the articulation of its conceptual structure. In other words, the superficial look of the cow is an accommodation to human sensory and cognitive representations of what it is to be a cow: the "deep meaning" of a statement.

Nothing that I have said so far about diaeresis goes much beyond ordinary experience. Socrates speaks, for example, about the forms of the virtues, of justice in particular. He also calls this form a model (*paradeigma*), that to which we look in attempting to state the definition of justice.[1] Such a definition would be impossible, or there would be contradictory definitions with no basis for rank-ordering them, if there were nothing but historically contingent individual conceptions of justice. Disputations and eristical arguments occur with respect to justice when the parties to the dispute are employing conflicting definitions that exclude or contradict one another. From a Platonic standpoint, the reason why philosophers have disagreed down through the centuries about the definition of justice is because they have not seen, and have even repudiated the very existence of, the form of justice. A dialectical presentation of justice, on the other hand, is based upon diaeresis, and so upon the formal structure that underlies, and is the goal of, our analytical speech. If the formal elements picked out by diaeresis are not differentiating marks of the nature of the item under analysis, then the result is not an Idea, or a sequence of Ideas, but a concept or conceptual structure. Modern analytical philosophy attempts to engage in what we may call diaeresis without forms, for which it substitutes concepts or predicates, in other words, linguistic entities. The quasi-mathematical structure of the syntax of a statement should not obscure the fact that the semantic content equates the form or look of things with subjective linguistic construction.

Dialectic appears for the first time in the *Republic* in the passage we are examining. I prefer to postpone a more detailed analysis until we arrive at the discussion of the Ideas. Suffice it to say for the moment that it refers to reasoning with pure forms. This is not true of diaeresis, which begins with perceptions or statements of ordinary experience and disassembles them into their constituent forms. Diaeresis is like classification; dialectic is reasoning. The latter contradicts eristical disputation by making use of the difference between reasoning with pure Ideas and reasoning with surface grammatical units or the conflicting meanings that convention assigns to individual statements, definitions, and arguments.

Glaucon and the others are being taught by Socrates to look away from the contingent surface of language to the actual intelligibility of what they speak about. Since they believe, or aspire to believe, that there is only one "look" to justice that covers all of its instances, they are prepared to visualize it as a kind of goddess who retains her identity throughout her various manifestations. To those who say that justice can be defined in many ways, Socrates would reply that it is always justice that is being defined variously, and so it must somehow be the same as ("look like") all of these definitions. Otherwise, it would not be justice that we were defining.

In sum, the general sequence of thought in this passage is from the shape or figure (*morphē*) of the body to the form of the soul. Socrates intends to claim that men and women have the same soul, and that this has been obscured by the difference between their bodies. In order to distinguish between two human beings for the sake of assigning them to the correct political class, we must employ the appropriate characteristics as differentiae. This process is called *diaeresis*, which Socrates clarifies with an example. Bald and long-haired men are opposite by nature, yet if bald men were shoemakers, it would be ridiculous to prevent long-haired men from being so as well (454c1–9). This absurdity arises if we fail to divide out all the natural properties of human beings in order to determine which ones bear upon the business or natural task of each person. Two characteristics of this procedure are immediately obvious. First: as was previously mentioned, the division we arrive at will depend upon the principle of division we employ at the outset. Second: if we divide up, say, the concept of shoemaking in order to determine which human attributes qualify us for the task, we must know in advance what it is to be a shoemaker. Otherwise we shall not know how to carry through the division, that is, which properties to eliminate, which branch of the diaeresis to follow. But in this case, the diaeresis is unnecessary.

It is also evident that the method of diaeresis does not lead to conceptual discoveries but clarifies what we already know from our ordinary experience. For example, if a man and a woman are both physicians, then we shall not say that the difference in sex bears upon the capacity to practice medicine. But it is by experience that we discover the aptitude of women for medicine, not by sorting out their properties. One such property is "capable of being a physician," but we know it by experience, and it is this experience that enables us to divide out the property from others. What, then, was the point of introducing in obscure terminology the art of diaeresis? The reference seems to carry the rhetorical weight of persuading Socrates's interlocutors to reconsider the conventional criteria by which women are separated from men. As is directly obvious, Socrates proceeds not by an actual diaeresis of the human soul but rather through an appeal to the common experience that he shares with the other interlocutors.

2

Socrates turns now to the question of whether there is any task in the management of the city that belongs exclusively to women. The first step is to offer a brief explanation of what it takes to be naturally suited for something. We require quickness of learning, retention in the memory of what has been learned, and the ability to discover for oneself much of what is involved, as well as subordination of the body to the discursive intelligence. It is obvious that Socrates begins with tasks that do not depend upon the difference between the bodies of the two sexes. He can all the more easily ignore these differences because he is going to abolish the family in the guardian class. No one could deny that the process of bringing a pregnancy to term, as well as nursing and rearing the infant, to mention nothing else, take up a woman's time and energy in a way that interferes with her progress in the development of other skills. In Socrates's city, these tasks will be reduced to the minimum.

Nothing can be done about the fact that women carry the child until it is born and that they are equipped to nurse it as males are not. These two features of the female body make it obvious that such is its natural function. But this function does not preclude the possibility that women can fulfill all three of the main roles in the operation of the city. As was already clear from the fact that the education of the guardians is primarily of the soul, we seem to be faced with an opposition between the female body, to which nature has assigned one kind of job, and the female soul, to which nature has assigned the same tasks as to the male soul, the performance of which is in conflict with the work of the body. This opposition between the body and the soul is different from the natural illness of a conflict within the soul between the desires and the intellect to which all human beings are subject. A good education in music and gymnastics will cure the soul of its sickness, but there is no education that will suppress the conflict between a woman's body and her soul. Women are thus divided in their own nature in such a way as to make them especially suited to play a leading role in the revolution against nature. Perhaps this thought is also behind the biblical story of Adam and Eve in the Garden of Eden.

The arguments by contemporary traditionalists against female emancipation are based upon the commitment to the preservation of the family. These arguments do not seem to apply in the present case. In order for them to do so, it must be shown that the substitution of the city, or rather the guardian class as a whole, for the private family has worse consequences for the just city than does the preservation of the traditional family. Perhaps the most general criticism of Socrates's innovation is Aristotle's remark that each is most concerned with his own; no one takes care of what is common to all.[2] In other words, as Socrates himself has emphasized, human beings love most their own productions, including their children. Where this ownership cannot be established, the basis for love of children and family is dissolved, and with it, the most important basis of patriotism.

Socrates's point is not so much that love of the city extends the love of one's own to the whole but rather that love of one's own is to be abolished as much as possible. The guardian is never to say "my" but rather "our." The political problem here is that love is by nature an extension of self-love and thus of privacy. People will by nature try to identify their own children, and whatever the laws, they will tend to feel more affection for those whom they know, or even believe, themselves to have produced. This difficulty is also visible in the lack of love on the part of the guardians for the moneymakers. A love for the institutions of the city that does not extend to love for the citizens is contrary to human nature, and love for the citizens is mediated by love for one's own family. We often refer to a generalized love of human beings as philanthropy, but this has no place in Socrates's thinking, which restricts our obligations to our fellow citizens, more precisely, to our own class.

The upshot is that one's class becomes one's family; the sought-for unity is not obtained, whereas we acquire many disadvantages, in particular, the dilution of affection that is the necessary consequence of the ideological multiplication of one's relatives to include the entire class. In addition, we would have to explore very carefully the question of the difference in character between those who have been raised in a traditional family and those who have been reared and educated by the ruling regime. To mention just one point, incest cannot be controlled in the Socratic city, as we shall see shortly. Despite certain crude precautions that are taken to duplicate family restrictions on sexual intercourse, Socrates in effect makes every citizen of one's own generation a legitimate sexual object. The precautions themselves indicate the impossibility of destroying the family in all of its forms. That is, they raise the question whether the sexual liberty of the guardians will not brutalize them rather than preserve the harmony of fierceness and gentleness upon which their work depends.

Thus far, Socrates has established that nature, as it manifests itself in individual entities, such as human beings, is so to speak multi-eidetic. This is so in two senses. First, the form of an entity may be constituted from a multiplicity of entities; which elements of this multiplicity we select for scrutiny depends upon our analytical intentions, but these do not relativize the natures of the elements themselves. Forms of this sort are referred to by Socrates as Ideas. Second, an entity may consist in a multiplicity of properties that do not themselves correspond to Ideas. One such property is sex. Sexual identity does not change in itself when viewed from different perspectives, but its significance is relative to the intention of the analyst. It seems to me that this is an awkward thesis to defend with respect to sex, but it is clearly what Socrates means by denying the decisiveness of sexual identity for membership in a particular political class.

Perhaps the same point can be restated somewhat more simply as follows. Each natural thing has many looks, and these must be separated from one another and classified according to their contribution to the existence of the being in question. For example, being long-haired makes no or very little contribution to the humanity of a person. Some human beings have long hair and others are bald, but neither alternative leads us any more quickly to the answer to the question "What is a human being?" To cut to the chase, the answer is not "bald-headed creature" but "rational animal." Hence Socrates's emphasis on the soul rather than the body, and even more narrowly, on the intellectual component of the soul. His conclusion, however, is not quite "the equality of the male and female soul." Glaucon and Socrates agree that there is no human concern in which the male class is not superior to the female class. In other words, whereas women can perform all kinds of tasks, some men will be able to excel in comparison even with the most capable women (455c4–d5). The point is not the perfect equality of men and women but the capacity of women to compete with men for any job at all. As Glaucon puts it, many women are better than many men in many things.

The interesting thing about women is that, in the traditional scheme, they are generally not erroneously classified in the way that men are (for example, cast into the moneymaking rather than the soldier class). Instead, they are divided off from the males and given their own separate work on the basis of their physical nature. For Socrates, this is unjust, not so much because the private rights of women are being violated as because the division is an essential component of the structure of the traditional family. The goal is the abolition of the distinction between "my" and "your," which abolition must be extended for the sake of patriotism to the distinction between "my wife" or "my child" and "your" wife or child. More fundamentally, "business," in the definition of justice as minding one's own business, is understood as "intellectual" or spiritual rather than corporeal. It is plainly the business of women to give birth and nurture to the infant. But Socrates wishes to say that this kind of business does not go to the heart of the matter. It is more like the difference between bald and long-haired men. To deny women the right to be assigned to one of the three classes of the just city is to accept the wrong property as the basis for explaining what it is to be a woman. Women are human beings, and as such, they have souls of varying degrees of intelligence, spiritedness, and desire.

The difficult thing about this whole argument is that both parties to the dispute, traditional and Socratic, seem to be correct. It is entirely correct, and even unavoidable, to distinguish between men and women on the basis of their bodily or sexual differences. But it is also undeniable that to do this is to prevent many if not all women from developing the best attributes of the soul. That this problem cannot be easily resolved is, I believe, evident from the enormous and heated disputes it has engendered in our own time. One difficulty is that there is no criterion, valid for the entire class of women, that permits us to decide which is more just: to emancipate every female, as much as possible, from the restrictions that are based on sexual characteristics or to let each individual woman decide for herself. This latter alternative, which might make sense even today, is out of the question for Socrates, for the reason that I have just given. The justice with which he is concerned is political, not private. This is in a way quite startling, since the entire discussion began for the purpose of deciding which is happiest, the just or the unjust life. But the acceptance of the analogy between the city and the soul has shifted us over to the public nature of justice, and we have simply taken it for granted that this is the same as the private nature.

Although he never raises it explicitly, Socrates forces us to consider the possibility that women are doomed to injustice by nature, not by a male-dominated society. In order to see the importance of this question, one could do worse than to ask men how many of them regard it as an injustice that they are not able to become pregnant, give birth, and suckle their own children. I shall risk the assertion that very few men believe themselves to have been treated unjustly by nature in this matter. Anecdotal though it may be, there is an old story that Plato thanked god every morning for having made him a philosopher, an Athenian, and a man. Such thankfulness is an acknowledgment of mercy toward oneself, and so of injustice toward another.

Socrates cannot possibly contend that, from the standpoint of diaeresis and dialectic, the difference between the sexes is at the same level as the difference between bald and long-haired men. But this is the implication of the use of this example to illustrate eristical uses of contradiction. Socrates has to drive home the point that the pursuit of justice demands that we treat the capacity to be a ruler, guardian, or moneymaker as more important than the ability to become pregnant or the lack of such an ability. Of course, this principle is applied only to the two top types; the women of the moneymaking class, so far as we know, will carry out the same roles they play in actual cities. Ironically, this will not make them moneymakers at all but rather housekeepers, mothers, and so on. What Socrates insists upon is that females born into the working class with the natural capacity to guard or rule must be moved up to their naturally appropriate class, just as those in the upper classes who are found best suited for moneymaking are moved down to the third class. At least in this respect, women continue to play their traditional roles in the just city, namely, to be treated unjustly.

Socrates draws his conclusion at 455d6: "There is no pursuit of the city's governors that belongs to woman as woman, nor to man as man." But there are certainly private pursuits that belong to women as women and to men as men. The criterion at issue is not so much that of nature as it is that of politics. More precisely, it is that of guarding the city. With allowance made only for differences in physical strength, women can perform the same tasks of guarding as can men. Incidentally, Socrates uses medicine here as an example; women can both conceive children and treat their diseases, but only the treating of diseases is significant for the assignment of an occupation. Also important: occupations are assigned on the basis of aptitude in the upper classes; they are not chosen by the private person in accord with his or her personal taste. Socrates seems to assume that those who are especially qualified for some job, for example guarding, will be marked by a love for its prerequisites, for example gymnastics (456a2).

Some women are apt at medicine, others are not. Some are apt at music, whereas others are by nature unmusical. Some love gymnastics and war, others do not; some are lovers of wisdom, whereas others are not, and so too some are spirited, and others are not. It follows that some women are by nature guardians. Socrates is not so much listing the attributes of potential guardians as he is making the point that only attributes like those mentioned are relevant to the process of deciding who is a natural guardian and who is not. The mention of medicine is especially curious in view of the previously noted ambiguity about the class membership of physicians. I think there is no doubt that physicians and judges, to mention only these, will come from the guardian class, which cannot be tended in these crucial ways by those who are naturally moneymakers and hence the political analogue to desire (456a1–12).

Socrates concludes that women who are suited to be guardians will receive the same education as their male counterparts, and that the relevant laws are not impossible or like prayers because they are in accord with nature (456b12–

c3). I remind the reader that this was shown thanks to the example of noble dogs, but also thanks to the assumption that there are natural differences between men and women that are not politically central. Socrates wishes to establish that his proposals are both possible and best. We may grant that they are possible, in the sense that they can be forced upon the city, but Socrates faces rather serious charges that this force is as much unnatural as it is natural. So at least I have argued. The question about their possibility is equally applicable to the question of whether these are the best proposals concerning the disposition of women, and so to the question of the abolition of the family.

Socrates uses a rather hasty argument to make his point. The guardians will consist in the best men and women (and here he includes rulers with the soldiers). The best possible thing for a city is to have within its citizenry the best possible men and women. These are produced by the gymnastic and musical education we have legislated. Therefore our proposals are the best. This argument begs the question. It assumes that the best possible men and women will all be guardians. Socrates has not yet proved that it is best for these men and women to be guardians. He would say that it is best for the city, but this is not what we set out to demonstrate. The question before us, although it has long since been obscured if not forgotten, is which life, the just or the unjust, is the happiest for the private person? Our definition of justice, minding one's own business, looks as if it is a direct expression of the individual or private person. But our business turns out to be what is best for the city, not for ourselves. And if any of us should have any doubts about this, they will soon be suppressed by the comprehensiveness of the public education. The doubts of Adeimantus about the happiness of the guardians remain valid.

One might defend Socrates by saying that what is best for the city is simply that each private person play the political role for which nature has best suited him or her. To this I repeat that my politically optimal function may have nothing to do with, or even contradict, my private happiness. And when it comes to happiness, it is always private. If I am unhappy, I gain no solace from knowing that I live in a happy city. No one could object in principle to the thesis that the most gifted should rule, but politics is the process of adapting principles to the exigencies of praxis. In order to guarantee the rule of the best, the city is transformed from a city of pigs into a city of slaves. The only place where one might stand a chance of finding happiness is, paradoxically enough, in the working class. Perhaps the major fallacy of Socrates's entire argument is the notion that one may force people to be happy by brainwashing them. We are not lacking in historical examples to demonstrate that this is a psychological absurdity. Socrates would have an easier case to make if he simply jettisoned personal happiness at the outset and claimed instead to be showing the consequences of the unmitigated desire for justice. But even this attempt runs into the obstacle of the conflict between justice and persuasion. I would of course agree that, up to a point, we must be persuaded or habituated to be just. Up to a point, I say, for past that point, there can be no justice through compulsion alone. Even if you know better than I do what is best for me, I must play a decisive role in choosing my own life or I am no longer a moral agent. If I am compelled to do what is just, it is not I who am just. Socrates's entire argument collapses at this point because it eliminates justice from the ostensibly just society, exactly as it eliminates happiness from the happy city.

And so we are asked to reaffirm the act that initially subjected us to ridicule: the women must strip for gymnastics. Whoever laughs at this sight does not know that "the beneficial is noble and the harmful is ugly" (*to men ōphelimon kalon, to de blaberon aischron*: 457b4–5). In other words, we are to look not at the bodies but rather at the spirit within, namely, the politically beneficial. For the women will be dressed in virtue, not robes. Thus, says Socrates, we have managed to escape a difficulty as though it were a wave that threatened to submerge us. But there is a bigger one ahead. Not only must women share the same education as men, "these women will all be common to all these men." Notice that Socrates does not say that all these men will be common to all these women; the priority remains with the male.

No woman will live in private with any man, nor will any parent know its own child, or vice versa (457c4–d3). Making every allowance for the apparent difference between upper-class Athenians and contemporary Europeans (to say nothing of other societies) on the importance of romantic love between the sexes, it would be impossible to say that the phenomenon of marital love is a social construction of late modernity. Not all love is "romantic" in the nineteenth-century sense of the term. Socrates's proposal is a big wave, that is, shocking, precisely because it abolishes private sexual arrangements. This has various religious and moral implications of a major kind, as I have noted previously. But once again, the key word here is "private." Citizenship is determined by political function, not bloodlines. Or in slightly different words, bloodlines are regulated by political function. It is obvious that the point here is to abolish love in the sense of a private attachment to the extensions of one's own body. Love is for the city or class, not for human beings, and certainly not for wives or children. As a consolation prize for this deprivation, Socrates bestows a kind of prudent promiscuity upon his guardians. It would be going too far to say that Socrates replaces virtue with pleasure, since the virtue in question is traditional or vulgar by philosophical standards. No single step in the entire argument reveals more clearly than this one how little Socrates is bound by conventional morality, and in fact by the traditional structure of Greek civilization. The willingness to recommend such a change is more important than the question of whether Socrates believes that the change is possible.

3

Glaucon demands that Socrates justify both the possibility and the beneficialness of having women and children in common in the guardian class. Socrates had hoped to be spared the necessity of proving that the arrangement would be the greatest good; instead, he asks permission to put the question of possibility to one side for the time being, and to proceed like daydreamers who imagine that what they want exists and indulge in enjoyable speculations about how they will make use of it. This is a kind of laziness or softness of the soul, to which Socrates says that he has himself succumbed (457e2–458b7). The passage is odd because it licenses two opposing inferences. On the one hand, it sounds as if it will be easier to prove possibility once we are convinced of the advantages of the community principle (as we might call it for the sake of brevity). On the other hand, Socrates seems to have expected that the advantages of the principle would be easier to establish than the possibility of acting on it.

However this may be, we are to assume that the community principle is in effect, and to show that it is the most advantageous for both the city and the guardians (458b5–6). As to the desirability of the guardian class itself, that has presumably been established by the earlier argument concerning the parts of the city, the analogy with the soul, and the principle of one person, one job. I should note that Socrates pays virtually no attention to the defects of the thesis that intelligence should rule in the city, a thesis with the corollary that it is just for intelligence to disregard not only what is preferred by spiritedness and desire but also the private preferences of the wise. Socrates more or less assumes that the most reasonable is politically the best. This is not an assumption that has been verified by experience. It depends instead upon what remains to be proved, namely, that the most reasonable is possible, and that Socrates is correct in his identification of the most reasonable. It might turn out upon closer inspection that it is more reasonable to take private preferences into account, even if this means in some cases that persons will not be matched perfectly with the task for which they are best suited by nature.

Otherwise stated, it is not so easy to separate the questions of desirability and possibility. What for example could it mean to say that a certain model of the city is the best, although it is impossible to bring into existence? Part of the excellence of a city is precisely its possibility; impossible models are models not of human beings but rather of wished-for creatures who dwell in imaginary principalities. I do not wish to repeat the entire argument, but to the extent that the Socratic regime must be imposed onto the citizenry, Socrates denies that in a genuine city the citizens rule and are ruled, or in other words, he denies that consent cannot be entirely replaced by ideological force or brainwashing. On these criteria, which are far from imaginary, the Socratic model is not that of a city fit for human beings but rather of one fit for pigs. In less violent language, its very impossibility makes it undesirable as a model.

No one objects to Socrates's proposal to divide his burden, and so he turns to the question of the benefits that accrue from the principle of community. It is assumed that rulers will wish to lay down commands and assign auxiliaries to carry them out. Some of the commands by the former will themselves be in obedience to the laws, but in other cases the rulers will imitate the laws, that is, express the spirit of the regime in new laws or unwritten customs (458b9–c4). This assumption, although obvious enough, is especially important as a preamble to the order to turn over the women of the appropriate nature to the men who have been selected as guardians. Again, the classification of men is prior to that of women; the men are not handed over to the women. Of course, Socrates is revising existing custom, in which men are entirely dominant, but the flavor of that dominance remains detectable within the construction of the model itself. Since we are daydreaming, why can we not imagine the establishment of the community to be initiated by the women? The fact is that the whole dialogue is a masculine daydream, or nightmare if you prefer, in which no women have a voice; even their emancipation is given to them by the men. The comedian Aristophanes is more radical; he writes of an imaginary rebellion by women who triumph by refusing sex to their husbands.

Now Socrates faces up to the problem of erotic necessity. Since all housing is in common, as is the gymnastic training, men and women will be drawn together into sexual mixing by an inner natural necessity that is much fiercer than geometrical necessity. In other words, eros predominates over mathematics. "But to have sexual mixing with each other in a disorderly manner, or to do anything else of that sort, is not holy [*hosion*] in a city of happy persons, nor will the rulers allow it." Glaucon agrees that it would not be just to do so (458c8–e2). Let us look at this more closely. Socrates refers here to a city of happy persons, not to a happy city. Second, he does not say that sexual promiscuity would make the guardians unhappy but says rather that it is not holy. This is obviously not the same as to say that it is not reasonable. We have to be very careful at this point. It is safe to say that Socrates regards promiscuity as unreasonable, but he does not make this argument because it would not prevail over erotic necessity. Otherwise put, only the rulers (if anyone) are reasonable; we must remember that the soldier-guardians are spirited, like Glaucon, only more so; one may easily imagine that they are also more erotic, but certainly not less so. The idea of having all women in common is entirely in keeping with the erotic daydreams of spirited men; I am not well situated to deny that this is also true of women, especially when the force of motherhood is subtracted from the impetus toward security and fidelity. But we can be sustained in our opinion about men by the story of the ring of Gyges, which exemplifies common opinion about the male sexual appetite, an opinion, incidentally, that seems to be confirmed by contemporary anthropological and biological doctrines.

Precisely because reason is too weak to control eros directly, Socrates must have recourse to traditional religious procedures. The rationalist monotheism of Book Two is silently dropped for reasons of political expediency. Marriages must be made as sacred as possible, "and those which are most beneficial will be sacred" (458e3–4). As Bloom points out, there is an echo here of the "sacred marriage" of Zeus and Hera. Of course, the rituals to be installed have been invented by the founding fathers, but the connection between marriage and holiness is intrinsic to pagan religion. Socrates defines "holy" as what is useful to the city, not what the gods wish. As his words imply, the most beneficial marriages are especially holy. These are understood by the model not only of the noble hound, that deus ex machina, but this time also of the nobly bred birds that Glaucon among others breeds in his home, as well as horses. The breeding of dogs and birds can be controlled by human beings through the simple expediency of keeping the animals isolated. But human beings cannot be kept in pens and coupled like animals. In the happy city, however, we can approximate to this "by a throng of lies and deceptions that our rulers will have to use for the benefit of the ruled" (459c8–d2).

This shows us what is obvious in itself, namely, that the natural proclivity toward promiscuity is constrained only by religious morality. In the Socratic city, religion becomes an instrument of lying, not truth telling. These new lies about marriage are the continuation of the noble lie that is designed to persuade us of our origin in the center of the earth (414d1ff.). This lie tells us that our remembered childhood was imaginary. If it takes effect, then each generation of citizens must be taught that there is a mysterious disjunction in human existence that begins at the latest in the moment of conception. We believe ourselves to have been born and reared on the surface of the earth, whereas the truth is that these events transpired underground. This makes it rather difficult to understand why our actual couplings should be subjected to such regulation if they are all illusory and children are manufactured by divine creatures. But the deeper point is the constant connection between eros and lying. We lie to our wives and husbands in our daydreams, on which point the story about the ring of Gyges is exemplary. We lie more concretely when we are actually unfaithful. And of course, in order to control us as much as possible like dogs, birds, and horses, our rulers lie to us for our own benefit, namely, to make us suitable guardians of the happy city, that is, a city that would make no one happy. We come back to the difference between erotic and geometrical necessity. Since the former prevails over the latter, we have to be tricked and controlled into believing that what makes us happy is what makes actual human beings sad, or produces happiness in us only as our natural appetites wane, as in the case of old men like Cephalus or philosophers like Socrates.

Precisely if sexuality is the desire for what one lacks, then it is oriented toward the future, and thus to wishing and dreaming. Of course, the entire model of the just city is itself a daydream, but it is a daydream about how to regulate sexual eros. In the *Republic*, the best city is the one that ostensibly fulfills us in the present, and it is the impossibility of such fulfillment that is the deepest reason for the impossibility of the city. Not even the recourse to philosopher-kings, steeped in mathematics and with their eyes presumably fixed upon the eternal Ideas, can bring human life fully into the present. On this point, namely, the future-oriented nature of human life, Heidegger is surely correct. Where he goes wrong, as I have shown elsewhere at great length, is in his analysis of the future, and so of temporality. Since there is no conceptual explanation of the present as present, the entire structure of temporality must be derived from an atemporal source that Plato calls "the Ideas," and others refer to as "heaven" or "God," whereas still others speak of concepts, sets, predicates, and logical structure. I shall return to these obscure notions later. Here I want to say only that the various lies told by Socrates on behalf of the founding fathers are noble because they attempt to explain the inexplicable, namely, the presence of eternity within time. But these lies are philosophically unsound; the correct procedure is to explain the presence of time within eternity.

After this brief flight into the empyrean, I come quickly back to earth. The drugs and lies that are required to regulate breeding are beneficial. They are not eternal but come into existence in connection with marriages and breeding (459d4–5). We need the best men to have intercourse with the best women as often as possible, and the worst to couple with the worst as seldom as possible. Furthermore, the children of the former group must be reared, whereas those of the latter group must not; in other words, they must be destroyed, in order for the flock to reach its highest point of development. Furthermore, that this is taking place must be concealed from everyone but the rulers, so that the herd of guardians is to be kept as free of factions as possible (459d7–e3).

This passage reveals a defect in the overall argument. The division of the city into classes is blurred at the edges; by this expression I mean to say that there are better and worse guardian natures, not a homogeneous group of highly developed spirits. It seems quite likely that this is also true of the rulers at one extreme and the workers at the other. The latter are not important to Socrates's argument, although one can easily imagine that highly gifted workers might be forced to remain in the lowest class yet be bright enough to cause trouble for the regime. As to the rulers, Socrates requires no fixed number and even suggests in one passage that there might be a single philosopher-king. But even so, this leaves a cadre of highly educated, spirited, and undoubtedly ambitious persons who are shut off from political influence and forced to live the life of a barracks officer. I see here the likelihood of stasis in all three classes. This potential stasis rises to the surface of the argument in the discussion of sexual eros and breeding. It is entirely unrealistic to assume that the rulers will be able to enforce the destruction of inferior progeny without the knowledge of the lower subclass of auxiliaries. The chances for stasis are therefore excellent.

In sum, the deviations within each major type of human soul are numerous enough to rupture the unity of each class. And nothing has greater potential for upsetting the political order than the attempt to treat human beings, in particular, guardians, like animals bred for war. In any event, Socrates tries to preserve that order by establishing festivals and sacrifices to sanctify the marriages of the guardians. We also learn that there will be poets in the city who will write marriage hymns (460a1).[3] The number of marriages permitted will be fixed by the rulers in such a way as to keep the size of the city steady. These marriages will be arranged by crooked lots; in other words, they will be rigged in advance to guarantee that the best men mate with the best women and the worst with the worst. And of course, since the unions are by lot, personal taste does not come into play. The purpose of these marriages is plainly for breeding, and although Socrates does not make a point of it, for satisfying the sexual appetites of the young. No doubt affection may follow cohabitation, but by separating marriage from affection, Socrates tacitly exaggerates the force of erotic appetite. The potential for trouble at the practical level is so obvious here that it is senseless to reply that we are discussing a model, not an actual city. The point of a model is to provide us with a goal for the construction of a workable actual city, not a blueprint for disaster.

Not only do the extraordinary male auxiliaries get to mate with the extraordinary females, excellence in war is to result in bonus copulations. Frequency of intercourse is thus acknowledged as a desideratum among the younger guardians. There is no reason to assume that the ordinary members of the class will not have sexual appetites as strong as those of their superior colleagues. Even if the blame for their lower number of sexual contacts can be attributed to chance, as will be their less desirable marriages, there is bound to be jealousy toward the winners, and in this way factions will eventually arise. As if this were not bad enough, the newborn infants are taken away from their parents and turned over to nurses, whereas the deformed and the children of the inferior parents will be "hidden away in a secret and invisible place," a euphemism for destruction. Socrates takes it for granted that no one will object to being deprived of his or her children. Neither does he seem to have any doubts that being raised by nurses in milk pens is the best way in which to rear superior children. Since schemes have to be contrived to prevent mothers from nursing their own children, we can assume that the instinctual preference for one's own remains potent in the beautiful city. At each point, the deception and ruthlessness shown by the rulers toward the inferior guardians mounts. It is an odd consequence of the new regime that the auxiliary guardians are subjected both to more supervision and more dehumanization than are the workers or moneymakers. The culminating point in this series is the callous acceptance of infanticide as necessary to guarantee the purity of the guardian class (460a8–c7). This coldness will eventually be exceeded when Socrates tells Glaucon that in order to found the city, all inhabitants of the area over the age of ten must turn over their children to the founding fathers and themselves be "rusticated" (VII. 540e5ff.).

Socrates next restricts procreation to the prime of life. In women, this occurs between the ages of twenty and forty. In the case of men, he is a bit more vague; the peak is fifty-five, but the beginning of the reproductive prime is the age when a man is no longer able to maintain top speed at running. As usual, there will be festivals and laws designed to regulate reproduction; should these be violated, the infant will be condemned. Socrates leaves it to us to infer that condemnation means infanticide. Here as elsewhere, it should be clear from experience that there will be exceptions, and perhaps many exceptions, to the assumptions underlying the regulation of sexual life. In particular, superior infants will be destroyed through the imposition of the very rules that are designed to keep the class pure. This shows conclusively the invalidity of the analogy between the city and the soul. It is manifestly unjust to the individual infant to be destroyed despite his or her own natural superiority. We can defend Socrates only by arguing that destruction is justified by the good of the whole class or city. This in turn requires us to say that there is no such thing as justice for the individual person, or perhaps that individual justice is different from communal justice. But the analogy is refuted in either case. If justice is minding one's own business, it cannot be the business of a natural ruler or soldier to be put to death at birth. For such individuals, justice turns out to be minding the business of the city, that is, doing what is good for others, in this case, undergoing an unjust death to avoid the risk of contaminating the entire class.

Those guardians who are over the age of legal reproduction may have intercourse with whomever they wish, with certain restrictions as to age, provided that they abort any resulting foetuses. This is a version of what is called in our own day "recreational sex," and its advocacy is a good sign of the radical separation between sexual pleasure and procreation in the just city. The underlying viewpoint is the reverse of the biblical injunction against spilling the seed in vain. Among the many consequences of Socrates's proposals is the encouragement of indifference toward one's own children. This may be understood as an attempt to placate the sexual instinct as a reward for the many restrictions to which it has been submitted. Despite the natural love of one's own, the guardians are to be seduced into identifying their family by its political function, in particular, by making war, rather than by the ties of flesh and blood. The pleasures of the body are a reward for the subordination of these pleasures to the love of the city. It thus turns out that the main enemy, against whom the guardians must defend the city, is themselves (461a3–c7).

The restrictions on free or recreational sex due to age are intended to avoid the threat of intercourse with one's children, grandchildren, parents, and grandparents and their ancestors. On the other hand, sex between brothers and sisters is permissible. It is not worth our trouble to analyze the liberties that would be granted by the vague definitions of family relations that Socrates gives. What is worth emphasizing is, first, that these restrictions are compatible with incest but, second, that Socrates finds it necessary to try to rule out sleeping with one's mother or father, grandmother or grandfather, children and grandchildren. This certainly implies that he regards the general repugnance toward incest as something natural to human beings, and not subject to brainwashing, with the exception of connections between brothers and sisters. Grandparents and parents have produced us, whereas we have produced our children and (by extension) grandchildren. Brothers and sisters, on the other hand, despite their being children of common parents, have not produced each other, either directly or by extension. In this precise sense, the sexual link between brother and sister is diluted, by comparison with the other relationships. On the other hand, since they are members of the same generation, they grow up in close contact all through the years of sexual maturation and are much more likely to have sexual relations with each other than with those who are much older or much younger than they (461c8–e4).

Having described the community of women and children, Socrates now turns his attention to showing that it is the best way for them to be organized. The guiding principle is as follows: there is no greater evil for the city than what tears it asunder and makes it many instead of one, and no greater good than what binds it together and makes it one (462a9–b2). If a single person is unified, then his intelligence governs his passions via the mediation of spiritedness. But the unification of a city leaves us with a multitude of individual persons, each of whom is unified in a different way, that is, via the predominance of intellect, spiritedness, or desire. A city is a unity of multiple unities; otherwise put, the unity of the individual is not the same as the unity of the city, because in the latter we retain the separation of the three classes or types of individual person. In addition, the city is all three types, whereas the individual person is dominated by just one attribute (although he or she of course possesses the others as well).

It is therefore a mistake on Socrates's part, given his own premises, to conceive of the unity of the city on the model of the unity of the individual person. The city is a harmony of three classes, whereas the person is a unity defined primarily by one attribute. Cities require persons who are intelligent, some who are brave, and others who love to make money; and these are *different* persons. No single person can be all three types of person. A completely unified city would therefore reduce to a monad, since it could be no one of the three types, for example a city devoted to making money, without losing the very harmony that for Socrates is the structure of the city. Socrates himself brings out the absurdity of his own analogy when he adds that "the community of pleasure and pain binds together, whenever all the citizens are gratified and pained as much as possible by the same generations and destructions" (462b4–6). The pleasure and pain of the person is always *my* pleasure and pain, because I am always separate from each of the others. The only way in which to make pleasure and pain entirely common would be by destroying the body — not a very efficient strategy. Socrates tries to do this as much as possible by unifying the thoughts and desires of the citizenry, but the thoughts of the rulers, even if they are the same as each other's, differ from those of the guardians and the workers, and so too with the other attributes of the soul.

Socrates concludes that the best-governed city is one in which everyone says "my own" and "not my own" about the same thing and in the same way, whereas the city is dissolved when this does not happen (462c3–8). This is a hasty inference, since it could apply to a complete tyranny in which everyone agrees with the tyrant as to what is theirs and not theirs. But there is another point as well. If everyone says "my own" about the same thing and in the same way, then we all become rivals for that one thing. In a harmonious city, I say "my own" only when no one else does. This is of course true only of things that cannot be owned by everyone or at least enjoyed by all simultaneously. The problem seems to disappear in the case of "ideas" (and also in the case of "Platonic Ideas"). All of us can be pleased by the idea or thought of "my" city without coming into conflict with the others. But we do not live in "ideas" (or "Ideas"); we live in the world of genesis; and in this world, each of us occupies a volume of space and time that is not occupied by everyone else. The existence of the body is the final limitation against the excessive because self-destructive attempt to unify the city. And this is no doubt why the city is itself compared by Greek thinkers, including Socrates, to the body, or let us say to a ship that carries the soul to its multitudinous destinations.

Socrates's conclusion is the exact opposite of my own, and Glaucon accepts it without hesitation. The best city is one that comes as close as possible to a single human being (462b10). For example, if I cut my finger, I feel it in my entire "community" of body and soul. So too if a single citizen of the best city experiences pleasure or pain, the entire city will share in it. To this one may reply that if I cut a finger on my left hand, I do not feel it in the right hand, or for that matter in my foot or stomach. Pains, like pleasures, are quite diverse with respect to the portion of the body or soul they affect. Still, it is I who feel the pain, not you. You may be pained that I am pained or pleased that I am pleased, but in both cases there are two distinct locations of the respective sensations. The situation does not change in the case of a spiritual pleasure like patriotism, or what we can call love of the city. You and I may feel the same love for the city and the same hatred or pain induced by our common enemy. But as felt, the pleasure or pain is my own; the unity is conceptual. That is, we are united because each of us knows that the other loves the city; we are not united simply because the emotion is abstractly speaking the same in both cases. If I may return to the point made by Socrates about the very origin of the city, it comes into being because of our individual neediness. It is not simply that I cannot fend for myself but that I know that I cannot do so. I know that I love the city because it preserves me from destruction by the enemy. You know the same thing, but it is your destruction, not mine, that sets the whole process of patriotism into motion for you.

This is the kind of knowledge that is peculiar to politics. It is not knowledge of the Platonic Ideas or of the sum of two and two; in cases like these, we can indeed know the same thing, but we shall be neither united nor separated by that knowledge, because the closer we come to the unity of the knowledge, the farther we are removed from self-awareness: the more we disappear. Knowledge becomes political when we can act on it, and in fact are forced to do so.

The knowledge that two and two are four becomes political in the thoughts of an engineer who needs to use this formula in the process of building a bridge, not in those of a mathematician.

4

To come back to the text, since there is no private property, there will be many fewer lawsuits. Socrates adds that there will also be no suits for assault or insult, since it is noble and just for young warriors to defend themselves personally in such cases (464d7–465a4). In other words, the guardians, as marked by spiritedness, will be subject to the same insults and injuries as are such persons in any polity, and their method of resolving these abuses will be to fight it out, very much like the Homeric heroes or, to go to the other end of the spectrum, contemporary street gangs. It is dubious to hold that the code of honor is superior to recourse to the courts, but the main point is that the root of factionalism has not been removed by the shift from the latter to the former.

After outlining the great peacefulness that will mark the lives of the guardians among themselves, an observation that seems to be contradicted by the reference to duelling, Socrates comes back to an earlier and controversial point. Since they have no private or personal property of any kind, they will be rid of all personal suffering, and so they will live a more blessed life than the most blessed of the Olympic victors. The latter are celebrated for a local triumph, and for a short period of time, but the guardians receive constant praise as preservers of the entire city, a praise that Socrates says extends to their children as well (465c9). Is this supposed to refer to the entire age group? If it does, the joy that we feel at the prosperity of our children will be considerably diluted; if it does not, Socrates seems temporarily to have forgotten that the guardians have no children of their own. In any event, the point is that the previous question as to whether we were making the guardians happy (465e5, 466a3–4) has now been answered. The life of the *auxiliaries* (*epikouroi*: 466a8) is much more beautiful than that of the Olympic victors; it is therefore not comparable to the life of the moneymakers. I emphasize the shift in terms. It reminds us that the rulers are part of the extended guardian class, in which they are distinguished from the soldiers. Since the happiness of the soldiers depends upon their being tricked and lied to by the rulers, it is hardly likely that the rulers will be able to arrange for their own happiness in the same way. The workers, as Socrates indicates, are out of the picture. As to the rulers, we do not yet know if they will be happy *as* rulers. This will depend upon whether they wish to rule and enjoy it more than anything else. They must, in other words, prefer ruling to philosophy and learning. We see here already a problem with the rulers; they are not focused upon one task, as are the soldiers and the workers. Instead, they have two jobs, philosophy and ruling. And there is no Hegelian *Aufhebung* of the two.

In short, the male and female guardians "must guard and hunt together like dogs, both while remaining in the city and when exiting it for the sake of war" (466c8–d1). The peak of human happiness is a dog's life. It is therefore appropriate that the next topic concerns the manner of making war. The first main point is that the guardians will lead the strongest children to war as observers, so that they can become familiar with the work for which they have been bred, and in particular, become skilled horsemen (466e1–467e8). Second, in addition to the usual arrangements to encourage bravery and discourage cowardice, if one of the guardians is taken prisoner, we shall make no effort to release him but shall present him as a gift to the enemy, to do with as they please (468a8–b1). I cannot refrain from wondering whether this custom does not interfere with the ostensible love of the guardians for one another. It may make the soldiers more desperate, but this is not the same as bravery or affection. The more we immerse ourselves in the details of the Socratic city, the more it looks undesirable and unworkable.

The third point in the present series has to do with postmartial erotics. Those who perform well in war must be crowned and kissed by each member of the campaign, youths and boys in turn. Presumably young women and younger girls are present, but they are mentioned only marginally with respect to kissing (468b12–c4). Glaucon is delighted with this arrangement, as we might have suspected. And the passage makes clear that the kissing ceremony is explicitly erotic (468c3: *erōn*), not just an expression of patriotic affection. Marriages, on the other hand, since their purpose is reproduction, are between male and female, as usual; and the brave man will be frequently favored by the marriage lottery. Sex is not so much restricted as it is transformed into a political weapon. I note, however, that nothing has been said thus far to endorse full-fledged pederasty or recreational homosexual intercourse. But that homosexual love will be present in the beautiful city is now clear. Note too that in keeping with the male orientation of the city, men compete for wives; it is not said that women compete for husbands.

Socrates turns from eros, and so from life, to death. Our dead heroes will be said to belong to the golden class (a reference to Hesiod's "golden age"; see Bloom's notes here). As they are to become friendly demons, we must ask "the god" how they are to be buried (468e4–469a6). It is striking that Socrates's commitment to a rationalist monotheism is blurred, if it does not quite disappear, at the three sacral points of human life: birth, marriage, and death. At these times we need traditional ceremonies, temples, demons, and other trappings of pagan mythology. And once more, the city we are constructing, although revolutionary, is nevertheless Greek. It rests upon a distinction between Greek and barbarian. For example, Greeks will be denied the right to hold other Greeks as slaves, but nothing is said against the enslavement of barbarians (469b8–c7). Our soldiers are required to spare those of Greek stock from slavery, because they will be required as allies against the great risk represented to Greek freedom by the barbarians. This is not a humanitarian or philanthropic but a strictly patriotic restriction. It exemplifies the definition of justice as doing good to one's friends and harm to one's enemies. And one's friends are the members of one's own pack, herd, tribe, or class.

Socrates continues by forbidding his auxiliaries the right to strip the dead (except for weapons), an act that is illiberal and greedy, as well as womanly and small minded (Griffith squeamishly translates *gunaikeias* as "cowardly"). Again we learn that there are temples in our city, to which the property of dead enemies, especially if they are Greeks, cannot be brought as votive offerings; for this would be a defilement of our own (Greek) stock, unless the god orders it to be done (470a3; cf 465a8). Socrates sounds very much here as if he is lecturing his contemporaries on actual politics, in particular, on the stupidity of Greek fighting Greek, when they are friends by nature but temporarily dislocated by sickness into factionalism. Greek and barbarian, on the other hand, are enemies by nature (470c5–d1). Once more, blood relationship defines one's own tribe, and friendship is restricted to members of the same people. One would assume that the same principle holds between individual persons, and the reason is that the discussion here is of war and politics, not philosophy. If a barbarian is capable of philosophy, that does not make him a philanthropist, any more than Socrates recommends friendship with barbarian sages. Friendship is restricted to one's own because nature makes universalism impossible. For example, although customs are not natural, it is natural for different people to have different customs, and the clash of custom leads naturally to war. One could also say that the conditions of existence are hard and that, in a pretechnical society, the struggle for survival makes foreigners automatically suspect. In my opinion, however, the deepest reason for the restriction of friendship is that we love ourselves and our children the most, and by extension, that we see ourselves as defined by our ethnic stock. The other is alien. As Socrates says, "The Greek family [*genos*] is with respect to itself its own and co-generated, but with respect to the barbarian, is foreign and alien" (470c1–3).

When Socrates asks Glaucon if ours is a Greek city, he replies, "It must be" (470e4–6). Glaucon and the others are open to the most extraordinary political innovations but not at all to the possibility that the new city could be barbarian (that is, not Greek). I want to emphasize that this is not simply a matter of philhellenism in a cultural or political sense. It is an expression of the blood, albeit one that is rendered articulate. Who else are we to love if not ourselves and our own? Nature has ingrained in our very mode of existence a preference for those who generated us, and whom we generate in turn. From that perspective, "multiculturalism" is for Socrates and his audience a principle of separation, not unification. The Greeks, says Socrates, are good and tame toward one another, in comparison to how the barbarians act toward us (470e3–8). In view of the violence with which the Greeks were destroying each other in the Peloponnesian War, even as Socrates was speaking, his remarks may seem absurd. But his point is that Greek violence to Greeks is a sickness, exactly like the violence of the desires toward the intellect in the soul of an individual person. When friends and relatives fight, this is called by him "faction," or the disruption of the harmony of the soul. Wars are fought between strangers and enemies.

It follows that the soldiers of the beautiful city must treat their fellow Greeks as kindly correctors. They will punish only those who are to be blamed for the differences between the two cities (471a12). Even this wording is suggestive, because it is taken for granted that in a war, our city is always on the side of justice. Glaucon agrees that the auxiliaries of the just city will behave toward Greek opponents as Socrates suggests, whereas toward barbarians they will behave as Greeks now do to one another. He further agrees that Socrates has shown the city to be desirable. But it is now time to terminate the listing of laws governing war and turn to the serious difficulty. Is this city possible? Socrates replies that Glaucon has just assaulted his argument by raising the third wave, which is bigger and more difficult than the first two. These waves were raised by the demand of Polemarchus and Adeimantus that Socrates explain in detail the principle of women having the same jobs as men and the principle of the community of women and children (457b7ff.). At that time, Socrates asked to be allowed to postpone the question of possibility and to show only the utility or desirability of the aforementioned community. But now he is forced by Glaucon to face up at last to the question of the possibility not simply of women and children in common but of the entire polity (*politeia*: 471e2).

PART Three

8

Possibility

I

Socrates begins his attempt to surmount the third wave by introducing the distinction between speech and deed. In doing so, he employs a term, *paradeigma*, that has appeared previously in the *Republic* but not in an obtrusive passage. Let us briefly review the senses of this term.[1] According to Liddell, Scott, and Jones, the two primary senses of *paradeigma* are "pattern" or "model" on the one hand and "example" on the other. There are two main kinds of model. The first kind can be constructed by human ingenuity to serve as a standard for producing something in a certain (more or less) definite manner. For example, a blueprint is a model of a house of such-and-such a kind; a sewing pattern is a model for a garment or quilt or something of that sort. The second kind of model is more difficult to explain. In this case, the pattern is not constructed or imagined by the human intelligence but discerned or perceived or even intuited as the expression of the essential nature of something that we encounter in our experience. Suppose I am a bird-watcher and I come across a hole-boled grebe. I may determine that this is a "perfect specimen" of its species. In other words, it corresponds to the criteria for being a grebe in an exemplary manner. Notice that human beings, say ornithologists, may have settled on these criteria, and in that sense produced the model. But they did not produce the grebes themselves, or what it is to be a grebe. The model is in these cases itself an approximation to the actual nature of the hole-boled grebe.

I doubt that there is a great controversy about the model or pattern of the hole-boled grebe. But in many branches of science, the search for superior models may appear to be endless. This is true of models of both types, produced and perceived. It is so widely true that the temptation becomes overwhelming to think of all models as human creations or interpretations of what it is to be a such-and-such. This leads to the view that the natural order is itself such an interpretation, or congeries of interpretations. In other words, the view just mentioned is an *interpretation* of the existence and intelligibility of human experience, and so a denial that there are any natural models or patterns, independent of our cognitive and perceptual powers. I shall come back to this question when we arrive at Socrates's official presentation of the doctrine of Ideas.

Meanwhile it is worth observing that a model is also in another sense an example. The architect's blueprint is both a model for making houses and an example of the class of models. What is a model from one standpoint is or may be an example from another. This is also true of Platonic Ideas. The Idea of justice is an example of a Platonic Idea, but in its function as this particular Idea it expresses what it is to be just, and not what it is to be a Platonic Idea. It is a model or pattern that appears in every example of justice. Here is a very important point. The perception of the Idea of justice tells us what justice is but not what it is to be an Idea; and so too with all the Ideas, with the possible exception of the Idea of the Good, which we shall have to examine later. For the time being, we can say that there seems to be a fundamental difference between a model in the everyday sense and a Platonic Idea. Ideas are not standards for human action but exhibitions of what makes each member of a particular kind a member of that kind. The Idea of justice does not have as its function causing us to act justly; rather, it underwrites or guarantees the existence of just acts, that is, it enables us to identify just acts as such, regardless of whether we perform such acts. In Aristotelian language, the Idea, as a model, is the essence of justice. I want to emphasize that the general definition of "model," say, "a standard for doing something," is not itself a model, because it does not tell us how to do something in particular.

To generalize, there are two kinds of model, which we may call active and passive. The first or active kind shows us how to act if we wish to do something. The second or passive kind shows us what it is to be something of a certain kind. Platonic Ideas are in this sense passive (again with the possible exception of the Idea of the Good, to which an active role is assigned). The distinction between active and passive is broader than that between models in the everyday sense and Platonic Ideas. There are limitless occasions in ordinary language when we say that something is "a model X" (for example, "a model child" or "a model gentleman") to describe the nature or behavior of someone or something that has already acted in such-and-such a way or is already a thing of kind X. If I point to a bird and say "that is a model robin," I do not mean that if I wish to become a robin, I must act in accord with the model. Nor is it right to say that in these cases the agent, for example the child or the bird, acted intentionally in accord with its model. I am using the term to identify the child or the bird as an example of the model that expresses the general consensus about an excellent thing of that sort. In these cases, we may often replace "a model X" with "a perfect X," for example "a perfect gentleman." Finally, models may be constructed by human reflection or perceived as ingredient in the nature of a class of objects. Although the terms are entirely anachronistic, it is tempting to refer to these as "epistemological" and "ontological," respectively.

When we appeal explicitly to an example, we are tacitly appealing to a model. The expression "for example" draws our attention to something in particular, say a statue, that satisfies the requirements built into an abstract concept like "classical Greek art." Statements like "this is an example of classical Greek art" tell us that the example exhibits but is of course not identical with the model. But statements like "Socrates is a model husband" do not mean that Socrates is the model itself (that is, of good or perfect husbands) but rather mean that he is an example of the model "good" or "perfect husband." So the distinction between example and model does not require that both be mentioned in the same statement. The point is that we have no way of identifying an example *as* an example of a certain kind, unless we know the kind; and this is to know the model. This deserves expansion.

In order to verify the statement "Socrates is [an example of] a model husband," we compare the behavior of Socrates to that of his wife, Xanthippe, with the properties that define model husbands. If Socrates exhibits those properties, then he is a model husband The definition of what it is to be a model husband must be known in advance before we can identify Socrates or anyone else as an example of that definition. Incidentally, Socrates sometimes complains against responding to requests for a definition with examples (as in the *Theaetetus*), but if the examples are correctly chosen, it is highly unlikely to be for any reason other than that we understand clearly at least part of what it is to be so-and-so, and hence have a kind of prediscursive awareness of the definition. We see that to be a so-and-so means to behave in such-and-such a manner; less awkwardly expressed, that to be a just man is among other things to honor one's contracts. If the model were totally inaccessible to us, we could identify no appropriate examples of it.

Another way to look at an example is to see it as an incompletely articulated model. Think of an architect's model of a house or a sculptor's preliminary casting of a statue he is about to produce. One may build many houses in accordance with the same pattern, and so too in the case of statues. In these cases, the results of attempting to produce an instance of the general definition exhibited by the model are examples; the pattern or model stands to its examples as the original to its images. The examples will inevitably fall short of realizing perfectly the model. But the model is as it were implied by the example. We can see that this particular house is an example of that particular blueprint, and in fact we must see the model or blueprint first, or discern from our inspection of the real house what kind of house it is, in order to identify the example as of that blueprint. The house is an imperfect reflection of the blueprint. As it becomes more and more perfect, it ceases to be a house. We sometimes speak enthusiastically of "a perfect house," but we know very well that only perfect people can live in perfect houses: in other words, only models or concepts in both cases.

Another interesting complication is that the model may itself be an imperfect conceptualization of the original inspiration of the architect or sculptor. Or it could be improved by a still more gifted artisan. Furthermore, the different approximations to the original pattern or model may each possess a unique value that leads us to speak of them as originals rather than copies. In one sense, then, the copy is not an example but an original; yet in another, it is clearly a variation on the model.

The distinction between model and example is relative to context. There is no one set of entities called models that never function as examples, and conversely, no set of examples of which none is ever a model. An example of a joke is a joke, not an abstract definition of a joke, but the joke works as an example if it renders a definition intelligible. Let the definition here be "a joke is a story that makes us laugh." We must know in advance of giving examples what it is to tell a story and why we laugh at those stories that strike us as funny. Then we are in a position to see that "joke" means something we already know. The same analysis applies to a mathematical equation. An example of a mathematical equation is precisely some particular equation that exhibits or makes intelligible what the definition of a mathematical equation tells us it is.

To sum up: we cannot explain in general terms what it is to be an example without giving an example . The purpose of the example we give is to cast light on the nature of examples, but if we do not know what it is to be an example, then we cannot give one. So examples are not definitions of some general entity. We can say that examples are not models or patterns, and in that precise sense, they are not originals. It is my grasp on a pattern or model that enables me to exemplify it. Socrates has prepared us to consider the nature of a paradigm by using the word earlier in the dialogue, for example at III. 409b1–d3, where it occurs three times. He speaks there of having a paradigm within our soul of a good or a bad man. These paradigms arise from experience, but obviously they are not simply a collection of examples. One cannot gather together examples under a single heading if one has no idea of what the heading is, and so which are its examples.

Furthermore, the case of the paradigm of the good or the bad man is not that, say, of a physical object that serves as the "pattern" for identifying copies of itself. What actually happens is something like this. By dint of long experience with particular actions of human beings that we have been educated to regard as good or bad, or which we believe to be such on the basis of some other criterion, whether it be moral intuition, divine revelation, or simple habituation (that is, brainwashing), we develop the ability to judge particular actors, with whose general behavior we are familiar, as examples of what we mean by "good" or "bad" men. I am of course not denying that we can give definitions of good or bad men. My point is that we can do this only after we have come to know what we regard as a good or a bad man, and we do not arrive at this knowledge by means of a definition. The definition itself is understandable if and only if we already understand why certain modes of behavior are good, and this in turn requires us to know what is meant by "good". This knowledge does not spring into our minds ex nihilo. It accumulates or, better, crystallizes out of countless experiences, most of them very simple, but all of them mysterious in the sense that we must ultimately grasp what it is to approve of something by calling it good, in order to acquire the experiences from which our definition crystallizes. This is enough to show that the word *paradigm* has a vague but not unintelligible sense in the passage we are examining. It is easy enough to say that the paradigm is what enables us to distinguish between good and bad men. But a definition of the paradigm is not enough to activate it in each particular case. On the contrary, we have to apply the paradigm to the individual case by an act of judgment. And there is no paradigm of how to judge.

Thus far I have indicated only some of the problems that arise when we try to sort out the meaning of *paradeigma* in its ordinary senses of model or example. The purpose of this exercise is not to solve the technical puzzle of these terms but to show the background complexity to what will shortly be introduced as the doctrine of Platonic Ideas. It is, I think, true that this doctrine arises from everyday use, and that it expresses something undeniable about the conditions of intelligible discourse. However we explain it, or fail to explain it, intelligible discourse exhibits formal structures about which we talk, and which are not simply random linguistic constructions of the spontaneous discursive process. It is no doubt true that language follows rules, but rules follow the kinds of things about which we speak, which are themselves either discovered rather than invented, or, if invented, then by procedures that preexist the act of invention and refer to formal patterns that are not invented but discovered in their very use.

2

We are now ready to return to the text. "If we discover what sort of thing justice is,[2] will we also require that the just man must not differ from justice itself [*autēs ekeinēs*], but be in every way such a thing as justice [itself] is? Or will we be glad if he comes as close as possible to it, and participates [*metechē*] in it more so than other things?" (472b7–c2). In the language of the preceding discussion, the just individual is an example of the pattern or model of what it is to be just. Examples are not and cannot be perfect instances of models; if they were, they would be the model itself. Human beings are flesh-and-blood copies of the perfectly just man; they "participate" in the model to one degree or another, just as circles on the blackboard participate to one degree or another in the perfect geometrical circle.

" 'It was therefore for the sake of a paradigm,' I said, 'that we investigated what sort of thing is justice itself [*auto to dikaiosunēn hoion esti*] and for the perfectly just man if he should come to exist, and as coming to exist, what kind he would be' " (472c4–6). Socrates gives no explanation for what will soon become technical terminology in the doctrine of Ideas. This terminology is understood because it emerges not quite from ordinary or everyday usage but from a modification of that usage. We often speak of perfect justice as something that cannot be found in this life, and we do so because we understand how individual acts of justice fall short of perfection. This in turn means that we have a clear if not fully analyzed picture of what it would be like to achieve perfect justice. By "justice itself" is meant perfect justice, with no shortcomings, and so that at which individual acts of justice aim. Just acts are the mark of the just man, and the perfectly just man is one who never acts unjustly. The one assumption made by Socrates is that we can infer perfection or completion from our observation of imperfection and incompleteness. But deciding on the basis of unjust acts what it would be to be a perfectly just man is not the same as inferring from a half-filled cup what a full cup would be like. The best we can do is to postulate or construct a model of perfect justice and measure human actions by its standard. This is not in itself a fatal difficulty for the doctrine of Ideas. What we need to know is that perfection is the goal that we can understand, even if we cannot agree on the definition of perfect justice, and furthermore that it is this goal that enables us to distinguish between just and unjust acts, or order just acts as a kind of progress toward perfection. But it has to be admitted that we see Ideas, or at least Ideas like justice, through a glass darkly, and not as precise quasi-mathematical structures. This reflection should also help us to see that for Plato, even constructed models are copies or images of perfect and natural in the sense of unconstructed Ideas.

What we want to know is not whether it is possible for the perfectly just or unjust man to come to exist but rather who is happier, the existing person who comes as close as possible to perfect justice or the reverse. We have been making "a paradigm in speech of the good city" as a painter might make a paradigm of the most beautiful man. The painting is no less good because the most beautiful man cannot be shown to exist. So too the good city is no less good if it cannot be shown to be possible. This passage implicitly compares making the city in speech with painting rather than with discovering the good city. It raises a problem that Socrates does not explicitly mention here but that will come up in the course of our analysis. Speaking makes use of an artificial language that is not a perfect exhibition of the natural order but a "model" or interpretation of that order. This means that the city in speech is also imperfect; we fall away from perfection, namely, the direct and complete apprehension of the city itself—not the model but the Platonic Idea or what Aristotle calls the essence—if, of course, there is such a thing as the Idea of the good, just, or beautiful city (472d4–e5). That this is a genuine concern to Plato is shown by the reference, in the *Republic* and elsewhere, to noetic intuition, that is, the pure mental apprehension of the being of existing things. As we shall see, the noetic intuition is not unspeakable; up to a point, at least, we can say what we have seen.[3] But *noēsis* is not in itself a process of producing propositions or *logoi*; this is called *dianoia*. We cannot see the Ideas (*noēmata*) perfectly if our access to them is filtered through *dianoia*. Perfect vision requires that noetic intuition be prior to, although not independent of, discourse. I mean by this that the content (*noēma*) of the intuition cannot be produced discursively, although once seen, it can be described. Discourse is about something other than itself. But knowledge is possible if and only if we can indeed describe what we have seen, and this seems to render intuition epistemically subordinate to *dianoia*. Even if I can see an Idea in itself, I need to communicate to myself and others what I have seen, in order to be able to claim that I know something. Pure silence is not knowledge.

There is, then, the following hierarchy in Socrates's distinctions. First, we have the perfect city, which cannot exist in speech or in deed but is a kind of limit toward which spoken models of this city converge asymptotically. Second, there is the spoken version of the perfect city that we are presumably being given in the *Republic* but that might be presented in quite a different form to a different audience and under different dramatic circumstances. Third, there are actual or (as we now say) historical cities, which are still more unjust and less good than the second kind, because they are subject to the full panoply of the contingency of human experience. As Socrates puts it, it is the nature of acting to attain less truth than speaking; we can come closer to the perfect city in speech than in deed (473a1–4). To this I add the Platonic point that it is the nature of speaking to attain less truth than being. At least this is so with respect to things of which there are Platonic Ideas.

If we restrict ourselves to the explicit statement of Socrates in the present passage, there is no reference to the perfect city beyond speech. But the description of the city in speech has been characterized as incomplete at more than one point; for example, the laws of the marketplace were left to the citizens to promulgate. Again, the city in speech depends for its possibility upon philosopher-kings, and these in turn depend upon the existence of Ideas. But as Socrates will tell Glaucon, he is incapable of presenting a full account of the doctrine of Ideas, just as he was previously incapable of presenting a full account of whether the soul does everything as a unity or via distinct parts. In fact, it is easy to see that no matter how much detail we fill in, we shall never be able to describe every aspect of life in the good city, because living cities are in continuous motion and change, and call for accommodations of rules, principles, and laws to the contingent particularity of everyday life. The general principles of the city in speech are enough to guide us in the task of filling in these details on the basis of each set of circumstances that we face, but not enough to tell us what we must actually do in each such set.

Let us for the moment reserve comment on the perfect city or perfect paradigm of the just man as entities existing beyond the full reach of articulate discourse. Socrates is now ready to indicate the one change that would be necessary to transform an actual city into the good city. He starts from the bottom and looks up to the city in speech. And this change is what he calls the third wave that threatens to capsize his argument in laughter. This wave is even more laughable than naked men and women wrestling together in the palaistra. "Unless philosophers are kings in the [actual] cities or those now called kings and rulers philosophize genuinely and sufficiently, and political power and philosophy should fall together into one and the same thing, and those natures who are now heading separately to one or another of these should be prevented from doing so by necessity, there is no end of evils, my dear Glaucon, for the cities, nor I think for the human genus, nor will the polity that we have just described in speech ever grow into possibility and see the light of the sun" (473c11–e2).[4]

It seems to be obvious that there is no point in forcing a king or ruler who is not by nature a philosopher to combine politics with philosophy. We are left with the need to force philosophers to combine philosophy with ruling. What should also be obvious, but is not usually mentioned, is that the philosophers in question must be those who accept Socrates's interpretation of the good city. There are no factions in this city, and therefore it is essential that there be one homogeneous and permanent philosophical teaching about politics. How much of Socrates's theoretical views must be accepted by the philosopher-kings is not yet altogether clear. What will shortly become evident is that by "philosopher," Socrates refers to persons of outstanding theoretical and practical gifts who have received a very specific kind of education. I note in passing the reference to the possible "growth" of the city into the sunlight. This metaphor is a preparation for the discussion of the Idea of the Good.

Socrates says that it will now be plain why he hesitated to discuss the question of possibility. We should remember that the term *philosopher* is relatively late and was apparently coined by Pythagoras, from whom Plato adopted it, to refer to those who aspire to wisdom but do not yet possess it. The educated Athenian would have difficulty in distinguishing between "philosopher" and "sophist," and would associate the latter not with justice or the capacity to rule but rather with word splitting, eristics, and making money by teaching others how to make the worse speech prevail over the better. Even those who were better informed would think of apolitical speculators like Parmenides and Heraclitus who had no political philosophy but were immersed in the study of being, nature, or genesis. Furthermore, despite or because of Socrates's virtual creation of political philosophy, the proposal to make philosophers kings is one that would be ridiculed by a large majority of Athenians. The magnitude of this "third wave" is also clear from the fact that Socrates and Glaucon do not refer to the first two waves about women and children. Glaucon alludes to them indirectly when he says that very many extraordinary men will strip for action against Socrates, but the cause of their outrage is the doctrine of the philosopher king, not the opening of all professions to qualified women or the principle of women and children in common. It looks as if the dislike by the many of philosophy is stronger than the difficulties raised by the natural difference between the sexes (473e6–474a4).

Socrates blames Glaucon for his present predicament, although it was Polemarchus and Adeimantus who interrupted him at the beginning of Book Five to demand a full account of the principle of women and children in common. Glaucon, however, has regularly taken the lead in encouraging Socrates to speak openly about difficult problems (e.g., 450b6–c5). Once again he offers to assist Socrates in repelling his many potential critics by supplying good will, encouragement, and perhaps more subtle answers than another might give to Socrates's questions. Socrates accepts the offer and suggests that they begin by explaining what is meant here by "philosopher." In making this suggestion, he also says that only those whom he is about to describe, that is, those who possess the proper nature, are to be permitted to philosophize or rule. In other words, there is to be no private profession of philosophy in the just city until the age of retirement from office by the philosopher-kings. It would of course be going too far to say that Socrates banishes philosophy as well as poetry from the beautiful city. But he restricts the practice of both on the basis of political exigency (474a5–c4). We should therefore guard against the too hasty conclusion that, despite the difficulty of the discussion of philosophy in the *Republic*, this one dialogue contains Plato's full account of its nature, something that is excluded by the Second and Seventh Letters.

3

The discussion of women and children illustrated both directly and indirectly the political problem of bodily eros. The innovative description of the nature of the philosopher begins with a reference to another branch of bodily eros, namely, pederasty. Part of Glaucon's suitability for the role of main interlocutor in the *Republic* is the fact that he is a dedicated pederast. Whereas women are free to be philosophers if they possess the proper nature, heterosexual love is not used as an orienting metaphor in the introduction of the erotic nature of the potential philosopher. I have suggested elsewhere, and shall repeat here, that pederasty is in the Platonic dialogues a sign of the detachment of eros from politics, as is most obvious in the massive fact that it cannot lead to sexual reproduction. Socrates goes to great efforts in his treatment of women to abolish the family, but he cannot suppress the necessity of sexual reproduction to the city and the preservation of familial relationships among members of different generations of guardians. The city is a family (or at least this is true of the extended guardian class). But homosexual relations are the opposite of a family; or at least they were until quite recently.

However, from a Platonic point of view, the contemporary desire of homosexuals to marry, or at least to live together in fidelity and love, even to raise children via adoption or artificial insemination, while it expresses something very important about political life, has nothing to do with the symbolic significance of pederasty for the discussion of philosophical eros. Indeed, from that standpoint, the desire to "normalize" homosexual relations is a sign of the triumph of politics over philosophy. In a striking sense, such normalization is an *unnatural* distortion of the inner philosophical significance of pederasty. That significance is rooted in a detachment from the city, even at the most literal level; pederasty was against the law in Athens, and as the comedies of Aristophanes suggest, it was an object of ridicule to the average citizen, not an activity to be lauded, as it was by a small proportion of the educated upper class. The second element (the first being the rejection of childbearing) in the symbolic significance of pederasty is that, in the classical Greek world, women were regarded as unsuited to philosophy, which was, in one form or another, an element in the education of adolescent males. Again the political dimension is paramount. Philosophy makes young women unsuited for preparing to assume the management of a house and the rearing of children. This is precisely why Socrates's proposals concerning women were so revolutionary. The ostensibly greater philosophical capacity of boys makes more plausible the transformation of bodily eros into love of the soul, and thence of the Ideas. Incidentally, the Athenians viewed philosophy as appropriate to youths but not to mature men, whose natural occupation is politics.

In the *Gorgias*, Callicles makes explicit the connection between philosophy and pederasty as seen from the standpoint of the statesman or politician. Glaucon, we should remember, is himself a youth, for whom the opposition between pederasty and politics has not yet arisen. I do not of course mean to suggest that no Athenian statesmen were pederasts. I am speaking entirely of the metaphorical role played by pederasty in the Platonic dialogues. Pederasty and philosophy are perversions of the political life, and this would be so even if every statesman in Athens were a fervent pederast. On this assumption, the pederasts would be forced to marry women and have children by them, even, so to speak, if their hearts were not in it.

This is the minimum background for appreciating the role of Glaucon in the present stage of the discussion. As to the substantive part of the discussion, Glaucon does not understand, and is apparently hesitant in admitting of himself (475a3–4), the characteristic of the extreme lover, namely, to love every boy, whether handsome or ugly. I am not prepared to verify this assertion; indeed, it strikes me as an extremely unlikely generalization. The more we love beautiful music, the more we detest ugly music. I suspect that the more we love beautiful human beings, the less we love ugly persons. There is an important exception, or apparent exception, to this rule. We may fall in love with someone who is ugly yet come to see this person as beautiful because of our feelings for him or her. But this actually substantiates the principle; what we are looking for is beauty, even the illusion of beauty if we must. This is why we say that love is blind.

Socrates plays upon Glaucon's comprehensive delight in boys to establish the thesis that whoever loves anything loves "the entire form" (*eidos*). His other examples are wine and honor; but the point of these examples is not that a lover of wine loves all kinds of wine, good and bad. It is rather that if the lover of wine is deprived of superior varieties, he will accommodate his appetite to inferior specimens. So too lovers of honor will settle for a lower office if the highest offices are denied to them (474d3–475b7). One could object that alcoholics love all wines, good or bad, just as over-sexed or mentally ill men may love, that is desire, every female. But alcoholism and satyriasis are illnesses or disorders of the soul, not paradigms for philosophy. Socrates infers from his examples that philosophers desire all of wisdom, not just some part of it. Thus anyone who loves only one or a few kinds of learning cannot be a lover of learning or a philosopher (475b8–c5).

Let us grant to Socrates that the philosophical nature loves learning of all kinds at the beginning of the educational process. As that nature matures, however, it must surely come to subordinate some forms of knowledge to others. For example, as we are about to see, the potential philosopher must concentrate for many years on the study of mathematics, and this requires him or her to neglect other branches of learning, such as poetry, medicine, law, warfare, and even shoemaking and carpentry. This is, after all, the principle underlying the tripartite structure of the good city. To indulge in an erotic metaphor, one may admire someone else's wife without attempting to seduce her. To put this in another and more general way, wisdom is not the same thing as learning, although there cannot be any doubt that those who seek the former are predisposed to the latter. But there is also no doubt that an excessive love of learning can be an obstacle to the love of wisdom.

One can be partially learned, but it is impossible to be partially wise. Perhaps we can say that partial wisdom is just philosophy, or the love of what one does not yet possess. There is of course a difficulty here that was emphasized by Hegel. How can we love something that we do not know? I suggest the following answer. There is a difference between a complete possession of wisdom and an anticipation of it. It is in fact quite possible to fall in love with someone at first sight, and so with someone whom one does not as yet know. What is essential is that we be acquainted with that person. Interestingly enough, the person whom we love need not even be real; we may have imagined her or him in our daydreams. Eros supplies us with the awareness of love, which guides us to seek out its human manifestation. Hegel did not become a philosopher only after he achieved wisdom; he must have known in advance the right direction in which to pursue it.

Glaucon himself raises the problem I introduced a moment ago. If philosophers are those who pursue every kind of knowledge insatiably, then in many cases the pursuit will actually prevent them from philosophizing. He mentions as examples lovers of sights and of hearing, by which latter he means those who run from one musical performance to another and so have no interest in listening to philosophical discussions. Socrates says that the genuine philosophers are lovers of the sight of truth. Glaucon agrees but demands clarification (475d1–e5). Before we study Socrates's reply, let us pause for a moment. The senses of seeing and hearing are cited as instruments for falling in love with sights and sounds. We can say that these are the most philosophical of senses because seeing provides us with the widest range of forms (as Aristotle notes), including written texts, and hearing enables us to follow the speeches of those who explain the forms that we see. In other words, seeing and hearing are closer to thinking than are touching, tasting, and smelling.

This is not without its qualifications, but it makes a rough and ready sense. What, however, does it mean to see the truth? We see colors, shapes, and forms, both separately and in various relations to one another. But truth is not an additional visible entity, whether separate from or attached to such entities, that can be seen to complete them in some way. We do frequently claim "to see the truth," but what we see is not a visible object of the sort just mentioned. Neither do linguistic propositions pop into our intellects with little signs attached to them marked "this proposition is true." The literal interpretation of such sensory metaphors is tedious, but it serves to bring out the inner obscurity of the claim to see the truth. We see other things, about which we think, and it is thinking, not seeing or hearing, that reveals the truth (or fails to arrive at it).

On the other hand, it seems to be impossible to address the question "What is thinking?" without recourse to sensory terminology. This is not simply because our senses furnish the intellect with "data" about which to think. Thinking itself is like listening to oneself speak, with the single crucial exception of those occasions when we suddenly understand something. This act of understanding is not itself speaking, or listening to speech, because discourse is propositional, and the meaning of a proposition is another proposition, not a sound or a sight. We seem to come closer to this universal experience by saying "I see" rather than "I hear you" (an extremely common phrase in contemporary American English). But I believe that the closeness is an illusion. This difficulty will soon become extremely important when we arrive at the doctrine of Ideas, which is expounded primarily in terms of the primacy of intellectual vision or intuition. I remind the reader of the Heideggerian critique of Husserl's perceptualism, continued by Derrida and others against all forms of "Platonist" preference for "presence" or complete visibility, as opposed to concealment, absence, and related notions of partial invisibility. My own view is that these doctrines are as closely wedded to the metaphors of sense perception as are their Platonist enemies. We cannot identify something as absent or concealed unless we see the context in which it should be present or unveiled. I shall develop these remarks at the appropriate moment. But the point required comment because it is already introduced in Socrates's initial presentation of what it is to be a philosopher.

Socrates has introduced the nature of the genuine philosopher as a lover of the sight of the truth, in contrast to the lovers of sights and sounds. We speak of seeing the truth, hearing it, and by extension, even of "tasting," "touching," or "smelling" it. And yet, it is plain that these are metaphors, however helpful, since truth is not a sensation, or even an object constructed of sensible properties, like a painting, a song, a person, a tree, a rock, and so on. The most obvious sense of truth is that which we utter in saying of something that it is such-and-such. But we could also be wrong or consciously lie in uttering such a statement. The statement must say of what is that it is, or of what is not that it is not, this or that property (cf. Aristotle). In other words, truth is not just talk but talk that tells us what is the case. Therefore we must know in advance what is true about something before we can truly say that it is so-and-so or such-and-such. Truth is not established by perceiving the correspondence between how things are and the statement that tells us how they are. In order to grasp this correspondence, we must already know the truth about how things are.

It thus looks as if what seemed to be the most obvious sense of truth is actually nothing more than the communication or affirmation of the truth that we know already, in a way that is prior to the correspondence between our propositions and the states of affairs they describe. In other words, we cannot define truth entirely in linguistic terms, for if the meaning of a linguistic expression is another linguistic expression, there will be an infinite regress of substitutions, no one of which is intelligible in itself or as it stands. In the process of assigning meanings, syntactic or semantic, to functions and words, we are not simply talking to ourselves but manipulating signs, and both the signs and the manipulations have already been understood. The fact that thinking is expressed in language in no way proves that it is identical with talking or listening (itself an extension of talking). We have to know what we are talking about, and this knowing is not simply more talking.

In order to explain what Socrates (that is, Plato) means by an Idea, it is not necessary to develop an exhaustive account of truth. One could rather say that the doctrine of Ideas is motivated by the impossibility of arriving at a noncircular analysis of the nature of truth. Socrates starts with the facts of ordinary experience: We are capable of distinguishing between truth and falsehood.

There is no way to doubt this experience except on the basis of assumptions that must themselves be taken as true. To mention only the most obvious, it must be true to say, "I do not know whether proposition p is true." But Socrates does not remain at the level of ordinary or everyday language. He takes the metaphors of sensation that we use to explain thinking the truth and goes on to show that they are unsatisfactory because knowing the truth is nothing like perceiving a sensory quality. Despite the proliferation of visual imagery in his description of thinking the Ideas, the point of that imagery is to enable us to understand that *what* we think cannot be sensations. The famous Socratic question "What is X?" does not ask for the names of separate properties and of sensations (color, smell, and so on) but asks rather for the *paradeigma*, the pattern of constituent elements that makes X what it is, rather than non-X or Y.

The problem, of course, is how we apprehend the entity that corresponds to the name "X" in any given case. As a preliminary formulation, let us say that this entity stands to thinking as does color to seeing and sound to hearing. But this formulation is quickly seen to be inadequate, since thinking X is nothing like seeing a color or hearing a sound. By "thinking" is meant here the process of grasping the aforementioned pattern. I refer not to Aristotle's *koinē aisthēsis*, which unites the sensed properties into an identifiable sensed object, but to the cognition that the unity we sense is an object of such-and-such a kind. *Koinē aisthēsis* may present us with a unified sensory object, but it does not tell us that the object is a so-and-so of such-and-such a kind. This last expression rather points to the unity, identity, and stability of X as nonsensuous. Sensory metaphors tell us what thinking is like, but not what it is. By the same token, they tell us what Platonic Ideas (paradigms) are like, but not what they are. And the same is true, of course, for the modern language of concepts. Whatever may be the exact contribution of the senses to the act of understanding a concept, that act is not sensuous. Perhaps the simplest way in which to say this is that the understanding of the concept makes sense out of the sensory information to which it directs its attention; "making sense" requires us to talk, but the thoughts that are presented to our discursive intelligence come from a zone of silence and darkness. But we are at a loss to describe silence and darkness except as privations. Trying to describe how the intellect moves from sense data and individual properties to a unified X of such-and-such a kind is like trying to describe the connection of causality in terms of perception. We are left with the statement that A always precedes B, and so on, but not with a description of the causal link itself.

In short, when I understand something, I can say what I have understood, but to take discursive thinking as the road toward understanding is not the same as actually understanding something. When you utter a proposition, I understand it not simply by hearing the words but by an unspoken act of apprehension that furnishes me with the meaning, which I can then communicate verbally. And the same is true of mathematical analyses of the nature of truth. I do not understand an equation by writing down another equation. I must first understand before I can write down anything relevant to the question of the meaning of that proposition. Understanding accompanies and guides perception and discursive thinking; it is not the same as these functions.

4

So much for preliminaries. Now let us turn to Socrates's exposition to Glaucon at 475e9. Socrates begins a bit abruptly, by establishing that the noble and the shameful (alternatively, the beautiful and the ugly) are each one thing, but taken as opposites (that is, as a two-term relation), they are two. "The same *logos* is true of the just and the unjust, the good and the evil, and all the forms (*eidōn*). Each is itself one, but by appearing everywhere in a community with deeds, bodies, and each other, each seems to be many" (476a4–7). This is the famous problem of the one and the many, which Socrates describes in the *Philebus* in more abstract and concise terms. An *eidos*, as has already been established by usage rather than analysis, is a family or kind that unites a collection of things each of which is the same such-and-such. The form is of course not itself the collection of particular instances but what each has in common with the other members of the collection. The instances of justice may differ in many ways from one another, but they are all the same with respect to the properties that qualify them for membership in the class of just things. It seems that the class or *eidos* itself cannot be included among just things; if it could be, we would generate a third-man argument, that is, we would require a metaclass of just things that includes the class itself as well as the members of the class, and so on indefinitely. This causes a number of difficulties for Socrates. For example, the class or form of beautiful things is also beautiful, and the same could presumably be said of the good. We have to find a way to speak, say, of the beauty of the Idea of beauty without dissolving the line between a class and its members. One possibility is to say that some forms exhibit the very property that they transmit to their instances. Good, beautiful, and just would be candidates for this way of speaking, whereas the form of the cow, for example, would not.

Socrates, however, is not now at that level of technical complexity. He makes the much simpler point that those who love sights and sounds love noble or beautiful instances of these, "but their discursive intelligence [*di-*

anoia] is unable to see and enjoy the nature of the beautiful itself" (476b6–8). He does not say that they are unable to see the form of sight or sound itself; to do so would make the discussion much too difficult for Glaucon. As it is, Glaucon raises no objection to references to the just, the beautiful, and the good in themselves. He has been prepared for these expressions by the long pursuit of perfect justice, that is, the paradigm of the just man. In everyday life, no one asks about the cow itself, only about cows and classes of cows (healthy, good milk givers, prime beef, and so on). But we do ask about justice itself, because there are so many specious claims to justice, and the genuine thing is indispensable for social and political life. And something similar could be said of the beautiful and the good. I regard this as a striking point; everyday life directs us toward forms like those of the just, beautiful, or good in themselves.

Socrates next compares seeing beautiful things, but not seeing the beautiful itself, to dreaming. Dreaming takes a likeness to be the thing itself; for example, I may dream of Napoleon, and so long as I am dreaming, I take him to be the historical personage. So too daydreamers take individual beautiful things to be beauty itself. Those on the other hand who perceive both beautiful things and the beautiful itself, in which the former participate, are awake, that is, not dreaming. Again, Socrates is sticking closely to everyday life. No sane person would confuse justice itself for a just man, for reasons too obvious to enumerate. But someone might very easily deny that there is a cow itself in which real cows participate, but which is in fact more genuinely "cow-ish" than real cows (476c2–d4).

The discursive intellect of the man who "knows" (in the sense of being able to identify: *gignōskontos*) beauty itself, is in the state of possessing knowledge, whereas the man who cannot distinguish between the form and its instances is opining, not knowing. Such a man will become angry with us when we try to correct him. We must find a way to soothe and gently persuade him, and to conceal from him that he is sick. The way proceeds as follows. We ask him whether someone who knows, knows something or nothing. Glaucon, who is deputed the task of answering for the man, says that we know something. Furthermore, we know what exists (*on*) or is something, for how could we know, in the sense of being acquainted with or identifying, what does not exist, i.e. is no thing at all (*mē on*: 476d5–477a1)?[5]

Once again, this is a commonsense assertion, not a statement of ontological principles. And yet, the "ontology" follows directly from common sense. *On*, the neuter singular participle of *eimi*, "I am," refers to anything at all, and hence to any particular thing that is a possible object of experience or content of thought. Socrates is here relying, as we all do, on the commonsense principle that to be is to be something in particular. There cannot be "something" that is not a "thing." At this level of analysis, the question of "being," in the sense of a general form that is different from but gives existence to the particular things that participate in it, does not arise. Such a question is not part of everyday life in the way that justice itself is. We do of course speak regularly of "everything" in the sense of the cosmos, but hardly of a form of everything, of which the cosmos is an instance. Words like "everything" and "being" lead us in quite a different direction from words like "justice" and "beauty." And the problem of reflexivity is especially visible in these two cases, since the form "everything" must itself be something in particular, just as "being" is a being.

In this context, then, "no thing" must be understood as the negation of "thing," that is, "something in particular," and not as the name of a mysterious metaphysical nonentity. Even in dialogues like the *Sophist*, which contains his fullest technical treatment of the problem of nonbeing, Plato remains true to father Parmenides and tries to avoid saying "absolute nothing" (*to mēdamōs on*) by interpreting "not" as a differentiating term, very much like Aristotle's understanding of negation, but which Plato calls "otherness." Once again, the principle holds good that to be is to be something in particular; hence not to be is always not to be this or that, but therefore to be something other. As Glaucon asks, in a Swiftian mood, "How could we know the thing that is not?"

Socrates infers from Glaucon's answers that what entirely exists (is an *on*) is entirely knowable, whereas what in no way exists (is no *on* at all) is entirely unknowable (477a2–4). This passage is excessively cryptic. To be "entirely" is not to come into and pass out of existence, and so not to exist in part. Socrates assumes that since "not to be" is the opposite of "to be," and what is not cannot possibly be known, therefore "to be" is identical with "to be knowable," the opposite of "cannot be known at all." But the conclusion does not follow. We still require a demonstration that being is by its nature knowable. Nothing excludes the possibility that some completely existing entity is partly or completely unknowable. The corollary to this assumption makes more sense, namely, the assertion that what is not fully, and so participates in both being and nonbeing, cannot be fully known. But this corollary does not depend upon the identity of being and knowability. It simply assumes that what is in some way, or to some degree, may be knowable, since there is something to know. With respect to the Platonic Ideas, each is fully what it is; therefore, we may assume, each could be fully known if our intellects were capable of grasping every manifestation of being.

Ignorance is therefore more intelligible than knowledge, odd as that may sound. It is easy to understand that we cannot know what does not exist, and so that what exists only partly is necessarily partly unknowable. But it is not necessarily partly knowable. By claiming that to be is to be knowable, Socrates sets up the necessary condition of extreme rationalism that sits uneasily by the side of his many professions of ignorance, not to mention the assertion that wisdom is inaccessible to human beings (a claim that I shall examine later, when we come to the allegory of the cave in Book Seven).

A genuine being, then, is what it is fully and permanently. Since generated things are imperfect, and there is presumably just one Idea or form corresponding to each way of being, the Idea is in each case the only genuine being of its kind. If there is anything that both is and is not (*einai te kai mē einai*), it will lie between pure being (*tou eilikrinōs ontos*) and that which is in no way a thing. How this can be so is not explained, but I assume that he means something akin to what I said a moment ago. To repeat, genesis is a mixture of being and nonbeing, that is, it exhibits itself in the process by which things move toward and away from what it is in the fullest sense to be a thing of that kind. As incomplete, that is, as coming and ceasing to be, they are imperfect images of the original form. "That which is in no way a thing" is not a thing or a form, and hence not the negation (or "other") of some other thing or form. It is no thing at all, hence nothing; and therefore it cannot be known or even be the object of belief or opinion.

Socrates continues: that which both is and is not, is between what is entirely and what entirely is not. Since knowledge is of what is, whereas ignorance is of what is not, there must be some cognitive condition that is in between knowledge and ignorance (477a6–b2). This is identified as opinion (*doksa*). Opinion is a *dunamis* other than knowledge (477b5). This word can be translated either as "power" or as "potentiality." These are not synonyms, because although power often means "potentiality," it is sometimes indistinguishable from actuality. For example, the king is actually the ruler of his country even if he is not at this moment performing an act in his official capacity. A boxing champion actually has the power to render me unconscious, even though he is simply standing in his corner, waiting for the bell to ring. In general, something is potentially X if it has the power to become X. In the present passage, *dunamis* refers to a mental faculty, a power that we have for apprehending objects of cognition in a certain way that is actually ours, even if we are not using it at the moment.

Socrates goes on to say that opinion is directed at something different from that to which knowledge is directed; the difference is in accord with their distinct powers. He asks whether knowledge does not refer by nature to being (a thing), that is, to knowing how things are (that is, exist), but instead of going on to opinion, he breaks off and says that at this point a distinction is necessary. Socrates proceeds to define powers as "a *genos* [family, class] of beings [*tōn ontōn*] by which we are capable of what we are capable," and so too with everything else. Sight and hearing are powers, "if you understand the form [*eidos*] to which I refer" (477b7–c4). "Form" seems to be used synonymously with "class." In other words, powers are one form or class of beings. Nothing is said here to cast light on the question of whether there is an Idea corresponding to this form or class. This is connected to the question, also not yet posed, whether there are Ideas of artifacts or of natural things only. Some powers are natural, but some are not.

Socrates goes on to provide an obscure account of powers. "I see neither color nor shape in a power nor any of the other things that I see in many other cases at which I look when I distinguish one thing from another for myself. In a power, I look only at this, at that to which it is directed and what it accomplishes" (477c6–d1: see Griffith's note). A power is not a physical object; hence it cannot be apprehended by sense perception. This shows us that the term *form*, previously applied to "power," has to be distinguished from "shape" (*morphē*). At least on this count, a power is like a Platonic Idea. Despite Socrates's use of "I see" or "I look," it is plain that he is referring to a kind of thinking that is not really analogous to sense perception.

Powers differ in accord with their objects and work. Since knowledge and opinion are different powers that accomplish something different, they must be directed toward different things. The power of knowledge is to know how being is (Griffith: "knowing things as they are"), while "opinion opines." But it cannot opine the same things that knowledge knows, nor can it opine the things that are not. The upshot is as follows. Opinion is neither as clear as knowledge nor as obscure as ignorance. Hence it lies between the two (477d7–478d4). Let us recall that opinion lies between knowledge and ignorance and its objects partake of both being and nonbeing. Opinion is the cognitive act appropriate to the dream state, whether waking or asleep, in which we take a likeness for an original. The likeness must reflect enough of the original to allow us to identify it as a likeness of this particular kind, for example a beautiful body. But it cannot reflect the complete original, since then it would be indistinguishable from it. The one who opines (as distinct from the knower) assumes further that the beauty in the particular body is the original. He does not see its inferiority to the original, nor has he asked himself how what he takes to be the original can be the same in many bodies, each of which comes into being and perishes, so that the beauty in each case did not exist at one time and will not exist at another. Belief or opinion thus takes the being of the copy as if it were the original, but forgets its nonbeing. Belief is genuine knowledge to the extent that it correctly apprehends the particular manifestation as of such-and-such a kind; but it is genuine ignorance to the extent that it does not and cannot know the nonexistent part of that manifestation. It does not see the original that is what it is at all times and in every manifestation. To look ahead, opinion does not see the Platonic Idea but sees only its instances. And these instances neither are (that is, fully or purely) nor are not (that is, completely).

Has Socrates answered the question why the objects of opinion cannot be the same as those of knowledge? He defines opinion as taking a likeness for the original. For example, we might take the beauty of a youthful body to be the genuine and complete manifestation of what it is to be beautiful. But the body ages, undergoes accidents, and deteriorates in various ways; this shows us that the beauty of the physical body is transient. Furthermore, we experience beauty in many different bodies, and whereas the manifestation of physical beauty will vary in its details, we recognize that each manifestation is beautiful. Let us say that physical beauty varies in time and place. But what does not vary is that each such manifestation is beautiful. What is common to all beautiful bodies is not itself a body. Modern philosophers would be inclined to refer to it as the concept of beauty, but this does not meet Socrates's point. It is not the concept of beauty that makes individual bodies beautiful. On the contrary, we can form a concept of beauty only after we have encountered the pure form or Idea of beauty itself. Since the Idea (paradigm, form) is neither an individual instance of beauty nor a concept but is beauty itself, which shows itself indirectly or as partially concealed by its physical manifestation, it is not the object of opinion. That object is the "in-between" instance of physical beauty. It is in between because it participates in both the being of physical existence and the nonbeing of the incompleteness of genesis.

If this reasoning is sound, it follows that there can be no opinion of an Idea. As Socrates presents the matter, the moment we recognize that transient instances of beauty are imperfect manifestations of beauty itself, we "know" the Idea. This kind of knowledge is not discursive, which is why Socrates regularly compares it to vision. There is an intellectual (noetic) act of recognizing the Idea that is somehow analogous to seeing. Let us call it intuition. Seeing in the usual sense is the perception of a particular body; intuition is the perception of the beautiful itself. Let us note carefully that each Idea, say that of beauty, is "general" in the sense that it covers all of its instances. But it is also "singular," that is, one particular Idea and none other. Still open is the question of whether there can be discursive knowledge of Ideas. Socrates will allude to this point later, when he introduces the method of dialectic. There cannot be any doubt that Socrates regards it as possible to state some of the characteristics of Ideas, and to argue for their necessity, whether or not we can know them scientifically in the Greek sense of that term, which of course excludes probability or belief and is indubitable as well as a permanent acquisition. As I pointed out above, in the *Republic* Socrates associates the noetic apprehension of pure

Ideas with the discursive intelligence. Unfortunately, he does not explain what can be known of an Idea and what cannot.

There is a very important corollary to the preceding results. There has been considerable debate in the scholarly literature about not only what Socrates means by an Idea but also whether he—that is to say, Plato—actually "believed" in their existence. My first response is that there cannot be a belief or an opinion about the Ideas, as we have just seen. To put it as concisely as possible, either we see them or we don't. The arguments that Socrates presents on behalf of the Ideas are certainly not rigorous, nor are they always logically valid. This, I think, is not a defect in his presentation but something demanded by the nature of the problem. Plato holds that being and intelligibility depend upon the formal properties that constitute what it is to be a thing of a certain kind. I think that this is undoubtedly true, and I have never seen a plausible, let alone convincing, refutation of the point. Even those who reduce being to genesis, and genesis itself to chaos, do so by making discursive use of the identifiable elements of the ostensible illusion of human existence. Once more stated with extreme concision, the absence of formal structure leaves us with nothing to talk about and thus nothing to say. Whereas it may be true that "things fall apart," it is not true that the formal properties by which we identify the things that are falling apart are themselves falling apart. They are present or absent, fully visible or partially concealed. But as partially concealed, they do not lose part of their existence. We are able to infer their full existence from the parts we can observe.

The problem is in the gap between intuition and sensory vision. Ideas have no sensory properties. This makes it very attractive to talk about them as though they were concepts. But I have already pointed out that concepts are themselves discursive artifacts rather than the genuine manifestation of the beings that we describe, or try to describe, with concepts. In other words, concepts are the product of *dianoia*, and they refer to what is apprehended by *noēsis*. To come back to the text, the objects of opinion lie between those of knowledge and ignorance.[6] Knowledge is of paradigms, forms, or Ideas; and these "are" in the full sense of being entirely what it is to be a thing of a certain sort. Ignorance is the complete absence of knowledge; hence it has no objects (a better way of putting the point than to say that ignorance is directed toward nonbeing, which sounds as if we are reifying nothingness). The objects of opinion both are and are not. That is, they are imperfect copies of what it is to be an object of that sort. A copy is not nothing; it is precisely a copy or image. But as a copy, it falls short of the original, and is not that original (478d5–12).

We must therefore find objects of the sort just described, namely, those that are objects of opinion. Opinions vary, or more precisely, particular instances of this or that nature can give rise to diverse opinions, depending upon how we consider them. What looks beautiful to one person seems ugly to another; what is just to one is unjust to another; and so too with the holy. Socrates gives another kind of example; the half can seem to be double; that is, two can be seen either as twice one or half of four; so too the light can appear heavy and the heavy light. Socrates does not give examples of objects like cows or trees. These differ from his own examples; we are able to misperceive or misidentify cows as horses or trees as persons, but a cow is not correctly seen as something other than itself, whereas it is not a mistake to see twice two as half of eight rather double the pair. The cow does not shift its form; half and double do (478e1–479c5).

The upshot is that all of Socrates's examples are ambiguous; one cannot say that they are one thing more than another. Socrates therefore suggests that we place them between being and not to be (*metaksu ousias te kai tou mē einai*: 479c7). Socrates varies his terms in this passage; the expression *paradigm* has long since been dropped in favor of *eidos* and (at 479a1–2) "the beautiful itself and an Idea [*idean*] of the beautiful." In the present passage, the infinitive replaces the participle in the expression denoting "not being," and *ousia*, a very difficult word to translate, replaces *on*. One has the impression that Socrates, in this statement, is shifting from thing language to a more general conception of being and nonbeing. Whether this is right or not, it is clear that he does not define his terms with technical precision but says just enough to elicit agreement with Glaucon.

Socrates concludes that we have now found that the many customary beliefs of the multitude "roll around somewhere between nonbeing [*mē ontos*] and pure being" (*tou ontos eilikrinō*: 479d3–5). In other words, they are moving, not standing still, as do knowledge and, in its own way, ignorance. This motion is the mark of their imperfection; they continuously exchange one identity for another. Such are the objects of opinion, namely, of those who do not see the beautiful itself and the Ideas (as we can now call them) of the other kinds. People of this sort believe but do not know. Those, on the other hand, who see the Ideas, know and do not opine. We shall be right to call the latter "lovers of wisdom" (philosophers) and the former "lovers of opinion" (*philodoksous*: 479e1–480a13).

Let us now recall that we set out to find the philosophers in order to show that it is not laughable (473c6–9) for them to be kings in the good city. Socrates will have more to say about the philosophical nature, but it is plain that the first and most important qualification is to "see" the Ideas. Unfortunately, the number of those who are able to do so is very small (476b10–11). Since the majority of human beings are, if not ignorant, at best lovers of opinion, we can safely say that they will regard the doctrine of Ideas as itself laughable.[7] And the auxiliaries or soldier-guardians, who do not qualify for the philosophical class, must be included among those who laugh. What, then, is the political point of the vision of the Ideas? What does it contribute to the actualization of justice?

The implicit claim is that the vision of the Idea of justice is necessary in order to guarantee just rule. The claim would be supported by the following argument. In order for an act to be just, it must participate in the Idea of justice. For example, if the king is deciding some point of law, say, the rules that govern commercial transactions in the marketplace, and has to choose between two courses of action, he will inspect them both in order to determine which is an image of the Idea of justice. But what if both alternatives participate in justice itself? Then the question becomes: Which alternative is practically superior? And this is a matter of practical judgment or prudence. One could say that at least the vision of the Idea has put us into the position of choosing between just alternatives. But I must say that I do not know what it means to decide whether a certain course of action is just by seeing whether the Idea of justice is exhibited therein. Statesmen look at actions, not Ideas, and the justice of actions is determined by their consequences in the city. No action is just in itself, only within a practical context. One could therefore argue that the Idea of justice appears in the act only after we have decided upon its justice. Surely we do not inspect each component of a political action to see if it participates in the Idea of justice. But there is an even more serious problem. We are said to have perfect knowledge of the Idea but only opinions about its spatiotemporal instances. If I look at an action, or some component of an action, I cannot have anything but an opinion about its justice. If I look deeper and now see the Idea of justice, my perfect knowledge of the Idea is not transitive to the case of the act that is its image, since these images lie in the domain between being and nonbeing. I am then in the paradoxical position of being certain of the Idea of justice but uncertain of the act that participates in that Idea.

To come at the same problem from another angle, knowing the Idea of justice gives me a definition of justice, not a judgment of what is just in the given case. That is, it is to know a general pattern that constitutes what it is to be just in any case whatsoever. But general patterns convey nothing of what specifically to do under such-and-such circumstances. I therefore cannot check through a pile of possible judgments or actions in order to see which is just until I know which pile of judgments or actions to inspect. And I know this only because I already am in a position, if not to define justice, to recognize it when I see it.

Let us take a specific example. Suppose I am trying to decide whether to vote for John McCain or Rudolph Giuliani as the Republican nominee in the American presidential election of 2004. In the first place, I cannot "see" my vote as an instance of the Idea of justice. The act of voting becomes just if and only if it is based upon just principles and is likely to have just consequences. But I cannot know in advance that my principles were soundly chosen, or that good consequences will definitely ensue. I have to see how each candidate would behave if elected. But I cannot see this until they actually are elected; and obviously enough, only one can be. I must therefore take a chance and act on my *opinion* that the choice of one of the two candidates will yield greater justice than the choice of the other. And since only one man can be elected, I shall never know if my choice was the better one. I can say that "my hands are clean" or that I acted with a good conscience and to the best of my judgment, and so I can claim to be just myself. But my vote is itself, and must forever remain, an opinion.

One arrives at the Idea of justice through purely formal reasoning, namely, that things cannot exist as something in particular or be known to be the kind of particular they are, unless there is a pattern or "formula" that expresses what it is to be a particular of that kind. It then becomes clear that the pattern is not identical with any of its images. Socrates therefore owes us an explanation of how the pattern "participates" in its images while retaining its separate identity and existence. This difficulty was made famous by Aristotle, and so far as I know, it has never been resolved satisfactorily. My own previous suggestions on this point in effect grant Aristotle that the separation thesis, which is defended in the *Republic*, must be abandoned. Ideas do not exist apart from their particulars but are fully present within them as what it is to be a particular of such-and-such a kind. The Idea is "demonstrated" simply by the existence of the particular as what it is. We run into insoluble problems when we try to say precisely what it is to be a particular of this or that kind. These problems are well represented by the Aristotelian doctrine of essence. In order to define an essence, we must know the essential attributes. But in order to know the essential attributes, we must know the essence.

Platonists must hold that we can be assured of the existence of Ideas by the very intelligibility of particulars. A particular is an imperfect manifestation of a pattern, that is, a paradigm or Idea. If these patterns themselves change constantly, then nothing can be identified as anything in particular, because to identify this particular is always to subsume it under a general formula, a formula that is not a concept but of which we can make a concept or discursive representation of what it is to be, in this case, just. This is what I shall risk calling an ontological argument. And it provides no basis for assisting us in determining which acts are just. What it does is to explain how it is possible for us to identify some act as just, once we have done so.

To say that it provides us with a basis for explaining how it is possible is itself a euphemism, or let us say an extremely incomplete metaphor. We can be certain that there are patterns or Ideas for the reasons that have now been sufficiently stated. But we cannot know these Ideas as if they were themselves things to be subsumed under, or to participate within, another Idea or pattern. And neither does Plato ever give, here or elsewhere, the slightest clue as to the *work* by which the Idea contributes being and intelligibility to the particular. He will in fact take up this topic when he comes to the Idea of the Good. But the entire discussion is admittedly inadequate, and it consists of an elaborate simile that compares the Idea of the Good to the sun. I shall reserve my analysis for the appropriate occasion. Meanwhile, I believe that we are forced to doubt that Socrates has contributed anything substantial to the question of why philosophers must be kings. The most he could be said to have shown is that they are lovers of the Ideas. But this hardly gives them practical knowledge, and hence it is not at all plain that it gives them justice. This objection, incidentally, is the tacit argument of Aristotle against his teacher in the *Nicomachean Ethics* and *Politics*.

9

The Philosophical Nature

I

Our discussion has now brought to light the philosophers and distinguished them from the nonphilosophers, although according to Socrates this would have been accomplished more adequately if we could have devoted ourselves exclusively to that one task. As it is, we have a great deal to do with respect to the original question of how the just life differs from the unjust life (VI. 484a1–b2). This opening passage in Book Six shows us that Socrates has had to accommodate his presentation of the philosophical nature to the needs of the broader investigation, which is neither precisely philosophical nor narrowly political, but starts with the question of the happiness of the life of the individual person and shifts to the happiness of the city. Otherwise put, the initial analogy between the city and the soul rules out the possibility that the individual person could be happy in an unhappy city, namely, one that is not organized in accord with Socrates's instructions. In this broad sense, the discussion is politicized. And this leads to a serious contradiction in the argument. On the one hand, the life devoted to philosophy is the best and happiest. On the other hand, even the philosopher must subordinate private happiness to political obligation. This amounts to a shift from happiness to justice.

In his résumé of our previous result, Socrates says that philosophers are those who are able to grasp what is always the same in every way, whereas nonphilosophers wander about in that which is many and various in all ways (484b3–7). The key point, however, is that the philosophers should be able to apply their vision of the one in many to the many itself, that is, as Socrates says, to guard the laws and customs of the city. Socrates speaks of guardians here rather than philosopher-kings, but the context shows that he is thinking primarily of the latter. Only those who are sharp-sighted can keep watch over anything. But there are two kinds of guardianship. One is characteristic of the soldiers, and for this type it is unnecessary to see the Ideas. Their sharp-sightedness lies in the ability to distinguish friends from enemies; otherwise, it would be better to call them loyal to the rulers. The ruler-guardians, on the other hand, are those who are not blind, in the precise sense that they have a clear paradigm in the soul of what they are to guard, namely, the giving and preserving of laws that are for the sake of the beautiful, the just, and the good. To this, Socrates adds, as though he had overheard my objections at the end of Book Five, that the ruler-guardians must not only have access to the paradigms but also possess experience and be in no way inferior to the nonphilosophers in any part of *aretē* (excellence or virtue: 484c6–d7).

The Socratic ruler combines both philosophy, that is, vision of the Ideas, and what Aristotle would call practical virtue.[1] The latter includes experience, and it reminds us of Aristotle's description of the *phronimos*, the person of prudence. But for Aristotle, the vision of the Ideas, or anything analogous to that vision, is not required by the statesman. I believe that there is no disagreement between Plato's Socrates and Aristotle about the need for philosophy in the task of constructing the paradigm of a just city. They differ on the need for philosophy on the part of the rulers of the already constructed city. To stay with Socrates, all other things being equal, the ruler is selected on the basis of the criterion of what Glaucon calls the most important gift, namely, vision of the Ideas. He accepts Socrates's claim that the ruler-guardians must see what it is to be each thing, and in particular, they must love the learning that makes clear to them the *ousia* that is always and does not wander about in genesis and destruction (485a10–b4).

I want to emphasize that none of this explains why the ruler requires vision of the Ideas in order to legislate and judge. If anything, it makes that requirement extremely dubious, since the philosophers will be fixated upon the eternal and unchanging order, and apparently they will spend as little time as possible "wandering around" in the domain of political life. It is tempting to say that Plato tries to overcome the dualism of theory and practice in his philosopher-kings, but a more accurate judgment, I believe, is that the philosopher-king exhibits perfectly the conflict between theory and practice. The writing and publication of the *Republic* is itself a revolutionary political act that sets into motion the historical dialectic of politics and philosophy. Plato expresses simultaneously the need of politics for philosophy and the danger of each for the other. If there is to be justice and happiness for human beings, philosophers must rule. But if philosophers rule, that is, if they carry through the demands of wisdom and compel the citizenry to be truly just, the result is injustice and unhappiness as well. One might infer from this that the correct procedure is to institute a moderate philosophical rule that applies wisdom prudentially to human affairs instead of going to extremes. Unfortunately, human affairs are not static; history shows the futility of instituting halfway measures. Contingent pressures would soon force the moderate philosophical rulers into one of two choices: to become ever more extreme or else to loosen their grip and allow increasing relaxation of the laws and customs.

I have suggested that the publication of the *Republic* is a kind of surrogate fulfillment of Plato's political ambitions as well as a dramatic illustration of the failure of his trips to Sicily. We are now in the domain of speculation, but not unreasonably so; the dialogue form requires it. What was impossible in Sicily in Plato's time may be possible in another time and place. So too with the claim that philosophers are unwilling to rule the city. For we also know that modern philosophers from Machiavelli and Bacon to Heidegger, Lukács, and Kojève have not been averse to engaging in politics, to say nothing of the efforts of those who mistake ideology for philosophy. What is ideology if not the extreme politicization of philosophy? And is not the *Republic* one of the most influential, perhaps *the* most influential, of the causes of the deterioration of philosophy into ideology? After all, it follows from Socrates's own statements that even he, were he offered power in a city ruled by philosophy, would be compelled to accept it, if that city were his own. But what city is the philosopher's own if not the philosophical city? And how can it be governed, if not by noble and medicinal lies?

None of these remarks is a simple contradiction of the claim that genuine philosophers would accept rule only under compulsion. The compulsion is precisely that of wishing not to be ruled by one's inferiors. Expressed positively, it is the desire to see wisdom prevail over ignorance. Without that desire, the *Republic* could never have been written; once written, its whole force is directed toward the production of circumstances in which the desire to rule overcomes the reluctance to seek political power. It is all very well to say that philosophical eros is directed toward the Ideas. We can leave it an open question whether the desire to suppress ignorance and injustice through wisdom and justice is itself an expression of philosophical eros or spiritedness, although I have already stated that the two cannot be radically separated. In either case, philosophers are not thinking machines but human beings. Socrates acknowledges this platitude by requiring the philosopher to submit to the compulsion of spirited reason. I believe that only considerations of this sort will explain why it is not unjust to compel philosophers to rule in the just city. On my reading, the philosophers compel themselves. It is part of the comedy and the tragedy of human life that this compulsion usually if not always leads to disastrous results. This is why it is not at all an exaggeration to say that justice leads to injustice. Finally, it is a strong confirmation of this interpretation that it alone allows for the possibility of the just city, since otherwise, according to Socrates, there would be no compulsion on philosophers in actual cities to engage in the founding of the new order. In sum, the reluctance, even the unwillingness, of philosophers to rule is embedded within a dramatic representation of the desire of philosophers to rule.

According to the literal sense of Socrates's argument, we are faced with the paradoxical need to select as rulers those who do not wish to rule but are pulled in another direction beyond the city, and so whose qualifications for ruling are suspect. Socrates proposes to show how the same persons can possess the attributes of both philosophical vision and the rest of virtue, as well as experience virtuous acts (485a1–2). What we really want from him, however, is a demonstration that the two sets of attributes are equally or jointly necessary for ruling. He begins by listing the attributes of the philosophical nature, of which the first is the love of the learning that makes clear the *ousia* of what is always (485a10–b3). We met with the Greek word *ousia* in the previous book. It is often translated as "being" and occasionally as "beingness." The word clearly refers to what Aristotle would call the "essence" of the things that exist, whereas *on* normally (but not always) refers to a particular "being" or existing thing.[2] Philosophers love not just the eternal Ideas but also their core or essential nature, in other words, that which is like a super-Idea or universal Idea in that it exhibits what it is to be an Idea. Socrates emphasizes that philosophers love all of this learning and not merely some part of it, just as lovers of honor love all of honor, however trivial, and lovers of boys love all boys. This statement is actually a qualification of the original comparison between pederasty and love of learning. Previously Socrates said that philosophers love every bit of learning (V. 475b4–c4), whereas here he says that they love all of the learning that discloses *ousia* (485b5–9). In other words, they need not love those parts of learning that pertain to genesis and practice. This is certainly a peculiar prerequisite for potential kings.

The next characteristic is that they are unwilling to receive a lie but hate it and love the truth. This passage should be compared to the discussion of lying in II. 377d4ff., where Socrates approves of noble lies for the good of the city but adds that everyone hates the genuine lie, namely, the one by which we deceive the best part of our soul about the best things (382a4ff). It cannot be the case that it is hateful for the citizens of the good city to receive a medicinal or noble lie in their souls. We must suppose that politics requires the rulers to lie to their subjects but not to themselves. Socrates adds that the same nature cannot be both a lover of wisdom and a lover of falsehood. By this he must mean that the philosopher does not desire to be deceived, whereas he is required to deceive others (485b10–d5)

The remaining attributes of the philosophical nature are as follows: (1) The desires of the lover of learning are drawn away from the pleasures of the body "toward the pleasure of the soul itself with respect to itself" (485d10–11). It follows immediately that the philosophic nature is temperate (*sōphrōn*) and in no way a lover of money (485e3o5). Otherwise put, the love of learning itself makes the soul temperate, whereas not all temperate persons are lovers of learning. The first kind of temperance is philosophical; the second kind is what Socrates will call at 500d4–8 "demotic" virtue. The epithumetic or appetitive part of the soul is thus represented in the present passage as subordinated to the love of wisdom or the intellectual part without the mediation of spiritedness, which will be alluded to subsequently. This seems to be contrary to the analogy of the city and the soul.

(2) The philosophical nature cannot be marked by "illiberality" (*aneleutherias*). "For pettiness [*smikrologia* can also mean "logic chopping"] is entirely opposed to the soul that is always about to stretch out to the whole and to everything that is divine and human" (486a4–6). "Liberality" has nothing to do with spending money (as it does for Aristotle) but refers to something that reminds us of Aristotle's "greatness of soul" (*megalopsuchia*). What I shall call Socratic greatness of soul has to do with speech, not deed, and with the erotic inclination toward comprehensiveness and depth of knowledge. In our time, this would often be given the pejorative characterization of asking "the big questions." Here Socrates condemns not careful analytical thinking but rather its trivialization through detachment from the genuine philosophical desire for completeness.

Socrates again applies what will later be a technical term in Aristotle's ethics: "magnificence" (*megaloprepeia*). In Aristotle, the term refers to the proper expenditure of large sums of money on splendid public buildings and the like, whereas liberality concerns spending small sums in the proper way.[3] For Socrates, on the other hand, the attributes in question are the mark not of a gentleman but of a philosopher, and so of someone who, in the just city, neither possesses nor spends money. Nor does Socrates distinguish between them in this passage; "greatness of soul" is immersion in great topics, namely, "contemplation [*theōria*] of all time and all *ousia*," and for such an intellect, human life is not at all a great thing. *Ousia* appears for the third time in this passage; it is closely connected with the "whole" or the "all," that is, with the essential nature not just of individual things but of everything, or with what it is to be anything at all. The magnificent person will therefore not fear death, since the loss of life is not a great matter. One sees Socrates's point, but it is worth mentioning that we must be alive in order to philosophize (486a8–b2). Socrates thus extends magnificence to cover the orderly soul that does not love money, is not illiberal, does not boast, is not a coward, is not hard to deal with, and, finally, is not unjust (486b6–8). The virtue of bravery will remind us of spiritedness, but in the case of the philosopher, its cause is rather different from that of the guardian-soldier's courage. In the latter case, the cause is eros for the city, or at least for one's class; one could therefore say that the soldier's courage is based upon a love for life, and in fact for one's own life, in the extended sense that the class is an extension of the individual soldier. In the case of the philosopher, on the other hand, courage before death is based upon a disdain for life as something too petty to cling to, or even to pay it much attention. Again, this is an odd attribute for a ruler.

(3) The philosophical nature will learn easily and possess an excellent memory. In addition, it will be musical and graceful, since these attributes draw it toward measure (*emmetria*), which is associated with truth. As Socrates glosses the term, a measured soul is led easily "to the Idea of each thing," thanks to its attributes of measure and charm (486b10–d11). He then summarizes the attributes of the philosophical nature: "a retentive memory, a good learner, magnificent, charming (*eucharis*), and a friend and kinsman of truth, justice, courage, and temperance" (487a2–5). There will be two more summaries of the philosophical attributes at 490c9–11 and 494b1–3. As we shall see, there are small variations from one list to another. In the present case, no explicit mention is made of seeing the Ideas or a dislike of moneymaking, which is perhaps represented by temperance, just as liberality is represented by magnificence. At 490c9–11, health is connected to justice, and both measure and charm are omitted. Finally, at 494b1–3, Socrates lists only facility in learning, memory, courage, and magnificence. I do not believe that these variations point to anything more than that Socrates is not being precise, but this in itself is an important point. A precise listing of the attributes of the philosophical soul is impossible. Underlying these lists is the question, previously raised as the most difficult of all, whether the soul performs each type of action with a separate faculty, or does everything as a unity.

At this point, Adeimantus intervenes, as he did at the beginning of Book Five, in order to level a charge that is frequently made against Socrates. Glaucon encourages Socrates to speak at crucial points in the discussion, but he is on the whole Socrates's guardian, not his accuser. Adeimantus was severe in his judgment of the poets in Book Two; now he associates himself with a common criticism of Socrates and of philosophers in general. No one could disagree with each single statement by Socrates. But everyone who hears Socrates talking as he is now believes that he takes advantage of their inexperience in questioning and answering, and that at each question he misleads them a little bit with his argument, so that, at the end of the discussion, when all the little slips are added up, they find that they have made a major error and said the opposite of that with which they began (487b1–7).

Adeimantus does not quite use the term, but he is in effect reporting a charge of sophistry against Socrates. No competent reader of the dialogues in general, and the *Republic* in particular, can miss the fact that Socrates employs an unusual number of faulty arguments. This presents us with two choices. Either Socrates is himself incompetent, or he has no hesitation in making use of persuasive arguments in order to obtain what he no doubt regards as salutary agreement. The first alternative is not affirmed by Adeimantus. Socrates's accusers have no doubt of his abilities, only of their own; they are afraid that Socrates is tricking them, not himself. I do not think it is wise for us to be more naive than Socrates's interlocutors. This leaves us with the second alternative. We are by now familiar with Socrates's position on medicinal and noble lies, and if we consult the *Phaedrus*, we can be left in no doubt concerning Socrates's understanding of philosophical rhetoric, which accommodates the truth to the understanding of his particular interlocutor and/or audience. It would be childish to deny that highly intelligent and well-educated persons often do the same, in particular with children or those of limited intelligence. What infuriates modern scholars is the thought that Socrates, or rather Plato, would lie to them. No one wishes to be deceived, perhaps not even "for one's own good," for this implies that we are of limited intelligence or character and hence not fit to hear the truth.

I myself believe that the evidence falls on the side of the second alternative. No one can completely avoid logical errors, but Plato's assignment of faulty reasoning to Socrates goes beyond the norm of inadvertent carelessness; nor is that defect sustained by the extraordinary care with which the Platonic dialogues are constructed, care even in portraying carelessness. And there is another consideration. Philosophers have always disagreed, and this situation has not changed in late modernity by the adoption of powerful mathematical and logical tools to analyze conceptual discourse. Formal structure is not the same as the soundness of one's opinions; even nonsense can be given a logical structure. Could it be that Plato believed all philosophical arguments to be faulty and incomplete, and that his portrait of Socrates is intended to illustrate this defect? This is compatible with Plato's statement in the *Letters* that the truth cannot be spoken or written. The last possibility is that Plato regarded himself as superior to everyone, and hence as entitled to employ rhetorical tricks for our own good. None of these possibilities is pleasant, but philosophers are paid to face up to the truth, not to delude themselves with gratifying rhetoric.

To come back to Adeimantus, he raises the objection that, although one might not be able to contradict Socrates at any step, it is nevertheless true that of those who practice philosophy beyond their youth, most become very strange, not to say entirely vicious, and even the decent ones are made useless to the city. Socrates accepts the truth of this charge and proceeds to justify his thesis of philosopher-kings with an image (487c4–488a1). The appeal to images is, I believe, due to the impossibility of giving an effective account of the corruption of potential philosophers that does not, like a play, evoke the process before our very eyes. A straightforward psychological or conceptual analysis cannot capture the full power of the phenomenon. This does not, however, release the commentator from the need to restate the image in a more prosaic and analytical form. To this I now turn.

2

Socrates instructs Adeimantus not to make fun of him for his use of images but to listen to this one "so that you will see still more how I cling to images" (488a1–2). Socrates puts into words something that he envisions or imagines, and that Adeimantus can himself see if he attends to the words. Even in the case of discourse there is a component of seeing what to say and, of course, what has been said. This is not a mere exchange of statements. In the present case, Socrates says that the fate of the most decent men (that is, the decent potential philosophers) in actual cities is like no other single thing; he will have to bring together traits from a variety of sources, just as painters do when portraying mythical or imaginary creatures (488a2–7).

In this image, the city is represented as a ship whose owner is taller and stronger than the crew and passengers but somewhat deaf and short-sighted, as well as knowing very little about seamanship. This seems to be the personification of the entire citizenry, as contrasted with particular classes and groups of individual citizens within the city, who are portrayed as sailors involved in a quarrel with each other as to who should be the captain. None of these persons has learned the art of piloting, but all say that it cannot be taught and are prepared to kill those who claim otherwise. All beg the shipowner to turn over the rudder to them; if one group succeeds, the others kill its members. Finally, the shipowner is drugged and put in chains, and the crew takes over, apparently collectively. They plunder the cargo and sail while drinking and feasting, and they praise the man who is clever at getting them the rule, whether by persuasion or force, whereas he who lacks this gift is regarded as worthless. In particular, the rebellious crew do not understand that knowledge of the heavens (the season, weather, position of the stars, and so on) is required in order to be a pilot. Nor do they believe it possible to learn how to take over the helm, whether the others desire it or not, while at the same time acquiring the knowledge just mentioned. The true helmsman will thus be accused of stargazing (associated with atheism; see Bloom's note) and be rejected as useless (488a7–489a2).

This passage has often been taken, and I think rightly, as a denunciation of democracies, by which, of course, Socrates envisions the rule of the mob, that is, the tyranny of the multitude. Less obvious but even more important for us is the fact that Socrates associates a certain kind of knowledge, of which the satirical exemplification is stargazing, with the art of piloting. But piloting is only metaphorically like governing; for example, the ruler of a city need not know meteorology or astronomy. But to what political arts does the image refer? In the context of the ongoing topic of discussion, namely, the feasibility of the philosopher-king, it is clear that Socrates is thinking of mathematics and dialectic, or in other words the study of eternity, not of the temporal changes of season, wind, and the rotation of the stars. One could perhaps sympathize with the citizens of a democracy for denying that stargazers make good statesmen, without denying the more general point that some kind of skill is required. Also striking is the hint that the true statesman can find it helpful to learn, in addition to the heavenly arts, how to take over the rule with or without the consent of the people.

Socrates's image is admittedly imprecise or constructed from heterogeneous elements. It is most effective in portraying the chaos of Greek democracies, and it presents a powerful evocation of the need for political knowledge. It is entirely less successful in indicating what that knowledge might be. Here, as on so many practical questions, we would do better to turn to Aristotle for advice. But Socrates is not engaging in Aristotelian prudence. He is defending the laughable and even mad proposition that philosophers, or people whose attention is exclusively drawn to being and eternity, should be kings. The rhetorical force of his image derives from its powerful and exaggerated portrayal of the weaknesses of actual cities. I say "exaggerated" because the image ignores the many splendid aspects of Athenian democracy, of which philosophy is not the least. Socrates may be correct in saying that the Athenians would laugh at his thesis of philosopher-kings, but the Athenians may be correct in so responding. The deeper we penetrate into the *Republic*, the more striking it becomes how little it has to do with actual politics, and the more plausible is the suggestion that the work is ironical or satirical. But what is being satirized, if not philosophy? On my view, the eccentric portrait of the philosopher-king is part of Plato's dual intention to indicate both the need for a complete reorientation of politics and the absurdities that follow from such a reorientation. We need those who love the Ideas more than the city, but it is this kind of love that leads to the rise of ideology in the reconstruction and governance of the city.

Socrates next asserts that the fault lies with the many, who do not call upon the philosophers to rule them. For it is incumbent upon the sick man to consult with the doctor, not vice versa, and philosophers, as we now know, are physicians of the soul. This of course assumes that actual citizens know that they are sick, and that they correctly identify the true ruler as a stargazer (489b3–c7). But since their sickness is rooted precisely in their ignorance of these facts, it is plain that they will never consult the philosopher-physician voluntarily, and so that the latter must use "persuasion" and force to acquire rule. Conversely, since Socrates claims that genuine philosophers have no desire to rule but are drawn away from the city by the heavens, there is virtually no chance that philosophers will become kings. And if a king should be born some day who is by nature a philosopher, he will either give up his rule or be forced to accommodate his philosophy to political exigencies.

So much for the uselessness of the few decent philosophers. Socrates turns next to the viciousness of the majority of those who profess philosophy. He reminds Adeimantus of the attributes requisite for the philosopher who aspires to be noble and good (that is, a gentleman). The first is the pursuit of the truth in every form, that is, the striving toward what each being is by nature, and hence not idling near the many things that are believed to exist, which would make his vision dull and terminate his eros. By having intercourse with genuine being (*migeis tōi onti ontōs*), he will generate intelligence and truth, and know and live truly, having been released from his labor pains (489d10–490b7). Again and again it is borne in upon us that the political usefulness of such a person is invisible not merely to the multitude but may be so to us as well. We should also notice that in carrying out his metaphor of the erotic nature of philosophy, Socrates says that "intercourse" with genuine being *generates* (*gennēsas*) intelligence and truth. I do not wish to press a single metaphor too closely, but the sentiment is quite different from the usual view that truth is discovered rather than produced. A second thought, however, suggests the difference between the eternal Ideas or things as they genuinely are, on the one hand, and the truth that is generated in the human soul by the vision of these genuine beings, on the other.

In the procession of truth, we find a healthy and just character, accompanied by temperance as well as the other attributes that we have already observed: courage, magnificence, ease in learning, and a good memory. This must be contrasted with the corrupted form of the philosophical nature. And Socrates emphasizes that, few though persons of a philosophical nature may be, they are faced with many sources of destruction (490c5–491b5). We may initially be surprised to learn that each of the virtues of the philosophical nature can serve as a source of corruption, and so too can things that are said to be goods, like beauty, wealth, and powerful relatives. To begin with, the best nature comes off worse than the mediocre one from a hostile or inadequate upbringing. This is true for the soul as well; the best nature becomes exceptionally bad if it receives a bad education. For a weak nature will never be the cause of anything great, whether good or bad (491b7–e6).

As is so often the case in the *Republic*, Socrates's generalization seems to be pointing toward a valuable truth, but in an exaggerated form. If the best persons are the natural philosophers, this must mean that they turn into the worst tyrants if brought up badly. I find this difficult to accept. Even Alexander the Great, whose tutor was Aristotle, seems to have possessed a nature totally different from that of the born philosopher. The tyrant is if anything the corruption of the love of honor or, if we follow Socrates's own analysis, as prefigured in the story of the ring of Gyges, of sexual eros. On the other hand, Socrates might claim that the love of truth can deteriorate into the love of honor as a result of the usual education received by the well-connected and politically ambitious sons of the aristocracy. To this we might add that if the young potential philosopher loses his love for the whole cosmos, it resurfaces as love for the whole city. This is, after all, the reversal of the transformation of the love of ruling the whole city into love of the cosmos. Philosophy is thus seen to be a kind of purified tyranny. Why not, then, think of tyranny as corrupted philosophy? Once again, we can argue the case pro and contra. On the one hand, the very attributes selected by Socrates to characterize the philosophical nature are those that remove him from political ambition. It would pay us to consider the case of Alcibiades in this context, who was attracted not so much to philosophy as to Socrates, and who turned aside from philosophy to politics despite Socrates, or as we can put it more accurately, who turned back to politics after his Socratic interlude. Are we to suppose that if Alcibiades had been raised by Socrates instead of Pericles, he would have become a philosopher rather than seeking to conquer Greece?

Conversely, suppose that Socrates had been raised by Pericles. Are we to believe that he would have become like Alcibiades? On the other hand, as I noted a moment ago, the twentieth century alone produced at least three major philosophical figures, Heidegger, Lukács, and Kojève, of whom the first sought political influence and the other two obtained it. And there is the example of Plato himself and his three trips to Sicily, albeit in the service of political views radically different from the two modern examples. If one swallow does not make a spring, neither do three. Yet one cannot deny that there is some kinship between the great-souled philosophical nature that aspires to the whole and the beneficent tyrant who wishes to rule the city or the nation. This is quite visible in the dogmatic arrogance of the most comprehensive thinkers, who seek to impose their views on the human race, an arrogance that is recreated in miniature by the minor philosophical figures of the professional world. What seems altogether dubious, however, is the claim that Alexander, Napoleon, Hitler, and Stalin would have become genuine philosophers had they received the proper education.

On balance, it seems reasonable to grant that a child of remarkable intellectual and spiritual qualities may be corrupted by the misuse of those very faculties, and in particular by the early onset of the love of honor. Socrates grants that this process is not inevitable in the case of the potential philosopher, if a god happens to assist him (492a5). He also shifts the blame for this corruption from the sophists to the multitude who gather in assemblies, courts, theaters, and army camps, among other places. It is this multitude, he says, that is the greatest of all sophists; it entirely overcomes private education through the constant uproar of approval and disapproval that excites the spirits of talented young men. Caught up by the crowd, they will adopt the same standards of nobility and baseness; if they should resist, they will be punished with dishonor, fines, and death (492b5–d8).

Once again, Socrates exaggerates, I think. He seems himself to be caught up at this point in a rage against the power of the multitude in a democracy. There is no doubt that some gifted youths will be carried away by the opinions of the many, but a good number will not be. Whether they are saved by the gods or their own nature, there is always a solid minority open to, and eager for, the defense of truth and virtue. The real problem lies in the cultivation by the multitude of a class of surrogate or pseudophilosophers, ideologists, and political rhetoricians, who could never aspire to philosophy, but whose cleverness and susceptibility to honor make them instruments of the mob. This result is facilitated by the rarity of the genuinely philosophical nature, which Socrates himself emphasizes, and which leaves plenty of room for charlatans, as well as inferior persons who may be persuaded of their own superiority, to fill the vacuum.

In sum, according to Socrates, the truth is not that the sophists are the teachers of the many but rather that they are its students. After a careful study of the "beast," they gather together all that they have learned about its behavior and call it wisdom; in particular, they define as good what delights the mob and as evil what angers it. Socrates extends this beyond political action to include the arts and crafts, among which he specifically mentions music and poetry (493a6–d7). The fundamental distinction is between those who see the Ideas and those who do not. Let us say that only the few can see the one true being in each case, whereas the multitude sees only the many images of each original. It is therefore impossible for the many to be philosophical, and this is why those who practice philosophy are blamed by the crowd, as well as by those persons who associate with the crowd and wish to please it (493e2–494a9).

The rule of the many is closely connected to the fact that only a few can see things as they are. Since the many can neither philosophize nor grasp the teaching of genuine philosophers, it should be clear that, if a just rule depends upon philosophy, the only way to acquire political power is by force. In the extreme case, the founders of the city must persuade the adults to turn over children under the age of ten to the philosopher-kings and themselves disperse in the countryside. But who will do the persuading? Are we sufficiently naive to suppose that Socrates could control the multitude on this radical point, when he is regularly presented in the dialogues as lacking the ability to persuade the many? How many of us would follow such a request? Everything therefore turns upon our attitude toward the thesis that justice requires the rule of philosophers (and not, of course, sophists, public intellectuals, or clever mediocrities). As to the possibility of the city, the question is how a few philosophers will be able to exercise the force needed to create the city, and whether the city, assuming it to be created, can withstand the internal strains that threaten to tear it apart from the outset by the enduring existence of the distinction between the few and the many.

Socrates rounds off his image of the difficulties faced by the potential philosopher in terms that suggest what must have been the youthful experience of Plato himself, who resisted that experience, and in a slightly different register, of Alcibiades, who succumbed to it. We should note especially 494c7–d2, where Socrates says that the extremely gifted and handsome youth who comes from a wealthy and noble family in a big city, "filled up with extraordinary hope, supposes that he will be capable of minding the business of Greeks and barbarians." Apart from its obvious reference to Alcibiades (and perhaps to Plato himself), the passage shows the difference between political ambition and philosophical justice. The former wishes to rule the whole civilized world, whereas the latter restricts itself to a single city, and a Greek city at that. Ambition is global, whereas justice requires the distinction between friend and enemy, that is, the intensification of the former and its protection against the corruption of the latter.

Socrates goes on to repeat the main points of his analysis of why so many of the best natures desert philosophy, which is then commandeered by persons of a worthless sort who disgrace it. I call attention to his striking simile at 495d1–e2: "Just like those who run away from prisons into temples" (that is, to gain sanctuary), "these men are delighted to escape from the arts into philosophy, namely, those who happen to be cleverest in their little art. For even though philosophy is faring thus, it preserves a more magnificent reputation than the other arts. Many who are imperfect by nature aim at this, men whose souls, just as their body has been damaged by the arts and crafts, have been mangled and enervated by engaging in vulgar handiwork." This is an especially difficult passage for the contemporary admirer of Plato, as it seems to speak to the worst form of pseudoaristocratic prejudice against what were once called the mechanical arts and, in general, working with one's hands. We can say on Socrates's behalf that the emancipation of *technē*, however admirable for other reasons, had the bad effect of dragging philosophy away from the "magnificence" of the theoretical love of the whole. At the risk of being regarded as a Luddite, I shall add that as philosophy has increased its technical apparatus, it has become progressively narrower in its vision and ever more inclined to dismiss as stargazers those whose love of wisdom reflects the liberality of the soul. On the other hand, it is perfectly correct to say that the Socratic school underestimated the connection between art and philosophy, a connection that is, ironically enough, already visible in the constructive approach to political philosophy that is not entirely concealed by the love of eternity in the *Republic* and is quite visible in the *Statesman*. To this, one may add that the restriction of constructivism to politics is due to a misunderstanding concerning nature itself, or put more fundamentally, to a failure to resolve the problem of the relation between being and time.

The "little bald-headed tinker" who has acquired some money and just bathed in a public bathhouse, in order to propose to his impoverished master's daughter (495e4–8), is the ancestor of the artists, craftsmen, farmers, merchants, and financiers who gradually work their way into nineteenth-century society and dissolve the still-functioning class structure that goes back to classical antiquity, and that serves as the paradigm for the just city. No one should be under the illusion that we can have this city without reconstituting the class structure that goes with it. This is why it is essential for us to think through the entire argument in the *Republic*, in order that we may be certain that the just city is actually just. The decision is not simply political but also theoretical: it depends upon the nature of philosophy, and therefore on the nature of nature.

3

The considerations raised in the beginning of Book Six have enabled us to draw the distinction between philosophers and sophists. To say that the city is a great sophist, and that the individuals to whom we give that name teach "the dogmas of the many" (493a8), is to state the incompatibility between genuine philosophy and the politics of actual cities. Under the right political circumstances, the philosopher may state with considerable frankness the nature of this incompatibility, as does Plato himself. Socrates provides us with a most eloquent account of the corruption within democracies of all but a few of the already small group of potential philosophers, but he does not draw our attention to the fact that it is only in the democratic Athens that he was able to bring philosophy down from the heavens to walk in the streets of the city. Nor can one imagine Plato's dialogues being written and discussed in Sparta or Corinth. As we noted some time ago, there is a connection between fevered and luxurious cities on the one hand and philosophy on the other.

And this gives rise to another observation. It is surely ironical that the *Republic* could not be written, and certainly not be widely discussed, in the so-called just city of which it speaks so glowingly. We may perhaps imagine frank discussions in private between a few potential philosopher-kings, but they would have to practice the esotericism of the medieval Muslim and Jewish philosopher-theologians. One could maintain that this was precisely the Platonic Socrates's conception of the ideal relationship between philosophy and politics, but the fact remains that the realization of the ideal depends upon its being ignored or repudiated in actual cities, in order that philosophers might arise who are capable of founding, in speech first and then in deed, the correctly constructed regime. Philosophy cannot conceal itself until it exists. The medieval esotericists had before them the public presentation of philosophy in ancient Greece. More generally stated, the original philosophers did not need to conceal themselves from the city because they did not discuss politics. One could hardly be more outspoken about the inadequacy of custom and belief than Parmenides, or about the stupidity of the many than Heracleitus.

As things stand, Socrates continues, only a few of those who are philosophical by nature manage to survive corruption by the many, as he has himself, thanks to his demonic sign (496c3–5). I suppose that the point is obvious, but let us note that Socrates here refers to himself as one of the elect and, indeed, probably the only one who has been preserved for philosophy by a divine agency rather than simply through his own nature. However this may be, Socrates is one of that small band of philosophers "who have seen sufficiently the madness of the many, and that no one so to speak does anything healthy when engaging in politics" (496c6–8). Rather than being torn to shreds by wild beasts, the philosopher accordingly minds his own business and tries to get through life by remaining quiet, like a man who takes shelter from a storm behind a little wall. That this cannot be literally true is shown by the existence of the *Republic* itself. Plato is the exception to the general rule; he dares to interfere with the contemporary political situation through the power and artistry of speech. On this point he differs sharply from his teacher and contradicts by example the political reticence expressed by Socrates. In so doing, he shows us that speeches are themselves deeds.

Adeimantus agrees that to spend one's life free of injustice and unholy deeds is no small accomplishment, but Socrates replies that it is not the greatest. The magnitude of one's achievements depends upon the suitability of the regime. In the right political environment, the philosopher "will increase in power and save the common things in addition to the private ones" (497a3–5). As the context shows, Socrates means by "suitability" his political utopia. And this contradicts Socrates's point concerning the reluctance of philosophers to participate in politics, which they do out of a sense of patriotism and justice. In so doing, they surely seem to restrict their philosophical powers rather than to augment them. We are left with a paradox. Political activity, or saving the common things, augments the philosopher's nature; but by taking him away from the contemplation of what genuinely is, and forcing him to devote many years to the care of the transient images of being, this activity is undesirable to the philosopher and must interfere with the development of his theoretical powers. I take this to be another sign of the inner conflict between theory and practice. It explains why the philosopher both turns away from and is tempted by rule in the city.

Socrates adds that no actual city is suitable for the philosophical nature, which is why philosophers who dwell in them are twisted and distorted, like a seed planted in alien soil. But if this seed ever takes hold in the best regime, then it will show itself to be truly divine, whereas the other types are merely human (497a8–c4). The representative of intelligence belongs to a species different from that of the representatives of spiritedness and desire, although he is closer to the former than to the latter. The philosopher's eros comes from above, not from below.

How then should philosophy be cultivated in the city? It should be done in a way that is the opposite of current practice. As things stand, philosophy is studied by youths who were only recently children, and they abandon it when they reach the age of starting a household and making money. Socrates adds that such students approach but do not arrive at the hardest part of philosophy, which concerns *tous logous*, literally, "the speeches," but probably better translated by Griffith as "reasoned argument" (498a3). In later life, they are willing to be entertained by philosophical discourse, but except for a few, they are no longer able to participate in the discussion themselves. In the proper approach, youths will prepare for philosophy by training their bodies to be their assistants in the subsequent philosophical education. When they reach maturity, they will receive a more intense gymnastic of the soul. As we shall see shortly, Socrates has in mind here a primarily mathematical preparation for the actual philosophical exercise of dialectic. When their strength no longer permits them to engage in politics and war, the members of the divine class should be left free to devote themselves entirely to philosophy, except for an occasional side activity (498b3–c4).

Adeimantus assumes that this speech by Socrates will arouse the enmity of the many and, in the first instance, Thrasymachus. But Socrates rebukes Adeimantus and tells him not to make an enemy out of someone who is now a friend, and who was never really an enemy (498c5–d1). Leo Strauss explains this friendship as Socrates's acknowledgment of the indispensability of Thrasymachus, that is, of popular rhetoric, to the founding of the city.[4] This is plausible up to a point, but it raises the question of the adequacy of the tripartite division of the city and the analogous structure of the soul. Thrasymachus is neither a philosopher nor a warrior, yet he must be employed to persuade the many to acquiesce in the founding of the good city. We saw earlier that there is some difficulty about locating technicians like physicians and judges in the correct class. This difficulty returns in the person of the rhetorician. If Thrasymachus is one of the many, or still more radically, the spokesman for the many, then he must persuade himself. But this contradicts the previously stated need to make the many, that is, the class dominated by moneymaking and bodily appetite, subservient to the philosopher-kings through the compulsion of the spirited soldiers.

We can summarize this problem by saying that Socrates must persuade the many through the persuasion of Thrasymachus. And yet, as Strauss notes, Socrates is incapable of persuading the many in deed, although he can persuade them (in the persona of Thrasymachus) in speech. I would rather say that Socrates has silenced or tamed Thrasymachus, that is, shamed him into silence before the gifted and well-to-do members of the audience; but there is no evidence that Thrasymachus has been persuaded, nor does he say anything to verify Socrates's claim that they are now friends and were never enemies. Nor is it ever clear in the *Republic* how the city is to be founded. I know of no serious argument to this end that is grounded in the details of Socrates's own presentation. In order to found the city, we shall need rhetoricians, but also soldiers; yet there cannot be rhetoricians or soldiers of the proper sort until the city has not only been founded but also has survived for at least a generation. The more we think about this, the clearer it should be that a philosophical revolution can succeed only by adapting its rhetoric to the taste of the many. This is to say that revolutions, in order to succeed, compromise their own principles and doctrines in the very act of taking power. It is true that military force is also required, but this is in itself the major accommodation to the crowd.

Socrates goes on to say that neither a man (the natural philosopher) nor a city will ever become perfect "until some chance necessity will compel those few philosophers who are not corrupted, those who are now called useless, to take over the care of the city, whether they want to or not" or, alternatively, until some existing king or his son receives the divine inspiration of philosophical eros. I note that this leaves room for political ambition on the part of philosophers. Socrates says that there is no reason why either or both of these alternatives is impossible. Otherwise we would be rightly laughed at for talking about wishes or daydreams (499b2–c5). My response, once more, is that the city as Socrates describes it is already a statement of the limitations upon philosophical rule. A founding act that requires us to kill everyone over the age of ten can hardly be the basis of justice; as to wisdom, the proposal seems to be more Machiavellian than "Platonic" in the traditional sense of that term. In short, one could go so far as to say that the *Republic* states clearly the internal paradox of the wish for philosophical rule. By acquiring power, it sacrifices the justification of that power. This is to say that one cannot establish the rule of philosophy by the means Socrates describes. In that sense, the city is impossible. What is called "philosophy" is in fact medicinal lying. In slightly different terms, genuine philosophy cannot rule in the city; it can rule only in the souls of genuine philosophers.

There is one other point of special interest in this passage (499c7–d6). If some necessity has in the past compelled, or will in the future compel, philosophers to take charge of a city, or if even now there is such a necessity "in some barbaric place," or will be later, then, Socrates says, the regime of the just city will come into existence. In his previous discussion with Glaucon, Socrates established agreement that the city would be Greek Here that restriction is quietly relaxed. There is no intrinsic reason why philosophy should not arise somewhere other than in Greece or among Greeks. Socrates takes it for granted that, should it do so, its practitioners will establish a city as well as the conditions for philosophy and in that sense will be genuine Greeks, regardless of their geographical location.

Socrates turns now to the task of persuading the many, whom he has just denounced in exorbitant terms as sophists and antiphilosophers who collectively constitute a raging beast. Here he assures Adeimantus that, taken as a whole, the many are gentle (500a5–7). He seems very quickly to have forgotten his recent description of the many and blames Adeimantus for indulging himself in quarreling with them. If they are treated gently, the multitude will respond by changing their erroneous opinion concerning philosophers. This blatant contradiction is one of many rough spots in the flow of Socrates's argument. Instead of describing the city as the teacher of the sophists, he now attributes the harsh disposition of the many toward philosophers "on those unsuitable persons from outside who rush in like noisy revelers, abusing each other and indulging in ad hominem attacks, thereby acting in a way that is least fitting for philosophy" (500b2–6).

Socrates appeals to the corrupt, sick, and mad behavior of the many to explain why genuine philosophy is politically useless, and he argues that the abuse of philosophy by the many is due to the corrupted and drunken boisterousness of false philosophers. In order to avoid contradiction, Socrates must hold that the genuine philosophers can detach the many from the seductions of the false. But this is extremely unlikely; in fact, there is no reason, on the basis of Socrates's own description of how the many respond to genuine philosophers, to accept the suggestion that their gentle rhetoric could penetrate the constant confusion, noise, irrationality, and viciousness that are said to characterize the great beast of the city. The clinching point is perhaps this: the claim that Socrates makes here contradicts the central image of the soul, in which the intellect is incapable of persuading and taming the desires without the mediation of spiritedness. Furthermore, the paradigm of the just city shows that the many are entirely excluded from the education and responsibilities of the ruling regime; it is the soldiers or auxiliaries who are persuaded by noble lies and who must keep the multitude in order.

Socrates next adverts to the lack of interest in human affairs that marks the philosopher, whose gaze is always directed toward what genuinely is, which he imitates, thereby becoming orderly and divine. This is an odd claim, since it is contradicted by the very work in which Socrates utters it. The claim is made in support of the assertion that philosophers feel no envy toward the multitude and do them no injustice. On the contrary, "if some necessity arises," in other words, if the philosopher is forced to accept the rule of the city, and to shape (*plattein*) the characters of human beings, both in private and in public, as well as himself, "do you suppose that he will be a bad demiurge of temperance, justice, and demotic virtue in its entirety?" "Least of all," Glaucon replies (500d4–9). As he does throughout the founding of the beautiful city, Socrates uses the language of production to describe the transformation of the human character. The philosopher can shape human beings in the image of the divine order; he cannot make them divine. The image is called "demotic," or vulgar, virtue, because genuine virtue is wisdom, and this cannot be injected into the souls of the many.

We come once more to what looks like a contradiction in Socrates's argument. If the three kinds of human being, which correspond to intellect, spiritedness, and desire, exist by nature, with the corollary that the difference between the few and the many cannot be suppressed, then how can human beings be so malleable as to be rendered temperate, just, and courageous by the philosopher? Furthermore, if the virtue that corresponds to the divine nature of the philosopher is the contemplation of eternal and unchanging being, how can the order of the cosmos serve as a model for demotic virtue? The more the philosopher introduces order, harmony, measure, and the absence of change into human affairs, the less human these affairs become. The philosopher aspires to be a god, as Aristotle points out in the first book of the *Metaphysics* and as is apparent in Socrates's own account of the philosophical life. But the gods of the demos are superhuman mortals, not Platonic Ideas.

Entirely apart from the conflict between the previous portrait of the bestiality of the multitude and the present claim of their docility, there is no reason to believe that they will acquiesce in the philosopher's intention to wipe clean the tablet of the city and the dispositions of the citizens (500d10–e4). This is just a softer way of making the point that everyone over the age of ten must be expelled from the city, and the more we think about it, the less soft it seems. No one who has lived through the twentieth century would dare to say that this "sanitary" cleansing is impossible, but that hardly makes it something that sensible persons will wish for. One thinks here of the famous statement by the American military officer who, in referring to a village in Vietnam, said that in order to pacify the village, it was necessary to destroy it. We should not be prevented by the sudden gentleness of Socrates's own rhetoric from perceiving the horrifying implications of the insistence on the part of the philosopher that the slate of the city must be wiped clean before the just city can be painted in its stead.

We must also emphasize the Socratic contention that human nature is malleable. Even the potential philosophers can be changed by the corruption of the many and their spokesmen. Whereas we may reject the brutality of the suggestion that the city be wiped clean like a painter's tablet, one cannot understand the Platonic account of human nature if one does not take seriously the constantly recurring terminology of construction and the images of demiurgy and painting. The same point recurs in the so-called late dialogue on politics, the *Statesman*, where weaving, a productive craft, serves as the central model of the royal art of politics. To reiterate, the statesman takes the two conflicting natures of the quick and the slow, which are by nature opposed to one another as enemies, and weaves them together into a city. It is not the city that exists by nature, but human types. In the *Republic*, Socrates claims that even the human types are "plastic." It becomes quite unclear how far the so-called natural differences between persons of one class and another actually hold. No doubt it is impossible to transform a wise man into a fool or a fool into a philosopher, but if the harsh may be made gentle and the gentle harsh or, differently stated, if the philosopher can start with a blank tablet and create citizens of virtue, albeit a demotic virtue, the range for improvisation is tolerably wide. In sum, the vulgar interpretations of Plato as paralyzed by a conception of glassy essences and so prevented from entertaining the idea of change in human life are at best a caricature.

The philosopher-king is now presented as a painter of cities, albeit one who looks to the divine exemplars of the just, beautiful, and moderate, and other such paradigms, in order to blend together human practice with the images of the natural originals (501b1–7). The purpose is to make human beings as divine as possible, as Socrates now puts it, with a favorable reference to Homer, and so as dear to the gods as possible. The accommodated nature of this passage is shown by the recognition of the authority of Homer and the allusion to the popular gods. And Plato attempts to soothe the reader's suspicions by repeating over and over the newfound gentleness of the many as they learn the true nature of the benevolent painter who is coming to destroy them, and to replace them with the philosopher-king's conception of good citizens of a just city. Adeimantus allows that the many will now be gentle to the painter of cities, if they are temperate (501c9). But this condition brings us back to the beginning.

Socrates allows himself to establish the persuasion of the many by the philosophers with one questionable assertion after another. He concludes: "Would you like us to say not that they are less angry but that they have become entirely gentle and persuaded, so that they will agree from shame if nothing else?" (501e7–502a2). "Most certainly," Adeimantus replies. With this facile discursive triumph attained, Socrates spends a page of the text in reiterating the possibility of each of the unlikely requirements for the existence of his city. The child of a king might be a philosopher by nature; he or she might escape corruption at the hands of the many, and the birth of one philosopher, "if the city has been persuaded, is sufficient to perfect everything that is now doubted" (502b4–5). Note the gap between the presence of an uncorrupted philosopher and the persuaded city. In the earlier account, the philosopher who escapes corruption does so by separating himself from the many, not by persuading them to be erased by his utopian sponge. This point is not cleared up in the later account, which instead substitutes gentility for bestiality in the character of the many. Now Socrates says that when the ruler sets out the laws and practices required for the new city, it is not impossible that the citizens will agree to carry them out. This of course depends upon their having been persuaded to obey the philosopher; yet it is hard to see how this could be accomplished *before* the laws and practices have done their work in producing obedient citizens. Socrates grants here only that it is hard for the city to come about, but not impossible (502c5–7).

4

We are now ready to turn to the question of how the philosophical natures will be educated. Socrates begins by repeating a point that he has made on several occasions: There will probably be only a few persons of this kind. One limitation on the number is that such a nature requires two kinds of qualities that are rarely found united in the same person. Those who are quick to learn, of strong memory, sharp-witted, and also high-spirited and magnificent are not inclined by nature to possess intellects that choose to live orderly, quiet, and extremely secure lives. The opposite is true; their acuteness carries them wherever chance leads, and they lose all steadiness. But steady characters that are not easily changed and are for this reason trustworthy and not easily moved by fear behave in the same way toward learning. They are hard to move here too; in other words, they learn with difficulty, as though they were stupefied and filled up with sleep and yawns whenever they have to study hard (503b7–d5).

This passage, as I noted previously, reminds us of a similar discussion in the *Statesman* (306c7ff.), in which the Eleatic Stranger develops the "strange" doctrine that courage and temperance, although both virtues, are in a way enemies and "by nature" (308b6–8) opposed to one another. He goes on to treat this opposition as between acuteness and quickness on the one hand and quietness and temperance on the other. It is the task of the statesman to weave these two disparate types into a city. In the present passage, there is also a natural opposition between acuity and quickness on the one hand, but not quite with gentleness and temperance on the other. The opposition is rather with those who are hard to move, whether in war or the classroom. At the beginning of Book Six, Socrates said that only those who combine knowledge of each being with experience of each part of virtue can be guardians (484d5–7). This is also not quite the opposition that he is now discussing. The steadiness that makes the slow learners immovable in the face of fear looks like the courage of the *Statesman* passage, but it is not obviously the same as experience in the various forms of moral virtue, justice, and goodness, or what Socrates calls "the demotic virtues."

The first passage in effect says that the two subsequent types of guardian, namely, the philosophers and the soldiers, coincide in their experience of demotic virtue, whereas the philosopher adds to this knowledge of the true beings, that is, the Platonic Ideas. The second passage says that acuity and quickness are to be combined with steadfastness and an incapacity for serious learning. But they cannot be combined in the same person; that is not just an opposition but a contradiction. There must be a difference between the quick and the steadfast even in childhood. On the other hand, it seems as if there cannot be, since Socrates says that they must combine in the nature of the philosopher, who is the guardian in the most precise sense of the term. It looks as though something has gone amiss here. That is, we require the art of weaving described in the *Statesman* to unite the quick and the steadfast, or the philosophers and the soldiers, into a single class of guardians, but a class with two distinct sets of human beings.

Socrates repeats that one must participate "well and nobly" in both natures, the quick and the steadfast, or one will not be permitted to have a share in the most precise education, or in honor and rule as well (503d7–9). And he is about to describe the education of the philosopher, which as we shall see consists for the most part in the study of mathematics—hardly a fit training for those who learn with difficulty or yawn their way through difficult subjects. What needs to be the case here is not that the philosopher combines both attributes, but that the class of guardians does. Alternatively, the potential philosopher must be steadfast but not deficient in understanding. We must therefore test the potential guardians in many studies, in order to determine whether they will be able to persevere bravely in the greatest ones, and so become one of the rare (503d11) persons who are suited to rule. Adeimantus asks which are the greatest studies. In reply, Socrates reminds him that when they talked previously about the four virtues of the soul, they had agreed to avoid the longer road for a shorter and less precise account (435d3). Adeimantus speaks for the others in assuring Socrates that the shorter responses were moderately satisfactory, to which Socrates replies that a measure in questions of this sort is entirely unsatisfactory if it falls short of completeness. The guardians cannot be content with the shorter way but must take the longer way in the exercise of many types of learning, to see whether they are capable of bearing the greatest studies (504a3–d3). The implication is clearly that the members of Socrates's audience are not competent to become philosopher-kings, since they are content with the shorter way.

Adeimantus infers correctly that the topics of the virtues of the soul and the education of the guardian class, as well as the topic of justice itself, are not the greatest studies. It is true that the discussion has been motivated by the question of whether the just or the unjust life is the happiest and most blessed. But this is a question about *human* life, and we cannot consider it properly without leaving it behind for the realm of the Ideas, that is, the *divine* life. Differently stated, human beings who lack the divine nature of the philosopher cannot be happy, except perhaps by chance, and in order to be a philosopher, one must take the longer way, a way that can be sketched (504d6–7) for persons like Adeimantus and Glaucon but cannot be stated fully and precisely. This rather strict statement must be modified by noting that the whole point of the Socratic city is to allow those who can only participate in philosophy indirectly, that is, by obeying the commands of the philosopher, to lead just lives as far as possible, and so to participate in happiness, as it were, in the second degree.

To continue, the guardians cannot be content with a sketch of the soul and its virtues, but all the less can we allow them to seek the goal of perfection by taking the shorter way in learning. The longer way takes us through the greatest study, which Socrates now identifies as that of "the Idea of the Good" (505a2).[5] His interlocutors have often heard him saying that it is through this study that other things, including justice, become "useful and beneficial" (505a2–4: *chrēsima kai ōphelima*). This short passage requires three comments. First: it is not yet stated explicitly, but the context and the continuation of the argument establish that we are to receive a sketch of the study of the Good, not the longer way itself. Second: there is a strong component of "utilitarianism" in Socrates's conception of the Good. In other words, we can take the first step on the longer way by recognizing that the Good is useful and beneficial without being nothing more than useful and beneficial. It would be contrary to our experience to say that the Good is useless and harmful, nor could we consistently characterize it as neutral, that is, neither helpful nor harmful. "Useful" and "beneficial" are ambiguous since both can be associated with the accomplishment of evil ends. But it would be hard to deny that something is useful or beneficial if it accomplishes a good end. If one thinks through this simple thought, one sees that there cannot be a definition of "good" that excludes utility or benefit, but also that there is something more than this to goodness. Third: Socrates has been using the word *idea* for some time now, without eliciting any questions from his audience. The interlocutors are presumably familiar with the so-called doctrine of Ideas, although in rather vague terms, or else they have been prepared to use it unreflectively by the terminology of "looks" and "kinds" that Socrates regularly employs. In any case, Socrates says that they have often heard him identify the Idea of the Good as the object of the greatest study, but that they have apparently forgotten or else wish to cause trouble for him.

Socrates reminds his listeners of the thesis that without knowledge of the Good, all other knowledge fails to be beneficial, just as no possession is beneficial in the absence of the Good. It is easy to see that "good" means "beneficial," and that Socrates counts what benefits us as "good." This is a circle, but no one has ever been able to avoid it. The argument that there is no Good in itself and that the meaning of the term varies from place to place or from time to time simply asserts that we disagree on what is beneficial, certainly not on the fact that the beneficial is good. No one knows better than Socrates that the same thing may be good in one context and evil or harmful in another; but it remains true that what we seek in each of the many differing contexts is *the Good*. As a preliminary formulation, we can say that Socrates's doctrine of the Idea of the Good corresponds to the commonsensical reasoning just noted. Everyone wants the good, and without it, nothing is worth anything. But no one can describe the good in a noncircular manner, that is, without employing terms like "beneficial" and "useful," to which we attribute in advance the characteristic of goodness. We cannot say what the Good is, not because there is no such thing or because we have to invent or define it arbitrarily but because, as human beings who are capable of discussing this subject, we already "know" the Good, or that we are impelled toward the Good even if we cannot say precisely what it is.

The thesis that there is such a thing as "good" seems to be distinct from the claim that there is an Idea of the Good. Many will be prepared to agree that we could not exist without distinguishing between "better" and "worse," and that this makes no sense except on the basis of a distinction between "good" and "bad"; but they would reject as absurd all talk of an eternal paradigm of goodness. My suggestion is that we take the minimal step, at least for the time being, of accepting that degrees of goodness, and the distinction between good and bad, are rendered intelligible only because all uses of "good" exhibit the same property. What varies from case to case is not the property "good" but what we identify as an instance of that property. And yet, it is not quite sufficient to refer to "good" as a property. If all instances of this property were to disappear, goodness would not disappear, so long as human beings or some other rational creature were able to deplore what is bad, that is, useless and harmful. Socrates asks us to take one more step: Even if there were no rational creatures to discern the Good, it would remain true that, were there any such creatures, the Good would be identifiable by them. In short, he holds that the Good does not simply appear within human experience and disappear under unfavorable circumstances but is intrinsic to the intelligibility of human existence. This is the easiest way in which to see what Socrates means by the "Idea" of the Good. There is a problem here, which arises because Socrates varies in his terminology from "the Idea of the Good" to "the Good." I shall take this up in due course.

It is, then, not metaphysics but common sense that drives us to the conclusion that we know what the Good is but cannot say what it is. In using terms like "useful" and "beneficial," we make use of our antecedent understanding that these are good. "Good" cannot be defined by means of terms that do not themselves imply goodness. Socrates indicates this at 505b5–c4. In the opinion of the many, the good is pleasure, whereas to the cleverer persons it is prudence. But this means good pleasures, not bad ones, and similarly, prudence about the Good, not about the bad. And there is a further point. Many would choose the appearance of justice and nobility, even if they were not actually just and noble. But the appearance of the Good is satisfying to no one (505d5–9). What Socrates means is not that one cannot profit from seeming to be good but that if to profit is good, there is nothing desirable about seeming to profit but not actually doing so.

The Good, then, is unique in that without it nothing else is worth having, and whatever we seek, it is for the sake of the goodness that we thereby acquire. And yet, we do not seem to be capable of defining this goal of all our desires in a noncircular manner. For example, it is not satisfactory to define the Good as what we desire, because we often desire bad things, that is, things that bring us harm. It then becomes obvious that we wrongly regarded that harm as in fact good. So the Good turns out to be what we desire because we regard it as Good. As Socrates puts it: "Every soul runs after [the Good] and does everything for its sake. It divines that the Good is something, but falls into an aporia and is unable to grasp sufficiently what it is, or to have a steady trust about it, as it has about other things" (505e1–3). A few lines later, Socrates says that he himself "divines" that no one will ever know the just and beautiful things before he knows the Good, and Adeimantus approves this as a noble divination (506a6–8). It is indeed divination to know something that we cannot put into words. This inability is the main reason, but not the only one, that we can love wisdom but never be genuinely wise.

In sum, the city will be perfectly ordered if a guardian looks after it who knows these things (*ho toutōn epistēmōn*: 506a9–b1). Socrates does not say that the philosopher-king must divine the Good and its relation to justice and beauty or nobility but says rather that he must know it. If this is taken literally, then we have another reason for regarding the Socratic city as impossible, because we have just shown that precise knowledge of the Good is impossible.

We can recognize it but not define it in terms of simpler elements that are not themselves good. Adeimantus does not pursue this point but comes close to it by asking Socrates whether the Good is knowledge, pleasure, or something else. In other words, Adeimantus is not content with divinations but wishes Socrates at least to state his suppositions about the Good. Socrates again indicates his reluctance and holds those who possess true beliefs without knowledge to be like blind men who are traveling the right road. He then asks whether Adeimantus would prefer that the discussants see ugly things, blind and crooked, when it is possible to hear bright and beautiful things from others. This sounds very much like an attempt to terminate the discussion of the Good; at least this is how it is taken by Glaucon, who intervenes with an oath: "By Zeus, Socrates, don't withdraw now, just as you are coming to the end!" (506b2–d3).

As usual, it is Glaucon who insists that Socrates pursue the most difficult issues. His enthusiasm is more effective than Adeimantus's questioning. He alludes to Socrates's earlier remarks about their having taken the shorter way and repeats that such a procedure will be satisfactory in the present instance. Socrates replies that he too would be satisfied to achieve the level of the discussion of justice, temperance, and the rest but fears that he will not be up to it and will disgrace himself. He then suggests that they put to one side for the time being the question of the Good itself (*auto tagathon*), since it is beyond the scope of their present thrust "to reach what I now believe it to be" (*ephikesthai tou ge dokountos emoi ta nun*), but he is willing to state "what seems to be an offspring of the Good and most similar to it" (506d6–e5). Whether for the reasons I have now given, or because Socrates regards even his opinions on the topic of the Good itself to be beyond the reach of his present audience, we are told explicitly that what follows will not be a precise account. As will soon become apparent, he means by an "offspring" of the Good an image, namely, that of the sun. This is not very encouraging, since he has just warned us that beliefs about and generated images of what is always, namely, the eternal, unchanging, and divine beings or Ideas, are crooked and ugly. Furthermore, when Glaucon says that he and the others will accept the offspring now, and that on another occasion Socrates will pay us what is still owed concerning the father, Socrates replies: "I wish that I were able to repay and you to receive, and not as now the interest only. Accept this interest and offspring of the Good itself. But be careful lest I deceive you unwillingly by giving a fraudulent account of the interest" (507a1–5).

Socrates presents himself as a blind man who may or may not be traveling on the right road. I mean this in two senses. First, it is highly likely that Socrates does not and cannot know the Good itself. He can only divine it.

Second, whether he knows the Good itself or not, he may defraud Glaucon and the others unwillingly by giving them a false version of his opinions, presumably for their own good. Glaucon, of course, is in no position to know whether what he is about to hear is a genuine offspring of the Good or a bastard. The only way to make sense out of this tangle of reservations and possible deceptions is to reiterate the accessibility of the Good to human beings in a prediscursive manner. I do not mean by this that we cannot talk about it; the image of the sun is exactly such a speech. But we cannot proceed from first principles, axioms, definitions, and logical deductions without first being aware of what is good, and so which principles, axioms, and definitions are pertinent. Socrates is not about to attempt to introduce Glaucon to something altogether unknown to him but rather to communicate something about what everybody knows, although the content of his communication is known only to a few.

10

The Good, the Divided Line, and the Cave: The Education of the Philosopher

I

In order to understand anything about the Idea of the Good, one must first know what Socrates means by an Idea. He does not use this word in the modern sense of a modification of consciousness, that is, a thought or some kind of cognitive act. In the language of modern philosophy, Platonic Ideas are objective, not subjective. We do not construct them; they are not artifacts of the perceptual and cognitive process. They are not points of view or perspectives, although we may and perhaps must apprehend them from one perspective or another. Neither could it be properly said that the Ideas, as apprehended, are "in" the intellect, any more than the tree of which we have a perception or thought is itself within that perception or thought. Plato nowhere explains, except by metaphors of vision, how the intellect apprehends Ideas. This is a problem separate from that of how the instances of an Idea participate in the Idea itself.

So much by way of introduction. Let us follow Socrates's own exposition, which builds upon his regular use of the word *idea* and its near synonym *eidos*[1] to refer to a paradigmatic exemplar of a look of a certain kind, and so of a family or class of things of that kind. Socrates begins by reminding his audience that there are many beautiful and many good things, and so on for the rest, and we distinguish them in speech. I note that this is possible only because we already understand what we mean by "beautiful" and "good." The act of identifying a number of things as beautiful or good is the same as classifying them together as instances of beauty or goodness. The act of classification produces a set of statements (*logoi*) that gives us a discursive explanation or definition of beauty or goodness but does not reduce them to discursive artifacts. The individual members of these two classes may vary from person to person, but we are able to disagree about such identifications only because we are both discussing the same general characteristic. Where this does not occur, no disagreement or communication of any kind is taking place.

It is worth mentioning at this point that Socrates does not say that all goods are the same, or that the same thing is good in all cases. What he claims rather is that heterogeneous goods all share the attribute of goodness. It is as true for Socrates as it is for Aristotle that "good" in one domain of experience or human action differs from "good" in another. We can name what is good in each case, but we shall always be identifying these different goods as instances of goodness. A much more serious problem is whether we can distinguish in everyday life the difference between sensible and foolish identifications of good things. One cannot prove the affirmative of this question by starting with the hypothesis of Ideas; on the contrary, our decision about whether experience is coherent or sheer chaos will itself determine whether we can take the next step from coherence to the Ideas. To say this in another way, many who reject the doctrine of the Ideas would be prepared to speak of predicates, classes, abstract properties, and, in general, *concepts*. But to do so is already to grant Socrates's crucial point. The concept (to take the most important example) is not itself a singular generated instance but a discursive representation of our recognition that we can classify particulars by certain properties that recur in singular generated instances. As for those who reject even abstract entities and concepts, they are left with the claim that life is unintelligible, since every attempt to arrive at formal structure entails generalization over particulars, or the construction of abstract entities like concepts. To put it mildly, this is not an easy case to defend coherently.

Socrates next explicitly states the procedure that he has been following for some time, without calling special attention to it. In addition to the many things that are beautiful, good, and so on, we also say that there is a beautiful itself, a Good itself, and so too in all cases in which we established a many; and again, we established that there is one Idea with respect to each many, and in each case we call this "what is" (*ho estin*: 507b5–7). In this very general statement, Socrates speaks as though there is an Idea for every case of a one-over-many, that is, for every collection of individual things on the basis of a single property which they all share. Artifacts are not excluded here. The main point is quite simple. Whatever is, must be something or other. It must have a definite nature, or else it could not be what it is but would be constantly changing or about to change, or be so indeterminate as not to be anything at all. One might object that many or all things change partly, without losing their identities, and of course Socrates would grant this. But he would add that there is a limit beyond which changes cannot take place without destroying the identity of what is undergoing change. In this case, the possibility of saying what it is that is changing no longer obtains. To repeat: the thing changes, but the kind of thing that is changing does not change. The qualities of the thing can all disappear, but the kind of thing that has suffered this dissolution does not itself dissolve. This is what makes it possible for us to say "everything changes" with respect to the many things of such-and-such a kind. The kind does not change just because some instance of that kind ceases to exist. If that were the case, then we could never say what it is from which the thing in question changed to something else. And to what else? In other words, if change lacked stability altogether, then there would be no change, and no speech about change.

The next point: "And [the many particulars] we say are seen but not thought [*noeisthai*], whereas the Ideas are thought but not seen" (507b9–10). This is more difficult. Let us start with an example. I see a beautiful vase, which is an item in the domain of genesis and is therefore accessible to my sensory equipment. If you ask me to identify the causes of its beauty, I shall point out various features of its shape as well as properties of its material constitution. But if you then ask me to point out the properties of the beautiful itself, I cannot point to the same things that allowed me to account for the beauty of the vase, because the beautiful itself is a property not of this vase alone but of all beautiful things. If the Idea of the beautiful has properties, these must be unique to the Idea of the beautiful; otherwise, that Idea would include in its own nature every beautiful thing in which its properties also inhere. We cannot therefore see the beautiful itself, although we can see beautiful things. Conversely, a beautiful thing, say, a vase, cannot be grasped by pure thinking, because it is an object of sense perception, whereas there are no sense perceptions of the beautiful itself, which has no sensory properties. It cannot have such properties, because they individuate what possesses them and make it take on the shape of this particular thing of such-and-such a kind. And this is impossible, since the beautiful itself belongs to all kinds of beautiful things.

This means, of course, that the constant reference to Ideas as visible, and so too the forthcoming image of the sun as the offspring of the Good itself, are entirely inadequate representations of Ideas. The situation gets worse when we realize that the very name *Idea* is inappropriate for whatever cannot be seen, since it means literally "look." But if the look of beautiful things is not itself visible, how can it be the look of those things? The look of beautiful things (beauty itself) is not the look of a vase, a person, or even a speech (if we may allow items belonging to hearing to fall metaphorically under "things seen," as when we say to someone who has just explained something to us, "I see what you mean"). Strictly speaking, the look of beauty itself is not a look at all; it is the pure thought that renders intelligible the existence of individual beautiful things. We naturally recoil from the thought of accepting such monstrosities, yet we are forced to do so by the consequences of their rejection. Up to a point, one could make the same case on behalf of "concepts." All the ironical criticism in the world against the existence of abstract entities does not alter the simple fact that a serious, strict nominalism is an absurdity, as is already shown by the name *nominalism*, which refers to the thesis that all concepts are just singular *names*. Singular each may be, but singularities are instances of generalities, in this case, of the general term *name*.

I turn now to the next step in Socrates's exposition. He first reminds Glaucon that we see with the sense of sight and hear with the sense of hearing, and so too with the other sensory capacities. The sense of sight, however, must be singled out for the following reason. In order to hear, we require only the sense of hearing plus an audible sound, but no third thing to bind them together. In the case of sight, on the other hand, we require a third thing, namely, light. This passage is of course not scientifically correct, since sound waves also require a medium through which to be transmitted to the hearing apparatus of a sentient being. But the Idea of the Good could hardly be compared to or represented by air, water, or earth, nor does the sense of hearing lend itself to the notion of rendering perceptible all generated items, most of which make no discernible or intelligible sound. It is only the speech about what we have seen that puts hearing into the picture. Furthermore, sound, or hearing, does not give life to speeches or make them "grow" in the way that sunlight does to all beings, speaking and silent (507b9–e5).

Since we are in the domain of imagery or poetry, the absence of precision can be forgiven. Let us therefore continue with the image of the sun. I quote Griffith's translation of 507e6–508a2: "In that case, because it involves a third thing of this important character, the link between the faculty of sight and the ability to be seen is something more valuable than the links between the other faculties and their objects. Unless of course light has no value." This is much easier to understand than Bloom's translation, but it is unfortunately inaccurate. Bloom translates: "Then the sense of sight and the power of being seen are yoked together by a yoke that, by the measure of an *idea* by no means insignificant, is more honorable than the yokes uniting other teams, if light is not without honor." There is a variation in the manuscripts between the dative and nominative of "significant Idea," but Griffith leaves the expression out, with no warranty that I can see. Bloom's translation is, I think, more accurate, but it is extremely obscure. The passage says that the yoke of vision and the visible is light, and that this yoke is more honorable than any other. The puzzle is what to do with the words *ou smikra idea*, and this is no doubt why Griffith omitted them. One would suppose that the expression is being used metaphorically to refer to sunlight. Socrates is saying that the Idea of the Good is at work here in making light, its metaphorical image, the most honorable yoke in the domain of sense perception or genesis.

That Socrates is indulging in rather flowery rhetoric here is further supported by his invocation of the sun as a god (508a4, a9). No doubt the reference is to Apollo, who in addition to being the god of clarity is also a physician, and is thus metaphorically associated with philosophy. Neither vision nor the eye is the sun, but the eye is the most sunlike of the sense organs and derives its power from the infusion of sunlight. And the sun is not sight but as its cause is seen by it. From this, Socrates draws the following analogy: the sun is generated by the Good, in a way analogous to itself. Just as the Good stands in the noetic realm to pure intellect and the intelligible things, so the sun stands in the visible realm to sight and the things seen (508b6–c2). Note that the analogy establishes that the Good does not cognize by pure thinking of the thought that is the original of the sight in the sensible world. Stated more simply, the Good does not see; it is not conscious, like the divine eye of Neo-Platonism and German Idealism.

There is a problem here. The sun generates in its realm, but there is no genesis in the realm of the Good. How, then, can the Good be the cause of being and truth? To borrow an expression from the *Timaeus*, genesis is the moving image of eternity. But eternity itself does not move. If motion or genesis is to be explained as an image of the Good, this explanation must be grounded in access to the original. We must in other words be capable of rising above temporality in order to compare the original to the image. In this case, we must already know the Good prior to identifying some changing item as an image of it. Finally, it is interesting that Socrates speaks, apparently interchangeably, of the Good and the Idea of the Good. As the first principle of the Ideas, the Good cannot be an Idea like all others.

Glaucon requires further explanation of the analogy between the Good and the sun. Socrates accordingly restates the previous point; just as the eye seems to lose its visual power in the dark, so too with the soul. Whenever the soul fixes its eyes upon what is lit up by truth and genuine being, "it engages in pure thought and knows it, and appears to possess pure intellect" (*enoēsen te kai egnō auto kai noun echein phainetai*).² Conversely, "when the soul directs its attention to what is mixed with darkness, namely, coming to be and passing away, it forms opinions and is dimmed, changing its opinions up and down, and seems now not to possess pure intellect" (*noun*: 508d4–9). The language suggests that the soul is the unifying identity of its various cognitive faculties; it is the agent that fixes its intellectual eye upon one kind or another of object. When attention is directed toward genuine being, pure intellect is able to function; when it is directed toward the changing and impure elements of genesis, it loses its power to see and sinks into the activity of forming opinions.

It would be dangerous to put too much pressure on the poetical language that Socrates is using in this passage, but we are certainly entitled, and even required, to notice the implications of that language. One such implication is that genuine being is entirely illuminated, whereas complete nonbeing is darkness without light. Thus the domain of genesis is a mixture of light and darkness. This passage is open to the claim by Heidegger and others that "Platonism" identifies being with presence, and this in turn with visibility. One must agree that even illumination cannot be complete; the difference between one thing and another, or the absence of a particular entity, inevitably introduces shadows, if not pure darkness, into the career of thinking. This problem is closely connected to the inadequacy of Plato's analysis of "the altogether not" as otherness. What is other than X is neither darkness nor absence, total or partial, but the presence of Y. And the presence of Y casts light on the absence of X by virtue of our ability to see that X is not present, or is partly obscured. This "not" is not the positive presence of Y. I think that Hegel comes closer to the mark by insisting that both the visibility and the invisibility of X depend not on Y alone but on the copresence of X and non-X. Y calls our attention to this copresence.³

Socrates continues: "Therefore say that what furnishes truth to the things known and the power [to know] to the knower, is the Idea of the Good. Since it is the cause of knowledge [*epistēmē*] and truth, you must conceive it as something known. But as beautiful as knowledge [*gnōseōs*] and truth are, you will be right to believe it to be other and more beautiful than these" (508e1–6). To begin with, I note that the Idea of the Good is here presented as an instance of something beautiful. Socrates does not discuss the point, but this must refer to the *koinōnia* or community of the Ideas. Second, the Good is not the activity of knowing or of self-consciousness. It is also not knowledge in the subjective sense but is rather the goodness of knowledge. But neither is it knowledge in the objective sense of the word, because what we know is the nature of this or that particular kind, not goodness. And similar considerations apply to truth.

Thus, for example, the sun is not a flower or the truth of a proposition about what it is to be a flower. It is (speaking loosely or metaphorically) the cause of the genesis of the flower, and it illuminates the flower so that we can learn the truth about its nature. Note that the sun is not the sole or total cause of the genesis of the flower; other factors play a role as well (earth, water, nutrients, and so forth). The sun makes it possible for us to acquire knowledge and truth by illuminating the flower, and so too the Idea of the Good functions in the intelligible domain. In short: nothing has been said as yet to allow the inference that the Good is the cause of the Ideas; this would be impossible in the ordinary sense of the term, since the Ideas are eternal. The only possibility here is that the eternal illumination of the Good is the causal factor in the eternal presence of the Ideas. In the case of the sun, on the other hand, it is indeed a partial cause in the existence of at least some things. So there is a disanalogy between the sun and the Good. But we are about to face a difficulty in this regard.

Socrates goes on to restate the point just examined and emphasizes that the Good is more honorable than knowledge and truth. Glaucon responds with admiration; interestingly enough, where Socrates speaks of honor, Glaucon speaks of beauty. Glaucon then asks: "But surely you are not referring to pleasure?" (509a6–8). This implies that the identification of the Good and the pleasant has not yet been entirely removed from Glaucon's mind. Socrates warns him not to speak blasphemy and goes on to the next characteristic of his image (509a9). "I believe you will say that not only does the sun furnish the power of being seen to what is seen, but also genesis, growth, and nurture, even though it is not genesis." Glaucon agrees, and Socrates continues: "Therefore say that not only is being known furnished to what is known by the Good, but also *to einai te kai tēn ousian*." Bloom and Griffith both translate these words as "existence and being." I do not believe that it will be possible to arrive at a precise and indisputable translation of these terms, but we must consider them briefly.

To einai means literally "the to be," which is intolerable in English but not quite as much in Greek. I see no reason why it could not be translated as "being." "Existence" is ambiguous, because it normally refers in English to items of genesis. *Eksistēmi* in Greek means to alter utterly, and by extension to degenerate from one's nature (Liddell, Scott, and Jones cite here *Republic* 380d8–e1, where Socrates speaks of "stepping out of one's Idea"). I have already discussed *ousia*, originally "property" or "wealth," as in the English phrase "a man of substance." If the expression were not so awkward in English, we could call it "beingness." But neither term allows for the inference that the Good causes to exist in the sense of bringing into being the Ideas. That would be disastrous to the entire doctrine.[4] Socrates must mean that the Good is a necessary condition for the being of Ideas, but a condition that always obtains. It would be very difficult to say exactly what this means, but I take the general sense to be this: Being (in the sense of beingness, not existence) is good; it is better to be than not to be, or, more cautiously expressed, it is better that the cosmos exist than that it not exist, for more than one reason but primarily because this makes philosophy possible, and it is philosophy that redeems and sanctifies life. On the other hand, if there were no life, such redemption would be unnecessary. Plato's view is very likely that philosophy itself justifies the existence of the cosmos.

The word *ousia* also occurs a few lines later at 509b9 in a passage that has become famous and is the object of conflicting interpretations. Socrates is saying that the Good is not itself *ousia* but is *epekeina tēs ousias*. The traditional translation of this phrase is "beyond being." If *ousia* refers to the nature of being altogether, then "beyond" must mean here either that the Good *is not*, that is, not only is it not a particular being (*on*), it does not exist in any sense of that difficult word; or else the Good does exist, that is, "be," but it also goes beyond *ousia* into some higher domain. The former case is unthinkable, since for Socrates we cannot think of what is not; the latter case seems to conjure up a hybrid entity like a centaur or hippogryph, one which both is and is not. In this case, it seems to be a member of the domain of genesis, the members of which wander between being and nonbeing. We are here facing one of those points in Plato that are too cryptic to be amenable to an entirely satisfactory explanation. My own preferred view is that the Good is "beyond" being in the metaphorical sense that it is neither this nor that of a separate and definable kind but is rather a property or set of properties of Platonic Ideas, namely, intelligibility, stability, and eternity.

Upon hearing the explanation of the analogy, Glaucon swears, "By Apollo, what a demonic excess!" Socrates characterizes this observation as "very laughably" made, but he does not say (as in Griffith's translation) that it made them all laugh. Socrates does not laugh in the *Republic*, whereas Glaucon does so frequently. Instead, Socrates blames Glaucon for insisting that he state his opinion about the Good. And in the continuation, he emphasizes that he is leaving out many details about the analogy between the Good and the sun, however unwillingly (509c1–10). We come now to one of the most famous passages in the *Republic*: the discussion of the "divided line." Especially since Socrates has just made a point of the incompleteness of the exposition, we would be foolish to look for anything more exact here than we found in the analogy between the Good and the sun. Let us look at the details, always bearing in mind that we are studying an image, not a chapter in a text on epistemology.

2

To begin with, we are to apprehend the being of two realms. The Good is the king of the noetic class and place (*to men noētou genous te kai topou*), whereas the sun is the king of the visible domain. The word *genos* means "race" or "family," and by extension a genus or collection of kinds (species or *eidē*). Here it refers to the collection of beings that are accessible to pure reason only, that is, the Ideas. "There are then these two *eidē*, the visible and the noetic." Socrates is not precise in his use of technical terms, and in the present passage the idiom is metaphorical, not technical. *Eidos*, *genos*, and *idea* are used interchangeably throughout the dialogue. That said, in the last sentence Socrates refers to the two kingdoms as contrasting unities, whereas previously he took account of their constitutive elements (509d1–4).

This is the preface to the divided line. Consider a line that is divided into two unequal segments and then cut each segment in two in accord with the same ratio. In other words, the line L is cut into two unequal parts A and B, and A is divided into parts c and d, whereas B is divided into e and f. A is to B as c is to d, and c is to d as e is to f. One of the first two parts stands for the visible domain, and the other for the intelligible domain, but Socrates does not say which is which, although he mentions the visible first. Commentators on this passage often assume that the larger part corresponds to the intelligible domain, presumably because the latter is the more important of the two. But it is equally possible that since there are many more items of genesis as well as their images than there are things that are cognized by pure intelligence alone, the larger segment of the first two should go to the visible realm. Let us see if Socrates's exposition gives us any assistance on this point. To anticipate, he will proceed from the cognitively lowest to the cognitively highest.

Thus in the segment corresponding to the visible domain, there will be a subsegment corresponding to images, that is, to shadows, reflections in water and mirrors, and so on. In the other subsegment are what I shall call with great caution the originals of these images, that is, the whole domain of natural and artificial things of which images, natural or artificial, are or can be produced. Glaucon then agrees with Socrates on the "truth-value" of each subsegment of the visible domain: as the opinable is to the knowable (*gnōston*: this term can mean "what we are acquainted with" and is not as strict in its meaning as *epistēton*), so the likeness (that is, the image) is to that of which it is the likeness (509d6–510b1).

Now we turn to the task of identifying the subsegments of the segment corresponding to the intelligible domain. Socrates's opening statement is very obscure and is not understood by Glaucon. Socrates begins once more with the subsegment of lower cognitive value. In this part of the intelligible domain, the soul uses the originals of images in the visible world as images of some cognitively higher original. Note that the soul was not mentioned with respect to the visible domain (but see 508d4–9). The soul is compelled to investigate the higher-order images (natural and artificial elements from the visible domain) on the basis of hypotheses and arrives at an end; that is, it arrives at a conclusion that is dependent upon the hypotheses just mentioned. Thus far the hypotheses are not further identified, but they are assumptions like first principles, axioms, and the like, which cannot be "discharged" but which remain as conditions upon the knowledge acquired. In the highest subsegment of the intelligible domain, the soul starts from a hypothesis but uses no images (that is, none of the objects of the visible world); furthermore, its hypothesis is discharged in the course of the investigation by way of Ideas alone.[5] In this case the hypothesis is presumably itself an Idea or eidetic structure, and dialectic confirms that identity. The conclusion of this kind of reasoning is a nonhypothetical beginning or principle, that is, an Idea (510b2–9).

Glaucon does not understand the account of the inferior kind of formal thinking. Socrates proceeds to clarify it by identifying the study in question as mathematics: geometry, calculation, and the like (510c2–3). The masters of these sciences assume that one knows the odd and the even, the different geometrical figures, the three kinds of angles, and so on. These are the hypotheses; they will retain their unproven or hypothetical status throughout the investigation and remain at the end as conditions upon the knowledge acquired. Furthermore, mathematicians use the "originals" of the visible domain, for example, by drawing a circle in the sand (or as we would say, on the blackboard). This image is not their actual target, which is rather the circle itself or the diagonal itself. According to Socrates, we cannot see the mathematical forms or intelligible originals except with the assistance of visible images. This claim would not be made by post-Cartesian mathematics, which reduces geometry to algebra, and algebra to set theory. But from the Greek standpoint, this reduction obliterates the genuine being of the pure geometrical entities.

To remain within the Socratic orbit, mathematicians use sensible objects as images of pure mathematical forms, in addition to failing to discharge the hypotheses upon which their reasoning rests (510c1–511a2). They are therefore associated with a subsegment of lower cognitive value than the one that corresponds to the philosophical master of dialectic. They study a class of noetic forms but do not arrive at unqualified formal knowledge. As Socrates reiterates, they cannot step outside their hypotheses to arrive at a pure unencumbered form that is itself a principle rather than a conditioned conclusion. This is reserved for the practitioner of dialectic, who corresponds to the highest segment of the intelligible realm. Mathematicians, in sum, study geometrical forms and kindred entities with the discursive intelligence (*dianoia*), because they move toward those forms through images, about which it is necessary to make speeches (*tous logous peri autōn poiountai*), even though the images of which they speak are not the primary object of their dianoetic thinking (510d4-5, 511a1).

Genuine *noēsis*, then, takes place only in the segment of the noetic domain that *logos* itself grasps through the dialectical power. I take the expression *autos ho logos* at 511b4 to refer to something different from the speeches made by mathematicians at 510d5. "*Logos* itself" functions with pure forms or Ideas exclusively, not with images. It is therefore not silence, as has sometimes been inferred, but purified speech. Its reasoning is not grounded in, deduced from, and so dependent upon, hypotheses. That is, it treats hypotheses not as principles (*archai*) whose conditioning authority is retained throughout the reasoning process but as beginnings or stepping-stones and springboards that will enable us to be free from their encumbrance, and so to arrive at the nonhypothetical principle of the all (*tou pantos*), that is, the Platonic Ideas. One other crucial point needs to be made. *Logos* itself cannot be simply discursive; if it were, the Ideas would be linguistic entities and the whole significance of the metaphor of the sun would be lost. Instead, pure *logos* speaks about what it has seen or grasped noetically. If there were no speech, we would not know what we had seen. But if there were nothing to see prior to speaking, we would not know what we are talking about.

This seems to confirm my suggestion about the hypothesis in dialectic. It must be an assumption that permits us to initiate the rational analysis of formal intelligibility but that is confirmed to be an Idea as the process continues. Since pure intellection makes no use of anything from the sensible world, I suggest that the hypothesis in question is the formal structure with which we begin our analysis of its elements, in a way that Socrates sketchily describes in the *Philebus* at 18a6-b4. It should, however, be mentioned that no one begins to think dialectically ex nihilo. That is, even though the noetic capacity may be functioning without our being aware of it, we have to recognize or, as Socrates sometimes says, recollect the Ideas from the world of images and empirical reasoning. Finally, let me reiterate what is perhaps the most important point in the passage. From the outset, *noēsis* is associated with *logos*. It is not used anywhere in this section of the *Republic* to refer to silent intuition, if by "silent" is meant the absence of discursive thinking.

When intellect has grasped the principle or form of the whole, it has discharged its hypotheses and is now in the domain of dialectic, that is, a process of reasoning that employs nothing but Ideas. Each link in the *logos* is an Idea that depends upon another Idea; to this we may add that if the number of Ideas is finite, then the structure of intelligibility is a circle of eidetic elements. Pure dialectic thus uses nothing but forms to proceed through forms; it begins, continues, and ends in Platonic Ideas (511b3–d5). Glaucon now claims to understand, but not adequately. He summarizes Socrates's statement in the following points. The science of being and of what is seen noetically is clearer than what is known through what are called the arts. These last use hypotheses as first principles. Therefore, even though the technicians use *dianoia* rather than the senses to observe the visible things, they start from a hypothesis and not from a genuine beginning (that is, an Idea), and so they do not possess and never achieve the understanding of *nous* (that is, pure intellect) with respect to these things that in themselves are noetic, provided that we start from the proper beginning. I note that Glaucon seems to collapse, or even to eliminate, the distinction between images and originals; he speaks only of hypotheses. He also blurs or leaves out altogether the difference between mathematics and the arts corresponding to the world of genesis. He overlooks the fact that *nous* is also said to use hypotheses, albeit of a totally different kind from that employed by *dianoia*. Finally, Glaucon says that Socrates calls the thinking of mathematicians *dianoia* but not *nous* (which is reserved for the dialecticians), and that he places it between opinion and *nous*. Here he leaves out the gnostic knowledge of the natural and artificial things that are the originals of the images of the doxastic realm. In other words, he collapses the subsegments of the visible world into one segment.

Socrates says that Glaucon's summary is adequate, but he proceeds to correct it without comment by reiterating that there are four parts to the divided line, corresponding to the four affections in the soul: *noēsis* at the top, *dianoia* in second place; the third we shall call *pistis* (trust), and the final one *eikasia*, "image making" or "imagination." These are to be arranged in a proportion, and their degrees of clarity correspond to the degrees in which their objects participate in truth (511d6–e4).

It is now time for our own summary of this extraordinarily difficult passage. I begin by calling attention to a peculiarity of the instructions issued by Socrates to divide the line. There is an excellent brief and clear note on this point in Griffith (511d5). I quote in part: "From the description of the line, a mathematician would be able to prove that the two middle sections, corresponding to thought and belief [in my translation, discursive thinking and trust], are invariably equal in length, regardless of the total length of the line and the location of its first cut." For example, if the line is nine units long and is divided at three, then the two main parts A and B must be three and six units, respectively. The subsegments of A, when divided by the same ratio of one to two, will be one and two units each. But in order for the subsegments of B to stand to one another in a ratio of one to two, they must be two and four units, respectively. "Whether Plato intended this fact to be significant is much disputed." Since we cannot be quite certain whether the line moves from the larger to the smaller part, or vice versa, as in Griffith's example (as well as at 509d6ff), we do not know which two parts are being equated. The least one could say is that Plato leaves certain ambiguities in his metaphorical account of the structure of the whole.[6]

Second, in his final summary, Socrates ranks the parts of the divided line in order of clarity and truth. In other words, the largest subsegment belongs to pure intellect, and so on down the line. On the other hand, the order of exposition is the reverse; Socrates begins with the realm that is lowest in clarity and truth. Neither of these corresponds to the beginning of actual experience, which takes its bearings by natural and artificial elements of genesis, not with their shadows and reflections.

Third, the sun, the so-called offspring of the Good, plays its role entirely within the domain of genesis and is an agent of generation as well as visibility. In order to preserve his analogy, Socrates must attribute to the Good the power to generate Ideas and thereby bring them into the light of reason. But this is strictly speaking incompatible with the eternal and unchanging nature of the Ideas. Instead of generation, we must have some kind of logical relation. For example, as I suggested above, we could say that the Good is not a genuine or definite Idea but rather stands for the stability, eternity, and intelligibility of the Ideas. If this is right, it would also explain why Socrates speaks sometimes of the Idea of the Good and sometimes of the Good. As a corollary to this point, the Good seems to function solely as what modern philosophers sometimes call an "ontological" agent. Despite the attribution to it of various laudatory terms, the Good has no ethical or political function, not, at least, as it has been described by Socrates thus far. This is somehow discomfiting, since the word *good* is normally used as one of the most important terms in ethical and political philosophy. The discomfort may be reduced when we recall that for Socrates, moral virtue, and indeed all virtues except wisdom, are classified together as "demotic" and are said to be closer to the body than to the soul (500d4–9 and VII. 518d9–e3). This is obviously a version of the standard Socratic thesis that virtue is knowledge.

The entire discussion raises an extremely difficult philosophical problem that is not considered directly by Socrates. We have been acquainted with four domains or degrees of clarity and truth that distinguish four kinds or degrees of being: images of the items of genesis; these items themselves, natural and artificial; mathematical forms, and Platonic Ideas. Items of genesis, and presumably also their images, share in being and nonbeing. But nothing is said about the difference, if any, between mathematical forms and Platonic Ideas. What differs is the procedure by which these are known. Thus, the mathematician uses images (figures drawn in the sand) and undischarged hypotheses, whereas the dialectician employs neither of these. But that in itself is not a reason for separating the mathematical forms themselves from the objects of dialectic. In other words, mathematicians seem to busy themselves with a subset of Ideas and to use a method that is inadequate to the perfect understanding of that subset. But could there not be dialectical knowledge of mathematical forms? Or is there something about the mode of being of Beauty itself, the Good itself, and so on, that sets these and the other examples of "genuine being," namely, Ideas, apart from the mode of being of the circle itself, the diagonal itself, and so on? I see no reason to assume that the Idea of a cow, or for that matter of justice, contains more being than the pure geometrical circle.[7]

The more one thinks about the doctrine of Ideas, including that of the Good, the more perplexed one becomes. In the present context, we should be especially perplexed by the question of the political significance of the doctrine. It is all very well to say that rulers of the city must see things clearly and distinctly (to borrow two key terms from the Cartesian version of Platonism). But there is an enormous difference between epistemic sharp-sightedness and justice. One may see things perfectly and still distribute them unjustly to one's subjects. One might suspect that the "demotic" virtues, which Socrates also attributes to the guardians, have more to do with their suitability to rule than do the epistemic virtues of dialectic.

To conclude: the (Idea of the) Good seems to be of little help to the philosopher-king, but its epistemic function is perhaps equally obscure. We acquire neither practical nor theoretical knowledge by gazing at the Good, and indeed, to look at it directly would seem to blind us, if the analogy with the sun is to hold. More precisely, we learn nothing in particular thanks to the Good; rather, the expression refers to the existence and intelligibility of particular Ideas and, through them, of the particular entities of genesis. To say that the Good is being and intelligibility is surely to cover too wide a ground to be useful in discriminating the worth of one action from another. As to why something is intelligible, that would seem to derive more from its nature or being than from an external source of illumination. Light is necessary to vision, but it does not produce what it illuminates. In other words, to become visible is not the same as to come into existence; things are what they are whether we see them or not, and this is especially true of the Platonic Ideas. And there is a further difficulty. If everything that exists is good, what, then, is evil?

3

In the image of the sun, Socrates attempts to provide Glaucon with a metaphorical account of the power of the Good. This power is directed toward the domain of Ideas; just as the Ideas give existence and intelligibility to the residents of the natural world, so the Good is the principle of the existence and intelligibility of the Ideas. The first image is thus devoted to the natural light of the sun and the supernatural light of the Good. In the second image, Socrates draws a correspondence between our cognitive faculties and the parts of a line. He refers to these faculties as "affections [*pathēmata*] of the soul" (VI. 511d6–e6), but the image of the divided line abstracts from those functions of the soul that are not concerned with the process of knowledge.

Let us say that the first image is primarily ontological whereas the second is epistemological. What is missing from these two images is human life. Nor does this seem unusual, since we are discussing the most difficult abstractions of philosophy

At first glance, this missing element seems to be furnished by the image of the cave. The image of the cave differs from its two predecessors in two main ways. First: the main topic is no longer the structure of being and cognition; instead, we are provided with a drama of how the human soul stands with respect to education and the lack of it (VII. 514a1–2). In other words, despite or thanks to the peculiar features of life in the cave, it is concerned with the human drama of the conversion to philosophy, as the first two images are not. Second, the images of the sun and the divided line give relatively little attention to the domain of reflections and shadows, whereas the image of the cave is primarily, although not exclusively, about shadows. Because of its subterranean location and dependence upon the shadows of artifacts cast by firelight, we may refer to the cave as the domain of the subnatural. The movement from the first to the third image is from sunlight toward darkness. It is true that the philosopher is shown to emerge from the cave, but he soon returns to it in an effort to release his fellow citizens from their bondage to the illusion that they are viewing the actual world.[8]

I interject a comment on terminology. The Socratic images (*eikones*) do not themselves belong to the domain of shadows and reflections of physical things (*eikasia*). But they are not accounts of originals. There is a shadowy character in every image that makes it difficult to classify them but distinguishes them from *logoi* or demonstrative arguments. Images do not demonstrate in this sense, but they "point out" (the literal meaning of *demonstrare*) or call to mind by means of hints, similarities, and poetic (as distinguished from logical) implications. An image in this sense is the presence of something that is absent but not invisible.

The cave image has often been taken by commentators to represent the city, in which human beings are enchained by custom until they are liberated by philosophy. There is obviously a case to be made for this interpretation, but it is not entirely satisfactory.⁹ To begin with, the cave is the domain of shadows, not of custom. One could say that custom is the shadow of the truth, but this would make the appearances in the cave shadows of shadows, not of custom. In any event, there are no customs in the cave, because there is no community.

If we measure it by the first two images, the cave represents *eikasia*, the lowest segment of the divided line, and not *pistis* (belief), the natural domain of *nomos*. The residents of the cave are bound in a ghostly existence that is in no way analogous to the life of the city. Prior to the philosophical liberation, there is no vestige of communal existence and so no politics. The cave dwellers begin to react to one another only as a result of the intervention by the former prisoner. The resulting debate is not about a transformation of the political arrangements in the cave, of which there are none, but rather the nonphilosopher's response to the philosopher's invocation to undergo a "turning around of the soul," that is, a journey from the darkness of artificial light and shadows up toward the sunlight. It would seem to be closer to the text to say that Socrates is describing the liberation of philosophers from politics altogether. And when the escaped prisoner returns to the cave, his purpose is not political but epistemological.

Considerations of this sort lead me to the following suggestion. If the image has a political message, it is surely that life in actual or nonphilosophical cities is a mere shadow of what politics would be like under the rule of philosophy. But there is another dimension to the image. The cave is subnatural and subpolitical, not a straightforward representation of actual cities in which *nomos* rules. And movement out of the cave is not movement into the city but rather movement into the sunlight. Finally, let us note that the release of the first prisoner is "by nature," not through human agency, whereas the returned prisoner's message to the cave dwellers is strongly resisted by them. There is a bifurcation within human nature that requires compulsion, whether through physical force, rhetoric, or the artificial construction of the city. Reason alone cannot persuade the nonphilosophers to give up their chains. This is the philosophical analogue to the need for compulsion in the institution of justice.

Whatever the political elements in the working out of the cave image, its function is precisely not to provide a rounded picture of prephilosophical life. As the story unfolds, it is clear that there is no intercourse at all among the residents of the cave, with the presumed exception of the puppet masters, to whom I will return shortly. The other residents of the cave are bound by chains on their legs and necks. These chains allow them to see only in front of them; they are "unable to turn their heads in a circle because of the chains" (514a6–b1). It follows that they can neither see each other nor reproduce themselves.

Their light comes from a fire that burns far above and behind them. "Between the fire and the prisoners there is a road above them, on which you must imagine [literally, 'see'] a wall built along it, just like the screens that puppet masters place between themselves and the audience, and over which they show the puppets." Glaucon is instructed to visualize other people carrying all sorts of equipment (artifacts) that project above the wall, as well as statues of human beings and other animals made out of various kinds of material. Some of the carriers utter sounds, obviously corresponding to the nature of their artifacts, whereas others do not (514b1–515a3). The chained residents cannot see themselves or each other, only their shadows cast by the fire onto the wall in front of them. And the same is true for the various implements and statues that the puppet masters are carrying along and behind the wall (515a5–b3).

I have already referred to the disanalogy between the cave and the city. Nevertheless, it is fair to say that for the philosopher, ordinary political life constitutes a shadow existence. Natural objects of the physical world can be considered shadows of their corresponding Ideas; so too with virtues like justice. One could refer to a doctrine of justice rooted in ignorance as a shadow of the real thing. The problem is that justice is not the theme of the image of the cave. In this image, our vision of actual objects is dependent upon our exit from the cave into the domain of the sunlight. This is obviously a repetition of part of the discussion about the Idea of the Good. "Goodness" in the political sense is not at issue. The so-called pedagogical representation in the cave image of our progress up the steps of the divided line is in fact lacking in any pedagogical guidance. Nor does it tell us how the necessary "turning round of the soul" takes place. If, however, we put to one side the concern for structural analogies between the divided line and the cave on the one hand and the cave and the city on the other, it is true and consistent with the portrait of philosophy in the *Republic* that cognitive progress draws us outside political life. In the highest sense, we learn what things truly are by exiting from the city and entering the heaven of Platonic Ideas, and this is certainly a strong point in the image of the cave. This remains true even if the exit from the cave is into the domain of belief associated with natural sunlight. In fact, we would have to pass through the natural world in order to understand what it is to be an artifact of any kind. This is interesting in its own right: The artificial is intelligible only in contrast to the natural.

I think it is a mistake to press the correspondences between the two images of the sun and the divided line and the image of the cave, just as it is wrong to press the correspondences between the city and the cave. On my reading, the cave represents various and not entirely consistent stages of the human soul. The discontinuities between this image and that of the city are another sign of the defect of the analogy between the city and the soul. Of course, it is also true that the soul is to some extent political, or that it finds its perfection, namely, philosophy, only in the city. This is why some aspects of the cave remind us of the city. But the fact remains that the direction of the ascent of the released prisoner is up, that is, beyond the city. I shall discuss the return into the cave in a moment.

Let us turn first to the puppet masters. It seems fairly clear that the puppet masters are not themselves victims but producers of illusion. If they are themselves real persons and not shadows, they must certainly know that they are deluding the chained prisoners, and since they are not themselves bound, they must be free to explore the entrance to the cave, and so to discover that another world lies outside its confines. On the political interpretation, the puppet masters are presumably the ruling class, but as I have pointed out, it is impossible to take the prisoners to be shadowy citizens. The absence of all contact between the prisoners, including that of awareness of each other's existence, is not a shadow of any intelligible political arrangement. It is hardly necessary to add that there can be no sexual reproduction in the cave, and so no preservation of the city. Not quite so obvious is the impossibility of educating the citizens to identify the shadows passing before them or to correlate the sounds they hear with the appropriate shadows. This impossibility is, however, implied by Socrates's hypothetical statement at 515b4–5 beginning "But if they were able to converse . . ."

In short, the main function of the image of the cave is to show that we all live in darkness, or that human existence is a shadow of the life that can only be lived by the philosopher-kings in the just city of the *Republic*. But the truly perplexing corollary is that the highest and purest human life is not at all a life for human beings. The genuine life that corresponds to pure sunlight is a perpetual *Wesenschau* or contemplation of Platonic Ideas. Life within the so-called just city is itself possible only through the use of compulsion, physical and psychological, and so through the promulgation of noble and medicinal lies. I repeat: life in the city ruled by philosophers is a life of darkness as well as illumination, and the illumination depends upon the darkness, if it is to be at all accessible to even a small number of human beings.

The image of the cave has been constructed to emphasize the radical discontinuity between wisdom and everyday life. It is in this context that I approach the question of the identity of the puppet masters. Despite the possibility of identifying them with the rulers of conventional cities, at a deeper level the identification makes no sense. For conventional statesmen are as much under the bondage of *nomos* as are the ordinary citizens. The puppet masters and their artifacts are parts less of a political than of a psychological image. They, together with their imprisoned audience, represent the affection of the soul that treats images as originals. On my reading, the two, masters and slaves, are not separate classes of persons but two aspects of each of us.[10] From this standpoint, the cave is the soul, it is not the city. The shadows are both cast and dissipated by our own inner enactment of the dialectic of master and slave. The freedom that we obtain in the achievement of political power is that of a puppet master; in other words, it is another form of slavery. More generally, the production of light is at once the production of darkness.

Socrates next considers a prisoner who is freed from and "healed" of the bad effects of his chains, namely, thoughtlessness (*aphrosunē*: 515c4ff). This person is released and forced to stand up suddenly "by nature." In other words, he is not released by the puppet masters, and certainly not by his enchained neighbors. I draw the further inference that there is no "method" or set of discursive arguments by which we shift from shadows to objects. This "shift" is an abstraction from the greater complexity of actual consciousness. It is performed instantaneously by nature. We may refer to this as the basis step of the ascent of eros, which was not visible at all in the chained condition. In other words, the real-life ability to shift from shadows to objects is already a consequence of the illuminative powers of the Good, although it is of course a much lower and more dim-sighted version of the ascent to the purely intelligible entities of mathematics and dialectic. The light of the Good is dimly visible in the artificial firelight of the cave, which is thus not entirely dark Even the ability to see shadows is a faculty of the power of sight.

In his first stage of liberation, the former prisoner is compelled not merely to stand up but to walk about and look at the light (obviously of the fire). Socrates says that he is not only dazzled by the light but also in much pain from his previous bondage. In his commentary to the *Republic*, Benardete notes that Socrates does not mention the pleasure associated with the release of the prisoner from his chains.[11] His explanation of why the release is painful is too complex to present in full, but it turns upon "the recovery of the body" from the domain of shadows. This of course assumes that life in that domain is incorporeal and painless. In this case, there would also be no pleasure. I take these useful observations to support my own interpretation of the cave as the soul in its prephilosophical enslavement. One problem with Benardete's reading is that the recovery of the body is apparently identified with the release from the chains, which takes place inside the cave. If that is Benardete's intention, then I think that he is wrong on this point.

We need not emphasize that the released person would hardly be able to stand or walk at all after a lifetime in chains. But Socrates is referring to the soul and its cognitive faculties, not to the actual body, and he attributes the impulse to nature, that is, to a spontaneous shift from one mode of quasi-cognition (the perception of shadows) to another (vision of the cave artifacts and, in the first instance, the fire). We are to imagine someone emerging from the first to the second stage; the ex-prisoner would be incredulous if he were to be told (by whom?) that he is now seeing more correctly, and that the artifacts projecting above the rear wall are more real than their shadows. Our hero would be blinded by the fire and would seek to turn back to the vision of shadows. Once again we are asked to suppose that he is dragged "by force" up the rough, steep, and ascending way to the outer world. When Socrates says that the shift is achieved by nature, he is referring to a compulsion (cf. 515c6, e1, and e6) of the philosophical soul to ascend toward the truth, and not to a rescue force of specially trained epistemologists who happen fortuitously to be present in the cave in addition to the prisoners and their puppet masters.

After the ex-prisoner becomes accustomed to the sunlight, his vision gradually sharpens, and he moves from shadows and reflections to the objects, natural and artificial, of the visible domain, and thus to heavenly bodies and, finally, to the sun and sunlight (516a5–b2). In this way he gradually acquires a correct picture of the physical cosmos and, with it, happiness that arises from comparing his present lot with that of the prisoners below. I note in passing that this is not the same as happiness caused by the release from bondage, and also that it expresses a certain self-satisfaction that is neither just nor, I think, unjust. He has no desire to return, even if he were to be included among those who receive honors and prizes for sharpness in making out the identities and sequences of the shadows of puppets (a possibility that contradicts the immobility of the bound prisoners and their ignorance of their neighbors). At this point, Socrates asks us to imagine that the ex-prisoner has descended back into the cave. No reason is given here for this step. The main point is that the free man would be blinded by the sudden (516e5; cf. 515c6) departure from the sun, and it would take a rather long time for his eyes to adjust to the domain below, so that he would be very poor at identifying the shadows and would be laughed at by his former companions, who would wish to kill the person responsible for our hero's release and apparent blindness.

It is not mentioned that in order to do so they would themselves have to be released from their chains. As I noted a moment ago, the prisoners are now assumed to be cognizant of their neighbors, as well as of the free man who has returned to their domain. More important, however, is the obvious allusion by Socrates to the probable fate of a philosopher who would attempt to free his fellow humans from their bondage to the visible domain. Here we do see an interesting link to the broader political argument. At each stage of ascent, compulsion is required; and the same is true of the attempt to "descend" in order to set free the prisoners below. Human beings do not wish to be liberated from their bondage.

In this stage of the account, it is clear that the structure and the sense of the image of the cave have undergone a dramatic change. Despite their chains, the dwellers in the cave (as distinguished from the puppet masters) are now aware of and able to converse with each other.

Although Socrates does not say so, they must be partially detached from their chains in order to possess these powers. As to the puppet masters, they play no role in this part of the story. There are no masters here, only slaves. The dialectic is now between the cave dwellers and the prodigal son who has returned to enlighten his former companions. Socrates next makes an explicit connection between the image of the cave and the discussion in Book Six of the Ideas, the Good, and the divided line. The domain of the sun is represented by the domain of the cave, which has two parts. The fire corresponds to the sun, whereas the shadows correspond to the images and reflections of the objects of the visible world (517a8–b4). This is compatible with the general understanding of the image of the cave as a metaphor for the ascent of the philosopher to the domain of the Ideas. And Socrates states that the cave represents the domain of the sun, not the city. He thereby reunites the epistemological or psychological elements of his presentation with the ontological foundation of the Ideas. The political dimension drops out entirely.[12]

4

Socrates has now completed his account of what he hopes (*elpidos*) concerning the Idea of the Good; only a god knows if it happens to be true.[13] The hope is then restated as follows: "In the knowable domain [*en tō gnōstō*], the last thing to be seen, and that with difficulty, is the Idea of the Good." A small but not uninteresting point: at VI. 510a9, Socrates uses the word *gnōston* to refer to the visible world of objects, as distinct from the noetic world (*tou noētou*) of intelligibles. Here *gnōston* (517b8) is used as a substitute for *noēton*. This is another indication of the fact that Socrates does not use his technical terms rigorously and univocally. To continue with his summary, once we see the Idea of the Good, "it must be agreed that this is the cause of everything correct and beautiful in all things. In the visible it produces light, and light's sovereign [that is, the sun]; in the intelligible domain, it is itself sovereign, and it furnishes truth and intellect" (*alētheian kai noun paraschomenē*: 517c4). At VI. 508e3, a passage which is echoed here, Socrates said that the Good is the cause of knowledge and truth. "Furnishing" is not quite synonymous with "causes"; we can furnish something to another that we have not ourselves produced. Within the obvious limitations of metaphorical speech, something extremely important is at issue here. If truth and intelligence are caused by the Good, then they are not eternal, unless the Good functions perpetually as their source. In this case, it would be better to say "furnishes" than "causes," and Socrates in fact makes this change. On the other hand, knowledge is caused by intelligence; as to truth, it is ambiguous, since it can apply in one sense to eternal beings and in another to the discursive knowledge produced by human cognition.

This problem will arise again in Book Ten, when Socrates refers to the Ideas as plants that grow in the garden of god (597d5–6). It is, incidentally, implicit in the myth of the soul told by Socrates in the *Phaedrus*, in which he says that even the divine souls that reach easily the roof of the cosmos, see the hyperuranian beings (that is, the Ideas) "through the medium of time" (*dia chronou*: 247c1–2, d3). Indeed, if Ideas are grown or produced, then they must be residents of time, and simply accessible to us through it.

This brings us to the final sentence in Socrates's summary of what he hopes to be true: "Whoever is going to act prudently in private or public must see [the Idea of the Good]" (517c4–5). In order for this to be true, the light of the Good must not only furnish beauty, intelligence, knowledge, truth, and existence but also make moral and political *goodness* visible and understandable. Nothing that has been said thus far casts any light on how this is possible. If we think about an action that has consequences for the person or the city, how does looking at the Idea of the Good establish the goodness or evil of that action? There is no Idea of the action, only of the Good. And the action is not a copy or imperfect representation of the Idea of the Good.

Even if we somehow saw that the Idea of the Good is the cause of, or furnishes, all the good things we have just enumerated, we would still have to know which act or judgment is the prudent, that is, the good one. Furthermore, there could be several possible responses to a given situation, all of them good to one degree or another. How does the Idea of the Good contribute to the process by which we rank-order the possible courses of action? Socrates has to maintain that this knowledge is conveyed by the "illumination" or radiance of the Idea of the Good itself. But what could we say to ourselves or to others to make intelligible the moral or political import of a particular view of the Idea of the Good as bathing a certain decision or intention in its radiance?

If the Idea of the Good illuminates everything, then it must illuminate immoral and imprudent acts and decisions as well as moral and prudent ones. Furthermore, many acts and decisions are sometimes good and sometimes bad. Since the light of the Good is perpetual, the goodness or badness of an act or decision must come from the act or decision itself, that is, from the particular circumstances of the given situation. In this case the light of the Good may allow us to see the act, but it cannot suffice to reveal its character. This has to be decided by practical intelligence. Whereas the Idea of the beautiful discriminates because it is the exemplar of beautiful things only, the Idea of the Good is responsible for everything and thus lacks the power to discriminate, or to allow us to discriminate, between good and bad. If we take into account Socrates's earlier remark at II. 379b15ff. to the effect that god causes the good only, then either evil does not exist or the Idea of the Good does not illuminate everything. Something is missing here: a serious doctrine of evil.

I believe that this lacuna is connected to the absence of politics and eros from the image of the cave. This absence is not compensated for when the cave image takes on a quasi-political appearance. For example, those who have escaped from the cave, which is ironically identified as the domain of visibility (whether by fire or sun), are unwilling to "mind the business of human beings" (*ta tōn anthrōpōn prattein*: 517c4–5). "Human business" is presented here as an epistemic or ontological error, not as an ethical or political one. Justice (IV. 433a1–b4) requires them to mind their own business. In this sense, justice is not political but theoretical, namely, allegiance to the private realm of intelligible beings. On the other hand, Socrates has just claimed that whoever is going to act prudently must first see the Idea of the Good. It therefore seems that justice depends upon the political activity of the philosophers, or a descent from the sunlight back into the cave. If this descent is attempted in actual cities, it will lead to the abuse and probable death of the philosophers, as well as deprive them of their greatest happiness. To the extent that the image of the cave is also a representation of the city, its import is clear: philosophy and politics are not at all harmonious but rather enemies. And yet, the just city depends upon the acceptance by the philosophers of political rule. Socrates will offer an argument to persuade the philosophers of his just city to rule, but this argument holds good only for those philosophers who have been born and raised in the city. Even if a philosopher in the actual world should somehow assume political power or an actual king be a philosopher, there is no reason to assume that they will found the Socratic city, even if they could overcome the obstacles to such an innovation. They are pulled in the opposite direction by the practice of philosophy, and since the city does not yet exist, they owe it nothing.

To recapitulate, the intelligent man distinguishes between disturbances of vision that arise when moving from light to darkness and those that come from a shift from darkness to light. He would not laugh at the soul that is a victim of the first disturbance but would regard it as happy because of what it had previously seen, whereas he would pity and perhaps laugh at the soul that comes from darkness to light and is thus unable to see. I take it to mean that philosophical souls are incapable of functioning properly in the world of non-philosophers and thus behave in a way that is laughable to those whose eyes are accustomed to the dark. The passage also sustains the inference that even if the conventionally just person is happier than the unjust one, the philosopher is happier than both, who are equally pitiful because they cannot see the light of the Good. In short, happiness comes from philosophical justice, or minding one's own business, namely, philosophy, and not at all from political life, not even from ruling the city. This is entirely compatible with the original request by Glaucon and Adeimantus that Socrates depict the happiest life for the individual person. It is also plain that Socrates's answer is limited and obscured by his shift from the individual soul to the city. By forcing the philosophers to rule, Socrates is saying that happiness depends upon making unhappy for a long period of time the very group that is capable of happiness. By calling the nonphilosophical or cave life pitiful, Socrates deprives it of happiness. The nonphilosopher is dazzled by the sight of the intelligible world; that is, he cannot actually see it because he is blinded by approaching its glare and can regain his vision, if at all, only by a return to the cave. The philosopher, so long as he remains within the cave, must accommodate his vision to artificial light, and so to shadows. The cave is thus the metaphorical expression of the correlativity of light and darkness in human existence. In order to exist within the domain of genesis and temporality, to which we are chained, we must produce the artifacts of illusion. In order to be free of those chains, we must ascend to the Platonic Ideas.

The image of the cave was introduced to illustrate the effect of education on our nature. The inference drawn by Socrates is that it is a mistake to conceive of education as putting knowledge into an empty soul, as though we could put sight into blind eyes. On the contrary, the power to learn is innate in the soul. By "power," Socrates seems to mean the eye of the soul, that is, the intelligence. Just as the eye cannot turn by itself toward the light but requires the movement of the whole body, so too "one must turn around with the whole soul out of the domain of genesis until it is capable of looking at being [*to on*] and the brightest part of being, which we call the Good" (518c4–d1). This is an interesting passage because it indicates that the apprehension of being, as well as of the Good (which is "beyond" being), does not depend simply upon an acute intelligence. In order for the eye of the soul to function properly, it must be facing in the right direction, and this requires the turning around of the entire soul toward the light of the good. The split between philosophical and vulgar virtue does not reduce the former to pure intellectual cognition; some traits of character, such as the purification of eros, are necessary as well. As Socrates puts it, the *technē* of the turning round of the soul is not one that produces sight within it (518d3–7). There is no *technē* for the production of intelligence where it does not exist innately, but we can loosen the hold of genesis upon the soul by various disciplinary and pedagogical procedures. One extremely important procedure of this sort is the mathematical education that Socrates will shortly describe, but we should include the entire guardian education in music and gymnastics as contributing to the same end: detachment from immersion in the realm of becoming.

Socrates alludes at this point to the demotic virtues (cf. VI. 500d4–8) by saying that "the other so-called virtues of the soul" are perhaps quite close to the virtues of the body, because, unlike intelligence, they are not present by nature (not inherent in being) but are produced by habits and exercises. The power of intelligence (*tou phronēsai*) is more divine and never loses its power but is either useful or harmful depending upon the way in which it is turned (518d9–519a1). What is unclear here is the degree to which the turning of the soul is dependent upon the "other" virtues. Socrates does say that some persons are vicious and wise; they see very sharply the things toward which they are turned, which shows that their vision is not weak but is compelled to serve evil (519a1–6). Presumably these persons will no longer be vicious if they are turned toward the Good, and Socrates does refer to eating and other pleasures that attach to the soul and turn its vision downward (519a8–b5). The general point seems to be that whereas intelligence is natural, it can be corrupted by bad habits and education, and this is in conformity with the earlier discussion of the corruption of philosophical natures.

In sum, those who lack the proper orientation to the Good, that is, experience of the truth, are unfitted to rule the Socratic city because they lack a single unifying goal—by which Socrates presumably refers to vision of the Good. On the other hand, those who spend their entire lives in self-education are unwilling to participate in political activity, since they regard themselves as already blessed. As founders of the city, we must compel the best natures to engage in the ascent to the vision of the Good, and when they have seen it sufficiently, they must be further compelled to go down again into the cave and to share the work and the honors of the chained prisoners (519b7–d7). Once more, Socrates brings out the fact that the best natures do not ascend to the Good spontaneously; they must be "compelled," whether by the proper education or, as in Socrates's own case, by a divine sign. Furthermore, those who remain in the cave cannot be released by the return of the philosopher, who is forced to accommodate himself to their "toils and honors." In this passage, the cave clearly assumes a political significance despite the lack of structural isomorphism with the city. But just as it was not politics that set the potential philosopher on the upward march out of the city and into the intelligible domain, so it is not philosophy that compels the philosopher to descend from the intelligible to the visible domain and to accept the rule of the just city.

At this point, the paradox that underlies the pursuit of justice emerges with special clarity. Glaucon objects that it is unjust to make the philosophers live a worse life when a better one is available to them. The motivation underlying the entire dialogue is not to build a just city but to determine which is the better life for the individual human being, the just or the unjust. We have constructed the city on the assumption that it is the soul writ large, but it is now evident (as it has been for some time) that what is just for the city is not the same as what is just for the individual person. The same point came up previously with respect to the happiness of the guardians, and Socrates reminded Adeimantus that their purpose is to make a happy city, not happy persons (IV. 419a1–420e1). This is of course nonsense; there are no happy or sad cities. Now the interlocutor is Glaucon, and Socrates reminds him that "it does not concern the law [*nomō*] whether one class in the city fares extremely well, but it contrives to bring this about in the whole city, harmonizing the citizens by persuasion and compulsion, making them share with each other the benefit that each is able to bestow upon the community. And it [that is, the law] produces such men in the city, not so that each is permitted to turn whichever way he wishes, but in order that it may use them in binding the city together" (519e1–520a4).

This statement makes it clear that the best natures in the city must sacrifice their happiness, or a substantial part of their happiness, to the city, and that Socrates could not have been referring to them, but rather to the auxiliaries, when he assured Adeimantus that the guardians would be happier than Olympic heroes. In that passage, Socrates warned Adeimantus not to give the guardians so much happiness as to prevent them from being guardians. Here he issues a version of that warning to Glaucon: do not make the philosophers so happy that they cannot be rulers. The entire education of the philosopher in the just city is thus not for the sake of his happiness but rather for that of the city (cf. III. 416b5–6: education guards the guardians). Now Socrates is about to claim that it is just to compel the philosopher to rule in his city. I shall address this in a moment, but first let us be clear that if the philosopher acts justly, as he must thanks to his vision of the Platonic Ideas, in particular of the Idea of the Good, then the price he pays for living justly is unhappiness. In other words, the individual happiness of the auxiliaries and the philosophers, the two crucial parts of the just city, is entirely subordinated to *nomos* and the sharing of benefits, that is, to the unity of the city. At the very best, Socrates has produced a unified city out of persons who could be much happier elsewhere and, in the case of the very best ones at least, are treated unjustly. The city supervenes over the individual, and in so doing, it obscures if not dissolves the original question of individual happiness. This is an ironical vindication of

Aristotle's remark in the *Nicomachean Ethics* that justice is virtue "for the sake of another" (V. 1130a2–5).

Socrates has defined justice as "minding one's own business." But this can hold good in two different spheres, the private and the public. The philosopher's business in the private sphere is clearly philosophy. If we follow the argument of Socrates in the *Republic*, the business of the philosopher in the just city is to rule, and his entire education has been designed with that in mind, not for the sake of his personal happiness. There is no obligation for the philosopher to rule in actual cities; in fact, there is no such possibility. Assuming the unlikely, namely, the possibility of the just city, the philosopher is compelled to spend his best years minding the business of others, in other words, enforcing justice, which is virtue with respect to others. The only argument that Socrates could offer to show that no injustice is being done the philosopher is to claim that he could not live the philosophical life in some other city, unhampered by the ruling regime. But this is clearly false, as Plato's own life demonstrates. Furthermore, philosophers have been able to survive even in tyrannies, so long as they keep to themselves or mind their own business. We should not, however, take our bearings by the extreme cases. On the whole, it is the nature of the philosophical life that it does not require its practitioners to assume political power. Evidence is plentiful that when philosophers enter into political rule, they do so at the expense of philosophy and not to its benefit.

Socrates would presumably reply that the full development of the philosophical nature depends upon its being cultivated in the proper regime (see VI. 491b7–492e5). But he has not yet mounted a convincing case for the claim that the just city is best for the philosopher. The argument is rather that the philosopher is the best ruler for a city that is to be unified, that is, free from faction (520d3). It is, says Socrates, fitting for philosophers in other cities not to participate in the government, because they have grown up spontaneously against the will of the regime in each and owe these regimes nothing for their rearing. But we have begotten our philosophers for themselves and the rest of the city, to serve as leaders and kings. They have been better educated than the others and are more able to participate in both the philosophical and the ruling life. "Therefore you must go down, each in his turn, into the common dwelling place of the others and accustom yourself to see the dark things" (*ta skoteina*: 520b5–c3).

Perfectly educated philosophers can live both the public life and the private life. But they have been produced specifically to live the public life. This is their main function, and once it is fulfilled, they are then permitted to step out of office and return full-time to their studies. This is surely problematic. It is entirely unclear why the particular education of the philosophers, namely, mathematics and dialectic, fits them above all others for political rule. It would seem rather to detach them from the realm of becoming, and hence from the city. But the justification for compelling philosophers to rule depends squarely upon the premise that they are best suited to do so. Why should we accept Socrates's contention that their previous education makes the philosophers, once they have become accustomed to the cave light, ten thousand times better able to see and identify the shadows in the cave than anyone else (520c3–6)? It would be more likely to disable them for effective cave vision. But even if the reverse is true, and Socrates is correct about this point, how are the philosophers to persuade the cave dwellers of the superiority of their own judgments? That they cannot persuade them is plain from the tripartition of the soul and the need to govern by persuasion and force, and in particular by noble or medicinal lies.

The preceding reflection brings us to the conclusion that justice depends upon forcing human beings to do what philosophers believe to be just. And of course, this includes the justice of forcing philosophers to rule. The conclusion is by no means implausible, since in actual life we are frequently compelled to do what we ought to do, rather than to follow our natural inclinations. In this case, however, justice is involuntary, that is, not natural but dependent upon compulsion. And this in turn brings us back to the initial arguments of Glaucon and Adeimantus, namely, that no one would choose to be just if it were possible to be unjust without detection or punishment. It is thus difficult to see why the just life, chosen voluntarily for its own sake, is the happiest, or at least happier than the unjust life would be if we were free to live it.

However this may be, Socrates claims that the philosophers, having seen the truth about the noble, just, and good things, will better see and identify their images, so that they and we will be able to govern the city in full wakefulness, not in a dream in which human beings fight over shadows and thus split into political factions (520c6–d1). And they will accept the injunction to rule because it is just; note that Socrates does not say that they will be happy to submit to this compulsion but says rather that they regard it as a duty they must discharge. Socrates implies that the task is not onerous, since the philosophers will be free to dwell in the intelligible realm for the greater part of the time (520d6–8). We shall come back to this observation when we examine the details of the education of the philosophical natures.

5

Those philosophers who are born and educated in the just city "must go down" (*katabateon*) into the domain of shadows and accustom themselves to seeing there, in order to rule the city, each in his or her turn (520c1–3). Socrates here unmistakably gives a political interpretation to the cave, which represents all cities, actual or imagined. The exit of the philosopher from the cave is not accessible to the nonphilosophers, who continue to be ruled by shadows, that is, by the laws and customs to be established by the rulers. We recall that the first word of the *Republic* is "I went down" (*katebēn*), which is often taken to indicate Socrates's own descent into the cave of the Piraeus. This makes sense to the extent that Socrates is detained by force and is thus compelled to introduce his revolutionary political teaching. On the other hand, the reference to force is largely playful; what should rather be said is that Socrates voluntarily descends to the Piraeus in order to see a novel religious ceremony but is diverted from his intention by the accidental encounter with Polemarchus. The long conversation follows from the initial conversation with Cephalus and could not have been foreseen. This shows the element of chance that enters into the initiation of political revolutions.

It also has an important bearing on the question of the willingness or unwillingness of the philosopher to rule. As I noted at the outset, Socrates is amazingly frank in his construction of the wished-for city. This frankness is itself something more than the founding of a city in speech; it constitutes a political act in its own right, a bringing down (and so a *katabasis*) of philosophy from the heavens into the city (not to mention the lower city). To exaggerate slightly but not misleadingly, the "masked philosopher" is more fully a resident of the just city than of Athens. With all due recognition of irony and concealment, frankness is a necessary attribute of the Socratic, and so too of the Platonic, enterprise. It is not, of course, the entire enterprise.

We are encouraged by the text and our own historical experience to wonder whether the reluctance of the philosopher to rule cannot be overcome under certain circumstances. In fact, this reluctance would seem to be more properly a feature of the imagined than of the actual city. In the city we are now constructing, the philosophers will be educated in such a way as to abstract them from any concern with human affairs. They will wish to spend their days in contemplation of the pure Ideas, not in statecraft. Furthermore, within the just city, there is no room at all for the introduction of political revolutions; the just city has been founded, and the philosopher-king's only task is to preserve it in its original form, so far as this is possible.

But the coming into existence of the just city depends upon philosophers, even those as apparently apolitical as Socrates, having dangerous conversations with politically active and well-educated persons. It is naive to suppose that these conversations could be entirely insulated from the public, and in fact it is impossible to suppose this once Plato publishes the *Republic*.

In sum: I offer the conjecture that the reluctance of the philosophers inside the just city to assume the rule is because they are not actual philosophers but rather a caricature or a part of philosophy that is allowed to represent the whole. In my view, their rule would be disastrous, since they have been carefully deprived of all the requisite training and are by nature uninterested in obtaining the relevant experience, although Socrates will allow a certain period in their education in which to acquire it. This feature belongs to what we can call the ironical or esoteric side of Socrates's presentation. In order to solve the political problem, we must have philosopher-kings. But genuine philosophers would not restrict themselves to preserving the current political order; there would soon spring up schools, factions, and competing ideologies. What we require, therefore, is politically sterile quasi-philosophers with no ambition to change the existing order, who wish to "go up" as soon as possible to the domain of the Ideas. The solution to the political problem is the production of a static society lacking in the most important political features, a kind of maimed society that is governed by political incompetents.

Those for whom such thoughts are too adventurous are encouraged to pass the previous paragraph by, provided that they can offer a serious interpretation of the *Republic* that makes political and philosophical sense. Such an interpretation, in other words, must jettison piety and show that the Socratic city is not only possible but also desirable. My thesis is that it is neither, and that there is no real solution to the political problem. But we must continue to act as if such a solution were possible, for that is the only solution, and it is the essence of the noble lie. In other words, it is not enough to reject Plato's version of the just city. One must explain how a consummate thinker and artist like Plato could have produced an acknowledged masterpiece that recommends an absurd course of action. Perhaps one should reread *Don Quixote* before approaching the *Republic*.

Socrates says that the existence of a well-governed city depends upon our identifying a life that is better than ruling for the very persons who are going to rule. This is the life of the philosopher, who seeks no political honors or power, and who agrees to rule "without desiring it" (*mē erastas*) only in order to avoid the factionalism that arises from the struggle of the rival nonphilosophers to acquire the rule that they love (520e1–521b5). As I have just pointed out, it is unclear how there can be factions within the Socratic city. The auxiliaries will have been educated as subordinates, not as rivals to the throne. Socrates takes it for granted that there will be no rival philosophical schools, or in other words, and putting to one side my adventurous hypothesis, that all philosophers born and educated in the just city will be Platonists who are immune to faction. Unlike Plato, however, they have no political eros. That this is, to say the least, extremely unlikely is shown by the disagreement among

Plato's immediate students, shortly after his death, concerning such central issues as the doctrine of Ideas. Plato himself may never have changed his mind (already a dubious assumption), but the same cannot be said for Platonists, not to mention their inability to arrive at a common understanding of the master's teaching. Presumably the philosopher-kings will put to one side their doctrinal disagreements in order to preserve the unity of the city. Socrates counts heavily on the homogeneity of the education to be received by potential philosophers. No doubt the general upbringing of the guardian class will contribute to uniformity of thinking among the auxiliaries, but if the kings are to be of the highest caliber, we must assume that they will be able to think for themselves and thus raise the likelihood of substantive disagreement. In order for philosophy to rule, it must transform itself into ideology. It thus turns out that my adventurous remarks were not quite as adventurous as they seemed.

There is nothing adventurous in doubting that those who do not wish to rule but are compelled to do so will perform at a higher level than those who are suited by nature for the political life. The tedious routine of everyday government can hardly engage the full attention of those who are accustomed to dwelling in the domain of the Ideas. To this must be added our doubts that the training we are about to discuss is appropriate for the production of the best rulers. Socrates apparently has no such doubts; in the passage under discussion, he refers to the philosophers as "those who are most prudent [*phronimōtatoi*] in the things through which a city is best managed" (521b8–9). And he turns next to the education that will "engender" (*enggenēsontai*) such persons. The education must draw the soul away from becoming and up to being (*to on*). This cannot be accomplished by music, gymnastics, or the arts, the last of which we have rejected as vulgar (*banausoi*). Yet, somewhat strangely, although we have exhausted the individual kinds of study, we find what we are looking for in that which is common to them all, namely, "the trifling matter of distinguishing the one, the two, and the three. To say it in general, I refer to arithmetic and calculation" (522c6–7).

Arithmetic studies the properties of numbers; calculation is devoted to the operations we perform with them. Every art and science is forced to participate in these two disciplines. We must of course refer to them as arts or sciences as well, but they differ from the others in that they take us away from the vulgar, corporeal, and particular, and so from the domain of generated instances of things of such-and-such a kind. Every thing whatsoever is *one* thing. This trifling observation is enough to exhibit the difference between a number and the object of any other art or science. Whereas the objects of each science differ from the objects of the other sciences in the kind of thing they are, the unity or oneness of every object in every science is the same. Each cow is different from every other cow, but also from every horse, human being, tree, flower, and so on. It is this difference that allows us to say "one" in every case. Thus oneness is itself different from the formal and material properties by which objects are differentiated. Unity or oneness is, so to speak, a form without features; it cannot be a body or possess a perceptible shape, even though it applies to bodies and shapes.

This is not the place for an exhaustive analysis of the concept of unity. Socrates is appealing to what are initially commonsense notions about numbers. Stated simply, a number is for Socrates a plurality of units. In a full account, we would have to distinguish between pure or theoretical numbers and counting numbers. The latter can be used to count objects of the domain of genesis, whereas the former cannot. Thus the number seven used to give the sum of the individual members of a herd of seven cows is itself made up of seven "cow" units, whereas the theoretical number seven consists solely of seven units. Socrates does not draw this distinction in the present passage. Instead, he speaks simply of numbers as universally applicable to objects of any kind. I should also note that the definition of *number* means that "one" is not a genuine number; it is instead the standard or basis step out of which numbers are generated as "so many units." Socrates follows common sense in assuming here that each collection of distinguishable things can be placed in one-to-one correspondence with a determinate number. This is how a general, for example, knows how many ships he has in his fleet or, at a more humble level, how many feet he possesses.[14]

According to Socrates, not only is it the case that every art and science, including the art of war, uses numbers and calculation, it is also true that if the arts of arithmetic were properly used, they would by their nature draw us toward pure intelligence (*noēsin*), that is to say, pure being or "being-ness" (*ousian*: 522d1–523a3). This is a very deep assertion. Socrates is implying that the physical world of genesis "participates" in an intelligible world of numbers, thanks to the fact that each item of genesis is one, a property that can be "summed" by human intelligence in a process we call "counting," without destroying the independence of each element in the sum. To take my standard example, each cow in a herd remains one cow, even though that one cow is an element in a herd of, say, seven cows. If any cow would cease to be a unit through the act of being counted, then the number of cows in the herd would diminish by one. Socrates never considers this as a serious possibility, although strictly speaking, no one can guarantee the regularity of the natural order. The "isomorphism" (to borrow a term from mathematics) of "being" and "unity," which is developed at great length by Aristotle, is here taken for granted as an item of common sense.

In sum, to be is to be this thing here of such-and-such a kind. The "kind" is the measure of the unity of the being; nothing can both be and not be a member of a definite kind. Now of course, a thing can be a member of more than one kind. But it is a matter of common sense that for each thing, there is a kind to which the thing belongs by its very nature, that is, by virtue of its being the *kind* of thing that it is: say, a cow. The kind *cow* consists of those properties and their ordering that are exactly the properties one must possess in order to be a cow, no more and no less. I believe that Socrates would grant the impossibility of knowing or listing precisely those properties and the order through which something is a cow, but he would nevertheless insist that the kind, or as he calls it, the Idea, of the cow is immediately given in the unity and intelligibility, and so the existence, of any cow whatsoever or, stated more cautiously, by our experience of cows.

Much the same point holds good with respect to unity and number. To be anything at all that is intelligible or, in an alternative formulation, that possesses the power to act and be acted upon, as being the very thing that it is, is a "one" or unity; it possesses the property of unity. This is why "being" and "one" can be used interchangeably: There is no being that is not a one. But there is also no being that is merely a one; that is, every being is also a many. A cow has more than one essential property. But we cannot say that "being" and "many" can be used interchangeably, because each item in a manifold is what it is by virtue of its unity. I can say that a cow has many attributes, but in order to say that it *is* a many, I must first see it as the unity of many elements. Being is of course both one and many, but unity is prior to multiplicity because each element of that multiplicity is itself a unity, and so too is the manifold itself. A manifold could not exist, let alone be intelligible, if it were not this particular manifold, of such-and-such a kind, consisting of definite elements of such-and-such a kind, and thus it is a unity in two different senses, both of which are the foundation or basis for its manyness.

To repeat a previous image, the cosmos of generated particulars is covered over with a web of units, a web of one unit for each existing item. By counting and calculating, we make use of this web and are thereby turned partly away from the domain of genesis. But how are we drawn to a thoughtful consideration of the mathematical structure of intelligibility? It is one thing to know that we each have two legs, and something else again to focus our attention upon the unity within each element of a manifold. Socrates approaches this question very generally by asking for the circumstances under which we supplement sense perception by the pure thinking of *ousia*.

Some sensations do not invoke intellect because they do not present themselves as their opposite. Socrates apparently means by this that where there is no confusion as to the identity of the perceived object, pure thinking (as opposed to the discursive intellect that calculates with respect to items of genesis) has no role to play. We simply do not notice what I called the web of units, even though we are sustained by it in our ordinary perceptual experience. But there are other cases in which sense perception is unable to present to cognition one stable identity. Socrates gives the example of the index, middle, and little fingers. Perception gives us each finger as a finger, and not at the same time as two opposite identities; hence there is no need to call upon pure thinking. But the same finger is long or short, thick or thin, and soft or hard, depending upon which *other* finger to which we compare it (523c11–524a5).

The sense of this passage is not immediately clear. If I compare my thumb with my index finger, it looks short, whereas if I compare my index finger with my thumb, it looks long. It would be unreasonable to assert that this simple experience is enough to invoke *noēsis*. But this is because we are not concerned with the precise definition of long and short; our calculation with the concept of length is, as it were, regulated and dominated by the stable identity of the two fingers or, still more simply, by my desire to see which of two definite fingers is longer, thicker, or harder than the other. Trouble arises if I begin to worry about how the same finger can be long and short or thick and thin.

But is the trouble not easily settled by noting that the same finger is short in comparison with one finger and long with respect to a different finger? In one sense this is true, but Socrates wishes to say that the trouble is not with respect to which of two fingers is longer, and so it is not regulated by the perception of the fingers *as* fingers but rather has to do with the identification of long and short, hard and soft, thick and thin, and so on.

The aforementioned qualities are *relatives*; that is to say, they do not define separate existing things of a definite kind, like a cow, or a definite part of some composite, which we identify with a proper name or noun, like a finger, but refer instead to qualities that are attributed to a thing with respect to something else. Nothing is hard in itself, long in itself, and so on, except with respect to another. Socrates must therefore be claiming that pure intellect comes into play when we shift from names to relations, or more precisely, to those relations that are invoked to explain sensory puzzles like the one in the text.

This puzzle arises because our perception of a finger does not in itself, qua perception of a finger, answer the question how the finger can be both hard and soft, and so on. At this point we have to turn away from the sensed object as such and look toward general properties of sensed objects. These general properties are in one sense perceived (I come into contact with a hard finger by touching it), but in another they are grasped in pure thinking, because they have no sensory properties. To say that this finger is a finger is to utter a tautology. But to say that it is hard is always to make a judgment, not simply about the finger but about a relation in which the finger in question is one term. And the relation itself is not a sensory property.

Socrates refers throughout this passage to the soul as that which summons sensation, calculation, and intellection to the task of identifying the cognized item. This is not merely a *façon de parler*. The soul is the underlying unity that directs and integrates distinct cognitive powers. Otherwise put, it is active in each but identical with no single power. The soul is a unity that employs calculation and intellect in order to investigate whether the two opposing perceptions it has received (for example, the finger is long and short) are one or two (524b3–5). It follows from this account that the soul seems to communicate with itself independently of its perceptual and cognitive faculties. I do not think that we should take this literally; it is intended to convey the function of the soul that coordinates perceptions and thoughts into the unity of experience. This is a role that cannot be played by perception or conceptual thinking. Furthermore, as the principle of life, the soul is connected to the body without being reducible to it. It can (partly) detach itself from the body by the exercise of pure thinking, and this detachment is prepared by the shift from perceived particulars to general properties, such as relations. There is a problem in this passage. In Book Six (511b3ff.), *noēsis* is said to be independent of perception (*aisthēsis*) and to make no use of icons. Here (524b10–c2), it is invoked in order to resolve a contradiction in the report of sense perception. This illustrates the impossibility of providing a precise analytical description of the structure of the soul and, in particular, of answering definitively the question of whether the soul performs all of its functions as a unity or through "parts" (that is, distinct faculties; see IV. 436a8–b3).

At IV. 436 b7, Socrates says that the same part of the soul cannot do or suffer opposites at the same time and in the same way. If this should seem to occur, then we know that what was taken to be one is in fact many. On the basis of the present passage, we have to refine the earlier statement. Sense perception produces the illusion of opposites occurring simultaneously; this has to be corrected by calculation and discursive thinking. The understanding of a relation, for example, in the case of the finger that is long in one sense and short in another, requires us to think the relata at issue; at least this is how Socrates now presents the matter.

Suppose once more that the soul receives two sense perceptions of the same finger, namely, that it is both long and short. Perception itself is unable to resolve this contradiction. The first step is to employ calculation and intellect in order to determine whether these perceptions are actually two or one. If each is one whereas both taken together are two, then the soul will regard each perception as a distinct unity. In the present case, it cannot come to such a decision, because the finger is the same in both cases, whereas "long" and "short" are not things in themselves but modifications of things like fingers expressing a comparison or rank-ordering with respect to the property of length. Socrates puts this as follows: calculating and thinking show the soul that long and short are each one and both together two. It follows that they cannot both attach to the finger at the same time and in the same way. That is, the intellect is forced to see big and little as two distinct things, not as mixed up together into a single thing. And this moves us for the first time to ask what it is to be long and short or big and little. In sum, sense perception is capable of grasping some things as they are in themselves (*auto kath' hauto*). When a perception contains a contradiction, it gives rise to calculation and thinking (524b1–d6). But we must not forget that these last two powers, although they act in a way that goes beyond the perceptions themselves, are invoked by them. We do not begin to think with purely intelligible entities.

6

This rather long discussion of fingers is the preparation for explaining the status of the one together with all numbers. The one cannot be seen in itself as separate from its opposite, the many; therefore this property of opposition belongs to all numbers, since seven, for example, consists of seven ones, but in such a way as to constitute a unity distinct from every other natural number. Note that Socrates is referring here to the defective character of the perception of unities that are at once a manifold, that is, to the sensed particulars of genesis. But the same problem could apply to purely theoretical numbers that consist of pure monads. And of course, it applies to Platonic Ideas as well, each of which is a one as the particular Idea it is but also a many, because in order to be intelligible, it must have distinct features. "One" and "many" can be distinguished analytically, that is, by pure thinking. But they cannot be grasped as separate in their very being.

For Socrates, the main point here is that the one and the many turn us away from sense perception to calculative thinking. They are thus useful for the potential philosophers, because they lead them toward the truth. As to the auxiliaries or soldiers, they need to know how to calculate in order to arrange their troops, weapons, and supplies. Arithmetic and calculation must therefore be basic to the education of the two parts of the guardian class, if for different reasons in each case, namely, war on the one hand and the vision of pure being on the other (524d7–525c7). Socrates differentiates the study and use of arithmetic and calculation as it is practiced by philosophers and soldiers from the way it is practiced by merchants. This must refer to the baseness of moneymaking rather than to any intrinsic difference between the use of calculation in war and in private activities like commerce (that is, in peace).

At this point, I would like to interpolate a remark that is of importance for the overall discussion of philosophy in the *Republic*. The emphasis upon the role of mathematics in war and as a preparation for philosophical dialectic is an obvious consequence of the central fact about Socrates's just city. In founding this city, Socrates concentrates on the guardian class in the broad sense of the term, namely, as including auxiliaries or soldiers and philosopher-kings. But we should not infer from the link between war and philosophy in the just city that philosophy is itself intrinsically polemical. In all actual cities, the goal of the philosopher is to live as peaceful a life as possible and, in the extreme case, to spend life in a state of contemplation that is as far removed from war as possible. In the Socratic city, the philosopher must spend much of his or her life preparing for and engaging in war. War is an essential ingredient of politics, not of philosophy. One must add at once that in actual cities the philosopher is at war in two metaphorical senses, first, in the attempt to conquer ignorance, an attempt that is regularly compared in the dialogues to hunting, wrestling, boxing, and, by extension, the "dialectic" that is a constant feature of Socrates's interrogations of those who claim to be wise or are unaware of their own ignorance.[15] The second sense is an extension of the nature of dialectic (here used to refer to Socratic conversations, not to the pure philosophical science of Book Seven). The philosopher must engage in a constant discursive polemic in order to protect philosophy from the hatred of the nonphilosopher. This polemic, however, often takes the form of the pursuit of agreement, and hence of peace. In this second sense, the element of war has to do with what I shall call the "international relations" of the philosopher with the nonphilosophers. It is of course important for the survival of philosophy, but of philosophy as peace. It is also true, however, that these two metaphorical senses of being at war underlie the very explicit inclination of philosophy toward the acquisition of political power.

To continue with the main argument, I alluded earlier to the difference between theoretical numbers and those that are used for counting collections of perceptible objects. Socrates now refers briefly to this distinction. Arithmetic and calculation of the sort practiced by soldiers (and, I add, merchants) make use of counting numbers, namely, those whose standard unit is a finger, a cow, an apple, or whatever is being counted. We are, however, concerned with numbers that are in no way attached to bodies, and so whose units are homogeneous monads that cannot themselves be cut up or multiplied into a many, as could, for example, the cow unit that serves as the standard for the construction of numbers used to count cows. Socrates does not allude to a problem that should at least be mentioned. If the monads of pure numbers were all homogeneous, then they could be used indifferently to compose any number. But in addition, as homogeneous, they could not be distinguished the one from the other. It is circular to say that the pure monads of, say, the theoretical number seven can be counted one by one until we reach the sum of seven. Such a calculation presupposes the distinctness of the homogeneous monads. In order to avoid this circularity, we must presume that the pure monads of seven are distinct from the pure monads of, say, six or eight. But they cannot be, if they are uniquely one, that is, homogeneous, and so indistinguishable the one from the other. Furthermore, the pure number six contains the pure numbers two, three, four, and five (to say nothing of one). But they seem each to be made up of a selection of six-monads (that is, monads constituting the number six). In this case, the monads of six are not unique to it; that is, there are no proper six-monads or monads of any other number.

These puzzles of Greek number theory are of interest to us because they show us that the Platonic Ideas cannot be numbers or, conversely, that numbers are not Platonic Ideas.[16] Each number greater than one contains at least two numbers (two contains two one's, three contains one and two, and so on). If each Idea is a number, then it will appear within an endless number of other Ideas. But whereas numbers are made up of homogeneous units (or are supposed to be), Ideas are not. Assume that two is the number corresponding to the cow. Then every number containing two will correspond to an Idea containing the Idea of the cow. This is clearly absurd.

Socrates next asks the pure mathematicians what sort of numbers they are talking about that are made up of purely homogeneous units. The reply is that they are referring to numbers that can be thought discursively (*dianoēthēnai*) only (526a6). It is not clear whether Socrates is using *dianoein* as synonymous with *noein*, or whether he wishes to distinguish between mathematical thinking and the thinking of pure Ideas. I think that the latter is the case; Ideas are apprehended or intuited by *noēsis*, but if one is going to analyze the structure of an Idea, then discursive thinking and calculation are both required, as in the eidetic arithmetic discussed in the *Philebus*. This is certainly true in the case of mathematics. Finally, the study of arithmetic is also desirable because it makes us quicker at all our other studies and requires more hard work than the rest (526a1–c7).

Socrates next takes up the study of geometry, using the same criterion as in the case of arithmetic. Parts of geometry are required for the art of war, but not the more advanced part of the science. In the case of the potential philosophers, advanced geometry turns us away from becoming and toward being, thereby enabling us better to see the Idea of the good (526d1–527c10). It is worth noting that Socrates does not raise the problem of the one and the many in the discussion of geometry. Whereas one geometrical figure may contain another (for example, a triangle may be inscribed within a circle or divided into smaller triangles), the figure of the circle cannot be perceived as a figure of a triangle as well. There may be misperceptions, but if the perception functions normally, there is no opposition within it of the kind that accrues to long and short or thick and thin. It is also interesting that no distinction is drawn between "counting" geometrical figures and purely theoretical ones. The geometrician as such studies what is always, not what comes to be and passes away (527b5–6). The use of geometry in practical calculations is thus different from the use of arithmetic in war and business, although why this should be so is not mentioned. Before leaving this passage, I call attention to 527c2, in which Socrates warns Glaucon to tell the citizens "of your beautiful city" (*kallipolei*) never in any way to neglect geometry. This is the only use of the Greek word *kallipolis* in the *Republic*, although its equivalent occurs at 543d1–544a1.[17]

Socrates next suggests astronomy as the third element in the philosophical education. Glaucon replies that this will be very useful for farming, navigation, and generalship. He apparently fails to see the connection for philosophers between astronomy and mathematics, perhaps because the former studies the visible heavens. Socrates chastises him for answering like one who is afraid of the many. He then asks Glaucon whether he is conversing with those who seek the truth with the eye of the intellect or those for whom such a proposal is meaningless. "Or is it for neither of these, but primarily for yourself that you make these speeches [that is, participate in these discussions], but without begrudging it if some one of these other persons would be able to benefit from them?" Glaucon replies: "I choose [the answer] that I speak mostly for myself, both in questioning and answering" (527d1–528a5). Exactly as in Aristotle, the individual person seeks happiness for himself; the happiness of others is a secondary consideration. This shows the weakness of Socrates's claim that we are seeking to make the entire city happy, not a part of it.

At this point, Socrates admits to a mistake in his exposition that was due to haste. The sequel to plane geometry is not astronomy but solid geometry. Socrates thus comes close to neglecting geometry, something against which he has just warned the residents of Glaucon's city. Socrates attributes the low stage of the development of solid geometry to the fact that it is not held in honor by any city, and because there is no one to supervise work done on the subject. Counting, calculating, and plane geometry are immediately useful in everyday life, as solid geometry, thanks to the current level of technology, is not. The passage makes three points. First, the activities of everyday life play a role in the development of the pure sciences. Second, the arts and sciences can prosper through the stimulus of organized research. This is the distant ancestor of the modern research team. Third, despite all obstacles, the study of solid geometry grows because of its innate charm (528a6–c8). This remark can be extended to the arts and sciences as a whole. It also raises a question as to the ability of the philosopher-kings to regulate technical progress in the beautiful city.

Astronomy is then the fourth in the list of educational requirements. But Socrates is not speaking of astronomy as it is usually understood. Contrary to Glaucon's revised statement, the study of visible patterns in the heavens does not turn the potential philosopher's sight away from becoming and toward the domain of true being. These patterns must be used as aids in the study of the purely intelligible motions in accord with genuine speed and slowness, as measured by genuine numbers, of the genuine stellar figures that are accessible not to the eye but only to *logos* and *dianoia*. This sounds something like a model of the visible cosmos, a model consisting of mathematical idealizations of physical planets and stars. Socrates, of course, is referring not to a model constructed by human scientists but to a genuinely existing intelligible expression of the structure of the visible cosmos. We note once more that this "model" falls within the scope of discursive intelligence (528e3–529d5). It is therefore presumably not a "likely story" like the one described in the *Timaeus*.

The fifth and last element in the philosophical study of mathematics is harmonics, the antistrophe to astronomy. The latter has its root in the eye, and the former in the ear. Just as astronomy studies, or should study, the pure motions of intelligible originals of which the celestial bodies are imperfect copies, so harmonics, we may presume, when properly pursued, studies the mathematical properties of "intelligible" sound. Socrates does not elaborate on this science but says that we shall consult the Pythagoreans for further details. This is the second time that an outside expert is called upon. The first time was in Book Three and concerned music; the expert to be consulted is Damon (400b1–2). All that need be mentioned here is that Socratic harmonics will study the ratios of numbers that produce sonic concordances, but not the sounds themselves (530d4–531c4).

This completes the "useless" education of the potential philosopher up to the study of dialectic. We must of course not forget the preliminary training in music and gymnastics, as well as the experience derived from war, but these are clearly useful. The question is whether they are useful for training rulers. Certainly a good case can be made for their utility, but not for their sufficiency as a preparation for the art of government. On the other hand, Socrates might claim that there is no formal preparation for prudence or sound practical judgment, and that this faculty will be developed in the fifteen years of practical experience that philosophers must negotiate before they are permitted to exercise royal authority. There is, then, political experience, but not a political *technē* akin to music and mathematics.

Socrates now indicates that the description of the mathematical education was a prelude to the main theme or melody (*nomos*). Glaucon agrees at once with Socrates that, with the exception of a very few, as he qualifies the point, those who are clever at mathematics are not dialecticians, which is the proper occupation of the genuine philosophers (531d7–e3). Why then was it necessary for the potential philosopher to spend ten years in the study of mathematics? The answer given by Socrates is that this study serves to detach the eye of the intellect from the transient objects of sense perception. It also makes quick learners still quicker, as well as accustoming them to intense intellectual exercise. As it seems, however, the detachment in question directs us to pure mathematical forms rather than to the so-called Platonic Ideas; those who reason with these forms make use of corporeal bodies as images and proceed by way of hypotheses that cannot be "discharged" at the termination of the process of reasoning. A special gift is required to detach one's intellect from the charm of mathematics and to allow it to ascend to the purely intellectual domain in which there are no images at all, only pure Ideas and hypotheses that are indeed discharged at the end of the process of reasoning.

Let me emphasize this important point. Just as the philosopher must spend many years in the exercise of power that he does not love, so too must he devote many years to the study of subjects that are not part of, and in fact turn most of its adepts away from, philosophy. Even in the just city, and perhaps especially here, the philosopher is not free to live an entire life of pure contemplation. In all cities, actual or wished for, to the extent that the philosopher participates in politics, whether in the derivative sense of educating others or the extreme case of ruling, war replaces peace for most of the philosophical life. In saying this, I do not retract my previous assertion that philosophy is intrinsically peace. The point is rather that there are insuperable obstacles to peace that are ingredient in human life. In order to retain its connection with human existence, the fantasies of the Socratic city must be regulated by those same obstacles. It is ironical but true that the very circumstances which, according to Socrates, produce the genuine philosopher serve also to restrict his or her access to that life. This is true in both a theoretical and a practical sense, and in both cases the liberating and restricting instrument is mathematics.

7

Mathematics is the prelude to philosophy; dialectic is the principal theme. The prelude acquires its utility for us if it brings the things we have studied thus far into community and kinship with one another, and if it can compute in what way they are related to one another. Otherwise, it is useless for our purposes, however helpful it may be in other contexts (531c9–d4). The peculiarity of mathematics, clearly indicated by Socrates, is that it serves both to draw us toward the domain of the intelligible and to obstruct our access to the Platonic Ideas. It is this peculiarity that leads to the odd relationship as well as opposition between mathematics and Platonism. In the long tradition of mathematical or mathematically influenced philosophy, one finds a strong current of Platonism, but also the use of mathematics in various ways to heap ridicule upon the Platonic Ideas. The pertinence of mathematics to philosophy is on the one hand undeniable but on the other sufficiently ambiguous to lead to a revision of the original doctrine, at least as we find it in the *Republic*. Stated as simply as possible, mathematical Platonism means the belief in the eternal existence of pure mathematical entities, such as the natural numbers or sets, as the actual objects of mathematical study. For the mathematician, the prelude *is* the principal melody.

This is not the place, nor am I the person, to enter into a technical analysis of the long and complex relationship between mathematics and philosophy. I do need to emphasize that Socrates is aware of the fact that proficiency in mathematics is usually an obstacle to dialectic as he understands it: The Platonic Ideas are either altered or rejected. Yet this is apparently a risk that must be run as a propaedeutic that turns the student away from genesis toward eternity. As to the main melody, it completes the initial ascent from the cave of shadows to the things that exist in, and are illuminated by, the light of the sun. Sight is the imitation of dialectic, which latter functions exclusively in the realm of the intelligible. As Socrates initially states the task of dialectic, it must be able to give and receive *logos* (531e4–5). Note that this requires the use of speech or argument (it proceeds *tōi dialegesthai*: 532a5–6), the *logos* through which, with no assistance from the senses, we attain to what each thing is itself and do not give up until we grasp what is good itself through *noēsis* alone, and thus arrive at the end of the noetic realm (532a5–b2).

In this passage, the distinction between *noēsis* and *dianoia* is not one between silent contemplation and discursive thinking but instead has to do with the nature of the entities considered by each. Socrates then draws attention to the fact that the ascent from the visible to the intelligible is expressed by the icon of the cave (532b6–d1). Glaucon assumes that Socrates can articulate the properties of the main melody, just as he did in the case of the prelude. This amounts to the request that Socrates replace the poetical representation of the highest form of intelligible thought by *logos*, as he did in the case of mathematics (although, we must add, not completely). But Socrates demurs. "My dear Glaucon, you will no longer be able to follow me, although there would be no lack of zeal on my part. For you would no longer see an icon of the things we are discussing, but the truth itself, as it now appears to me, whether genuinely or not, it is no longer worth insisting. But that there is something like this to see, that one must insist upon" (533a1–5). The passage is unclear, but the problem seems to be not that there are no words to describe the nature of dialectic but that Glaucon could not understand them. In other words, his general intelligence and previous education make it possible for him to grasp more or less what Socrates has to say about all aspects of the founding of the city except this one. Nor is that surprising, since he has not yet himself undergone the special education required for the task. Otherwise stated, whereas the entire discussion is in one way or another an accommodation to the intelligence of Glaucon, to say nothing of the other interlocutors, the treatment of dialectic is necessarily more evasive than what has preceded or what will follow.

Glaucon understands enough to agree that one must insist upon the truth of something like what Socrates says, namely, that there is a way of understanding what each thing is, a way that differs from all the other arts, even those of mathematics, which dream about being but are incapable of seeing it in full wakefulness (533b6–c1). He then recapitulates the four parts of the divided line: knowledge, discursive thinking, trust, and imagination (*eikasia*), which correspond respectively to Platonic Ideas, mathematical entities, the objects of genesis, and their shadows or icons. The one true form of knowledge is thus knowledge of the Ideas; mathematics is something between knowledge and opinion. The first two parts of the divided line are to be called *noēsis* (intellection) and the second two opinion. *Noēsis* is thus used here to signify the domain of the intelligible, of which mathematics, studied by *dianoia*, is a part. Being (*ousia*) is to becoming as intellection is to opinion; and as intellection is to opinion, so is knowledge to trust and thought to imagination. This is, as it were, the schematism of the structure within which objects are classified. Socrates declines to discuss the proportions of the things so classified (533e7–534a8).

There is some fluctuation in Socrates's terminology, of which the most important example is his use of *noēsis* to signify both dialectic and the domain of the intelligible that includes *dianoia* (see VI. 511d6–e4, where *noēsis* refers to the highest segment of the divided line and *dianoia* to the second or mathematical segment). Knowledge of the Ideas is the same as grasping what each thing is, and this in turn is the ability to explain it to oneself and also to another (*logon didonai*: 534b4). But the same discursivity seems to apply to the Idea of the Good, which must be distinguished by *logos* from everything else, "and just as in war," the dialectician must be able to escape from every obstacle so that "he comes through this with the *logos* still on its feet" (534c1–

2). This refutation of one's opponents is clearly discursive. The present passage also allows us to render more precise an earlier remark about philosophy and war. Refutation is like war, but the acquisition of knowledge and the contemplation of the genuinely intelligible or domain of pure being is like peace.

We are now finished with the discussion of the philosophical education, at the peak of which is dialectic. Now we must decide who shall be educated in this curriculum, and how it will be administered. The general answer to the first question has in a way already been given; we are to select the natures best fitted for ruling the city, namely, the potential philosophers (535a3–10). These were originally described as lovers of all of learning, truthful, attracted to mental rather than physical pleasure, not mean-spirited or avaricious, unafraid of death, and so on.[18] In the present passage, Socrates begins by mentioning steadiness, extreme courage, and insofar as possible, the best looking. Whether this last requirement is understood to be a sign of genetic excellence or simply a useful political trait is not stated. In the same group, Socrates includes persons of noble and virile character and those who are by nature most suitable for the education in question, namely, excellent learners with strong memories and the capacity to endure hard work. The potential student must love the truth and hate the willing lie (that is, the one that deceives for no good political purpose). We shall also require him to show temperance, courage, magnificence, "and all the parts of virtue" (536a1–2). These are clearly what Socrates called the "demotic virtues" at 500d7–9. It is evident that Socrates requires what Aristotle calls the practical as well as the theoretical virtues in the genuinely philosophical nature, much more evident than in Aristotle himself. Socrates might point to this requirement in replying to my doubts about the political utility of the technical education in mathematics and dialectic. The counterreply is that demotic virtue depends upon long habituation; experience is not the same as natural excellence. This apart, the utility of demotic virtue does not remove but rather encourages our doubts about the utility of mathematics and dialectic to the statesman.

At this point, Socrates breaks off the discussion of genuine and false philosophers and says that he has been behaving laughably. "I forgot that we were playing [*epaizomen*] and spoke too intensely. For as I was speaking, I looked at philosophy, and seeing her being spattered with mud undeservedly, I seem to myself to have been vexed and spoken too seriously as if I were angry with those who are responsible." Glaucon says that Socrates did not seem so to him, but Socrates replies that he seemed so to himself (536c1–7). This passage can be taken to refer to the entire discussion of philosophy, although it is more likely that it refers to the immediate discussion of the difference between genuine and spurious philosophers. In either case, however, two points follow. If the discussion of the philosophical nature, the peak of the dialogue, is play, the same must be true of the entire conversation. I do not mean by this that the conversation is trivial or a kind of jest. But it follows from the very characteristics of the philosophical nature that its possessor will not take human life too seriously. The second point is well captured by Nietzsche's maxim *keine Rache*. The philosopher does not take revenge, because he can do so only through a distortion of his own soul.

The immediate sequel contains an obvious commentary on the question of seriousness and play. The education that is required as a preparation for dialectic must be offered in a way that is free of compulsion; "the free man must not learn anything slavishly." Instead of compulsion, play must be used to educate the gifted children. In my opinion, this is one of the main reasons that Plato wrote dialogues. The drama is indeed a *play*, in which we ourselves are led to learning by enjoyment, not compulsion. "Serious" philosophy of the professional sort begins with Aristotle. The *Republic* is entertaining, as Aristotle's *Metaphysics* is not. The quarrel between the playful and the serious runs continuously through the history of philosophy. The playful, of course, run the risk of seeming frivolous in comparison to the hard-working technicians, whereas the latter are always in danger of becoming sclerotic and vengeful toward those whom they regard as not serious enough.

To continue, the course of studies is as follows. After the completion of the early education in music and gymnastics, the young students will be about twenty years old. At this point, their various studies, although acquired in no single order, must be arranged in a synoptic view that shows the relationship of one branch of learning to the other. The ability to do this is the greatest test of the eventual capacity for dialectic. Presumably those who acquire such an overview will then devote ten years to the study of mathematics, as one can infer from the fact that the training in dialectic begins at the age of thirty (537c9–d8). Since Socrates speaks in an unusually obscure way in this passage, it is also possible that the synopsis must be acquired after the study of mathematics, at the age of thirty, and serve as a test for those who are to be permitted to proceed with dialectic. It is very striking that Socrates does not allude explicitly to mathematics here, as he does to the other studies, including dialectic.

In either case, those who successfully complete the curriculum and acquire an overview of their studies will be permitted to spend five years in dialectical training, until the age of thirty-five, at which point the philosopher will be required to descend into the cave and spend fifteen years in governing the affairs of war and hold other offices suitable for young men. But Socrates does not pass directly from the stage of mathematics to that of dialectic. Instead, he interpolates a rather long excursus on the dangers that ensue from the study of dialectic by lawless and incompetent persons. The excursus takes the form of a story that seems to describe Plato's own experience. The philosophical nature is like a foundling who discovers, after he has grown up in a wealthy and powerful family surrounded by many flatterers, that those who raised him were not his real parents. This discovery causes him to shift his loyalty from his presumed parents and family to the flatterers. The point of the story is that the child grows up in the midst of convictions about justness and fairness, from which he is courted by the flattery of the pleasures of the soul. In other words, the dialectic of flatterers persuades the youth that the law is no more noble than it is base, no more just than unjust. He becomes an outlaw rather than an admirer of the ancestral (537e1–539a4).

This is why those under the age of thirty must be prohibited from participating in "arguments" (*logoi*), since young people abuse them, "employing them as though they were play" (539b2–4). This is an important modification of the earlier discussion of play at 536c1ff. Dialectic is the hard work and serious core of philosophy. Since dialogues are play, it is not surprising that Plato never gives us a detailed and extensive analysis of the nature of dialectic. It is a subject for which Glaucon, a young man of great political ambition, is not prepared. I do not need to emphasize the difference between Socrates's view on the study of and practice in arguments for young students of philosophy and the views of the present day. For Socrates, overindulgence in refutation leads to the loss of belief in what one formerly supposed to be true. An older man would not be so ready to participate in this madness but would imitate someone who is prepared to discuss and consider the truth, rather than to play the game of unlimited refutation (539c5–d1).

The training of the orderly and stable nature in dialectic will last five years, at the end of which the aforementioned descent into the cave is required. Note that the cave refers here not to the city, in which philosophers as well as nonphilosophers dwell, but to detachment from philosophy and absorption in the duties of ruling. The philosopher will spend fifteen years in gaining political experience through ruling in matters of war and other activities of young men. At the age of fifty, those who have shown themselves to be steadfast and best in everything, whether deed or knowledge, are brought to the end; that is, they are compelled to look at the Good itself "and, using it as a paradigm, to order the city, private men, and themselves for the rest of their lives, each in his turn. For the most part they spend their time in philosophy, but when their turn comes, they labor at politics and rule for the city's sake, not as though they were acting nobly but rather through necessity" (539e2–540b5). In other words, after fifteen years of gaining practical experience, the fifty-year-old philosopher becomes a full-fledged king, an obligation that he does not regard as noble and from which he is never entirely free for the rest of his life. The only period of uninterrupted philosophizing is the five years spent in dialectical training.

Now that the city has been constructed in speech, Socrates asks again whether it is not possible in deed, albeit hard, and so not simply a wish or prayer. As if the obstacles hitherto introduced were not hard enough, Socrates concludes that the founding fathers must send all those who are older than ten out into the country (*eis tous agrous*: "into the fields") and raise the remaining children in the manners and laws that have now been described (540e5–541a4). Glaucon agrees that this is the quickest and easiest way in which to establish the city. It is not hard to understand that this step could be taken only through the slaughter of all parents, but even if we take the statement literally, we must note that Socrates has no pity or concern for the expelled citizenry and no hesitation in depriving them of their children. In order to establish a just city, the ultimate act of injustice is required.

PART Four

11

Political Decay

1

We turn now to Book Eight. After summarizing the major elements in the foundation of the just city, Socrates refers back to the point at which they entered into the "digression" (543c5) concerning the status of women and children in common and the education of philosophers, as well as the main topics of the doctrine of Ideas, together with the images of the sun, the divided line, and the cave. The structure of the argument in Books Five through Seven shows that what we would today call the epistemological and ontological discussion of the middle books emerges directly from the claim that some women are by nature potential philosophers. The education of the philosopher is a key example of the abstraction from the body. But the exigencies of the body cannot be evaded indefinitely. As we are about to see, the inability to control the laws of sexual reproduction, the most fundamental expression of the principle of minding one's own business, leads to the deterioration of the just city.

Glaucon reminds us that Socrates was about to present the classification of the regimes and their coordinate lives at the beginning of Book Five, when he was diverted from the task by Adeimantus's demand to hear more about the community of women and children. Just previously (IV. 445d1–e3), Socrates had said that there are likely to be five types of soul corresponding to five distinct forms of regime. The first kind of regime is the one described in Books Two through Four, although it can be given two different names, depending upon whether there is one exceptional ruler or more: kingship or aristocracy. Socrates claims that the number of rulers in this regime will not affect the city's laws in any way worth mentioning. I am not sure that this is right, but we shall let it pass for the time being. The more important point is that this city is the only good and correct city and regime; the other four kinds and their associated souls are all bad and flawed (V. 449a1–5).

To come back now to the beginning of Book Eight, Glaucon says that Socrates previously called good and correct the city that he has described thus far, but that he "had a still more beautiful city and man to describe" (543d1–544a1). This more beautiful city is presumably the one that emerges from the digression (Books Five through Seven), but the passage has rightly bothered commentators. If we look back to the passage recalled by Glaucon (V. 449a1–5), Socrates identifies the just city as "good" and "correct," not beautiful, and he says nothing about having a still more beautiful city to describe. Socrates refers to the beautiful city as Glaucon's in the midst of the discussion in Book Seven of mathematical education. We cannot therefore unambiguously distinguish the city of Books Two through Four as Glaucon's beautiful city (527c2). It looks as if Glaucon is returning to Socrates the parentage of the city that Socrates has attributed to him.

The broad principles of the construction of the best city have been indicated by the end of Book Four (444a4–12). In Book Eight, Socrates distinguishes four defective regimes that govern actual cities; these are separated from the just city (543d1–544a2). Let us note that the four regimes are "the one that is praised by the many," which is found in Crete and Sparta, and then the oligarchy, democracy, and "noble" tyranny (544c1–7). Socrates does not identify the first of these regimes as an aristocracy; this term is reserved for the regime of philosopher-kings (544e4–545a1). Shortly thereafter, he repeats the names of the four inferior regimes, but this time he uses the word *timocracy* to designate the Spartan regime and refers to the timocratic man as the one who loves victory and honor (545a2–c5).

These passages show that Socrates does not refer to aristocracies when he discusses actual (and so defective) regimes. To paraphrase his own words, what the many call an aristocracy is not the rule of the best but rather the rule of military honor. If we inspect each of these regimes with respect to the justice of its associated life, we can then compare the life of pure justice (in the aristocracy or beautiful city) with that of pure injustice, in order to determine which is happiest (544b5–545c7).

We may disregard the frequently made objection to the order of the evolution of actual regimes as presented by Socrates. More interesting for our purposes is the replacement of aristocracy by timocracy. If the timocracy lies halfway between the aristocracy (that is, the just or wished-for city) and the oligarchy (547c6–7), then it must have been preceded by one or more types of decadent aristocracy. Socrates is silent on this point, no doubt because he wished to preserve "aristocracy" in its literal sense of "rule of the best" for his just city. This procedure leaves unclear how a timocracy could have evolved from an aristocracy immediately following the forgetting of the nuptial number. This becomes especially puzzling when Socrates explains the origin of the timocracy and its corresponding human type.

According to Socrates, a change of regime comes about only through the rise of factions in the ruling class. In the just city, this takes place between the ruling guardians and the auxiliaries. The process of decline begins when breeding is no longer conducted in strict conformity to the nuptial number, a complex and obviously ironical calculation that is designed to prevent sexual reproduction outside the boundaries of one's own class, in the wrong season, or with someone of the wrong age. The nuptial number is connected to the instruction of the Muses, in the first instance by a reference to Homer. Socrates asks Glaucon whether they should pray to the Muses to explain to us how the auxiliaries and the rulers divide into factions. "And shall we say that they speak to us in the tragic idiom, teasing and playing with us as though we were children, but pretending to speak seriously and in an exalted manner?" (545d5–e3). In a second passage, Glaucon's statement that the Muses necessarily say what is correct, is compromised by the fact that it is Hesiod who warns us that the Muses know how to lie as well as to tell the truth (546e1–547a7; *Theogony* 27–28).

Not even the philosophers are able continuously to regulate their reproductive function in accord with the cosmic order; eventually they will produce children at the wrong time (546a7–b3, c6–d3). Faction thus arises in the just city through impurities in the guardian and auxiliary classes. Socrates is obviously unwilling to refer to this stage of the no longer beautiful city as an aristocracy. It must therefore be a timocracy. As we are about to see, however, Socrates describes the origin of the timocracy from a previous regime, not further identified but certainly not the just city. I believe that some intermediate regime that is neither perfectly just nor perfectly timocratic must stand between these two, yet none is mentioned.

Although the impure children of the guardian class will neglect both music and gymnastics, it is clear that they come to regard the training of the body more highly than that of the soul. As a result, the guardians become unmusical and so less able to distinguish the three classes of children, whose souls, gold, silver, and bronze or iron, remind us of Hesiod's races of mortals. The mixing of these souls in breeding produces unlikeness and inharmonious irregularity, of which the consequences are war, hatred, and faction (546d2–547a5).

In the present context, it is the Muses, through Socrates' mediation, that are instructing us on the topic of faction, which, once it has arisen, pulls apart from each other the gold and silver souls on the one hand and the bronze and iron souls on the other. This formulation implies that in the beautiful city there is no faction and hence no separation of the classes. But that is of course quite false. The gold and silver people are entirely separated from the bronze and iron classes, with the single exception that the former rule; that is, they enforce order onto the latter. But this is not the same as unity. One topic that Socrates ignores throughout the discussion is the resentment that must arise among the workers and farmers toward the guardians. Socrates may perhaps assume that the lower classes will be content with peace and personal freedom, in a way like the view of eighteenth-century political philosophers that material prosperity and comfort mitigate against war. In his peculiar city, to be sure, the control of education must presumably extend to the bronze and iron children, but it is not very plausible to assume that these children, once they are adults, will be too docile to resist the authority of the guardians. After all, a dedication to material wealth and comfort leads inevitably to an exacerbation of the appetite, and there will surely be a resentment among the great majority of the city toward the nonexpansionist policies of their rulers.

In sum: Socrates holds that the struggle between the two main kinds of soul will arise only when the gold and silver class is diluted through miscegenation. But it is not very difficult to see that the tension between making money on the one hand, which is representative of the desire for privacy and personal freedom, and the inclination toward virtue and the tradition on the other constitutes the very structure of the beautiful city. Only if this were so, incidentally, could the decline from the best city to the first of the defective regimes take place after just one generation of faction, as seems to be implied by Socrates's account. In fact, the decline that Socrates is about to describe would surely take more than one generation in order to dilute the entire class of guardians. But this is a secondary issue. What I wish to emphasize is that the Socratic city does not resolve the problem of unity and difference; rather, it institutionalizes that problem. Socrates's fundamental premise, that the city should be as much like one man as possible, is itself entirely impossible. The tripartite division of powers attributed to the individual soul reveals the discontinuities and factions that are present in each of us by virtue of our very humanity. This becomes obvious when the parts of the soul are restated in political terms.

The conflict between virtue and money is then clearly visible in the structure of the just city. The decay that follows miscegenation unleashes the implied weaknesses of the separation of classes into a real conflict that ends, according to Socrates, in a compromise. The guardians introduce private property (land and houses: 547b8–c1), presumably among themselves, since the workers would already have possessed these. But they retain common meals and the care of gymnastics and war, as well as abstention from moneymaking, among the soldiers, that is, the auxiliaries. And they make the workers their slaves rather than those whom they freely guard out of friendship (547c1–4). One must therefore assume that the workers will be deprived of their own land and houses. Socrates is also silent on sexual arrangements, but we must again assume that the guardians will now have private liaisons, as well as wives and their own children.

The description of the transition from aristocracy to timocracy is incompletely and confusingly described. To repeat, since everything from the initial corruption of the just city to the establishment of the timocracy cannot itself be a timocracy, whereas it is also clearly not an aristocracy, are we to assume that it constitutes another form of regime? In fact, Socrates states that the timocracy, once it is established, will imitate "the preceding regime" (547c9–d2), by which expression he clearly refers to the aristocracy or just regime. But that leaves unidentified the nature of the regime between the aristocracy and the timocracy. As to the timocracy itself, perhaps its most striking feature is the lack of any mention of philosophy, which is now presumably an entirely private affair. The breakdown of sexual regulation leads to the disappearance of philosophy from politics. Therefore, the guardians choose as their rulers the spirited and simpler persons who excel at war and spend most of their time in pursuing it. To some extent, the timocracy resembles the warrior-aristocracies described in Homer. It is the Socratic version of a fall from the wished-for domain of the just city into the history of the evolution of actual regimes.

This evolution should more accurately be called a devolution; there is no sense of historical progress in Plato (547c5–548a3). Instead, as we know from the *Statesman* and *Timaeus*, there is a cycle of repetitions of political history, corresponding to the cycle of the genesis and destruction of the cosmos. We see in the present passage the beginning of a conflict between strength and wealth as the criterion of honor; the spirited and the desiring parts of the soul are released from the control of intellect. The story of the transformation from one regime to another is also the story of the deterioration in our understanding of honor. Desire triumphs over strength. Thus the timocratic man excludes the wise from rule and is himself secretly a lover of money, which enables him to satisfy his sexual desires behind the walls of his private residence, walls that conceal the decay of military honor (548a5–c2).

When Socrates asks for an account of the man who corresponds to the timocratic regime, Adeimantus answers that he must be like Glaucon in his love of victory. Socrates allows that perhaps this is so, but in other respects Glaucon is of a different nature. The man in question is more stubborn than Glaucon, and less apt at music. He is also a lover of ruling and honor; presumably, then, Glaucon, despite his eros, manliness, and love of victory, is not. But we should not forget the story that Glaucon was in fact eager to enter politics. Also unlike Glaucon, the timocrat is brutal to slaves but tame with free men and most obedient to his rulers. Finally, he regards himself as fit to rule because of his warlike deeds, and he is a lover of gymnastics and the hunt. Perhaps one could say that Glaucon's bravery is directed toward speeches rather than deeds; he fits neatly into neither the ruling nor the auxiliary class (548d6–549a8).

It is now time to study the faults of actual regimes, and the austerity and censoriousness of Adeimantus is well suited to this task. Glaucon will return when the discussion arrives at the character of the tyrannical man. Meanwhile, Socrates explains the decay of the pure virtuous man into a lover of money as due to not having acquired the guardianship of *logos* mixed with music. This alone, once it is born within the soul, is the savior of virtue throughout life (549a9–b7). *Logos* here refers to the faculty of reasoning, not to a philosophical doctrine. It needs no emphasis that music is closer to *logos* (argument, ratio, reason) than is gymnastic, which is still admired in this regime, but to no countervailing effect in the downward turn to corruption.

The next step in the argument is presented as a domestic drama in which those fathers who have preserved their virtue despite the decline of the guardian class avoid the honors, offices, and lawcourts of the city, even if it means that they must be content with less in order not to be troubled. These fathers are the best of the decadent descendants of the original guardians, and they preserve a sense of honor, but not of spiritedness. This means, incidentally, that they are not timocrats, because they are neither lecherous nor warlike. As I noted previously, Socrates never identifies their regime.

The wife of the good father complains to her son about the father's loss of station and wealth, which she attributes to his lack of courage. Adeimantus agrees that women are likely to have many complaints (549c2–e2). The son is subjected not simply to the complaints of his mother but also to those of the family servants, who encourage him to rectify his position in society. When he goes about the city, he sees that those who act like his father are belittled as fools, whereas those who behave in accord with his mother's advice prosper and are honored. There ensues a conflict within the son's soul; the calculating part (*logistikon*) is watered by his father and grows accordingly; whereas the other members of the household do the same for the desiring and spirited parts. The son is not a bad person, but he is drawn by both extremes and so ends up in the middle. He turns over the rule of his soul to the spirited element that loves victory. This is the evolution of the lover of honor (549e3–550b7).

Socrates defines oligarchy as rule based upon "value" (*timēma*), that is, the possession of sufficient property not to have to work for a living. We recall that the desire for wealth is already present in the timocracy, where it leads to concealment of one's net worth and the establishment of secret treasure houses (548a5–b2). In a society in which the highest value is honor, the desire for material wealth has the appearance of vulgarity; hence the need for concealment. In an oligarchy, concealment is not only unnecessary but is also counterproductive, since wealth is the basis for holding political office. The stage is thus set for the transition from timocracy to oligarchy. The rich citizens pass from private expenditures to a bending of the laws for their own financial advantage. They fall into competition with one another, and as in all contests, honor remains a strong factor. Even the poor multitude come to respect those who have acquired unusual wealth. The bestowal of honor upon wealth leads to the diminution in honor accorded to the virtuous and the good man. This is the remnant of timocracy in still more corrupted form. But the love of victory and honor that rules in the timocracy is now replaced by the love of money-making and money. I note that the love of making money is a pleasure separate from that of actually possessing it. It is also different from that of spending money. In an oligarchy, all three appetites combine. Eros has now descended from love of the Ideas to the love of honor, and then from the love of honor to that of the pleasures of the body. In other words, we have descended from the intellect through the spirited element of the soul to physical desire (550d8–551a10).

Adeimantus next asks what is the "manner" or "way" (*tropos*) of the oligarchy. Socrates begins by noting two major errors. First, the city chooses as its rulers not the most competent but rather the richest. Second, the city is divided into two, the city of the poor and that of the rich, "living in the same place, and always plotting against each other" (551d5–7). To these, Socrates adds the difficulty of conducting war through mistrust of the multitude and the unwillingness to make large expenditures on behalf of the armed forces. Finally, the same citizens engage in farming, moneymaking, and war, rather than each minding his own business. Socrates now promotes into first place among evils the permission given in oligarchies to one man to buy up all the property of another, leaving the latter a pauper and divested of any part in the regime. Where beggars are visible, there exist numerous hidden criminals. In short, the city is divided into the criminal few and the beggarly many (551a12–553a5). The next step is to describe the deterioration of the timocrat into the oligarch.

This is initiated when the son of a timocrat sees his father ruined by excessive expenditures and entanglement in lawcourts. The son repudiates the ways of the father and devotes himself to moneymaking. In the shift from aristocracy to timocracy, the wife and mother are presented as the first mover. In the shift from timocracy to oligarchy, however, the father takes the primary blame. But we should not forget that the desire for wealth is already present in the aristocracy — at least in actual aristocracies, if not in the Socratic version. Perhaps one can say that women in actual Greek cities could covet honor and wealth but were not free to acquire them through their own deeds. The mother urges her sons to act; the father ruins his sons through his own actions (553a6–c7).

In the oligarch, both the calculative and spirited parts of the soul are subordinated to desire or the love of money. Socrates devotes the balance of the passage to a list of the ways in which the oligarchic man resembles the corresponding city. The main point is that whereas the timocrat ruins himself through extravagance, the oligarch is miserly. It is this quality, we may suppose, that enables him to restrain his desires more frequently than he yields to them, at least when his own money is concerned. The worst aspects of the oligarch emerge from the manner in which he administers the money of others (553d1–555b1).

We have now studied the regimes that embody three different degrees of honor. The aristocracy honors the best, and the oligarchy honors money. Somewhere between them lies the timocracy, which honors military victory. One of the peculiarities of this narrative is that virtually nothing is said about the necessary difference between the aristocratic nature of the beautiful city and the character of actual aristocracies. Next we shall analyze Socrates's account of democracy, in which honor is replaced by freedom and diversity, or in other words, by the private life.

2

Oligarchies are transformed into democracies thanks to the insatiable desire on the part of the rulers for wealth. They refuse to discipline the borrowing and spending habits of the sons of the rich by passing the appropriate laws, in order that they themselves may become still richer by buying and making loans, and so eventually accumulating the property of others. The honoring of wealth thus leads inevitably to the loss of moderation. There is no law to regulate the use of one's property, nor is there any requirement to warn that all those who enter into voluntary contracts do so at their own risk The sons of the rich are thus corrupted in two main ways; they themselves become poor, or else, exhausted by licentiousness, they are unable to work or engage effectively in war. As a result, they are despised by the poor working class, the members of which are encouraged to overthrow them and seize power in the city. In slightly different terms, the sons of the oligarchy, whose fathers are busybodies because they farm, make money, and fight the wars, are transformed into do-nothings as soon as their all-consuming desire for money is extinguished by the complete loss of capital on the one hand and a failure to have learned any occupation but moneymaking on the other (553b3–556e1).

Let me underline the crucial point here, which is central to the process by which oligarchies deteriorate into democracies, out of which tyrannies arise. There are two main constituent types in an oligarchy: the stingy miser and the spendthrift. In Socrates's dramatic presentation, these types correspond very approximately to the fathers and the sons. By working to make and preserve money, the fathers retain something of the timocratic sense of honor. It is honorable to be rich; hence honor is able to suppress the bodily desires of the moneymakers more often than not. But the sons of the rich find it easy to avoid labor and to succumb to the temptations of their fathers' wealth. They become corrupt and are easily overthrown by the poor. Throughout this section of Book Eight, one sees at work an anticipation of Hegel's famous dialectic of the master and the slave, a dialectic that Socrates himself introduced into the dynamics of the soul. But the thrust of the dialectic in this passage is the reverse of that in Hegel. For Socrates, it results in the triumph of the tyrant, not the people. Hegel was of course no democrat, but he advocated a constitutional monarchy as a kind of synthesis of timocracy, oligarchy, and democracy that rises to the peak of political rationality. Socrates on the other hand condemns dramatic political change as an agent of decay. The dialectical inversions of rich and poor, old and young, and so on, lead to a dissolution of order and hence of justice and virtue. Everything comes to be permitted; this produces initial diversity and is attractive to women and children, as Socrates maliciously puts it. But the freedom of diversity leads to violent quarrels among the main factions of the many-colored democracy, each of which is vitiated by the others. The dialectical struggle for power terminates in the rule of the tyrant, not at all of his philosophical ministers and advisers.

To continue, the oligarchy soon falls into faction and the use of invited foreigners as military allies. Since the poor are more numerous than the rich and harder than the licentious sons who have squandered their patrimony in advance, they win the civil war between the rich and the poor and share political power with the survivors on an equal basis, frequently making use of the lot to distribute the offices of government. Oddly enough, Socrates does not explain why the victors of stasis do not reestablish an oligarchy, or perhaps even a tyranny of the proletariat. Perhaps the implication is that the experience of chaos arising from the decay of the timocracy and oligarchy through the fusion of the love of honor and money makes them unwilling to entrust the rule to any group smaller than the poor. However this may be, there is no love of honor in a democracy that is comparable to that in the previous regimes (556e3–557b3). The triumphant poor are now able to protect themselves against the rich, and one of the first consequences of this power will be the establishment of equality, that is to say, removal of obstacles in the path of the people to rule. No one is politically superior to anyone else. But freedom from the previous political hierarchies has two consequences that diverge from one another. The first is the aforementioned emancipation of the many, with a consequent lowering of standards in education and virtue. The second, however, is the license given to the expression of diversity, thanks to the absence of standards or rank-orderings of permissible and nonpermissible modes of behavior. The clash between uniformity and diversity is an unsettling force in the democracy. Socrates does not bring this point out with the desired sharpness, but it can be readily inferred from his analysis.

Socrates himself says that when we ask after the manner of the democracy, and so of the nature of the democratic man, the first two characteristics to be mentioned are freedom and diversity. On this point at least, the situation described by Socrates continues to hold good today. For Socrates, however, freedom of speech and permission to do whatever one wants is licentiousness (557b5, b8: *eksousia* means both power or authority and license or abuse), not the expression of justice or virtue. It would of course be absurd to call Socrates a democrat in his sense of the term, but many contemporary scholars are eager to claim him as a partisan of democracy on the grounds that it is most conducive to the study of philosophy. If we mean by "democracy" what Aristotle would call a "mixed regime," there is something to this claim, but it faces the overwhelming obstacle of Socrates's clear preference for an aristocracy of merit. Certainly those who see Socrates as an anticipation of the contemporary liberal have to explain away the entire political doctrine of the *Republic*. As to the thesis that the diversity of the human soul is more visible in a democracy than elsewhere, one should consider the difference between philosophy and politics, and in particular the fact that in Plato Sparta and Crete are presented as the best forms of government, not Athens.[1]

It is sometimes said that modern humanity differs decisively from the ancients in making freedom an unconditional good, whereas for the ancients, freedom is a virtue that belongs to the city, and so to the citizen, not to the individual or private person.[2] It is certainly true that ancient political thought recognizes the city, not the private person, as autarchic. The same is no doubt true for Socrates, with the possible exception of the philosopher, and even here it is difficult to see how philosophy could arise and flourish without the development of the city. But modern political theorists, including the champions of the natural rights of individuals as prior by nature to the laws of the state, recognize that the perfection of the individual depends upon a healthy government. To take only the most obvious example, the freedom of the individual from excessive state control depends upon the proper regulation of political power, including the presence of a police department sufficiently powerful to protect the privacy and other rights of the citizenry.

It cannot, however, be the case for Socrates that the health or sickness of the citizen is explained entirely in terms of the health or sickness of the regime. It is precisely this conventionalist thesis that custom is the king of all men that Socrates opposes in his doctrine of the three main kinds of human being. To say that the city is the soul writ large is to come close to saying that the soul is prior to the city and expands its inner structure to accord with our visual capacities. On the other hand, the defects of the analogy between the city and the soul stem from the obvious differences between the two, such as the decisive fact that the city cannot be a philosopher or for that matter take on any single occupation. As I put it earlier, there are no happy cities, only happy citizens. In a word, human nature is decisive for the formation of the character of the city, whereas the city cannot suppress the natures of the citizens through the regulatory chains of custom and education. The inability of the city to do this has the very consequences that we are now studying.

Let us not, then, exaggerate the degree to which Socrates or any other ancient political thinker subordinated the individual person to the city. We must keep firmly in mind that the just city is a construction of philosophers, who are not, as founders, themselves conditioned by their artifact. This conditioning process takes place *inside* the city, but it is imposed from the "outside." It is on the contrary modern historicism that transforms the individual citizen, including the founding fathers, into a product of the state or, in its extreme form, of the historical process. If this doctrine were correct, then there would be no explanation for the power of individuals to resist custom, law, and even ideological brainwashing. The truth seems, as is so often the case, to lie somewhere in the middle. Cities influence the formation of individuals, but it is the individual who determines the character of the city.

We also need to qualify the previous observation that both ancient and modern democrats value freedom and diversity above everything. This is no doubt true of the rhetoric of democracy in our day, and it certainly points to an important stratum of life in democracies, both ancient and modern. But just as Periclean Athens was not New York or Los Angeles, that is, a wild proliferation of licentiousness and extreme diversity, neither are New York and Los

Angeles the totality of the American democracy. The deterioration of post-Periclean Athens was not toward the extension of diversity but rather toward the coarsening of politics, as for example in the person of Cleon. No doubt the crowd came to power in a way that resembles Socrates's extreme portrayal, but the emergence of the crowd is not a triumph of freedom and diversity. As the preparation for tyranny, it takes the form of a narrowing of diverse views and a populist celebration of mediocrity. In sum, as Socrates tells the tale, the rule of the people deteriorates into the rule of the mob, and this both dissolves tradition and custom and gives rise to the emergence of "new men," but not to freedom so much as to the chaotic conflict of centers of power as well as the brutalization of desire. I can summarize this series of remarks by saying that Socrates portrays democracy very much as though it were synonymous with chaos, and nothing more than the preface to tyranny. But this is certainly an exaggeration, and it depreciates the value of freedom and diversity.

What Socrates is describing is a conception of democracy as the breakdown of political order, an order of the sort that is still visible in aristocracies, timocracies, and oligarchies. The love of honor, even when corrupted by the love of money, retains some connection, however diluted, with respect for the best. It leads either to a rank-ordering of actions that preserves even in deteriorated cases a basis for restricting the public manifestation of excessive licentiousness, as was plain in the timocracy, or to the mastery of bad by good desires most of the time, as is true in the oligarchy (554d9–e1). In a democracy, however, the highest virtue is the negative freedom from external restriction by the city, and so a liberty to do as one pleases in private. This is necessary, again, so that the poor, who have no time to devote to politics, will not be oppressed by the government. And in the case of the democracy, the dominance of privacy is not because of shame at one's lust or greed, but the exact opposite. Where everything is permitted, there is nothing of which to be ashamed.

It has to be emphasized that Socrates means by "democracy" the rule of the poor. This is not to deny that gradations in income will arise in such a city. But the character or manner of the city is determined by poverty, or let us say by the fact that, at least in classical antiquity, the poor are inevitably the majority. Rule of the poor means rule of the many, and this inevitably means a weak government. Indeed, the government must be kept weak so as to avoid the rise to power of a faction, which will then be transformed into tyrants, oligarchs, timocrats, or aristocrats. This in turn means that the energy of the rulers is directed not to accumulating political power but to the expression of their personalities in private life. Where there are few if any restrictions on private behavior, thanks to the love of freedom that is the same in principle as the desire for a weak government, then the innate diversity of modes of human behavior is encouraged to flourish. But this flourishing is in conflict with the unity or conformity that is a consequence of the transfer of power from the rich and better educated to the poor and ignorant.

The purpose of these remarks is not to repudiate democracy but to try to understand the underlying motivation of Socrates's analysis of it. It should go without saying that every sentence in the last two paragraphs has to be expanded by the recognition that, in actual democracies, there are consequences of the primacy of freedom and diversity that soon make the regime itself something much more complex than rule by the many or the poor. Socrates himself makes this point by saying that because of its license, the democracy contains all the species of regimes. He also says that it is probably the most beautiful of regimes, but that the judgment is ironical or pejorative is immediately indicated by comparing the democracy to a many-colored cloak that many boys and women would judge to be beautiful (557c1–9).

Someone might say at this point that the philosophical utility of the democracy lies precisely in its diversity of forms and human types.[3] In other words, the heterogeneity of the human soul is most clearly on display in a democracy. I personally believe that there is something to this claim, but there is no reason to assume that Socrates would accept it. We must not forget that the main purpose of the entire discussion, including the description of the philosophical nature in the middle books, is *political*, not theoretical. But we must also not forget that the political purpose, very far from being that of drawing up a plan for a possible regime to suit human beings in their actual diversity, is to show what we need to know in order to decide which is happier, the just or the unjust life. Socrates claims that in order to decide this issue we must construct a perfectly just city. Having ostensibly done so, he now intends to compare it with models of actual cities, all of which are corrupt and so unjust, in order that we may choose which life is happiest. The democracy is exceeded in its distance from the beautiful regime only by the tyranny. The freedom of licentiousness and its correlative diversity, if these are in any way useful to the philosopher, show clearly the conflict between philosophy and justice, not their coincidence.

The defense of democracy is thus entirely out of place in the dominant or political argument of the *Republic*. Furthermore, defenses of this sort inevitably confuse modern notions of democracy with the one employed by Socrates. None of this should prevent us from thinking through the problem of freedom and diversity. What it should prevent us from doing is trying to turn Socrates into a contemporary liberal. I do not, however, wish to suggest that either Socrates or Plato favored the transformation of Athens into Sparta. What they do is to show the tension between philosophy and politics, a tension that arises from the conflict between unity and diversity. Radical diversity, however, is simply another form of uniformity.

We seem to take it for granted today that happiness depends upon freedom, which in turn is understood to mean the ability to live one's life as one sees fit—at least up to the point at which this interferes with the freedom of someone else. Socrates might observe that the restriction, made famous by John Stuart Mill, is not a mere formality but grants the criticism of licentiousness. We are not free to do as we wish, because the private life intersects with the public. But this does not go to the heart of the matter. Socrates opposes the adoption of freedom as a first principle because it cannot be just or virtuous to allow every human type to flourish. He takes it for granted that some lives are better than others, and that lives can be rank-ordered in a way that sensible people will accept. If this is right, then justice demands that we encourage the better lives and discourage their inferiors. And the same holds good for the different kinds of regime. Late-modern advocates of freedom and the private flourishing of diversity no longer hold to the belief in an objective rank-ordering of human types or political regimes. But this in turn is contradicted by the widespread conviction that freedom and diversity are superior to restrictions on human behavior. What was once called "the open society" is widely believed to be superior to the "closed society." These views cannot both be correct, and if we think them through, we are on the way toward understanding the nature of the political problem.

To come back to the text, Socrates holds that in a democracy people are free to accept or reject political office, and so also to decide whether to participate in war (557e2–558a2). This is an exaggeration if it is applied to actual democracies, but again, Socrates is bringing out the inner sense of democratic license. If there is a complete democracy, then the private is superior to the public, and this is a contradiction of the nature of government. In modern democracies, particularly in the United States, the superiority of private freedom over strong government is usually advocated by "conservatives," whereas "liberals" advocate strong central government in order to impose equality as well as restrictions on private license (hence the many regulatory agencies). The odd result is that the liberal conception of democracy tends today to diminish private freedom and to enhance public authority. This shows us how dangerous it is to make direct comparisons between modern and ancient regimes.

It is also dangerous to make hasty generalizations about this or that regime, including the modern democracy. Let me give an example of a quite different tendency of modern liberal democracy that is more in keeping with Socrates's account of the ancient version. The pure form of democracy as understood by

Socrates is impossible. A life of complete freedom may be divinely sweet for the moment, as Socrates and Adeimantus agree, but not for long. The laxness in the enforcement of laws is well illustrated by extreme tolerance toward those who have been sentenced to death or exile. According to Socrates, these criminals are allowed to remain undisturbed in the city, as though no one cared about or saw their misdeeds. This is again an exaggerated expression of the consequences of refusing to participate actively in government. But it cannot be denied, and is in fact confirmed by contemporary democratic societies, that the emphasis upon privacy and the sanctioning of the expression of individual tastes goes together with a fastidious concern with the rights of criminals. Where diversity rules, everyone has his or her own "point of view" or "interpretation." Justice is then understood not as the firm application of the law but as the stringent restriction of the law against its excessive or rigid application.

To make a long story short, this is all in the service of civil liberties; that is to say, justice tends to be understood as liberty from the city. The liberal spirit in criminal law is thus almost the reverse of the same spirit in the regulation of commerce and industry. This is a fair representation of what Socrates is arguing in the present passage. Whereas we believe that erroneous applications of the law due to excessive strictness are in fact unjust and a threat to the freedom of all citizens, Socrates regards excessive lenience in the application of the law as a sign of the dissolution of government into factionalism, that is, the factionalism of the many, for whom one opinion is as good as another and the main thing is not to be disturbed from private leisure by the exigencies of politics. In short, we have both "liberal" and "conservative" tendencies in modern democracies. In his account of ancient democracies, Socrates shows that the advocacy of private freedom leads to consequences that resemble both of the aforementioned tendencies and cannot be reduced to one or the other.

3

In sum, democracy is "a sweet regime, anarchic and intricate, dispensing a certain equality to equals and unequals alike" (558c4–6). As the first step in identifying the private person who corresponds to the democratic regime, we must determine how he comes into existence from the son of the oligarch. Socrates begins by distinguishing between necessary and unnecessary desires. The necessary desires are those that we cannot turn aside and the satisfaction of which have beneficial consequences. The unnecessary desires are those from which we can rid ourselves by practice from childhood on, and which do no good but often cause us harm. It is assumed, as usual, that the fewer desires we indulge, the better we are; this is no doubt because of the proximity of desire to pleasure. Socratic puritanism is visible here in the inclusion of harmless desires within the category of the unnecessary. The distinction between "necessary" and "unnecessary" is much stricter than that between "harmless" and "harmful." The son of the oligarch will restrict the "unnecessary" pleasures as a waste of money; his miserliness is a kind of enforced virtue, as we saw a short while ago (558c11–559a6).

Socrates employs eating as an example of a necessary desire; that is, it is necessary if it serves our good health and condition. This can be satisfied by bread and (with a silent bow to Glaucon) relish. The desire for other kinds of food is harmful to prudence and temperance, and can be checked by training and education. Oligarchy is thus compatible with austerity and, on this point, with the nature of Adeimantus. One may suspect that whereas relish is sufficient for Adeimantus, it is the necessary minimum for Glaucon. However this may be, the "drone" or useless oligarch is ruled by unnecessary "pleasures and desires" (559c8–d2), whereas the stingy or moneymaking oligarch is ruled by necessary ones. This is the first point in the passage at which explicit reference is made to pleasure. The shift from oligarch to democrat begins when the stingy oligarch tastes the honey produced by the drone and becomes corrupted by unnecessary pleasures. What I called the enforced virtue of the oligarchy is now in the process of disappearing from the city. It will be replaced by the sweetness of license. The same analysis applies to the pleasure of sex and the other desires (559a11–e3).

The dialectic of necessary and unnecessary pleasures and desires within the soul of the young oligarch is the private counterpart to the political struggle whereby factions arise and allies are brought in from outside the city by both parties. Unnecessary pleasures and desires are "imported" into the soul to combat and corrupt its stingy element. Sometimes the oligarchic element triumphs, but the most frequent consequence is victory for the multiplying unnecessary pleasures, which storm the acropolis of the young man's soul and conquer it with the sweetness of democracy. "Pleasure" appears in this passage without the accompanying "desires." There is at least one crucial difference between a pleasure and a desire that is not mentioned here. Desires in themselves are painful, since they indicate a lack; it obviously makes no sense to speak of painful pleasures (although some experiences can be both).

In the absence of a beautiful educational regime, false and boasting speeches and opinions fill the void. Socrates undoubtedly has in mind here the rhetoric of freedom and diversity, with which he has identified democracy, and which stands at the opposite pole from his own beautiful city. This is indicated in the next passage; the boastful speeches guard the gates of the soul against the ingress of stingy troops. Shame is expelled as simplicity; moderation is called cowardice and spattered with mud. Insolence, anarchy, wastefulness, and shamelessness are called back from exile and renamed as good education, freedom, magnificence, and courage (559e4–561a4).

In the best case, if the new democrat is lucky and perhaps subdued in the violence of his desires by increased age, so that he does not admit all of the exiles, he lives his life with a certain equality of the pleasures. That is, he indulges in whichever one happens along. This is hardly restraint, but it is not fanaticism or extreme licentiousness. Let us call it a "sweet" self-indulgence lacking in all discrimination of the necessary from the unnecessary or the noble from the base. Those who deny that some pleasures belong to good desires and others to bad ones are in effect asserting that all are equal and must be nursed equally. This is obviously connected to the thesis that every form of life is equally good, which in turn derives from the licentiousness expressed in the view that nothing has authority over, or is superior to, anything else. Interestingly enough, Socrates sees this as leading to a kind of immoderate moderation, that is, an easygoing indulgence in everything. The democrat seems to be simpleminded in his advocacy of the equality of pleasure; he is not moved to triumph over the pleasures of others. "Everything is allowed" is for him a maxim of peace rather than war. Otherwise stated, the democrat is not yet the tyrant (561a6–c5).

Such, then, is the intricate soul of the man who is devoted to the principle of equality. In all his actions, private or political, he blows with the wind of inclination; there is neither necessity nor order in his life. This fair and multicolored creature is envied by many men and women, since it has within it the greatest number of political paradigms and manners of personal life (561c6–e8). We are left with the case of tyranny, which, it is plain to Socrates and Adeimantus, springs from the democracy. But apart from the fact that this follows from the order of Socrates's exposition, is there any reason to suppose that kings, aristocrats, and others cannot form a tyranny as easily as democrats and perhaps more easily, given the extreme permissiveness and indolence of the democratic character?

Socrates argues that when democrats become inebriated with freedom, they demand an ever greater amount, and punish those rulers who withhold it from them. Anarchy spreads throughout the city, into the private houses, and down to the very beasts. Fathers fear their sons, who in turn do not fear their fathers; these are the two sides of excessive freedom. Citizens, foreign residents, and strangers are all on a common level. The relations between fathers and sons are duplicated between teachers and pupils. The former fear their students and imitate them as charmingly as possible, so as not to appear despotic, whereas the pupils imitate and compete with their teachers, as if they were at the same level. The ultimate consequence of this anarchy is to make slaves as free as their owners, not to forget the effect that it has on the relations between the sexes. Finally, the lack of discipline extends to the dogs, and even to the horses and asses that refuse to move out of our way but jostle us when we encounter them on country roads (562c8–563d3).

The upshot of too much freedom, however, is too much slavery. At this point, Socrates slightly but noticeably alters his characterization of a democracy. Hitherto, he had emphasized the extreme tolerance, even lethargy and unwillingness, to enforce the laws of the city. Now he takes his bearings by the rulers in a democracy. Socrates compares them to drones, with or without stingers, who live in a beehive by appropriating the honey produced by others. The ones with stingers are the fiercest, and they grow in number and vigor, taking for themselves the role of ruler and leader. The stingless and less courageous drones swarm near the platform of public speakers and buzz loudly, preventing anyone else from saying anything sensible. These two tribes of drones are not the many but those who usurp authority in their name. There is another tribe distinct from the many, namely, those who are most orderly and so make the most money; in other words, this tribe includes the descendants who best retain the nature of the stingy oligarchs. They have the most honey, and it is they who serve as the garden for the drones (563e6–564e14).

The drones constitute one tribe, and the rich another. A third tribe is made up of the people (*dēmos*), who do their own work and avoid politics. They possess little, but collectively they are the largest and most sovereign tribe in a democracy. In other words, it is by their authority that the fierce drones rule and the stingless drones dominate public rhetoric. They themselves are unwilling to assemble as a sovereign body unless they are given a share of the honey squeezed out of the rich by the fierce drones (565a1–5). The rich in turn are forced to defend themselves against this extortion by addressing the people. They are then accused of making innovations, plotting against the people, and being oligarchs. When the people in their ignorance accept these slanders, the rich are forced, whether they wish it or not, to become oligarchs in fact. The result is a round of impeachments and lawsuits (565a6–c8).

Let us try to restate the political situation described in Socrates's elaborate metaphor, in which the transitions are far from clear. In the oligarchy, there is still to be found a kind of virtue that manifests itself as stinginess and hard work. In the democracy, however, the workers are poor and ignorant, and this mitigates against their exercising directly the political power that belongs to them as the majority of the citizenry. This power is usurped by the idle but ferocious minority that dominates the public assembly and sustains itself by squeezing the rich through taxes, assessments, rigged legal judgments, and so on. The fierce drones, as Socrates calls them, are enabled to assume power because of the previously described extreme anarchy in the city. The majority in a democracy wish neither to rule nor to be ruled. Hence there is a vacuum that can be filled by the most degenerate remnants of the oligarchy, namely, those who live for excessive pleasures and who arose because it is impossible to engender moderation in a city that exists for the sake of making money (see 555c7–d2). The drones are the ancestors of the licentious element in the oligarchy, but they are stronger in the democracy because they can assume effective political rule, whereas in the oligarchy they have been driven from power. And the richest members of the democracy are the ancestors of the nonlicentious element in the oligarchy. The confusions and reversals engendered within the democracy, with its diversity of human types and regimes, leads the members of this tribe to return to their oligarchic convictions, that is, to protect their wealth by overthrowing the power of the drones.

In sum, anarchy stirs up the various fragments of the oligarchy, but it cannot restore the oligarchy itself, which is dedicated to the virtues of moneymaking, however vulgarly manifested or inadequately pursued these virtues may be. The triumph of the poor against the rich, which was the origin of the democracy, mitigates against the reinstitution of a government that favors the rich. Furthermore, the desire of the poor for equality with the rich leads to the excessive emphasis upon freedom, and the ensuing celebration of diversity of types makes it all the easier for fragments of the oligarchy to resurface and in effect to take over political power. The people respond to this maneuver by selecting a single leader whom they make great. He in turn uses the obedience of the mob as a license to put to death members of his own tribe, thereby exciting the lust for human flesh among the mob, to which he also promises money and land. Plots against the leader now serve as an excuse for him to demand a bodyguard, and so too to confiscate the money of the rich on the grounds that they are enemies of the people and conspire to overthrow their leader. Such is the genesis of the tyrant from the diverse fragments of the corrupted oligarchy and democracy (565c9–566d4).

The tyrant begins his career as a friend of the people, to whom he distributes various benefits. But this cordiality and this generosity soon change, since the tyrant is constantly making war in order to guarantee that his own leadership is indispensable to the city. The many grow poorer as a result of having to finance the wars, and they are forced to neglect public affairs in order to tend to their own daily occupations. Dissidents are eliminated by being turned over to the enemy during the numerous wars; when the more courageous citizens, who helped the tyrant to achieve power, protest against these practices, they are also murdered. The net result is that the tyrant has neither friends nor foes of any worth whatever. Having destroyed the brave, the great-minded, the prudent, and the rich, he has purged the city of its best elements, thus reversing the practice of the physician, who purges the body of its worst elements and allows the better ones to remain. Socrates concludes that the tyrant must live with the worthless mob, or not live at all (566d5–567d4). From this standpoint, the tyranny expresses the extreme consequence of the leveling tendency of democracy. The outstanding leader of the many poor is already the anticipation of the tyrant.

This anticipation is also exhibited in the tyrant's need to hire mercenaries to defend him, but even more sharply in the freeing of the slaves and making them part of his armed guard. Once again the best are lowered and the worst are raised, if not to prominence, at least to a position of power. This is the reverse of the wisdom of the tragedians, in particular of Euripides, who claims that "tyrants are wise through intercourse with the wise," and who says that the tyrant is equal to a god. The initial decision to exclude the tragic poets from our city has thus been reconfirmed. Socrates claims that these poets gather large crowds in the Greek cities and draw the people toward oligarchy and tyranny. He adds that tyrants especially honor and pay the tragedians; democracies are next (567d5–568d3). In this passage, Socrates tacitly shifts the blame of associating with tyrants from the philosophers, who are frequently charged with this tendency, to the poets.

As a last step in the analysis of tyranny, Socrates takes up the question of how the tyrant supports himself. When the public treasury has been emptied and the money of his murdered enemies has been spent, the tyrant will compel the people that produced him to pay for his support. Socrates compares this to the case in which the father supports the son instead of the son supporting the father. The tyrant is thus prepared to strike his father, but only after he has taken away the father's weapons (568d4–569c9). In other words, the tyrant is the son of democracy. The camp of the tyrant is described as "beautiful, manifold, intricate, and never the same," or in other words, as a distillation of the constantly changing intricacy of the democracy in its prime (568d5–6; cf. 558c4–6).

4

Socrates begins Book Nine by saying that it now remains to describe the tyrannical man: how he emerges from the democrat and how he lives. It should be obvious that much of this work has already been done in the description of the tyrannical regime. And indeed, nowhere in his account has

Socrates sharply differentiated between regimes and types of human being. He does not provide us with a purely institutional or legal account of the four kinds of regime but rather provides us with a dramatic and psychological account of how human beings of a given type are driven to prepare the conditions for the deterioration of their regime into the next lower stage. The lack of sharp transitions from one regime to another, as well as the constant reappearance of earlier forms in deteriorated versions, exhibits the fluidity of political change, which is more like Hegelian dialectic than the mathematical models of positivistic social and political scientists.

Nevertheless, there is a very general alternation in the analysis from each regime to its representative psychological type. In turning to the tyrant, Socrates interrupts himself with the admission that something is missing from the exposition, to the detriment of the clarity of his account. We do not seem to have distinguished sufficiently the number and kind of desires. This was plain from the introduction in Book Eight (558d1ff) of the distinction between necessary and unnecessary desires. The distinction was unusually austere, as is evident from the subsumption of harmless (neither good nor bad) under unnecessary desires. That to one side, why does Socrates notice the absence of a thorough classification of desires as he is about to discuss the tyrant? One might suggest that this is because the tyrant exhibits a manifold of desires, which the timocrat and oligarch, in their pure form, do not. But this overlooks the intricacy and multiplicity of the democratic nature.

Socrates begins with the unnecessary pleasures and desires. I have already commented on the apparently insignificant shift between desire alone and desire together with pleasure. When reading Plato, however, it is better to err on the side of hairsplitting than carelessness. And there is a distinction between desire and pleasure. The former is the expression of a lack or emptiness, whereas the latter arises from the restoration of the natural condition, that is, of being filled up again (*Philebus* 42c–d). In the present passage, however, we are going to be given a fine analysis of the nature of pleasure and desire not from a physiological standpoint but from that of politics. Political psychology is something quite different from physiological psychology.

Some unnecessary pleasures and desires are "contrary to the law" (*paranomoi*). They presumably arise in everyone but can be extirpated in some cases, or limited to a few weak ones, "by the laws and the better desires, together with *logos*" (571b2–c1). In other words, we all suffer from these unnecessary pleasures; they are in fact natural and must be treated with compulsion and persuasion. What one could call their natural necessity is thus subject to modification by human artifice; some of us are capable of training, and so modifying, human nature. If the training is not regularly applied, we may presume that nature will reassert itself. These pleasures and desires illustrate very well the ambiguity of nature from a moral or political standpoint. It makes no sense to say simply that human beings should live in accord with nature. On the contrary, we are forced to judge nature by the standard of our own intelligence and experience. The standard is not in nature but in ourselves. To say that man is a natural being is to beg the question why other natural beings do not judge and change their natures in various ways. Socrates now identifies the pleasures and desires in question as those that spring up in sleep; more precisely, when the calculating, tame, and ruling part is asleep, the bestial and wild part seeks to rise up and satisfy its dispositions. These parts seem to be intelligence and desire, respectively; nothing is said of spiritedness until the immediate sequel. The desires in question are those of sexual intercourse with all kinds of persons, including not only one's mother but also gods and beasts. In the less precise division of necessary and unnecessary desires, food took precedence over sex. Here the force of sexual desire is given its full due. I suppose that mention must be made of the often observed anticipation in this passage of the characteristically Freudian discussion of dreams and sexuality. However, whereas Freud wished to analyze such dreams in order to bring out their latent psychological content, Socrates wishes them to be purged.

This purgation involves not consultation with an analyst but the performance of a certain procedure by the healthy and moderate man as he prepares for sleep. In this procedure, each part of the soul must be brought into the right condition. The calculating part is awakened and feasted on beautiful arguments and investigations until it arrives at harmony (*sunnoian*) with itself. The treatment of the desiring part of the soul is less clear. It must be fed in such a way that it is neither empty nor full (or, in the terminology of the *Philebus*, to the point at which it is not changing from one extreme to the other), so that it will not disturb us with its pleasure or its pain. Finally, spiritedness must not be aroused by thoughts of anger. According to Socrates, these exercises silence the other two parts of the soul and set the intellect into the motion of prudent thinking. In this case, the paranomic desires are least likely to appear in his dreams (571d6–572b1).

Socratic psychotherapy corrects the antipolitical desires and pleasures of nature with the discipline of argument and the better desires. It is obvious that this therapy will work only with those who are either already healthy and moderate or predisposed to be so. On the other hand, some form of lawless desire is to be found in every human being. One might reply that this is because we live in corrupt cities, but the counterreply is that we do so because we ourselves are corrupt. Nature provides us with both our own defects and the cognitive capacity to perceive these defects and to attempt to rectify them. In short, human nature is divided against itself. Socrates frequently refers to this division as an illness and to philosophy as the physician. But medicine is a *technē* and not a direct expression of nature. In this sense it is true to say that for Socrates and Plato, art rules nature. As Nietzsche puts it, man is the not yet finished animal.[4] When we inspect the roots, we find that the ancients and the moderns are not quite as opposed to one another as is often said to be the case.

Socrates reminds Adeimantus that the son of the oligarch is raised to appreciate the stingy or moneymaking desires but is corrupted by those clever men who are filled with the desires of the spendthrift. Since his nature is superior to that of his corruptors, he ends up halfway between the two kinds of desire and lives a life that is neither illiberal nor opposed to the law. This, of course, is the democrat. His own son is reared in accord with this intermediate character, but under the influence of the spendthrifts he is drawn toward opposition to the law, which his corruptors call complete freedom. The ensuing quarrel over his soul is settled in favor of the spendthrifts, who contrive to implant some sort of eros — a winged drone — into his soul, to serve as leader of his own spendthrift desires. The imagery is almost the reverse of that in the *Phaedrus*, where the soul is compared to a winged charioteer that rises up to the love of the Platonic Ideas. In the present passage, eros is a drone that drains the soul of the last vestige of decency and renders it tyrannical (572b10–573a2). But this is to say that it pulls the soul down rather than up, and that its conception of freedom is complete license or hostility to all laws. We have already had a glimpse of this tyrannical aspect of eros in the discussion of the violation of the nuptial number. The descent from aristocracy through the other regimes to tyranny is the political version of the reversal of the erotic flight of the soul as described in the *Symposium* and *Phaedrus*, which are both very much private or apolitical dialogues. What rules us in private is antithetical to what produces a healthy and moderate, that is to say just, city.

The son of the democrat thus loses his relatively moderate devotion to pleasures thanks to the sting of love, which, Socrates reminds us, has often been called a tyrant. Moderation is replaced by madness, and not at all by the divine madness of philosophical eros but by its exact opposite. In the just city, the correct eros is by nature temperate and musical, that is, the love of the orderly and beautiful (III. 403a6–8), whereas, as Glaucon testifies, there is no sharper or more manic pleasure than that of sexual love (*aphrodisia*: 403a4–5). Philosophy is characterized in the *Republic* as the temperate eros, and sexuality as the mad eros. Thus the philosophical nature is said to be a kinsman of truth, justice, courage, and moderation at VI. 487a2–5. A complete account of eros would have to take into account the private or manic as well as the public or temperate dimension. The main concern of the *Republic*, however, is to mitigate as far as possible the politically disruptive effects of eros. To mitigate — but not to deny. Just as the beautiful city is destroyed by the impossibility of regulating sexual eros, so the preparation of philosopher-kings is compromised by the eros of the philosopher for being, that is, for what is always (VI. 485a10–b4). In other words, the temperate eros as well as the manic eros are in tension, and even in conflict, with the exigencies of political justice. Since human beings cannot exist without eros and cannot achieve their highest form of existence without both kinds of eros, temperate and mad, and finally, inasmuch as eros is uncontrollable or intemperate in all but the few lovers of being, human life is seen to be fractured at its root.

According to Socrates, the mad and deranged potential tyrant tries and hopes to be able to rule gods as well as humans. But he becomes a tyrant in the precise sense of the term when, whether through nature or by his practices or both, he becomes drunk, erotic, and melancholy (see Bloom's note 1 on "melancholy": 573c3–10). Socrates emphasizes that whereas the tyrant is driven by many terrible desires, the principal stimulus is sexual eros (573b6–7, d4, e5–6). In order to obtain funds for a courtesan or favorite boy, the tyrant will strike his own father and mother and enslave them to his newly installed lovers (574b12–c6). When the pursuit of gratification causes him to liquidate his own income and the estate of his parents, the tyrant robs his fellow citizens and strips the public temples of their wealth. "Eros lives tyrannically within him in complete anarchy and lawlessness" (575a1–2). In other words, the man is like a city, and eros is its tyrannical ruler. In psychological terms, the tyrannical man is dominated by what Socrates has called the unnecessary or spendthrift desires, which are represented as stimulated, multiplied, and dominated by eros. I say "dominated" rather than ruled because anarchy and lawlessness do not constitute a government. The emancipation of desire is thus a more radical step than the rule of desire over intellect, which is still compatible with the enforced virtue of stinginess or the love of money. Tyranny, whether in the individual person or in the city, is the final step in the process initiated by the failure of the philosopher-kings to control sexual reproduction.

This last point is crucial to Socrates's argument, since it will allow him to attribute the greatest unhappiness rather than happiness to the tyrannical soul and city, which represent the extreme forms of injustice. The question before us is why an unjust man should be wretched rather than happy. In everyday life, there is much evidence to contradict this judgment, but evidence that is based upon the possession of external goods and their enjoyment. It is not entirely persuasive to say that whereas the unjust man seems to be happy, he is actually miserable. What Socrates requires is a demonstration of the inner misery of the unjust but apparently thriving person. The demonstration he offers us is the deterioration of eros in the four bad regimes and their correlative human types. Socrates begins with the assumption that the disorderly soul is sick, and that sickness, namely, the unchecked dominance of the desires, is the cause of injustice. This assumption is not self-verifying; it must be demonstrated by a close analysis of human nature. But in the last instance, all such demonstrations rest upon an interpretation of inner health. How are we to see into the soul? It is for this reason that Socrates introduces the analogy between the city and the soul. He claims, surely not without reason, that we can see something of the inside of a man or woman by observing his or her external behavior. This is precisely how we actually judge persons. But the procedure falls short of definitive proof, so long as we cannot see into the soul.

It is this inability, of course, that led to the repudiation of introspection in philosophy and psychology, as well as to the attempted reduction of consciousness to physiological processes. The dream of science is an extension of the dream of rationalist philosophies, namely, to turn the human being inside out, and so to replace privacy entirely by the public. But it is of course impossible to turn human beings inside out. What actually happens is that we replace the mysteries of the interior by public certainties, or what can be demonstrated in public. The ultimate consequence of this procedure is the suppression of happiness and unhappiness as criteria for judging lives, or the transformation of human beings into biological machines (almost a contradiction in terms). If, on the other hand, machines can be happy, it will only be because of their possession of a soul or interior and private experience. And this simply reproduces the original problem; the machines will have to be turned inside out.

In order to be happy, we must be self-conscious; in order to prove that someone who claims to be happy is actually so, we must see into the interior; "self" consciousness must be extended to the consciousness of others. No matter how we look at the problem, it is not susceptible of a final resolution. Therefore we rely upon deeds and speeches, and the evidence, both of our own responses and those of others, to the events of everyday life. To put this in another way, we know more than we can prove. It is not difficult for us to see that someone is dominated by lust or that cities suffer terrible wretchedness under tyrants. Unfortunately, it is also not difficult to see that whereas some people are miserable because of their dominance by desire, others are not. I would be the first to agree that even those who deny the existence of an interior or soul rely upon their ability to discern the character of a person, that is, his or her inner nature, and not just the external speeches and deeds. All investigations of human nature, including the investigation that seeks to reduce the human to the bestial and the bestial to the mechanical, are based upon introspection into oneself and one's neighbors. In order to reduce happiness to a certain physiological condition, it is first necessary to know what it is to be happy, and this knowledge we have acquired directly from within ourselves.

In his attempt to respond to the demands of Glaucon and Adeimantus, Socrates depends from the outset upon their ability to infer the inner order or disorder of the soul from external evidence. And this ability in turn depends upon the capacity of the two young men to see into their own souls. They "know" what it is to be happy or unhappy, and for all practical purposes they know the difference between justice and injustice. What they cannot see is the necessary connection between happiness and justice, on the one hand, and unhappiness and injustice, on the other. More precisely, they believe themselves able to see it, but they are not sure; there is unsettling evidence against their supposition. In a very real sense, they have anticipated Hume's problem about the impossibility of perceiving a causal connection. But in this case, the connection is "lived" rather than observed. Glaucon and Adeimantus are asking for the impossible; they want their lived perception to be transformed into the confirmation of an observed perception.

By shifting from the individual soul to the city, Socrates does not really abandon introspection or common human experience; he does not simply transfer the investigation from the inner to the outer. The transfer is itself based upon our common perception of the interiority or privacy of human consciousness. By painting the broader political canvas, Socrates supplies an illusion of objectivity. But it is an illusion, as is also shown by the aforementioned shift back and forth from private persons to public actions in his story of the decay of the regimes. Once we understand the purpose of the analogy between the city and the soul, its technical deficiencies are seen in another light. The analogy is an attempt to foster a salutary illusion, not to provide a technically sound basis to a deductive argument. And something similar is true of the account of the decay in the four regimes. Socrates wants to show how this decline follows the steady diminution in the control of the desires by intellect through the agency of spiritedness. If the account is taken literally and narrowly as an analysis of actual political processes, it is a failure. There is no historical evidence that cities always deteriorate in accord with Socrates's account. The political terminology is designed to give the sense of greater visibility to what is at bottom a psychological account of the quarrel between philosophical and sexual eros. In one last formulation, if we reject the Platonic Ideas, the emancipation of sexual eros is inevitable.

Socrates goes on to describe the private life of the tyrannical nature. The most important new point is that tyrants have no friends but are either one man's master or another's slave (576a4–6). The tyrannical eros is entirely distinct from *philia*. This point is closely related to the fact that tyrants are not free, despite their power within the city. On the contrary, they are continuously enslaved, or being transformed into the slaves of their desires, and they cannot trust anyone or keep their word to any associate, who must be seen as a potential rival for power. Such a man is then as unjust as anyone can be. And, what is crucial for the larger argument, he is the most miserable of human beings. In the midst of this exchange, Glaucon takes back the role of interlocutor. It would have been awkward for him to be the respondent in the sharp criticism of eros, given the previous emphasis on his own erotic nature.

In sum: the tyrannic man is like the tyrannic city, and so too in the other cases. Both the tyrannic city and the corresponding person are maximally miserable and unjust, whereas the happiest and most virtuous city is the kingdom founded by Socrates and his interlocutors (576c6–d5). Two small points: (1) Socrates says that the many will have many opinions about the tyrant; in other words, they may approve the tyranny, or wish it for themselves. (2) In this passage, Socrates speaks of virtue (*aretē*) rather than of justice. More striking, however, is the imagery he uses in cautioning Glaucon not to be overwhelmed at the sight of the tyrant, "but as we must, let's enter the city and view it as a whole, creeping in everywhere and looking, and then making clear our opinion" (576d8–e2). In the immediate sequel, Socrates applies this metaphor to the study of the tyrannic man: "Would I be right to impose the same demand concerning the [tyrannic] men themselves, if I think that the one who is best able to judge these things is the one who is able to use his intelligence to see into the character of a man" and does not, like a boy, judge the tyrant by his exterior pomp but is able to see through it into the interior (576e6– 577a5)? Socrates thus makes it explicit that in order to judge whether a person is happy or wretched, we must see into the individual soul and "creep about" into its hidden recesses. This procedure is obviously connected to, but it is also distinct from, the creeping about through the corners and recesses of the city. It is claimed that the city is the soul writ large, but the analogy is false to this important extent: the city is the exterior of the soul, and a large soul is just as much "interior" as is one of normal size.

The competent judge of the tyrant is someone who can see into the soul and thereby evaluate correctly his public experience of tyranny. Socrates proposes, and Glaucon agrees, that they pretend themselves to be judges of this sort. This passage is reminiscent of the beginning of Rousseau's Second Discourse, in which he says that he can affirm the truth of his interpretation of the natural human being because he has a special insight into the human soul. It is not my intention to ridicule claims of this sort; rather, my intention is to bring out the difference between them and claims that there is no "interior" or soul, and that all our knowledge of human beings must come from the study and measurement of their external speeches and deeds. This does not mean that introspection suffices. But our understanding of the feelings and intentions of others is based finally upon self-knowledge. There would be no other way in which to interpret exterior speeches and deeds, if we had no immediate understanding of the human significance of those external acts. Even those who say that there is no distinction between the inside and the outside, and so that the significance of speeches and deeds must be inferred from their public meaning, forget that there is no public meaning if the members of the public are robots.

Socrates now leads Glaucon through a review of the four regimes and their corresponding individual characters. Almost the entire tyrannical city, and all of its decent part, is enslaved to the worst element. So too with the individual of tyrannic nature. Both city and individual are poor, marked by insatiable desires and eros, full of suffering, and wretched. But the most wretched of all is not the private person; it is rather the tyrannical nature that actually obtains political power. Socrates refers here to the wealthy private person who is similar to a tyrant in that he rules over many servants and slaves (577c1–579b2).

12

Happiness and Pleasure

I

After a further review of the similarity between the tyrannical city and soul, in which no new points of importance occur, Socrates finally arrives at his conclusion, with much rhetorical fanfare. He serves as the herald of the news that Glaucon, the son of Ariston (the word means "best"), has judged the best and most just man to be the happiest, namely, the one who is kingliest and king of himself, and that the worst and most unjust man is the most miserable, namely, the tyrant (580b8–c5). Neither Adeimantus nor the other speakers are included in this agreement. This makes us wonder whether Thrasymachus, for example, is entirely persuaded, or only silenced, by the argument. This apart, Glaucon's preeminence among the interlocutors is shown by the fact that he figures in the statement of the conclusion to the long conversation about justice and happiness. We should also keep in mind that the happiest man is identified with the philosopher-king, not the monarch in the usual sense of the term. The philosopher who is a private citizen in an actual (and so not philosophical) monarchy will have more difficulty in preserving his soul under the rule of reason, but Plato is eager to maintain that such happiness is possible. This is one of the most important features of his dramatic character, Socrates. I doubt whether Plato was himself as "happy" as Socrates is presented to be.

Once again, it is not the actual monarch who is the happiest of mortals. Socrates does not discuss the monarchy or aristocracy in their historical forms but turns directly from the philosophical city to the timocracy (VIII. 544e3–545a4). One has the impression from this passage that "monarchy" refers to the rule of a single philosopher in the best city and "aristocracy" to the rule of several. As we recall, this city decays when the nuptial number is violated. The result of the decay is a timocracy; nothing is said about an actual aristocracy as the deteriorated form of the philosophical original. Something essential is lacking here, and we are given no hint why this should be so. Apparently Socrates collapses the (actual) aristocracy into the timocracy, which is ruled by victory and honor, "established in accord with the Laconian regime" (545a2). Perhaps he feels that the name is too exalted to apply to a defective historical regime. In any case, the identification of "kingly" with "aristocratic" is quite clear in 580a9–b4, where Socrates lists the regimes as "royal, timocratic, oligarchic, democratic, tyrannical."

So much for the demonstration of happiness. Socrates now claims that the tripartition of the soul will admit of another proof, that is, another proof about the superiority of justice to injustice. Whereas the first proof turned upon happiness, the second concerns pleasure. Socrates finds it useful to show that the life of the intellect is more pleasant than the life associated with the dominance of the other two parts of the soul. Many contemporary readers would find this even worse than an appeal to eudaimonism. I myself believe that the older view as represented by Socrates is more realistic. Who would choose a life of justice if it made us miserable and full of pain? But even further, what possible reasoning could demand that the just person be unhappy lest the desirability of justice for its own sake be compromised by the desire for happiness? Is this not unjust? And so too with pleasure; the superiority of justice to injustice derives from its effects on our soul, not from the carrying-out of a set of rules. It is not very convincing to be told that although we may be made happy or experience pleasure from being just, the two have nothing to do with one another.

We cannot settle this quarrel here, but it was necessary to say a few words in defense of the Socratic procedure, which has been subjected to much irrelevant criticism by Kant and his disciples.[1] Socrates is fully aware that justice is desirable for its own sake, but he also wants to claim that justice includes happiness and pleasure. He claims that we cannot be unhappy or live a life of pain if we are just. I think that this is almost certainly mistaken, but it is not immoral. On the contrary, Socrates is moved by the highest consideration for morality to unite happiness and pleasure to justice. As he sees it, it would be immoral to deny that justice is so united, and the political consequences of this denial are infinitely worse than those of its affirmation.

Socrates now claims that there is a tripartition of pleasures corresponding to that of the soul, as well as a threefold division of desires and kinds of rule. One part of the soul learns, a second part is the seat of spiritedness. The third and largest part is called by the general name of "desire" and is also referred to as the money-loving part, since the main desires are satisfied by money. I remind the reader that sex is the strongest desire; to associate it with money is to distinguish it from the love that characterizes friendship. Spiritedness is victory and love of honor, whereas the intellect, with which we learn, cares least for money and is always directed toward knowing the truth, and it may appropriately be called the love of learning and wisdom. In the cases of spiritedness and learning, Socrates does not employ *eros* to designate love but uses *philos* (friend) instead (580d7–581b11). But he does speak of the desires that characterize each of the three parts of the soul (580d8). In other words, *eros* and *philia*, despite their differences, both intersect with desire, and hence, with pleasure as well. Thus Socrates infers from what has just been said that there are three primary kinds of human being: *philosophon, philonikon, philokerdes* (581c2–3), that is, lovers or friends of wisdom, victory, and gain, respectively. As stamped by desire, *eros* and *philia* are in that sense interchangeable.

Each part of the soul has its characteristic pleasure, and therefore its own form of desire. If we were to ask each of the three in turn which of these lives is the most pleasant (*hēdistos*), they would each choose their own and ridicule or minimize the claims of the other two. This raises a difficult question. There are external criteria by which to judge competing claims of living nobly, shamefully, worse, or better. But pleasure seems to be entirely "inner" or, as we now say, subjective. How, then, can we judge which of the claims to being most pleasant is correct? Socrates develops at some length the reply that we must follow the judgment of the person who has had the most experience of the pleasures and combines this experience with prudence and argument. Stated as briefly as possible, the lover of wisdom has an experience of the pleasures of gain that is greater than the experience of the pleasure of learning possessed by the lover of gain, and so too with the case of honor. The first-named is also more prudent than the other two and altogether superior in the practice of argumentation. His judgment as to the most pleasant life must therefore prevail (581c8–583a3).

This argument is inconclusive because it might well be the case that the lover of wisdom is not capable of experiencing the pleasures of honor or money-making, which could actually be greater for their type of person than is the acquisition of learning for the person of strong intellect. Furthermore, we could be convinced by the lover of wisdom simply because he is superior to the other two kinds of men in prudence and capacity for argument; hence the significance of Glaucon's remark that the prudent man praises as a master praiser (583a4–5). John Stuart Mill uses a similar argument in claiming that the pleasures of Socrates are greater than those of the pig because Socrates is capable of experiencing both and prefers his own. These arguments show only that each of us, including the wise man, prefers what is peculiar to our own nature, and not that one kind of pleasure is intrinsically greater than the others. Finally, it is odd that Socrates employs an argument from the quantity of pleasure, since he normally argues that the choiceworthiness of pleasure depends upon the goodness of its source. In any case, Socrates wishes to show that the just life is not only happier but also more pleasant than the other kinds, and this is useful in arguing with people like Glaucon, although it may not be as effective with Adeimantus.

Socrates allows the intellect to continue as judge, and second place is awarded to the life of spiritedness and the pleasures of war and honor, whereas the love of gain places third and last. So much for the second argument. Socrates now presents a third argument on behalf of the superiority of the life of learning. This argument is more complicated than the first two, and we shall look at it carefully (See Bloom's footnote 7 for the reference to Zeus). We begin with the admission that pain is the opposite of pleasure. Second, there is a way of existing that is neither pleasant nor painful but something in the middle, which Socrates calls a certain rest or quiet of the soul. For example, when we are sick, we say that nothing is more pleasant than being healthy, but this had escaped us while we were healthy. And similarly, when we are undergoing intense suffering, we say that nothing is more pleasant than the cessation of suffering. The point of these examples is to show that cessation from pleasure and pain is itself neither genuine pleasure nor pain but rest or quiet. On the other hand, to a sick and suffering person, abstention from pain looks like pleasure, whereas to someone whose pleasure ceases, this cessation seems to us painful.

This argument is not entirely persuasive. It depends upon the premise that there are intermediate states during which we feel neither pleasure nor pain. This seems to be correct with respect to a specific pleasure or pain. If I have a painful sore throat and it heals, the previous pain disappears and is replaced, first, by the sensation of pleasure but, second, by what one can call the normal state of the throat, neither painful nor pleasant. It is, however, certainly not correct to say that the soul can be entirely at rest, since there are many pleasures and pains affecting it, at least when it is awake. I might also think about my previous pain and feel pleasure in its absence. Socrates claims in the sequel that there is nothing sound in these pleasures with respect to truth; they are fantasms or wizardry (584a7–10). He does not, and in my view cannot, explain the difference between a fantasm or illusion of pleasure and pain and the real thing. If I believe that I am in pain, then I am, even if the *source* of the pain is imaginary. An imaginary pleasure is neither a pain nor a state of rest.

That said, we can grant Socrates that there is a difference between a positive pleasure that we are now undergoing, say, the taste of a good meal, and what I shall call the negative pleasure of not being forced to eat a bad meal. But the sense of relief that accompanies the release from pain can hardly be called rest; in the case of recovery from a serious illness, the pleasure is exciting and liberating, not a return to quiet rest. And it can often be more pleasant than the so-called genuine or positive pleasures. The underlying difficulties here are, first, that it seems to be impossible to draw sharp distinctions between pleasure and pain and, second, that quiet and rest, like tranquility, are themselves pleasures, not illusions of pleasure. Socrates's own formulation of his argument is extremely confusing. Having just established that the intermediate condition of rest or quiet can be both pleasant and painful, depending upon whether it is being compared to the cessation of pleasure or of pain, he then says that what is neither pleasure nor pain cannot become both. Since pleasure and pain are motions, whereas rest is intermediate between the two and so is presumably not a motion, it must be an illusory pleasure or pain. I have already challenged this reasoning on the grounds that what seems to be pleasant is so when it seems so. To this I now add that the condition intermediate between two motions may itself be a motion. In a state of repose or tranquility, we do not literally cease to move, as is obvious from the fact that we enjoy the awareness of that tranquility (583c10–584a11).

In order to buttress his argument, Socrates turns next to pleasures that do not arise from the cessation of pain. He cites the example of a pleasant smell that suddenly occurs with great intensity, and without previous pain. It is no doubt correct to say that in most cases pleasant smells are not preceded by the pain of not experiencing them. Of course, someone could be deprived of his favorite smell and suffer the pain of absence, but Socrates has excluded these cases here. He does, however, refer to cases of a pleasant smell ceasing without causing us any pain, and asks us on that basis not to believe that release from pain is pure pleasure or that release from pleasure is pure pain (584c1–2). Socrates seems to be playing with words here. Let us grant that some pleasures are pure in the sense that their occurrence is not dependent upon a previous cessation of pain. But this in itself does not make the spontaneous pleasure, such as the smell of a flower, more pleasant than the pleasure that arises from cessation of pain, such as recovery from a painful infection or muscle sprain. An "impure" pleasure can certainly be more pleasant than a "pure" pleasure. Again, Socrates seems to be confusing the source of the pleasure or the conditions of its occurrence with the pleasantness of the pleasure itself.

Socrates now goes on to assert that most of the so-called pleasures that stretch from the body to the soul, in particular the greatest ones, belong to the family of relief from pain. He includes among them the pleasures and pains of anticipation that arise because of an expectation of future pleasures and pains. This leads to the elaborate formulation of the following point. The man who is inexperienced with respect to what is truly up, middle, and down will believe wrongly that when he is raised from the bottom to the middle and looks downward, he has arrived in the genuine upper region. On the other hand, if he is lowered from the middle to his starting point, he will suppose truly that he is back at the bottom. If we translate this back into the language of the middle and two extremes, whoever does not know genuine or pure pleasure will falsely identify it with the pleasures arising from cessation of pain. I very much doubt whether there is anyone who has never experienced what Socrates calls a pure pleasure. But even if we admit that there are many who lack sufficient experience to make the distinction between pure and impure pleasures, such persons are not thereby mistaken in enjoying what they take to be pleasure. That which is taken to be a pleasure *is* a pleasure. In saying this, I do not forget that the line between pleasure and pain can be very narrow, but that is a separate issue.

All of this logic chopping is in the tacit service of the wish to minimize the violent pleasures of the body, and in particular of sexual eros. But it has the absurd consequence that the pleasure of learning, if it is to be pure, is classified together with pleasures emanating from unexpected smells and tastes. We can grant Socrates that the lover of wisdom enjoys the toil of learning, but is this not in large part due to the pleasure of being released from ignorance, which ought to qualify as a painful state, and, indeed, to the anticipation of further release as we progress in wisdom? One other point here: those who descend from the middle to the bottom suppose truly that they are in genuine pain, whereas those who are raised from the bottom to the middle, if they are inexperienced in pleasure, suppose falsely that they are nearing fulfillment and pleasure. By putting the point in this way, Socrates deprives the middle position of the actual state of being pleased, but this begs the question. In addition, impure pain is taken to be genuine, whereas impure pleasure is not (584c4–585a5).

2

Let me briefly resume the main points of the previous discussion of pleasure. There are three parts to the soul, characterized by the love of learning, victory and honor, and money or gain. This last part is also called the *epithumetic* or desiring element in the soul. Strictly speaking, the other two parts also have desires, namely, for learning and honor; the desires of the money-loving part are those of the body, such as arise from food, drink, and, above all, sex. There are also three kinds of pleasure, one each for each part of the soul. It follows that there are also three kinds of person, one who loves learning above all, one whose greatest and defining love is honor and victory, and one who is primarily sexually erotic. This is not to say that any of these three types of person has none of the other elements but rather to say that each is defined by one element in particular. Nor are there three small persons or homunculi present within each of us and corresponding to the three parts of our soul. Among other defects, this interpretation of the soul would lead directly to an infinite regress of "persons" consisting of three small persons, each of whom is a person consisting of three small persons, and so on.[2] There is just you and me, that is, separate persons of a given type of nature. The description of these parts of the soul as themselves persons of a certain type is purely metaphorical; it is a dramatization of psychic faculties that define types of human beings. Whether these faculties can be sharply differentiated from each other is a serious problem, and the present passage, which attributes desire and pleasure to each of the parts of the soul, strongly suggests that they cannot.

The problem from our present perspective is that of the relation between eros or sexual desire, which is associated with the epithumetic or money-loving part of the soul, and the other kind of love, *philia*, also translated as "friendship," that appears in the expressions "lover of learning" and "lover of honor and victory." As Socrates says at 580d7–8, there are three kinds of desires, each of which corresponds to a distinct ruling principle in the three different types of person. This is crucial: Pleasure and pain are to be found in all three parts of the soul, and so too is desire. It is hard to define desire in a noncircular manner, but perhaps we can call it a nisus toward, or craving for, something that we lack. Borrowing terminology from passages we are about to discuss, desire is accompanied by pain so long as we do not possess what we seek, and by pleasure when we do. But Socrates does not discuss desire in this broader sense in any detail; he simply mentions it. Instead, he discusses pleasure and pain, which are defined from various perspectives but always in terms of possessing or being filled up and lacking or being empty.

Each of the three main types of person will claim that his or her preferred form of life is by far the most pleasant. This being so, we require some basis from which to judge the relative merits of these three claims. But there is no basis external to the three lives, since they exhaust the human race among them. Therefore we must appeal to the judgment of the person with the most experience, that is, the one who is capable of experiencing all three kinds of activity and their coordinate pleasures. Socrates assumes that this person is the lover of learning. Only he can appreciate the intense pleasure of learning, while he is also capable of experiencing the pleasures of spiritedness and moneymaking (that is, bodily desire). As I pointed out previously, this last claim does not follow with any necessity. Most men of learning would be very poor judges as to the intensity of the pleasures of honor and moneymaking. I believe that this consideration alone is enough to show the impossibility of rank-ordering lives by the criterion of pleasure. And in fact, Socrates does not really do so. His classification of pleasures (and pains) is based upon the assumption that what counts is the nature of the sources of our pleasure, not their effect on the soul. For example, the claim that knowledge is accompanied by a much greater amount of pleasure than victory or moneymaking is attractive only to someone who receives intense pleasure from learning. In other words, the entire argument is circular.

The passage in which Socrates classifies the pleasures is extremely obscure. In the first section of the passage, he distinguishes pleasure and pain as two discontinuous conditions that are separated by a middle state in which we feel neither pleasure nor pain but rather *hēsuchia*, rest or quiet (583c3–8). But we can mistake this middle or (as I shall call it) neutral state for pleasure if we arrive there directly through the cessation of pain; alternatively, we take it to be pain if we arrive through a cessation of pleasure. Socrates gives as examples of the former case a return to good health from illness and the cessation of an excruciating pain. We mistake this middle or neutral state for pleasure, simply because we have returned to the normal condition, which we would not even notice if we had not previously been ill or in pain. He gives no examples of the transition from pleasure to its cessation, which marks our entry into the neutral state that is neither pleasure nor pain. The point, once more, is that when one stops feeling pleasure or pain but does not immediately enter into another pleasure or pain, one may be deluded into thinking that the neutral state is itself pleasant or painful.

The reader must decide whether it is plausible to assert that relief from pain is in itself not a pleasure. Among the various problems with this assertion, I mention only the interaction of pleasures and pains within the continuum of life, and the subsequent near-impossibility of distinguishing the neutral condition with respect to one cessation of pleasure or pain from the neutral conditions associated with other such conditions. Perhaps we should also note that this assertion rules out Aristotle's subsequent claim that life is intrinsically pleasant. The distinction made by Socrates also requires that what seems pleasant to us may not be, and in fact is not if it is simply a return to the normal or neutral state. The theme of false or mistaken pleasures has rightly generated an extensive controversy in the secondary literature. I shall be very brief on this point. To say that I believe that I experience a pleasure but am mistaken is, I think, void of sense. It is not like saying that I believe that I perceive a human being but am mistaken: it is only a shadow or a trick of perspective. In the hypothesis of the false or illusory pleasure, there is nothing to correspond to the human being in the illusory perception. What I believe to be a pleasure *is* a pleasure, however much I may disapprove of the source or cause of that pleasure. The assertion boils down to the statement that "the pleasure that I feel is not a pleasure."

However this may be, the conclusion reached by Socrates is that the same thing, namely, the neutral state, can be both pleasant and unpleasant, depending upon the origin from which we reach it. This seems to contradict the point he has just established about the neutrality of the intermediate state. What Socrates means is that the neutral state seems to be, but in fact is not, both pleasant and painful: he asks whether it is possible for what is neither to become both, and accepts Glaucon's reply that this does not seem possible (583e7–8). Besides, he continues, pleasure and pain are both motions in the soul, whereas the neutral state is rest or repose.

Socrates needs to explain to us how we can be tricked by fantasms and magic into believing that we feel pleasure or pain when we do not (584a9–10). The key premise seems to be that relief from these two states is a negation rather than an assertion, so to speak; to cancel out one state of the soul is not in itself to replace it by its opposite. Otherwise put, the illusory pleasures and pains just considered were each preceded by a genuine pain or pleasure, respectively. We are now to consider pleasures which are not preceded by pain, although Socrates states that there are also pains which are not preceded by pleasures (584b1–3). The only example given is that of a pleasant smell which has no antecedent pain but arises instantaneously (*eksaiphnēs*) and can be extremely powerful. Socrates then indicates that this is an example of "pure pleasures," so called because they are not preceded by nor do they cause any subsequent pain (584b5–8). Presumably the illusory pleasures and pains are impure, but this is not stated explicitly.

Socrates might be on firmer ground if he were to hold that pleasures preceded by pains (and pains by pleasures) are impure but not illusory. This could be part of a more general argument that relief from pain is polluted by the immediately preceding pain, which continues to resonate in our memory, or even physiologically as the residue of the painful motion. Other questions remain; for example, we would have to ask whether an unsatisfied desire is painful, and if it is, whether that pain lingers in the pleasure experienced through the satisfaction of the desire. Nor is it clear to me, either on Socrates's hypothesis or my suggested emendation, why relief from an excruciating pain is any less pleasant than a powerful smell. Furthermore, it is not plausible to deny that the satisfaction of a desire is pleasant. What Socrates could properly claim is that the satisfaction of some desires is shameful, and that the pain of shame is stronger than or equal to the pleasure of the satisfaction. But even this premise holds good at most for persons of noble character, as Socrates will admit in the sequel.

Pure pleasure, then, is for Socrates not a release from pain. It is important for the transition to note that the example of the pleasant smell is of a pleasure that reaches the soul through the body. Socrates now says that the most numerous and powerful of the "so-called" (*legomenoi*) pleasures of this sort are a relief from pain (584c4–8). In accord with the previous definitions, these pleasures are both impure and illusory, and the same is true of anticipations of future pleasure through expected relief from pain. Socrates does not make it explicit immediately, but this entails that the pleasures of sex, food, and drink, to mention only the three most striking cases, are all illusions. And there is a deeper ambiguity. The apparently illusory pleasure arising from sex, eating, and drinking is not like that state which follows the return from sickness to health or the cessation of a pain in some part of the body. The pain in the case of the former examples is not that of the presence of something (sickness or a toothache) but rather arises from the absence of the satisfaction of a desire. Hungry people are in pain because they are without food, not (in this respect at least) because they are also ill or suffering from toothache. A hungry man could also be undergoing some other kind of pain, such as torture, but the removal of the torture would not satisfy his hunger. On the contrary, it would probably accentuate that desire, since he would no longer be distracted by the pain of torture.

There is one other problem with Socrates's analysis up to this point that I wish to mention. Let us take the case of the illusory pleasure that arises from the cessation of pain (for example, a toothache). Socrates never denies, and it seems to be required by what he does say, that the pain (for example, of the toothache) is a genuine pain and not an illusion. We recall that the only item called illusory is the pleasure that we mistakenly attribute to what is in fact the intermediate or neutral state of repose. It would make no sense to say that we have now arrived at this repose if we had not just been released from a painful motion. And the same would have to be true of a pleasure that disappears when we return to the intermediate condition of repose. These initial pleasures and pains, as I shall call them for convenience, are not pure, like pleasant smells, but neither can they be illusory, like the misinterpreted relief from pleasure or pain. Furthermore, what sense would it make to speak of pure pains? The onset of a toothache must be just as pure as the undergoing of a pleasant smell. It springs not from an antecedent pleasure but rather from the neutral state of the absence of pleasure and pain. But neither does its absence bring about a genuine pleasure; on the contrary, it returns us to the neutral state. Looked at in this way, the initial pleasures and pains must be pure. That is, the concept of the intermediate condition makes all pleasures and pains pure. As repose or rest, the intermediate condition cannot be or cause pleasure and pain. For how could what is entirely at rest generate a motion?

So much for problems of this sort. I trust that I have said enough to show the unsatisfactoriness of Socrates's analysis of pleasure and pain. Socrates now shifts to a variation on the metaphor of the intermediate state. There is in nature a "top, middle, and down" (as Griffith translates). Someone who has no experience of the upper region and who moves from the bottom to the middle will suppose incorrectly that he is now in fact in the upper zone. If this man were moved back to the bottom, he would suppose correctly that he had descended. Socrates says that this is the condition of those who have no experience of the truth about the genuine top, middle, and bottom (584e4–6). Socrates then applies this set of terms to the previous discussion of pleasure and pain. In a simple schema,

"Top" equals pleasure
"Middle" equals repose
"Bottom" equals pain

(1) Motion from the middle to the top equals genuine experience of pleasure.
(2) Motion from the middle to the bottom equals genuine feeling of pain.
(3) Motion from the bottom to the middle equals illusory pleasure.
(4) Motion from the top to the middle equals illusory pain.

Socrates affirms explicitly only (2) and (4), but he extends the general schema to include pleasure as well (584e7–585a5). Trouble arises when we move to the middle from the opposite extremes, or in other words come to rest, but not when we move away from the middle in either direction or are set into motion. It seems that "experience of the truth" is unnecessary for a true belief concerning (1) and (2) in our schema. It is easier to understand, or to interpret correctly, being set into motion than coming to rest. In this way, Socrates admits that what he calls "rest" (*hēsuchia*) is a problematical concept. If there is indeed such a state as that of repose, it must be like death rather than life, but a death that seems like life. Less melodramatically, it is a rest that seems like motion. In short, I can mistake one motion for another, as when some disturbance of the body during sleep makes me dream that I am flying. But I cannot mistake rest for motion or motion for rest. Someone might object that the motion of the earth seems to us to be rest, but in this case we have no immediate perception of the motion of the earth. We do not examine the moving earth and infer that it is at rest. But the assumption that sex is pleasant and a toothache is painful is based upon immediate sensation. If this can be wrong, then we have no way of evaluating our contact with perceptual reality.

3

Socrates now introduces a new reflection on the situation just described. This reflection turns upon the comparison of pleasure and pain to being filled up and emptied, respectively. Hunger and thirst are examples of the emptying of the body, while ignorance and imprudence illustrate the same condition of the soul. Similarly, eating and drinking are cases of filling up the body, while partaking of the nourishment of the soul (learning) and becoming intelligent are examples of filling up the soul. If the previous point about the middle state is to be sustained, we must assume that by "being filled up" (585b6–11, d7–10) Socrates is referring to the shift not from pain to its absence but rather from pain to pleasure in one continuous motion. This is an analysis of the shift from pain to pleasure different from the analysis we met with before, although the difference is not signaled. Unfortunately, not enough detail is supplied here for us to determine exactly what Socrates has in mind. He certainly seems to be presenting various stages in what he regards as a continuous analysis of pleasure; but the "filling up" image does not square with that of the top, middle, and bottom. Nor is it easy to see why being filled up in the case of eating and drinking is not like being in the normal or intermediate condition of repose, in which one is neither thirsty nor hungry. On the other hand, if thirst and hunger lead to pleasures in a sense totally different from that in the previous passage, then the overall argument is not consistent with itself, or requires further expansion in order to remove the appearance of inconsistency.

Instead of taking up questions of this sort, Socrates turns to a different aspect of the analysis of pleasure. Hunger and thirst are an emptiness of the body that is filled up with food and drink. Note that there is no question here of the need to fill up; life would be impossible without it. Also, there is a difference between filling up to the point needed for survival and the filling up of the gourmand who eats for the sheer (illusory) joy of eating. Analogously, ignorance and stupidity are the emptiness of the soul, which is filled up by the consumption of *nous*, literally, "intellect," but by extension, reason or good sense (585b4–8). Socrates does not contrast "knowledge" with the empty condition, but rather the faculty of acquiring knowledge. His next question is whether the truer fullness is of that which is less or more a being. The question does not seem peculiar to Glaucon; he answers without hesitation that the truer filling-up is of what is more a being (585b9–11).

In this passage, Socrates appeals to what has sometimes been called the principle of the degrees of being. To take the decisive example, a Platonic Idea is more genuinely a being than are the instances of genesis that participate in it. Socrates gives a parallel but different example. He asks Glaucon which kind of thing (*genos*) participates more in pure being, things like food, water, relish, and so on, or the form (*eidos*) of true opinion, knowledge, intellect, and, in general, all of virtue. Glaucon chooses the latter. This seems to establish the greater reality or participation in being of the soul, in contrast to the body (585d1–4). Throughout the Platonic dialogues, it is taken for granted that what is always and unalterably, is more genuinely a being, or participates more fully in being, than what is finite and changing. We have already seen this assumption at work in the case of the Platonic Ideas. The striking point in this passage is that since pleasures and pains are understood as motions, they cannot themselves be genuine beings. Differently stated, they come closer to genuine being through arriving at repose. So too the condition of being filled up must be closer to genuine being than is the condition of emptiness or the intermediate condition of filling up. Correlatively, the pleasures of knowledge and intelligence are superior to those of eating and drinking; this superiority derives not from the intensity of the pleasure but from the genuineness of the objects of understanding (585d7–10).

The crucial sentence reads (in Griffith's translation): "So if being filled with things appropriate to our nature is pleasurable, then that which is more genuinely filled, and filled with things which have more being, would make people more truly and genuinely happy, giving them true pleasure, whereas that which takes in things which have less being would be less truly and lastingly filled, and get hold of a pleasure which was less trustworthy and less true" (585d11–e4). Let me immediately underline the significance this passage has for the larger argument. Socrates holds that the just life is happier for human beings than the unjust life. Since justice is minding one's own business, the philosophers are the only people who can justly be filled up with what more genuinely is. In other words, genuine happiness is reserved for the philosopher, who is a special subset of the class of just persons. This is essentially the argument of Aristotle in the tenth book of the *Nicomachean Ethics*.

In its Socratic form, the argument rehabilitates pleasure. It is self-evident that the consumption of knowledge and understanding is pleasurable. But a moment's reflection also shows that we must keep the body in good condition if we are to be able to think and study. The pleasure of filling up the body with the necessary food and drink is thus a legitimate part of the happiest human life. What about sexual pleasure? Socrates does not mention it here, but we can infer from what he says about food and drink that it would be allowed in moderation, for the health of the body. From our immediate standpoint, the nerve of the argument is that pleasure is filling up (that is, being filled), and that what is itself most truly or fully, provides us with the most complete fullness.

Is this a reasonable assertion? At first glance it makes sense to say that the more substantial our nourishment, the more will our hunger be satiated. But difficulties soon arise. If the body is hungry or thirsty, it will not be filled up by gazing at the Ideas. And if we are not philosophers, then our souls cannot be filled up with truth but must have recourse to something else, say, poetry. Socrates interprets examples like these to establish that nonphilosophers are not genuinely filled up, but the reverse could also be defended. To be full is relative to one's capacity, and so too is the nature of the sustenance that fills us. As to the everlasting nature of genuine beings, this seems to be irrelevant to the question of fullness during life, but it should also be mentioned that philosophers continuously seek genuine nourishment; that is the nature of philosophical eros. Obviously, the grasp of some eternal beings does not suffice to fill up the intellect. Why then could the soul not achieve the same satisfaction from a steady stream of finite comestibles?

In some cases it is clear that those who consume the most perfect nourishment will receive the truest and most genuine happiness and pleasure. A rotten peach cannot please us as much as a ripe one. But the situation is less clear when we shift to sexual pleasure. One could say that a beautiful partner provides more pleasure than an ugly one, although this is far from universally true. What would be still harder to establish is that the intensity of sexual pleasure depends upon the moral character of one's partner. Socrates assumes that not intensity but genuineness, true being, is the paradigm for rank-ordering pleasures. Intercourse with an evil person is thus on his grounds a less genuine pleasure. But is it any the less pleasant? There are also difficulties with respect to the nourishment of the soul. Socrates takes for granted the edifying nature of the truth, and hence its pleasantness. But what if the truth is bad and painful? Does the pleasure of knowing the truth supervene over the pain of knowing sad truths? Socrates might point to our pleasure in tragedy as evidence for the affirmative response, but one could reply to this that tragedy is already an accommodation to sorrow, and that it would be much more pleasant if we were freed from death, disease, and poverty.

Socrates applies his previous analysis in order to conclude that the highest and best pleasures of the soul are pure, that is, unmixed with pain, whereas the lower degrees of pleasure, and in particular those corporeal pleasures that are so strenuously desired by the many, are mixed with pain and are phantoms and reflections of true pleasure. As the examples (food and sex) show, these mixed or impure pleasures are suitable for cattle. The pure pleasures are no longer illustrated by smells, as they were previously, but rather by the participation in what is genuinely true and a being in the fullest sense of the term. On this new account, smells must be impure pleasures, since they fill us up with transient odors emanating from residents of genesis (586a1–c6). In his analysis of pleasure, Socrates does not so much abstract from the body as argue for the superiority of the soul. But that superiority certainly directs us toward a life of bodily asceticism and psychic or intellectual Epicureanism. It looks as if one can never have too much intellectual pleasure.

At the same time, it would be absurd to rule out all bodily pleasure. Nor should we forget the love of victory and honor. The pleasures of bodily desire and spiritedness are impure in themselves; but to the extent that these desires are able to follow the pleasures of the prudential part of the soul, and with their assistance pursue and capture the pleasures that prudence permits, they too will possess the truest pleasures, to the extent that they are able to do so (586d4–e2). This is less clear than one would like, but it seems to be compatible with saying that there are quasi-pure or true bodily pleasures, permitted, either directly or indirectly, by the intelligent part of the soul. The situation within the soul is thus analogous to that in the city. So long as the other two parts of the soul obey intellect or philosophy, each minds its own business and enjoys its own pleasures justly, as well as enjoying the best and truest pleasures through following the orders of reason (586e4–587a1).

What is most distant from philosophy and reasoning (or argument: *logos*), namely, the control of the soul by the two inferior parts, leads to a kind of miscegenation of pleasures, in which these parts seek the wrong kind of pleasure. The erotic and tyrannic desires are farthest removed from law, order, and *logos*, whereas the kingly and orderly desires are least distant. It follows that the tyrant lives most unpleasantly and the king (presumably the philosopher-king) lives most pleasantly. Otherwise put, Socrates has now established to Glaucon's satisfaction that the most unjust life is the least pleasant and the most just life the most pleasant. Let us not forget that this is only one string on Socrates's lyre. The case for justice does not simply depend upon its pleasures, it depends also upon inner health or harmony. And pleasure is presented as a necessary accompaniment to harmony; it is never autonomous. As we have now seen at length, pleasures are pure or genuine if and only if they are proper to the nature of the person or part of the soul in question, and the degree of propriety is fixed by the degree of eternity and true being of the states or objects that cause pleasures (587a2–b10).

To say this in another way, the superiority of the just life is determined not simply by private harmony or pleasure but by the order of truth and being that is the precondition for harmony and suitable pleasure. Happiness itself is determined by "public" factors, in the fullest sense of the term *public*. In addition to knowledge of the Ideas, one should mention that not even the philosopher can be fully happy in an actual city. Whether the so-called beautiful city is seriously intended as the best regime or not, there can be no doubt that happiness depends upon the quality of one's political existence. One cannot possess a harmonious and healthy soul unless one has been properly educated, and a proper education is genuinely possible only in a city that is itself truly just.

Socrates now asks Glaucon if he knows how much more unpleasant the tyrant's life is than the king's. This prepares the way for another mathematical joke, reminiscent of the nuptial number. Socrates makes clear that the calculation to follow is not to be taken literally; it is difficult to say just how unpleasant the tyrant's life is, but perhaps it can be put as follows. The tyrant is third from the oligarch (in the series tyrant, democrat, and oligarch), who is himself third from the king (in the series oligarch, aristocrat, and king). Therefore the tyrant is separated from true pleasure by three times three, or the number nine. Socrates calls this a plane (as Bloom suggests, perhaps because a plane is determined by two numbers, length and width, here represented by three and three). Instead of stopping at nine, however, Socrates adds a reference to the solid and the cube and arrives at the result that the king's life is 729 times more pleasant than that of the tyrant (587a11–e4).

I will not belabor this calculation (see Bloom's notes on the passage). Socrates goes on to hold that the life of the good and just man is even more superior to that of the unjust man with respect to grace, beauty, and virtue than it is with respect to pleasure. He takes this as a kind of culmination of the entire discussion of the two lives and suggests that we are now in a good position to talk over our results with the person who initially defended injustice. This is presumably a reference in the first instance to Thrasymachus, but more broadly to those whom Thrasymachus represents (588a7–b8). In beginning this conversation, Socrates shifts from mathematical to mythical imagery. We are about to construct an image in speech of the soul, an image that is like the Chimaera, Scylla, Cerberus, and the other beasts that are said to have arisen through growing together many forms (*ideai*) into one. Our image is of a beast that has a ring of heads of tame and savage beasts, heads that it can change and make to grow out of itself. Next we need the form of a lion and, on a smaller scale, one of a human being. These three forms are to be joined in such a way that they grow naturally together with one another. This entire construction is then to be covered with an image of a human being, so that someone who cannot see inside will take the beast for a person (588b1–d9).

The mythical image is in one sense as fantastic as the mathematical image of the pleasure of the royal as opposed to the tyrannical life. But it is entirely superior in conveying a perception of the human soul. We see at once that the human being inside the outer shell is supposed to stand for the intellect, whereas the lion represents spiritedness and the remaining bestial heads are the various desires of the part of the soul that loves gain. There is of course no point-by-point analogy; to mention only the obvious, the inner human being presumably has a soul with three parts of its own. But the soul is more like a fantastic mélange of human and nonhuman loves and desires than it is like a ratio of numbers and geometrical forms (588d10–589b6).

After using the mythical image to illustrate the major points about the harmony and disharmony of the soul, Socrates concludes that praise of injustice is a lie; "for if we look to pleasure, good reputation, and benefit, the one who praises justice tells the truth" (589c1–3). In this statement, Socrates praises justice for its consequences, not for itself alone. To be sure, the main theme of Book Nine is pleasure, and the intention is to show that perfect justice is 729 times more pleasant than perfect injustice. But we have also determined that justice "in itself" is the good health or the perfect harmony of the soul, and it is hard to see why these should not count as benefits, nor are they separable from pleasure. The main point is perhaps the following. For Socrates, justice cannot be praised for itself alone, because it is, precisely as "itself," not alone. As I put it previously, justice is both inside and outside the individual human being. This is part, but only part, of what Aristotle means when he says that justice is virtue with respect to another. A person with a perfectly harmonious soul will always act justly, and it is impossible to imagine that this could be consistently misidentified by one's fellow citizens as injustice. Of course, the citizens might themselves be unjust, but then they would condemn the actuality of justice, not the appearance of injustice.

To this we must add Socrates's view that pleasure in particular as well as good reputation and benefits are all intrinsic to the just life. Those who follow Kant in criticizing eudaimonism too often adopt the heart of the position of Glaucon and Adeimantus in their initial demand that justice be praised for itself alone. We are told by the modern thinkers that it is immoral or unjust to praise justice for its consequences rather than for itself alone. But what is justice for itself alone if it is not health, harmony, pleasure, good reputation, and benefits? Who would be just or full of praise for it if it were painful, shameful, and harmful? There is no plausible way in which to conceive of inner health and harmony as entailing those consequences. As to the Socratic formula of justice as "minding one's own business," this is too cryptic to tell us anything important about the nature of justice. That is why the *Republic* is so long; one cannot mind one's own business except by minding the business of others. It is also worth noting that, according to Socrates, the person who blames justice does not err willingly (589c6). We have to persuade him gently, in other words, by education, not by force. Justice is by its nature something that human beings desire, but the training required to complete the education toward justice is extremely long; indeed, it extends over most if not all of our lives.

Socrates gives a number of familiar examples of how unjust acts lead to the enslavement of the best part of the soul to the most depraved. Speaking of the inferior parts of the soul, Socrates makes an important statement about justice: Those who represent the spirited or moneyloving lives "must be ruled by something similar to what rules the best life. We say that the [inferior man] must be the slave of the best man who has the divine rule in himself. It's not that we believe the slave must be ruled to his harm, as Thrasymachus supposed about the ruled, but that it is better for all to be ruled by the divine and the prudent" (590c8–d4). What we call freedom today is from the Socratic standpoint licentiousness, and so it is unjust rather than just. That is what is meant by "minding one's own business," not keeping quiet and staying out of the public eye but fulfilling the role that nature has assigned to us within the political regime. Put bluntly but accurately, justice is slavery of the worse to the better. Socrates is entirely outspoken here, which he is not in the numerous passages in which he speaks of persuasion. And of course, the same thing applies in the soul; the worse part is the slave of the better part. The relations between intellect and spiritedness are more complicated, but we can say that spiritedness is persuaded by intellect to enslave the desires of the body. We have now immersed ourselves sufficiently in the details of the *Republic* to see that, anachronistic as it might sound at first, Socrates conceives of human beings as divided against themselves, not merely as between the body and the soul but also within the soul itself. To be human is to suffer from what Hegel once called *innere Zerissenheit*, "inner tornness."

Socrates has now completed his defense of justice, and indeed of justice for itself, in the genuine sense that as itself, it cannot be separated from its beneficial consequences, such as pleasure, honor, and other benefits. This is not to say that the primary seat of justice is for Socrates in the body, not the soul. But the healthy and harmonious soul cannot do just deeds except through the medium of the body. Socrates then once more raises the question of the possibility of the beautiful city. Since the best human type in actual cities will regulate the desire for honor and possessions by determining whether these are truly beneficial for himself or herself, or in other words, for the philosophical life, he or she will cultivate the inner regime of the parts of the soul and not, as Glaucon points out, be willing to enter into politics. But Socrates punctuates his qualifying reply with an oath: "By the dog! In his own city [i.e., the beautiful city] he certainly will, but not perhaps in his fatherland [i.e., the actual or prephilosophical city], except by some divine chance" (592a7–9). Glaucon adds that the city of philosopher-kings is the one that has been founded in speech, "since I suppose that it is nowhere on the face of the earth." Socrates replies: "But perhaps a paradigm [of the best city] is laid up in heaven for the one who wishes to see it, and through seeing it, to found it within himself. For it makes no difference whether it exists or will exist. For he would be politically active in this city only, and not at all in others" (592a10–b5).

This is a much more qualified statement about the possibility of such a city than others we have noticed. The emphasis is upon the effort of the philosopher to order his or her soul in accord with the principles of the just regime, not to bring it into historical existence as an actual city. On the other hand, the statement is a bit more open concerning the philosopher's willingness to rule. This willingness, I suggest, increases to the degree that the actual city comes closer to the model of the city in speech. And this in turn leads to the temptation to make the two coincide in speech and deed.

13

The Quarrel between Philosophy and Poetry

I

The main theme of Book Ten is poetry. Socrates introduces the topic as an example of the correctness of the manner in which they have founded the city. In other words, it is not presented as a natural consequence of the last stage of the main argument, which is in fact finished. Nor is any reason given why Socrates chooses to deal with poetry rather than with some other example of proper founding. Some might even take Book Ten as a loosely attached appendix to the main dialogue, just as a number of scholars in the past have held that Book One was originally a separate dialogue. But a moment's reflection tells us that the first book is essential to the balance of the dialogue, not only as setting the scene for the full conversation but also in its presentation of traditional views of justice that Socrates is about to criticize, if not to reject altogether. The main part of Book One is taken up with the refutation of Thrasymachus, without which Glaucon and Adeimantus would not have been moved to register the challenge that leads directly to the founding in speech of the beautiful city. Stated positively, Book One shows us the various aspects of the traditional or commonsense notions of justice, which Socrates must take into account in presenting his new definition. If this were not done, Socrates would not respond to the queries of his interlocutors but be presenting them with a conception of justice that is a theoretical artifact.[1] But what is the inner connection between Books Two through Nine on the one hand and Book Ten on the other?

Let us begin to address this question as simply as possible. Plato was himself a great poet, whose dialogues exhibit a seamless web of dramatic and philosophical intricacy. It is now very widely accepted that one cannot understand Plato's philosophical teaching apart from the most careful consideration of its literary presentation. To take the primary example, the Platonic Socrates is not only one of the greatest dramatic heroes in Western literature, a kind of philosophical transformation of the Homeric Odysseus, but he is also presented as one who is able to shift from discursive prose to myth with the ease of a master of both idioms. And this is true despite his insistence throughout the *Republic* that he is not a poet but the builder of a city, to which is given the pregnant name "beautiful." Many readers of the *Republic* have been puzzled by Socrates's denunciation of poetry, which they take to be a straightforward presentation of Plato's own view. In addition, it has been objected that Socrates gives an oversimplified caricature of the nature of poetry as mimesis. This particular charge is not strictly faithful to the surface of the text, since Socrates contrasts mimetic with narrative poetry. But he spends most of his time discussing mimetic poetry, with which he finds both theoretical and practical fault, whereas narrative poetry, as long as it obeys the principles of the just regime, is admitted into the city. There is thus reason to believe that narrative poetry is not exposed to the theoretical criticism that takes up the first part of Book Ten.

Others have replied that Plato's (and Socrates's) criticism of poetry is strictly political and is not intended to provide a fair, detailed, and balanced account. The great power of poetry over our character and understanding of human life itself shows that the philosopher-king must take the place of the poet or, stated more cautiously, of the supervisor of those narrative poets who are allowed to remain, as for example the makers of noble myths (II. 377b11–c5; see also V. 460a1). This is to say that even the rule of philosophers cannot make do entirely without poetry. There is something that is plainly correct about this contention, but it has to be both modified and developed at some length. The first step in this process is to recognize that there is a difference between the role assigned to poetry within the beautiful city and its function in philosophical discussion in actual cities. The objections raised against poetry in the process of founding the beautiful city may not apply to poetry considered as an element of philosophy.

These objections are of two kinds, both moral and cognitive. In Books Two and Three, Socrates emphasized the moral argument. The traditional poets have produced a picture of the gods that is contrary to sound moral views, and they also portray wicked human beings in a manner so attractive as to make us sympathize with them. Interestingly enough, Socrates never says that wicked persons would not exist in the beautiful city, although it looks as if morally unsound theology is to be entirely extirpated. Since the poets who are permitted to remain in the just city are to be restricted in the content and form of their compositions, we have to assume that the city contains wicked and unjust persons whom the poets, if they were free to speak as they wish, would imitate. At the very least, they would be capable of inventing morally corrupting models, and the attractions of poetry are so much greater than those of the training and education furnished to the guardians that the discipline of the founding laws and customs, and so the morality and justice of the beautiful city, could not be preserved. In other words, poetry would soon counterbalance the rule of desire by spiritedness.

This argument can be restated as follows. There is one set of true principles for living a just, and therefore happy, life. No deviations from these principles are justified. Therefore, the natural inclination of human beings toward diversity must be restrained, at least in the guardian class (which includes philosophers and soldier-auxiliaries). Poetry celebrates the diversity of the human soul, but philosophy inculcates the correct principles of the best life. In this sense, poetry is like democracy whereas philosophy is like monarchy. Socrates himself cites the poets, and invents his own myths, when he is describing the radical diversity of the human soul in its natural condition. But once the city is founded and the medical treatment of its citizens begins, the restrictions on poetry go into effect.

I want to add that the portrait of philosophy in the *Republic* is also incomplete, and in a puzzling way, given the political context. The years spent in the study of mathematics serve to detach the intellectual perception of the best guardians from the world of genesis, and so too from the city. And this is only the preparation for the main business of philosophy, which is not political but that of contemplative absorption in the Platonic Ideas. That this is not a full picture of philosophy is plain from Socrates's own behavior in Athens, and for that matter, it is illustrated by the variety of themes in the Platonic corpus. What, then, is the political justification for this narrow and abstract representation of philosophy within the city? I believe that it is to purge the natural philosophical interest in the diversity of the human soul. The same medicine is prescribed within the beautiful city to philosophy and to poetry. But the medicine has side effects. In purging diversity, it detaches us from practice, and in particular from politics. The inner contradiction of the Socratic city is now evident. Far from being natural, the city is an unnatural construction. In order to produce rulers who are willing and able to enforce the uniformity of principles, and to restrict the kinds of particular cases to which the principles are to be applied, we must educate the best of the guardians in such a way as to disable them from exercising prudent political rule. In the city ruled by philosophers, there is no philosophical disagreement. But this means that philosophy itself is replaced by dogma and ideology.

One naturally wishes to know whether Socrates (and of course, Plato) was aware of this inner contradiction. Since Socrates does not explicitly draw the contradiction to our attention, we have to rely on our own judgment in this case. My view on this important matter, already indicated, is as follows. We can take Socrates (or Plato) as being quite sincere in his account of the procedures and institutions necessary for a just city. Human beings will do the right thing if and only if their desires are controlled by philosophy through the medium of spiritedness. Unfortunately, each theoretically correct step toward justice is a practical step toward injustice. The unification of theory and practice, or wisdom, is impossible. But this impossibility does not suffice to prevent philosophers from attempting to accomplish it, because that is the goal of philosophy. Such attempts may take the form of actual political intervention, or the more subtle form of writing a revolutionary book that advocates the intervention of philosophy in politics.

In sum, the *Republic* is a serious warning against the inner dialectic of philosophical rule. The cure for our illness is so strong that we run the risk of dying from its side effects. On the other hand, if we do not take our medicine, the chance of recovery is nil. The political philosopher has the duty of determining the right dosage.

To return to the argument of the text, in Book Ten Socrates emphasizes the cognitive deficiency of poetry (and the creative arts in general). We are about to study his account of this deficiency in some detail. The main point is that the truth, in the highest and fullest sense of the term, cannot be produced, only *reproduced*. Socrates embodies this point in an account at the beginning of Book Ten of the Idea of the bed. This account is initially puzzling, for two reasons. First, the reproductive capacity is assigned to the craftsman or artisan like the carpenter or vase maker, and not to the poet. Second, the account takes it for granted that there are Ideas of artifacts, a thesis that appears nowhere else in Plato. Stated as succinctly as possible, the bed produced by the carpenter is a reproduction of the original bed, that is, the Platonic Idea of the bed, whereas the artist reproduces the artisan's copy. The cognitive criticism of poetry thus carries with it the absurd attribution to the artisan of a perception of the Platonic Ideas.

We remind ourselves that the distance of the poet from the true beings is politically dangerous. The ruler of the just city must know the truth, in order to know what is appropriate to each kind of person. Socrates of course does not say so, but it seems to follow that the carpenter, who copies the original or ideal bed, is much better suited to rule the city than the poets or painters would be. In other words, the artisan should be at least an adjunct of the philosopher.

This is in a certain sense implied by the high status given by Socrates to technical knowledge, not only here but throughout the dialogues. However, the inference is weakened dramatically when we reflect that, after all, poets and painters do not achieve fame or display their peculiar gifts by copying beds and tables. Poets are judged by their insight into the human soul, and we recognize that they can exercise this insight even when, like Homer, they speak of medicine and generalship and other *technai* about which they know nothing. The cognitive criticism of poetry thus seems to be much weaker than the moral criticism. Poets may or may not perceive the Platonic Ideas, but if we assume that they do not, this in no way diminishes their excellence, which is the gift to express in beautiful speeches the deepest levels of the human soul and the most subtle nuances of human behavior. The poet can exhibit the full variety of the monster that is the human soul, and Socrates shows his own poetic gifts in the images he paints of it. This raises the question whether it is not also possible for philosophers to exhibit diversity. After all, is this not precisely what Plato does in the dialogues? One might reply on Plato's behalf that there is only one philosophy, the genuine kind that he espouses, and that shows diversity in order to bring out its dangers. In other words, the presence of Socrates, or the still more austere heroes of the later dialogues, is supposed to provide us with a sufficient inoculation against the charms of Alcibiades, a man who was so charming that Socrates himself professed to love him.

The second main section of Book Ten, which is devoted to the myth of Er, illustrates the general point perfectly. Here as elsewhere, Socrates or some other principal speaker tells a myth, usually about the individual soul or the cosmos as a whole, which is an imitation neither of a Platonic Idea nor for that matter of an artifact like a bed or a table. Nor, since it is a conjecture or product of the imagination, can it be compared to the precise veracity of mathematics, or the validity of a sound deductive argument. Plato's cosmic myths are what we call today "interpretations" of the structure of the visible whole, and they are based not simply upon such mathematical and astronomical evidence as may be available but also on speculations concerning the destiny of the human being within the physical cosmos. This is not the place to argue the point, but I believe that it is true even of dialogues like the *Timaeus*, which is not a treatise on cosmology any more than is Hesiod's *Theogony* but an interpretation of the cosmos as the residence of intelligence, in particular, of human intelligence. It will, I suggest, be the function of the myth of Er to reunite in a harmonious totality the moral and cognitive objections to poetry, but in such a way as to vindicate its nature as not just an adjunct or servant but an integral part of philosophy itself.

2

The next point that requires elucidation is that we were correct in not admitting into our city any part of poetry that is mimetic (595a1–4).[2] Let us recall the original distinction. Poetry is either simple or mimetic narrative. In the first kind, the poet describes the speeches and deeds of his characters in such a way as to distinguish his own voice from theirs. In the second or mimetic kind, the poet imitates the speakers directly; he speaks as if he were his characters (III. 392d5–393c1). This is dangerous because the skilled mimetic poet will imitate all types of human beings, good and bad, and even animals and monsters. The argument is not very forceful, since we could pass laws commanding mimetic poets to imitate good human beings only. But Socrates also maintains that mimetic poetry violates, and encourages us to violate, the main political principle of one man, one job. The straightforward narrator, on the other hand, does not pretend to be anyone but who he is. In the beautiful city, of course, he will be required to narrate only the speeches and deeds of good persons. But narrative as such is not excluded from the city.

Socrates is about to begin his criticism of mimesis, which, he says, mutilates the intellect of those who listen to its productions and do not have the medicine (*pharmakon*) of knowledge of what beings actually are. This last expression seems to refer to eternal and unchanging Ideas as well as to finite and changing things. The philosopher knows the difference between the two, albeit he does not know them in the same sense, since there is no genuine knowledge of the finite and changing things. In order for what we take to be our knowledge of genesis not to "mutilate" the discursive intelligence, we require philosophy; Socrates is thus not claiming that the domain of genesis is totally worthless and dangerous. We can suffice with opinion or belief in this domain, provided we have been inoculated with epistemic knowledge of the formal structure of intelligibility that supports genesis and gives it what reliability it possesses. Those who lack that knowledge are doomed to a life of sickness, in the sense that they cannot rely on their interpretations of the unstable and transient phenomena of genesis.

Socrates will explain this to Glaucon, although a certain affection and respect he has felt toward Homer since childhood makes him reluctant to do so. It is odd that Socrates did not express this affection and respect in Books Two and Three, where he developed at great length his harsh moral criticism of the poets, including Homer. Perhaps it is because there is a certain disharmony between affection and respect on the one hand and moral condemnation on the other. In any case, Socrates now states that truth must be honored above any human being, even the father and teacher of the entire domain of tragedy (595b3–c3).

After the moment of hesitation, the question is then posed: What is imitation? Socrates suggests that in attempting to answer, they begin in their usual way, namely, by setting up a single form (*eidos*) for each many, to which we apply the same name. It is not immediately clear why this is a good way to begin our explanation of mimesis. In everyday life, persons imitate other human beings, as in plays; painters and sculptors imitate their human models; children imitate adults; adults imitate those whom they admire, and so on. These are diverse operations; for example, imitating a brave act is not the same as painting someone's portrait. Again, some imitations produce genuine examples of a common kind; a brave act is no less what it is because it was undertaken in order to emulate an admired hero. Other imitations are originals not in this sense but possibly in some other. For example, a painting of some human model is a genuine painting, but it is not itself another human being. And no doubt there are other ways in which we could try to classify kinds of imitation. The proper procedure would seem to be to look for the attributes that are common to all acts normally designated as imitations.

We might begin in something like the following way: An imitation is a conscious attempt to make something that looks like something else but is not an identical duplicate of what serves as the original in the given case. This would have to be modified in various ways. For example, a master forger might be able to make an identical copy of a great painting, yet we would not normally say that the forgery is itself the same masterpiece, or for that matter, a masterpiece at all. To copy something, however perfectly, is not to create it but to pretend to do so. The forger, as it were, exists on the genius of others. To have a genius for forgery is not to be able to create a work of genius but to appropriate the inspiration of someone else. Imitation can of course be employed in order to create something original of genius; this happens, for example, whenever a brilliant playwright copies certain types of human beings, not in order to display them as quasi-photographs of the original but to bring them to life in a new situation, or a new rendition of a famous situation. Socrates would presumably disapprove of this example, since it is his goal to denigrate imitation, not to praise it. He wants to emphasize the fact that imitations are copies, not originals, and so are necessarily defective in comparison to the original. But beyond this, he wants to argue that the "original" originals, as it were, are the Platonic Ideas, or more broadly stated, the residents of eternity, and that the productions of poets are copies, not directly of these eidetic originals but of the instances of genesis that constitute a many, or a class of things all bearing the same name by virtue of the fact that they are themselves copies, that is, inferior and transient representations, of the unique original that corresponds to each such class.

It has often been asked what the one-many argument has in common with the arguments on behalf of Platonic Ideas in Books Five and Six. I think that this is a misleading way to pose the question, because it implies that there is a unified and well-elaborated doctrine of pure form and that all fluctuations by Socrates in the defense or explanation of this thesis are signs of carelessness or incompetence. In an important sense the doctrine we are about to study differs from the previous discussions: In Book Ten, god is compared to a gardener who grows or produces the Ideas, and there are Ideas not only of natural and conceptual entities but of artifacts as well. This not only contradicts the earlier presentations in the *Republic* but is also to be found nowhere else in Plato. Stated baldly, god is a poet in Book Ten; what is under criticism here is not divine or "ontological" but human poetry. The difference between the two presentations of the Platonic Ideas — if there really is a difference — can only be understood together with an understanding of the dramatic function of Book Ten.

Before we turn to logical and analytical subtlety, it is advisable to state as simply as possible why Socrates (or Plato) posits the doctrine of Ideas at all. As often stated by Socrates, the elements of genesis come into being, change, and disappear. Yet we are able to identify these elements and even in many cases to define their natures. If we call these identifications and explanations "concepts," then we hold that they are themselves productions, that is, full residents of genesis. One concept can always be replaced by another. In this case, however, it is not merely that all ostensible knowledge and being becomes opinion about becoming, it is also true that we cannot provide the standard by which we are able to distinguish changing elements of genesis, including our opinions. Opinions about a tree or a cow could not even achieve the status of an opinion, namely, a view of likelihood based upon the stable pattern of experience that unfolds as temporal and historical change.

To say that there is a one over many is thus to hold that the unstable identities and natures of the many residents of genesis can be classified as imperfect instances of an original, and that when something exists at all, or we can identify and understand it at all, what we are identifying and understanding is the original of which the instance is a copy. This is familiar from Book Five, and it is what Socrates refers to as our usual procedure at 596a6–7. Note that there may be more than one Idea that plays a constituent role in the original or paradigm of which particulars are ostensibly copies. This is addressed by the doctrine of *sunousia*, or "being-together," of Ideas; the point is also made with the use of the term *koinōnia* ("community").

There is no point in complaining about the many technical puzzles that arise from the doctrine of Platonic Ideas. No "theory" in the modern or contemporary sense of the term is being presented. We are not dealing with the logical and conceptual analysis of a finite area of experience or a determinate formal moment in the structure of intelligibility. I would almost call the doctrine of Ideas a myth, if I were not afraid that the expression would be misunderstood to mean that the doctrine is not seriously intended. The doctrine of Ideas, like all cosmological myths, is very serious; indeed, it is the most serious element in Plato's philosophical teaching. It is a likely story or safe hypothesis about how change can present itself in elements stable enough to exist at all and to be understood to one degree or another. In order to understand what Plato is after, we do better to think of Kant than any other modern philosopher; for Kant the domain of the transcendental is what Plato would call "a likely story" about the possibility of being and necessity. If the reader will allow a parenthetical exaggeration, the only difference between Plato and Kant on the carrying-out of their common motivation is that Plato knows that he is telling myths and either says so or makes it unmistakably clear from the dramatic context, whereas Kant pretends that he is developing a conceptual argument. But Vaihinger was certainly not mistaken in treating Kant's exposition as qualified by an "as if."

To come back to the one and the many, it appears in Book Five, for example at 477b9–c5, in conjunction with what is called in the secondary literature the argument from opposites. The latter expression refers to Socrates's claim that whatever has or may have an opposite does not fully exist, that is, does not fully partake of being. Thus what appears to be just to one person is unjust to another. Julia Annas points out that a man cannot be a not-man, and she generalizes to the conclusion that what does not admit of an opposite can be known, for example that Socrates is a man. She holds that Plato nowhere commits himself to the view that all particulars are always changing.[3] I find this unpersuasive in the face of Socrates's steady denigration of the instability of the domain of genesis; but the important point is that Socrates could not be a man unless there were a Platonic Idea of man. Socrates cannot be a not-man, for example a cow or a tree, because he is held together as the being he is, and this "holding together" is not logical but ontological.

To sum up, the big difference between the Platonic Ideas in Books Five through Seven and those in Book Ten is that in the latter context they are poems of god, whereas they are everlasting and unalterable in the former.

Socrates gives us no explicit reason for this shift; we have to figure it out for ourselves on the basis of our understanding of the implicit explanation of the dramatic structure of the *Republic*. I start with the observation that in both contexts the things of genesis are referred to as copies. In Book Five, the unique form (*eidos*) communes with many fantasies, which are compared to dreams, or taking a likeness for the original (475e6–476e2). There is no discussion of a creator god here; the copying process is not explained very adequately, but we may again call it "ontological" rather than "theological" inasmuch as it refers to the interaction between being and becoming. It is this process that Heidegger tries to explain entirely in terms of becoming, or as he would call it, historicity. This is not an irrelevant observation, since Heidegger is the most thorough of the descendants of what Socrates calls in the *Theaetetus* "Homer's army" (those who say that all things are changing, or that rest is a derivative of change). Heidegger thus replaces originals by transcendental structures of temporality; he is a Kantian but, precisely for that reason, a crypto-Platonist. On the other hand, he is anti-Platonist and anti-Kantian, since for him there are no copies and no Kantian phenomena, only originals, that is, unique moments of temporality. I add that Heidegger is in the same camp on this point as the analytic philosophers of language, who seem to think that being can be eliminated by the theory of predication, without seeing that in so doing they transform being into grammar.

Our first attempt to explain mimesis produced the suggestion that it is the conscious attempt to make something look like something else but, by virtue of that intention, not to produce the original itself. In imitating, we do not produce but rather reproduce. But even this way of putting the point can be misleading if we understand by "reproduction" an identical instance of the original. If such a thing were possible, it would be an act of creation, or what the Greeks call *poiēsis*. In the terms of Book Ten, it would be as if god had grown two (or more) Ideas of the bed. This is the sense of mimesis that obtains in Book Ten; in the ontological process of "dreaming" that a fantasy is the genuine thing, there are no intentions. But whether there is an intention or not, the underlying process is the same; the existence of the particulars of genesis is attributed to the unique form or Platonic Idea that stands over a collection of particulars and defines them as a class. What is new here is Socrates's choice of two artifacts, the bed and the table, as examples of a unique Idea (596a10–b5).

Socrates begins with the bed that we use in everyday life, which the craftsman produces after looking at the Idea, and so too with the table. The Idea is the one unique form that stands over and defines the family of humanly produced artifacts of a particular kind. To say that two things are of the same kind is to see the Idea, and this act of vision is signaled by the word *same*. This Idea, however, unlike its counterpart in Book Five, need not be eternal. In fact, if Glaucon remembers the previous discussion, he would have good reason to assume that the Idea toward which the craftsman looks is not the same as the Idea toward which the philosophers were previously looking. We do not normally think about it in the case of commonplace objects like beds and tables, but artifacts are not eternal. The first bed maker must have imagined an object suitable for reclining upon under circumstances like eating or sleeping, and in this way constructed the blueprint of what we now call a bed. The word *Idea* (*idea*) means literally "look" or "thing seen," but it carries no intrinsic sense of everlastingness and unchangeability. Without attributing modern psychology to Socrates, *idea* could here mean "what the first bed maker saw when he tried to make eating and sleeping more comfortable through the medium of an invention." As we say today, he had an idea of something that he could build for the efficient carrying-out of certain human intentions, and he happened to call it "bed."

One could reply to this that eating and sleeping are natural human functions that can be assisted by art, which, as Aristotle puts it, perfects nature. Whereas some craftsman was the first human being to conceive of, or at least to make and introduce into society, beds, the inventor did not create the bed ex nihilo but created it precisely by reflecting upon the various operations required by human life. In this sense, the blueprint made by the craftsman is a making visible the Idea of the bed that is implied in human nature. This reply makes Ideas potential rather than actual, as would also be the case if we take literally the notion of a creator god.

I bring up this possibility merely to emphasize the point that the Idea toward which the craftsman looks can be interpreted in various ways. When Socrates says that no craftsman can construct the Idea itself, he could be referring either to the just mentioned potential Ideas or to the immortal Ideas of the previous books. In short: at this point, Socrates attributes to artifacts an Idea that human beings cannot construct, but to which they look in producing the artifact in question. He has not ruled out the more familiar Ideas of natural kinds, logical relations, and moral attributes. We shall have to watch rather closely to see how far the example of the bed is intended to extend.

Now Socrates seems to change the angle of approach by asking Glaucon to consider what he calls a craftsman who makes all the implements that the other craftsmen make separately, but everything else as well: what grows from the earth, all living things, including himself, and furthermore earth, heaven, gods, and everything in heaven and Hades. Glaucon calls such a maker a most extraordinary sophist (596b12–d1). Socrates replies that in a certain way anyone, including Glaucon, could perform this feat, simply by carrying a mirror around and reflecting everything. We must assume that any of us could also carry the mirror down into Hades while still alive, but that is a triviality, as is the fact that the mirror cannot reflect itself without the assistance of other mirrors. The important point for Socrates is that the poet or in this case the painter functions like someone with a mirror when he portrays any of the objects that are available to him. In other words, Socrates is entirely ignoring what we would regard as the most important component of painting, namely, its originality or the production not of an imperfect and so inferior copy but rather of a new object or a new way of interpreting the object (596d2–e8). From our standpoint, the painter is not someone who copies real beds and tables, or for that matter real persons, animals, or heavenly and subterranean things, simply in an effort to come as close to the original as possible. But entirely apart from the fact that the Greeks, including Socrates, looked at art and what we call "creativity" quite differently from us, Socrates is not here concerned with the significance of the artistic activity or the purely aesthetic or even revelatory properties of the artwork. He is concerned with the ontological status of the work of art, represented here by a painting of a bed. By choosing a bed instead of one of his other examples, such as a person or a god, Socrates further trivializes art, and in choosing painting as the example of art, he picks the one case that is most easily reduced to the status of copying or reproducing an original.

The present discussion started with the craftsman and has now moved to the painter. It is an oddity of this account that there is no mention of the philosopher; instead, as I noted before, we get the still odder consequence that the artisan is credited with looking at the Idea, although we are not entirely sure which Idea he is looking at. It is true that the purpose of the account is to criticize mimesis, and so poetry, not to praise philosophy. In addition, as the criticism is directed primarily at the general act of mimesis, it is not even necessary to discuss the poet in this stage of the argument. The painter stands in for the poet; after all, for Socrates both are "makers" (the literal sense of *poiētēs*) and therefore related to the craftsmen (*dēmiourgoi*).

Glaucon might say that the painter does not truly make what he makes; yet in a sense, Socrates adds, he does make the bed. Glaucon replies: "Yes, he makes what appears to be [but is not truly] the bed." The word *phainomenē* can mean either that which shows itself or that which seems to be something but is not. Glaucon has in mind here the second sense (which could be stated more elaborately as "that which shows itself as seeming to be what it is not genuinely"). What is the point of the painter's activity? Is he a craftsman of optical illusions or imperfect imitations? Again, this is not Socrates's question. His point is that the painter cannot present us with the genuine bed or original of his copy, and so, whatever he may believe himself to be doing, he is contributing to an illusion that has detrimental consequences for the rest of us. Now no one in his right mind will mistake a painting, whether accurate or distorted, for a real bed. What, then, is the harm accomplished by painting?

I do not think that painting is the right art with which to make Socrates's point as clearly as possible. For that, he should have remained with poetry. But then the point about the nature of mimetic art would have been blurred. That to one side, Socrates's point can be restated generally. Works of imitation are like shadows of real things, but peculiarly useful and attractive shadows. They accustom us to dwelling in a world of shadows or reflections and trick us into taking these reflections for genuine beings. Even worse, these reflections cannot be explained in such a way as to preserve us from the dangers of what are today called subjectivism and relativism. The source of the stability in reflections is not itself a reflection, but it will never be accessible to us as long as we regard artists or makers as authorities on the natures of things.

In other words, mimesis is cognitively unreliable and, even worse, corrupting. Our picture of reality is produced not by those who have seen genuine beings but by those who are skilled imitators of things that are themselves copies of the genuine beings. Mimesis leads first to the replacement of knowledge by charm, second to philosophical corruption, and finally to moral and political despair that arises from the distraction of intelligence by a multiplicity of conflicting viewpoints. I have no doubt that this is an unfair caricature and criticism of poetry, in particular of the mimetic kind, but it is not entirely absurd. On the contrary, there is something in it that is deeply true. If we are hypnotized by imitations, then we lose touch with the reality that provides us with our only standard for evaluating imitations. But that is hardly to say that mimesis lacks all redeeming features. What Socrates should have said is, first, that just because poets pretend to be their characters, this does not mean that we have nothing to learn from them. Furthermore, whereas a complete surrender to mimesis is harmful, the activity becomes salutary when it is connected with the philosophical attempt to see the genuine beings and to employ them as standards for judging the work of imitation. What we want to avoid is the belief that persons are competent to imitate who have no knowledge of the originals.

There seems to be no reason why poets cannot also be philosophers, that is, why they cannot themselves perceive the genuine forms that are the originals of the particulars they imitate. And as we have seen, poets imitate not beds and tables but gods and human beings, in other words, their speeches and deeds, and through these, the natures of their souls. Whether or not poets imitate Ideas, they can still understand and communicate something of fundamental importance about the human soul. In some contexts, Socrates insists that no particulars can be understood in themselves; they can be understood only relative to an understanding of their Platonic Idea. But in Book Ten, the argument is different. The craftsman is now said to look toward the Idea in making an artefactual copy. But if the bed is a useful copy of an Idea, why cannot a great mimetic poem be a useful copy of the soul? No one can sleep in a mirror image of a bed, but it is certainly possible to learn something about beds from paintings, precisely because these are not mirror images but interpretations of the significance of their originals. The same fundamental point is true of mimetic poetry. We cannot engage with characters in a poem as we do with living persons, but the wisdom of poets like Homer, Sophocles, Dante, Shakespeare, and Goethe is none the less genuine, and one could argue that their understanding of human nature exceeds that of almost all philosophers in the narrower sense of the term. We are now in a position to conclude that there is something to understand in poetry that is different from a knowledge of the arts or professions practiced by the dramatis personae. This understanding may or may not be grounded in a vision of the Ideas. But it is not even necessary to believe in, or to have heard of, Platonic Ideas in order to possess the special understanding of the best poets, mimetic or narrative.

3

So far we have learned that the craftsman imitates the Idea by producing an implement, say, a bed, and the painter imitates the bed in his portrait of it. Let us note carefully that the painter is not said to imitate the Idea through the imitation of the bed. I have suggested that there is no reason to exclude this possibility. As is perhaps more obvious with other examples, such as the portrait of a human being by a master like Van Dyck, the painter brings to the act of each portrait an already formed understanding of what it is to be a human being, and with it, the ability to illustrate how the Idea of a human being is manifested in this particular case, as a human being of such-and-such a type. Painters do not arrive at a perception of the nature of humanity by looking at their model, nor is there one particular way in which human beings must look in order themselves to be instances of the Idea. I say "instances" because it is absurd to think of a real person as an imitation of the genuine original. The Idea of man is neither an ancient nor a modern, an aristocrat nor a peasant, a wise man nor an athlete, and so on. We do not say of an actual person that "he looks just like a human being" but, if anything, that he *is* a human being. We arrive at this knowledge not by staring at the Idea of man and then recognizing someone as a copy of it, nor do we say that the real person is an inferior version of what it is to be a human being. The actual situation is the reverse; we arrive at the Idea of man through our experience with real persons. And the mode of this "arrival" is entirely different from that of the craftsman to the Idea of the bed, or the painter to the actual bed.

Socrates goes on to say that the bed maker does not make what is (*ho estin*), namely, the Idea of the bed, but only something that is like the being (*ti toiouton hoion to on*: 597a4–5). This is entirely unpersuasive. The bed maker makes a bed, and beds are nothing like the Idea of the bed. We cannot sleep in the Idea, nor does it have a set of visual or physical properties of which the wooden rendition is a copy. What one could say is that each bed fulfils the function of the bed, the purpose for which it was invented. The Idea of the bed is not a genuine bed at all but the function or purpose of beds; in other words, it is genuinely and truly *not* a bed. One may thus seriously doubt whether it makes sense to talk about a bed that is fully and truly what it is to be a bed, as opposed to imitation beds of the sort that we use to recline on or sleep. What does make sense is to say that nothing can be a bed that does not fill the function or purpose of a bed, namely, to be something to recline on or on which to sleep.

Socrates then summarizes the situation. There are three beds. One is in nature, "which we would say, I suppose, has been made by a god." The second bed has been made by a craftsman, and the third by a painter. This gives us not just three beds but also three *forms* (*eidesin*) or kinds of bed (597b5–15). *Eidos* does not carry its technical sense here of "Platonic Idea"; there is obviously just one *eidos* in this sense. If there were three "forms" of bed, one of them the Idea, then we would have to posit some fourth kind of bed that expresses what is common to the first three types. And this leads to incoherence. Regardless of the difficulties involved, Socrates wants to distinguish the imperfect beds, built or painted, from the perfect or purely formal bed. This is why, for example, the craftsman had to look to the Idea in order to make his bed, and not to another already built bed. Socrates holds that we cannot look to the Idea in a produced or painted bed, because it is not and cannot be therein contained. If it could be, then we would not need to look at the Idea apart from its copies, and this is the reverse of what Socrates wants to establish.

According to Socrates, the god made just one bed in nature, that is, one Platonic Idea. Had he made two, the third man paradox would arise; that is, there would have to be a third natural bed in which the first two share, and so on perpetually. The god knows this, and furthermore he wishes to be the maker of the genuinely existing (*ousa*) bed, not of this or that particular instance. Socrates then asks: "Would you like us to call him the gardener of this bed or something of the sort?" And Glaucon agrees (597c1–d12). Ideas grow in the garden of being. This certainly sounds like an ascription of mortality to Ideas. Even if one argues that the language is metaphorical, it remains true that if there are Ideas of artifacts, then they must not all be always in bloom. Socrates, however, regularly moves from instances of a given kind in this world to the being of a unique Idea of those instances. Nowhere in Plato is there reference to Ideas that are actual in eternity but not exemplified in genesis. In the language of the garden, the gardener does not plant all his blooms in one initial season. Since there is no natural limit to invention, there are at any time an endless number of potential, not yet planted Ideas. Stated bluntly, there are infinite nonexistent Ideas. But this makes no sense at all. How can one nonexistent Idea, for which there are no instances, be distinguished from another? A potential Idea, finally, cannot be fully and truly what it is to be something of a certain kind, because it lacks the essential quality of being.

When Socrates first referred to the work of the craftsman, he said that the bed maker looked to the Idea in making a particular bed. This particular bed is not the genuine original but looks like it. The language certainly implies that what "looks like" that at which we gaze while making our own version of it is a copy of it. Are we to assume that Socrates presents the carpenter as an imitator (597a4–5)? Elsewhere, I have argued that this would be politically disastrous, since craftsmen would then be subject to the same fate as mimetic poets: exile. A city can subsist without poets, but not without carpenters.[4] Certainly Socrates never refers to the carpenter or craftsman as an imitator, and in fact, he carefully distinguishes these two kinds of reproduction. The carpenter is said to be the craftsman of the (actual) bed; nothing is said of mimesis. The title *imitator* is reserved for the painter, who is at the third generation from nature. Furthermore, it is one thing to imitate an Idea and something quite different to imitate imitations of Ideas. The difference between the carpenter and the poet is manifested in the bed itself. The carpenter must have seen something of the actual bed because we can sleep in the results of his vision, whereas poems and paintings are nothing like beds.

This argument would seem to fail as soon as we realize that poets and painters are not interested in beds as such. But such an objection misses the point. Socrates wants to support the banishing of mimetic poets from the city for political reasons, and these reasons do not obtain with respect to craftsmen. We can strengthen Socrates's argument by noting that craftsmanly "looking at" is not imitating but activating a function or power (*dunamis*). The bed does not look like its Idea, nor does it pretend to, as does the poem or painting. And it is essential that the bed not imitate the Idea, since the Idea itself does not look like a bed, any more than the Idea of a man looks like a man. In short, the "looking at" of the carpenter produces not an imitation of the Idea of the bed but a real bed. The "looking at" (if that is the right expression in this case) of the painter produces an imitation of a bed, not a real bed. The painter is like the poet, not the carpenter (597d1–e8).

As was noted above, the painter is said to try to imitate the bed of the craftsman, not that of the gardener. He cannot succeed, however, because his view of the bed is always from a certain perspective. Socrates could well have extended this point to perception. No one sees the bed as it is in its full spatiotemporal existence, but we must arrive at it by a kind of inference from the various perceptual glimpses that we can acquire (as in the case of Husserlian phenomenology). Socrates and Glaucon conclude that the painter does not imitate the being (for example, the bed) as it is but rather as it looks (*to phainomenon*) and is thus an imitator of a phantasm, not of truth (598b1–5). This is obviously absurd; neither the painter nor anyone else could present in a physical form a complete imitation of the full being of the bed, but even if he could, the painter would hardly regard this as the fulfillment of his intentions. The purpose of a painting, even a portrait of something as humble as a bed, is to provide an interpretation or a look at the bed as it appears from a certain perspective. The "truth" of the bed is exhibited, for those with eyes to see, in each of the perspectives from which we view it. If there are any nonperspectivist views, they can only be of the Idea of the bed. In another formulation, the truth of the bed painted by the painter is precisely perspectivist. That is the way we perceive solid objects in space and time. In any case, the entire point is trivialized by the assumption that the purpose of painting is to make quasi-photographic copies of things. This is plain from the next example, which is of a painter who could persuade children and fools into thinking that his portraits of various craftsmen, if seen from a distance, are real human beings (598b6–c5).

Socrates turns next to tragedy "and its leader, Homer." This is the more important target of Socrates's critique of imitation; the discussion of painting was intended to make points that are more plausible in the visual arts than in the discursive arts. In the former case, we can speak of a copy of a human being, but in the case of poetry, epic or dramatic, it makes no sense to refer to a character, say Achilles or Oedipus, as an imitation of someone, since these either never existed or have left no "copies" of their existence to the poets who, for all practical purposes, have invented them. And the same is even more true in the case of the gods. What the poet attempts to provide us with are persuasive representations of what a person like Achilles or Oedipus might have said or done under circumstances of such and such a kind, and to express this in language that is beautiful and evocative of significance for human beings at any time who face situations like those about which they read, or which they see performed on the stage.

There is one other important point that I would like to make about the criticism of poetry. Socrates says that the imitative poets imply by their copies of a variety of human types that they themselves know, or possess the expertise of, what their characters know or can do. What we do not realize is that these imitations are "third from what is and easy to make for those who do not know the truth" (599a1). And yet, Socrates as well as we are able to distinguish between good and bad poets, wise poets and fools. The criticism just noted implies that even good poems are easy to make for those who are ignorant of the topics discussed by their characters. If this is right, what is it about Sophocles that makes him superior to Agathon? One might be tempted to reply: "the language," but the truth communicated about human nature in the Oedipus trilogy is not a question of fine diction, intricate meters, and pertinent figures of speech, or more cautiously expressed, of these alone. Socrates makes no serious attempt to explore the central function of poetry, in particular of what he calls mimetic poetry. No one judges a poem to be superior if its dramatic personnel mimics the speeches and deeds of people who are known to us, and if we do not know them, we have no chance to compare the copy with the original. Finally, only a fool would turn to Homer or Pindar for instruction in carpentry, sailing, medicine, or any other particular art. Or to take a modern example, do we read Tolstoy's *War and Peace* in order to learn the military expertise of General Kutuzov?

We have to conclude that it is an entirely inadequate criticism of mimetic poets to say that they make what look like beings but are not (that is, phantasms: 599a2). On the other hand, it is entirely correct to say that the founders of a city like the one described in the *Republic* must be very seriously concerned with art, precisely because it is more effective than philosophy in teaching us about the human soul, and much more effective than philosophy in persuading us to behave, or to respond to behavior, in a particular way. Does this mean that Socrates falsifies the nature of art in general and mimesis in particular in order to justify rendering it subservient to the regime of the beautiful city? If so, it must be because he fears that the presence of mimetic artists in the city will overwhelm the monotonous suppression of diversity that is enforced by an appeal to entities (the Platonic Ideas) that no one can see, with the exception of a very few philosopher-kings, and whose political utility is dubious, to say the least. This is not to suggest that Socrates does not believe in the Ideas but to say that he has a realistic assessment of the limited appeal of philosophy. Hence the need to be unjust to its great rival. We have here another striking example of the deep truth that in order to have perfect justice, one must be unjust. Most scholars are unwilling to attribute what they regard as duplicity to Socrates, despite his praise of medicinal or noble lies. They are quick to point out the conceptual flaws in Socrates's account of the Ideas or the nature of poetry, but they see these flaws as mistakes, technical errors that are no doubt caused by the primitive state of logical and conceptual analysis in classical antiquity. I do not doubt that this approach is sometimes correct, but it strikes me as impossible for Plato not to have understood the shortcomings in his portrait of mimetic art, since it would obviously apply to himself and make all those dialogues in which he pretends to be his characters mere fantasies and farthest removed from the truth. And paramount among these fantasies would be the *Republic*.

Glaucon responds to Socrates's next question by saying that it would be a greater honor to leave many beautiful deeds behind one, rather than copies or phantoms. In particular, it is better to have governed a city and made people better, in public and private, than to have written accounts of those who did so. Thus Lycurgus, Charondas, and Solon are superior to Homer. Furthermore, Homer is credited with no innovations in the arts, nor did he found a school based upon a way of life, as did Pythagoras, which is still praised for the excellent character of its adherents. That this passage is ironical is evident from the mention of Protagoras and Prodicus, among others, who have won much honor by persuading their contemporaries that they could teach them how to govern their home and city (599b3–600d4). Certainly this could be no evidence for Socrates of the superiority of the sophists to the great poets. Nevertheless, the passage raises the interesting question of just what Homer and his fellow poets do teach us. A parallel question arises with respect to the philosopher, who is not a technician with a specific skill, like the carpenter, shoemaker, physician, or general. Socrates in particular professes to have no doctrine and to know only that he is ignorant. In what way is he superior to Homer? Are the Homeric portraits of prudent statesmen politically inferior to the largely metaphorical discussion of the Ideas?

In sum, Homer and all those who are skilled in making, are imitators of images of virtue and the other things they portray. The development of this inference leads to the following distinction. For each thing there are three arts; those of using, making, and imitating. The painter portrays the reins and bit but, as painter, understands nothing about them. The smith and the leather cutter know how to make them but not how to use them. This is known only by the horseman. Note that "use" is equivalent here to the function of the reins and bit; this confirms my previous observation that the Idea of something is not like a physical body that can be imitated but rather is the use and function of the entity in question, or what Socrates sometimes calls the "power" (*dunamis*) or capacity to do something.[5] He then asks: "Isn't it the case that the virtue, beauty, and correctness of each implement, animal, and deed is related to nothing but the use for which each thing was made or grew naturally?" And Glaucon agrees (601b9–d7).

The distinction between making and using is in general terms clear, but problems arise from its extension to "everything," including natural beings. The general context implies that this formulation is intended to apply to Ideas, which are grown by god. In this case, there seems to be no distinction between making and using. The divine gardener grows the Ideas as an essential precondition for the existence of the cosmos. Retaining Socrates's horticultural imagery, we can say that the gardener intends to create a beautiful and well-ordered garden. If the distinction between making and using holds here, then the gardener presumably intends to open the garden to the use of all living things, paramount among them the human being. But it would be impossible to say that the users of the garden understand it better than its maker. This point can be extended from god to nature, which produces but does not "use" what it grows, for example plants and animals. So the distinction between making and using seems to apply only to human artifacts and things grown by nature which human beings use for their own purposes.

In the case of human artifacts, the situation is mixed. There are many artifacts which we may use without knowing how to make them, and these range from the simplest, such as a plow, to the most complicated, like an airplane. Knowing how to use something is thus different from knowing how to make it, and I am not sure that it makes sense to say that one of these is closer to the truth than the other. If anything, it seems that knowing how to make something includes knowledge of what it is to be used for, that is, it includes knowledge of the function or capacity. To take an important example, Socrates may know how to make a just city, but this does not guarantee that he is especially competent to govern it. To say that philosophers must be kings is not the same as to say that *every* philosopher must be a king, although Socrates argues as if it were. We should not forget, however, that the philosophers raised within the city are entirely superior to those raised outside it.

Socrates next says that the maker will have a correct opinion about the beauty and badness of the artifact, thanks to his association with the man who knows how to use it, and who thus possesses exact knowledge (*epistēmē*). There seems to be no reason why the user could not communicate this exact knowledge to the maker, but the point is of secondary importance. The main conclusion is that the painter will have no knowledge and no correct opinion about the beauty and badness of what he imitates. I shall not repeat the weakness of this inference, but instead I note that there are some things about which the good painter must have at the least a correct opinion concerning their beauty. It is with respect to this opinion that we find some paintings beautiful and correct and others not. There is of course a difference between knowing what makes a beautiful painting and what makes a beautiful thing of the sort being painted, but they are not totally separate from one another.

Socrates, however, is not interested in the beauty of the painting as a painting, or rather he is defending the view that the beauty of the painting depends upon the beauty of its model. From this standpoint, only the portrait of a virtuous person could be beautiful and correct, and on Socrates's view the painter has no way to know the virtue of his prospective model. This is far-fetched, and I shall not dwell on it, except to observe that there can be beautiful and even virtuous paintings of evil people (601d8–602b4).

Having established the ignorance of the imitator concerning the beauty or the badness of what he copies, Socrates goes on to remind Glaucon of the coordinations between the three cognitive states of using, making, and imitating and the three parts of the soul. His first step is to introduce what in its developed form has come to be known as the distinction between primary and secondary attributes. Socrates points out that our vision fools us with respect to the relative size and distance of physical bodies, as well as with respect to their actual shapes. This is why we employ measuring, counting, and weighing. In short, seeing, the primary attribute of painting as Socrates presents it, is ruled by calculating, the primary attribute of the intellect. Especially here in the discussion of mimesis, but also elsewhere in the *Republic*, the intellectual intuition of pure Ideas is silently dropped in favor of the discursive and calculating powers. Incidentally, measuring, counting, and weighing are frequently, perhaps normally, of greater importance to *making* artifacts than to using them. The big exception is that of using devices of various kinds in order to carry out calculations. In this case using and making are on a par; it would certainly be difficult to argue that in these cases, using is a function of the intellect as making is not. In the present passage, Socrates does not connect making with spiritedness or the love of gain. Instead, he contrasts the rectification of errors of perception by calculation, and the resolution of contrary opinions that the former entails. He says that what resolves contrary opinions belongs to a part of the soul different from that which produces them. He does not name the part of the soul associated with contrary opinions but refers to it as one of the worst (602c4–603a9). We seem to be using a model of the soul here different from the initially posited tripartition.

Now the same point will be extended from sight to hearing, and with it we shift from painting to poetry. Socrates begins with a general definition of mimesis: "We say that the imitator copies human beings who perform actions either through force or willingly, and who as a result of the actions suppose themselves to have acted either well or badly, and in all these experiencing pain or enjoyment" (603c4–8). This definition, which has been formulated with poetry in mind, has three parts. First, imitation is restricted to human beings; there is no more talk of beds or other artifacts, but gods are omitted here as well. Second, there is no talk of imitating the body of a human being, or of trying to delude foolish people into taking the copy for the original, as was the case with painting. It is the actions (*prakseis*) of human beings that are imitated. Very surprisingly, Socrates does not mention speeches in general but restricts himself to judgments by the actors about whether they have acted well or badly. This puts the primary emphasis upon what we today call moral judgments, but in Plato the term *praksis* is normally contrasted with *theoria* and includes production as well as morality and politics, and we should follow his usage. The third part of the definition is stated a bit ambiguously, but it apparently means that the actors do experience pleasure and pain, not only from their actions but also from the judgments they pass on them.

In sum, mimetic poetry is the imitation of the deeds leading up to practical judgments, as well as of the pleasure and pain that these judgments cause. This definition may not be perfect, but there can be no doubt that it includes essential elements of poetry. There was no parallel definition of imitation with respect to painting, the discussion of which was inadequate, as I have tried to show. We must now see whether the sequel to the definition provides us with a satisfactory account of poetic imitation. We should, however, bear in mind that this discussion is about mimesis only, and hence not narrative poetry. Interestingly enough, as Socrates uses these terms, there is no such thing as narrative painting, whereas narrative poetry is certainly imitative to the extent that it describes, and in that sense copies within language, what others are doing or saying.

4

Socrates next reminds Glaucon that the soul is filled with myriad contrary opinions, which lead to faction within the individual person. His example is that of a good man who has lost a son, and who bears it with greater equanimity in the presence of others than when he is by himself. In the latter case, he dares to say and do things of which he would be ashamed if others could observe them. Within such a man there is an opposition between misfortune on the one hand and *logos* ("reason") and *nomos* (convention) on the other, which tell him to resist surrender to grief, and to deliberate on what must be done without being disabled by pain and the suffering itself. The best part of the soul is willing to follow the calculation of reason and convention, whereas the part that yields to suffering is unable to calculate (*alogiston*), is idle, and is a friend of cowardice (603c10–604d11). If we are to understand the tripartition model to be still valid, the second part to which Socrates refers can only be that of desire.

According to Socrates, the soul that shows outward signs of grief lends itself to much intricate imitation, whereas the prudent and quiet character is not easily imitated or understood, especially by the crowd that gathers in theaters during holidays. Certainly Greek poetry from Homer through the tragedians is filled with the lamentations of heroes and heroines, as well as of the chorus that represents the general citizenry. Grief is diversely expressed and appeals to the emotions of the many, whereas stoic self-control or judicious equanimity that goes about the business of life without succumbing to personal tragedy appeals only to the sensible few. For this reason, as the medium of diversity, mimetic poetry is directed toward the praise of the many, and so is drawn by nature not to the prudent and simple disposition in the soul but rather to the part that is irritable and various (604e1–605a7).

Is there any reason in principle why there could not be mimetic poetry about prudent, quiet, and simple persons who avoid a show of grief by responding to tragedy in the most sensible way possible, namely, by calculating the best response to some painful but irreversible event? Socrates does not mention any; instead, he attributes the actual practice of mimetic poets to their desire for glory among the many, and to the fact that it is easier to imitate persons who are grieving rather than those who are quiet. I see no way to demonstrate the point one way or another, but the actual practice of the best poets tends to substantiate the Socratic thesis. In general, sin is more interesting than virtue, and suffering stirs us as self-control does not. We would all reject as moral or political propaganda poems and dramas that repeated over and over again the superiority of virtue to vice and prudence to madness. If I may allude to the Aristotelian doctrine of catharsis, we go to the theater to be aroused to strong emotions, and to undergo their purgation by some sharp twist in the plot. If the "good guys" win from the outset, without undergoing any suffering or challenge to their very existence, there is nothing to arouse our interest. The celebration of constant virtue belongs in churches and patriotic festivals, not in the theater or epic poetry.

I think that, on balance, Socrates is right about this side of mimetic poetry, but that is not to endorse his evaluation as a whole. Such an endorsement requires us to accept the beautiful city as a desirable paradigm of justice and happiness, namely, one that requires the exclusion of the celebration of diversity that is so integral a part of human nature. Those who praise this city should at least face up to the fact that there is also no philosophical diversity within it; all its philosophers are Platonists, and in their public expression of Platonism there cannot be any unorthodox sects or factions. This is an essential corollary of the expulsion of the mimetic poets.

To continue: Socrates now summarizes the ways in which the poet corresponds to the painter. Both make things that are paltry in comparison with the truth, and both associate with a part of the soul that is inferior to the best. It is curious that Socrates does not name this part of the soul; one would suppose that he is referring to the epithumetic or moneyloving part, but the fit is not perfect. When it is stirred up by mimetic poetry, this part of the soul destroys the logistical element. The result is a bad regime within the individual person, dominated by the part of the soul that utters contraries, such as that the same thing is big and little. The contrast seems to be between two forms of cognition, one competent and the other not; the latter part is also clearly connected with the senses, which were previously said to make contrary statements until they are corrected by the part that calculates, weighs, and measures. It looks as though the division of the soul in Book Ten differs from that in the main body of the dialogue, although there are of course similarities as well (605a8–c5).

We should note that the calculative part of the soul does not simply rectify perceptual errors but is also concerned with the formulation of moral judgments. Socrates proceeds to develop this connection by describing how the mimetic poets mutilate even "the best of us" thanks to the attractiveness of their descriptions of excessive mourning. This shows quite clearly the great power of poetry over philosophy. The latter can rule only by force, whereas everyone, even the best of us, can be corrupted by poetry. In other words, we must force ourselves not to fall victim to mimetic poetry, and this can be done only by expelling it from our new city. In the case of tragedy, we fall victim to pity at the sufferings of others; on the other hand, when we give way to the pleasure derived from hearing jokes that we would be ashamed to tell ourselves, the result is comedy. And a similar story can be told about sex, spiritedness, and in general, the pleasure and pain of desire (605c6–606d8).

In the Socratic analysis, here as well as in Books Two and Three, poetry has no positive contribution to make to the intellect. It is useful for producing hymns to the gods and celebrations of good men. But if we admit "the honeyed Muse" into the city, whether in lyric or epic, "pleasure and pain will become jointly king instead of custom and reason, which has always been generally accepted as best." The attack on Homer is thus complete; he is the best of poets, but he corrupted rather than educated the Greeks (606e1–607a8). It goes without saying that this is heresy to Socrates's contemporaries, although neither Glaucon nor any of the other interlocutors protests. The conjunction of custom or law (*nomos*) and reason requires a word of comment. In actual cities, the poets themselves portray what is customary or legal; the philosophers are the agents of *logos*. But customs undergo a certain change, which is accelerated by the rule of pleasure and pain, and in particular of pleasure, the agent of novelty and diversity. Once we have established the laws certified by philosophical reasoning, any change in the subsequent customs must be for the worse. They must therefore be rigidly excluded; hence the close allegiance between custom and reason.

The same point is made by Socrates in slightly different words when he alludes to the old quarrel between philosophy and poetry (607b5–6). The poets condemn philosophers for disobedience to the city, that is, to custom. In so doing, they veil over their own loyalty to change, which is initially less binding than custom but finally more powerful because more charming, and so able to initiate or accelerate changes in custom. As Shelley puts it, poets are the unacknowledged legislators of society. To which Socrates would reply that their laws are progressively changing and becoming ever more diverse, that is to say, democratic. As Socrates says in the *Euthydemus* when the sophist accuses him of "still saying the same things," "Yes, and in the same way." Even those who reject the Socratic analysis of poetry as entirely inadequate would, however, do well to consider his central contention. Whether or not poetry has reasons of its own that reason does not know, the charm of production, which in our own time we see most clearly in technology, is more powerful than the safeguards we set up against the production of dangerous artifacts.

The edict to expel the poetry that follows pleasure and imitation will be withdrawn as soon as the poets can convince us that they deserve to dwell in a city with good laws. Some readers, distressed by the exile of charming poetry, have drawn solace from these words of a possible return, but this is surely a mistake, one induced by the very charm of poetry that Socrates acknowledges himself to feel (607c4–d2). The whole point of the discussion is that charm in itself is dangerous; it becomes healthy only when it is attached to, and so controlled by, virtuous objects. We shall listen benevolently to the argument on behalf of poetry because we have been prepared by "the rearing of the beautiful regimes to love it" (607e6–8). But if the case for the return of poetry cannot be made, we shall continue to reject it, even though such a rejection requires us to use force against ourselves.

This in effect completes the discussion of mimesis and the arts of painting and poetry. Nothing has been said about music as distinguished from poetry, no doubt because it would be much more difficult to identify what it is supposed to imitate. The obvious answer is "moods and emotions," or more generally, states of the soul. But it is not easy to describe or identify the originals in words, as it is in the case of painting and mimetic poetry. The next topic is the immortality of the human soul.

14

The Immortal Soul

I

Poetry has been sacrificed as an obstacle to the triumph of the good over the evil life. Otherwise stated, it is the good life that makes us happy, while we live it. But an entire life is as nothing when compared to all of time. It remains to be proved that the good, that is, the just, person will enjoy a happiness higher than that accruing to life itself, and the reverse must be true of the unjust or evil person. Socrates seems to drop a bombshell when he suddenly asks Glaucon: "Have you not perceived that our soul is immortal and never perishes?" He then tells us that "Glaucon looked at me and was astonished. 'By Zeus!' he said, 'certainly not I! Can you say that?'" Socrates says that he can and must, if he is not to do an injustice. He then assures Glaucon that he, too, can understand the immortality of the soul, for it is not difficult (608c1–d10).

It would take us too far afield to discuss in detail Greek views on immortality. Suffice it to say that Glaucon, whatever he has heard previously from the poets and philosophers, seems to be thoroughly unfamiliar with the idea. He does not say that he has heard this view before but rejects it, and certainly not that he accepts it. Equally interesting is Socrates's assurance that the argument is not difficult, as well as his observation that justice requires him to present it.

I shall not explore here the question of whether Socrates (or Plato) actually believed in the immortality of the soul. Certainly the claim is made in other dialogues. But our business is with the *Republic*, and it is safe to say that Socrates is about to give a popular version of the argument for immortality, just as he adjusted his account of the Ideas and the Good to the understanding of Glaucon and Adeimantus. This does not of course excuse us from the duty to inspect the argument.

The good, Socrates begins, is what saves and benefits, whereas the bad is what destroys and corrupts. To each thing, there corresponds something bad and something good, for example, opthalmia to the eyes, rust to bronze, and rot to wood. When one of these attaches itself to the appropriate thing, it makes its host bad and ends by dissolving and destroying it altogether. If there is anything that is not destroyed by its corresponding evil, nothing else can do so, for the good will certainly not destroy anything. If then we find something whose corresponding evil makes it bad but cannot destroy it, then we know that this thing is by nature incapable of destruction (608d13–609b8). This reasoning is now applied to the case of the soul. We have already discovered things that are bad for the soul: injustice, licentiousness, cowardice, and ignorance. But none of these dissolves and destroys the soul by separating it from the body. Since it is unreasonable (*alogon*) to assume that what is not an evil of the soul can destroy it, the soul must be immortal, for it cannot be destroyed by those agents that destroy the body (609b9–610a4).

In constructing this argument, Socrates assumes from the outset that the soul is separate from the body. He therefore never considers whether the dissolution of the body is not also the dissolution of the soul. Second, the evils of the soul listed by Glaucon and accepted by Socrates may not be the only kind. They constitute evils of vice but not of agents of destruction, and this does not prove that the soul is immune from evils analogous to those of rot, rust, or disease. What Socrates claims is that things fall apart for a reason. We can list the reasons in the case of the body, but we cannot do so with respect to the soul. These objections to Socrates, as well as his probable replies, are not conclusive. The objections rest upon the assumption of reductionism, that is, of the soul to the body; or let us say that they accept the view that the soul is the harmony of the body, a harmony that dissolves with the body. The replies rest upon a quite different pair of assumptions, namely, separation of soul and body, and the absence of destructive causes. Proofs of immortality are very much like proofs of the existence of God. The immediate evidence of the physical world, and indeed of human life, mitigates against immortality and God, but this evidence can always be turned aside with an appeal to the difference between the seen and the unseen, the testimony of faith, miracles, and so on.

The Socratic argument turns out to be easy, not because it is convincing but because it both oversimplifies and assumes what it purports to prove. There is, however, a strong advantage to the refuters, since any argument can be invalidated by the proper use of principles and the appropriate interpretation of the issue to be proved. In short, whereas injustice or moral vice may not dissolve a soul (and truth be told, how do we know that it does not?), some weakness in its construction may do so. The next stage of the argument is not as clear as the first part. Suppose someone claims that injustice gradually destroys the soul. Our claim, says Socrates, is that in this case injustice is like a fatal disease that kills sooner or later. To this, Glaucon replies that, if this is so, injustice will not be such a bad thing, since it kills those who suffer from it. But he believes rather that injustice kills others, not the one who is unjust, upon whom it confers added vitality and whom it keeps constantly awake. In other words, Glaucon denies the hypothesis that Socrates has just attributed to those who refuse to admit that the soul is immortal. The initial assumption that underlies Socrates's point is that if injustice kills, justice does not. However, Glaucon denies that injustice kills, and Socrates takes this as a confirmation of the thesis that the soul cannot be destroyed by its own evil, and so is immortal (610c6–611a3).

It follows, says Socrates, that there are always the same souls, neither more nor less, since none ever perishes. He then adds, somewhat mysteriously, that if any of the immortal things became more numerous, they would come to be out of the mortal, and everything would end up being immortal. I take this to mean that immortal things cannot generate at all, whereas the mortal cannot generate the immortal. If the latter were possible, gradually everything mortal would die off, leaving only immortal things. However, the argument is not very important. Much more interesting is the contention that the soul cannot have as its natural state complexity, as well as unlikeness and difference with itself. This thesis seems to go directly counter to the regular picture of the soul as at war with itself, and as consisting of conflicting parts. It is derived from the same objection to diversity that we saw with respect to poetry. In political terms, if there is faction within a city, it is no longer one city but many, and most of these "cities" (in fact, all but one at the most) must be bad, and hence unjust. This is hard to see if one observes the soul in its maimed form, thanks to communion with the body and other evils. One has to look instead to the love of wisdom in order to determine its kinship with the immortal as well as what it is truly like, including whether it has one or many forms, a remark that seems to allow us to doubt whether the soul has three parts, or whether this model covers all souls (611a4–612a7).

Socrates now claims that justice has been vindicated and shown to be superior to injustice even apart from the benefits it bestows upon human beings.

This being so (as he claims), it is now harmless to return to justice and the rest of virtue the wages that they procure for the human soul. Socrates indicates that the separation of justice from its benefits is impossible, but that it was granted for the sake of the argument, so that justice in itself could be compared with injustice in itself. This vindicates my own previous claim as to the impossibility of the aforementioned separation; even psychic health and harmony depend upon interaction with one's fellow citizens, as should be obvious from the analogy between the city and the soul. Whatever its defects, the analogy certainly expresses Socrates's conviction about the interdependence of justice in the city and the soul. I cannot mind my own business unless everyone else in the city does so as well (612a8–e1).

The language of the passage we are now studying has reintroduced the gods, who were replaced in Books Two and Three by *the* god, only to return in the subsequent discussion of birth and death. The discussion of death and immortality once more brings about a descent toward conventional religion. Thus Socrates says that whereas both gods and human beings honor justice, it does not escape the discernment of the gods at least as to who is just and who is not. He who is discerned to be just by the gods is dear to them and receives from them the best possible, except for some necessary evil that was due to him for mistakes in a previous incarnation (for Socrates is indeed referring to the doctrine of reincarnation). We must therefore assume that even if the just man becomes poor or sick, whatever evil befalls him will end in some good, while he is living or even when he is dead. This statement is based not upon the previous argument for the connection between inner harmony and justice but rather upon the assumption that the gods exist and reward justice with good things, all appearances to the contrary notwithstanding. We are now in the domain of the edifying, not that of *logos*. Socrates reverses the initial portrait of justice as stripped of its actual face and concealed behind the countenance of injustice. He now attributes to justice the very benefits that were assigned to injustice disguised as justice. In other words, Socrates maintains that justice cannot in the long run be mistaken for its opposite. He who aspires to divinity through justice and virtue is as much like a god as a human being can be. There is no mention now of the love of wisdom, to which Socrates referred only a moment ago. We are approaching the grand climax of the myth of Er. The dramatic itinerary of Book Ten thus shows us that politics depends not simply upon philosophy but upon myth or poetry as well (612e2–614a4).

2

The restitution to justice of its good reputation and external benefits is licensed by Socrates on the grounds that its true nature can be concealed from neither human beings nor the gods. If it seems that the just are afflicted with evils, we may rest assured that these will end in some good, either in the remainder of their lives or in the next world. It is unclear why Socrates asserts this conclusion so confidently. Certainly our experience does not confirm the proposition that the just are always rewarded in this life. As to the next life, if anything takes place there, it is contingent upon the will of the gods, and the assumption of their benevolence has not been verified by anything that has been stated in the dialogue thus far. It does not follow from the so-called proofs for the immortality of the soul, which are compatible with the presence of injustice in the next life. In general, the argument in Book Ten undergoes a rapid transformation that begins with the account of the Ideas as divinely created or grown and culminates in the myth of Er. In the closing pages of the dialogue, we have shifted from the domain of *logos* to that of myth. And yet, the main body of the dialogue is itself a myth, a conversation that probably never took place about the founding of a city that has never existed and almost certainly never will exist.

Let us say that the main part of the *Republic* deals with life, whereas the myth of Er deals with death. This is not quite precise enough, because death is of interest to Socrates only as it casts light on the shift from one incarnation to the next. Furthermore, the characters about whom Plato writes are already dead at the time of the composition of the dialogue and have been resurrected as articulate phantoms by the genius of the author. One way to summarize the accomplishment of the *Republic* is to say that it overcomes the dissolution and destruction of the soul through a concatenation of myths that are not imitations but recollections of the origin. Death is conquered by poetry. The more we think about it, the less the *Republic* seems to be an attack upon poetry and the more it vindicates philosophy's need for poetry. This is certainly true outside the beautiful city; that is, it is certainly true of the procedure by which Socrates (and so Plato) constructs the city and attempts to persuade us that it constitutes a possible solution to the problem of justice and politics.

Having described the advantages that will accrue to us from justice in this life, Socrates now goes on to complete his assignment by adding on an account of the prizes, wages, and gifts that await the just man in death (614a5–8). He does so in a kind of narrative poetry that could be admitted into the beautiful city. The story is of a strong warrior named Er who died "once upon a time" in war (see Bloom's and Ferrari and Griffith's notes for the various literary allusions in the opening of the myth). On the tenth day following, the corpses were gathered; Er's dead companions had already begun to decay, but his corpse was well preserved. On the twelfth day, when he was about to be buried at his home, he came back to life and recounted what he had seen in the next world (614b2–8).

I note first that Er is a warrior; nothing is said to suggest that he is also a philosopher. We may assume that philosophers do not require a mythical consolation against death. Their task is rather to improve upon the Homeric account of the descent into Hades that is presented in the so-called "Alcinous section" of the Odyssey, an account from which Socrates explicitly distinguishes his own story (614b2–3). Homer's shade of Achilles tells Odysseus that he would rather be a slave on earth than king of all the dead (XI. 488–91). This sentiment is clearly unacceptable within the Socratic city, and one of the main purposes of the myth of Er is to teach his students how to purge it from the souls of the auxiliary-guardians. Er is himself chosen without explanation by the underworld judges to return to the surface of the earth as a messenger of what occurs after death. The benevolence of the gods toward the just is thus demonstrated by their wish to rectify the desolate view of death attributed by Homer to Achilles. In this regard, it is interesting that whereas the live Odysseus descends into Hades and then returns to tell what he has seen, Er first dies in order to descend and is then resurrected by the gods in order to describe to the living the world below. Socrates excludes the appearance of the living in Hades or the dead on the surface of the earth. To that extent, his myth follows the order of nature more closely than does Homer. As to the resurrection itself, that is the work of divine judges; we may call it the surd of the imagination, that is, the indispensable condition for our coming to know what death is really like.

In the opening scene, the dead souls gather in a daimonic place where judges are supervising the transmission of souls. There are two holes leading up to heaven, and two more descending down to an unspecified place that is obviously the lower depths of Hades. Some souls are arriving from above, by a descent from heaven, whereas others appear from below. The recent dead are then judged and sent off to the appropriate place, namely, to heaven if they have lived a just life and to the depths of Hades if they have not. The other two openings are discharging recent arrivals from heaven in the one case or the lower depths in the other. These arrivals gather in a meadow and tell each other what they have seen in their previous habitat. The residence in the earth below takes up one thousand years and is plainly filled with terrible things, since those who have just completed it weep and lament as they recount their experiences. It is thus clear from the outset that the unjust are to be severely punished; the benevolence of the gods does not extend to forgiveness for our sins. Those who have come from heaven, on the other hand, tell of its good experiences and incredibly beautiful sights (614b8–615a4).

According to the testimony of the souls, each unjust deed is punished ten times over. More precisely, the stay below fills up ten times one hundred years;

a hundred years is taken as the length of human life. This allows time for ten punishments to be administered for each unjust act in a lifetime. The calculation is quite unclear, but one way in which to understand the myth is that there is a one-to-one correspondence in the duration of the unjust act and that of each of its ten separate punishments. The unjust man thus relives his life ten times over, with the pain he has caused others now converted into his own misery in each cycle. And good rewards are earned for the performance of good deeds in life, in the same measure, namely, tenfold. Nothing is said about those who mix evil with good in their lives and are thus alternately punished and rewarded. This would both complicate the task of routing the various souls to the appropriate destination and destroy the arithmetical tidiness of the myth. On the other hand, there is an indication that the size of the penalty is a function of the wickedness of the corresponding action. Those who, like the fictitious Ardiaeus, a Pamphylian tyrant of a thousand years ago, killed their fathers and committed heinous crimes of other sorts, are punished longer than the thousand-year norm, and some who are regarded as incurably evil are tortured, flayed and thrown into Tartarus. And the rewards to good souls are the antistrophes of these punishments (615a4–616b1).

It would be obtuse to analyze each detail of the myth or to try to paraphrase it into some coherent philosophical doctrine. The main point in the balance of the myth is the procedure by which the souls that have completed their thousand years (or more) of rewards or punishments choose the life that they will live in the next incarnation. In passing to the place in which the distribution is to be made, the souls see the shaft of light that stretches from above through all of heaven and earth, in the center of which are visible chains that stretch down from heaven and bind it in such a way as to hold the entire revolution together. From the extremities of the shaft of light the souls see the spindle of necessity, by which all the revolutions of heaven are turned. It thus seems that the structure of the physical cosmos is visible from the location of the accumulated souls. This location is somewhere between heaven and Hades, and it contains the entrance and exit to each of these domains. It is the scene of the shift from death to life, and so belongs exclusively to neither (616b1–c5).

We should not pass by without commenting on the peculiar admixture of necessity and contingency in the cosmos. The motions of the cosmos itself are bound by necessity, and nothing is said of a first mover or ruling intelligence in this connection. The fate of the souls is determined by the judges of what I am calling the intermediate zone, who are either gods or daimons. Since judgment of good and evil requires intelligence and perception of the individual soul, it cannot be explained by the chains visible in the shaft of light or by the spindle of necessity. One might wish to claim that the punishment of injustice and the rewarding of justice is an intrinsic necessity of the mythical cosmos, but it cannot have been established by chains and spindles. There must be two kinds of necessity, structural or cosmological on the one hand and psychic or juridical on the other. These two exist together, but no explanation is offered of how each fulfills its function without interference from the other. The various spheres of the fixed stars, the planets, the sun, and the moon, which are described here as whorls in the stem and hook of the spindle of necessity, constitute the structure of a cosmos of heavenly bodies but not of souls, divine or human (616c5–617b4). The image of weaving, which represents politics in the *Statesman*, is here applied to the structure of the entire cosmos.

The question of the two necessities, and a fortiori the relation between physics and politics, is not answered; rather, the mystery is deepened by the next step, in which Socrates boldly asserts the inner unity of the body and soul of the cosmos. "The spindle turns in the lap of Necessity." But there is no distinction between structure and life; in addition to one siren for each heavenly sphere, emitting a single note that accords with the other seven to produce a single harmony, Necessity is accompanied by her three daughters, the fates (*moirai*): Lachesis, Clotho, and Atropos. These figures are traditional representations of fate, but as Ferrari and Griffith point out in their note, "It was not traditional, however, to personify 'Necessity' " as is done here and again at 617d" (p. 339). This is Plato's bold resolution of cosmic dualism. Construction, and so the unification of theory and practice, is the work of the divine or cosmic forces. Hence the weaver of the city of humankind is an imitation of cosmic construction, not simply of the Ideas.

What one can call contingency or freedom is also required in order to make the soul responsible for its acts in the subsequent life, and this is done by allowing each soul, after it has completed its previous punishment or experienced one thousand years of blessings, to choose the life it will live next. The order in which the souls choose is determined by lot, but there are more than enough kinds of life available, so even the last to choose has the chance to select one that is not bad and will content him, if he chooses intelligently and lives earnestly (619b3–5). Although the choice is free, once it is made, each soul is bound to its selection by Necessity. The presiding prophet prepares the choices with the statement that each ephemeral soul is about to initiate another cycle of life that ends in death. "The demon will not choose you, but you will choose the demon . . . Virtue has no master. You will possess more or less of it as you honor or dishonor it. The blame belongs to him who chooses; god is blameless" (617d6–e5). The soul exists independent of the life it chooses to live. This is indicated by Socrates at 618b2–4 when he says that the lives on display are of every type, but "there is no order of the soul within them, thanks to the necessity that the soul becomes different depending upon which life it chooses."

This formulation raises difficulties that cannot be probed too closely without dissolving the point of the myth. Socrates warns Glaucon that we must devote ourselves to the assiduous investigation of the causes of a good or a bad life, just as has been described in the main part of the dialogue. How we live now will determine not only what our reward or punishment will be in the intermediate zone but also what kind of life we shall live in our next incarnation. If the soul is immortal and reincarnation is a continuous cycle (with rare exceptions that will be mentioned shortly), then the life we are currently living has been determined by the choice we made following our last thousand-year stay in heaven or Hades, and so on ad infinitum. We can be held responsible for this choice if and only if we have learned the correct lesson from our rewards or punishments. But this knowledge cannot be acquired without philosophy (619d1–e1). If this is right, it looks as though a truly happy life is reserved for philosophers. And the soul must already be philosophical prior to the choice of a particular life; this is required to enable it to make the correct choice.

On the other hand, if choice is a matter of chance, then moral responsibility is dissolved. The first soul to choose a life in the present lottery comes from heaven, "and he had lived in an orderly regime in his previous life, participating in virtue by habit without philosophy" (619c6–d1). Thanks to folly and gluttony, he hastily chooses a tyranny for his next life, without pausing to examine the pattern, which includes eating his own children and other evils. And of the others who make bad choices, not the least number of them have just arrived from heaven. Since they were in heaven thanks to having chosen correctly in the previous lottery, it is obvious that, except for philosophers, which life we choose is largely a matter independent of our previous choice.

That is, conventional or demotic virtue is not sufficient to guarantee continuous happiness. On the other hand, the punishment for a life of injustice makes the dwellers in Hades more cautious in their next choice. "For this reason, and thanks to the chance of the lot, there was an exchange of evils and goods in most of the souls" that had come from Hades (619d5–7). Socrates admits here that the lottery is not perfectly just; not every soul has a chance at a superior life in the next incarnation. One could also suppose that the effects of severe punishment are as efficacious as philosophy in determining the next choice. But Socrates goes even farther. If a man always philosophizes in a healthy way in this life, "and the lot for his choice does not fall out among the last," it is likely, from what we hear about the intermediate zone, that not only will he be happy here, he will spend his thousand years in heaven, and not below the earth (619d7–e5). This is quite different from the previous assertion that there are always plenty of good lives from which to choose. It seems that not even philosophy can guarantee happiness, which is partly a matter of luck The myth of Er thus suggests the following dilemma. If we enforce cosmological necessity on human souls, then the choice between justice and injustice disappears. But if we separate cosmological necessity from human life, chance figures at every level of the distribution of lives, and thus threatens the significance of free choice.

I call attention to the reference in the myth to Odysseus, who is one of a number of well-known persons observed in their choice of the next life by Er. It is Odysseus's lot to choose last. He is said to have recovered from his love of honor because of the labors of his former life, and so spends considerable time in looking for the life of "a private man who is not a busybody" (*andros idiōtou apragmonos*: 620c6–7). Odysseus says that this would have been his choice even if he had chosen first. Socrates thus closes the myth with one final rebuke of Homer, and in this way with the whole Greek tradition of justice. The praise of the quiet life is of course to be found elsewhere among the Greek writers, for example, in Herodotus, but it goes counter to the Greek love of glory, for which Homer is the most fluent spokesman, and which even Socrates ranks second to the pursuit of wisdom. As it turns out, the happiest life for the wise man is philosophy together with the quiet of the private life in which one minds one's own business. The Socratic city raises grave difficulties for the pursuit of such a life, if it does not render it altogether impossible. To this I add that the myth, in providing us with a pacific vision of philosophy, does not take into account the temptation of philosophers to enter into politics, if only through speech. The dialogue ends on a pious note of submission to fate and the gods.

3

Julia Annas regards Book Ten as an appendix, even as an excrescence. "We can see why Plato thought it relevant to the rest of the *Republic*; but the level of philosophical argument and literary skill is much below the rest of the book."[1] On the first point, I believe that Annas forgets how poor most of the arguments in the *Republic* were shown to be by her own very competent analysis. I have rather emphasized that the content of the arguments in Book Ten differs from that of the main books (Two through Nine) on two extremely important points. The Ideas are now said to have been produced by god, and the gods and legends of the traditional religion are reinstituted by the myth of Er. The proofs for the immortality of the soul fit well into this general context.

Whether this makes for a diminution of literary skill is in my opinion dubious; the other books vary widely from a literary standpoint, and none approaches the dramatic peak of Book One and the first part of Book Two.

What is not dubious is that Book Ten exhibits a piety that is absent from the other books, a piety that culminates in the edification of the myth of Er. Book One was much more tough-minded. Socrates descended into the Piraeus in order to observe a new religious festival. In other words, he was moved initially by a kind of theoretical curiosity, and he judges the barbarians to have performed as well as the Greeks. In Books Two through Seven, with the exception of the introduction of Apollo in connection with burial rites and the commemoration of the dead, the traditional gods disappear; they are replaced by the god of the philosophers on the one hand and the eternal Ideas on the other. At the same time, the open-mindedness toward the barbarians is replaced with the explicit assertion that the philosophical city is almost surely Greek, and that Greeks may enslave barbarians but not their fellow Greeks. Religion is not an issue in Books Eight and Nine; Socrates presents the account of the decay of actual regimes in purely psychological, that is to say human, terms. In Book Ten, eternity is replaced by the garden of being, and what one could call "ontology" becomes a branch of theology. The behavior of historical human beings is now explained as a consequence of the choices of ghosts. As one would expect, Socrates is unable to provide a rationally compelling account of the harmony between cosmological necessity and human freedom.

In Books Six and Seven, the Ideas are eternal. In Book Ten, they are grown by god, whereas the human soul is now immortal, something that was not mentioned previously by Socrates. Even further, the Ideas are trivialized by serving as the originals that are copied by technical artifacts; the critique of imitation has the odd consequence that craftsmen and artisans are closer to the Ideas than are poets, painters, and musicians. As to the immortality of the soul, it is required as the basis for the myth of reincarnation, in which no one, as Seth Benardete observes, chooses either the life of philosophy or the just life.[2] In Book Ten, philosophy is replaced by carpentry on the one hand and the life of a private man who minds his own business on the other. This antipolitical life is taken by Odysseus, who is the last to choose in the myth of Er.

These "reversals," if that is the right word, are too many, and they cut too deep to be explained as careless errors on Plato's part. I prefer a different hypothesis. In Book Ten, Plato engages in a carnival of retractions, to warn the reader with an eye for irony against taking too seriously the odd proposals that are presented in the main books of the dialogue. To say that these proposals are odd is not to say that they are false but rather to say that the unmitigated truth is too harsh to serve as a paradigm for human affairs. This is why the dialogue ends with a myth. I cannot demonstrate this hypothesis with geometric or erotic necessity, but it allows me to make sense of Book Ten for myself, and I invite the reader to consider it. Philosophy cannot function without poetry, and eternity is not accessible to human beings except through the diffusing lens of myth.

Epilogue

The general thesis of this study can now be stated as follows: In the *Republic*, Plato presents us with his most comprehensive portrait of the Socratic effort to bring philosophy down from heaven into the city. This effort faces the insuperable difficulty that, when philosophy completes its descent, it is sooner or later transformed into ideology. In order to survive, philosophy must preserve its heavenly residence. But this in turn depends upon the philosophical intervention in the affairs of the earthly city. The city must be made safe for philosophy, but philosophy must also be made safe for the city. If this dual responsibility is not properly discharged, the inner balance between theory and practice dissolves. The problem, of course, is to understand what is meant by "properly."

The unearthly character of philosophy is most famously expressed by Plato in his doctrine of Ideas. Our knowledge of these Ideas depends upon a never adequately described science called "dialectic," or reasoning by means of Ideas alone. We cannot, however, reason about the Ideas before we have encountered them, a procedure that Socrates regularly compares to the act of vision. We must say what we have seen, but we cannot say what we have seen before we see it. There is then a radical distinction between the few philosophers, who possess this mysterious power of intellectual vision, and the many nonphilosophers, who do not. According to Socrates, the political problem, which is best described as how to institute justice in the individual soul of the citizen, requires the rule of philosophers. Otherwise put, justice depends upon the rule of those who see the pure Ideas in their original heavenly form. But this in turn requires the use of rhetoric and force in order to persuade those who cannot see the Ideas. Politics is grounded in noble or medicinal lies.

The political status of philosophy in the *Republic* is represented by the difference between the exterior and the interior argument. In order to initiate a political revolution of the kind that Socrates describes, one must speak quite differently to the philosopher and the nonphilosopher. We would expect the argument for the nonphilosopher to lie on the surface of Socratic discourse, as for example when Socrates accommodates his account of the Ideas to the intellectual capacity of his audience, and in particular to Glaucon. Oddly enough, the surface political argument is much more radical and much more candidly expressed than we would expect. It is quite plausible to hold that there is no inner or esoteric argument in the *Republic*, at least certainly not with respect to politics, including, of course, the political activity of the philosopher.

The problems of interpretation that arise from this situation can be most easily and directly resolved, I have suggested, by assuming that Socrates is quite serious about his account of the best city, which is much too radical to serve as an accommodation to the many. The actual exterior of an argument for revolution must be expressed with considerable frankness to those who are to be enlisted as auxiliaries to the ringleaders. But one would not expect philosophical initiators of a political revolution to make fundamental recommendations that are either impossible or politically undesirable.

While admitting that his program would be difficult, perhaps impossible, to enact, Socrates never wavers from the endorsement he bestows upon it, which is also readily accepted by the two main interlocutors, Glaucon and Adeimantus. Nor has anyone presented a cogent explanation of why Plato might write a lengthy account to demonstrate the impossibility of acquiring true justice by praising without exception an absurd solution to the problem of justice, one that he knows to be self-contradictory and that would have been rejected by the Athenians as unjust and tyrannical. If Plato is showing, or attempting to show, that the excessive pursuit of justice leads to injustice, would it not have been simpler for him to recommend a sober and moderate regime in the manner of Aristotle? My suggestion is that Plato accepts the need to speak radically, that is, to contradict the prevailing *nomos*, and to state the need for philosopher-kings. This need is rooted in the criticism of the existing religious beliefs, the dissolution of the family, which is unjust to women, and the rigorous use of ideology and physical force in order to institute and preserve the rule of philosophers.

Still more precisely, Plato argues dramatically that the just city depends upon the rule of Platonism. At this point, the Straussian hypothesis comes into play, but in a revised form. It is not merely the case that the excessive pursuit of justice leads to injustice. The greater difficulty lies in the fact that justice is not the same for philosophers and nonphilosophers alike. We can of course reach a compromise between the conflicting claims to justice, but a compromise soon deteriorates into an ideological quarrel between the two disputants. One might wish the philosopher to find or construct a compromise that is fair to both parties and does not decay into conflicting ideologies. But even if one assumes that to be possible, it was nevertheless not Plato's intention. His intention was rather to state the extreme case for philosophical justice, and thereby to show that in order to institute justice for philosophers, we must suppress justice for nonphilosophers. Those of us who are not Platonists will want to add that he also suppresses justice for philosophers, as is most easily seen in the absence of non-Platonists from the rank of philosopher-kings. Plato would reply that this absence is perfectly just, because there is only one truth, and that is his truth. And so philosophy is covered over by the rhetorical battle of philosophers with respect to the nature of truth and who, if anyone, possesses it. In order to survive, the Platonist must become an ideologist.

In short, Socrates accommodates his discussion of the philosophical basis of politics, namely, the doctrine of Ideas, to the understanding of those who are by nature auxiliaries. But he does not accommodate the discussion of politics proper, that is to say, of the founding and defense of the just city. The founding fathers do not need to possess a precise understanding of the doctrine of Ideas, but they do require to know the precise structure of the city they are to found. I use the term *auxiliaries* here to designate not simply the soldiers but, more broadly, the inner circle of assistants to the philosopher-kings, such as Plato's two brothers, Glaucon and Adeimantus.

Those who cannot tolerate the suggestion of any duplicity on Socrates's part are forced to agree that the just city is impossible. Socrates says that those philosophers who are born and raised in any actual city (that is, any city other than the just city) will refuse to engage in politics. But one cannot have been born and raised in a nonexistent city, and the just city cannot exist unless it is founded by philosophers. Such a founding takes both many allies, including a sufficiently large military force, and time to establish the peculiar institutions of the city. That this is impossible is shown by Socrates's assertion that in order to found the city, we must expel everyone over the age of ten. But this action leaves the philosophers with no conceivable military force. I do not need to emphasize the likely outcome of any request by a few philosophers (or perhaps one) that the adults turn over their young children and accept voluntary rustication.

The impossibility of the just city in no way forces us to maintain that Socrates does not believe in the justice of the extreme measures he introduces in his political paradigm. Such belief is entirely compatible with the central premise that justice depends upon philosophy. But the philosopher requires auxiliaries who will put him into power, and there are none at the beginning of the political revolution. What is, however, quite likely is that the philosopher will acquire disciples whose grasp of the founding project is less perfect than that of Glaucon and Adeimantus. In order to take place at all, in the absence of already formed auxiliaries the revolution must turn to ideology. Prior to the existence of the wished-for city over a sufficient period of time, there are no properly educated guardians, and without guardians of various kinds, for example, physicians and judges in addition to soldiers, the city cannot exist at all.

As we know from the *Statesman* as well as the *Republic*, strict justice consists in obeying the instructions of the wise man. Faced with the difficulty, or rather the impossibility, of finding a wise man, we turn in the sphere of actual politics to the establishment of laws, written and unwritten. The absence of any detailed discussion of the laws of the just city in the *Republic* already implies its impossibility. In real cities, there must be laws and acknowledged interpreters of the laws. These interpreters rely upon what Aristotle calls *phronēsis* (practical intelligence). One of the great weaknesses of the Socratic city is that it never establishes the practical value of the intuition of pure Ideas. A moment's thought shows that the interpretation and enforcement of the laws have nothing to do with the grasping of the Idea of law, assuming that there exists such an entity. To mention only the most important deficiency of the Socratic argument, dialectic is reasoning with Ideas, including the Idea of the human soul, whereas politics is reasoning with particular empirical cases. This leads inevitably to the establishment of legal specialists, jurists, and a host of specialists whose judgment is pertinent to the particular instance under investigation. Under such circumstances, one of two things follows. Either there arises a multiplicity of quasi-philosophical ideologies claiming to exhibit the true spirit of the laws, or the spirit of the laws is separated from the variety of technicians or specialists by the conviction that there is no coherent spirit, in which case ideology is disguised as objectivity and the mastery of correct methodology in one *technē* or another.

It looks very much as if the entrance of philosophy into politics leads immediately to, or is identical with, the disappearance of philosophy in the Platonic sense from politics. I myself believe that this is the sensible inference to draw from Plato's *Republic*. The trouble starts with the assumption that justice is giving to each person his or her due, and that only the philosopher can know what is due to us. The defect in this assumption lies in the fact, noted by

Socrates in the *Phaedrus*, that human beings cannot be wise but at best are lovers of wisdom. Aristotle draws the correct inference from this doctrine. His solution to the political problem is to replace the philosopher with the gentleman. The modern (and postmodern) tradition begins with the ostensible replacement of the gentleman by the people. It remains to be seen whether this choice will endure. What Socrates calls the quarrel between philosophy and poetry has been transformed in our time into the quarrel between poetry and technique. We have to leave this complex issue with a question. Are poetry and technique not themselves parts of philosophy that have become detached from each other through the excesses instituted by the dogmatic rhetoric of the philosophers like Plato, whose warning to the philosophers and nonphilosophers alike has deteriorated into the very dilemma from which he proposed to save us?

I come now to my conclusion. The axis of the political argument in the *Republic* is the so-called analogy between the city and the soul, or the claim that the city is the soul writ large. This analogy has been subjected to considerable criticism, in particular with respect to its conceptual or logical cogency. I myself have contributed to this criticism in the present study. Since I subscribe to the charge of the formal defectiveness of the analogy, and have also claimed that Plato is quite serious about the desirability of the extreme measures Socrates claims to be required by true justice, the question arises whether Plato simply overlooked the formal defects of his analogy. If he did, the philosophical value of the *Republic* seems to be vitiated; the work is reduced to a historical curiosity of great but entirely misleading influence. If he did not, why then did he ground his political teaching in a formally defective manner?

Given the reticence of Plato and the nature of the dialogue form, it is not possible to give a decisive answer to this question. But a close reading of the text gives rise to more or less plausible hypotheses. By "plausible" I mean here hypotheses that save the phenomena of the text. One cannot save these phenomena except by going beyond the text, but one cannot responsibly go beyond the text except on the basis of a close consideration of the text itself. The reader will recognize this as a statement of the famous "hermeneutical circle," which is subscribed to in fact if not with full self-consciousness by all Plato scholars, regardless of their philosophical orientations.

My own hypothesis begins with the observation that it is entirely implausible to suggest that Plato believed none of the consequences of the argument he so carefully constructs. As to the charge that Plato was either logically incompetent or, somewhat less harshly, that formal reasoning had not developed sufficiently in his time to permit him to see his errors, whatever its merits, it leads to the unfortunate conclusion that the Plato scholar is wasting time, time better spent in reading more logically up-to-date authors. In order to reply to this conclusion, one must account for errors in reasoning as a necessary part of the general argument, or in other words, show that the errors are intentional. The most obvious way to do so is to note that we normally recur to bad arguments in politics, either because there are no valid political demonstrations or because they are politically useless, not to say harmful. This is, so to speak, a corollary of the need for noble and medicinal lies. The point can be established by a consideration of the main thrust of the argument in the *Republic*. Let us take as our example the analogy between the city and the soul.

As has been frequently noticed, this analogy appears only in the *Republic*. Thus the soul is presented in the *Phaedrus* by the image of the winged charioteer conducting a team of two horses, one white and one black. This image is itself peculiar, but we have no space to do more than remind ourselves that the horses represent the good and bad spiritedness, respectively, of the soul, whereas the charioteer represents the intellect. Nothing at all is said of any analogy between the soul and the city. But the *Phaedrus* is the reverse of a political dialogue; it is devoted to the fate of the individual soul in its effort to transform physical desire into love of the "hyperuranian beings" or Platonic Ideas. In this respect, the dialogue reminds us of the *Symposium*, which is concerned with the vision of pure beauty by the private person, although of course this vision can initiate creations of good political speeches. Again, there is no reference in the *Symposium* to an analogy between the city and the soul.

The *Republic* also begins (and ends) with the question of whether the just or unjust life is happier or more blessed for the individual person. In the *Republic*, however, this question is very soon transformed into the study of the soul through its analogy with the city. The point is obvious from the titles of the three dialogues just mentioned. "Phaedrus" is the name of a private person, "Symposium" is the name of a private drinking party, and "Republic" is the name of the ruling regime of the city (*politeia*). If we take our bearings by the natures of these three dialogues, rather than by hypotheses based upon how old Plato was when he wrote them (they all come from what is often called the same "middle" period of Platonic production), then we are led quite easily to the hypothesis that the political presentation of the soul by Socrates requires the aforementioned analogy, whereas the private presentation does not. To this I add that there is no tripartition of the soul in accord with three political classes in the *Statesman*, a dialogue of the third, or late, period, in which the argument is unfolded by the Eleatic Stranger as an exercise in dialectic or sound philosophical reasoning. As to the *Laws*, Plato's final dialogue, the presentation of the laws of the best practicable city, the analogy between city and soul is once more absent, and an Athenian stranger (the ghost of

Socrates?) replaces Socrates himself. It is widely agreed that the *Laws* presents Plato's second-best city. I shall not examine this belief more closely, except to note that the replacement of the best by the second-best, or of the theoretical by the practical, leads also to the absence of the analogy between the city and the soul.

In short, it looks as if the extreme statement of the views attributed by Plato to Socrates concerning the dependence of the happiness of the private person upon residence in the just city requires the analogy between the city and the soul. Let us recall once more the major steps in the reasoning that is implied by the identification of personal happiness with public justice. Justice is giving to each person his or her due; Socrates expresses this as "minding one's own business." But who knows the business of the individual person? Who knows what the person ought to do, as contrasted with what he or she desires to do? The answer can only be: the philosopher, in the special sense attributed by Socrates to that appellation. But there are very few philosophers, and the intelligence is not capable of regulating the desires without the mediation of spiritedness (police and soldiers).

Thus it follows that philosophers must become kings, and that their rule be implemented by the auxiliaries, who are themselves prepared for their task by a special education of gymnastics and music. In order to make certain that the guardian-auxiliaries do not deviate from the teaching of the philosopher-kings, their education must be controlled from birth by what we can only call brainwashing, or stated in a more genteel idiom, by staining their souls with the dye of the political doctrines of the philosophers. Once more to summarize: justice is the application to another of the philosopher's knowledge of what is good for another. The simplest and clearest exposition of this teaching is that philosophers tell noble lies to nonphilosophers. Since all philosopher-kings are Platonists, it is neither necessary nor possible to lie to them, whether nobly or ignobly.

As is also clear from the *Statesman*, the political rule of the wise man depends not merely upon the existence of such a person but more precisely on the application of his judgment to each individual case. The *Statesman*, which is more theoretical than the flamboyant *Republic*, makes it explicit that the rule of wisdom is impossible; hence we require laws. This is also no doubt why the doctrine of Platonic Ideas is not mentioned in the *Statesman* (and if it is present in the *Sophist*, appears in a form quite different from that discussed in the *Republic*). Differently stated, the minimal attention paid in the *Republic* to the promulgation of laws is closely connected to the "transcendent" or "separated" status of the Ideas. A claim to wisdom or dialectic cannot be verified by those who lack wisdom. If wisdom is to rule, it can only be through force and lying. But the philosopher is poorly equipped to develop a rhetoric that is suited for political purposes, and even if he were well equipped, reliance upon speech alone would lead sooner or later, and sooner rather than later, to a degradation in the philosophical rhetoric: in other words, to the creation of ideology. In this case, the expulsion of the poets would be in vain.

Theory, so to speak, depends upon praxis. The force of the argument for perfect justice, or as perfect a justice as possible, rests upon force, namely, the force applied by the auxiliaries, in the first instance upon the workers (the third class). For this reason, there must be a distinction between spiritedness and desire. Second, it must be the case, as Socrates contends, that spiritedness is by nature more inclined to reason than to desire, which is primarily sexual or directed toward moneymaking. If spiritedness is not distinguished from desire, it will be thoroughly infected by it. If spiritedness is identified with the intellect, we open the door to the subordination of intelligence to the will, which, if we think it through, results in the reconquest of the philosophers by the poets. Hence we arrive at the need for three parts to the soul. But this is to say that we postulate three main types of human being: the philosopher, the soldier, and the moneymaking partisan of (largely erotic) desire. Each type has its own work, which is to say that the structure of the city is articulated into three types or classes: rulers, soldiers, and workers.

Plato is thus in a position to assert that there is a formal analogy between the city and the soul. But this in no way requires that the analogy be formally sound. The form is that of poetry, not *logos* The logical deficiencies in the analogy show us the impossibility of solving the political problem by pure logic, diaeresis, or Platonic dialectic. Otherwise stated, this is why there is no Idea of the city. The conceptual structure of the city is internally incoherent. From the standpoint of logic, the analogy is destroyed by the simple fact that the residents of the just city have a tripartite soul as persons but a unified soul as citizens. Thus, for example, members of the worker class must be isomorphic to the component of desire in the individual citizen, whereas the individual citizen is not a unity but a harmony, a kind of ancestor of the Hegelian unity of opposites. Those who dislike Hegel may be satisfied with a more Platonic formulation: theory and practice are unified as a disharmony that is the not so secret interior of the philosopher's daydreams.

Notes

Introduction

1. For a similar thesis, see Seth Benardete, *The Argument of the Action* (Chicago: University of Chicago Press, 2000). It should be said in passing that, although I accept the authenticity of the Platonic Second and Seventh Epistles, I do not base any major points of interpretation on them. This is both in order to avoid useless controversy and because the individual dialogue must still speak for itself.

2. Friedrich Nietzsche, *Sämtliche Werke: Kritische Studienausgabe* (Munich: W. de Gruyter, 1980) vol. 6, p. 11.

3. H. G. Gadamer sees the unacceptability of this hypothesis (in its extreme form), but his own view seems to borrow from it. "Surely one must read the whole book as one grand dialectical myth. . . . Here, reading dialectically means relating these utopian demands in each instance to their opposite, in order to find, somewhere in between, what is really meant." See *The Idea of the Good in Platonic-Aristotelian Philosophy*, translated and edited by P. Christopher Smith (New Haven and London: Yale University Press, 1986), pp. 70–71. Would it not have been simpler for Plato simply to defend the "middle" position directly, as does Aristotle in his practical writings? And how do we arrive at the middle? What lies in the middle between the community of women and children and traditional families?

4. A summary of some of Strauss's observations on the dramatic form can be found in *The City and Man* (Chicago: Rand McNally, 1964), p. 56.

5. Strauss's interpretation of the dramatic setting of the *Republic*, especially as developed in unpublished transcripts of graduate seminars held at the University of Chicago, is unusually good, and my brief account draws heavily on his more extensive analysis.

6. Strauss, *The City and Man*, p. 63.
7. *Ibid.*, p. 91. See *Republic* II. 376d4ff. and III. 398a8.
8. *Plato: The* Republic, edited by G. R. F. Ferrari and translated by Tom Griffith (Cambridge: Cambridge University Press, 2000), p. 366.
9. Strauss, *The City and Man*, p. 78.
10. Ferrari and Griffith, p. 349.
11. I note that the division of the manuscript into ten books goes back to antiquity, although no one knows whether Plato himself or a later editor was responsible. I have consulted the translations of Bloom (*The* Republic *of Plato*, translated by Allan Bloom [New York: Basic Books, 1968]) and Griffith. Bloom is more literal, but Griffith is often much clearer. My own translations are usually taken from Bloom, sometimes modified, but sometimes I cite Griffith when Bloom's laudable attempt to stick to Plato's syntax and vocabulary lapses into excessive obscurity.

Chapter One: Cephalus and Polemarchus

1. For a different approach to the theme of descent, see Eva Brann, "The Music of the *Republic*," *St. John's Review* 39, nos. 1 and 2 (1989/90): 1–103.
2. For a more detailed discussion of Glaucon's nature, see my article "The Role of Eros in Plato's *Republic*," reprinted in *The Quarrel between Philosophy and Poetry* (New York and London: Routledge, 1993), pp. 102–18.
3. Jacob Howland points out that "at 527c1–2, Socrates speaks of 'the men in your [Glaucon's] *kallipolis*.'" See his article "The *Republic's* Third Wave and the Paradox of Political Philosophy," *Review of Metaphysics* 51 (March 1998): 640. The city is somehow dependent upon, and is thus partly an accommodation to, the political eros of Glaucon. That the highest reaches of philosophy are beyond his grasp, however, is made clear by Socrates in the discussion of the Ideas, in particular, the Idea of the Good.
4. Cf. Julia Annas, *An Introduction to Plato's* Republic (Oxford: Oxford University Press, 1981), pp. 72–73.
5. *Politics*, book III, chapter 4.
6. Once more I wish to point out that the best interpretation I know of the opening scene is by Leo Strauss, as developed in his unpublished lectures on the *Republic*. I follow him on many details, but my overall reading of the character of Cephalus, and the role played by his definition of justice, is somewhat different from that of Strauss. I also place more emphasis upon the symbolic significance of sexuality and death in the discussion with Cephalus.
7. See *Meno* 88c4–d3 and Monique Dixsaut's essay "Les sens platoniciens de la *phronēsis*," in *Platon et la question de la pensée* (Paris: J. Vrin, 2000), esp. p. 96. Cf. Xenophon, *Memorabilia* IV. 6.8.
8. Bloom and many recent scholars translate *kalon* as "fine." But there is a difference between saying "nobly done" and "fine" that is especially noticeable in contemporary English, and the same can be said for "beautiful," which has lost its connection with nobility. I prefer to retain the original echo.

Chapter Two: Thrasymachus

1. *The* Republic *of Plato*, translated by Allan Bloom (New York: Basic Books, 1968), p. 444.
2. This view is hardly peculiar to Thrasymachus. In the *Nicomachean Ethics*, VI. 1139b14 ff., *technē* is listed as one of the five truth-achieving faculties of the soul; as such, it is distinguished from those faculties that are capable of arriving at falsehoods. Cf. 1140a9–10: *technē* is a disposition concerned with making that reasons truly. This is not to say that the ancients were unaware of the endless perfectibility of technical artifacts and procedures. But this technical perfectibility is limited by the natural end that is served by each art. For example, the end of medicine is health, and the end of shoemaking is shoes. Once these ends are achieved, no further progress is needed. See *Politics* I. 1257b25ff. For a fuller discussion, see my essay "*Technē* and the Origins of Modernity," in *Technology in the Western Political Tradition*, edited by Arthur M. Melzer, Jerry Weinberger, and M. Richard Zinman (Ithaca, N.Y.: Cornell University Press, 1993), pp. 69–84.
3. Cf. Aristotle, *Nicomachean Ethics* V. 1034b5.
4. Angela Hobbs distinguishes between the argument for justice and the praise of (one's own) injustice. See *Plato and the Hero: Courage, Manliness, and the Impersonal Good* (Cambridge: Cambridge University Press, 2000), p. 167. This is sound, but the deeper distinction is between the possession or lack of a *technē* for justice.
5. *Nicomachean Ethics* VIII. 1, 1155a26ff.
6. Cf. Nietzsche's communication to Jacob Burkhardt of 6 January 1889 in *Sämtliche Briefe: Kritische Studienausgabe* (Berlin: Walter de Gruyter, 1986), vol. 8, pp. 577–78.

Chapter Three: Glaucon and Adeimantus

1. Socrates links Adeimantus to austerity at III. 398a8, in connection with the expulsion of poets, who imitate bad as well as good things.

Chapter Four: Paideia I: The Luxurious City

1. On this general point, consult the splendid study by Waller Newell, *Ruling Passion: The Erotics of Statecraft in Platonic Political Philosophy* (Lanham, Md.: Rowman and Littlefield, 2000).
2. See Leon Craig's shamefully neglected book *The War Lover: A Study of Plato's Republic* (Toronto: University of Toronto Press, 1994) for a detailed discussion on the connection between philosophy and war.
3. Angela Hobbs has a good discussion on the various senses of *thumos* in *Plato and the Hero: Courage, Manliness, and the Impersonal Good* (Cambridge: Cambridge University Press, 2000).
4. Hobbs refers to the portrait of Achilles in the *Republic* as *thumos* gone astray, ibid., p. 199.
5. All students of the *Republic* should consult the discussion of mimesis and the two genres of narrative and enactment in Stephen Halliwell, *Aristotle's* Poetics (Chicago: University of Chicago Press, 1998).

Chapter Five: Paideia II: The Purged City

1. Glossary to Ferrari and Griffith, *Plato: The Republic*, edited by G. R. F. Ferrari and translated by Tom Griffith ((Cambridge: Cambridge University Press, 2000), p. 352.
2. See my *Plato's* Sophist: *The Drama between Original and Image* (Carthage reprint, South Bend, Ind.: Saint Augustine's Press, 1999).
3. *Politics* I. 1261a15ff., 1264a26.
4. See Aristotle, *Politics* III. 1.

Chapter Six: Justice

1. This difficulty was first pointed out to me by Leo Strauss.
2. For further discussion, see Bernard Williams, "The Analogy of City and Soul in Plato's *Republic*," in *Plato's* Republic: *Critical Essays*, edited by Richard Kraut (Lanham, Md.: Rowman and Littlefield, 1997), pp. 49–59. Williams is effectively criticized by G. R. F. Ferrari in his *City and Soul in Plato's Republic* (*Lectura Platonis* 2, Macerata: Akademia Verlag/Sankt Augustin, University of Macerata, 2003). The main point of Ferrari's criticism is that the just city is not monolithic (composed exclusively of just citizens, p. 43) and that the relations of parts of the soul and classes of the city are metaphorical, not causal (pp. 60, 99).
3. Williams, "The Analogy of City and Soul," p. 57.
4. This passage militates against Ferrari's claim that the parts of the soul do not stand in a causal relation to the parts of the city.
5. Hobbs, p. 25, points out that at IX. 586c–d, the life in which the thumoeidetic element is brought to its fulfillment is said to be "without reason or sense" (*Plato and the Hero: Courage, Manliness, and the Impersonal Good* [Cambridge: Cambridge University Press, 2000]), p. 25. This passage seems to be at odds with the one we are now studying. But the later passage is referring to the complete corruption of *thumos* whereas the earlier passage presents the normal function of the soul. We must, however, remember that "normal" includes a range of responses, many of which may be "natural" but are not for that reason good or beneficial. Furthermore, the problem of the "rational" component of *thumos* is already visible in the earlier passage, as I have argued above.
6. Strauss, *The City and Man* (Chicago: Rand McNally, 1964), p. 115.
7. *Ibid.*, p. 116.

Chapter Seven: The Female Drama

1. For further discussion of paradigms, see my *Plato's* Statesman: *The Web of Politics* (New Haven: Yale University Press: 1995), chapter 5.
2. *Politics* II, 1262a33.
3. Cf. III. 398a1ff.

Chapter Eight: Possibility

1. For further discussion, see my *Plato's* Statesman: *The Web of Politics* (New Haven: Yale University Press, 1995).

2. Bloom translates "what justice is like," but this could imply that justice resembles something other than itself (*The* Republic *of Plato*, translated by Allan Bloom [New York: Basic Books, 1968] p. 152). I follow Griffith here (*Plato: The* Republic, edited by G. R. F. Ferrari and translated by Tom Griffith [Cambridge: Cambridge University Press, 2000]).

3. Cf. Monique Dixsaut, *Platon et la question de la pensée* (Paris: J. Vrin, 2000), pp. 64f., and Klaus Oehler, *Die Lehre vom Noetischen und Dianoetischen Denken bei Platon und Aristoteles* (Munich: C. H. Beck, 1962) pp. 104, 114f.

4. In his discussion of this passage, Bloom is right to emphasize that philosophy and politics do not come together by nature but must be forced to do so.

5. See Griffith, note 38. His translation is clearer in this passage than Bloom's.

6. I use "object" in its everyday sense of anything to which we do something or may refer.

7. Cf. Leo Strauss, *The City and Man* (Chicago: Rand McNally, 1964), p. 119.

Chapter Nine: The Philosophical Nature

1. This will have to be reconsidered when we reach 500d4–8.

2. *Ousia* is often translated by Aristotle scholars as "substance," which is the Latinate form of *hupokeimenon* in Greek. For our purposes we do not need to pursue further the ambiguities of this terminology.

3. *Nicomachean Ethics* II. 7.6.

4. Strauss, *The City and Man* (Chicago: Rand McNally, 1964), pp. 123–24.

5. From now on, whenever "the Good" is capitalized, it will refer to what is also called "the Idea of the Good."

Chapter Ten: The Good, the Divided Line, and the Cave

1. I agree with the assertion of H. G. Gadamer that the words *idea* and *eidos* were undeniably interchangeable in the Greek of Plato's time "and in the language use of the philosophers also." However, he correctly notes that Plato never says *eidos tou agathou* and then goes on to say that "*Eidos* always refers only to the object" whereas *idea*, which can also designate "object," gives greater emphasis to the viewing of something than to how something looks. See *The Idea of the Good in Platonic-Aristotelian Philosophy*, translated and edited by P. Christopher Smith (New Haven: Yale University Press, 1986), pp. 27–28. See also M. Dixsaut, *Platon et la question de la pensée* (Paris: J. Vrin, 2000), pp. 126–27, for whom *idea* in the *Republic* can mean either *eidos* (form) or (as in the case of the Good), "puissance de liaison." Dixsaut is right in trying to understand the nondeterminate nature of the Good, but in a general statement about the sense of *eidos* and *idea*, I think it is safest to start with their near synonymity. Socrates brings out the problem by sometimes speaking of the *idea* of the Good and sometimes just of "the Good."

2. Socrates anticipates the Spinozist maxim that to know is to know that one knows.

3. For further discussion, see my *The Question of Being* (South Bend, Ind.: Saint Augustine's Press, 2002) and *Metaphysics in Ordinary Language* (New Haven: Yale University Press, 1999). I shall take up the theme of light and darkness at greater length when I come to the allegory of the cave.

4. Something of this sort seems to happen in Book Ten, during the discussion of the quarrel between philosophy and poetry. I will discuss this in the appropriate place.

5. As usual, I translate *idea* with a capital *I* whenever the reference is to a Platonic Idea.

6. See also Pierre Aubenque, "De l'égalité des segments intermédiaires dans la ligne de la *République*," in *Sophiēs Maiētores* (Paris: Institut d'Etudes Augustiniennes, 1992). Aubenque takes the equality of segment *c* and *e* (in his notation, *b* and *c*) to refer to the mediation of mathematical entities between the Ideas and the domain of genesis, and so to weaken the status of *chōrismos* in Plato. Aubenque's analysis equates *pistis* and *dianoia* on the ground that they are mathematically interchangeable (p. 42) . I find this implausible, much though I agree with his rejection of separation between the intelligible and the sensuous.

7. These considerations seem to give support to the thesis of Aubenque, ibid.

8. Socrates refers exclusively to male philosophers and residents of the cave. This certainly has to do with the absence of any reference to sex or to human reproduction.

9. See Leo Strauss, *The City and Man* (Chicago: Rand McNally, 1964), p. 125. Strauss says flatly that "the city can be identified with the Cave," but his analysis ignores the details of the image that weaken the identification. For a more elaborate presentation of the view that the city is "nothing but shadows" (that is, represented by the cave), see Seth Benardete, *Socrates' Second Sailing* (Chicago: University of Chicago Press, 1989), p. 175.

10. Cf. IV. 444b4–5.

11. Benardete, *Socrates' Second Sailing*, p. 175.

12. For a more detailed analysis of the allegory of the cave, as well as of the reading of that passage by Martin Heidegger, see my Gilson Lectures, forthcoming from Presses Universitaires de France.

13. *Elpis* is also used at II. 369a8 to refer to the possible utility of the analogy between the city and the soul.

14. Those who desire a more elaborate discussion of Greek number theory than is here appropriate should consult Jacob Klein, *Greek Mathematical Thought and the Origins of Algebra*, translated by Eva Brann (Cambridge, Mass.: MIT Press, 1968). See also Julia Annas, *Aristotle's* Metaphysics, *Books M and N* (Oxford: Clarendon Press, 1976).

15. This side of philosophy is well captured by Leon Craig in *The War Lover* (Toronto: University of Toronto Press, 1994).

16. For a more elaborate discussion of this point, see my *Plato's* Sophist: *The Drama of Original and Image* (New Haven: Yale University Press, 1983; reprinted Notre Dame, Ind.: St. Augustine Press, 1999).

17. See Jacob Howland, "The *Republic's* Third Wave and the Paradox of Political Philosophy," *Review of Metaphysics* 51 (March 1998): 640.

18. See Ferrari and Griffith, *Plato: The* Republic, edited by G. R. F. Griffith and translated by Tom Griffith (Cambridge: Cambridge University Press, 2000), p. 244, n. 18, for a list of the passages in which these natures were previously described.

Chapter Eleven: Political Decay

1. David Roochnik develops the pro-diversity thesis in considerable detail in his *Beautiful City: The Dialectical Character of Plato's* Republic (Ithaca, N.Y.: Cornell University Press, 2003).

2. For an influential version of this argument, see Benjamin Constant, "The Liberty of the Ancients Compared with that of the Moderns," in *Constant: Political Writings*, translated and edited by Biancamaria Fontana (Cambridge: Cambridge University Press, 1988), esp. page 317.

3. On this point, see Roochnik, *Beautiful City*, for a detailed "dialectical" defense.

4. *Jenseits von Gut und Böse*, in *Sämtliche Werke: Kritische Studienausgabe*, edited by Giorgio Colli and Mazzino Montinari (Berlin: Walter de Gruyter, 1980), vol. 5, p. 81.

Chapter Twelve: Happiness and Pleasure

1. It would take us too far from our own investigation to do more than note the new fashion in scholarship that seeks to minimize the difference in the domain of ethics between Aristotle and Kant.

2. This problem was made famous in the secondary literature by Bernard Williams, "The Analogy of City and Soul in Plato's *Republic*," in *Plato's Republic: Critical Essays*, edited by Richard Kraut (Lanham, Md.: Rowman and Littlefield, 1997), pp. 49–59.

See the discussion in Julia Annas, *Introduction to Plato's* Republic (Oxford: Oxford University Press, 1981), pp. 142ff.

Chapter Thirteen: The Quarrel between Philosophy and Poetry

1. Cf. Julia Annas, *Introduction to Plato's* Republic (Oxford: Oxford University Press, 1981), pp. 16ff.

2. I remind the reader that in book three at 398a some mimetic poets are excluded from the expulsion.

3. Annas, *Introduction*, pp. 223–24; cf. p. 210.

4. See my Gilson Lectures, Lecture Two ("The Idea of the Bed"), forthcoming from Presses Universitaires de France.

5. Cf. Monique Dixsaut, *Platon et la question de la pensée* (Paris: J. Vrin, 2000), p. 127. In the *Republic*, she says, *idéa* replaces *eidos* when, as in the case of the Good, it is not possible to speak of a determinate form. *Idéa* in these cases means "puissance de liaison" of the visible (that is, intelligible) to the organ of vision (that is, the intellect). From my standpoint, this would be a subcase of the Idea as function or power ("puissance").

Chapter Fourteen: The Immortal Soul

1. Julia Annas, *Introduction to Plato's* Republic (Oxford: Oxford University Press, 1981), p. 335.

2. Sith Benardete, *Socrates' Second Sailing* (Chicago: University of Chicago Press, 1989), p. 229.

Index

Abortion, 191
Achilles, 97, 100, 368, 382
Actors, 102
Actual city: blueprint for, 189; and cave, 270, 277; and division of labor, 146–147, 182; growth of, 141; and happiness, 133; human behavior in, 147; and just city, 99; justice in, 95, 97, 104, 134, 169; models of, 138, 317; and philosophers, 9, 129, 230, 234, 241, 242, 281, 291, 348, 351, 391; and poetry, 353, 375; and political ambition, 62; regimes in, 306; rulers of, 53, 144, 208–209, 351; and speech, 351; and transformation to good city, 208; weaknesses of, 146, 235
Adeimantus. *See* Glaucon and Adeimantus; Justice
Aeschylus, 67, 117
Agathon, 103
Alcibiades, 99, 165, 237–238, 239
"Alcinous section" of *Odyssey*, 382

Alexander the Great, 237
Analysis of *Republic*, method of, 1–2
Anarchy, 321–322, 323
Anger, 155, 158
Animals, breeding of, 187
Annas, Julia, 386
Apollo: and music, 107; and philosophy, 259; and rituals, 20, 100, 139–140, 159, 387
Aptitude, 175, 182
Ardiaeus, 383
Aretē (excellence), 58–59
Argument from opposites, 360
Aristocracy, 163, 306–307, 309, 312, 334
Aristocracy of merit, 314
Aristophanes, 103, 171, 186, 211
Aristotle: on art, 47, 116–117, 362; on classes in city life, 116–117, 124; definition of political life of, 103; and democracies, 5, 235, 314; and essence, 230; on family, 179; and fanaticism,

Aristotle (*continued*)
  13; on friendship, 51, 162; and gentlemen, 393; on good, 62; on happiness, 281, 293, 345; and Ideas, 168, 207, 228; on justice, 349; magnificence in, 231; nature of, 237; and negation, 218; on philosopher as king, 226; and philosophers, 167, 246, 345, 393; and philosophy, 6, 299; Plato compared, 142–143; and pleasure, 340; on political dangers of harbors, 13; and practical intelligence, 292; and practical virtue, 228, 298; and principle of noncontradiction, 152; and prudence, 235; on sensory perception, 213, 215; and separation thesis, 225; Socrates compared, 9; and technical knowledge and practical judgment, 45, 49; on training, 85; on unity and being, 286; on virtue, 23. *See also specific titles of works*

Arithmetic and calculation. *See* Mathematics

Army, 82–83

Art: and arithmetic and calculation, 285; and character, 110; classification of, 33; genuine, 31; and hypotheses, 266; and moneymaking, 52; musical man, 55–56; ontological, 363–365; and organized research, 293–294; and philosophy, 240; and progress, 116–117; and science, 293–294; view of, 46–48

Artifacts: Ideas of, 355, 366–367; making and using, 371; producing, 45, 46–47, 48, 92

Arts and crafts. *See* Craftsmen and artisans

Asclepius and Asclepiads, 116–117

Astronomy, 293, 294

"Atheism" of philosophers, 68

Athenian Stranger, 173, 394–395

Athens, 20, 134, 169

Athletes, 41. *See also* Gymnastics

Attica, 151

Audience capacities, 3, 12, 167

Austerity, 7–8, 74–75, 79–80, 88, 99, 107, 165. *See also* Glaucon and Adeimantus

Autonomy, 111

Auxiliaries, soldiers: and arithmetic and calculation, 290, 291; brotherhood of, 127; burial and commemoration of, 20, 100, 387; and calculation, 290; communal life of, 129; and community of women and children, 27, 167–168; conduct after battle of, 196; and courage, 143; and death, 96–97; education of, 87–90, 95–96, 123–124, 126, 129, 284, 285, 395; erotic nature of, 187; expelling all over age ten, 7; and factions, 307; and gods, 139; and happiness, 280; and helpers, 125–126; and honoring gods, 95; and Ideas, 224, 228, 391; and laughter, 98; life of, 194; and myth of Er, 382; nature of, 249; and noble dog, 83–86; philosopher-kings versus, 126; and philosophers, 392, 395; and poetry, 354; and revolution, 390; role of, 38, 131, 132, 228, 391, 395, 396; and sexual relations, 189–190; soul of, 151; and spiritedness, 149, 150; and three parts of soul, 70; and timocracy, 309; treatment of citizens and enemies by, 197; women as, 186; work of, 94–95. *See also* Guardians

Barbarians and Greeks compared, 196–197

Beautiful and good things, 216, 255–258, 260

Beautiful body, 220–221

Beautiful city: and aristocracies, 306, 307, 312; and Book One, 163; and decay in customs of marriage and breeding, 7; and democracies, 320; enemies of, 134, 135; and factions, 308; and family, 190; founding of, 21, 50, 54, 148, 245–246, 308; and geometry, 293; and guardians, 34; and happiness, 348, 374; homosexual love in,

195; Idea of, 207; justice in, 161, 374; medicine and judging in, 120; and mimesis, 369; model of, 135; philosophers in, 166; and philosophy, 7, 354; and poetry, 210, 353–354, 381; possibility of, 351; purging luxury from, 116; and regulating sexual eros, 328; soldiers in, 197; and speech, 352, 357; technical progress in, 294; use of term for, 306

Beauty, 221, 372

Bed. See Idea of the bed

Being, 217–219, 223, 230, 262, 267, 297

Being-together *(sunousia)*, 360

Belief, 220–223, 357

Benardete, Seth, 273, 387

Bendis, 13, 19–20

Best city: construction of, 141, 306; decline from, 308; defined, 188, 193; human behavior in, 147; and monarchy, 334; paradigm for, 351; revolution for, 390; second-best, 395

Bewitchery, 125

Biblical hermeneutics, 93

Birds, breeding of, 187

Birth, 127, 178

Bloodlines and citizenship, 135

Bloom, Allan: on altered Homer passage, 117; on Aristophanes, 171; and attributes of character, 151; and body, limits on care of, 117; and challenging conventional opinion, 144; and combination of letters, 113; and contracts, 34; and *dogma*, 125; and existence and being, 261; on heroes as golden class, 195; and *kreittôn*, 40; on minding one's own business, 172; and myth of Er, 381, 391; on plane, 348; on sacred marriage of Zeus and Hera, 187; and stargazing, 235; and sun's image, 258–259; and writings, 112

Brainwashing, 128, 143, 183

Bravery. See Courage

Breeding. See Sexual reproduction

Brotherhood of soldiers, 127

Builders *(oikistai)*, 101

Burial and commemoration of soldiers, 20, 100, 387

Business dealings with tradesman and artisans, 136

Callias, 51

Callicles, 38, 39, 211

Cave, allegory of: and ascent to Platonic Ideas, 11; and education of philosopher, 269–283, 296, 299, 300, 305; as psychological, 127; and subnatural, 81; and theme of descent, 19, 20; and wisdom, 219

Censorship: of guardians' opinions, 125; of myths, 87–88; and noble and medicinal lies, 95; of poets, 28, 93–94, 96, 99

Cephalus and Polemarchus, 13, 14, 15, 19–37

Character, 26, 50–51, 110

Characters in *Republic*, identity of, 12–15

Charity, principle of, 69, 113

Charmides, 13

Charondas, 370

Children: acknowledgment of, 75; education of, 87–89; expelling all over age ten from city, 21, 246, 301, 391; and family, 178–179; games of young boys, well-ordering of, 136; infanticide, 190–191; limited number of, 73, 74; and myths, 87–89; production of, 73, 74, 128; rearing of, 168, 188, 190, 301; removal from parents, 135, 239; and spiritedness, 159; stories and songs for, 87–88; and war, 195. *See also* Community of women and children

Citizens, 27, 71, 124, 135, 184

City: and allegory of cave, 269–270, 271–272; basic elements, 73; and changing human nature, 97; and civil liberties, 319; classes in, 146, 147, 151–152, 159, 189, 192, 396; defense

City (*continued*)
of, 166; development of, 71–74, 79; and division of labor, 73; and eros, 26; expelling all over age ten from, 21, 246, 301, 391; and family, 179, 210; first, 73, 79–80; Greek versus barbarian, 196–197; and happiness, 143, 280; healthy, 75–76; and justice, 32, 87, 143; love of, 125; models of, 186, 192; neediest, 71–74, 75, 79, 82, 108; of philosopher-kings, 74, 79; of pigs, 75, 80, 81, 94, 108; as Platonic Idea, 71; and poetry, 101–102; power versus laws in, 43; practical difficulties of, 137; preservation of, 134–135, 137; reason for existence of, 71; roles in, 155, 183; second, 80; and selfishness, 73; and self-love, 125; sex and stability of, 128; as single human being, 193; size of, 134–136; of slaves, 183; and Socratic tyranny, 81; and soul, 22–23; in speech, 208; and warriors, 94; wealthy, 134; and women, 178, 182. *See also specific type (e.g., Actual city, Just city)*

City and soul, analogy of: and allegory of cave, 271–272, 280; and courage, 143–144; criticism of, 190, 271–272, 393–396; distinguishing soul from city, 155–156; and happiness, 131, 136, 278, 333; and harmony, 156–157; and injustice, 57; just city, 71, 99, 103, 146, 148, 245, 396; and justice, 69–71, 95, 99, 148–152; justice in, 22–23; ordering of parts of, 131; properties and functions of, 86; purpose of, 329, 330; as reflection of sickness in, 10; and temperance, 122; tripartite division of, 103, 148–152, 154, 156–157, 167, 308, 379, 394–395, 396

Civil liberties, 319. *See also* Freedom of speech

Class: Aristotle on, 116–117, 124; breeding between, 128; and children, 135; in city, 146, 147, 149, 151–152, 159, 189, 192, 240–241, 396; deviations within, 189; and family, 178, 179; love for, 179; stasis in, 189; types of, 396. *See also specific class*

Cleitophon, 44

Cleon, 316

Comedies and tragedies, 98, 102–103, 172, 346, 368

Community, 74, 360

Community of women and children: avoiding discussion of, 21, 137, 142; demand for clarification of, 164, 165, 305; difficulties with, 166; and guardians, 135, 167–168, 184–192, 197; and just city, 21; organization of, 191–193; and political problem of eros, 210, 211; possibility of, 197; procedure for, 184, 186; and regulation of sex, 135; and wished-for-city, 28

Compelling to be just, 63

Compounds (*ta suntheta*), 92

Concepts, 256, 359

Conceptual analysis. *See* Diaeresis

Contracts (*sumbolaia*), 34

Contrary opinions, 372, 373

Conventional morality, 67, 88

Cooking. *See* Food

Copy versus original, 70–71

"Correct" behavior, 31

Corruption: within democracies, 241; and philosophers, 247–248; and philosophical nature, 237, 241–242, 279; and poets, 67–68

Cosmos, 262, 294, 356, 383–384

Courage: and city, 143–145; and education, 109; and gentleness, 122; and guardian-soldiers, 95–97, 109, 143; and letters, 111–112; in members of all classes, 144; and nature of warrior, 82–86; and noble lie, 99; political, 144; political intelligence versus, 137; and spiritedness, 232; and temperance, 122, 160, 248; and wisdom, 86

Course of study for philosopher-kings, 299–301

Courtesans, 80
Craftsmen and artisans: ancestor of, 240; and arts, 46–47, 82; classification of professions as, 40; and description of founding of city, 89; and Idea, 362; and mimesis, 362–368; and musicians and gymnasts, 123; ruler as, 44–45; work of, 138. *See also* Moneymaking; Workers
Cretans, 172
Critias, 13, 14
Cultivation and tillage, 80
Cyclical nature of life, 6

Damon, 110, 111, 136, 294
Dasein, 30
Dead bodies, disregard of dignity of, 100
Death: fear of, 96–97, 99; and immortality, 23; interest in, 381; and metaphor of descent, 127; and old age, 24–25, 29; and religious tradition, 195; and self-love, 27. *See also* Er, myth of
Debts, paying, 30
Decadence, 4, 6, 7
Decency and order, 29–30
Definitions versus examples, 205
Democracy: Aristotle on, 5, 235, 314; and beautiful city, 320; and corruption, 241; denunciation of, 14, 235; regime of, 306, 312–323, 327; Strauss on, 14; treason against, 15; tyrant springing from, 313, 321
Demons, 100, 195
Demotic virtues. *See* Virtue
Derrida, Jacques, 213
Descent, theme of, 19, 20, 22, 127, 283, 382
Desire: control of, 63–64, 150, 152–155; and money-loving, 335; multiplication of, 82; necessary and unnecessary, 320, 325–327; nondesire versus, 152; to rule, 81; and soul, 335, 339; spiritedness compared to, 157; and workers, 149. *See also* Moneymaking
Diaeresis, 175–178, 181, 396

Dialectic: and allegory of cave, 273, 275, 282; and city, 7; and diaeresis, 175–178, 181, 396; and force, 51; hypotheses in, 265–266, 268; and justice, 30; and legislation, 138; master-slave, 163, 273; and mathematics, 28, 243, 264, 266, 268, 291; nature of, 291; and *noçsis*, 265; and philosopher-kings, 235; and philosophy, 291, 295–296, 299–300; and Platonic Ideas, 3, 45, 165, 221, 264, 392; and politics and philosophy, 229
Dialogues, narrative and performed, 11
Dianoia, 207, 222, 266, 296, 297
Diotima, 72
Discursive intelligence, 216–217, 221–222
Disputations and eristical arguments, 175–177, 181
Diversity, 354, 379
Divided line, 3, 8, 262–267, 269, 270–271, 275, 297
Division of labor (one man, one art): and actual city, 146–147, 182; and army, 83; and auxiliaries, soldiers, 124, 126, 137; basis of, 72; and city, 73, 137, 145; and happiness, 131–132; and imitation, 102–103; and minding one's own business, 71, 161; and soul, 149; and state of nature, 82
Do good to friends and harm to enemies: and defining justice, 31, 33, 34–37, 60–61, 164, 169, 172; and guardians, 106; and partial justice, 58; and philosophy, 85–86; and slavery, 196; and soldiers, 84; and unjust man, 66; and use of strength, 42
Do good to one friend while harming another friend, 60–61
Doctrine of Ideas. *See* Ideas, doctrine of
Dog. *See* Noble dog
Dogma, 125
Dogma and ideology, 355
Dramatis personae. *See* Characters in *Republic*, identity of

Dreaming, 217, 362
Drones, 322–323
Dueling, 194
Dunamis, 219
Dye of obedience, 144

Earned wealth, 26, 27
Eating. *See* Food
Ecclesiazusae (Aristophanes), 171
Education: and allegory of cave, 278; arguments and young students, 300; and falsehoods, 88; in fevered city, 94; gymnastics preparation, 159; of highest class, 40; of judges, 120; musical, 114, 159; of philosophers, 212, 249, 255–301; and philosophical nature, 248; and temperance, 160; of women, 171, 172, 178, 182–183, 184. *See also* Cave, allegory of; Education of guardians; Gymnastics; Music education
Education of guardians: and fear of death, 96–97; and freedom, 104; and honoring gods and ancestors, 95–96; and mathematics, 28; and noble lies, 87–94, 98–100; training for occupation of, 85; and women, 171, 172, 178, 182–183, 184. *See also* Gymnastics; Music education
Eidos, 92, 223, 255
Eleatic Stranger, 30, 248, 394
Emancipation of female. *See* Women
Epistemological images, 269
Epithumetic or appetitive part of soul, 22, 40, 231, 339. *See also* Desire
Equity, 30
Er, myth of, 11, 19, 65, 68, 356–357, 380, 381–387
Eristical arguments. *See* Disputations and eristical arguments
Eros: and cleverness and poverty, 71; and detachment from politics, 210; and hedonism, 118; and impossibility of full satisfaction, 81–82; and lying, 187–188; and music, 114–115; and pleasure, types of, 339; political and private, 68; praise and denunciation of, 25–26, 165; religious control of, 187–189; and *thumos* (spiritedness), 21, 25; as tyrant, 25
Erotic love of beautiful, 115
Erotic necessity, 186–187
Erotic soul and music education, 122
Eudaimonism, 349
Euripides, 117
Euthydemus, 376
Everyday life: activities of, 293–294; and Platonic Ideas, 205–206
Evil, 277, 378
Examples, 203, 204–205, 206
Excessive care of body, 117
Excessive cruelty, 100
Existence and being, 261–262. *See also* Divided line
Expelling all over age ten from city, 246, 301, 391
Extreme lover, characteristics of, 211–212

Factionalism, 284–285
Factions, 307–309, 379
False city, 80, 94
False images *(fantasma),* 92–93
False myths, 88
False pleasures, 341
Falsehoods, 5; and education, 88, 89. *See also* Noble and medicinal lies
Familiarity, 85, 86, 109
Family: abolishment of, 25, 127, 142, 180, 183, 210, 390; city substituted for, 179, 210; elimination in guardian class, 178; and private life, 24. *See also* Children; Community of women and children; Women
Fanaticism, 13
Farmers. *See* Workers
Father, role of, 127
Females. *See* Motherhood; Women
Ferrari, G.R.F., 15, 381, 384
Fevered city, 94, 241. *See also* Luxurious city *(truphôsan)*

Fierce drones, 322–323
Fierceness and gentleness, 85, 109, 123, 145, 150, 160, 172
Fine arts, 80. *See also* Art
Fingers, comparison of, 288–290
Flute, 123
Food: cooked food *(opson)*, 31, 75; cooking, 16, 31–33; meat eating, 32–33, 41, 74, 75, 80; regulation of food and drink, 159–160; with relishes, 32–33, 74, 75, 80, 116, 118, 320, 345; and sex, 116; simplicity of, 72
Force, 50–51, 57, 239, 390, 391
Foreign relations, 42–43
Forms: of beds, 366; desire for pure, 25, 168; and dialectic, 265–266; and *eidos*, 216; of entity, 180; imperfect images of, 219; justice, 176; and language, 149; model *(paradeigma)*, 176; of virtues, 114, 176
Founding fathers: and construction of city, 110; and doctrine of Ideas, 391; and education of guardians, 123, 144; and justice, 161; and noble lie, 88, 89, 98, 188; and regulating sexual conduct, 187. *See also* Philosopher-kings
Four kinds or degrees of being, 267–268
Four virtues of soul, 146, 249–250
Frankness, 3, 6, 13, 241, 283, 390
Freedom, 111, 350; and happiness, 318
Freedom of speech, 68, 104, 111
Freud, Sigmund, 326
Friedländer, Paul, 11
Friendship: among members of same people, 196; in city context, 74; definition of, 39; and familiarity, 85, 86; and family, 24; and force, 51; and justice, 51; mastery versus, 162; *philia*, 339; and temperance, 160; and Thrasymachus, 50. *See also* Do good to friends and harm to enemies
Future-oriented nature of human life, 188

Gadamer, H.G., 11
Gedankenexperiment, 169
Genesis, 259, 262, 263, 267, 278–279, 286, 345, 359
Genuine pleasures, 337
Geometry, 292–293
Glaucon and Adeimantus, 12–13, 14–15, 60–76
Gods: and education, 87, 95; existence of, 68; and false images *(fantasma)*, 92–93; as gardener who grows Ideas, 276, 359, 367, 371, 381; and good, 90–91, 95; guardians' beliefs in, 95; immortality, 380–381; injustice of, 66; intemperance, 100; and justice, 101, 380; and lies, 92–93, 98; mistreatment of parents by, 88–89; and myths, 87–89, 90; nature of, 90–91; playthings of, 173; plural gods, 96, 97, 139; and poetry, 91, 353–354; singing of, 74; singular god, shift to, 90–93, 139; Socrates's attitude toward, 20; and temperance, 94, 97; as unchanging and eternally truthful, 93; unity, goodness, and truthfulness, 93–94; as unjust, 66; and war, 88–89. *See also specific god or goddess*
Good: and allegory of cave, 271, 273; ascent to, 19, 279; and audience, 3; and beautiful things, 216, 255–258, 260; beneficial nature of, 34; beyond being, 262, 278; distinguishing among types of, 256; function of, 267; and generation of ideas, 267; and geometry, 292; and gods, 90–91; illumination by, 276–277; and immortality, 377–378; injustice and three goods, 66; and justice, 40; kinds of, 61–62; longer way to study, 250–254; and mathematics, 266, 267–268; self-interest, 54; and sun, 3, 258–262, 268–269; and unhappiness, 280; and utility, 33–34. *See also* Do good to friends and harm to enemies; Good city
Good character, 110

Good city, 141, 207, 209, 306
Good counsel (euboulia), 142, 143, 144, 159
Good life, examination of, 23, 95, 97
Good man, 105
Goodness. See Good
Gorgias, 38, 39, 51, 211
Governing. See Philosopher-kings; Rulers; Ruling
Grammar and art of ruling, 46
Grief, 373–374
Griffith, Tom: and analysis of pleasure and pain, 343; and auxiliaries, 196; and being and existence, 261; and divided line, 266–267; and Glaucon, 21; and idea, 259; and image of sun, 258–259; and laughter, 262; and myth of Er, 381; and necessity, 384; and power of knowledge, 220; and principle of degrees of being, 345; and reasoned argument, 243; and words, 113
Guardians: censorship of, 125; and demotic virtues, 268; and desire, 65; and dye of obedience, 144; and family, 178–179; female, 172; fierceness and gentleness of, 123–124; and founding of city, 21; and gymnastics, 115–116; and happiness, 23, 129–130, 280; and imitation, 102, 104–105, 110–111; impure children of, 307–308; and just city, 4, 291, 392; and justice, 34–35, 106; and male drama, 172; marriage of, 187–189; message to, 8; and music, 109–115; need for, 34–35; and noble dog, 83–86, 172; and philosophy, 167–168; and physicians and judges, 40, 121–122; and poetry, 118, 354; as prisoners, 195; and prudent promiscuity, 184; requirements for, 248; response to assaults or insults, 194; and rich cities, 134; role of, 131–132, 137, 195; and rulers, 124–126, 355; and sexual relations, 27, 116, 180, 187–190, 191; shortcomings of, 138; skill of, 142; soul of properly educated, 122–123; and temperance, 122; and timocracy, 309; types of, 83–86, 228, 249; and women, 182–183, 186. See also Auxiliaries, soldiers; Education of guardians
Guardian-soldiers. See Auxiliaries, soldiers
Gyges, ring of. See Ring of Gyges
Gymnastics: diet and drunkenness controlled by, 159, 160; and dye of obedience, 144; and educated soul, 120–122, 145; for guardian's education along with music, 87, 115–116, 122, 160, 183, 279, 294, 395; liking for end product of, 62; music considered primary to, 124, 136; for philosopher's education, 94, 299; reason for, 123; and women, 172, 186

Habits and exercises, 279
Hades, 11, 19, 96, 382
Happiness, 129–132; Aristotle on, 281, 293, 345; and auxiliaries, 280; and city, 143, 280; and freedom, 318; and guardians, 23, 129–130, 280; individual, 280–281; and just city, 55; and just or unjust man, 23, 58, 62, 70–71, 100, 136, 207, 304, 328–329, 345, 394; personal, 183–184, 395; and philosophers, 227, 280; and philosophical justice, 278; and pleasure, 333–351; and self-consciousness, 329–330; and transition from private, 55; and working class, 183
Harmonics, 294
Harmony: and disharmony, 130–131; and justice, 347; and rhythm, 105–106, 107; of soul, 132
Healing, 157, 163
Health and sickness: and analogy of justice, 162; soul, sickness of, 162; and unhappiness, 131; and work, 117, 118
Healthy city, 75–76, 79
Hearing, 213. See also Sensory perception

Hector, mourning of Priam for, 97
Hegel, Georg Wilhelm Friedrich, 212, 260, 313, 350, 396
Heidegger, Martin: and being, 260; and *Dasein*, 30; and dramatic form, 11; and future-oriented nature of human life, 188; and historicity, 361; and politics, 143, 229, 238; and sense perception, 213
Hera and Zeus, sacred marriage of, 187
Heraclitus, 209
Hermeneutical problem, 4, 55, 393
Herodicus, 116
Herodotus, 386
Heroes, 100, 195
Hesiod, 67, 88, 96, 195, 356, 397
Heterosexual love, 210
Hobbes, Thomas, 39, 41
Holiness and marriage, 187
Homer: criticism of, 67, 357–358, 375, 386; and descent into Hades, 382; and false myths, 88; and gods, 20; and heroes, 194, 374; and human nature, 3–4; on justice, 35; and love of glory, 386; and making human beings divine, 247; on medical practice, 117–118; and Muses, 307; and nuptial number, 307; and one man, one art, 103; respect for, 357; and spiritedness, 159; and style or diction, 101; and tragedies, 368; and tragedy, 368; and training, 116; and "unquenchable laughter of the gods," 175; warrior-aristocracies in, 309; wisdom of, 365
"Homer's army," 361
Homoiotēs, 70–71
Homosexual relations, 75, 195, 210–211
Honor, 66, 99, 339, 340, 347
Horsemanship, 47
Horses, image on *Phaedrus*, 394
Housing, 72, 186
Human nature, 3–4, 97
Hunger and thirst, 153, 344–346
Husserl, Edmund, 213
Hypotheses, 265, 266

Idea of beauty. *See* Beautiful and good things
Idea of human soul. *See* Soul
Idea of Justice, 63
Idea of justice. *See* Justice
Idea of man, 365–366
Idea of the bed, 355–356, 361–368
Idea of the Good. *See* Good
Ideas *(noēmata)*, 207
Ideas, doctrine of: and being, 219, 359–360; disagreement over, 284–285; knowledge of, 220–222; as laughable, 224; as myth, 360; and myth of Er, 11; and politics, 268, 391; problems with, 175–176; purpose of, 359; Socrates's belief in, 222; and speech, 208; and statutes, 65; terminology of, 206, 213–214; on truth of, 3; understanding of, 206–207, 255–258; and unearthly character of philosophy, 389. *See also* Platonic Ideas; *specific types (e.g., Good)*
Ideas of artifacts. *See* Artifacts
Ideology, 6, 9, 20–21, 236, 355, 389, 390, 391, 392
Ignorance, 85, 218–219
Iliad, 101
Illusory pleasure and pains, 341, 342–343
Images: comment on terminology of, 269–276; false images *(fantasma)*, 92–93; ontological images, 269, 363–365; of pleasure, 348–349; of ship, 234–235
Imitation, 104–105, 110–111. *See also* Mimesis
Imitator, 101–103
Immortality, 23, 27, 377–388
Incest, 25, 88, 179, 191
Individual soul, 22–23
Infanticide, 190–191
Inherited wealth, 26, 27
Injustice, 54–57; and analogy of city and soul, 57; and anger, 157–158, 164; attraction of, 164; and happiness, 70–71; and just city, 120, 122, 301; and

414   Index

Injustice (*continued*)
    laws, 64; perceiving, 158; and physicians, 33; pleasure, 334; portrait of perfect injustice, 65–67, 349; praise of, 49–50; as profitable, 54–55; punishment for, 29; rebellion of soul, 161; and soul, 161, 379–380; and superiority of justice, 61, 63; and temperance, 67; and three goods, 66; and women, 181. *See also* Just and unjust man; Thrasymachus
Intellect and desire, 153–154
Intelligence, 83, 85, 157–158, 159, 242–243, 278–279
Intelligible domain, 156, 206, 263–264, 275, 296. *See also* Divided line
Intemperance, 31, 67, 74, 100, 107, 121
Interest, 43–44
Intuition, 221, 222, 392
Isomorphism, 69, 148, 286

Judges, 119–123; appointing, 136; education of, 120; and guardians, 116, 121–122; in lawsuits, 146–147; physicians, connection with, 21; of souls in myth of Er, 383–384
Just, beautiful, and good, 216–217
Just and unjust man: and artists, 31–32; and better live for human beings, 280, 282; and claiming more, 55; concealed just man, 66; and happiness, 23, 58, 62, 70–71, 100, 136, 207, 304, 328–329, 345, 394; and harming enemies, 36; no just persons, 65; paradigm of, 217; and pleasure, 347; portrait as statues, 65–67; and praise of unjust life, 64; and punishment, 383; and strong, 54
Just city: analysis of, 2; and anti-Platonists, 6; and aristocracy, 306, 307; armaments in, 110; and audience capacities, 167; audience for, 12; auxiliaries in, 38, 197; and better lives in, 58; of cave, image of, 272; and class, 82, 240; cleansing of, 246; and community of women and children, 21; and compelling to be just, 63; constructing, 5, 30, 64, 95, 111, 166, 317; and cooking example, 32–33; erotic structure of, 165; expelling all over age ten from, 140; and factionalism, 284; and family, 179; founding of, 7, 10, 12, 15, 63, 68, 70, 124, 391; good in, 91; and guardians, 4, 26, 108, 111, 115, 291; and happiness, 55, 130, 143, 395; impossibility of, 391–392; and injustice, 120, 122, 301; institutions and procedures in, 355; and knowledge of human beings, 118; and laws, 392; limits on discussion in, 4, 241; and lying, 128; mathematics, 291; model of, 138, 148; and musical man, 114; nature of, 315; paradigm of, 8–9, 79, 228; of philosopher-kings, 38, 247; and philosophers, 143, 168, 169, 210, 230, 231, 244, 277, 279, 280, 281–284, 295, 315, 391; and poetry, 30, 354; possibility of, 4–5; and power, 57; practitioners of *technē* in, 40; regime for, 306–307, 309, 327; regulating sex in, 25, 73, 188, 191; rejection and analysis of, 284; and rule of Platonism, 391; rulers of, 103, 172, 281, 355–356, 371; and sexual reproduction, 25, 305; and soul, 22–23, 71, 99, 103, 146, 148, 245, 396; structures of, 7; temperament for, 327; theology, 118; theoretical presupposition of, 167; transforming human beings, 81; transition from private happiness, 55; tripartition of, 49; as unworkable, 4; virtue and money, conflict between, 309; and women, 174, 181, 182; workers in, 27
Justice, 139–170; appearance of, 62, 63; arguments in defense of, 62–63; and art of ruling, 53; and beautiful class, 62; beneficial nature of, 39, 40, 42–43, 48, 90–91, 350; Cephalus' definition of, 30, 31; compelling to be just, 63;

desirability of, 63; and excellence, 59; failing to define it, 60–61; and fellow citizens, 135; form of, 176; and freedom of speech, 68; and friendship, 51; and goodness, 40; and guardians, 34, 106; and happiness, 129–133, 333–351; and harmony, 62, 347; as human excellence, 36; Idea of Justice, 63, 202, 224–225; and injustice, 49–50; investigation of, 22; legal, 42; and liberty from city, 319; and lying, 31; model *(paradeigma)* of, 176; and noble simplicity, 106; and nonphilosophers, 391; partial, 58; and paying debts and telling truth, 30; perceiving, 158; perfect, 206–207, 217; and philosophers, 277, 391; and philosophy, 392; and pleasure, 30, 334, 348, 349; Polemarchus's definition, 31–37, 42–43, 60–61, 63, 84, 101, 172; and political problem, 289–290; as product of intelligence, 85; public and private nature of, 181; pursuit of, 22–23, 82; and reward, 381; sense of knowledge of, 44; as slavery of worse to better, 350; Socrates's belief in, 2–3, 8–10; switch from substantive to formalist doctrine of, 42; as technical knowledge, 56–57; and temperance, 67, 71, 100; Thrasymachus's definition, 38–59, 60, 64–65, 348, 352; utility of, 34. *See also* Do good to friends and harm to enemies; Minding one's own business

Kakia (privation of excellence), 58–59
Kallipolis (beautiful city), 293
Kant, Immanuel, 161, 334, 349, 360
Kēdemonas, 125
Kiene Rache, 299
King. *See* Philosopher-kings; Rulers
Knowledge, 44, 85, 86, 90, 141–142, 153, 220, 222, 260
Koinônia (community), 360
Kojève, Alexandre, 229, 237
Kronos, 88

Lacedaimonians, 172
Lachesis, Clotho, and Atropos (Fates), 384
Late dialogue on politics, 246
Laughter, 31, 98, 106–107, 169, 171, 172–174, 208, 262
Law *(nomos)*, 280, 375
Law and custom, 94
Laws: decisions prior to writing, 71; enforcing erotic uniformity, 128; and injustice, 64; and just city, 392; of marketplace, 208; need for, 30; observance of, 91; power versus, 43; and rich citizens, 311; ruling class, 41, 42–43
Laws, 173, 394–395
Lawsuits, 116, 194
Learning, 230, 278, 335, 340. *See also* Education
Leontius, story of, 154–155, 156
Letters, 234
Letters, words, and writings, 111–113
Lexis, 101
Licentiousness, 350. *See also* Eros
Logical nominalism, 152
Logically faulty arguments, use of, 1–2
Logismos (calculation), 153, 159
Logos, 61, 64, 155, 157, 158, 159, 265, 296, 297, 310
Love, 114, 211–212, 335, 339
Love of city, 125
Love of Ideas, 27
Love of truth, 27
Lovers of sights and of hearing, 216–217
Loyalty, 84, 85, 141
Lukács, Georg, 229, 237
Luxurious city *(truphôsan)*, 75, 76, 79–108, 109, 241
Lycurgus, 370
Lying, 26, 31, 93, 98–99, 126–129, 187–188, 230–231. *See also* Noble and medicinal lies
Lyre, 107
Lysias, 13

Madman, lying to, 30, 32, 37, 93
Magnificence, 231–232, 248

Making versus using, 370–371
Male drama, 171, 172
Malleability of human nature, 246–247
Man and city, analogy of, 148–149
Marriage, 135, 187, 189, 190, 191, 195; homosexual, 210–211. *See also* Community of women and children; Sexual reproduction
Master and slave, 273, 313
Mathematics: and divided line, 264–265; and education of philosophers, 212, 249, 297, 299, 354; and the Good, 266, 267–268; and image of pleasure, 348–349; and philosophers, 28; and Platonic Ideas, 267, 296; sameness in arithmetic, 149–150; scope of arithmetic and calculation, 285, 292–293; and war, 291
Medicinal lies. *See* Noble and medicinal lies
Medicine, 31–33, 46–48, 52, 56–58, 116–121, 177, 182, 327. *See also* Physicians
Memorabilia (Xenophon), 62
Memory, 125, 232, 237, 248
Men: classification of, 186; male drama, 171, 172; superiority of male class, 180
Merchants, 138, 290, 291
Metals, myth of, 98, 127, 129, 307–308
Metaphysics (Aristotle), 246, 256, 299
Might makes right, 39–43, 51, 162, 164
Mill, John Stuart, 318, 336
Mimesis, 357–376
Mimetic poetry. *See* Poetry and poets
Minding one's own business: and allegory of cave, 277; Bloom on, 172; and city, 183, 190–191; and city and soul, 380; and defining justice, 95, 132, 146, 157, 183, 345, 350; and division of labor, 71, 161; and judges, 147; and knowledge, 90; and noble dog, 85; and philosophers, 281, 395; and philosophy, 85–86; and sexual reproduction, 305; and temperance, 145

Miscegenation, 128, 308, 309, 347
Mistakes, 44–45, 46
Models, 201–207
Models of justice, 161
Modern constructionist philosophy, 99
Monarchy, 163, 333–334. *See also* Rulers
Money, 26–27, 29, 34, 66, 308–309, 310, 335
Moneymaking: art of, 46, 48, 52; and brutes, 172; class of, 123, 146, 396; and desires, 150; governing, 38; and guardians, 179; life of, 194; and musicians and gymnasts, 123; and pleasure, 340; and sexual pleasure, 27; soul of, 151, 396; virtue of, 160; and women, 181. *See also* Craftsmen and artisans; Desire; Workers
Monogamy, 74
Monotheism, 139, 195
Morality, 41, 334
Morphē, 92
Motherhood, 127, 187
Multiculturalism, 197
Murder, 88, 169, 171
Muses, 307, 308
Music: and melody, 107; and rhythm, 109–110; and temperance, 111–112, 145; and virtue, 113. *See also* Music education
Music education, 109–115; and decay of virtuous man who did not acquire, 310; and erotic soul, 122; for guardian's education along with gymnastics, 87, 115–116, 122–123, 137, 160, 183, 279, 294, 395; neglect of, 307–308; and philosophical nature, 232; prevention of innovation of, 136; primary to gymnastics, 124, 136; purging city through, 159; reasons for, 123; and sex, 159; and simplicity, 159; women, 172
Musical man, 55–56, 107, 114, 124–125
Myth of Er. *See* Er, myth of
Myths, 87–89, 93, 126, 348–349

Naked wrestling by women, 172, 184
Narratives, 11, 101, 103, 105, 357
Natural city, 80–81
Nature, 163
Necessary and unnecessary desires and pleasures, 320, 325–327
Necessity and contingencies in cosmos, 383–385
Needs and city, 71–74, 75, 79, 82, 83, 108, 125
Nicomachean Ethics (Aristotle), 23, 226, 281, 345
Nietzsche, Friedrich, 4, 6, 12, 41, 42, 129, 299, 327
Nobility of justice, 158–159
Noble and medicinal lies: for education and protection of young, 88, 233; for good of city, 8; and loving justice, 133; and marriage, 187; as military issue, 95; necessary to govern, 2, 54, 98–99, 111, 125–128, 144, 229–231, 282; by philosophers to nonphilosophers, 395; in political context, 93; scholars' view of, 233, 369; and Socrates's position, 2; as solution to political problem, 284; true lie versus, 92; and women, 128
Noble dog, 83–86, 109, 172, 183
Noble lie. *See* Noble and medicinal lies
Noēsis, 222, 265, 296, 297
Noetic intuition, 207
Nominalism, 258
Noncontradiction, principle of, 152
Nous, 266, 343
Numbers, 285–287, 290, 291–292, 294, 296, 348, 349. *See also* Mathematics

Oaths, 25, 31, 35, 51, 107, 136, 351, 377
Objections to Plato's political thought, 5
Occupations, 73, 182
Odysseus, 159, 382, 386
Oedipus, 368, 369
Old age, 22, 24–26
Oligarchy, 306, 311–314, 319–321, 322, 323, 327, 348
Olympians, 20, 90
"One man, one art," 73
One-many argument, 216, 290, 358–359
Ontological images, 269, 363–365
Opinion *(doksa)*, 219–221, 225, 297, 357, 372
Opinions, 222–224
Opposites, argument from, 360
Opson (cooked food). *See* Food
Oratory, art of, 49
Ordinary language, 149
Originals and images, 113–114
Otherness, 218, 260
Ouranos, 88
Ousia, 223, 230, 232, 261, 262, 287, 297

Pain and pleasure, 336–338, 340, 341–342; as compared to hunger and thirst, 344–346
Painting, 207, 247, 363–364, 365, 368, 372, 376
Paradeigma, 201–205, 206–207
Parents: removing children from, 135, 239; treatment of, 88–89. *See also* Motherhood
Parmenides, 209, 218
Patriotism, 26–27, 125, 179
Patroclus, 97
Pattern and model, 201–205
Peace, 81, 291, 295
Pederasty, 165, 195, 210–211, 230
Peloponnesian War, 20
Perfect city, 208
Perfect justice, 206–207, 217
Pericles, 237–238
Personal freedom and privacy, 308
Personal immorality, 127
Persuasion, 247–248
Phaedo, 98
Phaedrus, 8, 25, 233, 276, 393, 394
Philebus, 216, 265, 292
Philia (love), 335, 339

Philosopher-kings: absence of non-Platonists, 391; age of, 301; and allegory of cave, 272; Aristotle's view on, 142; assistants to, 391; and children, 239; and city, 74, 79, 208; and construction of city, 110; course of study of, 299–301; and doctrinal disagreement, 142, 285; education of, 137, 143; feasibility of, 235–236; and the Good, 268; and happiness, 333; and human nature, 104; just city of, 38, 247; need for, 25, 137, 390; and noble and medicinal lies, 95, 98–99; number of, 189; officers, 83; as painters of cities, 247; and philosophy as profession, 210, 227–254, 279, 281, 299; and Platonic Ideas, 168; and poetry, 353; possibility of, 7; role of, 138, 395; and soldiers, 126, 168; for solution of political problem, 284; and speech, 351; and type of regime, 306; and tyranny, 328; wisdom, 123

Philosophers: "atheism" of, 68; and auxiliaries, soldiers, 392; and compulsion to seek political power, 9; course of studies, 299–300; criticism of, 69; curriculum of, 299–300; education of, 212, 249, 255–301, 305; genuine and false, 298–299; and genuine happiness, 345; and geometry, 292; goal of, 291; as god, 246; and happiness, 280; impossibility of full satisfaction of philosophical eros, 81–82; just men as, 65; and justice, 277, 391; level of confidence of, 169; as lovers of sight of truth, 213, 214; obligations of, 54; origin of term, 209; and peace, 291, 295; and personal happiness and public justice, 395; and persuasion of many, 247; philosophical nature, 227–254, 279, 281, 299; and Platonic Ideas, 280; and poetry, 354; political activity of, 390; and political ambition, 165; political temptation of, 6, 10; potential, 126, 129, 165, 210, 212, 234, 237, 238, 239, 241, 246, 249, 279, 285, 290, 292, 294, 295, 298, 302; power to, 7; public life and private life, 281–284; and reproduction, 307; and ruling, 5, 209, 229, 230, 236, 277, 280, 281–282, 355; ruling by, 229, 390; and rustication, 391; understanding of term, 209–210; and war, 291. *See also* Cave, allegory of

Philosophical eros, 81–82, 154

Philosophical nature, 227–254, 279, 281, 299

Philosophy, 156–157; advertisement for, 8; and art, 240; competing desires on ruling, 166; and corruption, 241; and courage, 86; and dialectic, 291, 295–296, 299–300; and eros, 25; and Greeks, 244; and healing, 163; and justice, 7, 392; and pederasty, 211; and poetry, quarrel between, 2, 3–4, 6, 25, 30, 352–376, 393; political, 5–7, 241, 390, 392–393; practicing beyond youth, 234; psychiatric interpretation of, 156–157; and purpose of study, 389; and ruling, 285; seriousness and play, 299; soul of, 104; subordination to political compulsion, 166; as temperate eros, 327–328; in true city, 80; and tyranny, 5, 6, 9, 10, 281; unearthly character of, 389; and war, 94, 298; wisdom, temperance, gentleness, and orderliness, 123. *See also* Cave, allegory of

Phocylides, 117

Phoenician myth, 126

Phoenicians, 151

Phronēsis (practical judgment), 142

Phronimos (person of prudence), 228

Physicians: Apollo as, 259; class of, 21, 40, 46, 119, 120, 123, 182, 243, 392; and contracts for a fee, 31–32; and guardians, 116, 121; judging by, 120; and justice, 32, 33, 34, 37; and luxurious city, 80; need for, 116, 117, 118; requirements for, 118–119; and

technical knowledge, 31–33, 56; and usefulness, 33; women as, 177. *See also* Medicine
Piety, 91–92. *See also* Religion
Pigs, 88
Pilot, 33, 46, 48, 234–235
Pindar, 29, 30, 117
Piraeus, 13, 19, 22
Plato, writings of, 11
Plato and Socrates compared, 143
Platonic Ideas: and allegory of cave, 11, 271, 272; and aptitude, 175; ascending to, 278; in Books Five through Seven versus Book Ten, 360–361; city as, 72; and classification by particulars, 256; and degrees of being, 345; and dialectic, 3, 45, 165, 221, 264–266, 392; and everyday use, 205–206; and Idea of justice, 202; and intellect, 168, 265; introduction to, 62, 71; and knowledge, 218, 249; and mathematics, 267, 296; objective nature of, 255; and opinion, 221; as "original" originals, 112, 358–359; and philosopher-kings, 168; and philosophers, 3, 280; and philosophy, 354; and poetry, 355; and power, 220; result of reject of, 330; and soul, 394; terminology of, 64, 149; variation not allowed, 175, 193; and virtue, 111. *See also* Ideas, doctrine of
Platonic imitations, 101
Pleasure: Cephalus' interest in, 24; Glaucon's omission of, 67; happiness and, 333–351; temperance and, 29–30, 114
Pleoneksia (having more than one's share), 53, 55, 57, 67
Poetry and poets, 93–99; attacks on, 15; censorship of, 28, 93–94, 96, 99; and city, 74, 80, 101–102; and corruption, 67–69; criticism of, 71–72, 101–103, 139, 352–376; and death, 96–97, 381; and defining justice, 30; and education, 87; and gods, 91, 353–354; and hermeneutics, 117; and metaphor of sexual reproduction, 26–27; mimetic, 3, 103, 105, 357, 367, 368, 370; and music purge of regulation of, 108; and myth, 89; need for, 381; and patriotism, 26–27; and philosophy, quarrel between, 2, 3–4, 6, 25, 30, 352–376, 393; reconquest of philosophers of, 396; and riddles, 31; and soul, 104, 118

Polemarchus. *See* Cephalus and Polemarchus; Justice
Police, 34, 94
Political ambition: of philosophers, 165, 244; and philosophical justice, 239–240; of Plato, 229
Political compacts, 65
Political decay, 305–332
Political life, 81; and philosophy, 6–7
Political organization of sexual relations, 165
Political power, 67; by force, 239; to pseudophilosophers and ignoble sophists, 170
Political revolution, 390
Politics, 42–43; and allegory of cave, 270; late dialogue on, 246; and philosophers, 229; and philosophy, 5–6, 209, 241, 392–393; problems of, 284, 289–290, 318, 393; of suspicion, 69
Politics (Aristotle), 23, 116, 142–143, 226
Polupragmosunē (minding of everyone's business), 12, 146, 147
Polytheism, 140
Popper, Karl, 5
Possibility, 201–226
Poverty, 133–134
Power, 41, 66, 219–220; desire for, 53–54; of knowledge, 220; of multitude, 235; political, 67, 170, 239. *See also* Rulers; Ruling
Practical intelligence, 138, 392
Practical judgment, 45, 146, 224, 294–295
Priam, mourning for Hector, 97
Prisoners, guardians as, 195

Private property, 27, 53, 194
Procreation, 135
Prodicus, 370
Promiscuity, 184–187
Property. See Private property
Protagoras, 370
Prudence, 145, 228, 294–295
Pseudophilosophers, 229
Psychiatric interpretation of philosophy, 156–157
Puppet masters, 270–273, 274, 275
Pure pleasures, 337, 338, 341, 342, 343, 347
Purged city, 109–138
Pythagoras, 209, 370
Pythagoreans, 294

Quarrel between philosophy and poetry. See Philosophy; Poetry and poets
Quiet life, praise of, 386

Reading, learning of, 111–113
Realpolitik, 39
Reason, 157–158
Regimes, types of, 162–163, 305–311, 329, 332, 334. See also specific type
Reincarnation, 65, 381
Religion, 74, 139–140, 187–189, 195
Relishes. See Food
Respect for elders, 136
Rest or quiet of soul, 336, 337, 340
Revolution, 6–7, 8, 134; "ideology" of, 20–21; political, 390; in speech, 22; women's divided nature and, 178
Reward and punishment, 381–386
Rhetorical powers, criticism of poets', 68, 243–244
Rhythm, 109–110
Ring of Gyges, 65, 187, 237
Rituals for sexual relations, 187–189
Rousseau, 147, 331
Rule of mob, 235, 239
Rulers: of actual city, 53, 144, 208–209, 351; arts, use of, 48; as craftsmen and artisans, 44–45; division into factions by, 307; education of, 141, 294; as guardians, 124–126, 132, 355; judging lawsuits, 146, 147; minding business of others, 12, 146, 147; and mistakes, 44–45, 46; number of, 306; obedience of, 100, 102, 108, 160; and personalities, 316; property of, 53; role of, 194–195; selection of, 124–125, 228; and soldiers, 14, 126–127; upbringing of, 124; and women, 183; workers versus, 189. See also Philosopher-kings; Ruling; Tyranny and tyrants
Ruling: art of, 45–49, 52–53, 55–56; and guardian class, 142; intelligence, 159; and just city, 281; justice, 53; and philosophers, 5, 209, 229, 230, 236, 277, 280, 281–284, 390; technē, 53; temptation to, 6
Ruling class, 41–43, 272
Rustication, 21, 246, 301, 391

Sacred, nature of, 25
Sacrifice, 88
Sarpedon, 97
Scythians, 151
Seeing. See Vision
Self-interest, 54
Selfishness and city, 73
Self-love, 27, 125, 127
Sensory metaphors, 213–215
Sensory perception, 258, 288–289. See also Hearing; Vision
Sensual gratification, 27
Separation thesis, 225
Servants, 80
Sex and sexual relations: abolishment of private, 184; downplaying of, 73; and food, 116; as mad eros, 327–328; and money, 27, 66, 100; political organization of, 165; private versus use for political advantage, 67; promiscuity, 184–187; regulation of, 159, 160, 328; and reproduction, 167; rituals for, 187–189; sacrifice of, 167–168; as sexual weapon, 195; and soldiers,

189–190. *See also* Homosexual relations; Sexual desire; Sexual pleasure
Sexual desire, 172, 326, 335, 339, 396
Sexual eros, 53, 128, 187–191, 328, 338
Sexual pleasure: genuine pleasure and happiness, 346; and health of body, 346; and moneymaking, 27; reproduction versus, 191
Sexual reproduction: and age, 190–191; and allegory of cave, 270, 272; failure to control, 328; inability to control laws of, 305; metaphor of, 26–27; miscegenation, 128, 308, 309; necessity of, 210; and nuptial number, 307, 327, 334; and philosophers, 307; as political function, 165; regulation of, 188–190; role of men and women, 175; sexual pleasure versus, 191; in true city, 79
Sexual taboos, violation of, 25
Shadows, 269, 271, 272, 273. *See also* Cave, allegory of
Shape *(morphē)* of body to form of soul, 174–177
Shelley, Percy Bysshe, 376
Ship, image of, 234–235
Shoemaking, 46, 47, 48, 177
Shoemaking, example of, 133
Sicily, Plato's trips to, 6, 9, 129, 143, 229, 238
Sight and hearing, 258, 259, 296, 372
Simonides, 30, 31
Simple music, 122
Sisters, 127
Skopia (lookout point), 162
Slaves, 196, 273, 275
Socrates detained with cloak slave boy, 163–165
Soldiers. *See* Auxiliaries, soldiers
Solid geometry, 294
Solon, 370
Sophist, 218, 395
Sophistry, charge of, 233–234
Sophists, 370
Sophocles, 25

Sôphrosunē. *See* Temperance
Soul: and allegory of cave, 271, 273; civil war of soul, 156; and desire, 335; and enslavement by unjust acts, 350; happiness and pleasure, 333–351; Idea of human soul, 392; immortal, 377–388; and knowing one's own, 330; myth of, 276; in other works of Plato, 394–395; and perception, 289–290; pleasures and types of, 347–348; and pleasures peculiar to, 335–336; and political problem, 289–290; purging diversity in, 354; relationship to city, 147–148; sickness of, 162; struggles between main kinds of, 307–308; three forms of, 167, 373–375; three parts of, 69, 70, 123, 349, 396; turning of, 278–279; types of, 306; as underlying unity, 289–290. *See also* City and soul, analogy of
Soul and city. *See* City and soul, analogy of
Sparta, 80
Specialists, 40, 110
Speech: about human beings, 100; in beautiful city, 352; in city, 207–208; and deed, 201; education in, 87; and music, 107; as narration, 105; permissible and impermissible ways of speaking about human beings, 100; style and diction, 101; true and false, 87; with or without meter, 91
Spinoza, 93
Spiritedness: and anger, 155, 157–158; and auxiliaries, soldiers, 149, 150; and children, 159; and courage, 83–84, 85, 86, 232; desire compared to, 157, 396; directed by reason, 65; and gymnastics, 122; and intellect, 154, 159; and intelligence, 83, 85; mediation of, 64; and soul, 335, 394
Stargazing, 235, 236, 240
Stasis, 156
Statesman, 30, 246–247, 248–249, 309, 384, 392, 394, 395
Strangers, 85–86, 109

Strauss, Leo: on Book Five, 163; on democracies, 14; on force, 51; and narrative and performed dialogues, 11; on poetry, 15; on political consequences of rule of philosophers, 10; on popular rhetoric, 243; on Thrasymachus, 15, 166, 243; on titles, 11; view of, 5, 11, 81–82, 167

Street gangs, 194

Style, 105–106

Sun: and divided line, 263, 271; and the Good, 3, 226, 258–262, 268–269; image of, 19, 253, 254, 258–259; as offspring of the Good, 257, 267. *See also* Cave, allegory of

Suspicion, politics of, 69

Symposium, 25, 71, 103

Table, 356, 361–362, 363, 364

Tame and wild animals, 83–84

Tameness, 122

Technē: art of ruling not considered as, 53; and decision to use justice, 34; effect on philosophy, 240; as image of justice, 161; importance as theme, 142; as instrument, 56; and intelligence, 278; and justice, 37; and knowledge of good, 45; medicine as, 33, 327; and moneymaking, 52; musical, 56; obscuring difference between art and practical judgment, 49; and practical judgment, 45; practitioners of, 40; specialists required for, 110; and strength, 44, 49; Thrasymachus as champion of, 51, 57

Technical competence and expertise. *See* *Technē*

Temperance: and city, 135, 159; and class, 151; and courage, 248; courage compared, 145; defense of, 72; as demotic virtue, 231, 298; and Eleatic Stranger, 248; endorsement and praise of, 26; erosion of, 74; failure of, 81; and food, 320; and gods, 91, 94, 97, 139–140; and guardians, 108, 109, 138, 141; and harmony, 116, 137, 150, 159–160; and injustice, 67; and justice, 30, 67, 71, 72, 135, 160; and luxurious and feverish city, 95–96; and moderation, 99–100; and music, 110, 111, 112, 121, 159–160; and obedience to rulers, 102, 108, 160; and old age, 24, 25; and order, harmony, and simplicity, 159–160; and philosophers, 138, 237; and philosophic nature, 122–124, 231, 232, 237; and pleasure, 29–30, 114; quality of, 99–101; and soul, 130, 154; usefulness of, 29–30

Theaetetus, 361

Themistocles, 26

Theogony (Hesiod), 88, 356

Theology, 89, 90–92

Thetis, 97

Third man paradox, 366

Thirst. *See* Hunger and thirst

Thirty, the, 13–14, 15

Thracians, 151

Thrasymachus, 15, 38–59, 60, 64–65, 243, 348, 352

Three classes, importance of, 147, 151, 181

Three main human types, 151–152

Three parts harmonized, 161

Three points of soul, 158, 159

Thumos, 8, 21, 25, 155

Thus Spoke Zarathustra (Nietzsche), 12

Timaeus, 13, 294, 309, 356

Timocracy, 306–312, 313, 314, 334

Torch race, 13, 22, 24, 163

Tragedies. *See* Comedies and tragedies

Treason, 6

Tripartition of soul, 308, 334, 335–336, 338–339, 372

Triton ti eidos (a third kind of form), 62

True city, 74, 79, 80, 94

Truth, 5, 6, 27, 30, 214–215

Tyranny and tyrants: acts of, 57; career and life of, 51, 323–324, 328, 330–332, 333, 348; and complete injustice, 66; of multitude, 235; noble, 306; and philosopher-kings, 328; and philosophy, 5, 6, 9, 10, 237–238, 281; Plato criticized as fostering, 129; springing from democracy, 313, 321; of truth, 143; and vanity, 26–27

Unity or oneness, 286–288
Unjust man. *See* Just and unjust man
Useful, 36
Useful and beneficial, 250
Using, making, and imitating, 372
Utility, 28, 33–34, 41, 90, 161
Utopia, 163

Vaihinger, Hans, 360
Vanity and tyranny, 26–27
Virtue: and badness, 120; cardinals, 146, 149, 249–250; demotic, 65, 150–151, 231, 245–246, 247, 249, 267, 268, 279, 298, 385; forms, 176; four virtues of soul, 149, 249–250; money versus, 308–309; and music, 115; of philosopher and nonphilosopher compared, 23; philosophical virtue, 278; theoretical and practical virtue, 23, 228; and vice, 113–114, 160, 162, 176; vulgar, 246, 278
Visible domain, 263–264, 275, 296. *See also* Divided line
Vision, 213, 228, 255, 289; and intuition, 222
Voting example, 225

Wages, 53
War: arithmetic and calculation in, 290; as fundamental, 94–95; and geometry, 292; gods against gods, 88–89; guardians, 195; gymnastics as preparation for, 115–116; and luxury, 80; and mathematics, 291; and mating, 189; and philosophers, 291, 300; and philosophy, 94, 298; purpose of, 82–83
Warriors, 94–95. *See also* Auxiliaries, soldiers; Education of guardians
Wealth, 26–27, 133–134; and goodness, 28

Weaving: as image of cosmos, 384; as model for politics, 246–247, 249
Wet nurses, 80
Wild and tame animals, 83–84
Williams, Bernard, 150
Wisdom, 5, 86, 123, 141–142, 145, 150, 219
Women, 171–197; and abolishment of family, 210, 390; capabilities of, 180; and classes, 127, 180–181; classification of, 186; divided nature of and revolution, 178; doing tasks of male nature, 174–175, 197; education of, 171, 172, 178, 182–183, 184; effect of physical differences of, 174–175; emancipation, 178–179, 181; guardians, 172; and nature and injustice, 181; in neediest city, 73; and noble lie, 128; peripheral to discussion, 74, 75, 87; as philosophers, 210, 305; and philosophy, 211; possession of, 135; roles of, 178–179, 180–181; and superiority of male class, 180. *See also* Community of women and children; Family; Motherhood; Sexual reproduction
Words, letters, and writings, 111–113
Work and sickness, 117, 118
Worker-farmer-merchant class, 138
Workers: and courage, 144; and desire, 149; and happiness, 183; as moneymaking class, 27; need for, 73–74; need for supervision, 132; as political class, 69, 189; role of, 396; and temperance, 122; and timocracy, 309. *See also* Craftsmen and artisans; Desire; Epithumetic or appetitive part of soul; Moneymaking

Xanthippe, 203
Xenophon, 62

Youth, lost pleasures of, 25

Zarathustra, 4, 12
Zeus, 88, 97, 187